THE AMERICAN WEST

THE
AMERICAN WEST

A Treasury of Stories, Legends,
Narratives, Songs & Ballads
of Western America

Edited with an Introduction by **WILLIAM TARG**

Konecky & Konecky
72 Ayers Point Rd.
Old Saybrook, CT 06475

ISBN: 1-56852-534-6

Printed and bound in the U.S.A.

FOR Anne AND Russell

CONTENTS

Introduction, *William Targ*   **xi**

TALES AND LEGENDS

THE STORY OF THE LUCKY LOUSE, or, BLOOD WILL
   TELL, *G. Ezra Dane and Beatrice J. Dane*   3

THE PHANTOM FENCE RIDER OF SAN MIGUEL
   Henry Yelvington   16

MILLIONAIRES, *Mark Twain*   21

"SPEAKIN' OF COWPUNCHERS," *Charles M. Russell*   32

AN INGÉNUE OF THE SIERRAS, *Bret Harte*   37

THE SUN-DOG TRAIL, *Jack London*   54

THE TWO-GUN MAN, *Stewart Edward White*   67

THE BRIDE COMES TO YELLOW SKY, *Stephen Crane*   79

THE SQUARE PIANO, *Conrad Richter*   91

HIGHER EDUCATION, *Oliver La Farge*   110

GHOST OF THE CIMARRON, *Harry Sinclair Drago*   134

RIDING BOG, *Will James*   174

SPOIL THE CHILD, *Howard Fast*   187

WHEN A DOCUMENT IS OFFICIAL, *Frederic Remington*   199

A PIGEON HUNT, *Andy Adams*   207

THE COME-ON, *Eugene Manlove Rhodes*   212

BAR-NOTHING'S HAPPY BIRTHDAY, *Eugene Cunningham*   221

WE CAN'T ALL BE THOROUGHBREDS, *Irvin S. Cobb*   237

THE MYSTERY OF THE PALO DURO, *J. Frank Dobie*   249

A CALL LOAN, *O. Henry*   254

DON; THE STORY OF A LION DOG, *Zane Grey*   260

CORAZON, *George Pattullo*   282

NARRATIVES

THE FIRST COWBOY, *Frederick R. Bechdolt*   297

GENTLEMEN-ON-HORSEBACK, *Ruth Laughlin Barker*   318

THE EXPEDITIONS OF FREMONT, LEWIS AND CLARK, and Z. M. PIKE, *Henry Howe*   342

THE CAMP OF THE WILD HORSE, *Washington Irving*   363

LIFE AMONG THE TRAPPERS, *Henry Howe*   369

STAGE-COACH, *Captain William Banning and George Hugh Banning*   374

WINDWAGON, *Stanley Vestal*   393

COLONEL CHARLES GOODNIGHT—TRAIL-MAKER, *Dane Coolidge*   399

"STICK 'EM UP," *William McLeod Raine*   415

THE NAMING OF DEATH VALLEY, *C. B. Glasscock*   432

A PECCARY-HUNT IN THE NUECES, *Theodore Roosevelt*   447

DICK YEAGER, *Marquis James*   456

CRAZY AS A SHEEPHERDER, *David Lavender*   484

CUSTER, *Frederic F. Van de Water*   496

PIÑONES, *Haniel Long*   524

THE GRAND CANYON OF THE COLORADO *Robert Frothingham*   530

SONGS AND BALLADS

Collector's Note, *John A. Lomax*   537

A HOME ON THE RANGE   542

I RIDE AN OLD PAINT 543

WHEN BOB GOT THROWED 544

THE DREARY BLACK HILLS 545

SWEET BETSY FROM PIKE 546

SAGE-BRUSH 548

SAM BASS 549

BRIGHAM YOUNG. I 551

BRIGHAM YOUNG. II 552

THE BOOZER 553

AS I WALKED OUT IN THE STREETS OF LAREDO 554

THE TENDERFOOT 555

THE LONE STAR TRAIL 557

WESTWARD HO 559

WHEN THE WORK'S ALL DONE THIS FALL 560

WESTERN LIFE 561

THE COWMAN'S PRAYER 562

WHOOPEE, TI YI YO, GIT ALONG, LITTLE DOGIES 563

BILLY VENERO 564

THE COWBOY'S DREAM 567

WINDY BILL 568

THE COWBOY'S MEDITATION 570

THE COWBOY 571

THE RANGE RIDERS 573

THE GOL-DARNED WHEEL 574

THE TEXAS COWBOY 576

OLD TIME COWBOY 578

THE PECOS QUEEN 579

x　　　　　*Contents*

THE DYING COWBOY　　　　　　　　　　580

THE OLD CHISHOLM TRAIL　　　　　583

A Glossary of Western Words　　　　587

Acknowledgments　　　　　　　　　593

INTRODUCTION

IN THIS volume there is assembled a diversified collection of stories, songs, ballads, narratives and legends, in which is recorded some of the romance and spirit of the living drama of the West. There are stories here (some quite wonderful, I think) by native, tale-spinning old-timers, as well as by men renowned in the world of letters. Here are songs and ballads, relating of the Last Frontier, the Far West, the Golden West,—of the thundering herd, of lonely nights under cold prairie skies;—and tales of violent deeds in a day when law was administered from the holster.

You will encounter narratives here of the men and women who journeyed West, into the challenging desert, the unpathed mountain and forest, searching for food, for new homes and security, —some seeking escape, others adventure and gold. Here are the fugitives, pioneers, rangers, scouts, prospectors and the others, —the men of iron who won the West, blazed trails, fought, loved, hunted the buffalo, enriched the prairies, built cities. Here is the American Indian of the past and of today. Here are the quick-triggered gentry, the desperadoes, legendary and real, the man-hunters, who lived in the saddle in the midst of roaring guns. Here too is the West of the cowcountry as we know it today, presenting the cowman in his everyday life, hard-riding, witty, picturesque and colorful of speech.

The American West is a limitless source for the writer. It is a saga so prodigious that no single teller of tales, no poet, can hope to encompass its breadth. And the literature of the West, while voluminous beyond measure, continues to increase as new observers, historians, singers and story-tellers emerge.

The purpose of this collection is to capture, within the severe limitations of a single volume, some of the epic drama, the exciting color, the humor and flavor of the West, past and present,—the West comprising New Mexico, Texas, Arizona, Colorado, Wyoming, Montana, Nevada, Oklahoma and the remote regions of the Northwest. I have tapped only modestly the vast reservoir of Western literature but because of the diversity which I hope has been attained in my selection, I feel that the reader will come to experience a fuller understanding of this land and its people, and to savor its romance and grandeur. I hope, too, that this volume will help to introduce the reader to further adventures in Western literature. A large part of the contents is derived from full-length volumes, much of which is worthy of the reader's further acquaintance. (In the note preceding each selection, I have indicated the original source wherever possible.)

Here then, in prose and song, is the American West: a great land and people, interpreted by some of our finest writers and offered to you as a contribution toward a better understanding of our history and ourselves. This collection is offered, too, with the hope that it will provide you with many hours of reading pleasure.

My sincere thanks are due the many booksellers, librarians, editors, authors, publishers and agents, and my editorial associates, whose cooperation and enthusiasm for this work made its publication possible.

WILLIAM TARG

TALES AND LEGENDS

G. EZRA DANE and BEATRICE J. DANE

THE STORY OF THE
LUCKY LOUSE OR, BLOOD WILL TELL

An old-timer talks about the early gold-rush days, when prospectors paid for haircuts in gold dust, and the barber collected extra dividends after the day's work by "panning out the whiskers." He spins a yarn as fantastic as Mark Twain's famous "Jumping Frog of Calaveras County," and every bit as funny. This is the first of many equally diverting and richly vernacular tales of the ghost town of Columbia on California's Mother Lode, to be found in the book, *Ghost Town* (Knopf, 1941).

No SIR, nobody has a better right than me to set on this stump. I planted the old poplar myself on the corner here, near sixty years ago. It got to be three foot through at the ground, as you can see, and it must of been eighty feet high. But the roots begun to upheave the sidewalk bricks, and when the limbs would blow they'd brush the shakes off the awning of Mike Rehm's Pioneer Saloon, so the old tree had to come down.

Well, they must come an end to all things, no matter how great or how good. With men, and trees, and towns, it's all the same. And so it is with me. I grew up with this old town and I've come down with it.

Here I set like an old owl or fox amongst the boulders and think of the days and times that used to be. Them days and these! Them

3

days and these! It's like day and night, day and night. Oh, them was the days, I can tell you. Yes, sir, them was the days of great depravitation and plenty of whisky.

A fellow didn't have to travel, in them days, to see the world. The whole world come here then with samples of all kinds of humanity. The gold, that was what they all come for, of course. They followed the track of it, in '48 and '49 and '50, like you'll see chickens follow a trail of corn, pecking and scratching away after it, up the Stanislaus[1] River and ·the Tuolumne into these Sierra foothills, then along Wood's Creek, and acrost Shaw's Flat and up the main gulch here, that we called Miners' Avenue.

March 1850, that's when the first miners reached this flat—Dr. Thaddeus Hildreth and his party—and the five of them averaged fifteen pounds of gold a day for three days. Why, even a lazy man could do pretty well in diggins as rich as that. You take, for instance, one of these first comers, he was even too lazy to wash his drawers. To save himself the work of scrubbing them, he just tied them to a limb that overhung a little stream and let them dangle in the water. He figured, you see, that the current would wash them for him overnight. And the next morning when he come to fish them out, lo and b'God! he found his drawers gold-plated.

Well, with stories like that a-spreading, it's no wonder that Columbia's population grew from five men to six thousand in six weeks. A good many of them, of course, went out like they had come in—with the next rush to another new discovery. But others come that built, and made the camp a town, and the town a city. Yes sir, the greatest on the Mother Lode it was in its day, and they called it the Gem of the Southern Mines.

Well, that's the way it was. Columbia was born of gold; yes, and died of it. It practically ate itself up, the old town did. When the miners had scraped the land down to bedrock all around, then they begun to close in on the town itself. One house after another come down for the sake of the rich ground underneath. These few old buildings that still straggle along Main Street here, you see, either they've been mined under without falling down or they happened to be built in places where the bedrock come near the surface and the gold was scarce.

---

[1] Named in Mexican days for the renegade Indian chieftain Estanislao and therefore still pronounced *Stanislao* by the people of the region, in defiance of American map-makers.

So that's the way the miners come in, like a swarm of locusts. They stripped the country bare, right down to its poor old limestone bones, and then they left.

To look at the old place now, you wouldn't believe that it used to be as I remember it. I can set here and look down this street and see it as it was.

Towards the end of the afternoon the men would come in from the diggins in Matelot Gulch and from Miners' Avenue, and off Gold Hill and from Gold Springs and Murphy's Defeat and Texas Flat and the diggins out Springfield way, and down from French Camp and Italian Bar and Pine Log on the South Fork of the Stanislaus, and from Yankee Hill and from Martinez and Sawmill Flat. Say, that was a sight you ought to see! The street was so packed with people that a fellow could hardly cross. He'd just be carried along with the stream of humanity. The crowd would surge back and forth, and it was made up of all sorts and conditions of people from everywhere.

You'd see all kinds of dress, from frock coats and ruffled shirts and fancy vests down to red or blue flannel shirts with no coats or vests at all and old pants tucked into heavy boots. These pants would be held up, along with a pistol and knife and other hardware, by a good stout belt; and they'd be held together by patches. Usually the patches would be made from flour-sacks, each man advertising his favorite brand. Now you take, for instance, they was a fellow one time showed up with the label *Self-Rising Flour* right acrost the seat of his pants, and he was "Self-Rising Bill" from that day on.

Yes, and patches wasn't all they used the flour sacks for. A man didn't ever have to go without socks if he had a couple of flour sacks. He'd put his foot on the sack near one end and he'd fold the corners and the front end over the top of his foot, and then he'd bring the other end up in back over the heel and wrap it around his ankle and leg and pull his boot on over it; and that was called the "California sock."

Yes sir, and when the women begun to come in, they found the flour sack mighty useful, too. Old Mr. Bell that had the flouring mill down on Wood's Creek below Sonora—you can see his stone dam yet where the old mill stood—he used to tell how, time of the big flood at Sonora, when the creek overflowed and the women came squealing and splashing out of the houses with their skirts lifted up to their waists, of course they showed considerable of their home-made underwear, and under each lifted skirt the crowd could read: BELL's FLOURING MILLS. Yes sir, old Mr. Bell always said that was the best advertising he ever got, and it didn't cost him a cent.

So they was variety in the dress then at any rate, and a man could express his fancy, as well as his preference in grocery goods. One style that had its run was for white shirts with some threads drawn out and the rest caught up in patterns and designs—and showing through this fancy open-work, a red flannel undershirt.

You'd see head-gear of all kinds, too, and all shapes and varieties, from tall silk hats to sailor caps, but mostly black felts with wide brims and with crowns either creased or else conical and flat on top in Spanish style. And whiskers, say, you'd see all colors and styles of whiskers carved out in every pattern a man could imagine. It wasn't quite respectable then, you know, for a man to shave his beard off clean and let his face stick up bare out of his collar; it made him look like a gambler.

There wasn't any one style of anything, because these people, you see, they had come here from all parts of the world. Each nationality brought the ideas and customs of its own country and then they all got mixed up together, and each borrowed from the others until it was all just one grand conglomeration. Any evening on Main Street you could hear eight or ten different languages by the time you walked down one side and back the other: Spanish, and English of every brand from Cornwall to County Pike, and German, and French, and Italian, and Chinese, and Yiddish, and Kanaka, and a little Me-wuk Indian thrown in. And all the men you'd see was young. You'd never see a gray-haired man in the streets unless it was an old grizzled Indian or a Mexican. To get here then, you see, you had to come round the Horn or over the Isthmus or by wagon or horseback or afoot acrost the plains. It was just too hard for the old folks; they wouldn't attempt it. In the mining camps the ages ranged mostly from sixteen to thirty; anybody over thirty-five was decrepit.

Well, perhaps now you can repopulate this old deserted street from your imagination, like I can from my memory. You can picture the miners crowded in the stores waiting their turn to get supplies. At Pachoe's Exchange and at D. O. Mill's Bank that

Sleeper took over in '58 they'd be long cues of miners lined up to sell their dust. William Daegner, the first Wells Fargo Agent, kept his office open night and day to buy it. Why, of a Saturday afternoon I've seen a line of men from Knapp's store at the corner of Main and State the full block down Main Street, then acrost Fulton and up the stairs to Sleeper's Gold Exchange. Often a man would pay five or ten dollars to get a place near the head of the line.

Well, they'd march in and shake out the dust into the scoop, and old man Sleeper, he'd blow through the blower, to blow out the sand, you know. He wasn't too careful how hard he blowed, either, because any dust that spilled on the carpet they could clean up afterwards. That's like they say the barbers done; they'd shave the miners all day at a dollar a shave, and then in the evening they'd make another eight or ten dollars by panning out the whiskers.

Well, old Sleeper, after he'd finished with the blower, he'd weigh up what was left and give the man a tab with the value written on, and at the next window Charlie Sleeper—he was the old man's son—he'd pay out the exchange in gold and silver coin.

They had a sign in there: NO MISTAKES RECTIFIED AFTER YOU LEAVE THE COUNTER. And that sign meant what it said.

My father was purse-bearer for a company of miners, and one Saturday he went into Sleeper's Exchange to cash the week's clean-up. But when they come to divide it afterwards, they found they had two twenty-dollar pieces too much. So Father got in line again and when he come to Charlie Sleeper's window he says: "You made a mistake on my exchange," he says.

"No mistakes rectified after you leave the counter," says Charlie.

"Hold on!" Father says. "You give me forty dollars too much."

"Makes no difference," says Charlie. "That rule works both ways. Put it in your pocket," he says, "and don't hold up the line!"

Well, when they got their money, them as was working partners, they'd go out and declare dividends in the street, or in a saloon, or in somebody's house. Now you take for instance what old Mrs. Barron, a Cornish woman, used to tell. When first she come here in the fifties, she was a little girl then, and her family lived in Springfield. The Cousin Jacks—that's what we called the Cornish

miners—liked to come to their house for tea and saffron cake.
Well, they was four of them, partners, that when they cleaned up
their sluices, would come with their gold and borrow four tea-
cups in place of scales. They'd divide the gold in these four cups.
When they got it evened up the best they could by the eye, they'd
turn their faces to the wall and the little girl, she'd pick up the
cups and put one in the hands of each man. That way they could
be no disagreement, you see, if it turned out that one fellow had
a dollar or two more than another.

Then, when the miners had got their gold exchanged, and the
money in their pockets, the next thing was to pay debts. They'd
always have to pay the saloon-keepers first and in full, because
credit wouldn't last with them. Then they'd settle with the store-
keepers. What they had left, they'd set out to look for ways to
spend it. They's nothing burns the fingers like gold hot from the
mines, you know, and the miner has mighty tender fingers when it
comes to hanging on to it. Then too, they was always plenty of
fellows ready to oblige by helping to separate the miner and his
gold.

First of all, of course, was the saloons. About thirty of them
they was at one time, and the men would be lined up often five
and six deep at the bars. And in all the saloons you'd hear singing
—singing in every language—and that was singing, too! The fellows would get a few drinks, and then they'd begin to sing, and
more would join in until they'd be a regular chorus. Some of the
places would have violins and different instruments, and their
players would strike up and play for the boys.

Oh, they was excitement and turmoil all the time, but some of
the greatest excitements and the greatest turmoils was when Julia
Dean, the actress, come to town, or the famous Chapman Family,
or Junius Brutus Booth, or Kelly, the great violinist. Them was
extra occasions, that brought all the men in from the diggins. The
boys would be excited for two or three days before Julia Dean
come, and they'd go out and meet the stage miles away and escort
her into town. She'd bring her troupe with her and they'd play
for several days in Cardinell's Terpsichore Hall. That was a real
theater with a board floor and chairs and a stage. It was an
elegant place compared to some she had to perform in. In one
camp the troupe had to play in an old Mexican *pelota* or hand-

ball court with a dirt floor, where the miners staked out their places, just like they'd stake out claims, you know.

She was a mighty clever actress, Julia was, and such a pretty creature and so graceful, and they was so few pretty women here; the miners just went crazy about her. When she took her curtain call, the stage would be fair covered with buckskin purses. But the boys found they wasn't noise enough in the thump of these purses of gold dust to express their feelings, so they took to throwing silver dollars till they was hardly any left in town.

Then she'd have invitations from the owners of the different rich mines, like the Cannonade at Santiago Gulch, to come there and visit them and let them entertain her. They'd escort her out to their diggins and give her a pan of rich dirt to pan out, slipping in extra gold, you know, that they thought she didn't see. Of course she'd make an attempt to wash it, but she wouldn't know how to go about it, so some miner would take the pan to do it for her and maybe he'd slip in some more nuggets and a handful of dust; and all this went to Julia.

So besides all she took in at her performances, she'd get a lot more by visiting the miners' diggins; and my! this was considered a great honor, to be seen in the company of Julia Dean. Naturally she'd get proposals by the hundred. Why, when she played at Salt Lake, even Brigham Young wanted to marry her, but she told him: "No, Mr. Young," she says, "I'll have a whole man or none at all." Yes, she was wise, and they was fools.

Well, it was great times all right when Julia Dean come to town, but for wild excitement and real hair-raising they was nothing could match the bull and bear fights. They'd have them of a Sunday at the little plaza on State Street back of Ham and Hildreth's livery stable, in the bull-pen there.

Of course the men would bet on these fights, and thousands would go to see them; and when the bull and the bear would get to going good, goring and stamping and roaring and chawing and clawing and drawing blood, the people would get so excited that they'd bellow and roar louder than the animals. You could hear the men roaring clear acrost the flat, and the shrieks and screams of the Mexican women and the women of the town. My, oh my, what times they was!

I only saw one bull and bear fight, in the fall of '56, and that was the last we had, for by then the people was getting sobered down from the first wild days; they wouldn't allow these fights because they was so hideous, you know. So after that the men had no more bull and bear fights to risk their money on, but they was still plenty of ways that they could try their luck. Yes, sir, I've heard they was two hundred and forty-three faro banks operating in this town at one time with a capital all together of close on to two million dollars.

See that hole right acrost Main Street just cater-cornered to where we're sitting? Well, sir, that's all that's left of the greatest gambling house in all the Southern Mines—the Long Tom. It was Teen Duchow and Jack White jumped the ground and mined it out after the place burnt, along about '67. This Jack White, he was one of the regular gamblers there, and he knew that the gambling business had got so poor by then that the Mitchell brothers, who owned the place, they wouldn't build again. So they's been nothing but a hole there ever since.

But along in the fifties, say, that was a place to see! It was a big hall that run along the south side of Jackson Street from Main clean through to Broadway, with a door at each end. They was a string of tables along each side and an aisle between, straight through the building—twenty-four tables, two rows of them, twelve in a row, and a game going on at each one a good part of the time. In the evenings it was lighted by three big whale-oil lamps—bowls as big as a water bucket swung from the beams above the aisle, just higher than a man's head. They had wicks two inches thick and they made the place as bright as day.

To keep the house in order they had two doormen, one at each door, and two floormen inside, patrolling up and down the aisles. Anyone that come to the door the doorman would ask if he wanted to gamble or just to look on and see the sights. If he just wanted to see, it was: "All right, go ahead." But if he wanted to play, the doorkeeper would tell him: "Go over there to one of the floormen, and he'll show you to a table." So the fellow would go to the floorman and tell him what game he wanted and the floorman would find a place for him.

Of course, in them days, pretty near all the fellows that gambled had guns in their belts, and these floormen carried a big gun on each hip. They was the judges to settle disputes. The gamblers, you know, they wouldn't tolerate cheating from nobody. The minute they discovered that a man was cheating, the game was going to end right there. If the dispute got hot, and it begun to look like trouble, the floormen would pull out their guns and "bang" would go this light, and "bang" would go that light, and "bang" would go the other light, and the whole place would be dark.

At the same time the doormen would lock the doors. Then the floormen would take dark lanterns that would just throw a beam like a flashlight—they would take one of these lanterns in one hand and a gun in the other and would go to the table where the dispute was and find out what the trouble was about. If anyone was cheating, they would inquire: "How much money did you take by this fraud? How much did you win on that hand?" Maybe it would be fifty or a hundred dollars. "Well," they'd order him, "donate that money back to the men here that you took it from. Now if you people can go on peaceably with your game, all right; if not, leave the table and get out." But the fellow that was caught cheating always had to pay back before they'd let him go.

Then the floormen would rig up new lights and the games would go on as usual; and they *was* games, too. Often they'd be from fifty to a hundred thousand dollars on the tables there at once, and nearly all in gold—eagles and double-eagles and big fifty-dollar slugs, and sometimes raw gold dust.

Yes sir, many's the day's hard earnings passed over them tables from horny hands to soft ones. Why, they say the money changed hands so fast in the Long Tom that in the course of an evening a new-minted slug would get wore plumb smooth.

The sharpest gambler there in the Long Tom was Lou Alverson; he was number one. Then they was this Jack White, and Ad Pence, and Doc Johns—he was a professional gambler and a comic— and then Charlie Karp, the fan-tan man, and John Milton Strain, the fellow that found the thirty-pound nugget, and Gove'nor Hobbs. The last time I see the Gove'nor, poor devil, he was squirting sody water down at Oakdale, and he made me a milk shake. But they was still some sporting blood in his veins, for he says to me: "I been running to hard luck lately," he says, "but I'll shake with you for the price of that drink, double or none!"

These fellows, you see, they run the games themselves; the house just rented the tables and sold the drinks and the cards. Now you take, for instance, if I was dealing a game of monte, and wasn't having good luck, I might blame it onto the cards, and I'd buy a

new deck to change my luck; and cast-off cards would pile up on
the floor so you was wading through them by midnight.

Then in the morning they'd sweep the place out and us little
tikes would find two-and-a-half and five-dollar gold pieces, and
silver, just scads of it, in the sweepings, because money that was
dropped, they'd never stoop to pick it up. That was beneath
their dignity, because gold was so plentiful, you see. And sometimes a gambler would come to the door and stick his hand in
his pocket, and without looking to see what he had—gold or silver
or what—he'd fling a handful of it into the street to see the small
boys scramble.

Now I'm going to tell you something that happened in the
Long Tom that will show you what these fellows was like.

It was one day in the rainy winter of '54 and '55, and too wet
to work in the mines, so the boys begun to wander in early down
at the Long Tom. By noon all the tables was full and the gambling got more exciting as the day wore on. Some of the boys set
right there at the tables from morning through all the day and on
into the evening, without stopping except to take on a drink or to
make room for more.

If you once get the gambling fever, you know, in a place like
that, the longer you keep at it, the higher the fever gets. That
fever's catching and it'll spread through a crowd like any other
fever. So monte, faro, seven-up, and the different brands of
poker got too slow for some, and they begun laying bets on any
chance that offered. At some of the tables they was betting on
the turn of a card, and they was one crowd having a spitting
tournament at the stove. Then they was some fellows betting which
of two flies on the wall would move first, and others at the door
laying bets whether or not the next man to come in would be Irish.
But the greatest bet in betting history was laid that night by
young Ad Pence. An inspiration it was, no less.

"Boys," says Ad, pounding on the bar to get the attention of
the crowd, "Boys," says he, "luck's been agin me so far, but I've
got five hundred here that says I've a louse that can beat, in a fair
race, any louse that ever cut his teeth on any miner's hide."

He'd caught a good lively one and held him up for all the boys
to see.

"I say this louse is the champeen," says Ad, "for I've been

chasing him around my carcass for a week and I've only just caught up with him. Five hundred backs him against all comers."

Well, at that all the games stopped short, and everybody crowded up to the bar where Ad was showing off this champeen louse. But none of the boys would admit that he kept this kind of stock and it begun to look as though nobody was going to take the bet. Then a stranger, a big Irishman with a red beard, come elbowing his way through the crowd and up to the bar where Ad was standing.

"Will ye let me have a look at that louse?" he says.

So Ad held it out and the stranger squinted at it from one side and then from the other. "A dainty craycher indade he is," says he, "but I think he's no racer. His belly's too low and his legs are too short by a long ways. Now wait just a bit and I'll have something to show ye."

So the stranger put his hand inside his shirt, and scrabbled around in there for a minute, and when he pulled it out again, between his thumb and finger he held a struggling louse.

"Me boy," he says, "your five hundred is as good as gone. But before I take it from ye, I want ye to have a good look at *this* louse. Ye'll never see the likes of him again. Ye say yours is the champeen, but ye've only had him a wake, and he has not so much as a name. I say he's but a mongrel. Now *this* one is the greatest racing louse in all the world, and he has the most distinguished pedigray that ever a louse did boast. And I don't want to be taking your money under any false pretenses, so I'm going to tell ye his history, and when ye've heard it, if ye want to withdraw, I'll freely let ye do so.

"Just before me old grandfather died, back in Ireland, he called me to his bedside and he said to me: 'Grandson,' says he, 'I'm a pore man. I've no money to lave ye, nor any property. But there's wan threasure I have, Grandson,' says the old man, 'Katie, the finest little seam squirrel in all of Ireland, and a direct discindent of one that fed on Saint Patrick.

" 'Take her, Grandson,' says he, 'kape good care of her and fade her well, and she'll surely bring ye luck.'

"Now, me boy, this louse ye see here is Larry, Katie's great-great-great-grandson, and the blood of Saint Patrick himself runs in his veins, so he's bound to bring me luck. And to show the faith I have in him and in Holy Saint Patrick, bejayziz, I'll lay a thousand to that five hundred ye bet on yer mongrel louse! Now, do ye still want to make the bet?"

"I do," says Ad. "Your louse may be good, but I know what mine can do from long chasing of him, and my bet on him still stands."

So Ad and the stranger placed their stakes with Doc Johns, and side betting begun in the crowd.

"There can be no race without a racetrack," says the stranger, and he calls to the bartender. "Bring us a plate," he says. "Now, boys, the middle's the start, the edge is the goal, and the first little pants rabbit over the rim is the winner."

So the bartender brought the plate, and the stranger felt of it. "No louse," says he, "would ever set a good pace on this cold plate. Let's hate it up a bit, and then you'll see them kick up their heels and run."

So they heated the plate piping hot over the stove and set it on a table where all could see. And when Doc Johns counted off: "One, two, three, go!" each man dropped his louse in the middle of the plate and they were off, a-scrambling and a-jumping because it was so hot, you know. The boys was cheering and yelling and standing on chairs to see, and laying bets right and left.

Well, neck and neck it was at the start acrost the bottom of the plate, but Ad's louse pulled ahead a bit and he was the first to reach the rise of the rim. Then come the last hard pull for the edge. He started up the rise, but when he got about half-way up he lost his footing on the slippery rim and slid down again. So he backed up and he took another run for it, and got up a little further, but again he slid back. He was a game one, that louse was. He tried it again and again, but he couldn't quite make it. No sir, it was on that last hard pull up the rim of the plate that the blood of Saint Patrick begun to tell, for Larry, the stranger's lucky louse, he started up slow and careful, and he kept on a-pulling and a-scrambling and up and up he went and *over* the edge to victory and into his master's hand. A hero he was, for sure!

The fellows jumped down from the tables then and Jack White, he says: "Three cheers for Larry and the blood of Saint Patrick!" So the boys roared out the three cheers. And they *was* cheers too, for them young fellows didn't have no colds, nor consumption neither.

Well, then Doc Johns paid over the fifteen hundred dollars to the stranger, and Ad went up to shake his hand. "Stranger," he says, "it was a fair race, and the best louse won. The money's yours and I don't begrudge it to you. But I've one request to make of you, stranger, and if you'll grant it, I'll be forever grateful."

"And what may that be?" says the stranger.

"Just let me borrow Larry till tomorrow," says Ad.

"But what for?" says the stranger. "Why might ye be wanting to borrow me pet?"

"Why, man!" says Ad, "I want to improve my breed!"

HENRY YELVINGTON

THE PHANTOM FENCE RIDER OF SAN MIGUEL

This is a good story about a western good ghost who haunted only those who deserved it, and only when they deserved it, and kept strictly to himself the rest of the time. And I hope you don't feel, as some people do, that ghosts should stick to haunting houses exclusively. (From *Ghost Lore*, The Naylor Company.)

ANYONE who has ever been in the San Miguel country, down in McMullen County, Texas, especially up the San Miguel from where the Tilden road crosses the stream on to the old schoolhouse and graveyard which are on a hill out in a pasture, can easily imagine the narrative Old John Piedra tells of the phantom fence rider. This strip of country was some of the wildest of the old frontier during open range days and is still cattle country. A ranch house every four or five miles, except right near where the road crosses the stream, is all the sign of habitation you find there today. The valley is fertile, but narrow, and most of the inhabitants being ranchmen, very little farming is done. The San Miguel crossing is thirty-five miles from a railroad and there is no paving of any kind in McMullen County. In fact, there are only a few hundred votes in the entire county. The nature of the country is mostly rough and brushy hills with now and then a fertile valley.

16

Southward on to Tilden, the village county seat, some twenty miles away, it is the same kind of country and then going on south from Tilden one jumps into the wildest of the wild southwest, for there is nothing except hills and brush, coyotes and cattle, a panther now and then, some deer, houses about ten miles apart and graves marked by piles of stone or crosses. There are many graves too, not marked at all, and many more persons have been buried there whose graves have long been lost, for they were those without the law, who lived by their guns and when caught marauding or stealing cattle, were shot, and buried where they fell, unless they happened to be quicker than the rangers or posses of ranchmen who trailed them.

Coming on back to the San Miguel and the graveyard there where pioneers and members of their families are buried decently, let us consider its location. You leave the Tilden road about a mile before you reach the crossing, going south, and turn to the right at Tom Franklin's ranch house. Then you go a quarter mile or so, and go over a cattle guard, after which you pass the Henry ranch home, leaving it to the right. Then on for some distance through brush, you come suddenly to about two acres of fenced grounds. In the south side of the enclosure stands the schoolhouse where some five or six children of ranchmen get the beginning of their learning for a few months each year. In the northeast corner of the enclosure on the side of the hill, and fenced to itself, is the graveyard. Markers on the graves show that the first persons were buried in the plot some sixty years ago. People who have camped in the schoolhouse at nights, for it is the only shelter a person has in that locality unless they go to some ranch house, claim that many kinds of weird sounds come from the vicinity of the graveyard and that there is a constant knocking, and also murmuring as of distant voices. This present schoolhouse, which is a one-room affair, has not been there for more than twenty years, for the old building was burned. It stood nearer the graveyard. In fact, the back door was within fifty feet of the graveyard fence.

Old John Piedra is much older than the oldest grave in the graveyard. He went into that country in the early days, when the war of the open range and fencing was on in earnest. He was a rough and tumble cowboy who knew how to get the wildest cattle out of the thickets and was much in demand because of his ability

in that line. Old John speaks English brokenly, but I am going
to try and tell of the phantom fence rider as nearly in his words
as I possibly can.

"In dem days I talk to you about, not many fences. Just few,"
said John. "I work then most time south from Oakville, but I
have to go up on San Miguel to get some horses a feller buy from
ranchman there and send me for. It take all day to ride from
Oakville to Tilden road crossing. When I get to crossing it is
get dark and I start ride on to ranch house which is about seven
miles, I guess, up San Miguel. It been cloudy all day and thunder
some. Before I get mile away from crossing it start rain. I don't
have my slicker, only just my duck jacket and chaps. I think sure
I get wet. Before it start rain hard I come to graveyard and see
schoolhouse. I say to myself, maybe so I sleep here tonight and
go on to ranch tomorrow, I don't want get wet. I find schoolhouse
door close, but easy to open. I find good grass right by, to stake
my horse. I done water him at river crossing. I make camp in
schoolhouse. Pretty soon it begin rain hard.

"All night he rain, sometimes hard, sometimes not too hard.
All night, you bet, I stay wake. I can sleep not good. All kinds
noises. When I start sleep I hear somebody walk on floor. I look,
nobody there. I get near sleep again, somebody knock. I say 'who
you are, what you want, come in.' Nobody answer, nobody come.
Lightning flashes, I look out I don't see nothing but graves, but
maybe so look like they move. I say to myself 'graves he can't
move, dead mans, he don't hurt nobody.' I try go sleep. My horse
he snort like he see something. I look out window again, see just
graves. By golly I don't sleep. For sure I am glad when daylight
come.

"In morning it still rain. I don't be in big hurry, so I say I wait
till he quit raining. I sit in schoolhouse door and watch rain and
see my horse he eat grass. By golly, plenty good grass there. On
south of schoolhouse run string of barbed wire fence. Not many
fences in that time, but these fellow I go to for horses, we have
ranch fenced. This fence he come close to schoolhouse. Maybe so
fifty feet, maybe so sixty. Maybe so about ten o'clock I look down
fence I see man coming horseback. He ride big bay horse. He have
one wide black hat, black coat and chaps. He don't have on slicker.
He have Winchester in scabbard on saddle and romal hang on
horn of saddle. I see hatchet handle stick out of romal. I know he

fence rider. I think, maybe so this man one of dem fellows I go see for horses for that his pasture fence. When I get close I say 'hello.' He don't stop and don't look and don't say nothing. I say loud 'hello Compadre.' He just ride on. I say 'what hell the matter with you,' but he just ride on. I think maybe so this fellow he can't hear no time, poor fellow. He look all time at ground, just like he look for tracks.

"Maybe one hour, maybe more, I see this fellow he come back up fence line. I walk out to fence in rain, but it not rain too hard now, think I stop him. But when I look again this fellow he on my side of the fence. I think 'damn, how you get this side.' Then I think fence down here he ride across. But this fellow he not come back to schoolhouse. He turn and ride to graveyard and go down under hill. Last I see is top of his hat. I don't think nothing only this fellow he darn fool ride in rain, poor fellow he don't can hear.

"In maybe so two hours," continued John, "he stop raining. I saddle up horse and ride on to ranch house. When I get to house I find them mens all there. Old man and his five boys. They say 'rain too much, we don't work today.' I say 'that fence rider, he work in rain, what for?' The old mans he say 'what hell fence rider you talk about?'

" 'Don't you got fence rider these morning ride big bay horse, wear black hat, ride east by your fence and come back, come through gap, then ride down under hill by graveyard and go somewhere else?'

"When I say this these old man and all his boys they get excite. 'When you see that? How long he gone before he come back?' I think maybe so I got no business talk, I get trouble for somebody. But I done tell so I tell all I know about me not can sleep in schoolhouse and wait there this morning and see this fellow. This old mans he say 'get your guns, boys. We ride queeck.' He say to me 'you wait here' and all them fellows they get guns and saddle horses and ride fast back down fence line. He leave me at house, nobody else there. I think 'what in hell he matter with this country. Everybody go crazy. One mans can't hear, other mans no tell you nothing, just ran off.'

"I go in house and make cafe, and eat it somethings I find there. I wait there long time. When sun go down again, here come those fellow and have three Mexicans with hands tied behind, all riding on horses. I think 'what hell is thees?' "

John rolled a cigarette and then continued his narrative. "Them fellows they bring back all cow thieves. Old mans he tell me they take all to Oakville next day when go with horses. But me, I can't tell how he know cow thieves because this fellow ride fence. He not with these three fellows, he bring in. I ask old mans, 'is this fellow I see cow thief too an he get away?'

" 'Hell no,' say old mans, 'that fellow you see, he been dead ten years. He ghost.' I say 'damn, what hell all this?'

"Old mans he tell me fellow's name, I forget what it is. He say this fellow fence rider on ranch long time, ever since first build fence. He say ten years ago this fellow he ride fence, run across cow thieves cut fence and steal cattle and cow thieves he kill him. This man he buried down under hill in this graveyard. This fence rider, damn good fence rider, say old man and I say 'you betcher.' Old man say 'every time cow thieves cut fence this fence rider he ride down to where cut, then come back and go in grave. You tell us how long he gone, and what direction he go, and that how we know about where cow thieves cut fence. We go there find place, trail easy in mud and catch these fellows with one hundred five steers down near Frio.'

"You betcher," concluded Old John, "these San Miguel country damn funny country. Me I don't like him."

MILLIONAIRES

As a one-time prospector, Mark Twain knew well the hardship, humor and heartbreak of mining, and mining "paper profits." Perhaps only to the outsider was there any humor in the evanescent status in which the author found himself—a millionaire for ten days. (From *Roughing It*, Harpers, 1872.)

I NOW come to a curious episode—the most curious, I think, that had yet accented my slothful, valueless, heedless career. Out of a hillside toward the upper end of the town, projected a wall of reddish-looking quartz croppings, the exposed comb of a silver-bearing ledge that extended deep down into the earth, of course. It was owned by a company entitled the "Wide West." There was a shaft sixty or seventy feet deep on the under side of the croppings, and everybody was acquainted with the rock that came from it—and tolerably rich rock it was, too, but nothing extraordinary. I will remark here, that although to the inexperienced stranger all the quartz of a particular "district" looks about alike, an old resident of the camp can take a glance at a mixed pile of rock, separate the fragments and tell you which mine each came from, as easily as a confectioner can separate and classify the various kinds and qualities of candy in a mixed heap of the article.

All at once the town was thrown into a state of extraordinary excitement. In mining parlance the Wide West had "struck it rich!" Everybody went to see the new developments, and for some days there was such a crowd of people about the Wide West shaft that a stranger would have supposed there was a mass-meeting in session there. No other topic was discussed but the rich strike, and nobody thought or dreamed about anything else. Every man brought away a specimen, ground it up in a hand-mortar, washed it out in his horn spoon, and glared speechless upon the marvelous result. It was not hard rock, but black, decomposed stuff which could be crumbled in the hand like a baked potato, and when spread out on a paper exhibited a thick sprinkling of gold and particles of "native" silver. Higbie brought a handful to the cabin, and when he had washed it out his amazement was beyond description. Wide West stock soared skyward. It was said that repeated offers had been made for it at a thousand dollars a foot, and promptly refused. We have all had the "blues"—the mere skyblues—but mine were indigo, now—because I did not own in the Wide West. The world seemed hollow to me, and existence a grief. I lost my appetite, and ceased to take an interest in anything. Still I had to stay, and listen to other people's rejoicings, because I had no money to get out of the camp with.

The Wide West company put a stop to the carrying away of "specimens," and well they might, for every handful of the ore was worth a sum of some consequence. To show the exceeding value of the ore, I will remark that a sixteen-hundred-pound parcel of it was sold, just as it lay, at the mouth of the shaft, at *one dollar a pound*; and the man who bought it "packed" it on mules a hundred and fifty or two hundred miles, over the mountains, to San Francisco, satisfied that it would yield at a rate that would richly compensate him for his trouble. The Wide West people also commanded their foreman to refuse any but their own operatives permission to enter the mine at any time or for any purpose. I kept up my "blue" meditations and Higbie kept up a deal of thinking, too, but of a different sort. He puzzled over the "rock," examined it with a glass, inspected it in different lights and from different points of view, and after each experiment delivered himself, in soliloquy, of one and the same unvarying opinion in the same unvarying formula:

"It is *not* Wide West rock!"

He said once or twice that he meant to have a look into the Wide West shaft if he got shot for it. I was wretched, and did not care whether he got a look into it or not. He failed that day, and tried again at night; failed again; got up at dawn and tried, and failed again. Then he lay in ambush in the sage-brush hour after hour, waiting for the two or three hands to adjourn to the shade of a boulder for dinner; made a start once, but was premature— one of the men came back for something; tried it again, but when almost at the mouth of the shaft, another of the men rose up from behind the boulder as if to reconnoitre, and he dropped on the ground and lay quiet; presently he crawled on his hands and knees to the mouth of the shaft, gave a quick glance around, then seized the rope and slid down the shaft. He disappeared in the gloom of a "side drift" just as a head appeared in the mouth of the shaft and somebody shouted "Hello!"—which he did not answer. He was not disturbed any more. An hour later he entered the cabin, hot, red, and ready to burst with smothered excitement, and exclaimed in a stage whisper:

"I knew it! We are rich! It's A BLIND LEAD!"

I thought the very earth reeled under me. Doubt—conviction —doubt again—exultation—hope, amazement, belief, unbelief— every emotion imaginable swept in wild procession through my heart and brain, and I could not speak a word. After a moment or two of this mental fury, I shook myself to rights, and said:

"Say it again!"

"It's a blind lead!"

"Cal, let's—let's burn the house—or kill somebody! Let's get out where there's room to hurrah! But what is the use? It is a hundred times too good to be true."

"It's a blind lead for a million!—hanging wall—foot wall— clay casings—everything complete!" He swung his hat and gave three cheers, and I cast doubt to the winds and chimed in with a will. For I was worth a million dollars, and did not care "whether school kept or not!"

But perhaps I ought to explain. A "blind lead" is a lead or ledge that does not "crop out" above the surface. A miner does not know where to look for such leads, but they are often stumbled upon by accident in the course of driving a tunnel or sinking a shaft. Higbie knew the Wide West rock perfectly well, and the more he had examined the new developments the more he was satisfied that the ore could not have come from the Wide West vein. And so had it occurred to him alone, of all the camp, that there was a

blind lead down in the shaft, and that even the Wide West people
themselves did not suspect it. He was right. When he went down
the shaft, he found that the blind lead held its independent way
through the Wide West vein, cutting it diagonally, and that it
was inclosed in its own well-defined casing-rocks and clay. Hence
it was public property. Both leads being perfectly well defined,
it was easy for any miner to see which one belonged to the Wide
West and which did not.

We thought it well to have a strong friend, and therefore
we brought the foreman of the Wide West to our cabin that
night and revealed the great surprise to him. Higbie said:

"We are going to take possession of this blind lead, record it
and establish ownership, and then forbid the Wide West company
to take out any more of the rock. You cannot help your company
in this matter—nobody can help them. I will go into the shaft
with you and prove to your entire satisfaction that it *is* a blind
lead. Now we propose to take you in with us, and claim the blind
lead in our three names. What do you say?"

What could a man say who had an opportunity to simply
stretch forth his hand and take possession of a fortune without
risk of any kind and without wronging any one or attaching the
least taint of dishonor to his name? He could only say, "Agreed."

The notice was put up that night, and duly spread upon the
recorder's books before ten o'clock. We claimed two hundred feet
each—six hundred feet in all—the smallest and compactest organization in the district, and the easiest to manage.

No one can be so thoughtless as to suppose that we slept that
night. Higbie and I went to bed at midnight, but it was only to
lie broad awake and think, dream, scheme. The floorless, tumble-
down cabin was a palace, the ragged gray blankets silk, the furniture rosewood and mahogany. Each new splendor that burst
out of my visions of the future whirled me bodily over in bed or
jerked me to a sitting posture just as if an electric battery had
been applied to me. We shot fragments of conversation back and
forth at each other. Once Higbie said:

"When are you going home—to the States?"

"To-morrow!"—with an evolution or two, ending with a sitting
position. "Well—no—but next month, at furthest."

"We'll go in the same steamer."

"Agreed."

A pause.

"Steamer of the 10th?"

"Yes. No, the 1st."

"All right."

Another pause.

"Where are you going to live?" said Higbie.

"San Francisco."

"That's me!"

Pause.

"Too high—too much climbing"—from Higbie.

"What is?"

"I was thinking of Russian Hill—building a house up there."

"Too much climbing? Sha'n't you keep a carriage?"

"Of course. I forgot that."

Pause.

"Cal, what kind of a house are you going to build?"

"I was thinking about that. Three-story and an attic."

"But what *kind*?"

"Well, I don't hardly know. Brick, I suppose."

"Brick—bosh."

"Why? What is your idea?"

"Brown-stone front—French plate-glass—billiard-room off the dining-room—statuary and paintings—shrubbery and two-acre grass-plat—greenhouse—iron dog on the front stoop—gray horses—landau, and a coachman with a bug on his hat!"

"By George!"

A long pause.

"Cal, when are you going to Europe?"

"Well—I hadn't thought of that. When are you?"

"In the spring."

"Going to be gone all summer?"

"All summer! I shall remain there three years."

"No—but are you in earnest?"

"Indeed I am."

"I will go along too."

"Why, of course you will."

"What part of Europe shall you go to?"

"All parts. France, England, Germany—Spain, Italy, Switzerland, Syria, Greece, Palestine, Arabia, Persia, Egypt—all over—everywhere."

"I'm agreed."

"All right."

"Won't it be a swell trip!"

"We'll spend forty or fifty thousand dollars trying to make it one, anyway."

Another long pause.

"Higbie, we owe the butcher six dollars, and he has been threatening to stop our—"

"Hang the butcher!"

"Amen."

And so it went on. By three o'clock we found it was no use, and so we got up and played cribbage and smoked pipes till sunrise. It was my week to cook. I always hated cooking—now, I abhorred it.

The news was all over town. The former excitement was great —this one was greater still. I walked the streets serene and happy. Higbie said the foreman had been offered two hundred thousand dollars for his third of the mine. I said I would like to see myself selling for any such price. My ideas were lofty. My figure was a million. Still, I honestly believe that if I had been offered it, it would have had no other effect than to make me hold off for more.

I found abundant enjoyment in being rich. A man offered me a three-hundred-dollar horse, and wanted to take my simple, unindorsed note for it. That brought the most realizing sense I had yet had that I was actually rich, beyond shadow of doubt. It was followed by numerous other evidences of a similar nature— among which I may mention the fact of the butcher leaving us a double supply of meat and saying nothing about money.

By the laws of the district, the "locators" or claimants of a ledge were obliged to do a fair and reasonable amount of work on their new property within ten days after the date of the location, or the property was forfeited, and anybody could go and seize it that chose. So we determined to go to work the next day. About the middle of the afternoon, as I was coming out of the post-office, I met a Mr. Gardiner, who told me that Captain John Nye was lying dangerously ill at his place (the "Nine-Mile Ranch"), and that he and his wife were not able to give him nearly as much care and attention as his case demanded. I said if he would wait for me a moment, I would go down and help in the sick-room. I ran to the cabin to tell Higbie. He was not there, but I left a note on the table for him, and a few minutes later I left town in Gardiner's wagon.

Captain Nye was very ill indeed, with spasmodic rheumatism. But the old gentleman was himself—which is to say, he was kind-hearted and agreeable when comfortable, but a singularly violent wildcat when things did not go well. He would be smiling along pleasantly enough, when a sudden spasm of his disease would take him and he would go out of his smile into a perfect fury. He would groan and wail and howl with the anguish, and fill up the odd chinks with the most elaborate profanity that strong convictions and a fine fancy could contrive. With fair opportunity he could swear very well and handle his adjectives with considerable judgment; but when the spasm was on him it was painful to listen to him, he was so awkward. However, I had seen him nurse a sick man himself and put up patiently with the inconveniences of the situation, and consequently I was willing that he should have full license now that his own turn had come. He could not disturb me, with all his raving and ranting, for my mind had work on hand, and it labored on diligently, night and day, whether my hands were idle or employed. I was altering and amending the plans for my house, and thinking over the propriety of having the billiard-room in the attic, instead of on the same floor with the dining-room; also, I was trying to decide between green and blue for the upholstery of the drawing-room, for, although my preference was blue, I feared it was a color that would be too easily damaged by dust and sunlight; likewise while I was content to put the coachman in a modest livery, I was uncertain about a footman—I needed one, and was even resolved to have one, but wished he could properly appear and perform his functions out of livery, for I somewhat dreaded so much show; and yet, inasmuch as my late grandfather had had a coachman and such things, but no liveries, I felt rather drawn to beat him—or beat his ghost, at any rate; I was also systematizing the European trip, and managed to get it all laid out, as to route and length of time to be devoted to it—everything, with one exception—namely, whether to cross the desert from Cairo to Jerusalem per camel, or go by sea to Beirut, and thence down through the country per caravan. Meantime I was writing to the friends at home every day, instructing them concerning all my plans and intentions, and directing them to look up a handsome homestead for my mother and agree upon a price for it against my coming, and also directing them to sell my share of the Tennessee land and tender the proceeds to the widows' and orphans' fund of the typographical union of which I had long been a member in good standing. [This Tennessee land had been in the possession of the family many years, and promised to confer high fortune upon us some day; it still promises, but in a less violent way.]

When I had been nursing the captain nine days he was somewhat better, but very feeble. During the afternoon we lifted him into a chair and gave him an alcoholic vapor bath, and then set about putting him on the bed again. We had to be exceedingly careful, for the least jar produced pain. Gardiner had his shoulders and I his legs; in an unfortunate moment I stumbled and the patient fell heavily on the bed in an agony of torture. I never heard a man swear so in my life. He raved like a maniac, and tried to snatch a revolver from the table—but I got it. He ordered me out of the house, and swore a world of oaths that he would kill me wherever he caught me when he got on his feet again. It was simply a passing fury, and meant nothing. I knew he would forget it in an hour, and maybe be sorry for it, too; but it angered me a little, at the moment. So much so, indeed, that I determined to go back to Esmeralda. I thought he was able to get along alone, now, since he was on the war-path. I took supper, and as soon as the moon rose, began my nine-mile journey, on foot. Even millionaires needed no horses, in those days, for a mere nine-mile jaunt without baggage.

As I "raised the hill" overlooking the town, it lacked fifteen minutes of twelve. I glanced at the hill over beyond the cañon, and in the bright moonlight saw what appeared to be about half the population of the village massed on and around the Wide West croppings. My heart gave an exulting bound, and I said to myself, "They have made a new strike to-night—and struck it richer than ever, no doubt." I started over there, but gave it up. I said the "strike" would keep, and I had climbed hills enough for one night. I went on down through the town, and as I was passing a little German bakery, a woman ran out and begged me to come in and help her. She said her husband had a fit. I went in, and judged she was right—he appeared to have a hundred of them, compressed into one. Two Germans were there, trying to hold him, and not making much of a success of it. I ran up the street half a block or so and routed out a sleeping doctor, brought him down half dressed, and we four wrestled with the maniac, and doctored, drenched and bled him, for more than an hour, and the poor German woman did the crying. He grew quiet, now, and the doctor and I withdrew and left him to his friends.

It was a little after one o'clock. As I entered the cabin door, tired but jolly, the dingy light of a tallow candle revealed Higbie, sitting by the pine table gazing stupidly at my note, which he held in his fingers, and looking pale, old, and haggard. I halted, and looked at him. He looked at me, stolidly. I said:

"Higbie, what—what is it?"

"We're ruined—we didn't do the work—THE BLIND LEAD'S RELOCATED!"

It was enough. I sat down sick, grieved—broken-hearted, indeed. A minute before, I was rich and brimful of vanity; I was a pauper now, and very meek. We sat still an hour, busy with thought, busy with vain and useless upbraidings, busy with "Why *didn't* I do this, and why *didn't* I do that," but neither spoke a word. Then we dropped into mutual explanations, and the mystery was cleared away. It came out that Higbie had depended on me, as I had on him, and as both of us had on the foreman. The folly of it! It was the first time that ever staid and steadfast Higbie had left an important matter to chance or failed to be true to his full share of a responsibility.

But he had never seen my note till this moment, and this moment was the first time he had been in the cabin since the day he had seen me last. He, also, had left a note for me, on that same fatal afternoon—had ridden up on horseback, and looked through the window, and being in a hurry and not seeing me, had tossed the note into the cabin through a broken pane. Here it was, on the floor, where it had remained undisturbed for nine days:

Don't fail to do the work before the ten days expire. W. has passed through and given me notice. I am to join him at Mono Lake, and we shall go on from there to-night. He says he will find it this time, sure.

CAL.

"W." meant Whiteman, of course. That thrice accursed "cement"!

That was the way of it. An old miner, like Higbie, could no more withstand the fascination of a mysterious mining excitement like this "cement" foolishness, than he could refrain from eating when he was famishing. Higbie had been dreaming about the marvelous cement for months; and now, against his better judgment he had gone off and "taken the chances" on my keeping secure a mine worth a million undiscovered cement veins. They had not been followed this time. His riding out of town in broad daylight was such a commonplace thing to do that it had not attracted any attention. He said they prosecuted their search in the fastnesses of the mountains during nine days, without success; they could not find the cement. Then a ghastly fear came over him that something might have happened to prevent the doing of the necessary work to hold the blind lead (though indeed he thought such a thing hardly possible) and forthwith he started home with all speed. He would have reached Esmeralda in time, but his horse broke down and he had to walk a great part of the distance. And so it happened that as he came into Esmeralda by one road, I entered it by another. His was the superior energy, however, for he went straight to the Wide West, instead of turning aside as I had done —and he arrived there about five or ten minutes too late! The "notice" was already up, the "relocation" of our mine completed beyond recall, and the crowd rapidly dispersing. He learned some facts before he left the ground. The foreman had not been seen about the streets since the night we had located the mine—a telegram had called him to California on a matter of life and death, it was said. At any rate he had done no work and the watchful eyes of the community were taking note of the fact. At midnight of this woeful tenth day, the ledge would be "relocatable," and by eleven o'clock the hill was black with men prepared to do the relocating. That was the crowd I had seen when I fancied a new "strike" had been made—idiot that I was. [We three had the same right to relocate the lead that other people had, provided we were quick enough.] As midnight was announced, fourteen men, duly armed and ready to back their proceedings, put up their "notice" and proclaimed their ownership of the blind lead, under the new name of the "Johnson." But A. D. Allen, our partner (the foreman), put in a sudden appearance about that time, with a cocked revolver in his hand, and said his name must be added to the list, or he would "thin out the Johnson company some." He was a manly, splendid, determined fellow, and known to be as good as his word, and therefore a compromise was effected.

They put in his name for a hundred feet, reserving to themselves the customary two hundred feet each. Such was the history of the night's events, as Higbie gathered from a friend on the way home.

Higbie and I cleared out on a new mining excitement the next morning, glad to get away from the scene of our sufferings, and after a month or two of hardship and disappointment, returned to Esmeralda once more. Then we learned that the Wide West and the Johnson companies had consolidated; that the stock, thus united, comprised five thousand feet, or shares; that the foreman, apprehending tiresome litigation, and considering such a huge concern unwieldy, had sold his hundred feet for ninety thousand dollars in gold and gone home to the states to enjoy it. If the stock was worth such a gallant figure, with five thousand shares in the corporation, it makes me dizzy to think what it would have been worth with only our original six hundred in it. It was the difference between six hundred men owning a house and five thousand owning it. We would have been millionaires if we had only worked with pick and spade one little day on our property and so secured our ownership!

It reads like a wild fancy sketch, but the evidence of many witnesses, and likewise that of the official records of Esmeralda District, is easily obtainable in proof that it is a true history. I can always have it to say that I was absolutely and unquestionably worth a million dollars, once, for ten days.

A year ago my esteemed and in every way estimable old millionaire partner, Higbie, wrote me from an obscure little mining-camp in California that after nine or ten years of buffetings and hard striving, he was at last in a position where he could command twenty-five hundred dollars, and said he meant to go into the fruit business in a modest way. How such a thought would have insulted him the night we lay in our cabin planning European trips and brownstone houses on Russian Hill!

"SPEAKIN' OF COWPUNCHERS"

Charles M. Russell, artist and writer, tells us something about cowmen and quotes the disreputable anecdote about the eastern girl who asked her mother whether cowboys ate grass. "No, dear," said the old lady, "they're part human." Despite the irreverence of this anecdote, Russell knew and loved the West and was in turn loved by all who knew him and his work. (From *Trails Plowed Under*, Doubleday, Doran, 1903.)

SPEAKIN' of cowpunchers," says Rawhide Rawlins, "I'm glad to see in the last few years that them that know the business have been writin' about 'em. It begin to look like they'd be wiped out without a history. Up to a few years ago there's mighty little known about cows and cow people. It was sure amusin' to read some of them old stories about cowpunchin'. You'd think a puncher growed horns an' was haired over.

"It put me in mind of the eastern girl that asked her mother: 'Ma,' says she, 'do cowboys eat grass?' 'No, dear,' says the old lady, 'they're part human.' An' I don't know but the old gal had 'em sized up right. If they are human they're a separate species. I'm talkin' about the old-time ones, before the country's strung with wire an' nesters had grabbed all the water, an' a cowpuncher's home was big. It wasn't where he took his hat off, but where he spread his blankets. He ranged from Mexico to the Big Bow River of the north, an' from where the trees get scarce in the east to the old Pacific. He don't need no iron hoss, but covers his country on one that eats grass an' wears hair. All the tools he needed was saddle, bridle, quirt, hackamore, an' rawhide riatta or seagrass rope; that covered his hoss.

"The puncher himself was rigged, startin' at the top, with a good hat—not one of the floppy kind you see in the pictures, with the rim turned up in front. The top-cover he wears holds its shape an' was made to protect his face from the weather: maybe to hold it on, he wore a buckskin string under the chin or back of the head. Round his neck a big silk handkerchief, tied loose, an' in the drag of a trail herd it was drawn over the face to the eyes, hold-up fashion, to protect the nose an' throat from dust. In old times, a leather blab or mask was used the same. Coat, vest, an' shirt suits his own taste. Maybe he'd wear California pants, light buckskin in color, with large brown plaid, sometimes foxed, or what you'd call reinforced with buck or antelope skin. Over these came his chaparejos or leggin's. His feet were covered with good high-heeled boots, finished off with steel spurs of Spanish pattern. His weapon's usually a forty-five Colt's six-gun, which is packed in a belt, swingin' a little below his right hip. Sometimes a Winchester in a scabbard, slung to his saddle under his stirrup-leather, either right or left side, but generally left, stock forward, lock down, as his rope hangs at his saddle-fork on the right.

"By all I can find out from old, gray-headed punchers, the cow business started in California, an' the Spaniards were the first to burn marks on their cattle an' hosses, an' use the rope. Then men from the States drifted west to Texas, pickin' up the brandin' iron an' lass-rope, an' the business spread north, east, an' west, till the spotted longhorns walked in every trail marked out by their brown cousins, the buffalo.

"Texas an' California, bein' the startin' places, made two species of cowpunchers; those west of the Rockies rangin' north, usin' centerfire or single-cinch saddles, with high fork an' cantle; packed a sixty or sixty-five foot rawhide rope, an' swung a big loop. These cow people were generally strong on pretty, usin' plenty of hoss jewelry, silver-mounted spurs, bits, an' conchas; instead of a quirt, used a romal, or quirt braided to the end of the reins. Their saddles were full-stamped, with from twenty-four to twenty-eight-inch eagle-bill tapaderos. Their chaparejos were made of fur or hair, either bear, angora goat, or hair sealskin. These fellows were sure fancy, an' called themselves buccaroos, coming from the Spanish word, *vaquero*.

"The cowpuncher east of the Rockies originated in Texas and ranged north to the Big Bow. He wasn't so much for pretty; his saddle was low horn, rimfire, or double-cinch; sometimes 'macheer.' Their rope was seldom over forty feet, for being a good deal in a brush country, they were forced to swing a small loop. These men generally tied, instead of taking their dallie-welts, or wrapping their rope around the saddle horn. Their chaparejos were made of heavy bullhide, to protect the leg from brush an' thorns, with hog-snout tapaderos.

"Cowpunchers were mighty particular about their rig, an' in all the camps you'd find a fashion leader. From a cowpuncher's idea, these fellers was sure good to look at, an' I tell you right now, there ain't no prettier sight for my eyes than one of those good-lookin', long-backed cowpunchers, sittin' up on a high-forked, full-stamped California saddle with a live hoss between his legs.

"Of course a good many of these fancy men were more ornamental than useful, but one of the best cow-hands I ever knew belonged to this class. Down on the Gray Bull, he went under the name of Mason, but most punchers called him Pretty Shadow. This sounds like an Injun name, but it ain't. It comes from a habit some punchers has of ridin' along, lookin' at their shadows. Lookin' glasses are scarce in cow outfits, so the only chance for these pretty boys to admire themselves is on bright, sunshiny days. Mason's one of these kind that doesn't get much pleasure out of life in cloudy weather. His hat was the best; his boots was made to order, with extra long heels. He rode a center-fire, full-stamped saddle, with twenty-eight-inch tapaderos; bearskin ancaroes, or saddle pockets; his chaparejos were of the same skin. He packed a sixty-five-foot rawhide. His spurs an' bit were silver inlaid, the last bein' a Spanish spade. But the gaudiest part of his regalia was his gun. It's a forty-five Colt's, silverplated an' chased with gold. Her handle is pearl, with a bull's head carved on.

"When the sun hits Mason with all this silver on, he blazes up like some big piece of jewelry. You could see him for miles when he's ridin' high country. Barrin' Mexicans, he's the fanciest cow dog I ever see, an' don't think he don't savvy the cow. He knows what she says to her calf. Of course there wasn't many of his stripe. All punchers liked good rigs, but plainer; an' as most punchers 're fond of gamblin' an' spend their spare time at stud poker or monte, they can't tell what kind of a rig they'll be ridin' the next day. I've seen many a good rig lost over a blanket. It depends how lucky the cards fall what kind of a rig a man's ridin'.

"I'm talkin' about old times, when cowmen were in their glory. They lived different, talked different, an' had different ways. No matter where you met him, or how he's rigged, if you'd watch him close he'd do something that would tip his hand. I had a little experience back in '83 that'll show what I'm gettin' at.

"I was winterin' in Cheyenne. One night a stranger stakes me to buck the bank. I get off lucky an' cash in fifteen hundred dollars. Of course I cut the money in two with my friend, but it leaves me with the biggest roll I ever packed. All this wealth makes Cheyenne look small, an' I begin longin' for bigger camps, so I drift for Chicago. The minute I hit the burg, I shed my cow garments an' get into white man's harness. A hard hat, boiled shirt, laced shoes—all the gearin' known to civilized man. When I put on all this rig, I sure look human; that is, I think so. But them short-horns know me, an' by the way they trim that roll, it looks like somebody's pinned a card on my back with the word EASY in big letters. I ain't been there a week till my roll don't need no string around it, an' I start thinkin' about home. One evenin' I throw in with the friendliest feller I ever met. It was at the bar of the hotel where I'm camped. I don't just remember how we got acquainted, but after about fifteen drinks we start holdin' hands an' seein' who could buy the most and fastest. I remember him tellin' the barslave not to take my money, 'cause I'm his friend. Afterwards, I find out the reason for this good-heartedness; he wants it all an' hates to see me waste it. Finally, he starts to show me the town an' says it won't cost me a cent. Maybe he did, but I was unconscious, an' wasn't in shape to remember. Next day, when I come to, my hair's sore an' I don't know the days of the week, month, or what year it is.

"The first thing I do when I open my eyes is to look at the winders. There's no bars on 'em, an' I feel easier. I'm in a small room with two bunks. The one opposite me holds a feller that's smokin' a cigarette an' sizin' me up between whiffs while I'm dressin'. I go through myself but I'm too late. Somebody beat me to it. I'm lacin' my shoes an' thinkin' hard, when the stranger speaks:

" 'Neighbor, you're a long way from your range.'

" 'You call the turn,' says I, 'but how did you read my iron?'

" 'I didn't see a burn on you,' says he, 'an' from looks, you'll go as a slick-ear. It's your ways, while I'm layin' here, watchin' you get into your garments. Now, humans dress up an' punchers dress down. When you raised, the first thing you put on is your hat. Another thing that shows you up is you don't shed your shirt when you bed down. So next comes your vest an' coat, keepin' your hindquarters covered till you slide into your pants, an' now you're lacin' your shoes. I notice you done all of it without quittin' the blankets, like the ground's cold. I don't know what state or territory you hail from, but you've smelt sagebrush an' drank alkali. I heap savvy you. You've slept a whole lot with nothin' but sky over your head, an' there's times when that old roof leaks, but judgin' from appearances, you wouldn't mind a little open air right now.'

"This feller's my kind, an' he stakes me with enough to get back to the cow country."

AN INGÉNUE OF THE SIERRAS

The author of this tale wrote many great stories of the West. The present one was selected for this collection, first, because it is delightfully different and possesses, of all things in Western fiction, a protagonist in skirts; and second, because it is a little-known work and deserves a wider audience.

WE ALL held our breath as the coach rushed through the semi-darkness of Galloper's Ridge. The vehicle itself was only a huge lumbering shadow; its side-lights were carefully extinguished, and Yuba Bill had just politely removed from the lips of an outside passenger even the cigar with which he had been ostentatiously exhibiting his coolness. For it had been rumored that the Ramon Martinez gang of "road agents" were "laying" for us on the second grade, and would time the passage of our lights across Galloper's in order to intercept us in the "brush" beyond. If we could cross the ridge without being seen, and so get through the brush before they reached it, we were safe. If they followed, it would only be a stern chase with the odds in our favor.

The huge vehicle swayed from side to side, rolled, dipped, and plunged, but Bill kept the track, as if, in the whispered words of the Expressman, he could "feel and smell" the road he could no longer see. We knew that at times we hung perilously over the

edge of slopes that eventually dropped a thousand feet sheer
to the tops of the sugar-pines below, but we knew that Bill knew
it also. The half visible heads of the horses, drawn wedge-wise
together by the tightened reins, appeared to cleave the darkness
like a ploughshare, held between his rigid hands. Even the hoof-
beats of the six horses had fallen into a vague, monotonous, distant
roll. Then the ridge was crossed, and we plunged into the still
blacker obscurity of the brush. Rather we no longer seemed to
move—it was only the phantom night that rushed by us. The
horses might have been submerged in some swift Lethean stream;
nothing but the top of the coach and the rigid bulk of Yuba Bill
arose above them. Yet even in that awful moment our speed was
unslackened; it was as if Bill cared no longer to *guide* but only to
drive, or as if the direction of his huge machine was determined
by other hands than his. An incautious whisperer hazarded the
paralyzing suggestion of our "meeting another team." To our
great astonishment Bill overheard it; to our greater astonishment
he replied. "It 'ud be only a neck and neck race which would get
to h——ll first," he said quietly. But we were relieved—for he had
spoken! Almost simultaneously the wider turnpike began to glimmer faintly as a visible track before us; the wayside trees fell out
of line, opened up, and dropped off one after another; we were
on the broader table-land, out of danger, and apparently unper-
ceived and unpursued.

Nevertheless in the conversation that broke out again with the
relighting of the lamps, and the comments, congratulations, and
reminiscences that were freely exchanged, Yuba Bill preserved a
dissatisfied and even resentful silence. The most generous praise
of his skill and courage awoke no response. "I reckon the old man
wuz just spilin' for a fight, and is feelin' disappointed," said a
passenger. But those who knew that Bill had the true fighter's
scorn for any purely purposeless conflict were more or less concerned and watchful of him. He would drive steadily for four or
five minutes with thoughtfully knitted brows, but eyes still keenly
observant under his slouched hat, and then, relaxing his strained
attitude, would give way to a movement of impatience. "You ain't
uneasy about anything, Bill, are you?" asked the Expressman
confidentially. Bill lifted his eyes with a slightly contemptuous
surprise. "Not about anything ter *come*. It's what *hez* happened
that I don't exackly *sabe*. I don't see no signs of Ramon's gang

ever havin' been out at all, and ef they were out I don't see why they didn't go for us."

"The simple fact is that our ruse was successful," said an outside passenger. "They waited to see our lights on the ridge, and, not seeing them, missed us until we had passed. That's my opinion."

"You ain't puttin' any price on that opinion, air ye?" inquired Bill politely.

"No."

" 'Cos thar's a comic paper in 'Frisco pays for them things, and I've seen worse things in it."

"Come off, Bill," retorted the passenger, slightly nettled by the tittering of his companions. "Then what did you put out the lights for?"

"Well," returned Bill grimly, "it mout have been because I didn't keer to hev you chaps blazin' away at the first bush you *thought* you saw move in your skeer, and bringin' down their fire on us."

The explanation, though unsatisfactory, was by no means an improbable one, and we thought it better to accept it with a laugh. Bill, however, resumed his abstracted manner.

"Who got in at the Summit?" he at last asked abruptly of the Expressman.

"Derrick and Simpson of Cold Spring, and one of the 'Excelsior' boys," responded the Expressman.

"And that Pike County girl from Dow's Flat, with her bundles. Don't forget her," added the outside passenger ironically.

"Does anybody here know her?" continued Bill, ignoring the irony.

"You'd better ask Judge Thompson; he was mighty attentive to her; gettin' her a seat by the off window, and lookin' after her bundles and things."

"Gettin' her a seat by the *window*?" repeated Bill.

"Yes, she wanted to see everything, and wasn't afraid of the shooting."

"Yes," broke in a third passenger, "and he was so d——d civil that when she dropped her ring in the straw, he struck a match agin all your rules, you know, and held it for her to find it. And it was just as we were crossin' through the brush, too. I saw the hull thing through the window, for I was hanging over the wheels with my gun ready for action. And it wasn't no fault of Judge Thompson's if his d—d foolishness hadn't shown us up, and got us a shot from the gang."

Bill gave a short grunt, but drove steadily on without further comment or even turning his eyes to the speaker.

We were now not more than a mile from the station at the cross-roads where we were to change horses. The lights already glimmered in the distance, and there was a faint suggestion of the coming dawn on the summits of the ridge to the west. We had plunged into a belt of timber, when suddenly a horseman emerged at a sharp canter from a trail that seemed to be parallel with our own. We were all slightly startled; Yuba Bill alone preserving his moody calm.

"Hullo!" he said.

The stranger wheeled to our side as Bill slackened his speed. He seemed to be a "packer" or freight muleteer.

"Ye didn't get 'held up' on the Divide?" continued Bill cheerfully.

"No," returned the packer, with a laugh; "*I* don't carry treasure. But I see you're all right, too. I saw you crossin' over Galloper's."

"*Saw* us?" said Bill sharply. "We had our lights out."

"Yes, but there was suthin' white—a handkerchief or woman's veil, I reckon—hangin' from the window. It was only a movin' spot agin the hillside, but ez I was lookin' out for ye I knew it was you by that. Good-night!"

He cantered away. We tried to look at each other's faces, and at Bill's expression in the darkness, but he neither spoke nor stirred until he threw down the reins when he stopped before the station. The passengers quickly descended from the roof; the Expressman was about to follow, but Bill plucked his sleeve.

"I'm goin' to take a look over this yer stage and these yer passengers with ye, afore we start."

"Why, what's up?"

"Well," said Bill, slowly disengaging himself from one of his enormous gloves, "when we waltzed down into the brush up there I saw a man, ez plain ez I see you, rise up from it. I thought our time had come and the band was goin' to play, when he sorter drew back, made a sign, and we just scooted past him."

"Well?"

"Well," said Bill, "it means that this yer coach was *passed through free* to-night."

"You don't object to *that*—surely? I think we were deucedly lucky."

Bill slowly drew off his other glove. "I've been riskin' my ever-lastin' life on this d——d line three times a week," he said with mock humility, "and I'm allus thankful for small mercies. *But*," he added grimly, "when it comes down to being passed free by some pal of a hoss thief, and thet called a speshal Providence, *I ain't in it!* No, sir, I ain't in it!"

II

It was with mixed emotions that the passengers heard that a delay of fifteen minutes to tighten certain screw-bolts had been ordered by the autocratic Bill. Some were anxious to get their breakfast at Sugar Pine, but others were not averse to linger for the daylight that promised greater safety on the road. The Ex-pressman, knowing the real cause of Bill's delay, was nevertheless at a loss to understand the object of it. The passengers were all well known; any idea of complicity with the road agents was wild and impossible, and, even if there was a confederate of the gang among them, he would have been more likely to precipitate a rob-bery than to check it. Again, the discovery of such a confederate —to whom they clearly owed their safety—and his arrest would have been quite against the Californian sense of justice, if not actually illegal. It seemed evident that Bill's quixotic sense of honor was leading him astray.

The station consisted of a stable, a wagon shed, and a building containing three rooms. The first was fitted up with "bunks" or sleeping berths for the employees; the second was the kitchen; and the third and larger apartment was dining-room or sitting-room, and was used as general waiting-room for the passengers. It was not a refreshment station, and there was no "bar." But a mysterious command from the omnipotent Bill produced a demijohn of whiskey, with which he hospitably treated the com-pany. The seductive influence of the liquor loosened the tongue of the gallant Judge Thompson. He admitted to having struck a match to enable the fair Pike Countian to find her ring, which, however, proved to have fallen in her lap. She was "a fine, healthy

young woman—a type of the Far West, sir; in fact, quite a
prairie blossom! yet simple and guileless as a child." She was on
her way to Marysville, he believed, "although she expected to
meet friends—a friend, in fact—later on." It was her first visit
to a large town—in fact, any civilized centre—since she crossed
the plains three years ago. Her girlish curiosity was quite touching, and her innocence irresistible. In fact, in a country whose
tendency was to produce "frivolity and forwardness in young
girls," he found her a most interesting young person. She was
even then out in the stable-yard watching the horses being harnessed, "preferring to indulge a pardonable, healthy young curiosity than to listen to the empty compliments of the younger passengers."

The figure which Bill saw thus engaged, without being otherwise distinguished, certainly seemed to justify the Judge's opinion.
She appeared to be a well-matured country girl, whose frank gray
eyes and large laughing mouth expressed a wholesome and abiding
gratification in her life and surroundings. She was watching the
replacing of luggage in the boot. A little feminine start, as one
of her own parcels was thrown somewhat roughly on the roof, gave
Bill his opportunity. "Now there," he growled to the helper, "ye
ain't carting stone! Look out, will yer! Some of your things,
miss?" he added, with gruff courtesy, turning to her. "These yer
trunks, for instance?"

She smiled a pleasant assent, and Bill, pushing aside the helper,
seized a large square trunk in his arms. But from excess of zeal,
or some other mischance, his foot slipped, and he came down heavily, striking the corner of the trunk on the ground and loosening
its hinges and fastenings. It was a cheap, common-looking affair,
but the accident discovered in its yawning lid a quantity of white,
lace-edged feminine apparel of an apparently superior quality.
The young lady uttered another cry and came quickly forward,
but Bill was profuse in his apologies, himself girded the broken
box with a strap, and declared his intention of having the company
"make it good" to her with a new one. Then he casually accompanied her to the door of the waiting-room, entered, made a place
for her before the fire by simply lifting the nearest and most
youthful passenger by the coat collar from the stool that he was
occupying, and, having installed the lady in it, displaced another
man, who was standing before the chimney, and, drawing him-

self up to his full six feet of height in front of her, glanced down upon his fair passenger as he took his waybill from his pocket.

"Your name is down here as Miss Mullins?" he said.

She looked up, became suddenly aware that she and her questioner were the centre of interest to the whole circle of passengers, and, with a slight rise of color, returned, "Yes."

"Well, Miss Mullins, I've got a question or two to ask ye. I ask it straight out afore this crowd. It's in my rights to take ye aside and ask it—but that ain't my style; I'm no detective. I needn't ask it at all, but act as ef I knowed the answer, or I might leave it to be asked by others. Ye needn't answer it ef ye don't like; ye've got a friend over ther—Judge Thompson—who is a friend to ye, right or wrong, jest as any other man here is—as though ye'd packed your own jury. Well, the simple question I've got to ask ye is *this*: Did you signal to anybody from the coach when we passed Galloper's an hour ago?"

We all thought that Bill's courage and audacity had reached its climax here. To openly and publicly accuse a "lady" before a group of chivalrous Californians, and that lady possessing the further attractions of youth, good looks, and innocence, was little short of desperation. There was an evident movement of adhesion towards the fair stranger, a slight muttering broke out on the right, but the very boldness of the act held them in stupefied surprise. Judge Thompson, with a bland propitiatory smile began: "Really, Bill, I must protest on behalf of this young lady" —when the fair accused, raising her eyes to her accuser, to the consternation of everybody answered with the slight but convincing hesitation of conscientious truthfulness:—

"*I did.*"

"Ahem!" interposed the Judge hastily, "er—that is—er—you allowed your handkerchief to flutter from the window,—I noticed it myself,—casually—one might say even playfully—but without any particular significance."

The girl, regarding her apologist with a singular mingling of pride and impatience, returned briefly:—

"I signaled."

"Who did you signal to?" asked Bill gravely.

"The young gentleman I'm going to marry."

A start, followed by a slight titter from the younger passengers, was instantly suppressed by a savage glance from Bill.

"What did you signal to him for?" he continued.

"To tell him I was here, and that it was all right," returned the young girl, with a steadily rising pride and color.

"Wot was all right?" demanded Bill. •

"That I wasn't followed, and that he could meet me on the road beyond Cass's Ridge Station." She hesitated a moment, and then, with a still greater pride, in which a youthful defiance was still mingled, said: "I've run away from home to marry him. And I mean to! No one can stop me. Dad didn't like him just because he was poor, and dad's got money. Dad wanted me to marry a man I hate, and got a lot of dresses and things to bribe me."

"And you're taking them in your trunk to the other feller?" said Bill grimly.

"Yes, he's poor," returned the girl defiantly.

"Then your father's name is Mullins?" asked Bill.

"It's not Mullins. I—I—took that name," she hesitated, with her first exhibition of self-consciousness.

"Wot *is* his name?"

"Eli Hemmings."

A smile of relief and significance went round the circle. The fame of Eli or "Skinner" Hemmings, as a notorious miser and usurer, had passed even beyond Galloper's Ridge.

"The step that you're taking, Miss Mullins, I need not tell you, is one of great gravity," said Judge Thompson, with a certain paternal seriousness of manner, in which, however, we were glad to detect a glaring affectation; "and I trust that you and your affianced have fully weighed it. Far be it from me to interfere with or question the natural affections of two young people, but may I ask you what you know of the—er—young gentleman for whom you are sacrificing so much, and, perhaps, imperiling your whole future? For instance, have you known him long?"

The slightly troubled air of trying to understand—not unlike the vague wonderment of childhood—with which Miss Mullins had received the beginning of this exordium, changed to a relieved smile of comprehension as she said quickly, "Oh yes, nearly a whole year."

"And," said the Judge, smiling, "has he a vocation—is he in business?"

"Oh yes," she returned; "he's a collector."

"A collector?"

"Yes; he collects bills, you know—money," she went on, with childish eagerness, "not for himself—*he* never has any money, poor Charley—but for his firm. It's dreadful hard work, too; keeps him out for days and nights, over bad roads and baddest weather. Sometimes, when he's stole over to the ranch just to see me, he's been so bad he could scarcely keep his seat in the saddle, much less stand. And he's got to take mighty big risks, too. Times the folks are cross with him and won't pay; once they shot him in the arm, and he came to me, and I helped do it up for him. But he don't mind. He's real brave—jest as brave as he's good." There was such a wholesome ring of truth in this pretty praise that we were touched in sympathy with the speaker.

"What firm does he collect for?" asked the Judge gently.

"I don't know exactly—he won't tell me; but I think it 's a Spanish firm. You see"—she took us all into her confidence with a sweeping smile of innocent yet half-mischievous artfulness—"I only know because I peeped over a letter he once got from his firm, telling him he must hustle up and be ready for the road the next day; but I think the name was Martinez—yes, Ramon Martinez."

In the dead silence that ensued—a silence so profound that we could hear the horses in the distant stable-yard rattling their harness—one of the younger "Excelsior" boys burst into a hysteric laugh, but the fierce eye of Yuba Bill was down upon him, and seemed to instantly stiffen him into a silent, grinning mask. The young girl, however, took no note of it. Following out, with lover-like diffusiveness, the reminiscences thus awakened, she went on:—

"Yes, it 's mighty hard work, but he says it 's all for me, and as soon as we're married he'll quit it. He might have quit it before, but he won't take no money of me, nor what I told him I could get out of dad! That ain't his style. He's mighty proud—if he is poor—is Charley. Why thar's all ma's money which she left me in the Savin's Bank that I wanted to draw out—for I had the right—and give it to him, but he wouldn't hear of it! Why, he wouldn't take one of the things I've got with me, if he knew it. And so he goes on ridin' and ridin', here and there and everywhere, and gettin' more and more played out and sad, and thin and pale as a spirit, and always so uneasy about his business, and startin' up at times when we're meetin' out in the South Woods or in the far clearin', and sayin'; 'I must be goin' now, Polly,' and yet always tryin' to be chiffle and chipper afore me. Why he must have rid miles and miles to have watched for me thar in the brush at the foot of Galloper's to-night, jest to see if all was safe; and Lordy! I'd have given him the signal and showed a light if I'd died for it the next minit. There! That's what I know of Charley— that's what I'm running away from home for—that's what I'm running to him for, and I don't care who knows it! And I only wish I'd done it afore—and I would—if—if—if—he'd only *asked me*! There now!" She stopped, panted, and choked. Then one of the sudden transitions of youthful emotion overtook the eager, laughing face; it clouded up with the swift change of childhood, a lightning quiver of expression broke over it, and—then came the rain!

I think this simple act completed our utter demoralization! We smiled feebly at each other with that assumption of masculine superiority which is miserably conscious of its own helplessness at such moments. We looked out of the window, blew our noses, said: "Eh—what?" and "I say," vaguely to each other, and were greatly relieved, and yet apparently astonished, when Yuba Bill, who had turned his back upon the fair speaker, and was kicking the logs in the fireplace, suddenly swept down upon us and bundled us all into the road, leaving Miss Mullins alone. Then he walked aside with Judge Thompson for a few moments; returned to us, autocratically demanded of the party a complete reticence towards Miss Mullins on the subject-matter under discussion, reëntered the station, reappeared with the young lady, suppressed a faint idiotic cheer which broke from us at the spectacle of her innocent face once more cleared and rosy, climbed the box, and in another moment we were under way.

"Then she don't know what her lover is yet?" asked the Expressman eagerly.

"No."

"Are *you* certain it's one of the gang?"

"Can't say *for sure*. It mout be a young chap from Yolo who bucked agin the tiger[1] at Sacramento, got regularly cleaned out and busted, and joined the gang for a flier. They say thar was a

---

[1] Gambled at faro.

new hand in that job over at Keeley's—and a mighty game one, too; and ez there was some buckshot onloaded that trip, he might hev got his share, and that would tally with what the girl said about his arm. See! Ef that's the man, I've heered he was the son of some big preacher in the States, and a college sharp to boot, who ran wild in 'Frisco, and played himself for all he was worth. They're the wust kind to kick when they once get a foot over the traces. For stiddy, comf'ble kempany," added Bill reflectively, "give *me* the son of a man that was *hanged!*"

"But what are you going to do about this?"

"That depends upon the feller who comes to meet her."

"But you ain't going to try to take him? That would be playing it pretty low down on them both."

"Keep your hair on, Jimmy! The Judge and me are only going to rastle with the sperrit of that gay young galoot, when he drops down for his girl—and exhort him pow'ful! Ef he allows he's convicted of sin and will find the Lord, we'll marry him and the gal offhand at the next station, and the Judge will officiate himself for nothin'. We're goin' to have this yer elopement done on the square—and our waybill clean—you bet!"

"But you don't suppose he'll trust himself in your hands?"

"Polly will signal to him that it's all square."

"Ah!" said the Expressman. Nevertheless in those few moments the men seemed to have exchanged dispositions. The Expressman looked doubtfully, critically, and even cynically before him. Bill's face had relaxed, and something like a bland smile beamed across it, as he drove confidently and unhesitatingly forward.

Day, meantime, although full blown and radiant on the mountain summits around us, was yet nebulous and uncertain in the valleys into which we were plunging. Lights still glimmered in the cabins and the few ranch buildings which began to indicate the thicker settlements. And the shadows were heaviest in a little copse, where a note from Judge Thompson in the coach was handed up to Yuba Bill, who at once slowly began to draw up his horses. The coach stopped finally near the junction of a small crossroad. At the same moment Miss Mullins slipped down from the vehicle, and, with a parting wave of her hand to the Judge, who had assisted her from the steps, tripped down the crossroad, and disappeared in its semi-obscurity. To our surprise the stage waited, Bill holding the reins listlessly in his hands. Five minutes passed—an eternity of expectation, and, as there was that in Yuba Bill's face which forbade idle questioning, an aching void of silence also! This was at last broken by a strange voice from the road:—

"Go on—we'll follow."

The coach started forward. Presently we heard the sound of other wheels behind us. We all craned our necks backward to get a view of the unknown, but by the growing light we could only see that we were followed at a distance by a buggy with two figures in it. Evidently Polly Mullins and her lover! We hoped that they would pass us. But the vehicle, although drawn by a fast horse, preserved its distance always, and it was plain that its driver had no desire to satisfy our curiosity. The Expressman had recourse to Bill.

"Is it the man you thought of?" he asked eagerly.

"I reckon," said Bill briefly.

"But," continued the Expressman, returning to his former skepticism, "what's to keep them both from levanting together now?"

Bill jerked his hand towards the boot with a grim smile.

"Their baggage."

"Oh!" said the Expressman.

"Yes," continued Bill. "We'll hang on to that gal's little frills and fixin's until this yer job's settled, and the ceremony's over, jest as ef we wuz her own father. And, what's more, young man," he added, suddenly turning to the Expressman, "*you'll* express them trunks of hers *through to Sacramento* with your kempany's labels, and hand her the receipts and checks for them, so she *can get 'em there.* That'll keep *him* outer temptation and the reach o' the gang, until they get away among white men and civilization again. When your hoary-headed ole grandfather, or, to speak plainer, that partikler old whiskey-soaker known as Yuba Bill, wot sits on this box," he continued, with a diabolical wink at the Expressman, "waltzes in to pervide for a young couple jest startin' in life, thar's nothin' mean about his style, you bet. He fills the bill every time! Speshal Providences take a back seat when he's around."

When the station hotel and straggling settlement of Sugar Pine, now distinct and clear in the growing light, at last rose within rifleshot on the plateau, the buggy suddenly darted swiftly by us, so swiftly that the faces of the two occupants were barely distinguishable as they passed, and keeping the lead by a dozen lengths, reached the door of the hotel. The young girl and her companion leaped down and vanished within as we drew up. They had evidently determined to elude our curiosity, and were successful.

But the material appetites of the passengers, sharpened by the keen mountain air, were more potent than their curiosity, and, as the breakfast-bell rang out at the moment the stage stopped, a majority of them rushed into the dining-room and scrambled for places without giving much heed to the vanished couple or to the Judge and Yuba Bill, who had disappeared also. The through coach to Marysville and Sacramento was likewise waiting, for Sugar Pine was the limit of Bill's ministration, and the coach which we had just left went no farther. In the course of twenty minutes, however, there was a slight and somewhat ceremonious bustling in the hall and on the veranda, and Yuba Bill and the Judge reappeared. The latter was leading, with some elaboration of manner and detail, the shapely figure of Miss Mullins, and Yuba Bill was accompanying her companion to the buggy. We all rushed to the windows to get a good view of the mysterious stranger and probable ex-brigand whose life was now linked with our fair fellow-passenger. I am afraid, however, that we all participated in a certain impression of disappointment and doubt. Handsome and even cultivated-looking, he assuredly was—young and vigorous in appearance. But there was a certain half-shamed, half-defiant suggestion in his expression, yet coupled with a watchful lurking uneasiness which was not pleasant and hardly becoming a bridegroom—and the possessor of such a bride. But the frank, joyous, innocent face of Polly Mullins, resplendent with a simple, happy confidence, melted our hearts again, and condoned the fellow's shortcomings. We waved our hands; I think we would have given three rousing cheers as they drove away if the omnipotent eye of Yuba Bill had not been upon us. It was well, for the next moment we were summoned to the presence of that soft-hearted autocrat.

We found him alone with the Judge in a private sitting-room, standing before a table on which there was a decanter and glasses. As we filed expectantly into the room and the door closed behind us, he cast a glance of hesitating tolerance over the group.

"Gentlemen," he said slowly, "you was all present at the beginnin' of a little game this mornin', and the Judge thar thinks that you oughter be let in at the finish. *I* don't see that it's any of *your* d—d business—so to speak; but ez the Judge here allows you're all in the secret, I've called you in to take a partin' drink to the health of Mr. and Mrs. Charley Byng—ez is now comf-ably off on their bridal tower. What *you* know or what *you* suspects of the young galoot that's married the gal ain't worth shucks to any-body, and I wouldn't give it to a yaller pup to play with, but the Judge thinks you ought all to promise right here that you'll keep it dark. That's his opinion. Ez far as my opinion goes, gen'l'-men," continued Bill, with greater blandness and apparent cordiality, "I wanter simply remark, in a keerless, offhand gin'ral way, that ef I ketch any God-forsaken, lop-eared, chuckle-headed blatherin' idjet airin' *his* opinion—"

"One moment, Bill," interposed Judge Thompson with a grave smile; "let me explain. You understand, gentlemen," he said, turn-ing to us, "the singular, and I may say affecting, situation which our good-hearted friend here has done so much to bring to what we hope will be a happy termination. I want to give here, as my professional opinion, that there is nothing in his request which, in your capacity as good citizens and law-abiding men, you may not grant. I want to tell you, also, that you are condoning no offense against the statutes; that there is not a particle of legal evidence before us of the criminal antecedents of Mr. Charles Byng, except that which has been told you by the innocent lips of his betrothed, which the law of the land has now sealed forever in the mouth of his wife, and that our own actual experience of his acts has been in the main exculpatory of any previous irregularity—if not incompatible with it. Briefly, no judge would charge, no jury con-vict, on such evidence. When I add that the young girl is of legal age, that there is no evidence of any previous undue influence, but rather of the reverse, on the part of the bridegroom, and that I was content, as a magistrate, to perform the ceremony, I think you will be satisfied to give your promise, for the sake of the bride, and drink a happy life to them both."

I need not say that we did this cheerfully, and even extorted from Bill a grunt of satisfaction. The majority of the company, however, who were going with the through coach to Sacramento, then took their leave, and, as we accompanied them to the veranda, we could see that Miss Polly Mullins's trunks were already trans-ferred to the other vehicle under the protecting seals and labels of the all-potent Express Company. Then the whip cracked, the coach rolled away, and the last traces of the adventurous young couple disappeared in the hanging red dust of its wheels.

But Yuba Bill's grim satisfaction at the happy issue of the episode seemed to suffer no abatement. He even exceeded his usual deliberately regulated potations, and, standing comfortably with his back to the centre of the now deserted barroom, was more than usually loquacious with the Expressman. "You see," he said, in bland reminiscence, "when your old Uncle Bill takes hold of a job like this, he puts it straight through without changin' hosses. Yet thar was a moment, young feller, when I thought I was stompt! It was when we'd made up our mind to make that chap tell the gal fust all what he was! Ef she'd rared or kicked in the traces, or hung back only ez much ez that, we'd hev given him jest five minits' law to get up and get and leave her, and we'd hev toted that gal and her fixin's back to her dad again! But she jest gave a little scream and start, and then went off inter hysterics, right on his buzzum, laughin' and cryin' and sayin' that nothin' should part 'em. Gosh! if I didn't think *he* wuz more cut up than she about it; a minit it looked as ef *he* didn't allow to marry her arter all, but that passed, and they was married hard and fast—you bet! I reckon he's had enough of stayin' out o' nights to last him, and ef the valley settlements hevn't got hold of a very shining member, at least the foothills hev got shut of one more of the Ramon Martinez gang."

"What's that about the Ramon Martinez gang?" said a quiet potential voice.

Bill turned quickly. It was the voice of the Divisional Superintendent of the Express Company—a man of eccentric determination of character, and one of the few whom the autocratic Bill recognized as an equal—who had just entered the barroom. His dusty pongee cloak and soft hat indicated that he had that morning arrived on a round of inspection.

"Don't care if I do, Bill," he continued, in response to Bill's invitatory gesture, walking to the bar. "It's a little raw out on the road. Well, what were you saying about the Ramon Martinez gang? You haven't come across one of 'em, have you?"

"No," said Bill, with a slight blinking of his eye, as he ostentatiously lifted his glass to the light.

"And you *won't*," added the Superintendent, leisurely sipping his liquor. "For the fact is, the gang is about played out. Not from want of a job now and then, but from the difficulty of disposing of the results of their work. Since the new instructions to the agents to identify and trace all dust and bullion offered to them went into force, you see, they can't get rid of their swag. All the gang are spotted at the offices, and it costs too much for them to pay a fence or a middleman of any standing. Why, all that flaky river gold they took from the Excelsior Company can be identified as easy as if it was stamped with the company's mark. They can't melt it down themselves; they can't get others to do it for them; they can't ship it to the Mint or Assay Offices in Marysville and 'Frisco, for they won't take it without our certificate and seals; and *we* don't take any undeclared freight *within* the lines that we've drawn around their beat, except from people and agents known. Why, *you* know that well enough, Jim," he said, suddenly appealing to the Expressman, "don't you?"

Possibly the suddenness of the appeal caused the Expressman to swallow his liquor the wrong way, for he was overtaken with a fit of coughing, and stammered hastily as he laid down his glass, "Yes—of course—certainly."

"No, sir," resumed the Superintendent cheerfully, "they're pretty well played out. And the best proof of it is that they've lately been robbing ordinary passengers' trunks. There was a freight wagon 'held up' near Dow's Flat the other day, and a lot of baggage gone through. I had to go down there to look into it. Darned if they hadn't lifted a lot o' woman's wedding things from that rich couple who got married the other day out at Marysville. Looks as if they were playing it rather low down, don't it? Coming down to hardpan and the bed rock—eh?"

The Expressman's face was turned anxiously towards Bill, who, after a hurried gulp of his remaining liquor, still stood staring at the window. Then he slowly drew on one of his large gloves. "Ye didn't," he said, with a slow, drawling, but perfectly distinct, articulation, "happen to know old 'Skinner' Hemmings when you were over there?"

"Yes."

"And his daughter?"

"He hasn't got any."

"A sort o' mild, innocent, guileless child of nature?" persisted Bill, with a yellow face, a deadly calm and Satanic deliberation.

"No. I tell you he *hasn't* any daughter. Old Man Hemmings is a confirmed old bachelor. He's too mean to support more than one."

"And you didn't happen to know any o' that gang, did ye?" continued Bill, with infinite protraction.

"Yes. Knew 'em all. There was French Pete, Cherokee Bob, Kanaka Joe, One-eyed Stillson, Softy Brown, Spanish Jack, and two or three Greasers."

"And ye didn't know a man by the name of Charley Byng?"

"No," returned the Superintendent, with a slight suggestion of weariness and a distraught glance towards the door.

"A dark, stylish chap, with shifty black eyes and a curled-up merstache?" continued Bill, with dry, colorless persistence.

"No. Look here, Bill, I'm in a little bit of a hurry—but I suppose you must have your little joke before we part. Now, what *is* your little game?"

"Wot you mean?" demanded Bill, with sudden brusqueness.

"Mean? Well, old man, you know as well as I do. You're giving me the very description of Ramon Martinez himself, ha! ha! No—Bill! you didn't play me this time. You're mighty spry and clever, but you didn't catch on just then."

He nodded and moved away with a light laugh. Bill turned a stony face to the Expressman. Suddenly a gleam of mirth came into his gloomy eyes. He bent over the young man, and said in a hoarse, chuckling whisper:—

"But I got even after all!"

"How?"

"He's tied up to that lying little she-devil, hard and fast!"

THE SUN-DOG TRAIL

A master teller of tales relates here a harrowing and dreadful story of the Northwest—of pursuer and pursued, and in so doing, gives us an unforgettable picture of the indomitable will of man.

Sitka CHARLEY smoked his pipe and gazed thoughtfully at the newspaper illustration on the wall. For half an hour he had been steadily regarding it, and for half an hour I had been slyly watching him. Something was going on in that mind of his, and, whatever it was, I knew it was well worth knowing. He had lived life, and seen things, and performed that prodigy of prodigies, namely, the turning of his back upon his own people, and, in so far as it was possible for an Indian, becoming a white man even in his mental processes. As he phrased it himself, he had come into the warm, sat among us, by our fires, and become one of us.

We had struck this deserted cabin after a hard day on trail. The dogs had been fed, the supper dishes washed, the beds made, and we were now enjoying that most delicious hour that comes each day, on the Alaskan trail, when nothing intervenes between the tired body and bed save the smoking of the evening pipe.

"Well?" I finally broke the silence.

He took the pipe from his mouth and said, simply, "I do not understand."

He smoked on again, and again removed the pipe, using it to point at the illustration.

"That picture—what does it mean? I do not understand."

I looked at the picture. A man, with a preposterously wicked face, his right hand pressed dramatically to his heart, was falling backward to the floor. Confronting him, with a face that was a composite of destroying angel and Adonis, was a man holding a smoking revolver.

"One man is killing the other man," I said, aware of a distinct bepuzzlement of my own and of failure to explain.

"Why?" asked Sitka Charley.

"I do not know," I confessed.

"That picture is all end," he said. "It has no beginning."

"It is life," I said.

"Life has beginning," he objected.

"Look at that picture," I commanded, pointing to another decoration. "It means something. Tell me what it means to you."

He studied it for several minutes.

"The little girl is sick," he said, finally. "That is the doctor looking at her. They have been up all night—see, the oil is low in the lamp, the first morning light is coming in at the window. It is a great sickness; maybe she will die; that is why the doctor looks so hard. That is the mother. It is a great sickness, because the mother's head is on the table and she is crying."

"And now you understand the picture," I cried.

He shook his head, and asked, "The little girl—does it die?"

It was my turn for silence.

"Does it die?" he reiterated. "You are a painter-man. Maybe you know."

"No, I do not know," I confessed.

"It is not life," he delivered himself, dogmatically. "In life little girl die or get well. Something happen in life. In picture nothing happen. No, I do not understand pictures."

"Pictures are bits of life," I said. "We paint life as we see it. For instance, Charley, you are coming along the trail. It is night. You see a cabin. The window is lighted. You look through the window for one second, or for two seconds; you see something, and you go on your way. You see maybe a man writing a letter. You saw something without beginning or end. Nothing happened. Yet it was a bit of life you saw. You remember it afterward. It is like a picture in your memory. The window is the frame of the picture."

For a long time he smoked in silence. He nodded his head several times, and grunted once or twice. Then he knocked the ashes from his pipe, carefully refilled it, and, after a thoughtful pause, he lighted it again.

"Then have I, too, seen many pictures of life," he began; "pictures not painted but seen with the eyes. I have looked at them like through the window at the man writing the letter. I have seen many pieces of life, without beginning, without end, without understanding."

With a sudden change of position he turned his eyes full upon me and regarded me thoughtfully.

"Look you," he said; "you are a painter-man. How would you paint this which I saw, a picture without beginning, the ending of which I do not understand, a piece of life with the northern lights for a candle and Alaska for a frame?"

"It is a large canvas," I murmured.

"There are many names for this picture," he said. "But in the picture there are many sun-dogs, and it comes into my mind to call it 'The Sun-Dog Trail.' It was seven years ago, the fall of '97, when I saw the woman first time. At Lake Linderman I had one canoe. I came over Chilcoot Pass with two thousand letters for Dawson. Everybody rush to Klondike at that time. Many people on trail. Many people chop down trees and make boats. Last water, snow in the air, snow on the ground, ice on the lake, on the river. Every day more snow, more ice, any day maybe freeze-up come; then no more water, all ice, everybody walk; Dawson six hundred miles; long time walk. Boat go very quick. Everybody want to go boat. Everybody say, 'Charley, two hundred dollars you take me in canoe,' 'Charley, three hundred dollars,' 'Charley, four hundred dollars.' I say no; all the time I say no. I am letter-carrier.

"In the morning I get to Lake Linderman; I walk all night and am much tired. I cook breakfast, I eat, then I sleep on the beach three hours. I wake up. It is ten o'clock. Snow is falling. There is wind, much wind that blows fair. Also, there is a woman who sits in the snow alongside. She is white woman, she is young, very pretty; maybe she is twenty years old, maybe twenty-five years old. She look at me. I look at her. She is very tired. She is no dance-woman. I see that right away. She is good woman, and she is very tired.

" 'You are Sitka Charley,' she says. 'I go to Dawson,' she says. 'I go in your canoe—how much?'

"I do not want anybody in my canoe. I do not like to say no. So I say, 'One thousand dollars.' She look at me very hard, then she says, 'When you start?' I say right away. Then she says all right, she will give me one thousand dollars.

"What can I say? I do not want the woman, yet have I given my word that for one thousand dollars she can come. And that woman, that young woman, all alone on the trail, there in the snow, she take out one thousand dollars in greenbacks, and she put them in my hand. I look at money, I look at her. What can I say? I say: 'No; my canoe very small. There is no room for outfit.' She laugh. She says: 'I am great traveller. This is my outfit.' She kick one small pack in the snow. It is two fur robes, canvas outside, some woman's clothes inside. I pick it up. Maybe thirty-five pounds. I am surprised. She take it away from me. She says, 'Come, let us start.' She carries pack into canoe. What can I say? I put my blankets into canoe. We start.

"And that is the way I saw the woman first time. The wind was fair. I put up small sail. The canoe went very fast. The woman was much afraid. 'What for you come Klondike much afraid?' I ask. She laugh at me, a hard laugh, but she is still much afraid. Also she is very tired. I run canoe through rapids to Lake Bennett. Water very bad, and woman cry out because she is afraid. We go down Lake Bennett. Snow, ice, wind like a gale, but woman is very tired and go to sleep.

"That night we make camp at Windy Arm. Woman sit by fire and eat supper. I look at her. She is pretty. She fix hair. There is much hair, and it is brown; also sometimes it is like gold in the firelight when she turn her head, so, and flashes come from it like golden fire. The eyes are large and brown. When she smile—how can I say?—when she smile I know white man like to kiss her, just like that, when she smile. She never do hard work. Her hands are soft like a baby's hand. She is not thin, but round like a baby; her arm, her leg, her muscles, all soft and round like baby. Her waist is small, and when she stand up, when she walk, or move her head or arm, it is—I do not know the word—but it is nice to look at, like—maybe I say she is built on lines like the lines of a good canoe, just like that—and when she move she is like the movement of the good canoe sliding through still water or leaping through water when it is white and fast and angry. It is very good to see.

"I ask her what is her name. She laugh, then she says, 'Mary Jones; that is my name.' But I know all the time that Mary Jones is not her name.

"It is very cold in canoe, and because of cold sometimes she not feel good. Sometimes she feel good and she sing. Her voice is like a silver bell, and I feel good all over like when I go into church at Holy Cross Mission, and when she sing I feel strong and paddle like hell. Then she laugh and says, 'You think we get to Dawson before freeze-up, Charley?' Sometimes she sit in canoe and is thinking far away, her eyes like that, all empty. She does not see Sitka Charley, nor the ice, nor the snow. She is far away. Sometimes, when she is thinking far away, her face is not good to see. It looks like a face that is angry, like the face of one man when he want to kill another man.

"Last day to Dawson very bad. Shore-ice in all the eddies, mush-ice in the stream. I cannot paddle. The canoe freeze to ice. All the time we go down Yukon in the ice. Then ice stop, canoe stop, everything stop. 'Let us go to shore,' the woman says. I say no; better wait. By and by everything start down-stream again. There is much snow; I cannot see. At eleven o'clock at night everything stop. At one o'clock everything start again. At three o'clock everything stop. Canoe is smashed like egg-shell, but it is on top of ice and cannot sink. I hear dogs howling. We wait; we sleep. By and by morning come. There is no more snow. It is the freeze-up, and there is Dawson. Canoe smash and stop right at Dawson. Sitka Charley has come in with two thousand letters on very last water.

"The woman rent a cabin on the hill, and for one week I see her no more. Then, one day, she come to me. 'Charley,' she says, 'how do you like to work for me? You drive dogs, make camp, travel with me.' I say that I make too much money carrying letters. She says, 'Charley, I will pay you more money.' I tell her that pick-and-shovel man get fifteen dollars a day in the mines. She says, 'That is four hundred and fifty dollars a month.' And I say, 'Sitka Charley is no pick-and-shovel man.' Then she says: 'I understand, Charley. I will give you seven hundred and fifty dollars each month.' It is a good price, and I go to work for her. I buy for her dogs and sled. We travel up Klondike, up Bonanza and Eldorado, over to Indian River, to Sulphur Creek, to Dominion, back across divide to Gold Bottom and to Too Much Gold, and back to Dawson. All the time she look for something; I do not know what.

"She has a small revolver, which she carries in her belt. Sometimes, on trail, she makes practice with revolver.

"At Dawson comes the man. Which way he come I do not know. Only do I know he is *che-cha-quo*—what you call tenderfoot. His hands are soft. He never do hard work. At first I think maybe he is her husband. But he is too young. He is maybe twenty years old. His eyes blue, his hair yellow; he has a little mustache which is yellow. His name is John Jones. Maybe he is her brother. I do not know.

"One night I am asleep at Dawson. He wake me up. He says, 'Get the dogs ready; we start.' No more do I ask questions, so I get the dogs ready and we start. We go down the Yukon. It is night-time, it is November, and it is very cold—sixty-five below. She is soft. He is soft. The cold bites. They get tired. They cry under their breaths to themselves. By and by I say better we stop and make camp. But they say that they will go on. After that I say nothing. All the time, day after day, it is that way. They are very soft. They get stiff and sore. They do not understand moccasins, and their feet hurt very much. They limp, they stagger like drunken people, they cry under their breaths; and all the time they say: 'On! on! We will go on!'

"We make Circle City. That for which they look is not there. I think now that we will rest, and rest the dogs. But we do not rest; not for one day do we rest. 'Come,' says the woman to the man, 'let us go on.' And we go on. We leave the Yukon. We cross the divide to the west and swing down into the Tanana Country. There are new diggings there. But that for which they look is not there, and we take the back trail to Circle City.

"It is a hard journey. December is 'most gone. The days are short. It is very cold.

"We limp into Circle City. It is Christmas Eve. I dance, drink, make a good time, for to-morrow is Christmas Day and we will rest. But no. It is five o'clock in the morning—Christmas morning.

I am two hours asleep. The man stand by my bed. 'Come, Charley,' he says; 'harness the dogs. We start.' I harness the dogs, and we start down the Yukon.

"They are very weary. They have travelled many hundreds of miles, and they do not understand the way of the trail. Besides, their cough is very bad—the dry cough that makes strong men swear and weak men cry. Every day they go on. Never do they rest the dogs. Always do they buy new dogs. At every camp, at every post, at every Indian village, do they cut out the tired dogs and put in fresh dogs. They have much money, money without end, and like water they spend it. They are crazy? Sometimes I think so, for there is a devil in them that drives them. They cry aloud in their sleep at night. And in the day, as they stagger along the trail, they cry under their breaths.

"We pass Fort Yukon. We pass Fort Hamilton. We pass Minook. January has come and nearly gone. The days are very short. At nine o'clock comes daylight. At three o'clock comes night. And it is cold. And even I, Sitka Charley, am tired. Will we go on forever this way without end? I do not know. But always do I look along the trail for that which they try to find. There are few people on the trail. Sometimes we travel one hundred miles and never see a sign of life. The northern lights flame in the sky, and the sun-dogs dance, and the air is filled with frost-dust.

"I am Sitka Charley, a strong man. I was born on the trail, and all my days have I lived on the trail. And yet have these two baby wolves made me tired. Their eyes are sunk deep in their heads, bright sometimes as with fever, dim and cloudy sometimes like the eyes of the dead. Their cheeks are black and raw from many freezings. Sometimes it is the woman in the morning who says: 'I cannot get up. I cannot move. Let me die.' And it is the man who stands beside her and says, 'Come, let us go on.'

"Sometimes, at the trading-posts, the man and woman get letters. I do not know what is in the letters. But it is the scent that they follow; these letters themselves are the scent. One time an Indian gives them a letter. I talk with him privately. He says it is a man with one eye who gives him the letter—a man who travels fast down the Yukon. That is all. But I know that the baby wolves are after the man with the one eye.

"It is February, and we have travelled fifteen hundred miles. We are getting near Bering Sea, and there are storms and blizzards. The going is hard. We come to Anvig. I do not know, but I think sure they get a letter at Anvig, for they are much excited, and they say, 'Come, hurry; let us go on.' But I say we must buy grub, and they say we must travel light and fast. Also, they say that we can get grub at Charley McKeon's cabin. Then do I know that they take the big cut-off, for it is there that Charley McKeon lives where the Black Rock stands by the trail.

"Before we start I talk maybe two minutes with the priest at Anvig. Yes, there is a man with one eye who has gone by and who travels fast. And I know that for which they look is the man with the one eye. We leave Anvig with little grub, and travel light and fast. We take the big cut-off, and the trail is fresh. The baby wolves have their noses down to the trail, and they say, 'Hurry!' All the time do they say: 'Hurry! Faster! Faster!' It is hard on the dogs. We have not much food and we cannot give them enough to eat, and they grow weak. Also, they must work hard. The woman has true sorrow for them, and often, because of them, the tears are in her eyes. But the devil in her that drives her on will not let her stop and rest the dogs.

"And then we come upon the man with the one eye. He is in the snow by the trail and his leg is broken. Because of the leg he has made a poor camp, and has been lying on his blankets for three days and keeping a fire going. When we find him he is swearing. Never have I heard a man swear like that man. I am glad. Now that they have found that for which they look, we will have a rest. But the woman says: 'Let us start. Hurry!'

"I am surprised. But the man with the one eye says: 'Never mind me. Give me your grub. You will get more grub at McKeon's cabin to-morrow. Send McKeon back for me. But do you go on.' So we give him our grub, which is not much, and we chop wood for his fire, and we take his strongest dogs and go on. We left the man with one eye there in the snow, and he died there in the snow, for McKeon never went back for him.

"That day and that night we had nothing to eat, and all next day we travelled fast, and we were weak with hunger. Then we came to the Black Rock, which rose five hundred feet above the trail. It was at the end of the day. Darkness was coming, and we could not find the cabin of McKeon. We slept hungry, and in the morning looked for the cabin. It was not there, which was a strange thing, for everybody knew that McKeon lived in a cabin at Black

Rock. We were near to the coast, where the wind blows hard
and there is much snow. Everywhere were there small hills of
snow where the wind had piled it up. I have a thought, and I dig
in one and another of the hills of snow. Soon I find the walls of
the cabin, and I dig down to the door. I go inside. McKeon is dead.
Maybe two or three weeks he is dead. A sickness had come upon
him so that he could not leave the cabin. He had eaten his grub
and died. I looked for his cache, but there was no grub in it.

" 'Let us go on,' said the woman. Her eyes were hungry, and
her hand was upon her heart, as with the hurt of something inside.
She swayed back and forth like a tree in the wind as she stood
there.

" 'Yes, let us go on,' said the man. His voice was hollow, like
the *klonk* of an old raven, and he was hunger-mad. His eyes were
like live coals of fire, and as his body rocked to and fro, so
rocked his soul inside. And I, too, said, 'Let us go on.' For that
one thought, laid upon me like a lash for every mile of fifteen
hundred miles, had burned itself into my soul, and I think that I,
too, was mad. Besides, we could only go on, for there was no grub.
And we went on, giving no thought to the man with the one eye
in the snow.

"The snow had covered the trail, and there was no sign that
men had ever come or gone that way. All day the wind blew and
the snow fell, and all day we travelled. Then the woman began to
fall. Then the man. I did not fall, but my feet were heavy, and I
caught my toes and stumbled many times.

"That night is the end of February. I kill three ptarmigan
with the woman's revolver, and we are made somewhat strong
again. But the dogs have nothing to eat. They try to eat their
harness, which is of leather and walrus-hide, and I must fight
them off with a club and hang all the harness in a tree. And all
night they howl and fight around that tree. But we do not mind.
We sleep like dead people, and in the morning get up like dead
people out of our graves and go on along the trail.

"That morning is the 1st of March, and on that morning I see
the first sign of that after which the baby wolves are in search.
It is clear weather, and cold. The sun stay longer in the sky, and
there are sun-dogs flashing on either side, and the air is bright with
frost-dust. The snow falls no more upon the trail, and I see the
fresh sign of dogs and sled. There is one man with that outfit,

and I see in the snow that he is not strong. He, too, has not enough to eat. The young wolves see the fresh sign, too, and they are much excited. 'Hurry!' they say. All the time they say: 'Hurry! Faster, Charley, faster!'

"We make hurry very slow. All the time the man and the woman fall down. When they try to ride on sled, the dogs are too weak, and the dogs fall down. Besides, it is so cold that if they ride on the sled they will freeze. It is very easy for a hungry man to freeze. When the woman fall down, the man help her up. Sometimes the woman help the man up. By and by both fall down and cannot get up, and I must help them up all the time, else they will not get up and will die there in the snow. This is very hard work, for I am greatly weary, and as well I must drive the dogs, and the man and woman are very heavy, with no strength in their bodies. So, by and by, I, too, fall down in the snow, and there is no one to help me up. I must get up by myself. And always do I get up by myself, and help them up, and make the dogs go on.

"That night I get one ptarmigan, and we are very hungry. And that night the man says to me, 'What time start to-morrow, Charley?' It is like the voice of a ghost. I say, 'All the time you make start at five o'clock.' 'To-morrow,' he says, 'we will start at three o'clock.'

"And we start at three o'clock. It is clear and cold, and there is no wind. When daylight comes we can see a long way off. And it is very quiet. We can hear no sound but the beat of our hearts, and in the silence that is a very loud sound. We are like sleepwalkers, and we walk in dreams until we fall down; and then we know we must get up, and we see the trail once more and hear the beating of our hearts.

"In the morning we come upon the last-night camp of the man who is before us. It is a poor camp, the kind a man makes who is hungry and without strength. On the snow there are pieces of blanket and of canvas, and I know what has happened. His dogs have eaten their harness, and he has made new harness out of his blankets. The man and woman stare hard at what is to be seen. Their eyes are toil-mad and hunger-mad, and burn like fire deep in their heads. Their faces are like the faces of people who have died of hunger, and their cheeks are black with the dead flesh of many freezings. We come to where we can see a long way over the snow, and that for which they look is before them. A mile away

there are black spots upon the snow. The black spots move. My
eyes are dim, and I must stiffen my soul to see. And I see one man
with dogs and a sled. The baby wolves see, too. They can no longer
talk, but they whisper: 'On, on! Let us hurry!'

"And they fall down, but they go on. The man who is before
us, his blanket harness breaks often and he must stop and mend it.
Our harness is good, for I have hung it in trees each night. At
eleven o'clock the man is half a mile away. At one o'clock he is
a quarter of a mile away. He is very weak. We see him fall down
many times in the snow.

"Now we are three hundred yards away. We go very slow.
Maybe in two, three hours we go one mile. We do not walk. All
the time we fall down. We stand up and stagger two steps, maybe
three steps, then we fall down again. And all the time I must
help up the man and woman. Sometimes they rise to their knees
and fall forward, maybe four or five times before they can get
to their feet again, and stagger two or three steps and fall. But
always do they fall forward. Standing or kneeling, always do they
fall forward, gaining on the trail each time by the length of
their bodies.

"Sometimes they crawl on hands and knees like animals that
live in the forest. We go like snails—like snails that are dying
we go so slow. And yet we go faster than the man who is before
us. For he, too, falls all the time, and there is no Sitka Charley
to lift him up. Now he is two hundred yards away. After a long
time he is one hundred yards away.

"It is a funny sight. I want to laugh out loud, Ha! ha! just like
that, it is so funny. It is a race of dead men and dead dogs. It is
like in a dream when you have a nightmare and run away very
fast for your life and go very slow. The man who is with me is
mad. The woman is mad. I am mad. All the world is mad. And I
want to laugh, it is so funny.

"The stranger man who is before us leaves his dogs behind and
goes on alone across the snow. After a long time we come to the
dogs. They lie helpless in the snow, their harness of blanket and
canvas on them, the sled behind them, and as we pass them they
whine to us and cry like babies that are hungry.

"Then we, too, leave our dogs and go on alone across the
snow. The man and the woman are nearly gone, and they moan and
groan and sob, but they go on. I, too, go on. I have but the one

thought. It is to come up to the stranger man. Then it is that I shall rest, and not until then shall I rest, and it seems that I must lie down and sleep for a thousand years, I am so tired.

"The stranger man is fifty yards away, all alone in the white snow. He falls and crawls, staggers, and falls and crawls again. By and by he crawls on hands and knees. He no longer stands up. And the man and woman no longer stand up. They, too, crawl after him on hands and knees. But I stand up. Sometimes I fall, but always do I stand up again.

"On either side the sun are sun-dogs, so that there are three suns in the sky.

"After a long time the stranger man crawls no more. He stands slowly upon his feet and rocks back and forth. Also does he take off one mitten and wait with revolver in his hand, rocking back and forth as he waits. His face is skin and bones, and frozen black. It is a hungry face. The eyes are deep-sunk in his head, and the lips are snarling. The man and woman, too, get upon their feet, and they go toward him very slowly. And all about is the snow and the silence. And in the sky are three suns, and all the air is flashing with the dust of diamonds.

"And thus it was that I, Sitka Charley, saw the baby wolves make their kill. No word is spoken. Only does the stranger man snarl with his hungry face. Also does he rock to and fro, his shoulders drooping, his knees bent, and his legs wide apart so that he does not fall down. The man and the woman stop maybe fifty feet away. Their legs, too, are wide apart so that they do not fall down, and their bodies rock to and fro. The stranger man is very weak. His arm shakes, so that when he shoots at the man his bullet strikes in the snow. The man cannot take off his mitten. The stranger man shoots at him again, and this time the bullet goes by in the air. Then the man takes the mitten in his teeth and pulls it off. But his hand is frozen and he cannot hold the revolver, and it falls in the snow. I look at the woman. Her mitten is off, and the revolver is in her hand. Three times she shoot, quick, just like that. The hungry face of the stranger man is still snarling as he falls forward in the snow.

"They did not look at the dead man. 'Let us go on,' they said. And we went on. But now that they have found that for which they look, they are like dead. The last strength has gone out of them. They can stand no more upon their feet. They will not crawl, but desire only to close their eyes and sleep. I see not far away a place for camp. I kick them. I have my dog-whip, and I give them the lash of it. They cry aloud, but they must crawl. And they do crawl to the place for camp. I build a fire so that they will not freeze. Then I go back for sled. Also, I kill the dogs of the stranger man so that we may have food and not die. I put the man and woman in blankets and they sleep. Sometimes I wake them up and give them little bit of food. They are not awake, but they take the food. The woman sleep one day and a half. Then she wake up and go to sleep again. The man sleep two days and wake up and go to sleep again. After that we go down to the coast at St. Michaels. And when the ice goes out of Bering Sea the man and woman go away on a steamship. But first they pay me my seven hundred and fifty dollars a month."

"But why did they kill the man?" I asked.

Sitka Charley delayed reply until he had lighted his pipe. He glanced at the illustration on the wall and nodded his head at it familiarly. Then he said, speaking slowly and ponderingly:

"I have thought much. I do not know. It is something that happened. It is a picture I remember. It is like looking in at the window and seeing the man writing a letter. They came into my life and they went out of my life, and the picture is, as I have said, without beginning, the end without understanding."

"You have painted many pictures in the telling," I said.

"Ay,"—he nodded his head. "But they were without beginning and without end."

"The last picture of all had an end," I said.

"Ay," he answered. "But what end?"

"It was a piece of life," I said.

"Ay," he answered. "It was a piece of life."

STEWART EDWARD WHITE

THE TWO-GUN MAN

A two-gun man with an ironic sense of humor delivers Señor
Johnson's stolen cattle to him and collects the reward, but
Señor Johnson is no better off than he was in the first place.
This is an amusing tale, set against the colorful Arizona back-
ground Mr. White knows so well. (From *Arizona Nights*,
Doubleday, Doran, 1907.)

BUCK JOHNSON was American born, but with a black beard
and a dignity of manner that had earned him the title of
Señor. He had drifted into southeastern Arizona in the days of
Cochise and Victorio and Geronimo. He had persisted, and so in
time had come to control the water—and hence the grazing—of
nearly all the Soda Springs Valley. His troubles were many, and
his difficulties great. There were the ordinary problems of lean
and dry years. There were also the extraordinary problems of
devastating Apaches; rivals for early and ill-defined range rights
—and cattle-rustlers.

Señor Buck Johnson was a man of capacity, courage, directness
of method, and perseverance. Especially the latter. Therefore he
had survived to see the Apaches subdued, the range rights ad-
justed, his cattle increased to thousands, grazing the area of a
principality. Now, all the energy and fire of his frontiersman's
nature he had turned to wiping out the third uncertainty of an
uncertain business. He found it a task of some magnitude.

For Señor Buck Johnson lived just north of that terra incognita filled with the mystery of a double chance of death from man or the flaming desert known as the Mexican border. There, by natural gravitation, gathered all the desperate characters of three States and two republics. He who rode into it took good care that no one should ride behind him, lived warily, slept light, and breathed deep when once he had again sighted the familiar peaks of Cochise's Stronghold. No one professed knowledge of those who dwelt therein. They moved, mysterious as the desert illusions that compassed them about. As you rode, the ranges of mountains visibly changed form, the monstrous, snaky, sea-like growths of the cactus clutched at your stirrup, mock lakes sparkled and dissolved in the middle distance, the sun beat hot and merciless, the powdered dry alkali beat hotly and mercilessly back—and strange, grim men, swarthy, bearded, heavily armed, with red-rimmed unshifting eyes, rode silently out of the mists of illusion to look on you steadily, and then to ride silently back into the desert haze. They might be only the herders of the gaunt cattle, or again they might belong to the Lost Legion that peopled the country. All you could know was that of the men who entered in, but few returned.

Directly north of this unknown land you encountered parallel fences running across the country. They enclosed nothing, but offered a check to the cattle drifting toward the clutch of the renegades, and an obstacle to swift, dashing forays.

Of cattle-rustling there are various forms. The boldest consists quite simply of running off a bunch of stock, hustling it over the Mexican line, and there selling it to some of the big Sonora ranch owners. Generally this sort means war. Also are there subtler means, grading in skill from the rebranding through a wet blanket, through the crafty refashioning of a brand to the various methods of separating the cow from her unbranded calf. In the course of his task Señor Buck Johnson would have to do with them all, but at present he existed in a state of warfare, fighting an enemy who stole as the Indians used to steal.

Already he had fought two pitched battles, and had won them both. His cattle increased, and he became rich. Nevertheless he knew that constantly his resources were being drained. Time and again he and his new Texas foreman, Jed Parker, had followed the trail of a stampeded bunch of twenty or thirty, followed them on down through the Soda Springs Valley to the cut drift fences, there to abandon them. For, as yet, an armed force would be needed to penetrate the borderland. Once he and his men had experienced the glory of a night pursuit. Then, at the drift fences, he had fought one of his battles. But it was impossible adequately to patrol all parts of a range bigger than some Eastern States.

Buck Johnson did his best, but it was like stopping with sands the innumerable little leaks of a dam. Did his riders watch toward the Chiricahuas, then a score of beef steers disappeared from Grant's Pass forty miles away. Pursuit here meant leaving cattle unguarded there. It was useless, and the Señor soon perceived that sooner or later he must strike in offence.

For this purpose he began slowly to strengthen the forces of his riders. Men were coming in from Texas. They were good men, addicted to the grass-rope, the double cinch, and the ox-bow stirrup. Señor Johnson wanted men who could shoot, and he got them.

"Jed," said Señor Johnson to his foreman, "the next son of a gun that rustles any of our cows is sure loading himself full of trouble. We'll hit his trail and will stay with it, and we'll reach his cattle-rustling conscience with a rope."

So it came about that a little army crossed the drift fences and entered the border country. Two days later it came out, and mighty pleased to be able to do so. The rope had not been used.

The reason for the defeat was quite simple. The thief had run his cattle through the lava beds where the trail at once became difficult to follow. This delayed the pursuing party; they ran out of water, and, as there was among them not one man well enough acquainted with the country to know where to find more, they had to return.

"No use, Buck," said Jed. "We'd any of us come in on a gun play, but we can't buck the desert. We'll have to get someone who knows the country."

"That's all right—but where?" queried Johnson.

"There's Pereza," suggested Parker. "It's the only town down near that country."

"Might get someone there," agreed the Señor.

Next day he rode away in search of a guide. The third evening he was back again, much discouraged.

"The country's no good," he explained. "The regular inhabitants 're a set of Mexican bums and old soaks. The cowmen's

all from north and don't know nothing more than we do. I found
lots who claimed to know that country, but when I told 'em what
I wanted they shied like a colt. I couldn't hire 'em, for no money,
to go down in that country. They ain't got the nerve. I took two
days to her, too, and rode out to a ranch where they said a man
lived who knew all about it down there. Nary riffle. Man looked
all right, but his tail went down like the rest when I told him
what we wanted. Seemed plumb scairt to death. Says he lives too
close to the gang. Says they'd wipe him out sure if he done it.
Seemed plumb *scairt*." Buck Johnson grinned. "I told him so and
he got hosstyle right off. Didn't seem no ways scairt of me. I don't
know what's the matter with that outfit down there. They're
plumb terrorized."

That night a bunch of steers was stolen from the very corrals
of the home ranch. The home ranch was far north, near Fort
Sherman itself, and so had always been considered immune from
attack. Consequently these steers were very fine ones.

For the first time Buck Johnson lost his head and his dignity.
He ordered the horses.

"I'm going to follow that —— —— into Sonora," he shouted to
Jed Parker. "This thing's got to stop!"

"You can't make her, Buck," objected the foreman. "You'll
get held up by the desert, and, if that don't finish you, they'll
tangle you up in all those little mountains down there, and ambush
you, and massacre you. You know it damn well."

"I don't give a ———," exploded Señor Johnson, "if they do.
No man can slap my face and not get a run for it."

Jed Parker communed with himself.

"Señor," said he, at last, "it's no good; you can't do it. You
got to have a guide. You wait three days and I'll get you one."

"You can't do it," insisted the Señor. "I tried every man in the
district."

"Will you wait three days?" repeated the foreman.

Johnson pulled loose his latigo. His first anger had cooled.

"All right," he agreed, "and you can say for me that I'll pay
five thousand dollars in gold and give all the men and horses he
needs to the man who has the nerve to get back that bunch of
cattle, and bring in the man who rustled them. I'll sure make this
a test case."

So Jed Parker set out to discover his man with nerve.

At about ten o'clock of the Fourth of July a rider topped the summit of the last swell of land, and loped his animal down into the single street of Pereza. The buildings on either side were flat-roofed and coated with plaster. Over the sidewalks extended wooden awnings, beneath which opened very wide doors into the coolness of saloons. Each of these places ran a bar, and also games of roulette, faro, craps, and stud poker. Even this early in the morning every game was patronized.

The day was already hot with the dry, breathless, but exhilarating, heat of the desert. A throng of men idling at the edge of the sidewalks, jostling up and down their center, or eddying into the places of amusement, acknowledged the power of summer by loosening their collars, carrying their coats on their arms. They were as yet busily engaged in recognizing acquaintances. Later they would drink freely and gamble, and perhaps fight. Toward all but those whom they recognized they preserved an attitude of potential suspicion, for here were gathered the "bad men" of the border countries. A certain jealousy or touchy egotism lest the other man be considered quicker on the trigger, bolder, more aggressive than himself, kept each strung to tension. An occasional shot attracted little notice. Men in the cow-countries shoot as casually as we strike matches, and some subtle instinct told them that the reports were harmless.

As the rider entered the one street, however, a more definite cause of excitement drew the loose population toward the center of the road. Immediately their mass blotted out what had interested them. Curiosity attracted the saunterers; then in turn the frequenters of the bars and gambling games. In a very few moments the barkeepers, gamblers, and look-out men, held aloof only by the necessities of their calling, alone of all the population of Pereza were not included in the newly-formed ring.

The stranger pushed his horse resolutely to the outer edge of the crowd where, from his point of vantage, he could easily overlook their heads. He was a quiet-appearing young fellow, rather neatly dressed in the border costume, rode a "center fire," or single-cinch, saddle, and wore no chaps. He was what is known as a "two-gun man": that is to say, he wore a heavy Colt's revolver on either hip. The fact that the lower ends of his holsters were tied down, in order to facilitate the easy withdrawal of the revolvers, seemed to indicate that he expected to use them. He had furthermore a quiet grey eye, with the glint of steel that bore out the influence of the tied holsters.

The newcomer dropped his reins on his pony's neck, eased himself to an attitude of attention, and looked down gravely on what was taking place.

He saw over the heads of the bystanders a tall, muscular, wild-eyed man, hatless, his hair rumpled into staring confusion, his right sleeve rolled to his shoulder, a wicked-looking nine-inch knife in his hand, and a red bandana handkerchief hanging by one corner from his teeth.

"What's biting the locoed stranger?" the young man inquired of his neighbor.

The other frowned at him darkly.

"Dares anyone to take the other end of that handkerchief in his teeth, and fight it out without letting go."

"Nice joyful proposition," commented the young man.

He settled himself to closer attention. The wild-eyed man was talking rapidly. What he said cannot be printed here. Mainly was it derogatory of the southern countries. Shortly it became boastful of the northern, and then of the man who uttered it. He swaggered up and down, becoming always the more insolent as his challenge remained untaken.

"Why don't you take him up?" inquired the young man, after a moment.

"Not me!" negatived the other vigorously. "I'll go yore little old gunfight to a finish, but I don't want any cold steel in mine. Ugh! it gives me the shivers. It's a reg'lar Mexican trick! With a gun it's down and out, but this knife work is too slow and searchin'."

The newcomer said nothing, but fixed his eye again on the raging man with the knife.

"Don't you reckon he's bluffing?" he inquired.

"Not any!" denied the other with emphasis. "He's jest drunk enough to be crazy mad."

The newcomer shrugged his shoulders and cast his glance searchingly over the fringe of the crowd. It rested on a Mexican.

"Hi, Tony! come here," he called.

The Mexican approached, flashing his white teeth.

"Here," said the stranger, "lend me your knife a minute."

The Mexican, anticipating sport of his own peculiar kind, obeyed with alacrity.

"You fellows make me tired," observed the stranger, dismounting. "He's got the whole townful of you bluffed to a standstill. Damn if I don't try his little game."

He hung his coat on his saddle, shouldered his way through the press, which parted for him readily, and picked up the other corner of the handkerchief.

"Now, you mangy son of a gun," said he.

Jed Parker straightened his back, rolled up the bandana handkerchief, and thrust it into his pocket, hit flat with his hand the tousled mass of his hair, and thrust the long hunting knife into its sheath.

"You're the man I want," said he.

Instantly the two-gun man had jerked loose his weapons and was covering the foreman.

"*Am* I!" he snarled.

"Not jest that way," explained Parker. "My gun is on my hoss, and you can have this old toad-sticker if you want it. I been looking for you and took this way of finding you. Now, let's go talk."

The stranger looked him in the eye for nearly a half minute without lowering his revolvers.

"I go you," said he briefly, at last.

But the crowd, missing the purport, and in fact the very occurrence of this colloquy, did not understand. It thought the bluff had been called, and naturally, finding harmless what had intimidated it, gave way to an exasperated impulse to get even.

"You — — — bluffer!" shouted a voice, "don't you think you can run any such ranikaboo here!"

Jed Parker turned humorously to his companion.

"Do we get that talk!" he inquired gently.

For answer the two-gun man turned and walked steadily in the direction of the man who had shouted. The latter's hand strayed uncertainly toward his own weapon, but the movement paused when the stranger's clear, steel eye rested on it.

"This gentleman," pointed out the two-gun man softly, "is an old friend of mine. Don't you get to calling of him names."

His eye swept the bystanders calmly.

"Come on, Jack," said he, addressing Parker.

On the outskirts he encountered the Mexican from whom he had borrowed the knife.

"Here, Tony," said he with a slight laugh, "here's a *peso*. You'll find your knife back there where I had to drop her."

He entered a saloon, nodded to the proprietor, and led the way through it to a box-like room containing a board table and two chairs.

"Make good," he commanded briefly.

"I'm looking for a man with nerve," explained Parker, with equal succinctness. "You're the man."

"Well?"

"Do you know the country south of here?"

The stranger's eyes narrowed.

"Proceed," said he.

"I'm foreman of the Lazy Y of Soda Springs Valley range," explained Parker. "I'm looking for a man with sand enough and *sabe* of the country enough to lead a posse after cattle rustlers into the border country."

"I live in this country," admitted the stranger.

"So do plenty of others, but their eyes stick out like two raw oysters when you mention the border country. Will you tackle it?"

"What's the proposition?"

"Come and see the old man. He'll put it to you."

They mounted their horses and rode the rest of the day. The desert compassed them about, marvellously changing shape and colour, and every character, with all the noiselessness of phantasmagoria. At evening the desert stars shone steady and unwinking, like the flames of candles. By moonrise they came to the home ranch.

The buildings and corrals lay dark and silent against the moonlight that made of the plain a sea of mist. The two men unsaddled their horses and turned them loose in the wire-fenced "pasture," the necessary noises of their movements sounding sharp and clear against the velvet hush of the night. After a moment they walked stiffly past the sheds and cook shanty, past the men's bunk houses, and the tall windmill silhouetted against the sky, to the main building of the home ranch under its great cottonwoods. There a light still burned, for this was the third day, and Buck Johnson awaited his foreman.

Jed Parker pushed in without ceremony.

"Here's your man, Buck," said he.

The stranger had stepped inside and carefully closed the door behind him. The lamplight threw into relief the bold, free lines of his face, the details of his costume powdered thick with alkali, the shiny butts of the two guns in their open holsters tied at the bottom. Equally it defined the resolute countenance of Buck Johnson turned up in inquiry. The two men examined each other—and liked each other at once.

"How are you?" greeted the cattleman.

"Good-evening," responded the stranger.

"Sit down," invited Buck Johnson.

The stranger perched gingerly on the edge of a chair, with an appearance less of embarrassment than of habitual alertness.

"You'll take the job?" inquired the Señor.

"I haven't heard what it is," replied the stranger.

"Parker here ——?"

"Said you'd explain."

"Very well," said Buck Johnson. He paused a moment, collecting his thoughts. "There's too much cattle-rustling here. I'm going to stop it. I've got good men here ready to take the job, but no one who knows the country south. Three days ago I had a bunch of cattle stolen right here from the home-ranch corrals, and by one man, at that. It wasn't much of a bunch—about twenty head—but I'm going to make a starter right here, and now. I'm going to get that bunch back, and the man who stole them, if I have to go to hell to do it. And I'm going to do the same with every case of rustling that comes up from now on. I don't care if it's only one cow, I'm going to get it back—every trip. Now, I want to know if you'll lead a posse down into the south country and bring out that last bunch, and the man who rustled them?"

"I don't know ——" hesitated the stranger.

"I offer you five thousand dollars in gold if you'll bring back those cows and the man who stole 'em," repeated Buck Johnson. "And I'll give you all the horses and men you think you need."

"I'll do it," replied the two-gun man promptly.

"Good!" cried Buck Johnson, "and you better start to-morrow."

"I shall start to-night—right now."

"Better yet. How many men do you want, and grub for how long?"

"I'll play her a lone hand."

"Alone!" exclaimed Johnson, his confidence visibly cooling. "Alone! Do you think you can make her?"

"I'll be back with those cattle in not more than ten days."

"And the man," supplemented the Señor.

"And the man. What's more, I want that money here when I come in. I don't aim to stay in this country over night."

A grin overspread Buck Johnson's countenance. He understood.

"Climate not healthy for you?" he hazarded. "I guess you'd be safe enough all right with us. But suit yourself. The money will be here."

"That's agreed?" insisted the two-gun man.

"Sure."

"I want a fresh horse—I'll leave mine—he's a good one. I want a little grub."

"All right. Parker'll fit you out."

The stranger rose.

"I'll see you in about ten days."

"Good luck," Señor Buck Johnson wished him.

The next morning Buck Johnson took a trip down into the "pasture" of five hundred wire-fenced acres.

"He means business," he confided to Jed Parker, on his return. "That caballo of his is a heap sight better than the Shorty horse we let him take. Jed, you found your man with nerve, all right. How did you do it?"

The two settled down to wait, if not with confidence, at least with interest. Sometimes, remembering the desperate character of the outlaws, their fierce distrust of any intruder, the wildness of the country, Buck Johnson and his foreman inclined to the belief that the stranger had undertaken a task beyond the powers of any one man. Again, remembering the stranger's cool grey eye, the poise of his demeanor, the quickness of his movements, and the two guns with tied holsters to permit of easy withdrawal, they were almost persuaded that he might win.

"He's one of those long-chance fellows," surmised Jed. "He likes excitement. I see that by the way he takes up with my knife play.

He'd rather leave his hide on the fence than stay in the corral."

"Well, he's all right," replied Señor Buck Johnson, "and if he ever gets back, which same I'm some doubtful of, his dinero'll be here for him."

In pursuance of this he rode in to Willets, where shortly the overland train brought him from Tucson the five thousand dollars in double eagles.

In the meantime the regular life of the ranch went on. Each morning Sang, the Chinese cook, rang the great bell, summoning the men. They ate, and then caught up the saddle horses for the day, turning those not wanted from the corral into the pasture. Shortly they jingled away in different directions, two by two, on the slow Spanish trot of the cowpuncher. All day long thus they would ride, without food or water for man or beast, looking the range, identifying the stock, branding the young calves, examining generally into the state of affairs, gazing always with grave eyes on the magnificent, flaming, changing, beautiful, dreadful desert of the Arizona plains. At evening when the colored atmosphere, catching the last glow, threw across the Chiricahuas its veil of mystery, they jingled in again, two by two, untired, unhasting, the glory of the desert in their deep-set, steady eyes.

And all the day long, while they were absent, the cattle, too, made their pilgrimage, straggling in singly, in pairs, in bunches, in long files, leisurely, ruminantly, without haste. There, at the long troughs filled by the windmill or the blindfolded pump mule, they drank, then filed away again into the mists of the desert. And Señor Buck Johnson, or his foreman, Parker, examined them for their condition, noting the increase, remarking the strays from another range. Later, perhaps, they, too, rode abroad. The same thing happened at nine other ranches from five to ten miles apart, where dwelt other fierce, silent men all under the authority of Buck Johnson.

And when night fell, and the topaz and violet and saffron and amethyst and mauve and lilac had faded suddenly from the Chiricahuas, like a veil that has been rent, and the ramparts had become slate-grey and then black—the soft-breathed night wandered here and there over the desert, and the land fell under an enchantment even stranger than the day's.

So the days went by, wonderful, fashioning the ways and the characters of men. Seven passed. Buck Johnson and his foreman began to look for the stranger. Eight, they began to speculate. Nine, they doubted. On the tenth, they gave him up—and he came.

They knew him first by the soft lowing of cattle. Jed Parker, dazzled by the lamp, peered out from the door, and made him out dimly turning the animals into the corral. A moment later his pony's hoofs impacted softly on the baked earth, he dropped from the saddle and entered the room.

"I'm late," said he briefly, glancing at the clock, which indicated ten; "but I'm here."

His manner was quick and sharp, almost breathless, as though he had been running.

"Your cattle are in the corral: all of them. Have you the money?"

"I have the money here," replied Buck Johnson, laying his hand against a drawer, "and it's ready for you when you've earned it. I don't care so much for the cattle. What I wanted is the man who stole them. Did you bring him?"

"Yes, I brought him," said the stranger. "Let's see that money."

Buck Johnson threw open the drawer, and drew from it the heavy canvas sack.

"It's here. Now bring in your prisoner."

The two-gun man seemed suddenly to loom large in the doorway. The muzzles of his revolvers covered the two before him. His speech came short and sharp.

"I told you I'd bring back the cows and the one who rustled them," he snapped. "I've never lied to a man yet. Your stock is in the corral. I'll trouble you for that five thousand. I'm the man who stole your cattle!"

THE BRIDE COMES TO YELLOW SKY

There's a moral to this story: it seems that marriage has its compensations. And owing to one of them, a doubting bridegroom's life was saved. Mr. Crane wrote this after a visit to Texas, and it has a ring of authenticity that suggests fact more than fiction. (From *Twenty Stories*, Knopf, 1941.)

THE great Pullman was whirling onward with such dignity of motion that a glance from the window seemed simply to prove that the plains of Texas were pouring eastward. Vast flats of green grass, dull-hued spaces of mesquit and cactus, little groups of frame houses, woods of light and tender trees, all were sweeping into the east, sweeping over the horizon, a precipice.

A newly married pair had boarded this coach at San Antonio. The man's face was reddened from many days in the wind and sun, and a direct result of his new black clothes was that his brick-coloured hands were constantly performing in a most conscious fashion. From time to time he looked down respectfully at his attire. He sat with a hand on each knee, like a man waiting in a barber's shop. The glances he devoted to other passengers were furtive and shy.

The bride was not pretty, nor was she very young. She wore a dress of blue cashmere, with small reservations of velvet here and there, and with steel buttons abounding. She continually twisted her head to regard her puff sleeves, very stiff, straight, and high. They embarrassed her. It was quite apparent that she had cooked, and that she expected to cook, dutifully. The blushes caused by the careless scrutiny of some passengers as she had entered the car were strange to see upon this plain, under-class countenance, which was drawn in placid, almost emotionless lines.

They were evidently very happy. "Ever been in a parlour-car before?" he asked, smiling with delight.

"No," she answered; "I never was. It's fine, ain't it?"

"Great! And then after a while we'll go forward to the diner, and get a big lay-out. Finest meal in the world. Charge a dollar."

"Oh, do they?" cried the bride. "Charge a dollar? Why, that's too much—for us—ain't it, Jack?"

"Not this trip, anyhow," he answered bravely. "We're going to go the whole thing."

Later he explained to her about the trains. "You see, it's a thousand miles from one end of Texas to the other; and this train runs right across it, and never stops but four times." He had the pride of an owner. He pointed out to her the dazzling fittings of the coach; and in truth her eyes opened wider as she contemplated the sea-green figured velvet, the shining brass, silver, and glass, the wood that gleamed as darkly brilliant as the surface of a pool of oil. At one end a bronze figure sturdily held a support for a separated chamber, and at convenient places on the ceiling were frescos in olive and silver.

To the minds of the pair, their surroundings reflected the glory of their marriage that morning in San Antonio; this was the environment of their new estate; and the man's face in particular beamed with an elation that made him appear ridiculous to the negro porter. This individual at times surveyed them from afar with an amused and superior grin. On other occasions he bullied them with skill in ways that did not make it exactly plain to them that they were being bullied. He subtly used all the manners of the most unconquerable kind of snobbery. He oppressed them; but of this oppression they had small knowledge, and they speedily forgot that infrequently a number of travellers covered them with stares of derisive enjoyment. Historically there was supposed to be something infinitely humorous in their situation.

"We are due in Yellow Sky at 3:42," he said, looking tenderly into her eyes.

"Oh, are we?" she said, as if she had not been aware of it. To evince surprise at her husband's statement was part of her wifely amiability. She took from a pocket a little silver watch; and as she held it before her, and stared at it with a frown of attention, the new husband's face shone.

"I bought it in San Anton' from a friend of mine," he told her gleefully.

"It's seventeen minutes past twelve," she said, looking up at him with a kind of shy and clumsy coquetry. A passenger, noting this play, grew excessively sardonic, and winked at himself in one of the numerous mirrors.

At last they went to the dining-car. Two rows of negro waiters, in glowing white suits, surveyed their entrance with the interest, and also the equanimity, of men who had been forewarned. The pair fell to the lot of a waiter who happened to feel pleasure in steering them through their meal. He viewed them with the manner of a fatherly pilot, his countenance radiant with benevolence. The patronage, entwined with the ordinary deference, was not plain to them. And yet, as they returned to their coach, they showed in their faces a sense of escape.

To the left, miles down a long purple slope, was a little ribbon of mist where moved the keening Rio Grande. The train was approaching it at an angle, and the apex was Yellow Sky. Presently it was apparent that, as the distance from Yellow Sky grew shorter, the husband became commensurately restless. His brick-red hands were more insistent in their prominence. Occasionally he was even rather absent-minded and far-away when the bride leaned forward and addressed him.

As a matter of truth, Jack Potter was beginning to find the shadow of a deed weigh upon him like a leaden slab. He, the town marshal of Yellow Sky, a man known, liked, and feared in his corner, a prominent person, had gone to San Antonio to meet a girl he believed he loved, and there, after the usual prayers, had actually induced her to marry him, without consulting Yellow Sky for any part of the transaction. He was now bringing his bride before an innocent and unsuspecting community.

Of course people in Yellow Sky married as it pleased them, in accordance with a general custom; but such was Potter's thought of his duty to his friends, or of their idea of his duty, or of an unspoken form which does not control men in these matters, that he felt he was heinous. He had committed an extraordinary crime. Face to face with this girl in San Antonio, and spurred by his sharp impulse, he had gone headlong over all the social hedges. At San Antonio he was like a man hidden in the dark. A knife to sever any friendly duty, any form, was easy to his hand in that remote city. But the hour of Yellow Sky—the hour of daylight— was approaching.

He knew full well that his marriage was an important thing to his town. It could only be exceeded by the burning of the new hotel. His friends could not forgive him. Frequently he had reflected on the advisability of telling them by telegraph, but a new cowardice had been upon him. He feared to do it. And now the train was hurrying him toward a scene of amazement, glee, and reproach. He glanced out of the window at the line of haze swinging slowly in toward the train.

Yellow Sky had a kind of brass band, which played painfully, to the delight of the populace. He laughed without heart as he thought of it. If the citizens could dream of his prospective arrival with his bride, they would parade the band at the station and escort them, amid cheers and laughing congratulations, to his adobe home.

He resolved that he would use all the devices of speed and plainscraft in making the journey from the station to his house. Once within that safe citadel, he could issue some sort of vocal bulletin, and then not go among the citizens until they had time to wear off a little of their enthusiasm.

The bride looked anxiously at him. "What's worrying you, Jack?"

He laughed again. "I'm not worrying, girl; I'm only thinking of Yellow Sky."

She flushed in comprehension.

A sense of mutual guilt invaded their minds and developed a finer tenderness. They looked at each other with eyes softly aglow. But Potter often laughed the same nervous laugh; the flush upon the bride's face seemed quite permanent.

The traitor to the feelings of Yellow Sky narrowly watched the speeding landscape. "We're nearly there," he said.

Presently the porter came and announced the proximity of

Potter's home. He held a brush in his hand, and, with all his airy superiority gone, he brushed Potter's new clothes as the latter slowly turned this way and that way. Potter fumbled out a coin and gave it to the porter, as he had seen others do. It was a heavy and muscle-bound business, as that of a man shoeing his first horse.

The porter took their bag, and as the train began to slow they moved forward to the hooded platform of the car. Presently the two engines and their long string of coaches rushed into the station of Yellow Sky.

"They have to take water here," said Potter, from a constricted throat and in mournful cadence, as one announcing death. Before the train stopped his eye had swept the length of the platform, and he was glad and astonished to see there was none upon it but the station-agent, who, with a slightly hurried and anxious air, was walking toward the water-tanks. When the train had halted, the porter alighted first, and placed in position a little temporary step.

"Come on, girl," said Potter, hoarsely. As he helped her down they each laughed on a false note. He took the bag from the negro, and bade his wife cling to his arm. As they slunk rapidly away, his hang-dog glance perceived that they were unloading the two trunks, and also that the station-agent, far ahead near the baggage-car, had turned and was running toward him, making gestures. He laughed, and groaned as he laughed, when he noted the first effect of his marital bliss upon Yellow Sky. He gripped his wife's arm firmly to his side, and they fled. Behind them the porter stood, chuckling fatuously.

II

The California express on the Southern Railway was due at Yellow Sky in twenty-one minutes. There were six men at the bar of the Weary Gentleman saloon. One was a drummer who talked a great deal and rapidly; three were Texans who did not care to talk at that time; and two were Mexican sheep-herders, who did not talk as a general practice in the Weary Gentleman saloon. The barkeeper's dog lay on the board walk that crossed in front of the door. His head was on his paws, and he glanced drowsily here and there with the constant vigilance of a dog that is kicked on occasion. Across the sandy street were some vivid green grass-plots, so wonderful in appearance, amid the sands that burned near them in a blazing sun, that they caused a doubt in the mind. They exactly resembled the grass mats used to represent lawns on the stage. At the cooler end of the railway station, a man without a coat sat in a tilted chair and smoked his pipe. The fresh-cut bank of the Rio Grande circled near the town, and there could be seen beyond it a great plum-coloured plain of mesquit.

Save for the busy drummer and his companions in the saloon, Yellow Sky was dozing. The new-comer leaned gracefully upon the bar, and recited many tales with the confidence of a bard who has come upon a new field.

"—and at the moment that the old man fell downstairs with the bureau in his arms, the old woman was coming up with two scuttles of coal, and of course—"

The drummer's tale was interrupted by a young man who suddenly appeared in the open door. He cried: "Scratchy Wilson's drunk, and has turned loose with both hands." The two Mexicans at once set down their glasses and faded out of the rear entrance of the saloon.

The drummer, innocent and jocular, answered: "All right, old man. S'pose he has? Come in and have a drink, anyhow."

But the information had made such an obvious cleft in every skull in the room that the drummer was obliged to see its importance. All had become instantly solemn. "Say," said he, mystified, "what is this?" His three companions made the introductory gesture of eloquent speech; but the young man at the door forestalled them.

"It means, my friend," he answered, as he came into the saloon, "that for the next two hours this town won't be a health resort."

The barkeeper went to the door, and locked and barred it; reaching out of the window, he pulled in heavy wooden shutters, and barred them. Immediately a solemn, chapel-like gloom was upon the place. The drummer was looking from one to another.

"But say," he cried, "what is this, anyhow? You don't mean there is going to be a gun-fight?"

"Don't know whether there'll be a fight or not," answered one man, grimly; "but there'll be some shootin'—some good shootin'."

The young man who had warned them waved his hand. "Oh,

there'll be a fight fast enough, if any one wants it. Anybody can get a fight out there in the street. There's a fight just waiting."

The drummer seemed to be swayed between the interest of a foreigner and a perception of personal danger.

"What did you say his name was?" he asked.

"Scratchy Wilson," they answered in chorus.

"And he will kill anybody? What are you going to do? Does this happen often? Does he rampage around like this once a week or so? Can he break in that door?"

"No; he can't break down that door," replied the barkeeper. "He's tried it three times. But when he comes you'd better lay down on the floor, stranger. He's dead sure to shoot at it, and a bullet may come through."

Thereafter the drummer kept a strict eye upon the door. The time had not yet been called for him to hug the floor, but, as a minor precaution, he sidled near to the wall. "Will he kill anybody?" he said again.

The men laughed low and scornfully at the question.

"He's out to shoot, and he's out for trouble. Don't see any good in experimentin' with him."

"But what do you do in a case like this? What do you do?"

A man responded: "Why, he and Jack Potter——"

"But," in chorus the other men interrupted, "Jack Potter's in San Anton'."

"Well, who is he? What's he got to do with it?"

"Oh, he's the town marshal. He goes out and fights Scratchy when he gets on one of these tears."

"Wow!" said the drummer, mopping his brow. "Nice job he's got."

The voices had toned away to mere whisperings. The drummer wished to ask further questions, which were born of an increasing anxiety and bewilderment; but when he attempted them, the men merely looked at him in irritation and motioned him to remain silent. A tense waiting hush was upon them. In the deep shadows of the room their eyes shone as they listened for sounds from the street. One man made three gestures at the barkeeper; and the latter, moving like a ghost, handed him a glass and a bottle. The man poured a full glass of whisky, and set down the bottle noiselessly. He gulped the whisky in a swallow, and turned again toward the door in immovable silence. The drummer saw that the barkeeper, without a sound, had taken a Winchester from beneath the bar. Later, he saw this individual beckoning to him, so he tiptoed across the room.

"You better come with me back of the bar."

"No, thanks," said the drummer, perspiring; "I'd rather be where I can make a break for the back door."

Whereupon the man of bottles made a kindly but peremptory gesture. The drummer obeyed it, and, finding himself seated on a box with his head below the level of the bar, balm was laid upon his soul at sight of various zinc and copper fittings that bore a resemblance to armour-plate. The barkeeper took a seat comfortably upon an adjacent box.

"You see," he whispered, "this here Scratchy Wilson is a wonder with a gun—a perfect wonder; and when he goes on the war-trail, we hunt our holes—naturally. He's about the last one of the old gang that used to hang out along the river here. He's a terror when he's drunk. When he's sober he's all right—kind of simple—wouldn't hurt a fly—nicest fellow in town. But when he's drunk—whoo!"

There were periods of stillness. "I wish Jack Potter was back from San Anton'," said the barkeeper. "He shot Wilson up once—in the leg—and he would sail in and pull out the kinks in this thing."

Presently they heard from a distance the sound of a shot, followed by three wild yowls. It instantly removed a bond from the men in the darkened saloon. There was a shuffling of feet. They looked at each other. "Here he comes," they said.

III

A man in a maroon-coloured flannel shirt, which had been purchased for purposes of decoration, and made principally by some Jewish women on the East Side of New York, rounded a corner and walked into the middle of the main street of Yellow Sky. In either hand the man held a long, heavy, blue-black revolver. Often he yelled, and these cries rang through a semblance of a deserted village, shrilly flying over the roofs in a volume that seemed to have no relation to the ordinary vocal strength of a man. It was as if the surrounding stillness formed the arch of a tomb over him. These cries of ferocious challenge rang against walls of silence. And his boots had red tops with gilded imprints, of the kind beloved in winter by little sledding boys on the hillsides of New England.

The man's face flamed in a rage begot of whisky. His eyes, rolling, and yet keen for ambush, hunted the still doorways and windows. He walked with the creeping movement of the midnight cat. As it occurred to him, he roared menacing information. The long revolvers in his hands were as easy as straws; they were moved with an electric swiftness. The little fingers of each hand played sometimes in a musician's way. Plain from the low collar of the shirt, the cords of his neck straightened and sank, straightened and sank, as passion moved him. The only sounds were his terrible invitations. The calm adobes preserved their demeanour at the passing of this small thing in the middle of the street.

There was no offer of fight—no offer of fight. The man called to the sky. There were no attractions. He bellowed and fumed and swayed his revolvers here and everywhere.

The dog of the barkeeper of the Weary Gentleman saloon had not appreciated the advance of events. He yet lay dozing in front of his master's door. At sight of the dog, the man paused and raised his revolver humorously. At sight of the man, the dog sprang up and walked diagonally away, with a sullen head, and growling. The man yelled, and the dog broke into a gallop. As it was about to enter an alley, there was a loud noise, a whistling, and something spat the ground directly before it. The dog screamed, and, wheeling in terror, galloped headlong in a new direction. Again there was a noise, a whistling, and sand was kicked viciously before it. Fear-stricken, the dog turned and flurried like an animal in a pen. The man stood laughing, his weapons at his hips.

Ultimately the man was attracted by the closed door of the Weary Gentleman saloon. He went to it and, hammering with a revolver, demanded drink.

The door remaining imperturbable, he picked a bit of paper from the walk, and nailed it to the framework with a knife. He then turned his back contemptuously upon this popular resort and, walking to the opposite side of the street and spinning there on his heel quickly and lithely, fired at the bit of paper. He missed it by a half-inch. He swore at himself, and went away. Later he comfortably fusilladed the windows of his most intimate friend. The man was playing with this town; it was a toy for him.

But still there was no offer of fight. The name of Jack Potter, his ancient antagonist, entered his mind, and he concluded that it would be a glad thing if he should go to Potter's house, and by bombardment induce him to come out and fight. He moved in the direction of his desire, chanting Apache scalp-music.

When he arrived at it, Potter's house presented the same still front as had the other adobes. Taking up a strategic position, the man howled a challenge. But this house regarded him as might a great stone god. It gave no sign. After a decent wait, the man howled further challenges, mingling with them wonderful epithets.

Presently there came the spectacle of a man churning himself into deepest rage over the immobility of a house. He fumed at it as the winter wind attacks a prairie cabin in the North. To the distance there should have gone the sound of a tumult like the fighting of two hundred Mexicans. As necessity bade him, he paused for breath or to reload his revolvers.

IV

Potter and his bride walked sheepishly and with speed. Sometimes they laughed together shamefacedly and low.

"Next corner, dear," he said finally.

They put forth the efforts of a pair walking bowed against a strong wind. Potter was about to raise a finger to point the first appearance of the new home when, as they circled the corner, they came face to face with a man in a maroon-coloured shirt, who was feverishly pushing cartridges into a large revolver. Upon the instant the man dropped his revolver to the ground and, like lightning, whipped another from its holster. The second weapon was aimed at the bridegroom's chest.

There was a silence. Potter's mouth seemed to be merely a grave for his tongue. He exhibited an instinct to at once loosen his arm from the woman's grip, and he dropped the bag to the sand. As for the bride, her face had gone as yellow as old cloth. She was a slave to hideous rites, gazing at the apparitional snake.

The two men faced each other at a distance of three paces. He of the revolver smiled with a new and quiet ferocity.

"Tried to sneak up on me," he said. "Tried to sneak up on me!"

His eyes grew more baleful. As Potter made a slight movement, the man thrust his revolver venomously forward. "No; don't you do it, Jack Potter. Don't you move a finger toward a gun just yet. Don't you move an eyelash. The time has come for me to settle with you, and I'm goin' to do it my own way, and loaf along with no interferin'. So if you don't want a gun bent on you, just mind what I tell you."

Potter looked at his enemy. "I ain't got a gun on me, Scratchy," he said. "Honest, I ain't." He was stiffening and steadying, but yet somewhere at the back of his mind a vision of the Pullman floated: the sea-green figured velvet, the shining brass, silver, and glass, the wood that gleamed as darkly brilliant as the surface of a pool of oil—all the glory of the marriage, the environment of the new estate. "You know I fight when it comes to fighting, Scratchy Wilson; but I ain't got a gun on me. You'll have to do all the shootin' yourself."

His enemy's face went livid. He stepped forward and lashed his weapon to and fro before Potter's chest. "Don't you tell me you ain't got no gun on you, you whelp. Don't tell me no lie like that. There ain't a man in Texas ever seen you without no gun. Don't take me for no kid." His eyes blazed with light, and his throat worked like a pump.

"I ain't takin' you for no kid," answered Potter. His heels had not moved an inch backward. "I'm takin' you for a damn fool. I tell you I ain't got a gun, and I ain't. If you're goin' to shoot me up, you better begin now; you'll never get a chance like this again."

So much enforced reasoning had told on Wilson's rage; he was calmer. "If you ain't got a gun, why ain't you got a gun?" he sneered. "Been to Sunday-school?"

"I ain't got a gun because I've just come from San Anton' with my wife. I'm married," said Potter. "And if I'd thought there was going to be any galoots like you prowling around when I brought my wife home, I'd had a gun, and don't you forget it."

"Married!" said Scratchy, not at all comprehending.

"Yes, married. I'm married," said Potter, distinctly.

"Married?" said Scratchy. Seemingly for the first time he saw the drooping, drowning woman at the other man's side. "No!" he said. He was like a creature allowed a glimpse of another world. He moved a pace backward, and his arm, with the revolver, dropped to his side. "Is this the lady?" he asked.

"Yes; this is the lady," answered Potter.

There was another period of silence.

"Well," said Wilson at last, slowly, "I s'pose it's all off now."

"It's all off if you say so, Scratchy. You know I didn't make the trouble." Potter lifted his valise.

"Well, I 'low it's off, Jack," said Wilson. He was looking at the ground. "Married!" He was not a student of chivalry; it was merely that in the presence of this foreign condition he was a simple child of the earlier plains. He picked up his starboard revolver, and, placing both weapons in their holsters, he went away. His feet made funnel-shaped tracks in the heavy sand.

CONRAD RICHTER

THE SQUARE PIANO

Here is an intense story of feud, violence and beauty, written by one of our most able novelists and story-tellers, the author of *The Sea of Grass*. It is a tale with almost unbearable suspense, and it contains one of the strangest betrothal scenes in literature. (From *Early Americana*, Knopf, 1936.)

I NEVER thought that it would ever be gone, or that there would come a time when I would wish to see it again and could not: the dusty, frontier street of La Cruz as it lay that day in the spring sunshine with the railroad nearly a thousand miles away and all the wild brew of that raw land stirring in a young girl's veins.

I can close my eyes and see the muslin windows of the dark little Mexican shops a step down from the curbless sidewalks and the real glass panes of Tom Doan's trading post, unwashed since their long haul from St. Louis by wagon train. I can feel the strange alchemy in my young blood when the wind stirred the matted strands of the dry Ute scalp on the Lawler hide-and-wool warehouse like a motheaten hawk nailed to a barn. And sometimes, half asleep, I can still hear the Santa Fe stage as it passed my mother's house in town late at night—a clatter of hoofs, a rattle of spokes, and the rush of a lurching coach on rawhide springs, leaving in its wake something besides the small girl who lay with bare legs between the coarse, handmade sheets, breathing the faint scent of sage which my mother kept sprinkled on her folded bolster-cases.

But what I shall forget last is Valeria Wingate as she looked the day of what was to have been her betrothal night, the night of La Cruz's frontier show and dance. The Territory's Grand Musical Entertainment and Ball, it was called by Professor Freyburg, who rode horseback from Santa Fe once a month to teach pupils on the melodeon and violin, his dusty fiddle-case on his back, his leather music-roll tied to the saddle thongs, and his stirrups nearly touching the ground. It was to be a night of history in La Cruz, with Sadie Montgomery's long-overdue piano, the first in the territory, promised for the event, and a faint grim air starting to blow down the frontier street.

Early in the afternoon I felt the first touch of that air on my face. Twice I had run to the corner of the square to see if the piano had come, and for sight of Ewing riding in from our ranch on the Jicaritas. The first time, sitting in my red dress on a sack of oats on the Doan trading-post gallery, I noticed nothing. The next time I was aware of a veiled difference in the mood of the town.

Visibly, little had changed. The dusty red square and Jack Lawler's adobe corral still teemed with saddle-humped horses as usual, with steers in hand-made yokes, with slatted buckboards, white-sheeted wagons, and a small band of spotted Ute ponies packed with tanned buffalo hides to trade. Men moved in and out in heavy flannel shirts; in red, gray, and checkered linsey shirts; in shirts of fringed buckskin; occasionally in a blanket—and a sprinkling of women in sober cashmeres and brighter sunbonnets, in plaids and flowered calicoes, in black *rebozos* and in telltale cotton wrappers with high-heel shoes.

And yet there was something intangibly wrong; as when, during the past five years, I would ask my silent mother if anything were the matter and she would shake her head, but all the time I knew that there was. Turning home, I found tied to one of our front hitching-posts a familiar horse from the ranch—Andy Moffet's pinto, with the map of South America splashed on one hip. I ran through the solid pine gate and into the house the back way.

When I reached the sitting-room doorway, I saw my mother— a small, commanding person even in her great, post-oak chair—

basting a sleeve of the black percale dress she intended to wear to the entertainment that evening, and Andy Moffet standing in the center of the floor, a tall, inflexible figure, his powerful lips compressed into wrinkles like the mouth of a valise, his breeches gray with winter hair shed by his mount.

When he saw me, his long upper lip grew peculiarly uncommunicative.

"Yes, Miz Piatt, the brandin's a-goin' fine," he agreed steadily.

My mother's bright needle and thimble kept flashing as if nothing more important had been said before I came in, but my young eyes had caught the unmistakable print of sage I had seen but once in her cheeks since the day I had stood, a very small child, in the same doorway five years before when they had carried in my father—a huge man, with a shaggy head like a buffalo. I remember how the men had staggered with their burden and had with difficulty laid him on the long pine settee. His eyes, always an unsparing blue, were bright as if with fever, and when my mother would have hurried Ewing and me out of the room, he raised that massive head and his eyes glowed on us with a light I had never seen before in a man's face.

"Let them stay, mamma," he said. "I want Ewing to remember how a Piatt can die."

At the time it all seemed fated and inexorable as a scene out of the Old Testament which my mother read to us of a Sunday—the bleak faces of the men; the rigid young back of Ewing, only twelve, beside me; and my mother's incredibly steady hands as they pulled back my father's shirt and I saw with feelings that I cannot put into words where he had stuffed his handkerchief into his side.

Now with the mark of the sage again in my mother's cheek, it all came back to me like a bad dream of early childhood: the trouble of years' standing between my father and Jack Lawler; the green hide Lawler had hung on his plaza corral wall to dry with our brand, the Rafter P, turned out in a kind of insolent challenge which could be read more plainly those days than if printed in type; my father's slow, angered words: "Lawler's bought that stolen hide or stole the cow himself. Everybody in town knows I don't deal with him and is waiting to see what I'm goin' to do"; my mother's quiet plea: "Let it hang till tomorrow, Minor, before you claim it. Some Mexican will steal it during the night"; and the intense silence in the house next morning when Ewing reported that the hide was still there, and my father quietly took his gun belt from the bedpost and left for the square while my mother with strained hands set his accustomed place at the table.

That it had started over nothing of consequence such as sheep and cattle, range or water, but only a green hide, and had grown until nearly fifty men had taken sides did not seem strange to anyone then. Once someone had been killed, there was no stopping it until the last Piatt man had been felled. I thought with a sudden stab that Ewing was a man now, seventeen, with thick clustering hair, a blue eye that grew hard whenever he passed a Lawler man, and in his shadowed young face when it turned toward Valerie Wingate a light like his father's the day he lay on the settee and gazed at us children rigid in the doorway.

"I'm glad the spring work's coming along so well, Andy," my mother murmured without looking up.

They did not deceive me for a moment. From one of the two wide, walnut and convoluted steel frames on the wall, my father's fearless blue gaze looked down on me, but the eyes of my oldest brother, Ralph, held a gentle expression, as if they had entirely forgiven the hands that had held the fatal rifle barrel against him.

My mother glanced up with her gray eyes that could be so level and unreadable. "Don't you want to run down and see Vallie awhile, Cynthia Ann?"

I nodded, staring a moment, and slipped quietly out the way I had come. At the pump my shoes wanted to go the back way by our stable and corral, but something I remembered in my father's eyes sent me out the front gate.

A few more steps and I plunged into the square, telling myself that, no matter what had happened, the Lawlers would not hurt a little girl or my mother would not have sent me out. And yet I tried to walk as if I wasn't a Piatt and a little scared, as no Piatt should be. Down the square I went, a small, stiff figure with tightly braided pigtails sticking out behind me, the petticoats under my red plaid dress striking the ribbed stockings of my knees at every step. And when I passed the Lawler store and warehouse I felt in my back all the bullets that had found my father and Ralph.

At the alley by Kerr's saddlery shop I froze to the sandy soil to let Bill Parr pass, in a finely checkered green and blue linsey shirt and swaying on the saddle like a bag of oats. When I tossed a look over my shoulder he had stopped in front of the Lawler store and was throwing the barrel of his gun into the air to greet his companions inside.

With the shots echoing among the adobe walls of the square, I reached the house and shop of Ansel Wingate, gunsmith and surveyor. The sitting-room door stood open in the spring sunshine, and there was Valeria, aged sixteen, on her fringed red stool at the melodeon, practicing a new piece, printed in German, called, in English, *March and Evening Star from Tannhäuser*, which almost no one in La Cruz had ever heard before.

She did not hear my knock. Standing there at the door, I felt that no one could see her thus and soon forget her—her slender, resolute back in quaker-gray basque, her voluminous gray skirts rustling over the moving, carpeted organ treads, her hands already running with a sure touch through the new piece as if it had been one of Czerny's finger exercises. But what I admired most was her hair. The color of a new saddle, it held a burnished vigor, a hardy luster, unlike hair today. It was not simply an ornament, which it was, but a vivid expression of Valeria Wingate herself, alive with a quality I can still feel but cannot put into words.

Then she turned and saw me and was off the fringed stool in a moment.

"Are you and your violin ready for tonight, Cynthia Ann?" Valeria asked.

I nodded, hoping she could not tell that the muscles in the back of my neck were still rigid. Through the open door to the shop I could see Frank Dague, an armed guard to the Lawler wagons, throwing open the breech of a rifle and squinting through the barrel toward a window.

Valeria moved her fringed stool between me and the doorway. "Don't you want to sit over here, Cynthia Ann?" She indicated a heavy pine rocker covered with a fawn-colored burro skin and out of range of the shop.

I shook my head. I could see Frank Dague throwing the rifle expertly to his shoulder, his ragged mustache caressing the stock, his dark eyes like adamant glancing down the long barrel. He did it several times in quick succession, a rapid gesture that both fascinated and chilled me.

"You hear what happened last night at the lava beds, Ansel?"

he drawled. Then he moved out of sight, and all I could see were chisels, rasps, and mallets in racks on the workbench; foot lathe and three-legged transit in the corner; and on a stool the long figure of Ansel Wingate with black mustache and eyes more piercing than any tool in his shop, on the lap of his deerskin apron a long-barreled revolver with rough marks cut into the ivory handle.

"I heard at noon from my daughter," Valeria's father said quietly.

"I reckon you know what it means?" Frank Dague persisted. From the tone I judged that he was sighting the rifle through a window.

Valeria rose quickly before her father could reply. "Don't you want to hear my new piece, Cynthia Ann?" Without waiting for my reply she drew her fringed stool to the melodeon.

It was only a small box organ, varnished a light yellow, with few octaves and fewer stops, but when Valeria sat up to its carpeted pedals the gunsmith shop receded and pictures came on the whitewashed walls of the Wingate sitting-room.

And after a while the figure of the girl in the enlarged daguerreotype above the melodeon seemed to step out of its oval frame and sit in the room with us, a girl with the gentle bearing of a lady, in a dress graceful with many small bows, and with eyes that had never been accustomed to look on a rough, frontier world.

All I had heard of Valeria's mother from my own mother and Valeria herself seemed to float in the air about us: her father's great stone house in Pennsylvania; their garden that ran to the governor's mansion on the hill; her own square piano at a window overlooking a majestic river that never went dry like the Rio Grande; and the May morning white with apple blossoms when she had run away with a tall young surveyor with a black broadcloth cape swinging from his shoulders, and the fever of the West in his eyes.

But when Valeria's hands reached that part in her piece, "Oh, thou sublime, sweet evening star!" what I saw were the Jicarita Mountains towering over our wide ranch, and the golden cloud of autumn aspens lifting from the trees, and under them, walking up the rolling slopes, Valeria Wingate and my brother Ewing, hand in hand. But all the time through Ewing's misty outline I was conscious of Valeria's father's shop with revolvers hanging from pegs, and rifles and shotguns resting across black buffalo horns riveted to a wide plank erected from floor to ceiling.

Valeria kept playing one piece after another until the tinkle of the small bell in the shop told us that the customer had gone. Afterwards she glanced quietly at me in her direct, characteristic way.

"Has Ewing come yet, Cynthia Ann?"

I shook my head. "Are you going tonight, Vallie?"

Her brown eyes, strong with flecks of golden rust, searched mine as if to glimpse how much I knew. "If the piano comes and Ewing goes, I'll go," she said.

I told myself I didn't believe the piano would come any more that day. But half an hour later, when I went up the square, I heard a sound like a great pounding, the unmistakable signal of an approaching ox train. For a long time I stood under Sedillo's tamarisk while the reverberating linchpins in the unseen wheels grew closer. Presently a long file of slow-moving steers wound into the square, fourteen to the first wagon, yokes cracking against their horns, horn clicking against horn, chain clanking, shouts and whip-cracks rising from the bull-whacker.

The second wagon stopped at the red calico curtains of Dick Coors's Palace Dance Hall, four times a year seat of the district court and tonight scene of the Grand Entertainment and Ball. The air grew blue with curses, and a tremendous box was dragged sidewise into the hall. Mrs. Sadie Montgomery hurried up, suited and gloved, her bonnet feathered like no one else's in La Cruz. I could hear a great hammering and the portentous screech of drawn nails. Presently the long legs of the music teacher hurried across the square, his frock coat flapping, on his head his ancient beaver. And when I started for home I had heard for the first time in my life the momentous note of a piano, the monotonous striking of a single key, which I learned later was the professor tuning the steel strings after their long journey across the plains.

When I reached our hitching-posts the late-afternoon air had already turned chill, and Andy Moffet's pinto was gone. Our kitchen smelled hot and fragrant with burning piñon. A kettle, black without and copper within, steamed on the high stove. And the smaller of our wooden tubs stood on the kitchen floor attended by wash-pan and lard-bucket of soft soap on their accustomed bench.

My mother looked up from where she sat grinding home-parched coffee, the small, square mill held firmly between her knees. When I told her about the piano her face remained unchanged.

"Wash all over and dress. I'll get your clean things."

I peered into the sitting-room. "Hasn't Ewing come yet?"

"I told Andy to meet him on the trail and tell him to go back to the ranch."

The tub, I knew, had just come from the unheated storeroom, and I pulled it up to the stove and warmed its bottom for my feet with a dipper of hot water. Before I had rubbed my scant body dry with one of our huck towels, I could feel darkness settling implacably over the town. My mother lighted candles while I dressed in my clean, cold muslin underthings, but all the while I was thinking what people would say of Ewing if he stayed away from the show and dance.

Sitting wrapped in a warm blanket at my mother's orders after my bath, my ear caught the closing of our stable door. I glanced quickly at my mother. Then I saw that the table had been set with three places, that a fresh jar of mustang-grape jelly had been brought out on the clean, blue-checkered cloth, and that my mother was rolling the dough for half-moon apple turnovers, which she only made on important occasions.

In a minute or two the door pushed in, and Ewing's rugged young form filled the opening, his hat brushing the overhead, his best trousers pulled down over his boots, and Ralph's nugget stickpin in the tie on his blue flannel shirt. He smiled at me, but I had never seen his wind-tanned cheeks so flat.

I wondered at him. It didn't seem that he could be the boy who had stood with me in the sitting-room doorway five years before, but when he hung his hat on a kitchen peg I saw tonight how much he looked like his father—the same shaggy head like a young buffalo and unsparing eyes like a field piece deliberately trained.

"How are you, folks?" he greeted us quietly. For just a moment the youth in him broke through. "Apple turnovers!" he exclaimed; then the impassive curtain dropped back again.

I wanted to run up to him. He stood so reserved and alone, as if his road lay where no one could help or accompany him. But I stayed in my blanket and watched my mother's gray eyes turn to him through the smoky haze that hung in the candlelit kitchen.

"Are you hungry, Ewing?" was all she said.

I knew he must have ridden hard to get here in time to eat supper with us, but he nodded briefly, raised a boot to the wash-bench and started to take off his spurs.

"Didn't you see Andy?" she asked.

He glanced first at me to see if I were listening, then a silent look passed between them. "I told Vallie I was takin' her tonight," he answered.

"Vallie would understand," my mother said slowly.

He glanced down at his spur buckle, and a flinty look was in his eye. "I figure, mamma, I wouldn't be much of a man if I was scared of a Lawler."

My mother turned back to her stove.

"Are Taffy and her colt all right, Ewing?" I asked.

"Just fine, Cynthy Ann," he said, disengaging the other spur and tossing both into a corner. Tipping back a chair, he brought out his tobacco. At the familiar fragrance and an indefinable something else in the room, I could close my eyes and almost believe that my father and Ralph were there.

My mother was a little woman who never crossed the street or square to avoid a drunkard, Indian, or Lawler man, but I think she dreaded supper that night and put it off as long as she could. When at last we sat down to the table, it was a silent meal, with all of us watching the flicker of the candles.

Once my mother rose to replenish the platter of apple turnovers from the back of the stove, and I saw Ewing steal a lingering glance about the familiar room—at the huge wood- and chip-box he had often filled, at the shelf of medicines and remedies whose bitter taste he knew, at the nail on which hung the pine bootjack he had used and felt, and on its stand the water-bucket and floating dipper from which he had daily drunk.

When the eight-day clock in the sitting-room struck tinnily, he rose, and as he came back from his room I saw that he had put on a coat for the entertainment and dance. "I reckon I'll be goin' for Vallie," he said.

My mother had risen while he was out of the room and now stood beside him at the door. Her hair, black with a wide skein

of gray wound through it, came to his shoulder. I saw her hand
press his arm, then he turned quickly and went out. I remember
that before he reached the pump his tall form had already merged
with the darkness, then a square of candlelight fell across his moving back. He must have buttoned his coat in the interim. I could
see the outline of a heavy belt slanting downward toward the
front of his right hip, and long after the door had been closed I
noticed that my mother kept strangely listening.

I am sure tonight that if some grotesque power could set me
back in that vanished adobe house in La Cruz, I could still blow
out the candle on the sitting-room table and find my way unerringly to the front door in the darkness as I did that night
without stumbling over my mother's heavy post-oak chair or the
small pine table at which she often sat with the account books
for the ranch.

The moon had not yet risen, and I knew that we were outside
mainly by the cool fresh air in my face and the scent of town
piñon and cedar smoke in my nostrils. My mother closed the door,
and without benefit of lamp-post or match, with only a feeble
glimmer from an occasional window, we found our way out through
the solid pine gate in our earthen wall and down the narrow winding street toward where a dim nimbus marked the direction of the
square. The sidewalk twisted, rose and fell, now very narrow,
now obstructed in the very middle by the shaggy trunk of a giant
cottonwood, but never inconveniently to feet that knew every yard
of the way.

When we reached the square, cheerful rectangles of light glowed
from the Empire Saloon, from Doan's trading post, the Leavenworth House, and other places. Outside of Dick Coors's Palace
Dance Hall a yellow torch flared into the night, and across the
plaza groups of people were variously wending their way toward
it. Someone laughed. And suddenly I felt the tight pinch of my
small fingers relax on my bow and violin. There was, I realized,
entertainment ahead, a show, the exciting presence of a crowd—
above all, Sadie Montgomery's piano. And everything was all
right.

We stood presently with the blinding yellow glare in our faces
while our streaming black shadows shortened and lengthened behind us. Through the door I could see the professor making
change from his tall hat standing upside down on the chair beside

him. Behind him lounged protectingly the heavy figure of the
sheriff, a Lawler man who had done nothing about my father's and
Ralph's deaths, and I felt, rather than saw, my mother's tight lip
curl at his gun on either hip.

With his Spanish wife between us and the door stood Wes Gatlin,
owner of the huge W E S and father of two girls at convent school
in St. Louis. I knew it was he who had laughed. When he turned
to greet my mother I thought his massive face sobered for a
moment. Then he grew more jovial than ever, and I wished that
we might sit in his great, reassuring shadow and within the play
of his small, dancing black eyes.

We started down the aisle, and my blood tingled at the crowded
scene, at the hum of talk that rose from it, at the platform of
loose, planed boards laid on sawhorses and, on the floor in front
of it, a magnificent shape covered with a wagon sheet, which I
knew with a little thrill must be Sadie Montgomery's piano.

The first six or eight rows had been made up of chairs and
benches, after which planks had been laid across kegs and boxes,
all of which would be swept aside later for the dancing. The hall
was half full, but the best seats had by no means been taken,
everyone going to his respective station. I saw Mrs. Wes Gatlin
hesitating between the first and second rows. My mother displayed
no such uncertainty. She knew exactly where she was going and
marched there in short steps, bowing to acquaintances as she went
and taking two saloon armchairs on the aisle in the third row.

Ewing and Valeria were not there, and I twisted on my chair
to watch the incoming stream at the door: bushily bearded Doc
Stockton, who looked like General Grant and walked with one arm
behind him; the Claycombs, from the Carolinas, with their Negro
girl, who was given a solitary bench in a rearmost corner; teamsters in vivid black and white linsey shirts, finely checked; the
Maxwells, with nine children, the youngest in the arms of the
mother, who, I knew, would later consign eight of them to the first
and exuberantly join the dancing; Nick Holderness, the gambler,
in white bosom, collar and cuffs, a fine gold chain joining his pair
of studded stickpins; and the Widow Emms, who seldom sewed
but rather pinned, according to the latest style and fancy, her
overskirts and flounces, which, as she danced, were continually
coming down.

Cowhands and ranchers hung their buckled spurs on the row of square brass harness hooks adorning the rear wall, their gun belts, if they wore any, next, and their hats on top. But the Lawler men, I noticed, left nothing. They arrived separately, a little stiff-legged, yet very affable to everyone, not seeming to see one another until by accident they found themselves on the same or adjoining plank seats.

I knew them all: Earl Curran, with points in his eyes; Ellery Cox, with a sweeping cowman's mustache; Alex Gawthrop, very polished to everyone and with burned-out black eyes; Bill Parr, sobered up a little; Frank Dague, and others. But the one who riveted my eyes was Jack Lawler himself, a fine-looking, upstanding man with curling mustache very black against his pale skin. His eyes held a liquid generosity, and yet there was something about the man that terrified me.

It grew late. Valeria's father entered, his black broadcloth cape swinging from his shoulders. His piercing eye swept the hall, then with dignity he took a vacant chair across the aisle from us. Many rows had been completely filled. I began to believe that Valeria had succeeded where Andy Moffet had failed. Then without warning the rough hall seemed brighter and fresher, and there was Valeria with a roll of sheet music in her hand, standing as if on tiptoe at the head of the crude aisle, gazing with brilliant eyes over the lively scene, while Ewing, directly behind her, dug into a pocket to pay the beaming professor.

I remember that men on both sides turned their heads to stare at the picture she made, her long, blue velvet cloak thrown back from a new red silk dress trimmed with black lace, of which she had not breathed a word to me, her head gently bare, the sparkle of the lamps in her eyes and chestnut hair. She had at that moment the last drop of a young girl's admiration. And when Ewing came up and stood behind her, very tall, his somber face glowing over her shoulder, something tore at me under the bodice of my dress.

I turned to whisper their arrival to my mother. Before my recital had reached the black lace, the dress itself rustled in the aisle by us, and there was Valeria picking up her skirts to slip past my mother to one of the two vacant chairs beside me.

"It's very beautiful and becoming, Vallie," my mother praised, leaning across my lap. "Isn't Ewing coming up?"

"I wanted him to." Valeria gazed steadily at my mother, and something passed between them.

Turning quickly on my chair, I saw four Rafter P men in the back of the hall, all looking a little strange, among them the tall figure of Andy Moffet, who paid the professor while the others stood about joking with acquaintances on the last several rows. I had often eaten at the same table with them all: Uncle Jim Hatch, who wasn't my uncle at all, a stout little man into whose cheeks red apples came when he laughed; lanky Will Freyno, with white teeth smiling through his drooping yellow mustache; and Hoke Jones, one of whose eyes was very twinkling and the other expressionless, wide open, watching all that was going on.

With Ewing, tall and careless, in the lead, they came limping down the aisle in the awkward gait of men just off the saddle, laying an occasional warm hand on the shoulder of some friend along the aisle and finding room on three partially filled plank seats on the left side of the hall. I felt relieved that they had entered so genially.

Then abruptly I knew why they looked strange. All of them wore coats—even Uncle Jim Hatch, whom I had never seen more fully dressed than in a vest. A minute later I grew aware that the heavy form of the sheriff had utterly vanished from near the door, and that a peculiar tension was spreading over the hall, growing like the silence just before a long-awaited storm breaks on our motionless Southwestern hills.

My mother ordered me to sit forward in my chair, and I did in time to see Wes Gatlin turn his shrewd, massive face; then, rising as if by accident, he eluded his wife's restraining fingers and lumbered down the aisle, his voice raised in a remonstrating drawl that rolled over the entire hall:

"What are we waitin' for, professor—the railroad?"

A number of people laughed. I could almost feel the relief, and at once the drone of talk, scrape of feet, and epidemic of coughing revived. Behind us the Widow Emms leaned to whisper grimly across the aisle:

"Wes couldn't have done that if they'd brought their Irishman along—the one who shot it out with Jack Lawler's brother at the lava beds last evening."

In a moment Sadie Montgomery swept up the aisle, a sprightly, vivacious creature, bowing and smiling, wearing a marvelous fur cloak under which I caught sight of bare shoulders and arms and a bodice in a shade of silk I had never seen before, cut breathtakingly low. Her husband, twice territorial delegate to Washington, where he had met his wife, followed with blond Dundreary whiskers and silvery hair.

Presently the professor himself mounted the platform, his long nose and coat reminding me of a tall, bone-handled, loosely wrapped frontier umbrella silhouetted against the curtains.

"Wahoo for the professor!" Wes Gatlin yelled from his new seat in the rear, and a gust of handclapping and stamping ran through the hall.

"Ladies and gentlemen!" The Austrian professor beamed. "I feel the honor of all you to see here this wunnerful spring evening. A music festival first, then the dancing afterward, *gewiss?*" His face glowed. "The first number is a ballad, very beautiful, by a very beautiful lady." He beamed down at the Montgomerys.

Sadie Montgomery's whispering silk skirts were lifted to the platform, revealing high-top shoes adroitly laced down the inside, leaving as smoothly shod an ankle as I had ever seen. The professor opened his instrument case to accompany her, drew a sprightly bow on the violin tucked under his chin, and she made brilliant eyes at the audience while she sang: "Waltzing, swiftly waltzing. Oh, who will waltz with me?" at a certain bar in the chorus whirling prettily around as if in a man's arms. She fetched hearty applause, but Wes Gatlin fetched more and a faint red at the back of his wife's neck when he called:

"You can count on me, Sadie, for the first three-step."

The show now was fully launched. I had almost forgotten about Ewing. The professor placed in front of the curtains a small, marble-top table with a wicker cage containing a mocking bird. The bird sat with drooping wings while a whistled torrent of *Listen to the Mocking Bird*, every note vigorous and clear, filled the hall, brightening scores of faces and at the end winning a rousing thunder of clapping and stamping that would not be stilled until Wes Gatlin's repeated bawl: "Come on out, Matt, and wake up the mockin' bird!" had drawn Matt Clements, flushed and bowing, from behind the curtains.

A ladies' quartet as a lily, a daisy, a violet, and a rose sang *The Flowers in the Garden*, with their heads thrust through slits in the curtains. Then, with suppressed excitement in his face, the professor approached the massive, covered shape still looming in front of the platform. I knew before he had spoken a word that the dramatic moment of the evening had come, the unveiling of Sadie Montgomery's piano.

He laid his long arms on the draped object. *"Die Kraft und die Herrlichkeit!"* he exclaimed feelingly. Then he lifted off the wagon sheet.

A shuffle of feet sounded on the wide pine flooring as some rose to see better, and soon everyone was standing. Valeria encouraged me to stand upright on my chair, and I stared at a vast, magnificent piece of mahogany furniture with curved, claw legs, silver pedals, a name in gold, and a polish like a great dark mirror.

People grinned when Wes Gatlin yelled to the professor that his square piano was a fraud because it wasn't square, but I saw that Mark Leland, an English boy exiled at the Leavenworth House, looked at the piano long and feelingly, as at a familiar face from his native England; that Mrs. Claycomb's white-haired mother from the Carolinas furtively touched a black-bordered handkerchief to her eyes; and that Valeria never removed her gaze from the extraordinarily long and chaste keyboard.

A chill air struck at the back of my neck, and, turning, I saw the hall door standing open and coming up the aisle the rawhide face of Henry Madden, who had been a friend of my father's, and with him his brother, Tim, a Rafter P cowhand with a thin-skinned Irish face and taut, mocking air. People in the rear were staring at the latter with consternation, and after he squeezed in among the impassive Piatt men, spectators on adjoining benches began to edge off slowly, then, taking advantage of the standing crowd, tiptoed toward the square, while across the aisle others caught the contagion and began deserting their seats about the Lawlers.

More than a score had started toward the door when the professor first saw them and hurried to the platform.

"Ach, peoples, sit down!" he begged. "The best of the program still to come yet. I play for you myself on the piano after while. *Ja,* it's true my pupils never touch a finger to the piano, only the melodeon, but any mistakes, please excuse! The program goes on right away. Now the daughter of our popular gunsmith, Miss Valeria Wingate."

Except for the sibilants of departing feet, a profound hush had fallen on the hall. Even Wes Gatlin kept silent and, looking back, I saw that he had changed his seat. The Lawler and Piatt groups had become two isolated islands of men surrounded by a

small, glaring sea of empty benches. On her remote seat, the black
face of the Negro girl was a picture of hypnotic fright. But what
held my eyes was Ewing sitting quietly forward on his plank, his
hair curling about his head and on his face a little smile, as if
he were waiting for Valeria to play.

I knew that she could see everything because, with her roll of
sheet music crushed in one hand, she had risen to pass us into the
aisle. People were staring at her with mingled curiosity and pity.
But what I remember unforgettably is the piercing gaze of her
father as it fixed itself first on her marble face and then on her
slender young back moving above her wide skirts for the piano.

She seated herself rigidly, sweeping her skirts about her in the
familiar gesture of nearly three-quarters of a century ago. And I
thought how different Valeria's life was from her mother's, sitting
at the square piano in the great house of her father along that
peaceful Pennsylvania river of twenty years before. A few late
goers were still hurrying out. Valeria sat quiet, eyes on her music,
waiting for them to leave.

She waited so long I was afraid she couldn't go through with it.
Then, when the hall had grown tensely silent, she lifted her hands
and two notes rang in that grim adobe place like solemn bells.
As she went on, steadily feeling her way on Sadie Montgomery's
piano, I knew that she was playing—not her new piece, printed in
German, but the old, sad *Isle of the Sea*, which I have not heard
for many years and which no one seems to know any more.

I had heard the air a hundred times on our music box, but never
had it been wrapped around Ewing and Valeria as it was tonight.
A kind of mist seemed to rise from the piano into my eyes, and in
it I could see them both the first time they had gone anywhere
together, Valeria on Taffy, our *palomino* mare which Ewing had
led from the ranch for her use. I had wondered that day at the
look of pain in mother's eyes, but I understood it now.

And when Valeria's left hand began a gentle rocking movement
I could see the vast grassy sea of our Rafter P range, and Ewing
riding away on a strange black horse, motionless, silent, alone,
never looking back to where Valeria stood waving after him until
man and mount merged into the unknown.

A loyal roll of applause from the Piatt men met her as she rose
from the piano. As if that were the long awaited signal, she halted
with wide-torn eyes in the aisle. I heard behind us the heavy

chorus of men's boots on the pine floor, the crash of a plank bench. Then long-delayed lightning struck violently between the adobe walls of Dick Coors's Palace Dance Hall.

I remember such trivial things as a lamp-chimney rocking in its brass burner, Mrs. Wes Gatlin's single scream: "Wesley!" and the abrupt convulsive shudder in one of the muslin curtains, leaving a ragged hole that none of the ladies' quartet might thrust her head through. All around us, men and women had thrown themselves flat on chairs and floor. But I saw that Valeria had remained erect young marble and that my mother sat small and unquenchable on her chair, her chin like the rounded point of a rock, her only sign of emotion the pulse racing at her blue and gold brooch containing a lock of my father's wavy hair.

"Don't look back, Cynthia Ann," she warned me.

I froze on my chair until she herself had turned. When I looked, it was through a dark pall of smoke at the last of the Lawlers vanishing after their opening volley, leaving behind them an unforgettable scene. Planks, boxes, and kegs had been thrown about in the utmost confusion, reminding me of a room after small frontier boys I knew had played with their crude carpenters' blocks and now lay overtaken by sleep among their scattered playthings.

Sadie Montgomery quickly took my hand and led me up on the platform behind the curtains where Mrs. Wes Gatlin crossed herself and murmured in Spanish whenever a gun shrieked in the square. Sadie Montgomery's sheer green silk skirts were soiled where she had knelt on the floor, but her cheeks looked pink and her eyes brilliant with excitement. She kept patting my hand and telling me how much tonight I looked like a favorite niece in Baltimore, but all the time I knew she was doing it just because Ewing was dead.

The curtains parted and Colonel Montgomery appeared, his face bloodless. Even the silver in his hair seemed dulled. When several ladies begged him for the news, Sadie Montgomery drew me away, but I heard every word.

"It was Frank Dague's and Jack Lawler's last fight. Tim Madden has six or seven bullets in him, and they say Ewing Piatt is lying out in the street."

Someone said: "Sh!" but I had eluded Sadie Montgomery and was running through the curtains and down into the hall. I glanced

quickly away from the silent wagon sheet spread over the pine
floor and saw Doc Stockton, his coat off, an unlighted cigar in his
bearded mouth down on his knees beside the ghastly smiling Will
Freyno.

In front of the hall the huge form of Wes Gatlin blocked the
doorway. "They've forted up in the Lawler corral, Miz Piatt," he
was protesting awkwardly. "Ewin's lyin' right out in front of it.
I wouldn't go out in that square now if I was you—not till the
sheriff comes, anyway."

My mother just gave him a look and he moved out of her way
and Andy Moffet stepped up to go with her.

"They'd shoot you down like a dog, Andy," she said harshly.
"You were a party to this business. Now you can stay back and
take care of my child."

Valeria bent her white, steady face to mine. "Don't worry,
Cynthia Ann," she whispered. "Nobody would hurt your mother
or me. I'll bring her back in a few minutes."

With a crestfallen air, Andy had moved from the door. Together
he and I watched Valeria's sturdy young arm take my mother's
older one. Then they started out of the hall, red silk, black
percale, and stiff petticoats rustling, and all the rest of the square
lying silent in the dim moonlight, although I knew that eyes were
watching from a dozen darkened doors and windows. The sandy
creak of their steps steadily receded, and now I knew they must
be approaching the unsheltered ground in front of the Lawler
corral.

It seemed hours until they returned, breathing hard, a dark,
sagging length between them. As they broke into the lamplight, I
saw that Ewing's eyes were dully open. My mother's gray gaze
met the bearded physician's at the door.

"They want you in the Lawler corral," she said grimly.

Before the doctor left, he showed her one of two bullets gripped
in the end of what looked like a long, narrow, slightly rusty pair
of scissors. He forbade moving Ewing till morning. By midnight
everyone had gone, my mother for hot coffee and blankets, Will
Freyno to the Leavenworth House, and the other surviving Piatt
men back to the Jicaritas at my mother's sharp command. Sadie
Montgomery and the colonel had asked me along to their house
for the night, but I had stubbornly refused.

All the lamps had been blown out but one. It seemed no more

than a candle in the huge, cavelike room, throwing a sort of twilight over Ewing lying motionless on the floor in the shadow of the piano, Vallie's long, blue velvet cloak spread over him, his face haggard, but the hair still curling about his head like that of a young buffalo.

Most of the night his eyes remained closed. Once he opened them and I don't think he saw me on the piano stool in the dimness because there was something in his gaze that men seldom showed to a third person those days.

"I wanted to ask you tonight to marry me, Vallie." The words came out with slow distinctness in that silent, adobe place. "But I can't ask a girl to walk with her eyes open into what my mother's gone through."

Valeria said nothing for a little, just sat on her empty crackerbox beside him, in her red silk and black lace, gazing down at his face as from a great height. And in her eyes there was all that I can still see in the dusty frontier street of La Cruz as it lay that day in the spring sunshine with the railroad nearly a thousand miles away and all the wild brew of that raw land stirring in a young girl's veins.

"My mother used to say she wasn't put on earth to be scared of life, Ewing," she answered. Then she bent her head until the chestnut of her hair was softly golden in the glimmering lamplight.

And suddenly I realized that it was Valeria's betrothal night.

OLIVER LA FARGE

HIGHER EDUCATION

This is not a pleasant story, but in my opinion it is a significant one. It is written with the subtle skill and the craftsmanship characteristic of this Pulitzer Prize-winning author and authority on the American Indian. (From *All the Young Men*, Houghton Mifflin, 1930.)

THE door of the truck was hot to the touch. Even though it stood in the broken shade of poplars, the whole machine was a trap for heat more stifling than that which enveloped the sun-smitten road, the houses, the mesa. Looking northward, one saw the jumbled, garish country into which we were going, its harsh colours toned down without being softened by the over-brilliant light, its crazy shapes vibrating in the heat. The utterly silent landscape seemed to growl as one looked at it.

Joe Degler slouched over the wheel, his legs sprawling widely, his big, hairy arms lax. He was powerful, blond, unshaven; too big and hearty a man for the front seat of a truck on a June day in Arizona. He moved slightly, saying:

"Come in, Professor. We got a squaw ridin' with us. She's in seein' the agent. Soon's she turns up, we'll git goin'."

The name "Professor" is set in everyone's mind; I can't do anything about it. It annoys me, and so does the term "squaw," particularly from the lips of such as this big Texan, the aggressively *white* white men who give it always a downward intonation, by the brief word denying woman-kind to a whole race of women. I stood with my foot on the running board, seeing him stupid but well intentioned, tired momentarily of his friendship, and of tolerating him.

"Thanks, Joe," I said, "I don't want to climb into that oven of yours until I have to."

"Suit yourself. I'd as soon roast sittin' down as standin' up. She won't be real hot till we hit the sand by T'o Haskid; then you sure will wish someone'd invent water-cooled boots."

I looked in the back of the truck—mail-bags, assorted goods for up-country trading posts, my own bedroll and duffel-bag, and a new, bright, small trunk and imitation leather valise.

"Whose luggage?" I asked.

"Hunh?"

"Whose baggage?"

"Oh." He turned his head to stare at the objects. "That's what the Great White Father does for a squaw. It's hers."

"The woman who's coming?"

"Yeah. Just out o' school. Six years in California learnin' to stick her little finger out when she drinks tea, and then turned out to graze in the howlin' desert. Hell of a system, if you ask me."

I nodded. The trunk carried painted initials—L. N. L. for one of the flowery names the teachers give the children when they first come to school—wild-haired, frightened things, crowding together, their true names, their pride and ancestry ignored—Lucille or Lydia or Lilith or God knows what. N might be for an English surname, or some distorted fragment of a native word, half heard, truncated, misapplied. The letter teased, forcing vain speculation, *Nakai, Nadhani, Nditligh, Niltsi*—that struck a chord. Wind Singer was expecting his daughter back from school, he had told me. This might be she.

The cheap, showy, unsuitable luggage lay tiptilted with the other freight, forcing a superimposed mental vision of Wind Singer's camp, the hogahn of crude brush and sticks, the little bundles of goods and rolls of seldom-washed bedding, dogs and ashes and smoke and poverty of possessions in a home which could be moved without difficulty of packing as the grazing needs of the sheep dictated.

Joe said, "Here she is."

I noticed first the incongruous, pseudo-smart, tacky dress and the hat, already *passé* with its exaggerated angle which would not have been good even at the height of that fashion. Short skirts, and high-heeled shoes, and a stilted walk with pocket-book in hand shocked one who was used to Navajo women moving like queens, free-striding, with a swing of long skirts cut full enough to cover their legs when they ride astride. They are more perfectly at ease than most men, of any race, in the saddle, and majestic on the ground. This mincing, side-walk gait was an offence.

The face was Indian; not only the breadth of cheek-bone, fine long eyes and beautiful chiselling of a wide mouth, but the emptiness now drawn over it, the mask of absence which all Indians possess for protection in time of stress and which the school-children above all learn to use. She wore it now. One could not tell what looked through her eyes when she left school, but from then till now, on the train, re-entering the forgotten wasteland of her home, seeing the first of her own ragged people, meeting race-conscious Government employees, shunted about, disregarded, with the almost terror of her old way of life before her, she had put on the mask. She had been learning.

I knew Joe would not like it, I suspected that it was a poor idea, but there are some things one must do for his own sake. I lifted my hat, saying:

"Good morning. You'd better sit in front. I'll ride in back."

Joe was a Westerner; he could not let my gesture go without some attempt to equal it.

"Sure," he said. "Come in."

He did not move a muscle. His voice, his intonation, were hearty, but the reverse of the words ran undercurrent to them. She looked us over so quickly one could hardly detect the motion of her eyes.

"Thank you. I think I ride in back."

Joe said, "Wall, let's git goin'. Hop in, Professor. *Vamos.*"

That's what smugness accomplishes. I had demonstrated my high principles for my own benefit and so provided the girl with a snub, a reminder of her position, which otherwise would have remained in abeyance. Of course she had read Joe's feelings easily enough. How much better if I'd kept my trap shut and let her get in the back without that small fuss. Perhaps I was exaggerating. I didn't think so. I've known mean Indians, and stupid ones, but never one who was thick-skinned.

The car jolted and bounced and grew hotter. Dust settled upon us, little drifts of fine, grey powder and coarser, bright sand lay in the folds of the mail-sacks. The girl sat limply, resting against my bedroll. She ought to have plenty to think about; every mile of desert, every jounce, was a warning of the completeness of this, the second shattering change in her life. The first was years ago when she received whatever name L stood for, dressed in a dowdy uniform, and her young wildness was broken to the machine-like routine of an institution half penitentiary, half orphanage. How many times can the substance be shattered and yet re-create itself?

We got stuck in the sand at T'o Haskid, as per schedule; otherwise the trip was extremely dull. The road was empty. We passed a few shepherds with their flocks; altogether we saw about half a dozen hogahns at different places. The girl stared at them, and at the women. When we stopped to deliver mail at Tsaychee trading post, she stayed in the car, shrinking from the curiosity of whites and Indians alike. It was well past lunch time when we finally drew up in front of Luke's post at Kin Bukho.

Joe said: "Wall, here we are. You're lucky; I got to go on to Cheelcheen right now, or I'll lose my damn contract." He turned to the back of the truck. "All right, sister, here's your home town. I guess your folks are around here somewheres."

Bert Luke came out of the post to meet us, cordial as usual in his quiet, word-stingy way.

"Go on back," he told me, "I guess the old woman can fix you up some grub. You'll stay tonight?"

"Thanks, I'd like to. How are my animals?"

"Fat and sassy."

I took my bedroll and bag on my shoulder, and went around the corner of the post. From the front, one saw a sort of low, stone barn with a door and narrow windows appearing dead black against the glaring sunlight on the wall, trampled sand and a few tin cans for foreground, a couple of lounging Indians, some tethered ponies, a wagon. It looked like a store at the tail end of nowhere, and yet, taking up Joe's phrase, I reflected that the shopping centre of that girl's home town was even bleaker and more remote. Rounding the corner, one passes through a gate onto a narrow strip of real grass which Mrs. Luke waters and tends minutely. The back porch is covered with Virginia creeper, and two big cottonwood trees cast shade upon it. It is an oasis, a credible home.

Mrs. Luke was just coming through the gate. She hailed me with "Hello, Professor, you're packed up like a mule, ain't you?"

I said, "Sure, and likely to buck."

"Well, throw down on the porch and make yourself at home. Wind Singer and his wife are here. Did their girl come?"

"I guess so. Some girl did. She's out there, kind of lost."

"I'll bring her in."

The porch was cool. I dropped my burdens, sighed, and threw my hat down before shaking hands with the medicine man and his wife. They were quiet, constrained, and anxious; their smiles as our hands touched faded again while they sat watching the gate. I seated myself in a rocking-chair and made a cigarette.

Luke came through from the kitchen to join us. A devout Mormon, he did not smoke. The four of us sat, pretending to be natural. Mrs. Luke came into view with the girl in her pathetically unsmart clothes following at her side as though the older woman's bigness had caught her up and was cradling her along. Here at last was someone of remembered kindness, unchanged, a first stable point in a quicksand world. I saw Mrs. Luke pat her arm, and the girl smiled.

Luke said, "*Kodi, sikiso*," and gestured towards the path.

The two Indians rose, Wind Singer's Wife gathering her blanket around her shoulders, and went down onto the lawn. Mrs. Luke came past them with a brief word and a smile, and joined us on the porch. Her smile had disappeared; she looked at her husband and me gravely.

Wind Singer stopped a few yards from his daughter and her mother went forward alone. The girl stood still, her head hanging. The old woman moved slowly and we could see that her half-outstretched hands were trembling. Now they were close to each other, and Wind Singer's Wife was touching her daughter's shoulders. There was an agony of longing on her face. She said something, and the girl's head was bowed yet lower.

Mrs. Luke whispered through unmoving lips, "She don't remember any Navajo."

Wind Singer's Wife touched the girl's face lightly, fleetingly, with her hands, and the girl shrank. Then the old woman stepped back, and seemed for the first time to take in the strange clothes, the half-bare arms and neck, the short skirt. With the same slow, gentle motions she took off her blanket—it was moderately clean —and cast it about her daughter's shoulders. The girl took the edges in a curious, hypnotized fashion and drew them together. She did not shrink from the heavy wool, rather it seemed as though in complete despair she had ceased to mind. The mask on her face was so perfect that it now cried out, betraying its secret. Her mother spoke to Wind Singer; the three of them turned together and walked slowly, all with bowed heads, out of the gate.

Luke said "Damnation!" which was unusual for him.

"What does L stand for?" I asked.

"Lucille," Mrs. Luke said. "Her true name's *Zhiltnapah*, but they used to call her Running Girl because she was so lively."

Luke rose. "I got to get back to the store. Ruth, I reckon the Professor ain't had lunch." At the door he stopped, one hand on the jamb, and said, "Hooray for Uncle Sam and higher education."

"What are they going to do now?" I asked Mrs. Luke.

"Drive back with her to Lukhahutso. They came in their wagon."

"She'll sleep in the hogahn tonight, then?"

"I guess so, if she sleeps. You goin' there tomorrow?"

"Yes. I've got to stop by Show-Off's though."

"If you started right now you could spend the night at his place."

"Thanks. Not when I can get next to your cooking."

Show-Off had the trading post nearest to Lukhahutso, a lonely place, the farthest outflung store to the north of a chain owned by a Denver firm. We called him Show-Off after the name the Navajos gave him, *Bedaylahi*, which means someone loud and too smart and annoying. I did not know his right name. Although I disliked him, I had to use his post as my base while I worked in that district, and we got on all right. He was a big man, handsome in a flashy way, with curly black hair, a quick smile, and over-hearty handshake. He was industriously two-fisted, hairy-chested, he-man, hundred per cent and all the rest of it.

Leaving Luke's in the middle of the next morning, I reached Show-Off's early in the afternoon, and went in to let him know I was back and to get supplies. There were some six or eight Indians, men and women, in the store, mostly just loafing and talking, having finished trading. He urged me to stay for dinner and spend the night, but I said I had to get back to my camp.

Just about as I had my grub together, Show-Off said, "For Gawd's sake!"

I turned towards the door. Wind Singer and his daughter were coming in. She had discarded her hat, and wore a blanket loosely over her shoulders, but she still carried her pocket-book, her costume was still incongruous. I noticed that her expression seemed dazed, possibly resigned. There was nothing positive.

Her father came over and spoke to me. "Are you coming out to your camp?"

"Yes. I'll be there by sundown, I think."

"Good." He hesitated. "We have come here to buy cloth. She is going to make proper clothes, and put those things away."

I was glad to hear that, it sounded hopeful, but when I looked at the girl I was not so sure, and I wondered again, how often can the substance be shattered and re-create itself? She was dazed, there was a mechanical quality about her actions. Her father joined her at the counter, to help her pick out her materials. He was solicitous, quietly tender, and faintly proud as she talked with Show-Off in English.

He kept them waiting till he had given me the last of my grub, and rolled a cigarette, then he faced them.

"Just back from school, eh?" he said.

"Yes, sir."

"What do you want?"

"Calico. That there, and that, twelve yards of each, please." She continued, ordering the velveteen and rick-rack braid and thread, and a fringed Pendleton blanket.

Show-Off slapped the goods down before her in a tumbled pile. "Will you pay for them, or do I put it on your old man's ticket?"

"I pay for them."

He told her the price. She gave him some bills from her pocket-book. He made change at the cash register, and threw the change towards her, the coins sliding along the counter and ending all scattered.

"Better get a necklace or some earrings, hanh?"

"No, thank you. Will you wrap the things up, please?"

He stopped still, put his hands on his hips, stared at the girl and then at me.

"My God," he said, "the airs these squaws put on nowadays!"

She winced. Most of the Indians present knew enough English to understand the general meaning of what had been said. There was a period of utter silence while she gathered up her purchases, and then a man said his name in a low voice, pronouncing each syllable with slow, mocking clarity, and not addressing anyone at all, "*Be-day-la-hi.*" There was a snicker all round the store, and Show-Off flushed deep crimson. Wind Singer and the girl departed. I took my supplies and went to the corral, packed my mule and got going.

I passed close by Wind Singer's hogahn where the trail crossed the wagon-road but decided not to call there. That family might desire to be alone, it ought to be tired of white men just now. I rode up the cañon to my camp, checked over my cache of goods, threw down and turned my animals out to graze. Then I walked a few hundred yards to the cave, to make sure nothing had been disturbed. All was as I left it, a nice little ruin of the earliest period, with my test trench, half completed, running across it. I figured that I'd do another week's work on it before moving on, and that next year when the University gave me a regular expedition again —the funds were promised—I'd excavate this place thoroughly. This year I was simply scouting, enjoying the frequent changes of camp, and finding it a relief not to have any students to take care of.

The sun was low. I went back, built a fire and cooked supper. Camp again, the restful little cañon, the sharpness of night air adding to my pleasure in the fire, the big sky, the irregular, jerky clanging of the bell on my lead horse as he grazed, all good things of which one does not tire.

Hearing a single, barely audible footstep, I peered out of my circle of light. Wind Singer became visible in the darkness. He stepped up to the fire and warmed his hands, then sat down, remarking, "My wife said you came by."

"Yes, I got in sooner than I expected. I came faster than you, I think."

I passed him coffee and the makings. He rolled a cigarette slowly, and juggled with a live coal to light it.

When he had taken a few puffs, he asked, "What did Show-Off say that time?"

"He was rude."

"How?"

"Well—you know, in those stores by Wide Water, where your daughter was, they wrap things for you in paper, they tie them with a string. Nobody does that here. Your daughter asked him to wrap up her goods, and he was rude about it. It's stupid, I think."

Wind Singer grunted. "That's the way he is. Now she feels badly. She was not happy anyhow; now she is worse."

"It will take a little time, you know. Everything is different here, she cannot get used to it right away. Just give her time. How long was she at that school?"

"Six years."

I nodded. She must be about seventeen; she had not seen anything remotely suggesting this country or this life for that time. Wind Singer stared at the fire, and then spoke quietly, with deep feeling behind his level voice. His lined, kindly face was grave.

"She has all but forgotten our language, just a few words have come back to her since she returned. I can talk with you more easily than I can speak to my own daughter." He paused, making a small, desperate gesture with his hand. "She turns her face from us. Her brother went a little while to the school here at T'odnesji, he speaks English to her, he does what he can, but she will not look at him, either." He shifted his position. "What is this? We are men, we People. We think well of ourselves. We want our children to have what we have. We want them to learn English and writing and those useful things, but not to forget everything white men do not know, everything that has made us strong.

"I can understand a man like Show-Off; there are plenty of bad Navajos, too. But what is this other thing? What kind of man orders it?

"We know we are poorer than white men. We are ragged and dirty, I suppose. We live simply, a hard life. But we are not ashamed. We are strong, we are men, we have beauty. There is not one of us who would lower his face before any man. But my daughter comes back from that school at T'o Ntyel, where they sent her because she was the best in the school at T'odnesji, and she is all shame and fear. At night, when she thinks we are asleep, she cries."

He stopped. I wished I could change my colour, my skin, my race.

Wind Singer said, with less tension in his voice: "Perhaps if we have a ceremony for her, it will help. We should like her to marry Strong Hand—you know him well, I think."

"Yes, a very good man." I considered. "Don't do anything about it yet, either that or singing for her. Go slowly, let her become accustomed. Right now she is upset by the strange things, she is thinking about things, so that she cannot see the trail. Give her time, that is all."

"Perhaps you are right." He glanced upward. "It is late."

He rose, tall, spare, white-haired, dignified for all the shabbiness of his costume. He was well-to-do, but like many medicine men he didn't care much what he wore. His wife used his jewelry. He walked off, Navajo fashion, without any farewell. I finished another cigarette. Luke was right. Hooray for Uncle Sam and higher education.

I hadn't covered my grub properly. While I slept, a coyote got under the tarpaulin, and in the morning I found myself robbed of bacon, and my sugar had been spilled out of the sack into a hopeless mess of sand and ants. I tracked the beast for a mile, and lost its trail, so I breakfasted in bad humour and then saddled up to ride to Show-Off's and re-stock. It was still early when I reached the post, and there were no customers. Show-Off seemed pleased about my accident.

"Ain't you got a gun?" he asked.

"Sure I have, but I was asleep. Never heard him."

"That's right, you wasn't expectin' no thieves. But the coyote finally fooled you."

I let his remark pass by. He always resented the fact that the Indians, who stole from him when they could, let me wander unguarded among them without taking anything. Let it go.

When he had weighed out the sugar, he said, "Stop and have a smoke, Professor. Hell, thar ain't no hurry," and shoved tobacco towards me.

The store was still cool, and the day outside was hot. I leant against the counter and made a cigarette.

"Say, you kind o' didn't like the way I talked to Wind Singer's girl the other day, did you?"

"No, frankly, I did not."

"Wall, I guess you was right. I hadn't ought to of done it. But here she come in in them civilized clothes, and then would she give me a tumble? No, sir. Jest looked at me like I was a slot machine

she was a-goin' to get gum out of, and then she tells me to wrap
it up. I got kind o' stampeded."

This was more grace than I thought was in him. "It was a pity,"
I said. "Hard enough on the girl, coming back from school like
this, without adding onto it."

"Yeah, that's right. I didn't mean to. I'm sorry, that's truth.
Tough on her, being kicked back into the blanket. And she's a
cute little trick, too."

I glanced at him suspiciously. "I hadn't noticed," I said, although now he spoke of it I saw what he meant.

He seemed to feel a need to justify himself. "You know what
I mean. It's the way she was dressed, partly. Hell, I ain't seen
a girl dressed snappy in mor'n a year. Too bad she's goin' to put
on them Navajo clothes. It's a kinda relief to look at something
else sometimes."

"More than a year?" I asked. "Haven't you been out at all?"

"Not at all, barrin' one trip to Tuba to see the Agent. Since
Buck took sick and went out I been alone here. Can't leave. They've
promised to send a man in to relieve me, but they're damn slow
about it. I'm achin' to get drunk and have me some fun."

I nodded. "That's a long spell. But I bet you've got whiskey here."

"Sure I have, only I don't dare get rightly stewed, nor hand
any out. The Gov'ment's strict as hell. And it is lonely."

"Yes. Well, I hope you get out soon. Meantime, don't try to
fix yourself up with any Navajo women; it isn't safe."

"That's right, Professor. No squaw-trouble in mine. All I
meant was that girl looked cute, see, and no harm in being friendly.
And it is a pity she's got to go back into them Injun clothes. Anyway, I don't want to lose her folks' trade, so if you can say anything to 'em, I wish you would."

"All right. Well, I've got to be going. So long."

"So long. Come in some evening and have a drink."

"Thanks."

I was back at camp by noon, and spent the rest of the day extending my test trench in the ruin. While I worked, I kept thinking about the girl, and her family, and Show-Off, and Strong
Hand who was my particular friend. Show-Off's dangerous, because he's both stupid and smart. Hope he goes on leave soon. Well,
what the devil, this isn't my affair. I can't settle it, it only makes
me feel bad.

Ordinarily, I should have dropped in on Wind Singer after supper, since no one came to my fire, but I thought better not to. Instead I damned the whole situation and the Great White Step-Father, turned in, and had considerable difficulty going to sleep.

I slept late, waking to find it broad daylight and the sun about to rise. Someone was near me. Rolling my eyes, as I lay still flat in my bedroll, I saw red moccasins and above them familiar leggings of blue calico, right behind my head. Looking steadfastly forward, I sat up, yawned and stretched. Then with my eyes still on the trees beyond my feet, I said,

"*Ahalani, sitsili*—hello, younger brother."

Strong Hand laughed. "Hello, sleeper."

"Light the fire," I said, pulling on my trousers.

By the time I joined him he had a good blaze going. He had breakfasted, he said, but he would take some coffee. We talked about this and that, idle remarks, bits of small news. There seemed to have been nothing much new since we last saw each other. Our unimportant conversation was merely the vehicle for our pleasure in being together.

Finally I said, "Wind Singer's daughter is back."

"Yes, I saw her last night. I went to their hogahn. I thought you would be there, too."

"I was tired, so I just went to sleep. What do you think of her?"

He looked at me keenly. "You know what they were talking about, before she came?"

"About you and her? Yes, I have heard something."

"I went to see what she was like."

He rubbed his forefinger and thumb together. I passed him tobacco and papers. When he had his cigarette lit, he spoke again.

"It made me angry, what I saw. I was angry with all white men, even you, my friend."

He was a big young man, strong, intelligent. His friendship was good; I thought I would not care to have his enmity. He must have read my face, for he smiled, a flash of even teeth in a wide mouth, saying,

"I did not stay that way."

Then the smile faded.

"What was she like before?" I asked.

"I was older than she, I was beginning to be a man and she was still just a child, but one liked her. She was very lively, and she had that which pulls at people, Running Girl. Everyone liked her. I was looking for that last night, and all I could see was pain in her. She was pitiful. So were her parents." He dug in the sand with his fingers. "But she was most so. Then I did see it, a little, I think. Way down inside her is some of what she was, but frightened almost to death. She would be beautiful, too, I think, if she could take the cloud off her face.

"I wanted to help her. It made me want to fight. She was afraid of me, too."

He finished. I hesitated, then said, "You like her."

"Yes. I don't know why."

"What was she wearing?"

"Navajo clothes. She had just finished making them."

"It is a matter of time," I said. "If they will go slow, let her learn again, she will be all right, I think."

I stood up, gathering my notebook and tools.

"Perhaps," he said. "I don't know. Are you going to dig in the Old People's house there?"

"Yes."

"I'll watch you, if you aren't going to bring up any bones."

"I don't think so."

He stayed till lunch, making amusing remarks about the sandals, bits of pottery and so on that I uncovered, and in general being excellent company. Then he went away without further reference to Running Girl. That's enough of that, I thought. If I get involved in the subject again I'll scream. It has a horrid fascination.

The girl herself turned up just before sunset, while I was cooking supper. I saw her coming with no pleasure, although she looked infinitely more attractive in the dignity and real style of her native costume. She had chosen her colours well. The full skirt was rather a bright blue, with two green lines of braid around it near the bottom, matching her green velveteen blouse. A new, fringed blanket lay across her shoulders, and she wore a necklace of many strands of coral, undoubtedly a present from her father.

I did not know just what etiquette to follow, so I sat like a dumb lump, stirring my stew with a big spoon, until she was right by the fire.

"I am Lucille Niltsi," she said. "I came up with you in dat car."

I rose awkwardly, took off my hat and shook hands. "Won't you sit down? Excuse me if I go on cooking."

A long and painful silence ensued. I remarked that it had been a nice day, and got no answer. More silence. Then I asked her please to look in the Dutch oven and see if my bread was baked.

She said, "I don't know how you open it."

My God, I thought, and I bet she's had every known form of Domestic Science.

"Take this stick and poke it through the handle on the lid."

She did so, and managed to raise the cover and look in without spilling more than a few coals on the bread.

"I guess it's done."

"Then will you take it off the coals, please? Thanks."

Silence again, while she twisted and untwisted the blanket fringe in her fingers.

"Will you have some supper?"

"No, thanks. I got to eat pretty soon, over dere."

"Some coffee, then? Here's sugar and canned milk."

She took that. I knew she didn't get milk at Wind Singer's.

Had she been a normal Indian, I should have made no effort to talk, knowing that in time, out of silence would emerge whatever she had on her mind. But she was not normal; maladjusted education had left her with neither the poise for talk nor the faculty of gracious quietness. She fidgeted.

"That was a long, dusty ride we had in the car," I offered.

"Yes."

More braiding of the fingers in the fringe.

"How long is it since you were home last?"

"Six years. I was ten."

"Then you're sixteen?"

"Yes."

"You went to Riverside?"

"Yes."

"Did you like it?"

"Not at first. Dey treated us pretty rough. Only since dat new Commissioner came in, it was better. I liked it pretty good, den. It ain't goin' to do me much good."

Superimposed upon her native Navajo accent was the bad English of her under-educated teachers.

"I should think you could get a lot of good out of it."

"How can I? My people—dey live like savages. I got to live like a savage. Dere ain't nothin' else for me to do. I didn't want to come back, I asked to get a job. Dey couldn't get me one. I had to come. Now I can't get away."

"With your education, you could do great things for your people."

"I can't even talk to dem."

"You'll remember that soon."

"I guess so." She said these last words in a tone of utter misery.

"Is it so bad, Lucille?"

"Yes it is—" She hesitated.

I really wished she would go away and not burden me, but I did feel sorry for her, and I saw she wanted to talk.

I said, "Tell me about it."

"My fader says you're a good man. I thought maybe you would understan'. Dey can't. My broder can't. It's everything. Dese Inyan clothes I got to wear."

"They're handsome."

"Maybe. But I want nice, pretty things like white girls have. I don't like to sleep in my same clothes on de groun', an' get up an' not wash, an' go on like dat. I like clean things, an' change dem—an' you know, like you see in de movies, pretty things underneath. De blankets an' sheepskins are dirty, an' de food ain't no good, an' my fader an' moder, dey spit an' scratch demselves— pretty soon I guess I'll be scratchin' myself, too. An' den, dere ain't nothin' I know how to do. I spent five years learnin' to cook real good, on a stove. What can I do here?"

I nodded. "Of course it's hard. But if I can learn to live and work in camp, and even get so that I love it, so can you. You're thinking about the things your people haven't got yet—fixed houses, beds, baths. You can't have those things when you run sheep in a desert. But they will come. You like the movies and lace underwear." She started when I said that. In her prim, over-religious school world men did not speak casually of underwear. I went right on. "Those things don't make life. You forget what your people have—strength, intelligence, pride, skill, beauty, character, and a magnificent religion."

She interrupted me. "Ain't you Christian?"

"Not that way. I believe in God and Our Savior, yes, but I see more of Them in the Navajo religion than I do in any of the missions around the Indian schools." I was getting the effect I wanted, I was startling her narrowed mind into fresh thinking. "Do you remember what *bik'é hozhoni* means?"

"Well—kind of. Trail of beauty, ain't it?"

"Yes. But find out what it really means; get to understand it. Then you'll know something you never could learn at school."

She looked at me dubiously.

"I know, you're up against a tough situation. Remember this: you belong to about the only tribe of Indians that has a chance to continue and be really great, instead of being destroyed. Make them your business, become one of them, and with your education you can make yourself great through them."

"But de Inyans, dey don't think much of me because I can't do nothin'. An' de white people, dey hold it against me, some of dem, because I'm Inyan."

"Only some," I said, "they're fools. We aren't all like Show-Off, you know."

"Oh, him," she said. "He didn't mean no harm. I guess he was just feelin' cross."

It was my turn to be surprised.

"I went dere yestiddy with my broder to trade on some things. My fader he thought I could get a better price, because I can read and do arithmetic, you know."

I nodded. I had a feeling, without explanation, that this was what she really wanted to talk to me about.

"I got a good trade, too. He was real nice, Mr. McClellan, and he said he was sure sorry."

McClellan, I thought, so that's his name. *Mister* McClellan. "Well, that's good, but don't trust him. He's a bad man."

"Is he? I—I kind o' thought he looked—well, sort of like Ramon Novarro, you know."

My God, I thought, is this the Navajo country? Heaven defend us! "Maybe he does, but all the same, he's a cheap skate."

"Oh." She paused. "Well, I got to go back dere now. Thank you Mr. — I don't know your right name."

"Fayerweather."

"Mr. Fayerweader. I'll remember what you say about dat— *bik'é hozhoni*, you know."

"All right. I'll see you again."

"Yes, sir. Good night."

I poured myself some more coffee. My God! Heaven above! There can't be anything in it, but—subject for a Ph.D. thesis, "The Influence of the Cinema in Aboriginal American Life." Holy Moses!

About a week after that I packed up and moved to Nahki Tees Cañon, where there was an "open site" ruin I wanted to test. I was relieved to get well away from Wind Singer and his family's problem, although in the last days when I visited there I thought the girl seemed more at ease and almost cheerful. The old man told me that, on account of her knowledge, she was a remarkable trader and got him many bargains. He said he always knew Show-Off had cheated on those pieces of paper he used, but had never been able to do anything about it before. I said that was good, and I wondered, until, in the saddle once more and driving my mule and spare horse, I shoved the whole thing out of my mind.

Save for the two cottonwoods where I camped, from which the cañon took its name, Nahki Tees is a bare, bright expanse of sand and adobe between two low, red walls of rock, unshaded, empty, and harsh, but beautiful in its own strange way. Where I dug, it was like working on top of a stove. I prolonged the siesta hour. There were no near neighbours, but a main trail passed close by, so I seldom lacked for company at meals. The ruin I was exploring was interesting; the moon, approaching full, made the whole place a liquid silver glory at night, and I enjoyed myself.

One day Strong Hand dropped in for lunch. It was pleasant to see him. While I was cooking he made fun of me for doing a woman's work, and thence got into a direct, Rabelaisian, and very Navajo line of kidding about the disadvantages of being single.

"You, too," I said. "It is past time you left your mother's hogahn."

"I don't know. Perhaps I shall never marry."

"Why?"

"Oh, nothing. Only I may never marry."

I let that pass and dished up the grub. Something was on his mind.

When we were finished, he said: "I have been seeing that girl again. I have been there two or three times."

"Yes."

"You were right, what you were thinking when we talked before. I like her. Very much I like her." He stopped.

"Then, in the end you will marry, I think."

"Perhaps not."

"Why?"

"She might marry Show-Off, I think."

I grunted.

"You know how she makes such good trades with him? I was there one time when they were trading, I saw them. They like each other, I think. He gives her things, he does it just for her—and she knows it, I think. That is how it seemed to me, that time."

He paused. I waited.

"Yesterday her mother finished a blanket. She said she could get a better trade at Red Mormon's." (He meant Luke.) "She said she knew the way all right, so she went alone. She would have to be gone all night—Broad Woman" (that is Mrs. Luke) "would give her a place to sleep. So she went." He fiddled with his bow-guard while he talked, not looking at me. "I followed her, a little distance behind. Her tracks went right to Show-Off's, but she did not come home last night." He picked up a handful of sand and let it fall through his fingers, watching it. "I said 'marry,' I meant just sleep with him. Then what? I don't know."

We must have sat, thinking, for about a minute.

"What do you think of Show-Off?" he asked.

"I don't like him."

He looked square at me. "My friend, by that which stands up within you, would you be sorry if he were dead?"

I'm a white man, and we were speaking about a white man, but I had to tell the truth.

"No."

"All right. Lend me your rifle."

I took time to think before I answered. "No. You are not sure. Perhaps she did go on to Red Mormon's. Perhaps he honestly wants to marry her. There is much we do not know. Besides, one must not kill people. Those days are over. No."

It was plain to see his thoughts going beyond my answer. In the last analysis, I was just like other white men. We stood together, regardless of all else. He thought he could resolve a bad situation cleanly, in an old way, but my help ended where my race began.

"Wait," I told him. "Have patience a little. Your bullet might land in Show-Off. But even if she were safe in her hogahn, it might reach her heart too—yes, and in the end, yours." I sounded pompous and unconvincing to myself.

He grunted. The idea was hostile to him, but worth considering.

"It's going to rain soon," he said. "You'll have a wet camp here."

Strong Hand was right about the rain. It came in mid-July, concentrated thunderstorms, sometimes lasting a minute or two, sometimes an hour. Grass began to show in the valley, individual, pointed spears of green scattered through the sand. Because of my feeling about Show-Off and what I suspected he was doing, I had kept postponing going after supplies until now I was clean out of grub and there was nothing for it but to saddle up and visit the post.

Travel was better with clouds in the sky to temper the sun. My animals found grass at noon. About three I reached T'o Tletsowi Wash, to find it way up, a boiling flood of brown water from bank to bank. Nothing to do but wait. The crest of the flood went by shortly, and in about an hour it looked safe to cross. Just as I was mounting, Jake Barnett arrived in his car, an old, battered Dodge.

Jake is an old-timer who runs a trading post way up on the edge of the Pah-Ute Strip, whence he emerges once a month to get supplies and mail at Luke's. I had worked in his district one season, and knew him fairly well.

"Howdy, Professor," he said, "where's your boys?"

"Hello, Jake. Haven't any this season, just me myself prospecting. How's Mrs. Barnett?"

"She's fine as ever. You fixin' to cross?"

"Yes."

"Well, I'll let you scout it. See if you can find hard bottom for me."

"All right."

I snubbed my mule's lead-rope round my saddle horn and started across, working my way cautiously over the new-spread, treacherous mud. The going seemed good, with only one soft place. From the farther bank, I shouted instructions to Jake. He came over slowly but steadily, the car splashing up great showers of mud and water, until where it began to climb the bank it stuck fast.

For about thirty seconds he just swore, without any special objective, then he directed the stream of his profanity more specifically, upon the Navajo country and Navajo roads, the rain, the creek, automobiles in general, and finally at me for sitting in the saddle and grinning at him like a God damn laughing jackass. Then he smiled.

"Well, hell," he said. "Come on and help me dig out."

We dug, and I put my rope on the front bumper and pulled with my horse. Finally the car struggled free.

"Thanks," he said. "It's gettin' late. Looks like I'd have to spend the night at Show-Off's. You headin' thar?"

"Yes. I'm out of grub."

"Fine. If I get stuck again you can help me. That horse pulls good. If I get thar first I'll tell him you're comin'."

"All right. Bet you stick."

"How much?"

"Four bits."

"Taken."

I caught up with him again just at sunset, bogged down in an adobe flat about a mile from the post. It took us a good hour, digging, laying brush and using all my animals to get the car out. By then we were tired, wet, and coated with mud. The day had been cool, the night was going to be cold.

"Stick your pack in the car," he said, "then you can make time. Show-Off's an ornery son-of-a-gun, but he's got a stove, anyway."

With my mule unloaded I came along fast, arriving at the post just after Jake did. A light showed in the store windows, but he was getting no answer to his knocking.

"Isn't he here?" I asked.

"Sure he's here. I seen him. He don't want to let us in, by God. Show yourself at that window, Professor, let him know we know he's thar."

I had a sudden horrid idea of why he didn't want to let us in.

"Look here," I said weakly, "if he feels that way, I don't want his hospitality. Let's camp."

"Hell, no! I'm goin' to set by his stove if I have to kick his God damn door in. Rap on that window."

I dismounted and rapped. Sure enough, Show-Off was in the store, standing well back in the shadows, away from the lamp. I shouted and nodded to him. He came forward slowly to open the door, and as he did so, tried to place himself so that he blocked the entrance, saying, "I thought you was Injuns."

Jake said, "Sure, I'm Sittin' Bull in person," and brushed past him. I followed.

"Come in," Show-Off said. "Come in. I wish you'd 'a' got here earlier. I've finished supper and the stove's out. But pick yourselves some grub. Here's plenty canned stuff; what'll you have?"

He moved towards the food shelves, talking, hanging onto us with words, greatly desiring that we should stay in that room, afraid.

Jake was bristling. "We'll start a fire," he said, "and pick out our grub later. Come on, Professor."

Show-Off stepped over to the cash register where he kept his revolver handy on a shelf under the counter, but whatever wild idea he may have had of holding us up, he was too late. Jake was through the door already and I went after him automatically, not knowing if I wanted to or not. Just over the threshold of the kitchen-living-room he stopped short, and I came up alongside him.

Lucille—Running Girl—*Zhiltnapah*—sat opposite us in the one armchair, frozen with terror, her eyes wide and pitiful. She wore some kind of very frilly, elaborate negligee, pink in colour, and high-heeled slippers with big, feathery tufts on them. She had long, un-Indian earrings, and with the natural colour drained out of her face, it was plain to see that she wore make-up. I wondered what movie star she thought she looked like.

Jake took off his hat, saying, "Beg pardon, ma'am." Then we backed out and returned to the store together. Coldly and shortly, Jake told Show-Off. "Our mistake. We come to the wrong place." When we reached the door he turned to add, "You're sure playin' with fire, Show-Off. Or are you fixin' to marry?"

The man stood rigid, his hands resting on the counter just above his gun, looking at us and hating us. He was sullen and afraid and dangerous. We went out.

"We can camp up by that tank on the mesa," Jake said. "Thar's plenty wood, and I guess I got enough grub."

When we had the fire going and there was a smell of coffee in the air, we relaxed slightly.

"Who's the girl?" Jake asked.

"Wind Singer's daughter. She just came back from school."

"Damn them schools! You mean the medicine man from Lukha-hutso?"

"Yes."

"I know that family. They're fine people. Damn it all. Damn him." Jake spat. "Do you figure he give her them fancy clothes?"

"I think so. I talked with her one time; she's a movie fan. She hates dressing like an Indian. I guess he found out what she wanted and ordered it from Flagstaff; the Indian schools don't issue that stuff. She thinks he looks like Ramon Novarro."

"Who? Oh, yeah. I seen one o' his pictures once. Yeah. Ain't that hell now? It sure makes me sick to think of a Navajo gettin' full o' that stuff. I've lived with these people thirty years. The God damn, dirty—"

The coffee boiling over interrupted him.

"Well," I remarked, "as you said, he's playing with fire."

"Sure, but even if they get him, that won't help her none. The school mixed her up bad enough, but now she'll never get out o' the wire." He began dishing out the food.

I thought for a while. "Jake, Wind Singer and his wife are good friends of mine. And do you know Strong Hand—*Billah Betseel?*"

"Big, handsome young feller, Tahchini clan?"

"Yes, that's the one."

"Sure. He's a particular friend of yours, ain't he?"

"He certainly is. And he's in love with her, wants to marry her. Well, now, if all those people were white, and I liked them so well, and I saw this going on, I'd do something. But now I don't feel as if I could. What is it?"

"Wall, I dunno. Or maybe I do. Thar ain't many of us on this reservation, and forty thousand Navajos, let alone how many Hopis and Pah-Utes and so on. Suppose one white man sets the Injuns against another, or like we did what we'd ought to and bend a rifle barrel over Show-Off's head on account of an Injun? Suppose we got that started once? Well, all us white folks ain't always friendly. In the end the Injuns'd get up on their own hook.

Then what? Troops—fightin' and sheep killed and cornfields
burned and damn fine Injuns defendin' their country and gettin'
killed or goin' to jail for it. I ain't just imaginin', you know that.
It ain't but a year since Scar Face was killed and his Pah-Utes
rounded up, and not so damn long since the troops was into Ho-
tevila.

"It's just like that business with Skinny McGinnis and Yucca
Chief's wife. We tried to warn Skinny, but he wouldn't listen, no
more'n Show-Off would. That kind o' bastard thinks he ain't a
man if he ever fails to make use of a woman. He don't think, he
tells himself smokin'-car stories and believes 'em. Well, Yucca
Chief's wife. We tried to warn Skinny, but he wouldn't listen, no
prove it on him. Nobody holds it against him, he's a good citizen
right now. But we had to keep out of it."

He stared at his plate. "It's cock-eyed. It don't make sense.
But thar it is. We can split on each other, and if we know an Injun's layin' for a man, we got to warn him, even help him. We got
to. Maybe that's what makes us strong, I dunno. Only sometimes
it don't seem worth while."

I nodded. "I guess you're right. But I feel sort of sick of being
white."

"Yeah. I often do, livin' out here. You goin' on to Luke's?"

"Yes."

"Well, you may have to pull me out of some more mud tomorrow. Let's turn in."

I got back to Nahki Tees three days later, and had been there
two days more when Strong Hand appeared again, just as I was
washing the breakfast dishes. His face was set, his eyes seemed
deeper in his head; after we had touched hands he said nothing
until I was through with my chores. At length, reluctantly, I sat
down opposite him, passed over tobacco, and waited.

"You know Adudjejiai?" he asked.

The question was curious. "You mean that cañon with the
straight sides, where the woman threw herself over?"

"Yes."

"I know it."

"Now she has done it, too. That same place—that woman long
ago, and now—now she."

I made no answer. There was nothing to say.

"I feel bad about it. I feel a pain for her and her family. I think it would do me good to go hunting. I know about a coyote that I want to kill. There is nothing to wait for now; we know it all. Lend me your rifle for a day or two."

I thought for a long time. White man, the white man's burden. To hell with white men! Anger and sorrow and shame began to move within me, and this my friend sitting before me, demanding the means to do that which cried aloud to be done. I lend him my rifle, and he will go and shoot Show-Off. Fine. White man, I cannot compound with my soul for having failed to prevent tragedy, by helping my friend to a murder. I thought hard, with some difficulty, finding a whirlpool of feelings turbulent in my mind.

If Strong Hand had been white, he would have kept his eyes on me, trying to force me with the strength of his own intentness. Being Indian, he allowed me to be alone and to think for myself. There was only one conclusion, it was inevitable and I hated it, for itself, and for the opinion of this man whom I loved. I brought it all together in one piece, finally; I saw it and nerved myself to speak.

"I cannot." I heard the words unforgettably, as though someone had said them into my brain, the wretched inflection of my own voice making finality. *"Do bineishe'an*, I cannot." I dug my hands into the sand, watching my fingers bury themselves. "I cannot. I am going to pack up now, I am going to leave this country. It is not just because of what has happened, but also because of what I cannot do."

We sat for some little time. At length Strong Hand said, "I shall help you catch your horse." He took out his tobacco and papers and tossed them over. "It is pleasant to smoke."

I bent low while I made my cigarette, to hide my face. When I passed the makings back, I said the word which is so rarely used in Navajo, *"Kehey,* thank you." It is a humble word, implying deep gratitude and the laying aside of pride.

HARRY SINCLAIR DRAGO

GHOST OF THE CIMARRON

Mr. Drago (who is also Bliss Lomax and Will Ermine) writes this story of gun-men in the best "shootin' " tradition of current Westerns, combining sure characterization with excellent plot, and building up to a hair-raising climax that will leave you breathless. (From *Fifty Thrilling Wild West Stories*.)

FROM across the open prairie they approached the main-travelled road into Pawnee. The hour was late and the moonlit Kansas night was very still. Protected by the shoulder of a little knoll, they pulled up their ponies.

"We'll wait here for him," said one. "He ought to be along in fifteen, twenty minutes."

The tall, gaunt man who had spoken was Luke Coffey. The others did not question his judgment. Silent, alert eyes fastened on the road, they waited. They were several hundred yards from it, but in the moonlight they could see it uncoiling over the rolling treeless plain like a silvery ribbon.

The minutes dragged by and only the champing of their ponies broke the stillness of the night. Finally Luke glanced at his watch. "Almost midnight," he observed quietly.

The others nodded. One said: "We couldn't have missed him, Luke?"

"No. The road is deep in dust. It'll muffle the sound of a team. We'll see him before we hear him."

His observation satisfied them. Even among these hard-bitten men, with whom he rode tonight, Luke Coffey was accounted a man of parts, a tried and true hand at this business which engaged them. His lean, stony-eyed face, sharpened with an unrecognized tension, was an imperturbable mask.

But that was true of the others, too. There were six of them: Flint Tanner, who once had ridden with Butch Cassidy and the Wild Bunch; Ike Patrick and Dutch George, left-overs from Bill Doolin's long-riders; Reb Sontag, the last of the Sontag gang; Luke Coffey and the Kiowa Kid, a smiling, blue-eyed man, with an unruly shock of flaxen hair.

In point of years, the Kid was the baby of this outfit; he was also a newcomer to it. But the law already had grudges enough against him to recommend him to the men with whom he was riding now. His forays into outlawry had been uniformly disastrous, however; a fact which kept recurring to Luke and one or two others. They didn't dislike the Kid; he had a crooked smile that was hard to resist. Neither could they forget that his record was against him; that he was either a reckless fool or a hoodoo; and one was as dangerous as the other in their eyes.

Having expressed themselves frankly, the Kiowa Kid knew exactly where he stood with them. He had continued to smile and he smiled tonight, though they were over a hundred miles north of the Oklahoma line and had two railroads between them and the security of the jungle-like brakes of the Cimarron. Tomorrow, they were to rob a bank. The fact seemed to rest very lightly on him. He rolled a cigarette deftly and reached for a match. Luke was watching him. "If you got to smoke, Kid, climb down out of that saddle and hug the ground before you strike a light," he said sharply. "We're a long ways from home."

The Kid grinned. "Sure enough," he agreed. He slid down effortlessly and cupped his hat over the match before he struck it. Without seeming to, Luke continued to regard him. He couldn't figure the Kid out. No matter how sharply you brought him up he never seemed to resent it. It passed belief in Luke's mind.

Dark-visaged Reb Sontag edged his pony up beside Coffey. He was leading a saddled horse, a long-legged sorrel. The stirrups had been dropped over the horn to keep them from flapping against the animal's sides if they had to get away in a hurry. A canvas bag hung from the horn, too. Reb had a similar bag on his own saddle. It was filled with cartridges for their rifles. The canvas bag on the led horse appeared to contain nothing more ominous than a lightning rod.

"Sunthin's happened to him," Reb jerked out. "It ain't Doc's way to stall along like this. I'm for ridin' back to that last town and locatin' him."

"Take it easy," Luke advised. "Someone comin' now. It'll be Doc, like as not."

They waited three or four minutes as the two-horse team approached. It was hitched to a light rig, such as Doc had said he'd get.

"It's Doc, all right," Ike Patrick declared. "I'll give him the call." Cupping a hand over his mouth he produced an excellent imitation of the sand crane's long-drawn cry. As it floated across the still night air the man in the rig raised his whip over his shoulder. It was the signal they had agreed on.

"It's Doc, sure enough," Luke announced. Unconsciously, there was a note of relief in his voice. "We can ride down to the road."

The little man in the buggy saw them coming and he let the team amble along at an even pace. He was sixty if he was a day; and that's old for an outlaw. Of course, he had not been outside the law all those years. That was just as true of the men he led; at one time or another, all had been cowboys. For five years, though, he had been darting out of the wild, uninhabited Cherokee Strip to stick up trains and hoist banks in Kansas, Oklahoma and, on rare occasions, in New Mexico and the Texas Panhandle.

Heck Short, the United States Marshal for Northern Oklahoma, had first dubbed him The Ghost of the Cimarron. It was no mean compliment, coming from a man-hunter of Heck's recognized ability. Running Doc Johnson to earth had kept him and his deputies busy for several years now. Four or five times they had had him trapped apparently; somehow he had eluded them.

If the truth must be told, little Doc, with his puckered brown eyes and slow, whimsical smile, had come to enjoy this tilting with the law, beyond all other things in his life. It still thrilled him to be able to ride into a town in broad daylight and cow it by the very fact of his presence, sometimes without firing a shot, simply because he was Doc Johnson, the notorious outlaw; the allegiance of such men as Luke Coffey, Reb Sontag, Flint Tanner, had not ceased to warm something in him; the excitement of sticking up a train, of robbing a bank, had not palled on him; the thrill in the endless hide-and-go-seek with the law.

He had been an outlaw too long to have any illusions left about how it would end. Neither was he fooling himself that there was any profit to be winnowed from this business. At best, it was a game of wits, and he accepted it as such.

For two weeks he had planned this raid into Kansas. So far, he had not made a mistake. He had brought his men to within a few miles of Pawnee without man or woman catching sight of them. He had crossed railroads, avoided a score of towns, crept by farmhouses and ranches. It had meant travelling by night and seeking cover by day. But those were only the preliminaries; the hours that lay ahead should test his resourcefulnes. He looked forward to them with quiet confidence.

Earlier this evening he had walked into the little hamlet of Arcola and purchased a team and rig. He would need it in Pawnee. The big sorrel that Reb Sontag led belonged to him. The bag that hung on the saddle horn contained not only several samples of lightning rods, but catalogues, order blanks and the other advertising matter that a pedlar of lightning rods—common enough in that country in that day—would have in his possession. It was in such guise that he intended to drive into Pawnee and size up the bank. He had even thought to equip himself with a pair of gold-rimmed spectacles, and, back in Arcola, he had bought himself a black Derby hat and a green carpet bag. Strange equipment for an outlaw.

Glasses and hat, plus a fresh shave, had produced a change in him that Luke and the others found little short of amazing.

"You look almost like a preacher," Flint Tanner declared with a chuckle.

"You said it!" the Kid laughed. "Heck Short himself wouldn't know you in that get-up, Doc."

The little man cut the merriment short.

"Did you git here without bein' seen?" he asked.

"Yeh," Luke answered. "Didn't come close to runnin' into anyone . . . The Kid says we're about five miles south of Pawnee."

"So I judge, from what I learned in Arcola," Doc observed. He turned to the Kiowa Kid. "You're still sure we can find cover between here and town? I'm depending on you; you know this country."

It was not often that he had to put himself in another man's hands in a matter as delicate as this. But he liked the Kid; trusted him. Otherwise, Kiowa would never have ridden with them.

"I'm as sure as I ever was; and that's positive," the Kid answered. "You stick to the road; the rest of us will get back on the prairie. Go about two miles; you'll see the place then, an abandoned house burned down years ago. You turn in; you'll see the old barn then, back some distance from the road. We can put the horses in there and lie out in the brush."

There was confidence in the Kid's tone. His story was exactly the one he had told several times before when Doc was making his plans.

The little man said: "All right. Toss that bag into the back of the rig, Reb, and let me have my rifle. You can git along then. You'll be there ahead of me. Just be awful sure you got that barn to yourselves when you ride up to it. You see to that, Luke; don't take anythin' for granted. If you find things okay, one of you come back to the road and hail me as I drive by."

In a few minutes the night had swallowed them. Doc picked up the reins and drove on, his rifle on the seat beside him.

He had the road to himself. He let the horses make their own gait. Twenty minutes later he began to scan the country off to the right of the road for sight of the barn. The prairie was treeless, and he had no difficulty locating the building. Once abreast the old farm he could see the ruins of the house, just as the Kid had described them. The road that led into it was high in weeds.

He was almost upon it before he heard himself called. He recognized Luke Coffey's voice.

"It's all right," said Luke.

Doc pulled up the team and handed his rifle to him. "I'll go right along," he declared. "I don't want to drive into town too late." He bent down and opened the carpet bag, exposing a pair of .45's. He left the bag open, so that he could get to his guns in a hurry if he needed them.

"When do you suppose we'll be seein' you?" Luke asked.

"About noon, I'd say. I want to look things over awful care-ful. I'll go to the hotel and git a room when I git in. I'll be up early. If things work out, we'll walk into the bank about half-past two. I want to make it as late as I can so we won't have so long to go until dark."

Luke nodded. "Better locate this Cass Chilton, the sheriff of this county. There's no bluff about him, Doc."

"Don't worry; I'll tend to all that," the little man observed drily. He picked up the reins. "By the way, Luke, if I ain't back by one o'clock, don't wait no longer; I won't be comin' back. You understand?"

"Yeh," Luke muttered woodenly. They had been together a long time. In all his turbulent life the tall man had never liked anyone so well as he did little Doc Johnson. "So long," he said.

"So long," Doc called back as he drove on. The moment had a strange drag for him, too.

In Pawnee, he put his team in the hotel barn and walked into the office. He signed himself as John Black, of Emporia, and was shown to his room.

Ten minutes later, a ruddy-cheeked man walked into the hotel and glanced at the register.

"You're up late, Cass," the clerk said.

"Just getting ready to turn in," was the easy answer.

"A lightning rod salesman," the clerk explained as he saw the sheriff glance at the signature of the late arrival. "You acquainted with him?"

"No," Chilton laughed. "You can't know all these lightning rod fellers."

He went out presently, but he did not go home. Frank Ross, his chief deputy, was asleep in a chair in the sheriff's office. Chilton awakened him.

"Well, he's here Frank," he said. "Got in a few minutes ago."

Ross rubbed the sleep out of his eyes.

He said: "We better grab him, Cass. Why take a chance of waiting?"

"We'll wait," Chilton said grimly. "We'll grab the whole bunch tomorrow."

II

"Don't do that!" Reb Sontag rasped as Luke snapped his watch open for the tenth time within an hour. "Do you have to look at that timepiece every five minutes? . . . . We got hours to go yet!"

Luke glared at him angrily and turned away muttering to himself.

Reb was known to be nerveless in a pinch; he had proved it on a score of occasions when his life hung in the balance. Now the snapping of a watch case was enough to startle him. It was indicative of the tension that gripped them. The Kiowa Kid's smile had not deserted him, however. He seemed the least troubled of all. It was strange, considering that he was a tenderfoot compared with Luke and the others. They had been through similar hours of waiting, of dreadful expectancy, often enough to have become used to them, it seemed. But, of course, there are some things men never get used to when they have a price on their heads.

It was after ten now. All morning, farmers had been driving by, on their way into Pawnee. Their passing pulled the six men to sharp attention. Luke had punched a hole in the rotting front door of the barn, and he watched the road with never-ending suspicion.

He heard a wagon approaching now. He hurried across the barn floor and with his eyes to the hole watched the wagon until it was gone. Turning, he found the Kid standing beside him. Through slitted eyes he regarded Kiowa coldly. "What's on your mind?" he asked.

His unfriendliness was wasted on the Kid. "That swell to the north, Luke—you could see almost all the way into Pawnee. A man could crawl through the brush and reach it easy enough."

Luke shook his head emphatically. "We're stickin' right here!" he said. "Don't make any mistake about that, Kid!"

"All right," the other grinned. "It was just an idea."

Together they walked back into the brush at the rear of the barn where a blanket had been spread. Dutch, Ike Patrick and the others were sprawled out around it. On the blanket itself lay their rifles and the bag of ammunition. Earlier, they had played cards. The game had died for lack of interest. There was nothing to do but wait now, and the minutes were crawling like hours.

Eleven o'clock came. Finally it was noon. There was no sign of Doc. Flint Tanner jerked himself to his feet and began to pace back and forth, his lean, hard face corded with anxiety.

"Flint, will you stop it?" Reb growled at him. "Pull yourself together! There ain't nothin' to worry about. Doc said he wouldn't be back until noon. . . . You drive a man nuts!"

"It's noon, and he ain't here," Flint muttered. "I don't like it. I got a hunch there's somethin' wrong. I can feel it."

"You've had that hunch ever since we left the Strip," the Kid chided. "If you'd had your way, we would've passed up this chance to get our hands on some real money."

"You bet we would've passed it up!" Flint blazed back at him. "And that goes for the rest of us, too! You sold Doc this damnfool idea; it's on your account we're here!"

Kiowa refused to get angry. "Things have worked out as I said they would, ain't they?" he inquired without raising his voice.

"I don't know whether they have or not!" Flint muttered fiercely. "I'll tell you better when I see Doc ridin' in. . . . And I won't be sure even then."

There was an insinuation here that the Kid could not ignore. The others were listening, faces shadowed with their thinking.

"Why not call your shots, if you've got somethin' on your mind?" the Kid queried, a thin smile on his lips.

Flint Tanner glowered at him murderously. "I'll call my shots with you—any time! I'm tellin' you now that I'm damn sick and tired of your smilin,' grinnin' mug. You can't mesmerize me like you have Doc. I know what we're facin'. If we're lucky enough to ride out of Pawnee without a shot bein' fired, we'll still be in the soup up to our necks. . . . Railroads, telegraph wires, a hundred miles of open country! You can't beat a combination like that! Some of us have taken our last look at the Strip."

"Doc's got all that figgered out," said Luke. "Don't worry about the getaway. Doc never overplays his hand, Flint."

"You're right; he's always got a trick up his sleeve," Ike Patrick agreed. Dutch George nodded. Reb grumbled sceptically to himself and got up. Giving his gun belt a hitch, he walked to the barn, his step nervous, hurried. He was back in a minute.

"Don't see nothin' of him yet," he complained. "Minutes clickin' away, too. . . . Good God, look at your watch, Luke!" he burst out violently. "What time is it?"

"Eleven minutes past twelve," said Luke. He didn't try to hide his concern. "He should have been here by now."

"You bet he should!" Flint rasped. "I been tellin' you that for an hour! It don't take him all mornin' to size up a bank—"

"You wait here," Luke interrupted. "I'm goin' up the road and have a look."

He was gone only three or four minutes when they saw him running back. They stiffened in their tracks.

"It's okay," he told them; "I see him comin'. He's takin' his time. Ever'thin' must be all right."

They sighed their relief. The Kiowa Kid dared to laugh.

He said: "I told you this would work out, Flint."

"You just be sure it does work out!" Tanner shot back at him. It sobered the Kid in a flash.

"What do you mean?" he demanded, the blood draining away from his face.

"You asked for it, so here it is," Flint answered stonily: "Things have a habit of goin' wrong when you're around. I can give you the names of half-a-dozen men, all under the sod today, who were connected with you."

"Yeh?" Kiowa muttered thinly. "Accidents happen—"

"Don't let one happen today," Flint warned. "I'll be keepin' my eye on you, Kid. One phony move out of you and it will be your last."

The Kid stood transfixed for a moment, a steely glitter in his blue eyes. He was quick with a gun, but the odds were all against him here. A flash of sense cut through the red curtain of his rage. "Hell," he muttered, with a tight little laugh, "I ain't goin' to let you burn me up now. This thing will keep."

"Both of you shut up!" Luke ordered. "This ain't no time for flyin' off the handle."

Doc drove in a few minutes later. There was a twinkle in his eyes, proof enough that everything was all right. Accordingly Luke started to scold him.

"You sure took your time," he said. "You got any idea of what we been goin' through here, wonderin' what had happened to you?"

"Well, business is business," the little man declared without the vestige of a smile. "I sold four orders of rods. . . . Mighty neighbourly people round about Pawnee—"

"Come on, Doc, let's have it!" Flint cut in. "How do things look?"

"They couldn't be better," the little man declared, with sudden gravity. "The Kid had everything sized up just as I found it." He gave Kiowa an approving nod. "This bank is wide open for a touch. Plenty of money there, too. It didn't take me long to git every-thin' located."

"Why were you so late then?" Flint demanded.

The man's impatience was thoroughly understandable to Doc. "Well, I heard that the sheriff was goin' over to Argenta on the noon train," he explained. "I hung around to see if he would go. He did and two of his deputies went with him. They can't git back before evenin'. . . . That makes it just about perfect for us, don't it?"

Even Flint had no fault to find now. Doc had brought out some food. He got it from the buggy and they sat down around the blanket and ate.

His presence, plus the promise of action, unloosened their snarled nerves. Doc himself seemed as imperturbable as ever. Secretly, he studied the Kid. He knew how the others would stand up, once they reached town. Kiowa had recovered his poise. Still, he had less to say than usual.

"There won't be any difficulty about this, Kid," Doc observed encouragingly. "We won't be in Pawnee more than ten minutes. Just keep a cool head and do what you're told. I figger there's a chance we can hoist this bank without firing a shot. That's the way I want it if it can be accomplished."

"You won't have to be doin' any worryin' about me," Kiowa assured him.

"There won't be any time for worryin'," the little man reminded pointedly.

"You goin' to leave the team and ride in with us?" the Kid asked.

"No, I'm goin' to drive back." Doc had his plans all worked out. He called them around him. "I'll go back in the rig," he said. "We'll put the rifles in the buggy and cover them up with this blanket. There's a hitch-rack at the side of the bank. I'll leave the team there. You boys will be behind me all the time. If you're careful, you can ride up to the rack a few seconds after I get there."

"It's takin' a chance, puttin' all the rifles in the buggy," Luke objected. "If anythin' happened—"

"We won't let nothin' happen," Doc declared grimly. "And it's worth somethin' to us if we can git into town without our guns showin'."

He got out an old envelope and, splitting it, drew a map of the bank corner.

"This is the road as it enters town," he explained. "We cross the railroad tracks, and the bank is on the next corner, right here.

Dutch will lead my hoss. When we get to the rack, he'll gather up the reins of all of 'em and stay right there. . . . You got that, Dutch?"

"Yah, I unerstan'," Dutch George nodded.

"There ain't a window on the side of the bank," Doc went on, "but there's a back door. . . . Ike, you'll keep that back door covered. Just stand at the corner of the alley. Don't let no one come out. That plain?"

"Sure," Ike muttered. "Nobody gits out the back door."

"Right! Now look here," Doc continued, and his pencil travelled along the side of the bank to the corner; "Luke and me are goin' into the bank. Reb will make his stand at the front door; Flint, you take the corner; Kid, you'll go on across the street and sit down on the hotel porch. You'll have a grandstand seat. Don't let no one come out. If we get into a jam, you drop back to the bank corner." He looked them over at length. "Is that all clear to everyone?"

Luke was ready with a question.

He asked: "That makes five of us who'll be walkin' to the corner. Are we walkin' up together?"

"No," Doc told him. "The Kid will start first; he's got the farthest to go. You and me will follow him. Reb and Flint will be behind us. You'll take your rifles out of the buggy as soon as you hand your hosses over to Dutch. Flint can git my rifle and shove it in my saddle boot. . . . Anythin' else?"

There were other questions. Doc had a ready answer for each. He told them how they were to close in after Luke and he came out of the bank; how they were to leave town. No detail seemed to have escaped him. He went over everything several times, and when it seemed that they could not possibly have failed to grasp what he expected of them, he drilled them once more.

"Remember," he cautioned them, "don't use your guns unless there's no other way out. If we can knock this bank over without any bloodshed it will dull the edge of any pursuit that's organized to run us down. Stealin' money from a bank is one thing; killin' innocent citizens is another."

It was two o'clock when he told them to put their rifles in the rig. He went into the barn then and looked the horses over carefully. They were going to play an awfully important part in the hours to come.

"Guess you can throw your saddles on 'em, boys," he said. The Kiowa Kid was the last to enter the barn. Doc gave him an encouraging slap on the back. "This ain't nothin', Kid," he protested. "Let's hear you laugh once."

A mirthless, perfunctory grin was the best the Kid could manage. "I'll do my laughin' tomorrow," he muttered, his blue eyes flinty as he hurried on.

There was something vaguely forbidding in his tone that pulled Doc up. He stared after him for a moment wondering whether to call him back or not. He decided to let it go. "Nerves," he told himself. "He'll snap out of it when he gits movin'."

He climbed into the rig. He was still wearing the Derby and the glasses. He took the hat off and was about to toss it into the brush when he changed his mind. "Better wear it," he told himself. "I hate the damn thing."

Luke came out of the barn, leading his horse.

"Luke, you hold your watch on me," Doc said. "Give me five minutes, then you boys pull out, two at a time. Don't be more than a hundred yards behind me when I cross the railroad tracks."

He had no more to say. Raising a hand to Luke, he drove away.

First making sure that there was no one on the road, he turned into it and let the team jog along. The carpet bag that held his .45's rested on the floor of the buggy. He opened it, and unbuttoning his coat, shoved the guns into his belt.

He had time now to go over his plans and all that had been said. He could find nothing he would have changed. Only that remark of the Kid's came back to trouble him. He tried to dismiss it, but it stuck in his mind.

"Funny, he should have said it just that way," he thought. "I wonder what he had in his mind."

III

Though Pawnee was rapidly putting its cow town days behind it and becoming a thriving farm centre, it was still no unusual sight to see three or four cowboys riding into town from the ranches to the south-west.

Doc was counting on that to help him get his men to the bank before the real reason for their presence was discovered. Every second that suspicion could be delayed was precious.

The railroad was just ahead. He glanced back. Luke and Ike were not more than a hundred and fifty yards behind him. The others were only a short distance in the rear. They couldn't have timed themselves better.

"Workin' out nice," he told himself.

Once across the tracks, he did not look back again: his attention was all on the street ahead of him now. Something queer about it struck him; something that narrowed his eyes to even sharper attention. When he had ridden out of Pawnee that noon the street had been lined with teams. The hitch-racks were deserted now. Only a handful of people were on the sidewalks; all of them men.

"Strange," he thought. "Maybe it don't mean a thing, but it looks queer. They couldn't have cleared out any cleaner if they was expectin' us." But that was preposterous. "Why, shucks, there can't be nothin' to that," he argued. "I been too careful."

He drove on, every inch of him keyed up to a piercing alertness. Reaching the bank corner, he turned the team into the side street and headed into the hitch-rack. He hadn't been there ten seconds when Luke and Ike Patrick rode up beside him. Their faces were tense, pinched.

"Did you notice that street?" Luke demanded in a breath. "Somethin' wrong!"

"There can't be," Doc insisted. "We're goin' through with this play."

He was out of the buggy as the others rode up. Their faces were sharp with sudden suspicion of trouble. Flint Tanner was watching the Kid like a hawk.

"Git movin'!" Doc ordered before they could voice what was in their minds. "Everythin' will be all right!"

The Kid had grabbed his rifle and was walking back to the corner. Dutch had gathered up the reins. Ike was heading for the alley at the rear of the bank. Luke fell in beside Doc as he walked briskly back to the main street. Reb and Flint were only a few feet behind them.

The very air had suddenly become charged with an electric tension. A stillness that was not unlike the hush that precedes a storm had settled on Pawnee.

The Kid had reached the hotel porch opposite the bank by the time Doc and Luke arrived at the corner. Their attention was not on him, but Flint Tanner was following every move he made. He saw Kiowa start to take a chair beside the hotel door. With cat-like quickness then, the Kid leaped through the door.

"Doc, he's gone!" Flint cried. "He's got inside! The rat has sold us out!"

Doc stopped in his tracks. Before he could speak, Ike Patrick came running back from the alley. His grizzled face was damp with excitement.

"There's a posse down that alley, Doc!" he burst out. "Seven, eight men! For God's sake don't stand here! We'll be shot down like sheep!"

The little man needed to hear no more. "Git back to the hosses!" he jerked out. "We'll follow this side road out! Make it quick!"

They had not taken two steps before the muzzles of three or four rifles were thrust through the open window of the hotel. Instantly, they spurted flame. The four men leaped to the protection of the bank wall. Reb Sontag was a little too slow. Without a sound he swung around on his heels and let his gun fall. Luke tried to grab him, but Reb fell forward on his face, dead when he hit the sidewalk.

"He's gone!" Ike yelled as he saw Doc start to bend down. "You can't do nuthin' for him! That bunch in the alley will be at us in a second!"

The horses were rearing. The firing from the hotel grew more violent. The four men swung up into their saddles with difficulty. Doc Johnson reached down and untied the team. Flint and Ike had their rifles to their shoulders and were banging away at the snipers in the hotel.

"What do you want of the team?" Luke shouted at Doc.

The little man didn't stop to answer. He grabbed the off horse by the bridle and pulled the team in motion.

"Come on!" he cried to Luke and the others. Reaching the alley, he turned the team into it and sent them crashing into the posse that was dashing toward the street.

The alley was narrow. The possemen, seeing themselves bottled up, flung up their guns and fired. Somehow, Doc weathered the first blast, but before he could wheel his horse a slug crashed into his knee, shattering the bone.

Suddenly weak with excruciating pain, he grabbed his saddle horn, and as he did, a man opened the rear door of the bank and shoved out a gun. It was Cass Chilton, the sheriff, who should have been in Argenta, forty miles away.

"Throw up your hands, Doc! I got you!" Chilton cried.

The words were no more than off his tongue when Flint shot the gun out of his hand. The sheriff leaped back to safety.

"Hang on, Doc!" Luke shouted. "We got to get outa here!"

"Let go my hoss! I can make it!" the little man flung back. "Up this road and across the tracks when we git out of town!"

His knee was a grinding torture, but his head was clearing. He threw his big sorrel into a gallop.

Crossing the mouth of the alley, another hail of lead met them. The snipers who had been firing from the hotel had run out into the street. Their slugs were kicking up the dust all around the fleeing men. Ike and Flint turned in their saddles and pumped their rifles as fast as they could work the bolts.

Flint had been hit. The bullet had carried away his hat. Blood smeared his face. Ike had fared even worse. The whole front of him was a gory mess.

Dutch still led the horses that Reb and the Kid had ridden into Pawnee. It slowed him up. Luke grabbed one of the ponies. They couldn't afford to turn the extra mounts adrift until they were out of town. If one of their ponies went down, an extra horse would be priceless.

They were taking it at a dead run now. Open country beckoned them on. Little Doc swung to the south, across the railroad. The others were at his heels. Looking back they could see no sign of a posse; but they would be pursued; that was inevitable. By telegraph, no matter how roundabout the way, the country ahead of them would be warned of their coming. Wanted men, they knew they were riding for their lives.

They cursed the Kiowa Kid as they raked their ponies with the spurs. It was plain enough how he had sold them out to Cass Chilton. The deal had evidently been made before the Kid showed up in the Strip and won Doc's confidence. Just to live and be able to square their account with him was all they asked now.

They, at least, had always regarded the Kid with suspicion; Doc had trusted him. That made this black hour of treachery even harder for him to bear. He understood now what was in Kiowa's mind when he had said he would do his laughing tomorrow. Indeed, a hundred little things came back to him with new understanding.

No wonder the Kid had been so untroubled on the long ride up from the Strip; he knew where he was going; that they could have ridden down the main street of the towns they avoided and had no hand raised to stop them. Undoubtedly, Chilton had tipped off his brother peace officers to look the other way and wait for him to get The Ghost of the Cimarron and his gang dead-to-rights.

Doc glanced at Ike. The man's face was as grey as ashes. He had seen men die before, and he knew that Ike didn't have long to go. His own body was racked with agony. From the hip down he had lost all use of his right leg. He could hear the blood sucking up and down in his boot. It made him wonder what his chances were. Flint Tanner's wound was trifling. Luke and Dutch didn't have a mark on them. But this was only the beginning.

They were half a mile out of Pawnee before they saw any sign of the expected pursuit.

"Bunch of 'em comin'!" Luke called.

Doc nodded. "Let 'em come. They'll think twice about it before they try to close in on us in this open country. . . . It's shoot to kill now, boys. Some of us have got to come through this mess. You know why."

"You bet we know why!" Flint rasped. "I hope I'm the one lucky enough to meet up with him!"

The road they had followed into town lay before them. They crossed it and struck into the barren, rolling prairie to the west of it.

Doc kept glancing at Ike. The man rode slouched over in his saddle, hands grasping the horn.

"Ike—are you good for another hour?" the little man asked anxiously. "We're goin' to pull up when we reach that hill where I left you boys when I went in to buy the team."

"I can make it—and that's about all," Ike got out with an effort. "Don't let me slow you up, Doc. It's keno for me this time."

"You hang on; we'll fix you up," Doc lied valiantly. He raised his voice. "Boys don't push the hosses so hard! Let's see if that bunch wants to close in on us!"

It became apparent in a few minutes that the posse was content to keep them in sight and stay out of range.

"I thought so," Doc explained. "They figger they can make us run our ponies into the ground and that they'll git fresh mounts, and maybe some help toward evenin', and have us where they want us. . . . We'll play it smarter than that. When we reach the hill we'll hole up until dark. We can stand off fifty men from there."

There were no counter suggestions; if anyone could get them back to the Strip, he could. They knew he was badly wounded. It encouraged them to find him so full of fight.

In that land of few hills they could not miss the one they sought. With the posse always in sight, though not a shot was exchanged, they approached it. They started to swing around it, only to suddenly send their ponies up the slope.

Cass Chilton was a shrewd man. He sensed the move they were making and he and his men opened fire in a vain attempt to cut them down. In a minute or two the tables were turned and the posse had to drop back.

There was a light depression on the crest of the hill. It was deep enough to protect the horses. Both Ike and Doc had to be lifted down from their saddles. Luke tore up a shirt and bound the little man's knee. There was nothing they could do for Ike. Flint Tanner refused attention. In his bitterness he had a snarl for all of them.

Doc said: "I know how you feel, Flint. This is all my fault and I ain't denyin' it. I didn't think a man could fool me; but the Kid got under my skin; I liked him—trusted him."

"You don't hear me kickin'," Ike Patrick murmured. "You thought you was right. If we didn't like the set-up we could have pulled out before we left the Strip. You gave us the chance."

"I ain't blamin' no one but myself," Flint growled. "I had the hunch, and I didn't do nothin' about it. That's what burns me!"

They didn't have a drop of water. It was hot on the hilltop. As the sun began to drop toward the horizon, Ike begged for a drink. At times, he was delirious.

"He won't last till dark," Luke whispered to Doc. The little man could only agree. And yet, when night fell, Ike was still alive. The cool, evening breeze seemed to revive him.

"The moon will be up early," Flint declared woodenly. "How much longer are we waitin' here?"

Ike overheard the question and he took it on himself to answer. "You better go purty soon," he said. "It won't git no darker. When you're ready, put me on my horse. Tie my legs so I won't fall off. I'll take the extra horses and ride down the hill and pump my gun as long as I'm able. That'll give the rest of you a chance to git away."

"No; we can't do that, Ike," Doc protested. "You're goin' with us."

The others objected just as strenuously. Ike only smiled wanly. "Don't be fools," he murmured weakly. "I'm at the end of my string, and I'm goin' out tryin' to do somethin' for my pals. You can't deny me that favour, boys. Just git the Kid some day. That'll square everythin' for me and Reb."

In the end, he had his way. When they had tied him in his saddle, Luke put a rifle in his hands. Ike fumbled with his fingers as he tried to find the trigger.

"There it is," he muttered. "I got her now."

Doc edged his horse up beside him. The others were mounted and waiting. "Ike—I ain't goin' to say so long er anythin'," he murmured heavily. "I'd trade places with you in a second if it made any sense—"

"But it don't," Ike replied. "You'll lose that leg perhaps, but you'll git by; I can't. Just git these horses movin' for me, and pull your freight."

Luke Coffey's face was grim in the darkness as he slapped the lead horse into a gallop. Over the crest and down the slope they dashed. They carried Ike's pony along with them. His gun began to spit flame.

"Come on," Doc jerked out harshly, "and don't forget what happened here."

IV

Los Alamitos was just a little 'dobe mining town, nestling in a cup of the barren, tawny hills of Old Mexico, two hundred miles south of the Rio Grande.

In the blinding white sunshine of mid-day it was squalid, unlovely, as only Mexican towns can be. But there was always an hour or two in the evening, after the sun had dropped behind the San Jacinto peaks, when a great peace seemed to settle on it; the hills lost their harshness and the town itself seemed to lose its ugliness. To little Doc Johnson it was the pleasantest time of the day.

He and Luke had been in Los Alamitos for almost three years.

They had bought a claim above town and built themselves a comfortable shack. If their mine had not begun to pay dividends, it was perfectly all right with them. At least, it gave them an excuse for their presence, and that was enough.

They were situated high enough to give them a commanding view of the valley. Doc liked to sit out in front of the house and watch the purple shadows deepen as evening came on. He was out there this evening, after supper, his pipe going and his wooden leg propped up on a bench of his own making.

He was only a shadow of the wiry man he once had been. Pain had dimmed the reckless light that had burned so brightly in his eyes. For years he had been packing a slug wound around in his back. The old wound, plus the loss of his leg, was dragging him down now. He never complained, though he knew he was riding a downhill trail; and as the weeks slipped by he talked more and more of going home. Not to Oklahoma; but to the land of his boyhood. In his time, he had roamed over all of the West. Not even to Luke did he indicate which particular part of it was really home to him.

With the supper dishes out of the way Luke joined him this evening. For an hour they sat and smoked, with hardly a word passing between them. Twilight faded into night. Below them the lights of Los Alamitos began to prick the darkness. Doc watched them for a long time.

"A man ought to be contented here," he murmured quietly, "we're safe; this mine will make a living if it's worked right; the climate's fine. Don't seem like a person should be wantin' to be somewhere else all the time."

"It's better than bein' in the pen," Luke observed bluntly. Through old Texas newspapers they knew that Flint and Dutch had run foul of the law. "If I was you, I'd think that over considerable before I made up my mind to go back to the States."

"I've given it a lot of thought, Luke. I don't want to die in prison. The law's got a number of grudges against me, but somehow I figger I won't be picked up. I've never been photographed. That'll be in my favour. I've changed some, too; and I've lost a leg since the law had its last look at me."

"Don't talk nonsense," Luke grumbled. "Men like Heck Short would know you at a glance. Course, I know you ain't thinkin' of going back to Oklahoma; but I don't care where you go, they'll have your description, and they'll pick you up."

Luke was not as convinced of the soundness of his prophecy as he pretended, though he had voiced it from the moment Doc had first intimated he was thinking of returning to the States. But he did not want to be left alone in Mexico, and he was ready to take any stand that would keep the little man there with him.

"I don't know that you're right," Doc argued. "I been away from my home range for seventeen years.... That's a long time. There can't be so many left who used to know me. As for any printed description of me that's been sent out—well, I'll take my chance on it. I'm goin' back the first of the month, Luke."

Luke was silent for several minutes, his face grey in the moonlight. "You always was stubborn," he muttered. An idea occurred to him that pulled him up in his chair. "Doc, is all this talk about goin' home only a stall? Are you really aimin' to git back so you can pick up the Kid's trail?"

The little man shook his head thoughtfully. "No, I'm afraid that's somethin' that never can be squared now. I know Flint and Dutch wouldn't be where they are today if they hadn't tried to run him down. I figgered at first that we might bump into him down here."

"So did I," Luke monotoned. "But he ain't in Mexico; we'd have been tipped off by now, if he was, after the money we offered for word of him. It's a cinch he didn't only square himself with the law but had a piece of change handed him, too. It takes money for a man to drop out of sight as neat as he did."

"There's never been any argument about that," said Doc. "And the money didn't come from Chilton; the railroads or banks put it up, and I reckon the federal marshals had a finger in it." He shook his head sadly. "How long ago that all seems!"

Luke studied him for a moment. "What'll you do if you happen to run into the Kid?"

"What I've always said I'd do," Doc answered, without turning his head. "Time don't dim that a bit.... But about you, Luke. The mine is yours. You can git somebody up here to help you work it. The vein looks purty good."

"I'll sell the mine first chance I git," Luke muttered. "I couldn't stand bein' here alone."

"I know," the little man murmured. "I know exactly how you feel. I don't like to leave you; but I don't give myself over a year. I'd rather go this way; in a few months I won't be able to git around much. . . . You've got a lot of livin' ahead of you yet. Maybe that's why you can't understand this feelin' that's draggin' me home—"

"Oh, I want you to go," Luke exclaimed. "Your mind is set on it; don't think I'd try to keep you. And don't worry about me; I'll git along all right; I'll drift down to Guaymas or Mazatlan and find somebody that talks my lingo."

He got to his feet, his hard-bitten face motionless.

"Night's turnin' cold," he said; "you better be comin' in." His tone was sharp, petulant. Doc understood.

"I'll be in as soon as I finish my pipe," he told him. His pipe had been out for fifteen minutes. It hurt him to see Luke take his going this way. He could hear him shuffling around in the kitchen, his step leaden. He wanted to say something, but he was strangely without words for such a moment as this. And yet, he was deeply touched. They had been together a long time, and whatever else they were, they had been brave men. Between them there had always been unselfishness, loyalty, gruff kindliness and a faith in each other that few ever know.

The first of the month was only four days away. They were a long time passing. Doc had few things there that he wanted to take with him. When it came time for him to go, he was ready in a few minutes. There was a stage down the mountains to Hermosillo, where he could catch a train for the border. Several hours before the stage was due to leave, Luke and he appeared in Los Alamitos and repaired to their favourite cantina.

After the third round of tequila the world took on a rosier hue, and by stage-time both were beyond remembering why they were in town this evening, which was exactly what they wanted. The driver of the stage had presence of mind enough, however, to round up his prospective passengers. When he came for Doc, the little man did not protest; neither did Luke. In fact, the night was gone and the following day well along before either realized that half the length of Sonora lay between them.

From Arizona, Doc's way lay west. Days later, he stood on a station platform, gazing with fond remembrance at Tularosa, the little Nevada town he had not seen in seventeen years.

"It sure looks good!" he told himself. "I could find my way around with my eyes shut!"

V

Opposite the depot, where the old Nevada House had stood, he could see the blackened stumps of the foundation. A fire had levelled the place. Nothing else had changed much. The court-house, with the sheriff's office and the jail at the rear, still stood on a little square of its own, five or six feet above the level of the street. Farther along, he could see familiar signs on the buildings. Even the old Index Saloon was still doing business.

"It sure looks good," he repeated, his gaze wandering to the coalyard beyond the station. The sign still read: C. P. Haskins, Coal and Ice. There was a man at the scales, but it wasn't C. P.

He started down the street, peering here and there as he clumped along. It was only two blocks to the Index. Only once or twice did he see a face that looked familiar. It rubbed some of the eagerness out of his eyes. But there was Espinosa, the saddle maker, still working at his bench, turning out as fine a saddle as man ever made. It heartened him, and he turned into the Index with head up. A bartender slid a bottle of rye toward him. The man was a stranger.

Doc dashed off his drink before he spoke. "Billy Krinkle still run the Index?" he asked.

"Krinkle?" the bartender laughed. "Billy's been laid away ten years or more. Sam Kelting runs the place now. . . . You a stranger here, eh?"

"I used to live here years ago," Doc said as he poured himself a second drink and invited the barman to join him. "Punched cattle all over this county."

He asked after four or five old acquaintances. The man had heard the names before, but they were no longer around Tularosa. Vic Rossman still owned the bank; Mose Eberhardt still had the big store. But they had never been buddies of his; it was the boys who had stormed into Tularosa at the steer-shipping, or at the end of the month, pockets bulging with uneasy wages, and turned the town inside out in their frantic haste to catch up with pleasures long denied, that he had come a-seeking.

There was one for whom he had not inquired yet. Dreading the worst, he had held that name back. With unconcealed trepidation, he was about to voice a question concerning him, when a tall, broad-shouldered man pushed back the swinging doors of the saloon and looked in. There was a star on his vest, and he had the indefinable something about him that told the returned prodigal that he was face to face with the sheriff of the county.

He found something vaguely familiar about him. That he was there, seeking him so soon, Doc doubted. But now he saw the sheriff eye him with sudden interest; interest that deepened to frank surprise.

The sheriff let the doors bang behind him as he strode into the Index. The years had greyed his hair; his long moustache was streaked with silver. His eyes had not changed, however, and they wrinkled into a smile now that the little man at the bar would have recognized in China.

"Kim! Kim Younger!" he cried. "It's you as sure as shootin'."

The sheriff grabbed his hand and started to pump it. "Drew Johnson!" he grinned. "After all these years! Why, you dang little runt, where you been? And what's the meaning of this wooden leg?"

Little Doc—or Drew, to give him his real name—had foreseen these questions, and he had his answers ready. He had been in South America, mining; he had lost his leg in a blast.

"I was almost afraid to ask about you, Kim," he said; "the others all seem to be gone."

"Oh, they ain't all gone. Some of them have moved away, but I hear from them now and then."

"And your boy, Billy?" Doc asked.

"Big as I am!" Kim declared proudly. "He'll be twenty this birthday. Wait till he learns you're here! He's never forgot you, Drew."

Little Doc shook his head. "A man—and to think I used to ride him on my knee."

They had too much to talk about to tell it all there. Arm in arm they went up the street to the sheriff's office, and Doc, who had been looking askance at jails and peace officers for a number of years, overcame his uneasiness and settled down in solid comfort.

According to his story, he had made money and lost it several times. He was back in Tularosa to stay now; he had enough to keep him in comfort and wanted to get a little cabin, somewhere on the edge of town, so that he could keep a horse.

Kim knew just the place for him. Before noon came, Doc was settled. The sheriff had been a widower for many years. That evening the two had supper together, with Kim doing the cooking—the first of many meals they were to share. If from that first evening together Doc carried home anything to worry him, it was the fact that Kim was now serving his third term of office, a period covering the years in which the law had marked him as a wanted man.

"But there ain't a trace of suspicion in his mind," Doc told himself. "I'd feel it if there was."

The following day he had Espinosa fix up a saddle for him, with a stirrup made to accommodate his peg leg. Before the saddle was finished he had acquired a roan gelding. He could get around now, and it became the usual thing to see him riding into town from his cabin and hitching his pony in front of the sheriff's office. Often the animal stood there all day, while its owner lounged in one of Kim's comfortable chairs.

Even though he had not been told, Doc would have known before he had been back in Tularosa twenty-four hours that the life of the town had changed. Once it had depended solely on cattle and sheep. Sheep were still important, but the big cow outfits belonged to the past. Sheep had crowded them out. The range had changed; the grass was gone. But of even greater moment to Tularosa had been the discovery of rich veins of gold ore in the Santa Rosita Mountains, forty miles to the north. It was rich compensation for the passing of the cattle era. A small army of men had taken to the hills, and from the big National mine, the Charleston and a score of others, Tularosa reaped a harvest.

There was not a draw or cañon in those hills with which Doc was not familiar. Untold times he had rolled up in his blanket for the night at the base of the very dike where the National strike had been made.

This mining activity had brought problems of its own to Kim Younger. There once had been a time when he knew just about who was out in the hills. But that was beyond him now; too many new men had drifted in. There had been several robberies already; payrolls on their way to the mines. An attempt had even been made to rob a bullion wagon.

These tales had a peculiar interest for Doc Johnson. Where

there were robberies the law became active, and that was a menace
to his safety, for if suspicion ever caught him in its web he could
not hope to hide his past. Cautiously, he drew the sheriff out on
what he knew about the bandits.

"Two of 'em," Kim told him; "both masked. They seem to know
when the money is going up to the National. I tried to trap 'em
last month; laid out in Singer Cañon with my deputies all night;
they crossed me and grabbed the payroll down below at Cottonwood Creek Crossing."

"Likely place for a stickup," Doc mused. "Coon Flat is another."

"No, the Flat's too near the mine," Kim argued. "If a man was
fool enough to stage a robbery there, where would he go to get
away? Over the summit and across the Owyhee Desert?" Younger
shook his head confidently. "I don't believe it; the going would
be too hard, and a stranger would get lost."

Doc let it go at that. In his days of outlawry he had always
done the unexpected, and the Owyhee would have served him in this
instance.

Kim expected his boy in over the week-end, but Saturday and
Sunday passed and young Billy did not put in an appearance. Kim
was as disappointed as Doc.

"He'll surely be in next week," Younger insisted. "I'll get word
to him if I hear of anyone going over toward Antelope Springs."

Antelope Springs was across the Santa Rosita range, at the
edge of the Owyhee. Doc said it was too far to bring the boy in
just for a visit. "No hurry," he insisted; "a week or two more
don't matter."

Kim puffed his cigar for a moment. "I wish I could get him to
give up this wild horse idea," he declared soberly. "He's been at
it all summer and hasn't made a cent. I could get him a job at the
National; but that don't appeal to him; he wants to be out in the
open, he says."

"I don't blame him for that," Doc observed. "He comes by it
natural, Kim, bein' your son."

"Maybe," Younger murmured thoughtfully. "I guess I was wild
at his age, too; but I picked my friends a little more careful. I
didn't want him to throw in with this fellow Williams, who put
this idea of running broomtails into his head. If you want to make
anything out of wild horses it takes a big outfit—five or six men

—and even then, when you divide up it don't leave anything more than poor wages."

Tex Williams' name had come into their conversation before. Kim had always spoken disparagingly of him. Doc asked a question or two about him now.

"No, I won't say he's a bad egg," the sheriff answered. "You can't help liking him; but he's shiftless, Drew. He's been around here two years or more, and I never knew him to have a job. Billy thinks he's the salt of the earth. . . . I can't understand it."

"Well, he must have had some money to get the old Quigg place at the Springs," said the little man.

"He didn't put up a cent," Kim told him. "The Springs failed completely two years running, and Quigg gave up the place. There's a little water there this year, but the trees are all dead; nothing but sand and sage-brush as far as you can see."

Doc thought no more about it as the days passed. The following Saturday morning Kim and he were sitting in the shade in front of the office when two horsemen turned the corner and rode toward them.

"Here's Billy now!" Kim exclaimed. And then, with sudden loss of enthusiasm, "Tex Williams is with him."

Billy was in the lead. Doc searched his face in vain for some familiar feature. In this lean, bronzed six-footer there was nothing left to remind him of the little lad he had known.

Kim read his thought. He said: "You wouldn't know him, eh, Drew? . . . And, of course, he'll only remember your name, nothing more."

The two men slid out of their saddles and Billy turned the ponies over to his friend, who stopped to tie them. Doc's attention was focused only on the boy.

"Billy, I got a surprise for you," said his father. "You see this little runt here. Know who he is?"

There was only blank question in the boy's eyes.

"It's Drew Johnson," said Kim.

The name unlocked some vague but treasured memories in Billy Younger. He shook Doc's hand warmly. "Pop and I have always wondered what became of you—and here you are back in Tularosa. Where have you been all this time?"

"Oh, South America—Mexico—"

"You have?" Billy beamed. "That's swell! My pal, Tex Wil-

liams, has been down there. I've heard all about it." He turned to
call Williams. "Tex, come here! I want you to meet an old friend
of mine!"

Tex Williams turned and started toward them, a smile on his
lips and his step jaunty. Suddenly his face seemed to go grey,
and he half turned, as though about to run. Whatever his hidden
impulse, he overcame it, and walked up to them, his good-looking
face an expressionless mask.

Unnoticed by Kim and his son, Doc's expression had changed,
too. For a split second his eyes had narrowed with a lethal hatred.
He had himself in hand now. He was face to face with the Kiowa
Kid.

He had sworn to kill him on sight. He had a gun on him; here
was the target he had sought; but the Kid was safe for the moment.
The little man had put two and two together in a hurry. Many
things were plain to him now that Kim Younger had not been
able to fathom . . . robbery—two masked men—a boy with a wild
streak in him led astray by a human wolf—a strange knowledge
of when money was being sent to the National; of where the sheriff
and his deputies would be waiting.

It was very simple, Doc told himself.

"Tex, this is Drew Johnson, one of the best friends I ever
had," young Billy was saying. "He's been away about seventeen
years. Been down in your country. Shake hands with him."

The Kiowa Kid hesitated, but Doc stuck out his hand. It took
nerve to do that, loathing the Kid as he did.

"Glad to meet you," the Kid muttered.

"Glad to meet anybody who is a friend of Billy's," said Doc. "I
understand you been in South America."

"Yeh—" the Kid nodded.

"Then we ought to have somethin' to talk about," Doc said
evenly. "Look me up. . . . I'll be expectin' you."

VI

It was almost noon before Doc mounted his pony and rode
down Tularosa's main street. Instead of going to his cabin, he
struck off across the sage-brush flats; he wanted time to think
things over before he settled down to wait for the Kid to come.

He knew that Kiowa would come, sooner or later, the time depending on how long it took him to convince himself that he was in no immediate danger of being shot down in his tracks. Doc even dared to believe he knew the line of reasoning the Kid would follow in arriving at such a decision.

"He knows I'll kill him for the rat he is, if I ever git the chance to do it and keep myself in the clear," he thought; "but he'll also be smart enough to figger that he's got so much on me that I'll be mighty careful about startin' anythin'. Then it'll occur to him that he can use Billy to tie my hands; and that's just about the truth. If he's got anythin' on the boy, he'll use it as a club on me."

The thought was enough to whip him into a cursing fury for a minute. With unseeing eyes he stared at the brown Humboldt that flowed along silent and treacherous on its twisting course down the valley.

"It would kill Kim if he ever learned that the boy was mixed up in those robberies," he muttered fiercely. "The Kid will think of that, too, damn him! He heard enough this mornin' to know I'll never let that happen if I can prevent it."

And yet, he had only to think of Reb Sontag, of Ike, of Dutch and Flint Tanner, grinding out their lives in prison, to gaze at the wooden stump that served him for a leg and realize how numbered were his own days, to promise himself that the Kid should die for his treachery.

Before he headed back to town he had resolved on his course. He'd give the Kid a few days to break with Billy. Then he and Kiowa would leave Tularosa together. In some lonely cañon, death would catch up with the latter.

Arrived at home, he left the door open and took a seat inside that permitted him to watch the approach from town. The afternoon wore on without bringing the Kid.

"He'll come," Doc muttered imperturbably.

Toward evening he saw a rider turn off the main street and strike across the vacant lot toward the cabin. It was the Kid.

"Come in!" Doc called out stonily as the other pulled up at the door.

Kiowa dropped his reins over his pony's head, and taking off his gun-belt, draped it over his saddle horn. Unarmed he strode into the cabin.

Seconds passed as they stared at each other. Doc was in no hurry to speak, and the Kid was silent, too.

"Kid—you know where you stand with me," the little man said finally.

"Skip it," Kiowa muttered. "We got other things to talk about. Before you open up, get this: I ain't afraid of you, Doc. I wouldn't be here if I was. I've got a card up my sleeve, and you know it. You won't start any gunplay with me; and you'll do no talkin'."

"You got it all figgered out, eh?" Doc inquired flatly. A thin, contemptuous smile hovered over his mouth. "You ain't afraid, but you was awful careful to leave your guns outside."

"My way of being smart," the Kid flung back, with a sickly grin. He couldn't forget that he was standing up to The Ghost of the Cimarron—an experience that had put fear in the hearts of better men than he.

"The same kind of smartness that makes you think you can save your rotten carcass by hidin' behind Billy Younger," the little man ground out forbiddingly. "You're goin' to warn me that I can't touch you without smearin' him."

The Kid found himself beaten to the punch, and it disconcerted him momentarily.

"You figger it will stop me cold," Doc drove on; "that to keep Kim Younger from learnin' the truth I'll let you back me into a corner!"

"It'll stop you," the Kid blurted out viciously.

"No, it won't stop me, Kid; I wouldn't draw the line at lettin' you have it right where you stand, unarmed or not. You wrote your ticket when you sold us out in Pawnee. You may figger I'd have some explainin' to do that I couldn't git away with. . . . Well, you can forgit that part of it. I came back here to die; it don't matter much to me whether I go now or a few months from now. But I'd like to keep this town's good opinion of me; and I aim to do it. I'm goin' to give you three days to break with Billy. I don't care what excuse you give him. When the three days are up you and me are leavin' this country together."

"That's what you think," the Kid jeered. "Let me tell you somethin'; I'm stickin' right here! I've got things fixed. If anythin' happens to me, Younger and Dan Strickling, the superintendent of the National, will know in twenty-four hours who it was that got those payrolls."

Wooden-faced, Doc glared at him for a moment. He said:

"Kid, you're lyin'; you ain't that clever!"

From somewhere the Kid found courage to meet him eye to eye. "If you think I'm lyin', make the most of it!"

He didn't wait to say more.

"Three days!" Doc called out as Kiowa swung up into the saddle.

"You'll wait a long while," the Kid sneered, riding away.

Doc had not bothered to come to the door. For the better part of an hour he sat in his chair, pursuing his thoughts. He had issued an ultimatum, and he knew in his soul that he never could make it stick. Undoubtedly, the Kid was bluffing about having arranged things so that Kim and Strickling would discover the truth about Billy.... Undoubtedly; but that wasn't being sure; and Doc realized he was helpless until he could be sure.

"And that'll be never," he brooded. "The only way to find out is to step into the trap, and then it'll be too late to do anythin' about it."

He considered other plans of action, but always young Billy was left open to suspicion. Any thought of speaking plainly to the boy met his prompt veto. There was more to this than just covering up Billy's mistakes; he wanted to see the boy put back on the right trail.

Doc was down town that evening. There was nothing about his manner to suggest that anything was amiss. On the street, he encountered Kim. They walked back to the office together. Kim volunteered the information that Billy and Williams were down the street.

"What do you think of the man?" the sheriff asked.

"Oh, I don't dislike him," Doc declared casually. "Little harebrained, of course."

"He was out to see you, eh?"

"Yeh. Had quite a talk. I wouldn't try to turn the boy against him if I was you, Kim. This fellow Williams is a rolling stone; he'll pull out of this country without warning some day, and that'll be the end of it."

"I hope he goes soon," the sheriff muttered. "I don't like him. He's dug up a little money from somewhere; he and Billy are spending it."

"We did the same thing a thousand times," Doc laughed. "We never minded being broke."

"I know we didn't," Kim grumbled. "It don't mean a dang thing when you see your boy making the same mistakes you made. I want to see him buckle down and get ahead, amount to something, Drew. I swear I'd rather see him in his grave than to turn out as worthless as some of the boys around town. . . . You know he's all I got."

Doc nodded. He thought he understood fully what was in Kim's mind. His face was grim in the shadows where he sat, outside the office. "I wouldn't worry about him," he murmured quietly. "He's a fine lad, and he'll make a man you'll be proud of. Take my word."

He sat around with Kim until almost midnight, without seeing anything more of the Kid or Billy.

"You have Sunday dinner with us," the sheriff invited as Doc was leaving. "There'll be just the three of us. I'll arrange that."

Back at his cabin, Doc did not turn in at once. He placed a great significance on the fact that the Kid was beginning to spend money.

"He won't keep that up very long before somebody will be askin' questions," he said to himself. "Whatever it is that I do, it can't be put off very long."

He thought of things that Younger had said that evening. It fortified him in his resolve to close the Kid's mouth forever, as speedily as he could find a way. Kim had been the best friend he had ever had. That alone would have been warrant enough for what he proposed to do.

"I've done a lot of things in my time that was wrong," he muttered. "This will be one thing that was right. Maybe it'll help to balance my slate and take a load off my mind as well."

Kim Younger's cottage was only a block from the office. Doc had just turned the courthouse corner the following noon when Billy overtook him. They walked to the house together.

Kim was in the kitchen. He was really an excellent cook. "You and Billy sit down and talk for a few minutes," he said. "Dinner's about ready."

"Sure," Doc answered; "take your time."

Without seeming to, he studied the boy as they sat on the porch, and the feeling grew on him that under his calm surface Billy's nerves were tight as a drum; that a tense preoccupation gripped him. Several times Doc had to repeat a question. When asked about their plans for the wild horse round-up, the boy's answers were vague, perfunctory.

Doc knew what was worrying him. It was something that only a man who had lived outside the law could appreciate. The little man found his own conversation drying up, and he was glad when Kim called them to eat.

Before dinner was finished the sheriff made an announcement that pulled Doc up sharply. "Dan Strickling is in town," Kim said. "The payroll is going out Tuesday. Dan figures by sending it along a little early it will be safer."

Doc flashed a glance at Billy. The boy had not looked up from his plate. And now Billy said:

"I wondered why Strickling didn't try something like that. But chances are he won't be stuck up again in a year."

"I'm going to make sure he won't this time," Kim declared. "I'm going to lay out at Cottonwood Creek Crossing and I'll have two or three deputies planted in Singer Cañon. We'll slip out of town tomorrow afternoon and get ourselves fixed before daylight."

"That ought to do the trick," Billy remarked, reaching for his coffee. The cup tipped over. "Damn it!" he snapped irritably. "Look at that mess!"

Kim passed it off with a laugh. Doc's eyes were empty as he buttered a slice of bread. It was all very plain to him.

"I'd watch Coon Flat," he said guilelessly, eyeing the boy. He saw the pulse in Billy's neck beat faster; knew he was hanging on his father's answer.

"That's foolish," Kim said. "I've told you so before. If you could look at this as a bandit would—and that's the way to look at it—you'd agree with me. The first thing they figure on is a way out. . . . No sir, I'll divide my men between the Crossing and Singer Cañon!"

Doc didn't press the point. Billy's relief was evident to him, and that was what he had been angling for. To a certainty he knew that the Kiowa Kid and the boy would be in Coon Flat to hold up Strickling.

The little man told himself he wanted to be alone to decide what he was to do; but twenty-four hours passed and he was still as far as ever from finding a course that would accomplish his ends.

Early Monday afternoon he was at the sheriff's office. He had spent a sleepless night. Stepping into the office he found Kim and Tiny Albers, his chief deputy, with their heads together.

"I didn't know you was busy," he apologized, starting for the door.

"Come in," Kim insisted; "no secrets from you." He leaned back in his chair and laughed quietly. "Dan Strickling was just here, Drew. I mentioned your hunch about Coon Flat to him, and he thinks enough of it to send a man out to the mine with word to have four or five of the boys planted down there by daylight to-morrow morning."

"He does, eh?" Doc queried, as he sought a chair. In his casual tone there was nothing to suggest what this bit of information meant to him.

"I told him to go ahead," Kim went on. "I couldn't miss a chance like that to put you in your place, Drew."

Doc pretended to find it amusing. He asked about Billy, and learned that the boy and the Kid had left Tularosa an hour ago for Antelope Springs.

"No!" Doc exclaimed tensely. "That's too bad—" His concern was genuine enough, though it did not spring from the reason that Kim Younger supplied.

"Frank Stock has been wantin' me to spend a day or two at the ranch," the little man went on. "I figgered I'd ride out with Billy and his friend. . . . I suppose they're goin' around by way of the South Fork."

"They always do," said Kim. "If you're ready to go you can overtake 'em; they'll waste an hour at the Willow Point stage station."

"Well, if that's the case, I think I will tag after 'em. I'll see you in a day or two, Kim. . . . So long, Tiny!"

Once he had reached his cabin, he tarried only long enough to get his guns. He set a course across the sage-brush then that would take him into the hills several miles west of Willow Point. It was not in his mind to meet up with the Kid and Billy. By striking through the mountains he could reach Antelope Springs well ahead of them. That was what he proposed to do.

"A shame I can't let the Kid ride into this and git his carcass pumped full of lead," he brooded. "But I got to think of Billy; I got to put him in the clear. And I can't wait now. No matter what comes of it, I've got to call the Kid's bluff."

VII

Twilight was turning the grim, grey Owyhee into an undulating purple sea by the time Doc got his first glimpse of the dead poplars that stood like sentinels around the tumble-down house at Antelope Springs.

Leaving his horse out in the brush, several hundred yards from the house, he approached it warily. The long ride had been an ordeal for him. It made him realize how fast he was slipping.

He convinced himself in a few minutes that he had arrived ahead of Billy and the Kid. The door was not locked. He walked in and looked the place over. Save for a table, a couple of chairs and the bunks, it was bare. In the gloom, he found a lantern on the wall, above the table. He knew they would make a light as soon as they arrived. That meant they would come in the door and go directly to the table. Taking that into consideration, he explored an unused bedroom. Dragging one of the chairs into it, he half closed the door and settled down to await their coming.

The better part of an hour passed before he heard horses approaching. Voices drifted in to him, and he knew it was the boy and the Kiowa Kid. They were at odds about something, their tones sharp, acrimonious.

"You'll go through with this, Billy," the Kid said flatly as they pulled at the door. "It'll give us about ten thousand, altogether. You can do what you please with your end of it; me, I'm goin' to drift."

Doc saw them enter, black against the door. The Kid was in the lead. He went to the table and took down the lantern. A match flared in his hand. Presently, he had the lantern going. He started to straighten up.

"Stand where you are—both of you," Doc called out. There was a dreadful finality in his voice. Billy's eyes went round with surprise. The Kid sucked in his breath noisily.

"Now up with your hands," the little man commanded.

Slowly they obeyed.

Stepping into the room, Doc said: "Billy, your friend knows I'll bust him without battin' an eyelash. Don't you make the mistake of thinkin' there's any nonsense about this. The two of you turn your faces around now; I want to get your guns."

When he had disarmed them he told them to sit down on the bunk. The smoke-blackened lantern cast its flickering light on them. The Kid's face was murderous; Billy could only stare his amazement.

"We're goin' to have a little talk, boys," Doc said. "I know you're due at Coon Flat in a few hours. You needn't worry about it; we'll take care of that little stickup."

Billy didn't protest his innocence nor pretend not to understand this talk of stickup at Coon Flat. Doc liked him better for it.

"I warned you not to start anythin' with me!" the Kid whipped out. "That still goes!"

"It goes in the discard with me," Doc got out tonelessly. "Bluff or not, I'm callin' your hand tonight. And just so Billy will understand what we're talkin' about, we'll start from scratch. We'll put all the cards on the table." He broke off to gaze at the boy for a moment. "Billy," he said softly, "have you ever heard of Doc Johnson, the outlaw—sometimes called The Ghost of the Cimarron?"

"I've read about him in the papers," the boy acknowledged. His face was bloodless in the flickering light.

"Well, you're lookin' at him," the little man monotoned. "I'm Doc Johnson—"

"Oh, don't take that way of handing it to me," Billy burst out desperately. "I know you've got me, Drew. You don't have to invent any story—"

"I'm Doc Johnson," the other went on, ignoring the interruption, "and this skunk, that you call your friend, used to ride with my bunch. His name wasn't Tex Williams in those days. We called him the Kiowa Kid—"

Incredulity began to fade out of the boy's eyes, and as Doc went on relating step by step the tragedy and treachery of that day in Pawnee, the dead level tone rising to a horrible hammer beat, he knew he was hearing the truth. It seemed to put a spell on him, and, speechless, his gaze went from Doc to the Kid and back again in pathetic amazement.

As for the Kid, his eyes were as venomous as an adder's as he sat muttering and cursing to himself.

Doc brought his story up to his return to Tularosa and his talk with Kiowa.

"Drew, will you believe me, when I tell you I got mixed up in that first holdup before I knew what I was doing?" Billy burst out. "I got information from Pop that this rat wanted. I passed it along to him, and then he threatened to give me away if I didn't go through with the job. . . . After that he had plenty on me."

"And I got plenty on you now!" the Kid ground out. "You'll be awful careful that nothin' happens to me."

Doc said: "Shut up! Nothin' you can say will change this play a bit." He addressed himself to the boy again. "You know what it'll do to your father if he finds out."

Billy nodded miserably. "Been driving me mad," he murmured.

"Well, I figger he won't know. If I'm wrong, it won't help this rattler none. . . . Where is the stuff you got off Strickling?"

Billy jerked his head at the Kid. "He buried it."

"Where?"

"Under the horse trough."

The Kid ripped out an oath. "I suppose you're goin' to return it," he sneered. "That's rich; Doc Johnson handin' over a bunch of jack like that!"

"Stranger things have happened," the little man droned. He told them about Strickling's altered plans; of the trap that awaited them at Coon Flat. "I wish I could have let you ride into that, Kid. But no matter; I've got somethin' better fixed up for you." He turned to the boy. "Now rip up that bedtick, Billy; I'm going to tie up both of you. I'll leave you here. Me and the Kid are goin' to stick up Strickling tomorrow mornin'."

"No, Drew!" Billy protested. "You'll be killed!"

"Not both of us," said Doc. "You git the tick ripped up. And git this; it's your story: I been around here, under cover, for three months. You never was sure about it until tonight. You been passin' information on to the Kid. It hit you all at once this evenin' what you had been doin'. You tried to stop us, and we knocked you cold and left you here. . . . You just stick to that. It will work out okay."

Billy tried to object, but in the end he did as he had been told.

"Now you stretch out on the floor, Kid," Doc ordered. "Be damn sure you lie still."

"If you want me on the floor you'll have to put me there!" the Kid growled defiantly.

Doc raised his gun an inch or two. A slug burned the Kid's

cheek. "Will you git down as I asked?" he demanded without inflection.

Slowly the Kid obeyed. His hands were bound behind him. Doc then bound the boy hand and foot and pushed him over on the trunk. "I got to mess you up a little," he said flatly. He made a thorough job of it.

After picking up the Kid's guns he told the latter to get to his feet. "Git outside now and git on your horse. One wrong move out of you and it'll be all over."

The Kid mounted.

"Head for the little arroyo beyond the corral," Doc ordered. "My pony is there."

Ten minutes later they were moving into the hills. Doc looked back once. He could no longer see the light that burned in the house. "Kid," he muttered dismally, "I hope Reb and Ike are watchin'. They been waitin' a long time for this."

The Kid had no words in him.

Daylight found them stretched out on a rocky shelf, about fifteen feet above the trail Strickling must take on his way up to the National. A spur of the Santa Rositas, dwindling away to ragged little hills, had brought them to where they lay. In a narrow ravine, to the rear of them, they had hidden their ponies.

In the lemon yellow dawn little Doc scanned the country round about. A mile or more below him he could see the fringe of trees at Cottonwood Creek Crossing. Kim and one or two men would be there, scanning the trail even as he was. To the north, Tiny Albers and his companions would be watching from their ambush in Singer Cañon. Presently, Dan Strickling would come riding by, and then the final scene in this little play would hold the stage for a brief and bitter moment.

Doc's gaze returned to the Kid stretched out five or six feet away. They had not spoken in hours. There was nothing to be said. When a man stands on the scaffold, the noose about his neck and the black cap drawn over his face, the world about him standing still, waiting, he knows it is too late for words.

It was like that with the Kiowa Kid. He was all bad, and he had a wide streak of yellow in him, but he did not whine nor beg. Not because he was above whining; he knew it was too late for that; that it had been too late ever since that afternoon in Pawnee.

If the Kid's mouth twitched; if his eyes were wide, staring, it was not strange; he had a taste in his mouth that was like ashes; he was gazing at something beyond the understanding of man.

The yellow sky warmed to rose, and the dawn wind sprang up. Somewhere off in the malpais a coyote bayed his obeisance to the wonder of the new day; and then a little speck came bobbing along the trail. It was Dan Strickling, a rifle across his saddle bow and four thousand dollars in coin in his saddle bags.

It does not take a man long to cover a mile when he is astride a good horse. The Kid heard the patter of the pony, and he looked. For ten seconds he looked, and he marvelled at how fast the man came. And then the Kiowa Kid put his face in the dust and groaned.

And now Dan Strickling was riding by.

"Kid," Doc whispered, "this is where you git it."

The little man's hand was steady, and his aim was true.

A shudder or two, and the Kid lay still. But Doc was not watching. He was pumping his guns in the direction of Dan Strickling. If he failed to score a hit it was no accident.

The superintendent of the National flung his rifle to his shoulder and fired several times. Then he used his spurs, just as Doc had known he would.

The little man watched him go. Then he removed the Kid's bonds and put a gun in the stiffening fingers. All he had to do now was to get back to his horse and hope he could win across the Owyhee. Kim would find the Kid. How reasonable it would be to suppose that one of Dan Strickling's shots had killed him.

Time was precious; the shooting would have been heard at the Crossing. Doc began to run, his wooden stump banging on the rocks. He had gone only a few yards when he fell. He scrambled up, but before he could take a step a gun roared. Clutching his stomach, he tumbled forward.

It was Kim and his deputies, trying to keep abreast of Strickling. The sheriff had found a fresh trail, and it had led him to the two ponies.

Ten hours later Doc opened his eyes. He was in the little hospital in Tularosa. Men who have been shot in the stomach with a .30-.30 rifle do not get better.

The nurse stepped out of the room and a man entered. It was Kim Younger. He sat down beside the bed. For a long time he and Doc gazed at each other. There was great understanding in that steadfast meeting of the eyes. In itself it made all things right between them. But Kim had been waiting there for hours, hoping he might be able to say a word or two.

"Drew," he murmured softly, "I want you to know I appreciate what you did. I know all. . . . Billy told me."

Doc shook his head weakly. "Why did he have to do that?" he murmured. "I didn't want you to know, Kim——"

"He couldn't keep the truth back. I went to the Springs and found him trussed up, just as you'd left him. He showed me where the money was." Kim sighed heavily. "It's broken me all up, Drew —finding this out. I never dreamed the boy was mixed up in these robberies——"

Doc's eyes were sharp again for a moment. "Anyone else know?"

"No—only me."

"That's good. . . . No one must ever know."

Kim shook his head grimly. "They've got to know! I've got to tell 'em, Drew! I couldn't let 'em go on thinking that you were a thief. It would be different if you had never had a black mark against you."

Little Doc studied him with veiled eyes. Kim had said he knew all, but it was plain enough that he was mistaken; that Billy's story had not disclosed the fact that Drew Johnson and The Ghost of the Cimarron were one. It silenced the little man for a minute or two; he wanted to be awfully sure that he said the right thing now.

"Kim," he said at last, "an hour or two is all I've got left. . . . Oh, that's all right," he insisted as the other would have denied the obvious. "I ain't kickin' a bit; but you can't deny me the last favour I'll ever ask. What people think of me after I'm gone don't matter. You know I tried to cover up for the boy. I don't want to kick off knowin' it was all in vain. . . . You've got to let folks think that holdup was on the level."

Unnoticed, Billy had entered the room. His eyes were bleak as he approached the bed.

"Drew, I heard what you just said," his voice seemed to stick in his throat. "I can't let you cover up for me. I made a mistake, and I'm ready to pay for it——"

Doc's fingers searched for his hand. A ghost of a smile softened his chalk-like face. "It's all right, my boy; you've begun to pay for it already; and you'll keep on payin' as long as you're on the level with yourself. . . . I gave you a story to tell your father. You could have stuck to it and no one would ever have questioned you. But you wouldn't take that way out; you admitted your mistake; and if there was one thing I had to know about you to prove that the wild streak in you ain't a bad streak, it was that."

"I had to play it that way," Billy got out brokenly, unashamed of his misting eyes, "I had to tell Pop. . . . I hope you aren't sore about it, Drew—"

Little Doc shook his head faintly. "I ain't sore about nothin' now, Billy. For the first time in years everythin' is all right with me. . . . I'm restin' easy."

RIDING BOG

Will James, like that other authentic native son, Will Rogers, is a plain-spoken, richly endowed story-teller and observer. James is concerned with horses and cowmen, in prose and in drawing. In this selection, from his novel, *Home Ranch* (Scribner's, 1935), we have an illuminating portrayal of one of the less romantic aspects of ranch life. But there's a good deal more than "pulling bog" in this delightful chapter. And, while the author's syntax may not be according to the best usage, it possesses much flavor and a natural flow that somehow never "thins down."

WHO in samhill was it said how the cowboy's life was so grand and glorious?"

"I don't know, but I think it was the same feller who said something about beautiful snow."

"Well, whoever it was has never 'pulled bog' and never rode in wet snow."

This kind of talk was going on between two cowboys. There was about thirty feet of rope between 'em. One was on his horse at one end of the rope and the other, the loop end in his hand, was knee deep in sucking slushy black mud trying to find the horns of a cow that had bogged down.

He wanted to put his loop end of the rope around them horns. The cow had been fighting in trying to get out after having her drink, and the sucking mud had got her deeper as she fought, till only about half of her body showed. The cow being on the "prod" (fight) as they usually are when bogged down that way had fought at the sight of the two riders and tried to get at 'em, with the result that she got on her side, throwed her head until, in her struggling, she'd throwed it back and there she lay breathing hard, both her horns stuck deep in the mud.

There wasn't a part of her showed where a loop could be throwed so it would catch a hold. So there was nothing to do but for one of the cowboys to wade in the mud, get her horns and place the loop around 'em. Then as her head was straightened and she struggled some more to get at the cowboy who was near her, the other cowboy on the bank pulled with his horse, and all together she was soon brought to solid ground, there to show her gratitude only by trying to hook the men and horse that had saved her life.

But that's the nature of the range critter and the cowboys didn't pay much attention to that, there'd been such doings all day long. The cowboy who'd pulled her out rode safe of her horns' reach, left the slack of his rope drag, and as she run into it he speeded his horse and the mad cow soon found herself upside down to lay.

By that time the other cowboy had got on his horse, rode to where the cow had been layed, took the rope off her head and rode on. As the two looked back after they'd rode a ways, they seen that the cow was up and shaking her horns at 'em but they was now too far away for her to bother taking after 'em.

"Doggone it, Sol," says the cowboy who'd took the rope off the cow, "I been in the mud three times today and here you are riding high and dry as a mesquite bean."

The cowboy, Sol, grinned, "Shows that you're a better hand on foot than you are on a horse," he says.

The two, riding along the creek, was headed for the ranch. Their day's work was about done, for about half a mile ahead of 'em was the first fence surrounding the ranch and they didn't think there'd be any more bogged cattle on the way to that fence, from there on "inside" riders was doing the work.

It was early spring, heavy clouds hung low, a cold wind was blowing over a blanket of four inches of snow which come sudden after a couple of weeks of summer-like weather. It had been cold before, and the cattle being hardened to it had weakened when the warm weather came. Snows melted, and the watering places that had been solid footing along the creeks and water holes had turned soft and boggy and many weaker cattle layed in the bogs until riders come to pull 'em out. If none came they would stay there.

That's what such riders as Sol and the other had been doing for the past two weeks, riding every day and "pulling bog." Then come the spring snow and more cold, but the bogs was still mighty soft, and the cold made the work all the harder.

Sol looked at the shivering rider alongside of him.

"Try and keep your eye-teeth in, Gat," he says, "you'll soon be alongside of some fire."

Gat just grinned a little and says, "nice weather, ain't it?" and kept his horse on a stiff trot (riding at a trot is more warming than riding at a lope, especially against a cold wind).

The heat of home fires wasn't bothering Gat much, nothing ever bothered him much, for it was all in a day's riding. He'd done many of 'em, and when he'd remarked, while at the bog and up to his knees in mud, "Who in samhill was it said the cowboy's life was so grand and glorious," it wasn't with the feeling that he was disgusted or tired with the life, it was the joke of it that struck his funny bone, and if it'd been a lot worse he'd grinned and most likely passed some other such like remark. For, with the true cowboy, the old saying is "if you don't like it pick up and quit." Gat hadn't quit in all his life of riding.

But even tho Gat and Sol took it all as in a day's riding, they'd figured they'd done that day's riding well, and the sight of the top poles of the corral gates over a low ridge sure looked mighty good to 'em. For the top poles of the corral gates they was seeing was the first signs, from that direction, of the headquarters of the outfit they was riding for, the Home Ranch of the old Seven X's.

Topping the low ridge a spread of corrals and buildings come to sight, and sort of stringing along the big cottonwoods that growed natural along the near river-size creek was a row of low dirt-roofed log buildings, some scattered here and there, and to one side, sort of by itself was the low, rambling main ranch house where old John B. Mitchell, the builder and owner of the outfit, lived with his wife and little family of a grown daughter and son, and the son's family of a wife and little boy of ten. There was

also a very full grown female cook. The whole gathering of buildings and all was the size and had the appearance of a small town.

Gat and Sol rode on in, into a big corral and to a long log stable
where they fed their horses good hay and unsaddled. They'd feed
'em grain later, for these was "winter horses," and being there
was only two for each rider, one horse for one day and the other
for the next, and plenty of hard riding every day they had to be
hardened in, kept under good shelter and well fed.

They was better taken care of than the cowboys, who worked
just as hard as they did, with no day's rest between, and took
many chances besides, for when Sol and Gat rode it was, as with
about every day, middle afternoon when they got back and they
would have to wait till supper time before they would get anything
to eat. Their horses would be filling up on good blue joint hay in
the meantime.

But a cowboy sure never begrudges that, and as Gat and Sol
walked into the cold bunk house and started a fire it was with the
contented feeling that their horses was storing up feed and resting
for when they'd need 'em again. As for themselves, the going without the noon meal didn't bother them any. They was used to that,
for while riding from the ranch or different line and cow camps
they started of mornings for a certain work to do and didn't return
till that work was done. The average day's work from ranches
or cow camps is from sun up till middle afternoon, and the *cowboy*
don't pack no lunch nor canteen; if one did he'd just as well ride
bare headed, roll his sleeves, and say "my gracious" when he's
mad. He'd be snickered at and look as out of place as an orchid
amongst cactus blossoms.

As riders are very much cut down in numbers during winter
months there was only four other riders at the home ranch besides
Gat and Sol, two riding bog on the outside and two sort of old
pensioners riding the big pastures that went to make up the ranch.
There was, of course, a few more riders scattered at different
winter camps over the range, also at ranches where hay was put
up and where the riders culled out weaker stock and brought 'em
in for hay shovelers to feed.

The two old cowboys who rode the pastures wouldn't be back
till near supper time, for their daily rides didn't take 'em many
miles away and they could be at the ranch for their noon meal
and siesta, so they rode later. The other two outside riders would

ride zig zag and pull bog on to a near winter camp, fifteen miles away, where they'd stay for the night and then ride back to the ranch, covering every bog hole again on the way.

The ranch hands would also be out at their work with teams and hay forks till about supper time, so Gat and Sol was alone in the cowboy's bunk house and warming it up. There was another bunk house for the ranch hands.

A hunk of pitchy pine in the box stove and it wasn't long when the two riders turned their backs and took a step away from it. Gat's water soaked boots was oozing muddy water and he'd liked to change to another pair, but he didn't have another pair, he'd overdrawed on his wages when he'd went to town and celebrated the fall before and then he'd bought a new saddle which set him back so that the old boots, most always wrapped in gunnysack while riding, had to do for the winter. But wages or no wages he'd have to have a new pair of boots before roundup started, and being, like all cowboys, he wore made to order hand made boots and it would take a month to get them, so he decided that late afternoon, while his feet was cold and wet, that he would write out an order right after supper and hand it to old John B. to have it mailed when the first chance come. Another half a month's wages shot.

On account that the cook house, which was held down by the roundup cook, was quite a few hundred yards away, Gat had never thought of pulling his boots off. It would of been quite a job anyway, being they was so wet, specially putting 'em back on, and he sure didn't want to walk thru the snow to the cook house and back in his stocking feet. That might be all right for them who dive in icy pools during winters but the cowboy wouldn't see much sense to that, he gets plenty of weather anyway without hunting for it.

The order for the new pair of boots was made up after supper that evening, and being the two old riders was around by then and with their usual joking remarks to keep the air from getting stale, one of 'em, after watching Gat taking his foot measurements with a tape, asks:

"What size do you wear, Gat?"

"I don't know," says Gat. "I don't put down the size when I order boots, just measurements, you know that. But I bought a pair of shoes once, daggone 'em anyhow, I was in town for a winter, and I think they was six and a half."

"Yeh," the old cowboy says, sort of dry, "six hides and a half a keg of nails."

Regular good bunk house joking went on for a while and till the order was about made up, then the other old rider chirps up:

"Expect you'll be ordering fancy inlaid tops on 'em and wearing 'em outside your pants so's you can show 'em off to June when she gets back from her school learning."

"You bet," says Gat, looking up from his order, "and there won't be no cock-ankled broomsticks inside of 'em either."

The old rider couldn't let that pass. "Well," he says, looking down at his legs, "it's better to be a has-been than a never-been, and if your legs ever get around as many tough horses as these have you'll wonder how come they ain't plum gone or all twisted up." He went on before Gat could say a word to that. "Anyway, you won't be here when June gets back, you'll most likely be with the wagon (riding on roundup outfit) and the pretty tops of your boots will get all dirty. What a shame that will be."

"Yeh, maybe that's all so," says Gat, "but she don't like things that's new and pretty, she likes what's been around some, had experience and knows something and where the beauty lays deep. Of course," he adds on, "I have some of that on the surface, too."

He stuck his nose to the order blank and didn't try to compete with the remarks he'd brought on to himself. They came three ways, for Sol had joined in with the old cowboys, and they fitted to where he was about as beautiful and useful as the shadow of a burro on a pile of tin cans.

Gat could only grin, and he didn't say a word till one of the old riders sort of changed the subject a bit by saying how John B. didn't want his girl gallivanting around with no cowboys anyhow. He'd heard him say so, how he wanted her to be refined and fitting to refined company——

Gat was kind of surprised and got hot under the collar of a sudden and he didn't want to hear no more of that. "Yeh," he says, sarcastic, "I've seen some of such refinery, all combed and slicked up and trained to manners, but the manners I've seen some of 'em use with wimmen if they ever get 'em to one side would either make you want to hunt a hole for shame or perforate their slick hides with a forty-five, but cartridges are sort of expensive to waste on such land——"

"Now, now," Sol chips in, half grinning at Gat's peeved talk, "don't let yourself get away from yourself. What does June care what you think of the kind that's been curried below the knees? Besides you know yourself there's been some mighty fine fellers amongst the stiff collared gentry, as fine as you'll find anywhere."

"Sure," says Gat, cooling down some, "but I'm afraid of the skunks among 'em, for her sake. Because June is a mighty fine girl and I don't give a good godamighty doggone if she wouldn't even spit or look at me, I'd always think the same of her and act according."

"Them's mighty fine sentiments, cowboy," says one of the old riders, "and I hope no woman ever spoils 'em."

The talk getting kind of sentimental and serious that way didn't set so well with the other old rider and he kind of mumbled to the stove during a quiet space of time. "What's the use of Gat worrying about June, he's got less chance with her than I have with the moon. Just imagine, a forty-dollar-a-month bog rider with no eddication, never even seen a school book and learned to read only by brands on hides of critters, having the nerve to even think of that young lady, June, the daughter of old John B. hisself. Why old John B. would shoot any cowboy on sight if he thought for one second that cowboy had any inkling that way concerning that daughter of his. Besides," he went on, like it had just come to him, "you might never see her again, because John B. said something not so long ago about sending her to some place in Europe to finish her, or have her finished or something like that, whatever that means."

Gat lost his peeved feeling as the older rider talked. He knowed that it all was to stir him up and that about the girl going to Europe was most likely made up, so he hardly listened to what was said. He seen that, from past experiences, the only way to fight such talk was with the same, and with a grin. He raised his eyes to the smoked up ceiling and putting a hand over his heart he done his best to look soulful while he said "Love will find a way."

That near bucked the old rider off his chair, for he'd looked for Gat to get peeved again. But Gat did get half serious after his piece of acting, and as he sealed his boot order he turned to the old rider.

"What *is* old John B. to be so huffed up about so he don't want a cowboy to look at his daughter? The old son of a sea cook had nothing but a saddle and a 'long rope' when he started, and even tho he's been good since he come north and built this spread, you all know that he don't dare go back to Texas and pack the same name he did there."

That was all agreeable, but there was another opening.

"Well," says one of the old riders, "he done hisself proud anyway, and I sure don't blame him for not wanting his daughter to take interest in any reckless and drifting cowboy like he was at one time." As a good dig to Gat he went on to remark, "not many cowboys ever amount to anything anyway."

Gat wasn't slow taking up that opening and he aimed at both the old riders as he spoke.

"Like you two for instance," he says. "Here you are, you old decrepits, four times old enough to vote, all stove up, and you still ain't got nothing but wore out saddles and still wearing five and a half size hats."

That sort of riled the old boys up some, and Gat and Sol sort of leaned back to enjoy the show of emotion they knowed would come— The old riders realized, but too late, that they'd left Gat too good an opening, and now it took 'em a spell to get their wits stringing out for a good comeback. When they spoke their first words come together.

But one of 'em finally got the lead on the other, and after calling Gat a few cuss names and winding up on such as "pigeon-toed scorpion" and the like he went on. "Why I had three good holdings in my time. Two of them holdings was saloons, and goldern good ones too. I made a good stake and went back to cows, bought me a good outfit, then a hard winter come and cleaned me out—"

"Overgrazed your range, I bet," Gat managed to edge in.

The old rider didn't seem to hear him. "I mortgaged my ranch and what little stock I had left to the hilt then and stocked up again, and bought more cattle on shipment payment. I done fine for a few years and got to running up to five thousand head when another hard winter come on the tail of a mighty dry summer, and I was cleaned out again. We didn't cut or stack up any hay in them days, but we done a lot of riding."

Another good opening for Gat. "Yep, rode all winter with your feet against the stove."

The old cowboy flared up a little at that, even tho he knowed well that Gat was only egging him on. "No, by gad," he says, "I rode every daggone day that winter and some nights too, when sometimes I couldn't see my horse's ears for sixty mile an hour winds pushing thick hard snow.

"My men worked hard, too, but, well, when spring come I just turned my outfit over to the bank. I'd only paid off a little of the mortgage on account I'd been stocking up instead of paying on it. I wanted to count my cattle on my ten fingers, one thousand head to the finger. I'd been satisfied then and be a-sitting near as good as old John B. is sitting to day."

"And then you'd wanted ten thousand more," from Gat again.

"But," the old rider went on as a wind up, "if there'd been a daughter in my married life I wouldn't of let her marry a cowboy either if I could help it, they're born too durn free."

"Well," says Gat, getting to reason a bit on the subject, "there's cowboys and cowboys. You had about the same chance old John B. did, and then," he went on, "who is our governor and senator but a couple of born-in-the-leather cowboys who didn't know there was anything but cattle and horses on this earth till they was near thirty!"

That sort of stumped the old rider. He rolled a cigarette and all was quiet for a spell, a quiet that hinted for the other old rider that now was his chance to start telling what he'd done for hisself. But what all had just been said had got him to thinking things over, he'd got to thinking he didn't do so well with the chances he had either, and he wondered if he should tell of 'em.

It was Sol that finally spoke up and started him out. "Well, Lou, how many cows did you steal in your time?" he asks.

The old rider, Lou, didn't smile when he said, "Just enough for beef," and he went on from there. "But I have made some pretty good stakes, boys, and that's no corral dust. Mine was on horses, good horses. I'd picked up a few good bunches during a stretch of years when times was mighty hard, during a panic, and a dollar wasn't worth two bits, you couldn't sell or give a horse away and few bothered with branding 'em, but I figured there'd be a need of 'em some day and I gathered me some for keeps.

"Well, as I'd figured, it wasn't so very many years when the East begin to swarm over parts of the West, and by japers I got to selling some three-year-old unbroke colts for $400 a span. Of course they was big horses, and by that time I was running close onto eight hundred head of 'em.

"I sold out in fine shape and took a few years' time doing that. I didn't keep a hoof because I figured again that horses would go down in prices soon as the emigrating rush was over, and they did.

"Well, boys, I sure made me a stake, the biggest one I thought I'd ever make and big enough for any man, yes, any man with two families and for two life times. But I never was a family man. I went into horses again then, not good big draft horses like I had before and which run on the range the year around, but slim-bodied, spindle-legged, mesquito-looking daggone things that had to have private apartments, had to be washed and rubbed and coaxed to eat, and they'd pass a cow without seeing 'er, but boys how they could pass, pass most anything. They was race horses.

"I took my horses to wherever there was big races, in U. S.A. here, Mexico, the Island, and even England. I made fifteen thousand on one of my horses in one race and turned around and sold him for twenty thousand. I figured I had others coming up that was just as good or maybe better. It turned out that I did have.

"I done better than well for some years, my stake swelled up and I made so much money that it got to mean nothing to me. I had good stables and trainers and raised good fast horses. Them horses and me was well known with all the racy folks, and there was plenty of doings set up for me wherever I went, society circles and all kinds of circles and capers. It was sure a steady round of pleasure, and being I don't like to do things halfways, I didn't over-look none.

"But my most satisfying pleasures was being with my horses and I was with them as much as I could. But again, with the steady rounds of doings which I felt sort of obliged to take on on account they'd be in my honor and so on, I didn't get to do many things I really wanted to, and even tho I got sort of bloated on all of that and tried to squirm out many times there was many such doings I couldn't squirm out of.

"I was raised a horse's height from the ground, not on hardwood floors, and as I got to hitting the 'soogan' at about the end of the 'grave-yard shift' every night, year after year or doings after doings, that begin to tell on me, because I'd already spent thirty

years or so with the habit of crawling in during 'cocktail hours.'
Cocktail hours have a different meaning with race horse folks, or
any other folks for that matter, than ours have. It can be any
hour in the twenty-four, all depending on your craving and capacity.

"Well, as I already said, that begin telling on me. I'd chopped
off too quick on plenty of action and hard riding, went to riding
the easy overstuffed riggings instead, and to using my rope arm
to hoist a glass in place of a rope.

"Finally come a time when I didn't care to be with my horses
or see how they was being trained any more, and when a cowboy
gets that far gone he's sure far gone. I got to where I didn't want
to do anything but go gallivanting around and play nighthawk
in swallow tails. I done that well and got to thinking I was some
smart because my horses kept a-winning pretty steady, then I
figured I wasn't needed at the stables any more.

"That went well with me at the time. I went on to betting on my
horses, and drinking the way I was, I naturally thought I was
wise when I really didn't know what the samhill I was doing. Consequences is I was gypped right and left, my jockeys was bought
to pull my horses to lose, and I was gypped out of some of my
horses too.

"Then come the big bet, covering every horse, stables and all I
had. I hadn't seen my horse, the one I'd staked everything on, for
months. I went to see him, but I don't remember seeing him. I
guess I just sort of identified him in my mind and, being it was
him, felt sure I would win.

"Well—I didn't."

The old cowboy was quiet for a spell, he just sat and stared at
the stove, then he raised his head, and looking at the three other
riders he added on, "and by gad I'm durned glad I didn't."

Somehow, thru Lou's talk, neither Gat nor Sol looked or thought
for any opening to chip in a joking dig at him. Maybe it was because the story had to do with horses. Besides, even tho' the old
cowboy was mighty sincere in the telling of making and losing his
big stake, he seemed too ready to take on a joke good-natured if
one came his way. That had taken the hanker to joke out of 'em.

But, according to them, the story hadn't ended quite right as to
their idea of how it should. Old Lou sort of sensed that as he looked

at 'em, and he just about figured what remark to expect from either of 'em. He grinned.

"About the old race track loser's saying, 'slow horses and fast wimmen,' that combination has sure enough ruined many a man. Some of them fast ticks stuck around me aplenty too, they got a lot of fun out of me and I got a lot of fun out of them, it was a fifty-fifty break there. But I'll tell you what did buck me off, boys, and made me lose my stake, the only thing that did— It was old John Barleycorn."

Well, that was more of an ending, and, as old Lou figured, a sort of warning to Gat and Sol. Them two riders took it that way too, but they wasn't worried much about that or losing any stakes, for they hadn't made nothing but wages so far and they'd never thought of hitting on the trail of making a big stake. That could come later, and all they cared about for the time being was to perfect themselves in their riding and roping and knowing of the cattle game, which all always leaves room for more learning and improving, no matter how experienced a man a cowboy might be.

The talk got to thinning down, remarks got further apart as wits begin to dull. Gat yawned a couple of times, rolled another smoke and begin pulling his boots off. His first try proved that that was going to be a hard job on account of them being wet and soggy and sticking to his instep and heels like they was his own hide.

The cowboy don't bother making boot jacks or packing one around with him. His regular boot jack is his spurs which he keeps on his boots steady, and by pressing down on the shank with one foot he can usually get his boots off pretty well.

But that didn't work with Gat on days when his boots got wet, and no boot jack of any kind would of worked. At such times, Sol would help him out, straddle one of his boots, and grabbing it with both hands, Gat would push on his hind quarters till, with a lot of straining and twisting, the boot would come off.

When that was finally done that night, all of the four riders was ready to hit the soogans. Sol went outside, the whole ranch was dark, a wet snow was falling and the cold wind of that day was still blowing.

"Br-r-r-r," Sol shivered as he came back in and closed the door tight, "I'd hate to be bogged down to night. You'd ought to've kept your boots on, Gat, because they're going to be hard to put on in the morning and mighty hard to pull off again tomorrow night, and with this fresh wet snow, I'm thinking there'll be some slippery bogs to pull tomorrow."

But it was only an average March night, and the next day would only be an average March day on the old Seven X range, average, all but for the unexpected which sometimes comes and happens mighty fast, any time, anywhere.

HOWARD FAST

SPOIL THE CHILD

The author of this story has concerned himself with the delineation and interpretation of American life in all of his works. He is one of our most gifted novelists and short story writers. In "Spoil the Child," we have a profoundly moving drama, simple, restrained, embodying the essence of the hardship of travel over the plains in a day that is now history. (From *The Saturday Evening Post,* August 6, 1938.)

THE first morning pa was gone, I tried to ride one of the mules. I didn't think that would hurt, because the mules were unharnessed anyway. But Maude told ma, and ma licked me. Ma was in the wagon, and she wouldn't have seen. I told Maude I'd remember.

Pa left about six in the morning while ma still slept. "Goin' after meat?" I asked him. He had his rifle.

He nodded.

"Kin I go?"

"Stay with ma, sonny," he said. "She ain't well."

"You said I could hunt——"

"You stay with ma, sonny."

Maude got up a few minutes after that. I could see pa like a black dot out on the prairie. I pointed to him.

I said: "That's pa out there huntin'."

Maude was combing her hair, not paying a lot of attention to me. Then I tried to ride the mule. Pa would never let me ride his horse. It was only half-broken, cost four hundred dollars. Ma was always saying we could have lived a year on what that horse cost.

Maude woke ma. My mother was a tall, thin woman, tired looking. She wasn't well. I could see that she wasn't well.

"Dave, get off that mule," she said. "Where's pa?"

"Went out to hunt."

"Come here. Can't ever get it into your head to behave." I went over, and she slapped my face. "Don't bother them mules. When'll he be back? We can't stay here."

"He didn't say."

"Get some chips for a fire," ma told me. "My land, I never seen such a lazy, shiftless boy." But she didn't say it the way she always did, as if she would want to bite my head off. She seemed too tired to really care.

I guess ma licked me every day. She said I was bad—a lot worse than you'd expect from a boy of twelve. You didn't expect them to be bad that young.

"You learn to leave the mules alone," Maude called.

"You shut up," I told her. Maude was fifteen, and pretty. She had light hair, and a thin, delicate face. Ma said that someday Maude would be a lady. She didn't expect much from me. She said I would be like pa.

I walked away from the wagon, looking for chips. By now, pa was out of sight, and where he had gone the prairie was just a roll of yellow and brown, a thread of cloud above it. It frightened me to be alone on the prairie. Pa laughed at it, and called it a big meadow. But it frightened me.

We had been on the prairie for a week now. Pa said in another few weeks we'd reach Fort Lee, due west. He said that if he had cattle stock, he'd settle down right on the prairie. This way, he'd cross the mountains, grow fruit, maybe, in California. Ma never believed much he said.

I went back to the wagon and started a fire. Ma had gone inside, and Maude sat on the driver's seat.

"You might gimme a hand," I told Maude.

"I don't see you overworking," Maude said.

"You better learn to shut up."

From inside the wagon, ma yelled: "You hold your tongue, Dave, or I'll wallop you!"

"You're a little beast," Maude said.

"You wait," I told her.

I went to the keg, drew some water, and set it up to boil. I could tell by the sound that there wasn't a lot of water left in the keg. Pa had said we'd reach water soon.

When I came back to the fire, I glanced up at the sky. It was an immense bowl of hot blue, bare except for a single buzzard that turned slowly, like a fish swimming. I guess I forgot. I kept looking up at the buzzard.

Ma climbed down from the wagon slowly. "You're the same as your pa," she said. "Lazy an' bad." Her face was tight-drawn. For the past few weeks she had hardly smiled, and now it seemed that she wouldn't smile again.

"And fresh," Maude said.

I put the water on the fire, not saying anything.

"Spare the rod and spoil the child," ma said.

Then her face twisted in pain, and she leaned against the wagon. "Well, don't stand there," she told me. "Water the mules."

I went to the keg. I knew there wasn't enough water for the mules. I hoped pa would come back soon; I had a funny, awful fear of what would happen if he didn't come back soon. I kept glancing out at the prairie.

Pa had an itch in his feet. Ma said I would grow up the same way—having an itch in my feet. She was always sorry that she had married a man with an itch in his feet. Sometimes she said that the war had done it, that after the war between the North and the South, men were either broken or had to keep moving, like pa. Always west.

We lived in Columbus. Then we moved to St. Louis; then to Topeka. Pa couldn't stop, and ma got more and more worn out. She said that a wild land was no place to raise children. It was hard on ma, all right. Pa didn't do much, except when we were moving west, and then he would be like a different person. Ma never complained to him. She licked me instead.

I gave the mules enough water to cover the bottoms of their pails.

Ma came over, said: "That's not enough water."

"There ain't a damn sight more."

"Don't swear!" ma exclaimed. She clapped a hand across my head.·

"He's always swearing," Maude said. "Thinks he's grown up."

Ma stared at me a moment, dully; then she went over and prepared breakfast. It was gruel and hardtack.

"Fresh meat would be good," ma said. She looked over the prairie, maybe looking for pa. I knew how much she cared for pa. She would talk a lot about itching feet, but that didn't matter.

After breakfast, I gave the mules some oats, and Maude cleaned up the dishes. I kept glancing at Maude, and she knew what I meant. She didn't care, until ma went back into the wagon. It hurt me to look at ma.

"He'll be back soon, I guess," ma said. Then she climbed into the wagon. It was a big sixteen-foot wagon, the kind they called freighters, with a hooped top, covered with dirty brown canvas.

Maude said: "You leave me alone."

"I'll leave you alone now," I told Maude. "I gotta leave you alone now. Maybe you know what's the matter with ma?"

"That's none of your business," Maude said.

"It's my business, all right."

"You're just a kid."

I went to the back of the wagon and pulled out pa's carbine. It was the one he had used during the war, a short cavalry gun.

Ma saw me; she lay inside, and I could hear her breathing hard. She said: "What're you up to now; pa back?"

"Not yet."

"Well, you tell me soon as he gets back. And don't get into any mischief."

"All right."

In front of the wagon, I sat down on a feed box, and cleaned the gun with an old rag. Maude watched me. Finally, she said: "I'm gonna tell ma you're fooling with pa's gun."

"You keep your mouth shut."

Ma groaned softly then, and we both turned around and looked at the wagon. I felt little shivers crawl up and down my spine. Where was pa? He should have been back already. I put down the gun and walked around the wagon. In a circle, the prairie rose and fell, like a sea of whispering yellow grass. There was nothing there, no living thing.

Maude was crying. "Why don't pa come back?" she said.

I didn't answer her. I guess it occurred to me for the first time that pa might not come back. I felt like crying. I felt like getting into a corner and crying. I hadn't felt so small for a long time. It would be a comfort to have ma lick me now. You get licked, and you know you're a kid, and you don't have to worry about anything else.

I said to Maude: "Go inside the wagon and stay with ma."

"Don't you order me around."

"All right," I said. I turned my back on her. I didn't hold much with girls when they're that age.

Then Maude went inside the wagon. I heard her crying, and I heard ma say: "You stop that crying right now."

I loaded the carbine. I untethered one of the mules, climbed onto it, and set out across the prairie in the direction pa had taken. I didn't know just what I'd do, but I knew it was time pa came back.

It wasn't easy, riding the mule just with harness straps. Mules have a funny gait. And we didn't go very fast. I was glad ma and Maude were in the wagon, otherwise ma would probably lick the pants off me.

In about a half hour, the wagon was just a tiny black dot. It might have been anything. I kept glancing at the sun to remember the direction I had taken. Then a swell hid the wagon. I kept on going. I knew that if I stopped, even for a little while, I'd cry my head off.

I saw a coyote. He stood like a dog and watched me. An antelope hopped close, and I might have shot at him. But I couldn't bring myself to fire a rifle there. It would have done something to me.

I found pa. I guess I had been riding for about an hour when I saw him, over to one side. A buzzard flapped up, and I felt my throat tighten until I thought it would choke me. I didn't want to go over to him. I got down from the mule, and I walked over slowly. But I didn't want to; something made me.

He was dead, all right. Maybe it was Indians and maybe it wasn't; I didn't know. He was shot four times, and his gun was gone.

The buzzard wouldn't go away; I shot the buzzard. I didn't cry. The carbine kicked back and made my shoulder ache. I was thinking about how pa always called me an undersized, freckled little runt. He said I wouldn't grow up. Maybe that's why I didn't cry.

I went away a little distance and sat down. I didn't look at pa. I tried to remember where we were, what pa had told me about going west. When I thought of ma, I had a sense of awful fear. Suppose it happened now.

The mule walked over and nuzzled my shoulder. I was glad the mule was there then. If he wasn't, I don't know what I would have done.

Pa had to be buried. I knew that men had to be buried, but I couldn't do it. The prairie was hard, baked mud. I went back to pa and stood over him; I guess that was the hardest thing I had ever done in my life. I straightened his clothes. I pulled off his boots. Men in the West were always talking about dying with their boots on. I didn't know how it meant anything, one way or another, but I thought pa would be pleased if he didn't have his boots on.

Then I climbed up on the mule and started back for the wagon. I tried not to think that I was twelve years old. If you get to thinking about that, then you're no good at all. When I got back, ma would lick me plenty.

The mule must have found its way back, because I didn't pay much attention to that. I let the reins loose, holding onto the harness straps, and I kept swallowing. Then I saw the wagon.

I thought: "I can't tell ma now—maybe later." Nobody had ever told me about a thing like that, but I knew it wouldn't do to tell ma now. I guess I only felt it instinctively, but I knew that the importance wasn't in pa any more. All that was important was life, and life was just a fleck of dust in the prairie. It was like a nightmare to think of the distance of the prairie, and how we were alone.

I rode up to the wagon, and Maude and ma were both standing next to it. I could tell from ma's face how worried she had been about me.

"There he is!" Maude screamed.

Ma said: "I guess there ain't nothing a body can do with you, Dave. Get off that mule."

I slipped off, tethered the mule. My whole body was twisted up with the strain of keeping what I had seen off my face. I came over to ma.

"Where you been?" she demanded.

"Hunting."

"I reckon there's nothing else for a little loafer like you. Spare the rod and spoil the child. Come here."

I went over and bent down, and she walloped me a bit, not too hard. She wasn't very strong then, I guess. I cried, but I wasn't crying because of the licking. I had had worse lickings than that and never opened my mouth. But it seemed to break the tension inside of me, and I had to cry. I went over and sat down with my back against one of the wagon wheels.

Maude walked past me and said: "I guess that learned you."

I just looked at her, without answering. I took out my jackknife and began to pare at one of the wagon boards. Then my eyes traveled to the water keg.

I got up and went around to ma. She was still standing there, staring off across the prairie in the direction pa had gone.

Without turning, she said to me: "Seen anything of your pa?"

"No."

The sun was westward now, a splotch of red that blazed the whole prairie into a fire. I could get a little of how ma felt; I could see the loneliness.

"Get a fire going," she said. "He ought to have enough sense to come back early. Stop that whimpering. God help a woman when a man has itching feet."

I gathered chips and started the fire. When I took water from the keg for mush, the keg was just about empty. I didn't mention that to ma. She went about preparing supper slowly, awkwardly, and Maude watched her, frightened.

Ma kept glancing at the west.

"Be dark soon," I said.

"Guess pa'll be here any minute," ma said dully. I could tell that she didn't believe that.

"I guess so," I nodded.

We ate without speaking much. Ma didn't eat a great deal. As soon as we had finished, she went into the wagon.

Maude was saying: "I don't see how I can clean dishes without water. You fetch some water, Dave."

"There ain't no water," I said.

Maude stared at me, her eyes wide and frightened. She had heard stories, just the same as I had, about pilgrims who ran out of water. She opened her mouth to say something.

"What about ma?" I asked her quietly, nodding at the wagon. "Why don't pa come back?"

"Ain't no sense thinking about pa if he ain't here. What about ma? I guess it won't be long."

She shook her head.

"You don't need to be scared," I muttered. "It won't do no good to be scared. I reckon the worst part of this trip is over."

"Where's pa?" she whispered. "What happened?"

"How do I know what happened? You girls make me sick. I never seen anything to beat you girls."

I got up and went over to the water keg. I shook it, hoping, without having any reason to hope. I knew it was just about empty. We had plenty of food—dried meat and meal and dried beans—enough to last a month, I guess. But ma would need water.

Maude was crying.

"Why don't you go to bed?" I told her.

"Don't order me around."

"Well, you go to bed," I said. "Go in and sleep with ma. I'll stay out here."

"You're not big enough to stay out here alone," Maude said, but I knew she was afraid to stay inside the wagon with ma. I knew how she felt, and I didn't blame her for the way she felt, she was such a kid, with ma petting her all the time. We couldn't talk it over between ourselves, and that would have made it a lot better. But we couldn't.

"I'm plenty big enough," I said.

Inside the wagon ma groaned, and out on the prairie a coyote was barking. There's nothing like a coyote barking to make your insides crawl. I was all shivers, and I could see that Maude wanted to stay close to me. But that wouldn't have made it any better.

"Get in the wagon, damn you!" I cried. I was glad ma couldn't hear me swear. Ma would lick me good and plenty when I swore like that.

Surprised, Maude stared at me. Then, without a word, she went into the wagon.

I stood there, outside, for a while. It had grown quite dark. In the sky there was a faint reflected light of the sun, but it was quite dark. I walked over to the wagon and picked up one of the mule blankets. It was a warm night, summertime; I decided to put the blanket under the wagon and lie down on it.

I heard Maude saying her prayers in the wagon, but no sound from ma. I couldn't say my prayers. Usually, ma saw to it that I did, but tonight I couldn't say a word aloud. I tried, opening my mouth, but no words came out. I thought them, as much as I could. I tried not to think about pa. Spreading the blanket, I lay down on it, holding the carbine close to me. It seemed a part of pa and all that was left; I hugged it.

I couldn't sleep. I tried for a long time, but I couldn't sleep. It was quite dark now, with no moon in the sky. The mules were moving restlessly; probably because they wanted water.

I think I dozed a little. When I opened my eyes again, the moon was just coming up, yellow and bloated. I felt chilled thoroughly. Bit by bit, what had happened during the day came back, and now it was all more real than it had been in the daytime. While I lay there, thinking about it, I heard horses' hoofs; at first not noticing them, and only becoming aware of them when the horses bulked out of the night, two men riding slowly.

They were in the moonlight, and I was hidden in the shadow of the wagon. They didn't see me. They stopped just about a dozen yards from the wagon, sitting on their horses and eyeing the mules. The mules moved restlessly.

When I realized they were Indians I couldn't move, just lay there and watched them. They were naked to the waist, with their hair in two stiff braids to their shoulders. They both carried rifles.

I thought of pa. I thought of screaming to wake Maude and ma. I thought: "If they shot pa—"

They were cutting loose the mules.

I felt for the carbine, twisted around, so I lay on my belly. One of the men had dismounted and was coming toward the wagon. He held his gun in one hand and had drawn a knife with the other. I sighted the center of his breast and fired.

I remember how the sound blasted out the silence of the prairie. In the wagon, someone screamed. The Indian stopped, seemed to stare at me, swayed a bit, and crumpled to the ground. I remember the sharp pain in my shoulder from the blow of the recoil.

The mounted man's horse had wheeled about. He pulled it back, and fired at me. The shot threw sand in my face. I had a few cartridges and caps in my pocket, and I tried frantically to reload. The cartridges slipped through my fingers.

Then the Indian was gone. He had taken the other horse with

him, and I heard their hoofs thundering across the prairie. I dropped the carbine. My shoulder ached terribly. Inside the wagon, Maude was whimpering, my mother groaning.

I climbed from under the wagon. The Indian lay on his back, his face hard and twisted. I stood there, looking at him.

Maude climbed down out of the wagon. "What is it?" she cried. Then she saw the Indian and screamed.

"All right—I shot him."

She stood there, holding her hand to her mouth.

"You get back in the wagon. I guess he killed pa, all right. Don't tell that to ma."

She shook her head. Ma was groaning. "I can't go back," Maude said.

"Why?"

And then I knew. I should have known from the way ma was groaning. I went up to Maude and slapped her face. She didn't seem to feel it. I slapped her again.

"Get in there with ma."

"I can't—it's dark."

"Get in there!" I yelled.

We had lanterns on the outside of the wagon. I took one and lit it. I wasn't trembling so much now. I gave the lantern to Maude, who was still standing the way she had been before.

"Go inside," I said.

Maude climbed into the wagon, taking the lantern with her. Then I cried. I crouched under the wagon, clutching the carbine and crying.

Finally, I went over to the Indian. I forced myself to do that. He lay half across the rifle he had carried. I pulled it out, and it was my father's rifle, all right.

I don't know how long I stood there holding the rifle. Then I put it under the seat, along with the carbine. I didn't want to look at the wagon.

I walked over to the mules. It was hard to harness them. When it was done, I ached all over, and my shoulder was swollen where the carbine had rested.

I climbed to the driver's seat. The curtains were down, and I couldn't see into the wagon, but the light still burned. Taking down pa's whip, I let it go onto the mules' backs. I had seen pa do that and sometimes he let me try. The whip was fourteen feet long and I couldn't do much with it, but I got the mules moving. They had to keep moving. We had to find water.

At night, under the moon, the prairie was black and silver at the same time. Somehow, it didn't frighten me, the way it had during the day. I sat there thinking, I guess, of nothing at all, only awfully aware of the change inside me.

We drove on like that. I kept the mules at a slow pace, so the freighter wouldn't roll much. I was very tired, and after a while I didn't use the whip at all.

Then Maude came out of the wagon, sat down next to me. She looked at me and I looked at her, but she didn't say anything. She pressed close to me.

I whistled at the mules.

Inside the wagon something was whimpering. It made me tremble to hear that.

"Reckon we'll find water soon," I told Maude.

She nodded mechanically. Her head kept nodding and I dozed, myself. I guess I kept dozing through the night, fell asleep toward morning.

Maude woke me. The wagon had stopped, and the sun was an hour up. The mules had stopped on the bank of a slow, brown stream, lined with cottonwoods as far as I could see.

Maude was pointing at the water.

"Don't you start crying now," I said, rubbing my eyes.

"I won't," Maude nodded.

Ma called me, not very loud: "Dave, come here."

I climbed inside the wagon. Ma was lying on the bed, her arm curled around something. I peered at it.

"Do you know?" she said.

"I reckon I do. I reckon it's a boy. Girls ain't much use."

Ma was crying—not much; her eyes were just wetting themselves slowly.

"Where are we?" ma asked me.

"We been traveling through the night. There's a river out there. I guess we don't need to worry about water."

"All night—pa back?"

I said slowly: "I killed an Indian last night, ma. He had pa's gun."

Then she just stared at me, and I stood there, shifting from one foot to another, wanting to run away. But I stood there. It must have been about five minutes, and she didn't say anything at all. The baby was whimpering.

Then she said: "You harnessed the mules?"

"Uh-huh. Maude didn't help me—"

Ma said: "You don't tease Maude. You don't tease Maude, or I'll take a stick to you. I never seen a boy like you for teasing."

"Uh-huh," I nodded.

"Just like your pa," ma whispered. "It don't pay to have a man whose heels are always itching—it don't pay."

"No use cryin'," I said.

Ma said: "What are we going to do?"

"Go on west. Ain't hard now to go a few hundred miles more. Reckon it won't be hard. Pa said—"

Ma was staring at me, her mouth trembling. I hadn't ever seen her look just like that before. I wanted to put my head down on her breast, hide it there.

I couldn't do that. I said: "Pa told me. We'll go west."

Then I went outside. I sat down on the wagon seat, looking at the river. I heard the baby making noises.

I said to Maude: "A man feels funny—with a kid."

FREDERIC REMINGTON

WHEN A DOCUMENT IS OFFICIAL

This quietly told tragedy of an unimportant man is high-
lighted with ironic humor. The author is of course well known
in other creative arts, and as sculptor and painter, as well as
writer, he has established himself as an able interpreter of the
American Indian and cowboy. (From *Men with the Bark On.*)

WILLIAM or "Billy" Burling had for these last four years
worn three yellow stripes on his coat-sleeves with credit
to the insignia. Leading up to this distinction were two years
when he had worn only two, and back of that were yet other
annums when his blue blouse had been severely plain save for five
brass buttons down the front. This matter was of no consequence
in all the world to any one except Burling, but the nine freezing,
grilling, famishing years which he had so successfully contributed
to the cavalry service of the United States were the "clean-up" of
his assets. He had gained distinction in several pounding finishes
with the Indians; he was liked in barracks and respected on the
line; and he had wrestled so sturdily with the books that when his
name came up for promotion to an officer's commission he had
passed the examinations. On the very morning of which I speak,
a lieutenant of his company had quietly said to him: "You need
not say anything about it, but I heard this morning that your

commission had been signed and is now on the way from Washington. I want to congratulate you."

"Thank you," replied William Burling, as the officer passed on. The sergeant sat down on his bunk and said, mentally, "It was a damn long time coming."

There is nothing so strong in human nature as the observance of custom, especially when all humanity practices it, and the best men in America and Europe, living or dead, have approved of this one. It has, in cases like the sergeant's, been called "wetting a new commission." I suppose in Mohammedan Asia they buy a new wife. Something outrageous must be done when a military man celebrates his "step"; but be that as it may, William Burling was oppressed by a desire to blow off steam. Here is where the four years of the three stripes stood by this hesitating mortal and overpowered the exposed human nature. Discipline had nearly throttled custom, and before this last could catch its breath again the orderly came in to tell Burling that the colonel wanted him up at headquarters.

It was early winter at Fort Adobe, and the lonely plains were white with a new snow. It certainly looked lonely enough out beyond the last buildings, but in those days one could not trust the plains to be as lonely as they looked. Mr. Sitting-Bull or Mr. Crazy-Horse might pop out of any *coulee* with a goodly following, and then life would not be worth living for a wayfarer. Some of these high-flavored romanticists had but lately removed the hair from sundry buffalo-hunters in Adobe's vicinity, and troops were out in the field trying to "kill, capture, or destroy" them, according to the ancient and honorable form. All this was well known to Sergeant Burling when he stiffened up before the colonel.

"Sergeant, all my scouts are out with the commands, and I am short of officers in post. I have an order here for Captain Morestead, whom I suppose to be at the juncture of Old Woman's Fork and Lightning Creek, and I want you to deliver it. You can easily find their trail. The order is important, and must go through. How many men do you want?"

Burling had not put in nine years on the plains without knowing a scout's answer to that question. "Colonel, I prefer to go alone." There was yet another reason than "he travels the fastest who travels alone" in Burling's mind. He knew it would be a very desirable thing if he could take that new commission into the officers' mess with the prestige of soldierly devotion upon it. Then, too, nothing short of twenty-five men could hope to stand off a band of Indians.

Burling had flipped a mental coin. It came down heads for him, for the colonel said: "All right, sergeant. Dress warm and travel nights. There is a moon. Destroy that order if you have bad luck. Understand?"

"Very well, sir," and he took the order from the colonel's hand.

The old man noticed the figure of the young cavalryman, and felt proud to command such a man. He knew Burling was an officer, and he thought he knew that Burling did not know it. He did not like to send him out in such weather through such a country, but needs must.

As a man Burling was at the ripe age of thirty, which is the middle distance of usefulness for one who rides a government horse. He was a light man, trim in his figure, quiet in manner, serious in mind. His nose, eyes, and mouth denoted strong character, and also that there had been little laughter in his life. He had a mustache, and beyond this nothing can be said, because cavalry-men are primitive men, weighing no more than one hundred and sixty pounds. The horse is responsible for this, because he cannot carry more, and that weight even then must be pretty much on the same ancient lines. You never see long, short, or odd curves on top of a cavalry horse—not with nine years of field service.

Marching down to the stables, he gave his good bay horse quite as many oats as were good for him. Then going to his quarters, he dressed himself warmly in buffalo coat, buffalo moccasins, fur cap and gloves, and he made one saddle-pocket bulge with coffee, sugar, crackers, and bacon, intending to fill the opposite side with grain for his horse. Borrowing an extra six-shooter from Sergeant McAvoy, he returned to the stables and saddled up. He felt all over his person for a place to put the precious order, but the regulations are dead set against pockets in soldiers' clothes. He concluded that the upper side of the saddle-bags, where the extra horseshoes go, was a fit place. Strapping it down, he mounted, waved his hand at the fellow-soldiers, and trotted off up the road.

It was getting towards evening, there was a fine brisk air, and his horse was going strong and free. There was no danger until he passed the Frenchman's ranch where the buffalo-hunters lived;

and he had timed to leave there after dark and be well out before
the moon should discover him to any Indians who might be viewing
that log house with little schemes of murder in expectance.

He got there in the failing light, and tying his horse to the rail
in front of the long log house, he entered the big room where the
buffalo-hunters ate, drank, and exchanged the results of their
hard labor with each other as the pasteboards should indicate.
There were about fifteen men in the room, some inviting the bar,
but mostly at various tables guessing at cards. The room was hot,
full of tobacco smoke and many democratic smells, while the
voices of the men were as hard as the pounding of two boards together. What they said, for the most part, can never be put in your
library, neither would it interest if it was. Men with the bark on do
not say things in their lighter moods which go for much; but when
these were behind a sage-brush handling a Sharps, or skimming
among the tailing buffaloes on a strong pony, what grunts were
got out of them had meaning!

Buffalo-hunters were men of iron endeavor for gain. They were
adventurers; they were not nice. Three buckets of blood was four
dollars to them. They had thews, strong-smelling bodies, and
eager minds. Life was red on the buffalo-range in its day. There
was an intellectual life—a scientific turn—but it related to flying
lead, wolfish knowledge of animals, and methods of hide-stripping.

The sergeant knew many of them, and was greeted accordingly.
He was feeling well. The new commission, the dangerous errand,
the fine air, and the ride had set his blood bounding through a
healthy frame. A young man with an increased heart action is
going to do something besides standing on one foot leaning against
a wall: nature arranged that long ago.

Without saying what he meant, which was "let us wet the new
commission," he sang out: "Have a drink on the army. Kem up,
all you hide-jerkers," and they rallied around the young soldier
and "wet." He talked with them a few minutes, and then stepped
out into the air—partly to look at his horse, and partly to escape
the encores which were sure to follow. The horse stood quietly.
Instinctively he started to unbuckle the saddle-pocket. He wanted
to see how the "official document" was riding, that being the only
thing that oppressed Burling's mind. But the pocket was un-
buckled, and a glance showed that the paper was gone.

His bowels were in tremolo. His heart lost three beats; and

then, as though to adjust matters, it sent a gust of blood into his head. He pawed at his saddle-bags; he unbuttoned his coat and searched with nervous fingers everywhere through his clothes; and then he stood still, looking with fixed eyes at the nigh front foot of the cavalry horse. He did not stand mooning long; but he thought through those nine years, every day of them, every minute of them; he thought of the disgrace both at home and in the army; he thought of the lost commission, which would only go back the same route it came. He took off his overcoat and threw it across the saddle. He untied his horse and threw the loose rein over a post. He tugged at a big sheath-knife until it came from the back side of his belt to the front side, then he drew two big army revolvers and looked•at the cylinders—they were full of gray lead. He cocked both, laid them across his left arm, and stepped quickly to the door of the Frenchman's log house. As he backed into the room he turned the key in the lock and put it under his belt. Raising the revolvers breast-high in front of him, he shouted, "Attention," after the loud, harsh habit of the army. An officer might talk to a battalion on parade that way.

No one had paid any attention to him as he entered. They had not noticed him, in the preoccupation of the room, but every one quickly turned at the strange word.

"Throw up your hands instantly, every man in the room!" and with added vigor, "Don't move!"

Slowly, in a surprised way, each man began to elevate his hands—some more slowly than others. In settled communities this order would make men act like a covey of quails, but at that time at Fort Adobe the six-shooter was understood both in theory and in practice.

"You there, bartender, be quick! I'm watching you." And the bartender exalted his hands like a practised saint.

"Now, gentlemen," began the soldier, "the first man that bats an eye or twitches a finger or moves a boot in this room will get shot just that second. Sabe?"

"What's the matter, Mr. Soldier? Be you *loco*?" sang out one.

"No, I am not *loco*. I'll tell you why I am not." Turning one gun slightly to the left, he went on: "You fellow with the long red hair there, you sit still if you are not hunting for what's in this gun. I rode up to this shack, tied my horse outside the door, came in here, and bought the drinks. While I was in here, some one stepped out and stole a paper—official document—from my saddle-pockets, and unless that paper is returned to me, I am going to turn both of these guns loose on this crowd. I know you will kill me, but unless I get that paper I want to be killed. So, gentlemen, you keep your hands up. You can talk it over; but remember, if that paper is not handed me in a few minutes, I shall begin to shoot." Thus having delivered himself, the sergeant stood by the door with his guns levelled. A hum of voices filled the room.

"The soldier is right," said some one.

"Don't point that gun at me: I hain't got any paper, pardner. I can't even read paper, pard. Take it off; you might git narvous."

"That sojer's out fer blood. Don't hold his paper out on him."

"Yes, give him the paper," answered others. "The man what took that paper wants to fork it over. This soldier means business. Be quick."

"Who's got the paper?" sang a dozen voices. The bartender expostulated with the determined man—argued a mistake—but from the compressed lips of desperation came the word "Remember!"

From a near table a big man with a gray beard said: "Sergeant, I am going to stand up and make a speech. Don't shoot. I am with you." And he rose quietly, keeping an inquisitive eye on the Burling guns, and began:

"This soldier is going to kill a bunch of people here; any one can see that. That paper ain't of no account. Whatever did any fool want to steal it for? I have been a soldier myself, and I know what an officer's paper means to a despatch-bearer. Now, men, I say, after we get through with this mess, what men is alive ought to take the doggone paper-thief, stake the feller out, and build a slow fire on him, if he can be ridden down. If the man what took the paper will hand it up, we all agree not to do anything about it. Is that agreed?"

"Yes, yes, that's agreed," sang the chorus.

"Say, boss, can't I put my arms down?" asked a man who had become weary.

"If you do, it will be forever," came the simple reply.

Said one man, who had assembled his logistics: "There was some stompin' around yar after we had that drink on the sojer. Who-

ever went out that door is the feller what got yer document; and
ef he'd a-tooken yer horse, I wouldn't think much—I'd be lookin'
fer that play, stranger. But to go *cincha* a piece of paper! Well,
I think you must be plumb *loco* to shoot up a lot of men like we be
fer that yar."

"Say," remarked a natural observer—one of those minds which
would in other places have been a head waiter or some other
highly sensitive plant—"I reckon that Injun over thar went out
of this room. I seen him go out."

A little French half-breed on Burling's right said, "Maybe as
you keel de man what 'ave 'and you de papier—hey?"

"No, on my word I will not," was the promise, and with that
the half-breed continued: "Well, de papier ees een ma pocket.
Don't shoot."

The sergeant walked over to the abomination of a man, and
putting one pistol to his left ear, said, "Give it up to me with one
fist only—mind, now!" But the half-breed had no need to be
admonished, and he handed the paper to Burling, who gathered it
into the grip of his pistol hand, crushing it against the butt.

Sidling to the door, the soldier said, "Now I am going out, and
I will shoot any one who follows me." He returned one gun to its
holster, and while covering the crowd, fumbled for the key-hole,
which he found. He backed out into the night, keeping one gun
at the crack of the door until the last, when with a quick spring he
dodged to the right, slamming the door.

The room was filled with a thunderous roar, and a dozen balls
crashed through the door.

He untied his horse, mounted quickly with the overcoat underneath him, and galloped away. The hoof-beats reassured the buffalo-hunters; they ran outside and blazed and popped away at the
fast-receding horseman, but to no purpose. Then there was a
scurrying for ponies, and a pursuit was instituted, but the grain-
fed cavalry horse was soon lost in the darkness. And this was
the real end of Sergeant William Burling.

The buffalo-hunters followed the trail next day. All night long
galloped and trotted the trooper over the crunching snow, and
there was no sound except when the moon-stricken wolves barked
at his horse from the gray distance.

The sergeant thought of the recent occurrence. The reaction

weakened him. His face flushed with disgrace; but he knew the
commission was safe, and did not worry about the vengeance of
the buffalo-hunters, which was sure to come.

At daylight he rested in a thick timbered bottom, near a cut
bank, which in plains strategy was a proper place to make a fight.
He fed himself and his horse, and tried to straighten and smooth
the crumpled order on his knee, and wondered if the people at
Adobe would hear of the unfortunate occurrence. His mind
troubled him as he sat gazing at the official envelope; he was in
a brown study. He could not get the little sleep he needed, even
after three hours' halt. Being thus preoccupied, he did not notice
that his picketed horse from time to time raised his head and
pricked his ears towards his back track. But finally, with a start
and a loud snort, the horse stood eagerly watching the bushes
across the little opening through which he had come.

Burling got on his feet, and untying his lariat, led his horse
directly under the cut bank in some thick brush. As he was in the
act of crawling up the bank to have a look at the flat plains, a
couple of rifles cracked and a ball passed through the soldier's
hips. He dropped and rolled down the bank and then dragged himself into the brush.

From all sides apparently came Indians' "Ki-yis" and "coyote
yells." The cavalry horse trembled and stood snorting, but did not
know which way to run. A great silence settled over the snow, lasting for minutes. The Sioux crawled closer, and presently saw a
bright little flare of fire from the courier's position, and they
poured in their bullets, and again there was quiet. This the buffalo-
hunters knew later by the "sign" on the trail. To an old hunter
there is no book so plain to read as footprints in the snow.

And long afterwards, in telling about it, an old Indian declared
to me that when they reached the dead body they found the ashes
of some paper which the soldier had burned, and which had
revealed his position. "Was it his medicine which had gone back on
him?"

"No," I explained, "it wasn't his medicine, but the great medicine of the white man, which bothered the soldier so."

"Hump! The great Washington medicine maybeso. It make
dam fool of soldiers lots of time I know 'bout," concluded "Bear-
in-the-Night," as he hitched up his blanket around his waist.

A PIGEON HUNT

This sketch—it is anecdote more than story—derives its charm and appeal from the casual, leisurely manner in which it is written, and from the tantalizing vision it conjures up of pigeon pie shared with mutual devotees. (From *A Texas Matchmaker,* Houghton Mifflin.)

GLENN GALLUP arrived at the ranch on New Year's eve. He brought the report that wild pigeons were again roosting at the big bend of the river. It was a well-known pigeon roost, but the birds went to other winter feeding grounds, except during years when there was a plentiful sweet mast. This bend was about midway between the ranch and Shepherd's, contained about two thousand acres, and was heavily timbered with ash, pecan, and hackberry. The feeding grounds lay distant, extending from the encinal ridges on the Las Palomas lands to live-oak groves a hundred miles to the southward. But however far the pigeons might go for food, they always returned to the roosting place at night.

"That means pigeon pie," said Uncle Lance, on receiving Glenn's report. "Everybody and the cook can go. We only have a sweet mast about every three or four years in the encinal, but it always brings the wild pigeons. We'll take a couple of pack mules and the little and the big pot and the two biggest Dutch ovens on the ranch. Oh, you got to parboil a pigeon if you want a tender pie. Next to a fish fry, a good pigeon pie makes the finest eating going. I've made many a one, and I give notice right now that the making of the pie falls to me or I won't play. And another thing, not a bird shall be killed more than we can use. Of course we'll bring home a mess, and a few apiece for the Mexicans."

We had got up our horses during the forenoon, and as soon as dinner was over the white contingent saddled up and started for the roost. Tiburcio and Enrique accompanied us, and, riding leisurely, we reached the bend several hours before the return of the birds. The roost had been in use but a short time, but as we scouted through the timber there was abundant evidence of an immense flight of pigeons. The ground was literally covered with feathers; broken limbs hung from nearly every tree, while in one instance a forked hackberry had split from the weight of the birds.

We made camp on the outskirts of the timber, and at early dusk great flocks of pigeons began to arrive at their roosting place. We only had four shotguns, and, dividing into pairs, we entered the roost shortly after dark. Glenn Gallup fell to me as my pardner. I carried the gunny sack for the birds, not caring for a gun in such unfair shooting. The flights continued to arrive for fully an hour after we entered the roost, and in half a dozen shots we bagged over fifty birds. Remembering the admonition of Uncle Lance, Gallup refused to kill more, and we sat down and listened to the rumbling noises of the grove. There was a constant chattering of the pigeons, and as they settled in great flights in the trees overhead, whipping the branches with their wings in search of footing, they frequently fell to the ground at our feet.

Gallup and I returned to camp early. Before we had skinned our kill the others had all come in, disgusted with the ease with which they had filled their bags. We soon had two pots filled and on the fire parboiling, while Tiburcio lined two ovens with pastry, all ready for the baking. In a short time two horsemen, attracted by our fire, crossed the river below our camp and rode up.

"Hello, Uncle Lance," lustily shouted one of them, as he dismounted. "It's you, is it, that's shooting my pigeons? All right, sir, I'll stay all night and help you eat them. I had figured on riding back to the Frio tonight, but I've changed my mind. Got any horse hobbles here?" The two men, George Nathan and Hugh Trotter, were accommodated with hobbles, and after an exchange of commonplace news of the country, we settled down to story-telling. Trotter was a convivial acquaintance of Aaron Scales, quite a vagabond and consequently a story-teller. After Trotter had narrated a late dream, Scales unlimbered and told one of his own.

"I remember a dream I had several years ago, and the only way I can account for it was, I had been drinking more or less during the day. I dreamt I was making a long ride across a dreary desert, and towards night it threatened a bad storm. I began to look around for some shelter. I could just see the tops of a clump of trees beyond a hill, and rode hard to get to them, thinking that there might be a house amongst them. How I did ride! But I certainly must have had a poor horse, for I never seemed to get any nearer that timber. I rode and rode, but all this time, hours and hours it seemed, and the storm gathering and scattering raindrops falling, the timber seemed scarcely any nearer.

"At last I managed to reach the crest of the hill. Well, sir, there wasn't a tree in sight, only, under the brow of the hill, a deserted adobe *jacal*, and I rode for that, picketed my horse and went in. The *jacal* had a thatched roof with several large holes in it, and in the fireplace burned a roaring fire. That was some strange, but I didn't mind it and I was warming my hands before the fire and congratulating myself on my good luck, when a large black cat sprang from the outside into an open window, and said: 'Pardner, it looks like a bad night outside.'

"I eyed him a little suspiciously; but, for all that, if he hadn't spoken, I wouldn't have thought anything about it, for I like cats. He walked backward and forward on the window sill, his spine and tail nicely arched, and rubbed himself on either window jamb. I watched him some little time, and finally concluded to make friends with him. Going over to the window, I put out my hand to stroke his glossy back, when a gust of rain came through the window and the cat vanished into the darkness.

"I went back to the fire, pitying the cat out there in the night's storm, and was really sorry I had disturbed him. I didn't give the matter overmuch attention but sat before the fire, wondering who could have built it and listening to the rain outside, when all of a sudden Mr. Cat walked between my legs, rubbing himself against my boots, purring and singing. Once or twice I thought of stroking his fur, but checked myself on remembering he had spoken to me on the window sill. He would walk over and rub himself against the jambs of the fireplace and then come back and rub himself against my boots friendly like. I saw him just as clear as I see those pots on the fire or these saddles lying around here. I was noting every move of his as he meandered around, when presently he cocked up an eye at me and remarked: 'Old sport, this is a fine fire we have here.'

"I was beginning to feel a little creepy, for I'd seen mad dogs and skunks, and they say a cat gets locoed likewise, and the cuss was talking so cleverly that I began to lose my regard for him. After a little while I concluded to pet him, for he didn't seem a bit afraid; but as I put out my hand to catch him, he nimbly hopped into the roaring fire and vanished. Then I did feel foolish. I had a good six-shooter, and made up my mind if he showed up again I'd plug him one for luck. I was growing sleepy, and it was getting late, so I concluded to spread down my saddle blankets and slicker before the fire and go to sleep. While I was making down my bed, I happened to look towards the fire, when there was my black cat, with not even a hair singed. I drew my gun quietly and cracked away at him, when he let out the funniest little laugh, saying: 'You've been drinking, Aaron; you're nervous; you couldn't hit a flock of barns.'

"I was getting excited by this time, and cut loose on him rapidly, but he dodged every shot, jumping from the hearth to the mantel, from the mantel to an old table, from there to a niche in the wall, and from the niche clear across the room and out of the window. About then I was some nervous, and after a while lay down before the fire and tried to go to sleep.

"It was a terrible night outside—one of those nights when you can hear things; and with the vivid imagination I was enjoying then, I was almost afraid to try to sleep. But just as I was going into a doze, I raised up my head, and there was my cat walking up and down my frame, his back arched and his tail flirting with the slow sinuous movement of a snake. I reached for my gun, and as it clicked in cocking, he began raking my legs, sharpening his claws and growling like a tiger. I gave a yell and kicked him off, when he sprang up on the old table and I could see his eyes glaring at me. I emptied my gun at him a second time, and at every shot he crouched lower and crept forward as if getting ready to spring. When I had fired the last shot I jumped up and ran out into the rain, and hadn't gone more than a hundred yards before I fell into a dry wash. When I crawled out there was that d——d cat rubbing himself against my boot leg. I stood breathless for a minute, thinking what next to do, and the cat remarked: 'Wasn't that a peach of a race we just had!'

"I made one or two vicious kicks at him and he again vanished. Well, fellows, in that dream I walked around that old *jacal* all night in my shirt sleeves, and it raining pitchforks. A number of times I peeped in through the window or door, and there sat the cat on the hearth, in full possession of the shack, and me out in the weather. Once when I looked in he was missing, but while I was watching he sprang through a hole in the roof, alighting in the fire, from which he walked out gingerly, shaking his feet as if he had just been out in the wet. I shot away every cartridge I had at him, but in the middle of the shooting he would just coil up before the fire and snooze away.

"That night was an eternity of torment to me, and I was relieved when someone knocked on the door, and I awoke to find myself in a good bed and pounding my ear on a goose-hair pillow in a hotel in Oakville. Why, I wouldn't have another dream like that for a half interest in the Las Palomas brand. No, honest, if I thought drinking gave me that hideous dream, here would be one lad ripe for reform."

"It strikes me," said Uncle Lance, rising and lifting a pot lid, "that these birds are parboiled by this time. Bring me a fork, Enrique. Well, I should say they were. I hope hell ain't any hotter than that fire. Now, Tiburcio, if you have everything ready, we'll put them in the oven, and bake them a couple of hours."

.   .   .   .   .

It was after midnight when we disposed of the first oven of pigeon pot-pie, and, wrapping ourselves in blankets, lay down around the fire. With the first sight of dawn, we were aroused by Mr. Nathan and Uncle Lance to witness the return flight of the birds to their feeding grounds. Hurrying to the nearest opening, we saw the immense flight of pigeons blackening the sky overhead. Stiffened by their night's rest, they flew low; but the beauty and immensity of the flight overawed us, and we stood in mute admiration, no one firing a shot. For fully a half-hour the flight continued, ending in a few scattering birds.

EUGENE MANLOVE RHODES

THE COME-ON

No anthology of Western tales would be complete without
at least one account of a poker game, and here it is—one of the
author's best. I am indebted to Mrs. Rhodes for her consent to
use it here. (From *The Saturday Evening Post,* November 23,
30, 1907.)

STEVE THOMPSON had sold his cattle. El Paso is (was)
the Monte Carlo of America. Therefore—the syllogism may
be imperfectly stated but the conclusion is sound. Perhaps there
is a premise suppressed or overlooked somewhere.

Cash in hand, well fortified with paving material, Thompson
descended on the Pass City. At the expiration of thirty-six blame-
less hours he perceived that he was looking through a glass darkly
in the Business Men's Club, intently regarding a neatly-lettered
placard which ambiguously advised all concerned in this wise:

IF DRINKING INTERFERES
WITH YOUR BUSINESS
STOP IT

A back-room door was opened. A burst of merriment smote
across the loneliness. A head appeared. The tip of its nose
quivered.

"Hey, old-timer! Will you walk into my parlor?" it jeered.

Steve walked over with dignity and firmly closed the door—closing it through sheer inadvertence from the inside. A shout of welcome greeted him.

With one exception—the Transient—they were all old friends: the Stockman, the Judge, alike darkly attractive; the supple-handed Merchant with curly hair and nose; and the strong, quiet figure of the Eminent Person. A wight of high renown and national, this last, an ex-sheriff, who had attained to his present bad Eminence through superior longevity. As he was still in the prime of life, it should perhaps be explained that his longevity was purely comparative, as contrasted with that of a number of gentlemen, eminent in the same line, who had been a trifle dilatory at critical moments—to them final.

The Merchant, sometime Banker-by-night as now, began evening up chip-stacks. "How much?" he inquired, as the Judge and the Eminent Person hitched along to make room between them.

"I'm not playing tonight," Steve began. He was cut short by a torrent of scoffing advice and information.

"Only one hundred to come in—all you got to get out."

"Another victim!"

"Bet 'em high and sleep in the streets!"

"Table stakes. Cutter goes for aces and flushes."

"Just give us what you can spare handy and go to bed. You'll save money and sleep."

"Straight flush is the best hand."

"All ties go to the sweaters."

"A man and his money are soon parted!"

"You play the first hand for fun, and all the rest of the night to get even!" Thus, and more also, the Five in hilarious chorus.

"Any man caught bluffing loses the pot," added the Eminent Person, gravely admonitory. "And a Lalla-Cooler can only be played once a night."

"Nary a play play I," said Steve aggrievedly. "I stole just one measly horse and every one's called me a horse-thief ever since. But I've played poker, lo! these many years, and no one ever called me a gambler once. The best I get is, 'Clear out, you blamed sucker. Come back when you grow a new fleece!' and when I get home the wind moans down the chimney, 'O-o-o-gh-h! wha-a-t have you do-o-one with your summer's wa-A-a-ges!'"

"Aw, sit down—you're delayin' the game," said the Stockman. The Banker shoved over three stacks of patriotically assorted colors and made a memorandum. The Five howled mockery and derision, the cards danced and beckoned luringly in the mellow lamplight, the Judge pulled his coat-tail, the Major Premise tugged. Steve sat down, pulling his sombrero over his eyes.

"He that runneth after fools shall have property enough," he quoted inaccurately. "I'll have some of your black hides on the fence by morning."

The cards running to him, it was not long before Steve doubled his "come-in" several times on quite ordinary hands, largely because his capital was so small that he could not be bluffed out. The betting was fierce and furious. Steve, "on velvet," played brilliantly. But he was in fast company—too fast for his moderate means. The Transient seemed to have a bottomless purse. The Stockman had cattle on a thousand hills. The Merchant habitually sold goods at cost.

As for the Judge—his fine Italian hand was distinctly traceable in the frenzied replies to frenzied attacks upon certain frenzied financial transactions of his chief, a frenzied but by no means verdant copper magnate to whom he, the Judge, was Procurator-General, adviser legal and otherwise. The Judge took no thought for the morrow, unless his frequently expressed resolve not to go home until that date may be so regarded.

The Eminent Person, a Republican for Revenue Only, had been awarded a remunerative Federal position as a tribute to his ambidextrous versatility in the Life Strenuous, and his known prowess as a "Stand-Patter."

Upon all these things Steve reflected. With caution, some caution, and again caution, a goodly sum might well be abstracted from these reckless and capricious persons; provided always that he had money on the table to play a good hand for what it was.

For long his luck held good. Having increased his gains manyfold, he was (being quite a natural person) naturally incensed that they were not more. Yielding to his half-formed resolve, he dug up his herd of cattle and put them on the table.

"I am now prepared to grab Old Opportunity by the scalplock," he announced.

He played on with varying success. Presently, holding aces up, and being persistently crosslifted by the Eminent Person and the Judge, after a one-card draw all around, he became obsessed with the fixed idea that they were both bluffing and afraid to show down. When this delusion was dispelled, he noted with chagrin that the spoils of Egypt had departed, taking with them some plenty of real money.

That was the turning-point. By midnight he was hoarse with repeating, parrot-wise, "That's good—give me another stack." His persistent losses won him sympathy, even from these hardened plungers.

"Bad luck, old man—sure!" purred the consolatory Stockman, raking the pot. "I drawed out on you. Sometimes the cards run against a fellow a long time, that way, and then turn around and get worse."

"Don't you worry about me," retorted Steve. "You're liable to go home talking to yourself, yet, if the cards break even."

In the early stages of the game Steve had been nervous and restless from the fever in his blood. Now he was smiling, easy, serene, his mind working smoothly, like a well-oiled machine. Collecting all his forces, counting the chances coolly, he played a steady, consistent game.

The reckless plunging ceased so far as it was against him. The others, for most part, merely called his tentative bets with wary respect. Men of his type are never so formidable as in defeat. Things had come to such a pass that many good hands netted him little or nothing. Then came a rally; his pile crept slowly up until he was nearly even.

With twenty dollars each in a jackpot, the Eminent Person dealing, the Stockman modestly opened for two hundred. The Transient stayed, as did the Merchant and the Judge—the latter mildly stating that he would lie low and let some one else play his hand. Steve stayed.

"Happy as the dealer in a big jackpot," warbled the Eminent Person. "And now we will take an observation." He scrutinized his cards, contributed his quota and raised for double the amount. "I'll just play the Judge's hand for him," he remarked blandly. The Stockman cheerfully re-raised five hundred.

The Transient, momentarily low in funds, stayed for all he had before him. "I've got a show for this much," he said, pushing back the side money. "*And* a pretty good one. Bet your fool heads off! You've got to beat a hectic flush to finger this pot!"

The Merchant laid down three sevens—of diamonds, spades, clubs. "Any one got the seven of hearts?" he wondered. The Judge called. Steve, squeezing his hand carefully, drew out the seven of hearts, flashed it at the Merchant, replaced it, and stayed.

The Eminent Person, after due consideration, saw the five hundred and raised it to a thousand. "To dissuade you-all from drawing out on me," he explained, stroking his mustache with deliberate care.

The Stockman called without comment. The Judge hesitated, swore ferociously, and finally called.

Steve squeezed his cards with both hands for a final corroborative inspection, scratched his head and rolled his eyes solemnly around the festal board.

"Eleven hundred dollars of my good coin in there, now, and here I sit between the devil and the deep, blue sea. One thousand bucks. Much money. Ugh! One thousand days, each day of twenty-four golden hours set with sixty near-diamond minutes! Well! I sure hate to give you fellows this good gold!"

"Steve's got one of them things!" surmised the Stockman.

"A fellow *does* hate to lay down a bobtail straight flush, when there's such a chance for action if he fills," chimed in the Eminent dealer.

"It's face up, Steve. You'd just as well show us. My boy, you ought to wear a mustache," said the Judge, critically. "Your lips get pale and give you away when you try to screw your courage up. Of course, you've got a sweet, little, rosebud mouth; but you need a big, ox-horn mustache in this vocation."

"Don't show it, Steve," advised the Stockman. "I judge that His Honor's got one of them same things his black self. You might both fill—and you don't want to let him see how high yours is."

"If I only don't fill the wrong way," said Steve. "Want to split the pot or save stakes with me, Judge?"

"That would be a foolish caper. If I fill—I mean," the Judge corrected himself hastily. "I mean, I've got the money won now, unless you draw out on me. And that's a 52 to 1 shot."

"Me, too," said the dealer. "We both got it won. But I'll save out a hundred with you, Steve. That'll pay your bills and take you home."

"That'll be nine hundred to draw cards for a chance at nine thousand and action on what I got left. . . . Faint heart never won a jackpot. Here goes nothing!" said Steve, pushing the chips in. "One from the top, when you get to me. If I bet after the draw, you-all needn't call unless you're a mind to."

"Got that side money and pot straight?" queried the dealer lightly. "All right?"

He stretched out a long left arm and flipped the cards from the pack with a jerk of the wrist.

"Cards and spades? (I'm pat, myself, of course.) Cards to you? None? Certainly. None to you, and one to you, one to you, none—"

Steve's card, spinning round as it came, turned over and lay face up on the table—the three of hearts. (Laymen will please recall that, as already specified, a straight flush was, in this game, the Best Hand.) As the dealer was sliding the next card off to replace it, Steve caught the thin glint of a red 8 on its corner.

With a motion inconceivably swift he was on his feet, his left hand over the pack.

"Hold on!" he cried. "Look at this!"

He made a motion as to spread out the four cards he had retained, checked himself and glared, crouching.

"Sit down, Steve. Don't be a fool," said the Stockman. "You know you've got no right to an exposed card after the draw; and you know he didn't go to do it."

Steve bunched his four cards carefully and laid them on the table, face down.

"Certainly not. Oh, no! He didn't go to do it. But he did it, just the same," he said bitterly. "Now, look here! I don't think there's anything wrong—not for a minute. Nothing worse'n dumb, idiotic thumb-hand-sidedness. I specially don't want no one else to get mixed up in this," with a glance at the Stockman. "So you and the Judge needn't feel called on to act as seconds. But I'm vexed. I'm vexed just about nine thousand dollars' worth—likely much more, if my hand hadn't been tipped. *Mira!* Look!" he addressed the dealer, who sat quietly holding the pack in his left hand, his right resting on the table. "I've a right to *call* for my card turned up, haven't I?"

"Sure thing!" said the dealer equably.

"All right, then. One bad turn deserves another. But—plenty *cuidado*! Look out! If any card but the eight of hearts turns up, protect yourself or somebody's widow'll be in a position to collect life insurance, and *I* ain't married! Turn her over."

He leaned lightly on the table with both hands. Their eyes met in a level gaze.

"Let her zip!" drawled the Eminent Person.

Without hesitation he dropped the card over. No slightest motion from either man, no relaxing of those interlocked eyes. A catching of breaths around the table—

"The eight of hearts!" This in concert by the quartette of undisinterested witnesses.

The two Principals looked down, then. That the Eminent Person's free hand had remained passive throughout bore eloquent testimony to nerve and integrity alike. Nevertheless, he now ran that hand slowly through his hair and wiped his forehead.

"That was one long five seconds—most a week, I guess. Did you ever see such a plumb damn' fool break in your whole life?" he said appealingly to the crowd.

"I guess," Steve said sagely, pushing the eight-spot in with his other cards, "if you'd separated from a thousand big, round dollars to draw a card, then got it turned over, *you* wouldn't have cared a whoop if your left eye was out, either. It *is* warm, ain't it?" He sat down with a sigh of relief.

The Stockman bunched his cards idly and tapped the table with them. The Judge was casually examining the chandelier with interest and approval. Presently, he looked down and around.

"Oh, thunder! What are you waiting for, Thompson? I pass, of course!" he said testily.

Steve shoved in his pile.

"As I mentioned a while ago, you're not obliged to call this," he said demurely. "Just suit yourselves."

One card at a time, with thumb and forefinger, the Eminent Person turned over his hand with careful adjustment and alignment. After much delay, he symmetrically arranged an Ace-full, face up, and regarded it with profound attention.

"That was a right good-looking hand, too—before the draw," he remarked at last, sweeping them into the discard.

"Ye-es," assented the Stockman, mildly dubious. "It might have taken second money—maybe."

He tossed in four deuces.

The Transient spread out a club flush.

"Do you know—" he said confidentially "—I was actually glad to see that hand when I first picked it up?"

"Won't you fellows *never* learn to play poker?" demanded the Judge, severely. "Why don't you stay out till you get something?" He laid his hand down. "Four tens and almost five! The Curse of Scotland and Forty Miles of Railroad! *For*-ty miles, before the draw—and gone into the hands of a deceiver!"

"Oh!" Steve leaned over and touched the ten of spades lightly. "So *that's* why I couldn't fill my hand!" he remarked innocently.

"Get out!" snorted the Judge. "No use throwing good money after bad. I wouldn't call you, not if I had five tens!"

He slammed in his hand. The Eminent Person thoughtfully took out the hundred he had saved.

"Some one press the button and I'll go do the rest," said Steve.

He removed the side money, placidly ignoring the "pot" of some fifteen hundred dollars, for which the Transient, having his money all in, was entitled to a showdown.

The Transient's jaw dropped in unaffected amazement. Dealer and Stockman drummed their fingers on the table unconcernedly. Then the Judge suddenly saw a great light.

"You, *Thompson*!" he roared. "Turn over that hand! I feel that you have treated this Court with the greatest contemptibility!"

He pawed the discard with frantic haste, producing the—*seven of hearts*.

"Why, you pink-cheeked, dewy-eyed catamaran! What— What *have* you got, anyway?"

"Why, Judge," said Steve earnestly, "I've got a strong case of Circumstantial Evidence."

He turned over the eight of hearts; then, after a pause, the ace, king, queen and jack of spades. He resumed the stacking of his chips.

"I discarded that seven of hearts," he said, smiling at the Merchant.

A howl of joyous admiration went up. The Transient raked in the pot.

"The Crime of the Century!" bellowed the Judge. "I'm the victim of the Accomplished Fact! Cash my checks! I'm going to join the Ladies' Aid!"

"Aw, shut up," gasped the Transient. "No sleep till morn where Youth and Booty meetsh! Gi' ush 'nother deck!"

But Steve, having stacked his chips, folded the bills and put them in his pocket.

"What's the matter with you, you old fool?" demanded the Eminent Person affectionately. "You can't quit now."

Steve rose, bowing to right and left, spreading his hand over his heart.

"Deeply as I regret and, as I might say, deplore, to quit such a good, easy game," he declaimed, "I must now remove myself from your large midst. For a Lalla-Cooler can only be played once in one night. Besides, I've always heard that no man ever quit ahead of the game and I'm going to be the exception to prove the rule. I will never play another card—never no more!"

"What? Not in your whole life?" said the Stockman, chin on hand, raising his eyebrows at the last word.

"Oh—in my whole *life*!" admitted Steve.

EUGENE CUNNINGHAM

BAR-NOTHING'S HAPPY BIRTHDAY

There's a lot of humor, racy dialogue and suspense in this story of a Texas Ranger. Celebrating his twenty-seventh birthday was a mighty serious matter to quick-triggered, swaggering red-head "Bar-Nothing" Ames, as you will presently see.

SIX DINGY wall tents among the giant cottonwoods at Bloody made the camp of Captain Hewey's ranger company. Down the sandy slope a quarter-mile to the south, the rangers could see the wide ribbon of silver that was the shallow Rio Grande. They could watch—and cover with their Winchesters—Bloody Ford. It was by this crossing that Garcia, *El Bufalo*, might be expected to come into Texas.

"Bar-Nothing Red" Ames, sprawling comfortably in the shade of a tent with three companions, was staring down at the river from beneath the wide rim of his Boss Stetson.

"Reckon the Buffalo really aims to come see us?" he drawled, without looking at the other rangers. "Here we are, imitating a bunch of old Dominecker setting hens, all because the Buffalo sent word to the folks in Pease City that he's coming and he's coming a-smoking. Seems to me if the hairpin's coming at all, he oughtn't to put it off like this. He ought to fog up like a decent

221

scound'l so's we could bury him and hightail it for a damper climate."

"You don't mean damper; you mean wetter, you hollow-laigged sponge," Step-and-a-Half Carstairs corrected him, grinning. "But we have been hunkered here longer'n X Company gen'ally decorates one spot. We come in on the fourth and here it is the twenty-sixth, today."

Bar-Nothing came with a snaky wriggle to stand staring.

"Twenty-sixth!" he yelled. "Step-and-a-Half, you wouldn't fool a man, now? But, now I come to think of it, you don't own brains enough to make up a lie . . . "

"Of course it's the twenty-sixth," Step-and-a-Half told him with dignity. "I just pass over kind of contemptuous your remarks about my brains. Everybody knows it ain't that I can't lie with the best of 'em. It's just I got high religious principles against lying to jugheads that wouldn't know enough to cut out a lie from a whole herd of truth."

But Bar-Nothing was gone, moving as rapidly as the rocking of high heels permitted in the sand toward that tent where Captain Hewey, big, dark, quiet, headquartered.

"By Gemini!" Bar-Nothing said amazedly to himself. "If I didn't come inside a short inch of missing her. First time I ever forgot since I can remember; since I was just a button cowboy. I— Ah, hell! Cap'n's got company."

For out of Captain Hewey's tent voices carried to him. He moved up to hunker beside the canvas wall and wait the commander's leisure. Through the open flap he saw a big, tousled youngster in stained and shabby overalls and ancient boots, twisting a battered black Stetson in his two hands as he faced Captain Hewey.

"And so," the boy was saying, "now I come to be twenty year old, I guess it's time to make my throw at getting into the Rangers like I always wanted to all my life."

"Ah!" said Hewey in his deep, smooth voice. "Ah!"

Bar-Nothing shifted position until he could also see his commander, a big, immaculate figure in blue silk shirt, gray wool trousers and polished tan boots of alligator hide.

"I—don't know," Hewey drawled. "I'm just afraid— What have you been doing lately? Is that—can that be—calf dip that I smell on you? Surely not!"

"Why—yes, sir," the boy admitted nervously. "I been working with the calves all week. Dipping 'em, you know."

"Working!" Hewey cried. His tone held amazement, alarm—disgust. "Did I hear you say working? Just how long has that been going on? When did you begin this—what was that word?—working?"

"Ever since I was big enough to spin a loop in my twine and haze a calf, I reckon. I—I really am a hard worker, too!"

"My son," Hewey told him sadly, "I am very much afraid that all your dreams of becoming a Texas Ranger have been destroyed by one word—work. Automatically, you're disqualified. Rangers, my boy, never work! No ranger would even think of it. You—why, probably you've so hardened yourself in the awful habit that you couldn't break it. So—"

"But I sling the Mex' lingo like I was a chili-picker myself," the cowboy protested plaintively. "And I heard 'em say, over at Pease City, you needed to enlist a man could spiel it."

"Too, there are other qualifications to be considered. Let's see . . . . Suppose you had to lay out a man with your Colt. Would you strike him with the butt or the barrel?"

"With the barrel! Pa taught me that. You know he was in the Rangers with you thirty year back. He always says: Hold onto the cutter-handle and slam 'em with the barrel. Because you might have to shoot the *batardo* after all!"

"Right!" Hewey nodded solemnly. "If you were lone-wolfing it on the trail of five desperate outlaws, wanted dead or alive, how would you bring them into camp?"

"Well, if orders said 'dead or alive' I'd just bushwhack 'em and load 'em onto their horses," the boy said simply. "Pa always says: They pack better, dead!"

"Right! Now, where do you live these days?"

"Up the road a whoop and a holloa; on the Box A between this and Pease City. Ten mile up, I reckon."

"Well, I think we can enlist you, if you'll promise faithfully not to work any more. Sit down over there while I talk to the gentlemen here."

Bar-Nothing's sandy brows lifted. Could Captain Hewey be referring to him? He half-rose, but an irritable voice in the tent, coming from someone invisible to him, checked the motion.

"Well, if you got done monkeying with Sim Cook, Cap'n, I

would appreciate you taking my complaint about my blaze-faced sorrel being stole."

"Certainly," Hewey agreed. "When did you miss it?"

"Two days ago. I got word that it was tied to the hitch-rack in Pease City the day after it was stole. Some of that sticky loop gang of old Jay Bird Pease, they done the stealing. That damn' rustling old sidewinder! There he sets, saying he's the town and the town's him; he ain't only the justice of the peace, he's everything else in Pease. If I take my foot in my hand and fog it into town, trying to get back my horse, Jay Bird'll just wink at somebody and a gun'll go off accidental. Then Jay Bird'll prop my carcass up and try me for disturbing the peace and contempt of court and fine me whatever I got in my pockets and my horse and saddle."

"As bad as that?" Hewey drawled, black eyes twinkling.

"Likely, worse!" the robbed one cried. "So, I can't go and the sheriff, he won't go! I talked to him yesterday and he's sorry as hell he's got anyhow six months' work ahead before he can take on any new complaints. That sorrel's worth three hundred of any man's money. I want him back!"

"We'll certainly have to look into this," Hewey said thoughtfully. "Bar-Nothing! Something you want?"

"Oh, nothing much," Bar-Nothing answered. He got up and loafed into the tent. "It's just my birthday, Cap'n. I thought I'd like to drift over to Pease—it's just a short twenty mile—and buy myself a birthday present. Life-time habit of mine."

"Oh!" Hewey grunted. "You know, Red, we're supposed to be here because of Buffalo? That's why I've kept you wild buckaroos out of Pease."

"Yeh, of course. But, Cap'n! Birthdays make a lot of difference. Take me, now: If I hadn't started out with a birthday—right in the very beginning!—I couldn't be here with you watching for the Buffalo!"

"All right, then," Hewey surrendered. "You can go to Pease. But you're due back not later than nine tomorrow morning. You heard what Mr. Hawley said about his sorrel horse? Well, bring it back with you. Bring the thief, too, if you run into him. Take Sim Cook, here, with you. It will be experience for him. But, remember! Don't you get organized and start a riot. From what

I've heard, Pease is quite—a—salty—community. You go in like a lamb, Red."

"I don't mind a bit going in like a lamb," Bar-Nothing said gravely, "if I don't go out like a light. From what I heard Mr. Hawley say, if I recover that horse of his, some kind of riot is mightily apt to start itself. You want me just to lie down under it?"

"That would be a lot to ask of a red-headed man," Hewey said with the flicker of a smile. "Particularly when that red-head is known from the Panhandle to the Big Bend as 'Bar-Nothing' Ames. What I mean is, don't you look for any trouble."

"Now I think of it, I never had to!" Bar-Nothing drawled.

It was a clean, extremely neat, Sim Cook who rode out from the Box A with Bar-Nothing. He had scrubbed himself in the horse trough and put on new black Stetson, new blue flannel shirt, new waist overalls. His half-boots, his Colt and holster belt, the .44 Winchester carbine beneath his leg in saddle scabbard, even the stamped swellfork hull and one-ear bridle, were also brand-new.

"You see, I been saving up and getting things ready for my coming into the Rangers," he explained shyly to Bar-Nothing. "I certainly am glad Cap' Hewey took me! But he had me boogering for a spell, hurrahing me from behind that solemnous face."

He rode with admiring eyes upon Bar-Nothing's easy, efficient figure. For the name of this tall, swaggering, happy-go-lucky red-head was known from border to border of Texas—and fairly well in adjoining states—as one of the deadliest two-gun rangers in the Frontier Battalion and as a puzzle-buster, a criminal-catcher, towering in the very front rank.

"So this Jay Bird Pease, he's the lil' tin curly wolf with red stripedy legs," Bar-Nothing grunted, as they saw before them the "wide place in the road" which was Pease "City," with its lean rows of gray adobe and grayer frame buildings making "Main Street's" twin borders.

"He is that!" Sim Cook assured him earnestly. "He's been here since there wasn't nothing a-tall on this flat. He claims when he got here there wasn't ary mountain yonder—he planted 'em! Railroad coming by made the place and made him. Yes—sir! He rods Pease City from A to Big Casino. He's Big Auger."

"Railroad helped? How-come? I wouldn't guess Pease'd have a canary bird pack of stuff to ship out. Most of the ranches front on the West Spur and load out over there."

"It's the passengers," Sim explained, grinning. "Train stops ten minutes. Passengers look out and see Jay Bird's sign: *Cold Beer and Justice of the Peace.* They come a-racking it. Jay Bird, he reaches down and pulls out some bottled beer out of the wet sand under the bar. He slams it and his six-shooter on the bar. Beer ain't cold, but it's damp. Colt's staring right at the customers. Nobody's kicked yet about warm beer. Passenger gives Jay Bird maybe a ten dollar bill.

"Well, Jay Bird's Mex' kid runs out with the bill, hunting change. Passenger waits. Mex' boy don't show up. Train whistles —*toot-toot!* Still no Mex' boy; no change. (Jay Bird, he just can't figure how-come!) Conductor yells—*all aboard!* No Mex' boy showing. (Jay Bird's awful sorry.) Engine bell's a-ringing— *whangety-clang!* No Mex' boy yet. (Jay Bird do' no' what to do.) But that passenger, he has got to run so's not to miss his train. So he hightails, talking non-Sunday School lingo. Minute the train's down the track, out comes the Mex' boy from under the porch where he's been smoking cigareets. He hands over the five —or ten, or even twenty, to Jay Bird."

"Dear me, Suz!" Bar-Nothing cried, as they fox-trotted up Main Street toward Jay Bird Pease's thirst-and-justice head-quarters. "That's not altogether downright honest, Sim. Maybe we can look into it. Well—no sorrel at this hitch-rack."

"One across the road, yonder," Sim contributed, shifting in the saddle. "But he ain't got a white hair on him and Hawley, he said his horse was blaze-faced and had four stockings."

Bar-Nothing's first glance at Jay Bird Pease gave him instant and complete dislike for the squat, wizened old man. Jay Bird had whitish hair, the few straggling locks of it looking as if they had been stuck sparingly at random on his shiny, egg-shaped skull. His eyebrows were of a mustard-tinted gray and so shaggy that they almost hid the tiny, shifting reddish-black eyes. His nose was like a buzzard's beak overhanging a huge, loose-lipped mouth in which showed a scattering half-dozen of yellow fangs.

"*Buenas dias!*" he cried as Bar Nothing *cling-clumped* in with Sim Cook at his elbow. "*Como 'sta?*"

"*Muy bien*—very well," Bar-Nothing grunted. "*Muy bien.*"

Then he turned with artistic expression of bewilderment:
"Thought you said it was a white man, Sim—kind of . . ."

Malevolent rage twisted Jay Bird's face. One hand disappeared
from the bar. The tiny black eyes glittered like a sidewinder's. But
Bar-Nothing, standing with air of blandest innocence, had both
thumbs hooked in crossed shell-belts . . .

"Smart Aleck, huh?" Jay Bird snarled. "Well, you better
sabe this, right now: I'm Pease! I'm the town and the town's me!
Folks that look for grief around here—they locate it!"

Bar-Nothing leaned over the bar until his face was hardly more
than a foot from Jay Bird's.

"I have got just two questions to ask," he drawled. "First, what
the hell are you talking about? Second, what the hell do I care?
My name's Ames. I'm a ranger sergeant. Out of Hewey's X Company that's camped at Bloody Ford. I sing palpitating tenor when
I sing, but I howl a lot better than I sing. I go where I'm a mind
to go and I stay until I'm plumb ready to rattle my hocks. I ask
for what I want, then see that I get it. And right now I want a
drink!"

Jay Bird jumped at that sudden, unprefaced bellow. For there
was a blaze in Bar-Nothing's blue eyes that failed to match the
grin stretching his wide mouth.

"A' right! A' right!" he growled. "No call to be a bellowing
around here like that. You can have your drink. Nobody aims
to keep you drouthed up. But I don't like folks making remarks."

"Oh, me neither!" Bar-Nothing assured him. "Makes me fit
to tie—and I never found the man, or men, could tie me."

He put a silver dollar on the bar, but stared at Jay Bird.

"Li'l' words have come floating to me, about the way you make
your prices skip up and down, all-same the giddy gazellaroo. Now,
me, I just don't like such. But I never massacreed a barkeep yet
for charging me two-bits a throw."

"Two-bits is all right," Jay Bird told him sullenly—but with
a furtive stare at the door behind the rangers. As if he expected
—or hoped for—some relief from that direction, Bar-Nothing
thought.

"Here's looking at you, Simmy," he said, when two tin cups of
whisky were before them. "Look at her while she's red—"

"Can't," the boy disagreed, rolling a narrowed eye at Jay Bird.
"Can't look at the liquor, account I got to keep looking at that

door. Couple of good friends of Jay Bird's—couldn't you smell
'em; li'l' bit stronger'n a skunk?—they've been peeking in, trying
to make out what Jay Bird means by all his funny motionings and
eyebrow wigglings."

"I've been eyeing 'em, too, in that old mirror back there.
Wouldn't it just be too sad, if something they tried to pull got
poor old Jay Bird killed dead? Down her and take another."

They drank formally and Bar-Nothing refilled the cups, grinning cheerfully at the furious Jay Bird.

"Gullup that'n' and we'll ramble out where the air's fresh. I
like to celebrate my new birthdays where things smell clean. Oh,
Jay Bird! What'd you and the rest of your petty larceny thieves
do with Mr. Hawley's sorrel horse, huh?"

"Never knowed Hawley owned a sorrel," Jay Bird snarled,
choosing to ignore the bulk of the question. "Did he?"

"Says he did. Kind of sorrelish animal with a mane and—oh,
yes, a tail!—and a leg sticking down towards the ground from
each corner. Critter lived off grass and corn and hay and stuff
like that. What'd you say you did with him?"

"I said I never knowed Hawley owned a sorrel!" the baited Jay
Bird yelled. "And you looky here, young fellow! I told you before,
I'm Justice of the Peace. Ranger or no ranger, you run no sandy
around here, onto me!"

"You-all put him—where?" Bar-Nothing inquired, scowling.
"I didn't just make out what place you said. Well, ne' mind! Ne'
mind! I'll stumble onto him—always do. Then you'll be sorry,
Mister Jay Bird, your tail in a crack and all!"

"Better watch you don't stub your·toe trying," Jay Bird mumbled, as they turned toward the door. Bar-Nothing laughed.

"Any more juice-joints?" he asked Sim Cook. "I don't love to
throw all my tremendous-tremens trade to one place, specially not
a dump like Pease's. What-for a community is this, anyhow, that'll
suck up its red-eye over a bar like that? Why, you'd think it'd
sour on their stomachs! Me, I like to be happy and don't-give-a-
hoot, all-same li'l' bitsy bluebird. You never catch me off in a
mourning· corner sucking a bottle of nothing. *Nunca! Jamás!*
Never! I'm a sweet soul natural."

Approached, now, a citizen of the place who seemed to have
suffered that souring of the stomach he had mentioned. It was a
very tall man, six and a third feet in height. And he could not

have weighed thirty pounds over the hundred. His dark hatchet face was marked by V-lines from hooked nose to savage gash-thin mouth. He stalked down the dirt sidewalk squarely in their path, gaunt arms swinging, one huge hand slap-slapping his pistol holster, glowering ferociously.

> "Her pay-rents don't like me,
> They say I'm too pore,
> They say I'm unworthy
> To enter her door.
> They say I drink whisky—
> Well, my money's my own
> And them that don't like me
> Can leave me alone!"

Bar-Nothing's tanned face was boyishly happy as he moved forward, his chin a trifle lifted, his head swaying gently in time with *Jack of Diamonds.* So he and the tall man met toe-to-toe and stopped short.

"Where the hell you think you might be going?" the townsman demanded. "Think you can hog the road in Pease, huh? Well—"

"Well?" Bar-Nothing repeated softly. "Flea bite you, or something? Family troubles, maybe? Old lady won't let you sleep in the house account of your Peasey smell? Or—could it be just growing pains, you not having your weight yet?"

The tall man made a wordless, rasping sound and flicked his hand to low-swung Colt. Sim Cook jerked out his new Colt with all the speed he could manage. But Bar-Nothing's hands twitched like nothing in the world so much as striking snake-heads. He slapped the tall man on one cheek with the right-hand gun-barrel, on the other with the left-hand Colt. His victim seemed to forget that he had begun to draw. He staggered backward with an agonized grunt, both hands up with palms out. A deft blow across the temple dropped him.

"Hey! You red-head!" a squat man yelled from across the street. "Cut that out! Don't you hit Casselberry no more!"

He came panting over to them. Bar-Nothing spun his Colts on the trigger guards. The butts slapped into his palms; twirled again so that they stared at the star-wearer—as he stared.

"I'm city marshal," the stocky man blustered. "You can't—"

"You can't . . ." Bar-Nothing repeated softly. "Seems to me

that's the pet saying around this gawdforsaken village. And—know what's funny? I have been doing it, whatever it is, all the time! Now, my good advice to you is, ram that cutter back into the scabbard and quit trying to howl like a wolf! Good idea to file off the front sight of the hogleg, too: Because if a gunfighter comes along and takes it away from you and rams it down your neck, you won't get scarred up so much!

"I'm a sergeant in the rangers. This folding contraption on the ground come interfering with me in the execution of my doings. According to the statutes made and provided, I discussed that interfering with him in the way and the fashion I figured his intellects would understand best. Perfectly simple!"

"Casselberry interfered? How-come? Execution of what?"

"Celebrating my twenty-seventh birthday! And don't you think for one minute that's not a serious doing! Come on, Sim. We are turning over the prisoner to the city authorities. Now that he understands what's what, he's going to save—a—heap—of—trouble."

They went on, leaving behind them a silent marshal—pistol reholstered—bending over the unconscious Casselberry.

At the far end of the town was an ancient and bullet-pocked 'dobe house with the customary "gallery" along its street-front. A dingy tin sign bearing a faint likeness of a billygoat hinted of beer inside. They entered, to face a brown, still-faced man with sun-squinted gray eyes. He looked flashingly at Sim, then watched Bar-Nothing steadily.

"Hi, Pegleg!" Sim greeted the saloonkeeper. "Touch paws with Bar-Nothing Red Ames of the rangers. I'm a ranger, too, since today. Red, this-here's Pegleg Scott. He'll do!"

"Howdy," Pegleg drawled, relaxing. "I been watching out for some of that coyote-crew of Jay Bird's. They went racking past last night and shot some more nicks into my wall. But when they scallyhooted back to try it over, me and Bill Jameson the blacksmith and Squeaky Conner the freighter, we happened to be all out at the end of the c'ral a-cleaning our Winchesters—except me, being I al'ays favor a Sharps .50 buffalo gun. It made us so skittery when they got to howling that our long guns went off accidental-like and we come close to rubbing some of 'em out. Happened some of us did kind of buttonhole Hognose Judd, that trifling swamper at Jay Bird's wagon yard. Plumb killed the horse he was forking. Kind of sad, how it happened."

"They—bother you any, after?" Bar-Nothing asked owlishly.

"Not as I recollect, no. Of course, that nitwit marshal did come this way a li'l' piece yelling some kind of foolishness about me surrendering to the law up at Jay Bird's. He was yelling in English, too. He speaks tol'able Mex', too. Most of Jay Bird's thieves do. Handy for 'em. Lets 'em lie in two languages. But I couldn't just make out what he wanted. So I went around the Widow Jenk's c'ral to hear better and I motioned him to come closer. He must've mistooken my intendings because he singlefooted right away from there. Maybe I was waving at him with the hand I had my Sharps rifle in. What'll it be?"

"Beer and—who plays that fiddle? It's my birthday, Mr. Scott. So I just pine for happiness."

"I'll call Old Black Joe. He's asleep out back. Got a pickaninny, too, can double-shuffle and buck-and-wing."

At his yell an ancient negro appeared, grinning, to get the battered fiddle from the wall. He sawed the bow across the strings and swept into *Sugar in the Gourd.* A tiny black boy stole in, teeth splitting his face with a white crescent. His twinkling pink heels slapped a tattoo on the rough floor. Bar-Nothing fished a harmonica from his pocket and joined in.

Then, suddenly, a rapid rattle of shots carried to them, followed by raucous, high-pitched howl. Bar-Nothing jerked the harmonica from his mouth and swore irritably as he moved to the door and looked out.

In front of Jay Bird Pease's saloon a man was reloading his pistol, howling wolfishly the while. His hand jerked and again the Colt was emptied in air.

"I wish he wouldn't do that," Bar-Nothing said plaintively. "It plumb sends the shivers down my spine—that howl."

He went quickly along Main Street. Sim Cook trailed him, tight-faced, hand on Colt. The howling one was pulling more shells from his belt when Bar-Nothing stopped before him.

"What's the idea of these vulgar noises?" Bar-Nothing demanded coldly. "You just trying to bother people?"

"When I feel like howling—" the celebrant thrust stubbled, liquor-swollen face out belligerently "—howling's what I do!"

To Sim Cook was presented a sort of dust-wreathed Punch and Judy show accompanied by sounds as of applauding hands. It continued for only a minute or so, then Bar-Nothing stepped back with a sigh and the ex-howler began slowly to get to his feet. There were faces at every opening of Jay Bird's place. Bar-Nothing, seeing everything, stepped quickly in and twisted the man's right hand behind him. Holding that wrist and the left arm, he hustled him into Jay Bird's door.

"Pease!" he called grimly. "You have been bragging about being a justice. A' right! I'm not only a ranger, I'm a man with an ear for music. On both counts I give this two-legged tomcat into your custody for disturbing the peace. I certainly expect you to take charge of his case!"

"'*Sta bueno*," Jay Bird mumbled, without meeting Bar-Nothing's glare. "I—I'll take him in charge."

"Better see that you do," Bar-Nothing advised him.

Back in Pegleg Scott's place, he waved at the fiddler.

"Now, let her rip!" he cried. "I'm not in right good practice, Joe. You get so far ahead of me that I need spec's to make out what you're playing. Let's try *Going Up Cripple Creek*!"

Again the bow sawed frantically and Bar-Nothing, setting down his beer glass, wiped his mouth and lifted the harmonica.

"*Oooeeee! Yip! Yip! Yip!*" came to them from downstreet.

"Coyote's out again," Pegleg said gravely. "Believe I'd tie a knot in his tail this time, Red—a hard knot. But—that gang's likely ribbed up something, this trip. You could easy slide up behind this row of buildings and—whisper in his ear . . . "

"Can happen!" Bar-Nothing agreed, grinning one-sidedly.

A quick, barehead glance from the front door showed heads in Jay Bird's windows, figures in his doorway. Then, trailed again by the faithful Sim, he ran awkwardly down the room and through Pegleg's back entrance. They trotted up the rear walls of this row until at the corner of a store neighboring Jay Bird's 'dobe —but separated by a space of two yards—they could look at the howling figure in the street.

"Ah, he ain't coming, Harrigan!" someone in Jay Bird's yelled. "Yellow's up in his neck. Heave some lead in the air!"

Bar-Nothing turned to look at the half-dozen horses standing "hitched to the ground" behind the saloon. He crossed to them, looking at the ropes on the saddles. With quick, tight grin he took down a coil of slim rawhide *riata* and shook out a loop. Sim grinned, also, as Bar-Nothing came back to him.

"Now, I'll show you I used to be a right tol'able buckaroo before my health gave out and I had to quit work and go to rangering," Bar-Nothing grunted. "This is a California string; sixty-footer. Just what Doc' Ames would've ordered. A Texas thirty-two foot manila wouldn't reach our Howling Harrigan, but—"

He went quietly along Jay Bird's side wall to stop at the corner. The loop went up and out snakily, settled around Harrigan's neck and tightened. With a ferocious Comanche yell Bar-Nothing hauled in the slack hand-over-hand. Harrigan was dragged to him and he stooped to loosen the choking noose. He jerked the strangling man up, half-pushed, half carried him out and to Jay Bird's door.

"Back you go, you mangy fices!" he snarled at the audience. "I wouldn't trust one of your cur-faces behind me!"

He had one Colt out and sullenly they surged into the saloon before its muzzle—and Sim Cook's.

"Now, you Jay Bird!" Bar-Nothing snapped at Pease. "You listen to me prophesy and you listen good and hard: I'm tired of this pet sack of wind of yours and if I hear anything louder'n a Number Two whisper out of him, there's going to be more trouble around this skunk-den than your clothes'll stand. You *heah* me? I'm telling you in the solemnest tone I've got to lock him up until he's sober or plumb out of howls. You *heah* me?"

"I—I'll take care of him," Jay Bird promised, with downward glance, longing glance, at something behind the bar, but without moving either dirty hand out of Bar-Nothing's sight.

Once more they returned to Pegleg Scott's. But this time they had hardly passed through the door when Harrigan popped into the street. He had a pistol in each hand, Sim reported—Bar-Nothing had gone quietly on to the bar and motioned twice, once at the beer, again at the sawed-off shotgun hanging conveniently in Pegleg's rear. Six shots sounded, then a howl.

"He's keeping one loaded," Sim called. "Rammed her in his bellyband; loading the other one. You certainly got to get out from under your hat to his stubborn gall!"

Bar-Nothing drank his beer deliberately and bought one for Black Joe. Then he accepted the shotgun from the still-faced

Pegleg and made a second departure through the back door. This
time he and Sim ran through the litter of tin cans and bottles behind the buildings until they could cross Main Street at that end
of town farthest from Jay Bird's. They came back in the rear of
the buildings on that side, crossed again while the men in and
around Pease's looked toward Pegleg's place, or watched that
corner from which Bar-Nothing had roped Harrigan.

They slipped soundlessly into Pease's rear door and the crowd
at the front had no warning of their presence until Bar-Nothing
clicked back both shotgun hammers and yelled savagely:

"Yup! Yup! Grab your ears or grab a harp! Over to the wall,
all of you polecats; my patience has come unraveled. If 't wasn't
I promised Cap'n Hewey I'd be tender as a barbecued calf, today,
I swear I'd take you nine at a time and I'd sweep this county clean
with you. Sim! Dab a loop on that laughing jackass, huh?"

"Looky here!" Jay Bird yelled shakily. "I'm justice and—"

Bar-Nothing let the shotgun slide to the crook of his left arm.
His right hand flashed down; came up with a Colt. The slug
jangled a pyramid of tin cups on the bar at Jay Bird's very
elbow. The old man made a squeaking noise and jumped two yards
to the side, hands uplifted.

"Was a man, once," Bar-Nothing remarked casually, "got
himself a lot in Boot Hill, talking when he ought've been listening.
What's it, Sim?"

Sim, at the front door, steadied his new Colt against the frame.
He let the hammer drop and, blending with the bellow of it, a yell
half-startled, half-pained, came from Harrigan. Sim moved outside, pistol easily at hip-level.

"Just wondered could I shoot it out of his fist," he called back.
"Come on, Harrigan. Singing school's done shut up. We have
got language to pour into your long, dirty ears."

"Which is your goat?" Bar-Nothing demanded, when Harrigan
came meekly inside, shaking his bleeding gunhand.

"Big black out behind," Harrigan mumbled. "I—I never meant
no harm, Sergeant. I—It was just the whisky. I'll hightail!"

"You bet you'll hightail—right out to camp with us. Come
along. Jay Bird—and all the rest of you—if there's anything
happening as we rack out of this, Pease City's going to look like
a Kansas twister hit her. Only way you can stop us is to down us,
both. If that was to happen, Cap'n Hewey and the boys'd cer-

tainly enjoy piling up the carcasses of everybody that Sim and me left for 'em. Cap'll likely have a word or two to say to you, anyhow, time he hears what kind of justice you are."

While Sim prodded Harrigan ahead of him through the back door, Bar-Nothing watched with ready shotgun. Then he backed out and saw Harrigan climb into the saddle of the tall black.

"Why, that's the hull I took the California twine off of," he told Sim. "Bring our horses around, will you? I'll wait."

When Sim reappeared with their mounts, they swung up and jogged quietly toward the road. Pease City was sullenly quiet behind them. But within a mile they met the city marshal, riding out of a pasture. He gaped at them.

"What's all this?" he blustered. "You rangers needn't to think you can take a man out of town without seeing me first—"

"Take that gun out—slow!" Bar-Nothing commanded, gesturing with Pegleg's shotgun. "Get it, Sim. Now, my homely friend, just turn around and side us. I sort of want to hear what Cap'n Hewey will have to say to you. It'll be as good as reading a big, thick book, for you. It'll be a talk on how to live a lot longer'n you figure to last, way you've been heading. Come on!"

So, with the silent prisoners leading, they went toward Bloody Ford at the long, mile-eating hard trot. The sun was sliding toward the western horizon; the air grew noticeably cooler. It was nearly sunset when they came to the tents of X Company.

"What's this, Red?" Captain Hewey inquired from his door. "Prisoners? Did you recover Mr. Hawley's horse?"

With the question and sight of Hawley behind the captain, Bar-Nothing made a vague, self-reproachful sound.

"Blamed if I never forgot all about that bronc' in the arguring! We looked the place over and he wasn't in sight and then that skunk Jay Bird set this coyote to howling and—"

"That's my horse!" Hawley bellowed, surging out. "They colored up his nose and his stockings and hairbranded him, but I raised him from a colt and I'd know him in a million in the dark. And—And you, Ed Welch! You was riding him!"

With which he hauled the city marshal from the saddle and fell to committing assault, battery and minor mayhem upon him. Bar-Nothing swung down and separated them—after a time.

"This Harrigan," he told Captain Hewey, "he was disturbing the peace and every time I'd arrest him Jay Bird'd turn him loose and give him another drink and start him out again. So I packed him out here. I do think you'd enjoy talking to Jay Bird and Welch about the way they handle the law in Pease."

"I'll talk to Jay Bird, all right," Hewey said ominously. "As for Welch, we'll hold him on a charge of horse-theft. As for Harrigan—" he looked long and thoughtfully at the silent, glaring prisoner "—we'll keep him, too. Oh! Have a good time?"

"Worst birthday in my life! Them Peasers are half-skunk and half-coyote. Run a white man crazy."

From a hip pocket the captain drew a leather case. Out of it came a sheaf of folded papers. He riffled them, selected one and held it out to Bar-Nothing, whistling softly. Bar-Nothing unfolded the printed notice—and Harrigan's ugly likeness was there, under twin lines of heavy Gothic capitals—$1500 REWARD— MURDER—HIGHWAY ROBBERY—

"Happy birthday, Red," Captain Hewey drawled.

"Fif-teen hun-dred dollars!" Bar-Nothing breathed reverently. "Thanks, Cap'n! Thanks! She certainly is. She— She's a gen-u-ine P-cutter of a birthday!"

IRVIN S. COBB

WE CAN'T ALL BE
THOROUGHBREDS

Some men have a way of overlooking their past, but according to Mr. Cobb's tale, it can't be done without provoking the
dead. Characterized by the author's special brand of sardonic
humor, this story is sure-paced in the telling, and sure-fire in
the punch. (From *Faith, Hope and Charity*, Bobbs-Merrill,
1934.)

AMONG his own people his name signified "The One Who
Laughs." But his smile was imminent danger and his laughter
it was death. There was sudden destruction in it and also there
was shuddering, lingering torture. He laughed at burning homes,
at mutilated corpses and—when he had the leisure for such di-
versions—at the agony of victims dying by slow torments at the
stake or where they were spread-eagled and pegged down on ant-
hills to be eaten piecemeal.

For years on end, through a drawn-out campaign which endures
in our history as the cruelest and almost the bloodiest epic in
our Indian-fighting age, this gay red murderer laughed at pursuit.
Finally he was captured and lived out his time on an Oklahoma
reservation as the caged ward of a forgiving and beneficent government, a tiger with its claws drawn, selling his autograph at
a dollar a throw to tourists whose scalps he lovingly would have

237

lifted and whose eyelids he would have been proud to shear from their living eyeballs. To call him by his white man's name which is a Spanish name, he was Geronimo, the spindly scourge of the old but not so very old Southwest.

Under his wily leadership, a stripped-down and painted-up war party closed in, one burning forenoon, on a settler's isolated cabin of 'dobe and wattles in what is now the state of Arizona and not many miles north by east of the National Boundary. The raiders came afoot as was their way, silently sliding like so many side-winders through the scanty desert herbage and over the naked alkali smears.

This was a district where the mountains met the table-lands which the band had not invaded until now. This, then, was their first foray across this particular flat.

The head of that remote household was a shiftless young Irish-man whose name doesn't matter and indeed long since has been forgotten; and he was away from his home-place that day. He was ill-fitted to play the dry-farmer's game on these lonesome high plateaus. But he was the life of the party at any frontier saloon. In the cabin were his wife and his baby: the wife a homely, grubby-looking little Saxon of twenty or thereabouts, an immi-grant recently come from overseas, as her husband had; the baby a lusty man-child some six months old.

The woman had a short warning; not that it did her any good. A Mexican herder, fleeing for his life, checked and cried out to her as she, hearing the quick thump of hoofs, came to the door and, shading her eyes with her hand, looked out across the hot glare. Then he dusted on down the trail, riding hell-for-leather to the nearest settlement. He could not have taken her along with him, anyhow. His lathered pony already was carrying double, his own woman riding behind him and she gelatinous with terror.

The German girl didn't know what the Mexican said but she knew what he meant, all right. She ran back into the shanty and caught up the sleeping babe from his flour-barrel crib and, with him in her arms against her breasts, darted into the greasewood and the chaparral and the sage-brush at the rear of their claim.

Two hundred yards back, she faced west, being minded to head for the gap between the snaggled peaks yonder. If she made it, she would have a better prospect of hiding in the broken ground there than here on her own mesa, where a cactus plant was the tallest thing in view and a mesquite bush the densest.

She never made it. Probably she never could have made it. The slim swift figures moving in on the homestead from all four quarters were, as any old soldier out of our old army will tell you, the shrewdest trackers and the keenest-eyed tribesmen on this continent. Perhaps she knew that; her actions would seem to indicate as much.

Even so, none of the trotting enemies sighted her until she had sighted a brace of them. Squatting a moment for breath in the small shelter of a clump of mesquite she saw, three hundred yards away, bobbing up over a small dip like the obscene black-and-red blossoms of some poisonous poppy, two heads of long slick hair, each bound around with a gay turban of traders' cloth.

As I say, the flankers hadn't seen her yet. Did she bide on where she was, motionless and mute, there was, let's say, one chance in a thousand for her. Because from the time the fugitive quitted the 'dobe, either instinctively or by design, she had been traveling upon an upthrust strip of lava which almost was free of sand and on which her feet left few or no prints.

Now then, this drab piece of steerage fruit did a thing of stark heroism. Deliberately she threw away her one faint hope of salvation for the sake of her baby. She thrust the little moist warm bundle that was he in among the roots and the stems of that mesquite. Then on her hands and knees she crawled a few rods farther along the narrowing gritty outcrop. Then, turning herself about at right angles, she boldly stood up and ran south at top speed.

Actually she covered more than a quarter of a mile before one of the slender pursuers overhauled her and sank the blade of his war hatchet deep into her skull. Without tarrying to scalp her, he hurried off to join the other bucks in the rapid looting of the shack and the lean-to horse shed behind it. Well for him that he did, the child slept on until the Apaches were gone, as very soon they were gone. Strike fast and get away fast—that would have been skinny old Geronimo's motto, if grinning old Geronimo ever had any mottoes.

A troop of sun-finished regulars, with a squad of friendlies to scout for them and a handful of civilians to reenforce them, reached the ravaged shack before dark that same evening. They were in a hurry, naturally. So the woman's body was buried where they found it, and one trooper who had repute for piety said the Lord's Prayer over the shallow hole before they hastily shoveled her under and, for her, that was that and that was all.

About the time the burial was finished, somebody heard something mewing in the undergrowth and searched about and found the famishing baby in his brushy cache. After a brief but highly alcoholic period of mourning, the child's father sloughed off his domestic obligations and went away drunk and went away for good. A well-meaning couple named Jacobs took his abandoned offspring and gave that hungry derelict a place among their own increasing progeny.

These Jacobses weren't so happy in that land of mirages and massacres. They moved on to southern California and bought a quarter-section for practically nothing and as one of their brood, and under the name of Renfrew Jacobs, the adopted orphan grew up out of infancy into boyhood. When oil was struck on their property, he, being then of an age suitable for the higher education, shared in the sudden prosperity which came to the family.

He was sent off to college and took a course in mining and was graduated with honors, since he was smart and a good student and ambitious, and began the career which, by the time he was fifty, had put him in the front rank of the conspicuously wealthy and conspicuously strong business magnates of North America. Long before that, though, he had proved to an admiring world and an envying profession that he was a great engineer.

Being translated from field-work to office-work, he next proved that likewise he was a great and most scientific executive. Along about then it seemed a proper season for him to take unto himself a wife and start rearing a dynasty. Both of which, in the order named, he straightway did.

At forty he had been president of Interhemispheric Copper. At fifty he was chairman of the board and even by the Mellons and the Morgans was indeed very highly thought of. And at fifty-one he died of a highly fatal combination, to wit, as follows: rich living, overwork and just one tiny blood clot on the motor area of the left lobe.

The widow who survived him and who mourned his loss for substantially nine lively months before she remarried herself to a refugee prince from Russia, a land where princes appear once to have abounded in the utmost profusion, was a daughter of an old Knickerbocker stock, a stock that had been rooted in the friendly Manhattan schist for several snooty generations, and so she had come to his bosom handsomely dowered with the semi-regal tradition and that air of a true and inborn culture which so often is counterfeited but so rarely with success. To match with this lady's almost royal lineage, Renfrew Jacobs had, right from the beginning of his financial and social prominence, fashioned out of somewhat shoddy materials a fine blue studbook for himself.

He knew the early facts about himself and about his immediate forebears. In confidence, when he was old enough to understand and, as they mistakenly trusted, to appreciate the measure and the beauty of his real mother's supreme sacrifice, his foster-parents had told him who and what he was. With a precocious wisdom, having first sworn them to secrecy, he chose for ever after to bask in the shade of a blossomy and fragrant although, as you will perceive, an almost purely synthetic family tree.

Another man might have been proud to the point of boasting over so gorgeous a maternal heritage. Curiously, Renfrew Jacobs was not built that way. Besides, he was busy at shaping himself according to a different and a more refined model. Before the flattering mirror of his inner soul and to some extent before the eyes of the admiring multitude, he became a sort of glamorous fiction character, a craftily constructed acting part; and in times to come, if posterity only does right by our great captains of industry, will be one of an immortalized constellation of Aryan myths.

As a background for this grand future rôle, he created, or he suffered to be created, a common assumption that he was the result of the mating of scions of two old southern lines. Well, in a way of speaking, he was an all-southern product—South German on one side, South of Ireland on the other. But once the elder Jacobs had passed on, no living soul save Renfrew Jacobs knew that. You bet he wasn't passing the news around. The hidden truth burned inside of him like a little warm spot of shame.

Such gross vanities as he had—this especial one among the rest—might have made a lesser man ridiculous. But in this fair republic a man who piles ninety millions into one heap never can be made ridiculous by anything or anybody.

He was at the very height of his material leadership and of his seeming health, neither he nor any one else suspecting he was about to be snatched up to everlasting glory by what the attending physicians—eight in number at the final consultation—would diagnose as apoplexy, when a staff representative called by appointment at the Jacobs summer home in Lenox to question him on behalf of *Dynamic Individualities,* an inspirational monthly, and subsequently to write for the pages of that valued publication what would be in part a personality sketch, a study rather, and in part the consolidated tale of a massive succession of achievements.

The pair of them—the grateful interviewer and the graciously interviewed—sat on the latter's veranda looking out over an estate big enough for a barony, and presently the eager author put this one to the blandly majestic proprietor:

"Mr. Jacobs, what romantic incident—something like that makes a good starter for an article such as this is going to be— what picturesque or thrilling episode was there that occurred in your early life or, better still, in your childhood?"

Mr. Jacobs gave an inner guilty start. "And why do you ask that—of me?" he demanded suspiciously.

"Oh, it was just a vague idea of Mr. Laidlaw's, our editor, that's all." The caller's tone was most respectful, in fact almost humble. "He thought that inasmuch as you came from the Far West, and were born and brought up there at a period when the last wave of the crude but gallant pathfinding element was pushing its way out to the Coast, maybe it was possible that in your own youth there had been something exciting—something in the nature of an adventure or an experience which would make good copy, sir."

"Ah, I see," said Mr. Jacobs, now completely reassured, and he smiled a gentle smile betokening regret that the publishers and their subscribers must be disappointed. "I'm sorry to say, young man, that unless I should draw upon my fancy—which is not my habit—I can not gratify your readers in this regard. My people could hardly be called home-seekers, or even Argonauts, much less pioneers. True, they went from the South at what seems now a comparatively remote age in our country's development, but they went from refined and cultivated surroundings to an environment which, while possibly primitive in some respects, was yet immediately invested, as it were, with a translated refinement.

"I might add—if it is of any popular interest—that for at least a century before that my people had been part and parcel of the old South as it was in the ante-bellum days and on back into the Colonial days. In a community of gentlefolk, slave owners, plantation owners, luxury-loving people—that was where I was born. There is, I believe, some Huguenot blood in my veins, and some of the strain of the Cavaliers also.

"My mother, now——" Through a well-spaced and finely dramatic moment he paused, meanwhile looking out with softened eye upon his formal gardens and upon the only slightly less formal terraces, all ornated and groomed, which fell below, and then in a mildly sentimentalized tone of reminiscence continued: "My mother, now. She was the daughter of a rather famous soldier in the Confederacy—a brevet brigadier, a Kentuckian out of the Blue Grass regions but of Virginia descent.

"She passed away when I was a small boy. But I faintly remember her. Very small and fragile, I recall, and always wearing a bit of fine lace at her throat. Ah, me!" His small sigh was so cleverly done that it achieved genius—a thing so beautifully theatrical that it didn't sound theatrical at all.

Perhaps it was by coincidence that at this precise moment a cock pheasant crowed derisively from somewhere quite close by down the landscaped slope. It was, however, a common barnyard cock which gave similar proof to Apostle Peter that the prophecy touching on *his* words of betrayal had been fulfilled.

Mr. Jacobs, now pacing to and fro along his veranda, went on: "However, I hold that a display of pride in honorable and even— ahem—distinguished ancestry, however laudable it may be on some occasions and under some conditions, has no place really in a story such as I gather you propose to write. If you insist on mentioning it in passing, that is your own concern.

"To be born right is something; to be reared right is better still —granted. But the point I would make and emphasize—you may quote me here in full—is that the opportunities for rising to commercial supremacy in this splendid country of ours are open to those who spring from the most—how shall we phrase it?—well, the most prosaic, the most commonplace circumstances and often from the lowliest of parentage.

"Take, for example, the late lamented Andrew Carnegie, a man without benefit of early advantages, and yet look at his record.

Take my dear friend, Charley Schwab. Take Mr. John D. Rockefeller, Senior. Take almost any one of my recent or present contemporaries in the realm of big business." He said almost sadly, as though grieving for sundry ones: "No, my worthy young friend, we can't all be thoroughbreds, can we?"

"Quite so, sir. Thank you, sir. And now, sir, not changing the subject, but for the inspiration of our youth of to-day, to what do you ascribe, primarily and basically, I mean, your own pre-eminence?"

"In a word," answered Mr. Jacobs, meaning by that a considerable number of words—"in a word, to hard work. To keeping the faith with all men and all women regardless of the consequences. To punching the time clock on the dot always. To never watching the hands of the clock. To telling the plain truth, no matter what the cost . . ."

And so on and so forth for ten elaborating minutes—right out of the old copy-book. But good stuff for the younger generation —splendid stuff.

In the printed column or even in the rough proofs, Mr. Jacobs would have been greatly pleased to scan—that would seem to be the proper word, or anyhow the stylish word—to scan that which this talented young man went back to the office and wrote. Unhappily such pleasure was to be denied him. Six weeks later, when the subject-matter was going into type for the magazine and the magazine people would be ready pretty soon now to close up that number, Mr. Jacobs had his untimely stroke and lay unconscious until the end.

It so befell that the issue of *Dynamic Individualities* containing the write-up came out only two days before his death and less than a week before the funeral. So the rewrite men on the newspapers drew upon it freely; and what had been meant for a condensed biography ironically served the posthumous purposes of obituary.

The published list of clubs to which Mr. Jacobs belonged was a compendium of the worth-while clubs of Manhattan Island. The published list of the pallbearers, active and honorary, read like several important pages out of the Directory of Directors. In a bronze and marble mausoleum which cost ninety thousand dollars, and which is a conspicuous feature of a marcelled vista in

what the ribald-minded call "Millionaires' Row," he rests in trust,
sleeping the sleep which knows no waking, at the most exclusive,
the most conservative, the most fashionable of all up-town ceme-
teries—a cemetery having so exclusive a membership that unless
the candidates' remains really belong, they'll blackball 'em out
the very minute they come up before the admissions committee.

Irrigation has reclaimed much of the mesa lying just under a
certain notch in the range, so that alfalfa ripples where the savage
mesquite once sprouted and a lone 'dobe shack once squatted in
the midst of a fearsome desolation. In a strip of still unwatered
and therefore arid silt between two of the cultivated grass-fields,
a gang of Mexican laborers were excavating foundation trenches
for a proposed addition to the Pinto Buttes Dude Ranch when
about four feet down, the pick-point of a worker tinked against
something solider than the light ash-like subsoil.

Under direction of the foreman, a few minutes more of careful
digging revealed a human body, a woman's body, which, lying
for no telling how long in that moistureless altitude and shielded
beneath layers of that dry volcanic loam, was mummified, the
parchmented skin being here corrugated and there drawn as tight
as drumheads over the fragile but still intact framework.

For fear of breaking some of those brittle bones, the foreman
wouldn't let his Mexies lift the cadaver out of the hole. He got
down in the hole himself and with his fingers scooped up the coarse
dirt and flung it out so that the entire shape was exhibited, and
with it some crumbling fragments of the heavy woolen cerements
in which obviously the dead crudely had been shrouded.

He left the grim find thus and went to the main ranch house to
give in the word. With the morbid little crowd of hands and guests
who followed him back to the spot came Daddy Lem Doolittle,
spraddling along on his bowed and unsteady old legs like a set
of animated calipers.

Daddy Lem was an octogenarian relic of the early times, a
surviving bit of local color retained by the management to be
picturesque and quaintly philosophical all over the place, and
most of all to regale paying pilgrims from the East with tales
that were as high, wide and handsome as the views of this, his
original habitat—in other words, the official hired liar of the

establishment and, considering his age and the amount of liquor he had in his day consumed and his advanced stage of decrepitude, a very good liar, resourceful, ready, dependable.

This ancient's present mood, though, was not a mood for romancing. He squinted down into the opened grave, and then broke in on a babble of exclamations and theories and surmises coming from natives and visitors as well.

"You-all are all wrong," he stated decisively. "This here ain't no squaw. It couldn't be no squaw. Injuns never buried their female folks in no sich fashion ez this. 'Sides, the hair wuzn't dead black, to begin with. It's bleached out a heap and faded, but you kin tell yit that it must 'a' been light brown or mebbe yaller.

"So this here must be a white woman's body you boys have done oncovered." His voice, already shrill with age, grew shriller: "And, by Tunket, now I know who that white woman wuz! It comes back to me: The sorry feller, that she wuz his wife or leastwise his woman—I furgit his name, though, ef ever I knowed it—he had a claim staked out right in this here identical spot. She wuz a Dutch gal, but he wuz Irish and no durned good neither, I've heared tell.

"And the day the 'Paches come through this district, slaughterin' and stealin' and ravishin'—not the last time they come but the time before the last—he wuz off from home somewheres that day. And she—this here very Dutch gal that I'm tellin' you about —she tuck out acrost the desert with her baby in her arms and she dropped her kid in the bushes and kept runnin' till one of them onmerciful little devils run her down and knocked her skull in with a tomahawk.

"Why, jist look, you-all, and you kin see where the wound wuz, there in the back of her——" The shock of a new and strange discovery made Daddy Lem break off. "Who's been messin' about with her?" he demanded. "Who's been disturbin' that poor thing's molderin' remainders?"

"Not nobody," answered back the foreman. "I'm the only one touched her and I didn't move her none, neither—jist cleared out the hole."

"Then whut's she doin' restin' that way?"

"Way I found her, I'm tellin' you. But it does look funny, don't it? I been wonderin'."

"It looks dam' funny!"

All the others were silent, harkening to these two. The foreman hazarded a guess: "Maybe—maybe it might have been that whoever it was stuck her away was in such confusion they accidentally tumbled her in upside down?"

"Not nary a chanct. You're talkin' now, son, to somebody that knows whut he's talkin' about. You're listenin' to Arizony history, boy. Fur while I wuzn't here myself, my older brother, the late Pierce Doolittle, deceasted, he wuz here. He come in here with the posse that come in here with the soldiers that same evenin'. That wuz when they found the gal with her brains all spilt out on the ground and found the baby mouty hungry and terrible sunburnt but still livin'.

"Somebody or other taken the kid fur to raise. And ef I heared Pierce say it onct endurin' his lifetime, I heared him say it a hundred times, that whilst they wuz all set to light out and ketch up with them 'Paches before they could do some more fresh devilment, still they taken the time to lay the woman away decent and proper and Christian-like—foldin' her hands on her breast and wroppin' her up in a saddle blanket offen one of the cav'rymen's spare mounts—by Tunket, onless I'm mistaken, and I ain't, that's whut's left of the blanket still folded around her—and even coverin' up her face with a handkerchief off of somebody's neck to keep the dirt out of her face."

A fascinated and awe-stricken listener put in his oar: "Had you thought of this? Wouldn't it be possible that she was still breathing —that they buried her alive and in her struggles, poor thing, she wriggled and rolled over until she was face downward?"

"Huh!" The aged historian was very scornful about it. "You never knowed no 'Paches when they wuz in their prime. Ef a 'Pache ondertaken a job of killin' somebody, no matter how big a rush he wuz in, he finished that there killin' job before he quit—nary record of ary failure there! Nur you seemin'ly don't know whut layin' out in Arizony sunshine all day would do to you, let alone your skull bein' split plum' wide open behind."

"Well, then, what's your explanation?"

"Me, I ain't got none. I'm jist sayin' it's dam' funny—'scuse me, I furgot about there bein' ladies present. . . . Hold on, boys, I got me kind of a loose idee! It mout be foolish but sich ez 'tis, I've got it: Ain't you never heared 'em say it, jokin'-like, I'll admit, but still and all sayin' it, that ef a dead person has been laid away in the silent tomb and somebody, no matter how many years afterward, deliber't'ly does that there dead person dirt—I mean to say, does their memory dirt—that then that there dead person will turn smack over in the grave?"

"Surely you don't believe that, Daddy Lem?" asked a tourist.

"I ain't sayin' ez how I believe it, neither I ain't sayin' ez how I disbelieve it," answered Daddy Lem. "Till this minute I ain't never given it nary thought nur study. The older I git the less inclined I am to be certain shore about ary thing in this world or the next. But jist the same"—and he pointed a long fleshless finger into the hole—"jist the same, look down there and tell me ef this here thing ain't damnation funny!"

J. FRANK DOBIE

THE MYSTERY OF THE PALO DURO

The following factual account has all the elements of the mysterious and the occult. The logical explanation is a fascinating illustration of the way the subconscious mind works. (From *Coronado's Children*, 1931.)

LIGHTHOUSE CANYON is a tributary of that strange and wonderful cleft across the Panhandle Plains of Texas known variously as Prairie Dog Creek, Red River, and the Palo Duro. Coronado doubtless wandered over the region while in quest of the chimerical Gran Quivera. Long after him the *Comancheros* —Spaniards and Mexicans who traded with the Comanches—were familiar with it.

In Lighthouse Canyon itself was born in the year 1850 Jesus Ramón Grachias. He became a man of marked intelligence, fair education, and wide experience. At the age of seventy-six he happened one day while hunting burros to enter the camp of a college professor who was taking his vacation in New Mexico, and there he related one of his experiences.

"I lived in Lighthouse Canyon until my father died in 1854, and then my mother brought me away. My remembrances of those four years are very dim. More than thirty years later I was working on the Fort Worth and Denver Railroad then building into Am-

arillo. As I was thus again on Palo Duro Canyon, and as I had
some money saved up, I decided to visit the place where I was
born and where my father was buried. I put my wife, baby, and
camp things into a wagon and started west.

"We traveled slow. The country was still wide—ranches,
ranches, ranches. I did not know if there was a road into Lighthouse Canyon. I only knew that it was west. After two weeks I
came upon a Mexican who was trapping lobos for the J A Ranch.
He guided me to within ten miles of the place I wanted to go and
then, after telling me how to take the wagon, turned back.

"Many times my mother had described the place to me: the
great pillar projecting up from the center of the canyon almost
to the level of the plains like a lighthouse; the strange markings
on the walls of rock; the fine spring of water; the shaggy old
cedars around whose gnarled roots I used to play; the herds of
buffaloes and antelopes that came into the breaks for winter; the
owls and panthers and lobos that made their cries in the night.
Remembrance of all these things helped me locate the spot where
my father had built his *jacal* nearly forty years before. The
place was still wild and there was not one sign of former habitation, but when I unloaded the wagon and put up a tent, I knew
I would sleep that night on the spot where I was born.

"Many times I had promised my mother that some day I would
come back here and put a cross over my father's grave. I found
two flat stones lying near each other on the ground. When I
turned one of them over, I saw the letters J. R. G. They were
roughly cut. They stood for my father's name, my name also,
Jesus Ramón Grachias. The stones had marked his grave and had
very likely been pushed over by cattle or buffaloes. Also, my
mother had told me that the grave was fifty feet east of an old
cedar. I found only the burned stump of a cedar, fifty feet away
in the right direction. Accordingly, I heaped up a hill of earth
between the stones, set them in place again, and made a cross.

"The night after I had accomplished this I had a dream. I saw
in this dream someone digging near the stump of the burned
cedar. As I had myself dug there to get earth to put on the grave,
and as I had, moreover, dug in several other places to find fishing
worms, I did not regard the dream as very unusual. But the next
night the dream came again, and this time I heard very distinctly
these words: *'Dig fifteen feet east of old cedar tree.'*

"All the next day I was disturbed, thinking that my mother had perhaps said the grave was fifteen feet east of the cedar instead of fifty feet east and that I had maybe marked the wrong spot. I was much troubled, for now that I was on the ground I could not bear to leave the exact spot of my father's remains unmarked. Then I determined to make another mound fifteen feet east of the cedar tree and put a cross on it also. I measured off the distance and began to work. But the voice of the dream kept ringing in my ears: *'Dig fifteen feet east of old cedar tree.' 'Dig,'* it said. *'Dig.'*

"If I dig, I thought, I can tell if the earth has ever been disturbed. So I began digging. At first the ground seemed no softer than any other ground. Then very soon my spade struck something hard, something of iron. Quickly I uncovered it. It was the lid of a chest, about eighteen inches wide and thirty inches long. More quickly yet I uncovered one end and prized it up. The chest was about eighteen inches deep. With the help of my wife I now got it out of the ground. We were very excited. I had to break the clasps of the lid. We opened it. It was full of coins. They were all Spanish and were all dated before 1821, the year of Mexico's independence.

"The grave of my father was after all properly marked. We could now leave. I backed my wagon up to the chest and dug little trenches for the hind wheels so that the rear end of the bed would be low. Thus I managed to load the chest. I drove up the canyon to its head and topped out upon the plains. I had no desire to go back east. I made for Santa Fé. It took us ten days to arrive. The banker there was a friend to the family of my mother. He counted the coins and gave me credit for $7600.

"I do not know which was bigger in me, the joy or the mystery. My mother was still alive and I at once traveled to her to tell her all things and to take her money. She could not understand the meaning any more than I could. We talked and talked. She told me much about my father that I had never known or had forgotten. You will see if what I learned explained anything.

"When the Texans whipped Santa Ana, a great many Mexicans living in that state left. My father was among them. He and four other Mexicans set out for Santa Fé over a country they did not know even by report. There were no roads. Winter overtook them on the plains. They camped in a deep canyon—Lighthouse Canyon

—well protected. They made friends with the Comanches; game was everywhere. Early in the spring all their horses but two got away with the mustangs. On these horses two men left for Santa Fé to secure aid. Those messengers never returned. My father and his companions stayed, hunting and living on the country. I think they were happy.

"In the late summer of 1841 a body of Texas traders and soldiers—the Santa Fé Expedition—came among them, lost. The Mexicans joined them as guides. It is well known how the Texans were made prisoners and sent to Mexico City. My father was made prisoner also. He was kept for four years. Then he was released and came back to Santa Fé.

"There he married my mother. She was thirty-five years old; this was in 1849. He was twenty years older. As soon almost as they were married, he loaded a wagon with goods and set out for the plains of Texas. He told her that he was going to hunt buffaloes, but she said he seemed to hunt nothing but canyons. At last they came to the place he had been looking for. It was Lighthouse Canyon. 'I once lived here,' he said. 'I will live here again.' He died there, as I have already told you, in 1854.

"For a day before he died he seemed out of his head. He kept talking wildly to my mother of fights, of gold coin, of escapes, of enemies, of friends—of many things that she did not understand, for he explained nothing. He had never explained anything to her. The last hour of his life was calm. She was holding me over him to see if he would take notice when she heard, 'Buried fifty feet east of old cedar tree.' I recall only being lifted up and looking at him.

"So my mother with her own hands dug a grave fifty feet east of the big cedar tree, just as she supposed my father had directed. Then alone she got the horses, which were hobbled in the canyon, hitched them to our wagon, and drove with me to Santa Fé, leaving forever the lonely Palo Duro."

It has been said that the narrator—this finder who was not a searcher—was a fairly well educated man. The activities of the subconscious mind have long interested many people who make no claims to education. Jesus Ramón Grachias was quite averse to being regarded as superstitious.

"I do not believe in spirits," he said. "I do not believe in voices of the dead. Now listen. My mother was even when she married slightly deaf. What my dying father said to her was probably this: 'Dig fifteen feet east of old cedar tree. It is buried fifteen feet east of old cedar tree.' My mother, failing to catch the first word of his command, thought he was talking of his grave and heard 'fifteen' as 'fifty.' At the same time, although I was too young to attach any meaning to the words or to store them away in my memory, my subconscious mind registered the sounds. More than thirty years later when I returned to Lighthouse Canyon and rested in the shade of the cedars around which I had played as a child and drank from the spring that my little mother as a bride used to dip from and stepped on the soil where my father's feet had worn a trail and where he had died—then old associations stirred the subconscious mind to activity. My nerves were all active, my imagination was alive. It was natural for me to dream a dream in which the subconscious mind brought to the surface those words stored away so long ago, 'Dig fifteen feet east of old cedar tree.'

"The real mystery to me is how the money came to be there. Was my father at some time a robber—some time before 1821, for no coins were dated later than that year? Why did he live for years beside the money without using it, without telling his wife of it? Was he awaiting the return of some confederate? I do not know. I only wish that all the money were not spent now."

A CALL LOAN

O. Henry, "Caliph of Bagdad," was also Caliph of the Far West, and some of his finest stories are of that region. In this story of cattlemen and bankers, we are given an example of a particular Westerner's moral and business code—one to which few Eastern businessmen would subscribe. (From *Heart of the West*, Doubleday, Doran, 1907.)

IN THOSE days the cattlemen were the anointed. They were the grandees of the grass, kings of the kine, lords of the lea, barons of beef and bone. They might have ridden in golden chariots had their tastes so inclined. The cattleman was caught in a stampede of dollars. It seemed to him that he had more money than was decent. But when he had bought a watch with precious stones set in the case so large that they hurt his ribs, and a California saddle with silver nails and Angora skin *sudaderos*, and ordered everybody up to the bar for whisky—what else was there for him to spend money for?

Not so circumscribed in expedient for the reduction of surplus wealth were those lairds of the lariat who had womenfolk to their name. In the breast of the rib-sprung sex the genius of purse lightening may slumber through years of inopportunity, but never, my brothers, does it become extinct.

So, out of the chaparral came Long Bill Longley from the Bar Circle Ranch on the Frio—a wife-driven man—to taste the urban joys of success. Something like half a million dollars he had, with an income steadily increasing.

Long Bill was a graduate of the camp and trail. Luck and thrift, a cool head, and a telescopic eye for mavericks had raised him from cowboy to be a cowman. Then came the boom in cattle, and Fortune, stepping gingerly among the cactus thorns, came and emptied her cornucopia at the doorstep of the ranch.

In the little frontier city of Chaparosa, Longley built a costly residence. Here he became a captive, bound to the chariot of social existence. He was doomed to become a leading citizen. He struggled for a time like a mustang in his first corral, and then he hung up his quirt and spurs. Time hung heavily on his hands. He organized the First National Bank of Chaparosa, and was elected its president.

One day a dyspeptic man, wearing double-magnifying glasses, inserted an official-looking card between the bars of the cashier's window of the First National Bank. Five minutes later the bank force was dancing at the beck and call of a national bank examiner.

This examiner, Mr. J. Edgar Todd, proved to be a thorough one.

At the end of it all the examiner put on his hat, and called the president, Mr. William R. Longley, into the private office.

"Well, how do you find things?" asked Longley, in his slow, deep tones. "Any brands in the round-up you didn't like the looks of?"

"The bank checks up all right, Mr. Longley," said Todd; "and I find your loans in very good shape—with one exception. You are carrying one very bad bit of paper—one that is so bad that I have been thinking that you surely do not realize the serious position it places you in. I refer to a call loan of $10,000 made to Thomas Merwin. Not only is the amount in excess of the maximum sum the bank can loan any individual legally, but it is absolutely without endorsement or security. Thus you have doubly violated the national banking laws, and have laid yourself open to criminal prosecution by the Government. A report of the matter to the Comptroller of the Currency—which I am bound to make—would, I am sure, result in the matter being turned over to the Department of Justice for action. You see what a serious thing it is."

Bill Longley was leaning his lengthy, slowly moving frame back in his swivel chair. His hands were clasped behind his head, and he turned a little to look the examiner in the face. The examiner was surprised to see a smile creep about the rugged mouth of the banker, and a kindly twinkle in his light-blue eyes. If he saw the seriousness of the affair, it did not show in his countenance.

"Of course, you don't know Tom Merwin," said Longley, almost genially. "Yes, I know about that loan. It hasn't any security except Tom Merwin's word. Somehow, I've always found that when a man's word is good, it's the best security there is. Oh, yes, I know the Government doesn't think so. I guess I'll see Tom about that note."

Mr. Todd's dyspepsia seemed to grow suddenly worse. He looked at the chaparral banker through his double-magnifying glasses in amazement.

"You see," said Longley, easily explaining the thing away, "Tom heard of 2000 head of two-year-olds down near Rocky Ford on the Rio Grande that could be had for $8 a head. I reckon 'twas one of old Laendro Garcia's outfits that he had smuggled over, and he wanted to make a quick turn on 'em. Those cattle are worth $15 on the hoof in Kansas City. Tom knew it and I knew it. He had $6,000, and I let him have the $10,000 to make the deal with. His brother Ed took 'em on to market three weeks ago. He ought to be back 'most any day now with the money. When he comes Tom'll pay that note."

The bank examiner was shocked. It was, perhaps, his duty to step out to the telegraph office and wire the situation to the Comptroller. But he did not. He talked pointedly and effectively to Longley for three minutes. He succeeded in making the banker understand that he stood upon the border of a catastrophe. And then he offered a tiny loophole of escape.

"I am going to Hilldale's to-night," he told Longley, "to examine a bank there. I will pass through Chaparosa on my way back. At twelve to-morrow I shall call at this bank. If this loan has been cleared out of the way by that time it will not be mentioned in my report. If not—I will have to do my duty."

With that the examiner bowed and departed.

The President of the First National lounged in his chair half an hour longer, and then he lit a mild cigar, and went over to Tom Merwin's house. Merwin, a ranchman in brown duck, with a contemplative eye, sat with his feet upon a table, plaiting a rawhide quirt.

"Tom," said Longley, leaning against the table, "you heard anything from Ed yet?"

"Not yet," said Merwin, continuing his plaiting. "I guess Ed'll be along back now in a few days."

"There was a bank examiner," said Longley, "nosing around our place to-day, and he bucked a sight about that note of yours. You know I know it's all right, but the thing *is* against the banking laws. I was pretty sure you'd have paid it off before the bank was examined again, but the son-of-a-gun slipped in on us, Tom. Now, I'm short of cash myself just now, or I'd let you have the money to take it up with. I've got till twelve o'clock to-morrow, and then I've got to show the cash in place of that note or—"

"Or what, Bill?" asked Merwin, as Longley hesitated.

"Well, I suppose it means be jumped on with both of Uncle Sam's feet."

"I'll try to raise the money for you on time," said Merwin, interested in his plaiting.

"All right, Tom," concluded Longley, as he turned toward the door; "I knew you would if you could."

Merwin threw down his whip and went to the only other bank in town, a private one, run by Cooper & Craig.

"Cooper," he said, to the partner by that name, "I've got to have $10,000 to-day or to-morrow. I've got a house and lot here that's worth about $6,000 and that's all the actual collateral. But I've got a cattle deal on that's sure to bring me in more than that much profit within a few days."

Cooper began to cough.

"Now, for God's sake don't say no," said Merwin. "I owe that much money on a call loan. It's been called, and the man that called it is a man I've laid on the same blanket with in cow-camps and ranger-camps for ten years. He can call anything I've got. He can call the blood out of my veins and it'll come. He's got to have the money. He's in a devil of a— Well, he needs the money, and I've got to get it for him. You know my word's good, Cooper."

"No doubt of it," assented Cooper, urbanely, "but I've a partner, you know. I'm not free in making loans. And even if you had the best security in your hands, Merwin, we couldn't accommodate you in less than a week. We're just making a shipment of $15,000 to Myer Brothers in Rockdell, to buy cotton with. It goes down

on the narrow gauge to-night. That leaves our cash quite short
at present. Sorry we can't arrange it for you."

Merwin went back to his little bar office and plaited at his quirt
again. About four o'clock in the afternoon he went to the First
National and leaned over the railing of Longley's desk.

"I'll try to get that money for you to-night—I mean to-morrow,
Bill."

"All right, Tom," said Longley, quietly.

At nine o'clock that night Tom Merwin stepped cautiously out
of the small frame house in which he lived. It was near the edge
of the little town, and few citizens were in the neighborhood at
that hour. Merwin wore two six-shooters in a belt and a slouch hat.
He moved swiftly down a lonely street, and then followed the
sandy road that ran parallel to the narrow-gauge track until he
reached the water-tank, two miles below the town. There Tom
Merwin stopped, tied a black silk handkerchief about the lower
part of his face, and pulled his hat down low.

In ten minutes the night train for Rockdell pulled up at the
tank, having come from Chaparosa.

With a gun in each hand Merwin raised himself from behind a
clump of chaparral and started for the engine. But before he had
taken three steps, two long, strong arms clasped him from behind,
and he was lifted from his feet and thrown, face downward, upon
the grass. There was a heavy knee pressing against his back, and
an iron hand grasping each of his wrists. He was held thus, like
a child, until the engine had taken water, and until the train had
moved, with accelerating speed, out of sight. Then he was released,
and rose to his feet to face Bill Longley.

"The case never needed to be fixed up this way, Tom," said
Longley. "I saw Cooper this evening, and he told me what you
and him talked about. Then I went down to your house to-night
and saw you come out with your guns on, and I followed you. Let's
go back, Tom."

They walked away together, side by side.

" 'Twas the only chance I saw," said Merwin, presently. "You
called your loan, and I tried to answer you. Now, what'll you do,
Bill, if they sock it to you?"

"What would you have done if they'd socked it to you?" was
the answer Longley made.

"I never thought I'd lay in a bush to stick up a train," remarked

Merwin; "but a call loan's different. A call's a call with me. We've got twelve hours yet, Bill, before this spy jumps onto you. We've got to raise them spondulicks somehow. Maybe we can—Great Sam Houston! do you hear that?"

Merwin broke into a run, and Longley kept with him, hearing only a rather pleasing whistle somewhere in the night rendering the lugubrious air of "The Cowboy's Lament."

"It's the only tune he knows," shouted Merwin, as he ran. "I'll bet—"

They were at the door of Merwin's house. He kicked it open and fell over an old valise lying in the middle of the floor. A sun-burned, firm-jawed youth, stained by travel, lay upon the bed puffing at a brown cigarette.

"What's the word, Ed?" gasped Merwin.

"So, so," drawled that capable youngster. "Just got in on the 9:30. Sold the bunch for fifteen straight. Now, buddy, you want to quit kickin' a valise around that's got $29,000 in greenbacks in its in'ards."

ZANE GREY

DON: THE STORY OF A LION DOG

A graphic picture of lion hunting in the West, this is also the story of a dog who loved freedom. It is sensitively and beautifully told, and is one of the comparatively few short stories by the most popular of all writers of Western American fiction.

IT HAS taken me years to realize the greatness of a dog; and often as I have told the story of Don—his love of freedom and hatred of men—how I saved his life and he saved mine—it never was told as I feel it now.

I saw Don first at Flagstaff, Arizona, where arrangements had been made for me to cross the desert with Buffalo Jones and a Mormon caravan en route to Lee's Ferry on the Colorado River. Jones had brought a pack of nondescript dogs. Our purpose was to cross the river and skirt the Vermilion Cliffs, and finally work up through Buckskin Forest to the north rim of the Grand Canyon, where Jones expected to lasso mountain lions and capture them alive. The most important part of our oufit, of course, was the pack of hounds. Never had I seen such a motley assembly of canines. They did not even have names. Jones gave me the privilege of finding names for them.

Among them was a hound that seemed out of place because of his superb proportions, his sleek, dark, smooth skin, his noble head, and great, solemn black eyes. He had extraordinarily long ears, thick-veined and faintly tinged with brown. Here was a dog that looked to me like a thoroughbred. My friendly overtures to him were unnoticed. Jones said he was part bloodhound and had belonged to an old Mexican don in southern California. So I named him Don.

We were ten days crossing the Painted Desert, and protracted horseback-riding was then so new and hard for me that I had no enthusiasm left to scrape acquaintance with the dogs. Still, I did not forget and often felt sorry for them as they limped along, clinking their chains under the wagons. Even then I divined that horses and dogs were going to play a great part in my Western experience.

At Lee's Ferry we crossed the Colorado and I was introduced to the weird and wild canyon country, with its golden-red walls and purple depths. Here we parted with the caravan and went on with Jones's rangers, Jim and Emmet, who led our outfit into such a wonderful region as I had never dreamed of. We camped several days on the vast range where Jones let his buffalo herd run wild. One day the Arizonians put me astride a white mustang that apparently delighted in carrying a tenderfoot. I did not then know what I was soon to learn—that the buffalo always chased this mustang off the range. When I rode up on the herd, to my utter amaze and terror they took after me and— But I am digressing, and this is a dog story.

Once across the river, Jones had unchained the dogs and let them run on ahead or lag behind. Most of them lagged. Don for one, however, did not get sore feet. Beyond the buffalo range we entered the sage, and here Jones began to train the dogs in earnest. He carried on his saddle an old blunderbuss of a shotgun, about which I had wondered curiously. I had supposed he meant to use it to shoot small game.

Moze, our black-and-white dog, and the ugliest of the lot, gave chase to a jack rabbit.

"Hyar, you Moze, come back!" bawled Jones in stentorian tones. But Moze paid no attention. Jones whipped out the old shotgun and before I could utter a protest he had fired. The distance was pretty far—seventy yards or more—but Moze howled piercingly and came sneaking and limping back. It was remarkable to see him almost crawl to Jones's feet.

"Thar! That'll teach you not to chase rabbits. You're a lion dog!" shouted the old plainsman as if he were talking to a human.

At first I was so astounded and furious that I could not speak. But presently I voiced my feeling.

"Wal, it looks worse than it is," he said, with his keen gray-blue eyes on me. "I'm usin' fine birdshot an' it can't do any more than sting. You see, I've no time to train these dogs. It's necessary to make them see quick that they're not to trail or chase any varmints but lions."

There was nothing for me to do but hold my tongue, though my resentment appeared to be shared by Jim and Emmet. They made excuses for the old plainsman. Jim said: "He shore can make animals do what he wants. But I never seen the dog or hoss that cared two bits for him."

We rode on through the beautiful purple sageland, gradually uphill, toward a black-fringed horizon that was Buckskin Forest. Jack rabbits, cottontails, coyotes and foxes, prairie dogs and pack rats infested the sage and engaged the attention of our assorted pack of hounds. All the dogs except Don fell victim to Jones's old blunderbuss; and surely stubborn Moze 'received a second peppering, this time at closer range. I espied drops of blood upon his dirty white skin. After this it relieved me greatly to see that not even Moze transgressed again. Jones's method was cruel, but effective. He had captured and subdued wild animals since his boyhood. In fact, that had been the driving passion of his life, but no sentiment entered into it.

"Reckon Don is too smart to let you ketch him," Jim once remarked to our leader.

"Wal, I don't know," responded Jones, dubiously. "Mebbe he just wouldn't chase this sage trash. But wait till we jump some deer. Then we'll see. He's got bloodhound in him, and I'll bet he'll run deer. All hounds will, even the best ones trained on bear an' lion."

Not long after we entered the wonderful pine forest the reckoning of Don came as Jones had predicted. Several deer bounded out of a thicket and crossed ahead of us, soon disappearing in the green blur.

"Ahuh! Now we'll see," ejaculated Jones, deliberately pulling out the old shotgun.

The hounds trotted along beside our horses, unaware of the danger ahead. Soon we reached the deer tracks. All the hounds showed excitement. Don let out a sharp yelp and shot away like a streak on the trail.

"Don, come hyar!" yelled Jones, at the same time extending his gun. Don gave no sign he had heard. Then Jones pulled trigger and shot him. I saw the scattering of dust and pine needles all around Don. He doubled up and rolled. I feared that he might be badly injured. But he got up and turned back. It seemed strange that he did not howl. Jones drew his plunging horse to a halt and bade us all stop.

"Don, come back hyar," he called in a loud, harsh, commanding voice.

The hound obeyed, not sneakingly or cringingly. He did not put his tail between his legs. But he was frightened and no doubt pretty badly hurt. When he reached us I saw that he was trembling all over and that drops of blood dripped from his long ears. What a somber, sullen gaze in his eyes!

"See hyar," bellowed Jones. "I knowed you was deer-chaser. Wal, now you're a lion dog."

Later that day, when I had recovered sufficiently from my disapproval, I took Jones to task about this matter of shooting the dogs. I wanted to know how he expected the hounds to learn what he required of them.

"Wal, that's easy," he replied curtly. "When we strike a lion trail I'll put them on it—let them go. They'll soon learn."

It seemed plausible, but I was so incensed that I doubted the hounds would chase anything; and I resolved that if Jones shot Don again I would force the issue and end the hunt unless assured there would be no more of such drastic training methods.

Soon after this incident we made camp on the edge of a beautiful glade where a snow-bank still lingered and a stream of water trickled down into a green swale. Before we got camp pitched a band of wild horses thudded by, thrilling me deeply. My first sight of wild horses! I knew I should never forget that splendid stallion, the leader, racing on under the trees, looking back at us over his shoulder.

At this camp I renewed my attempts to make friends with Don.

He had been chained apart from the other dogs. He ate what I fetched him, but remained aloof. His dignity and distrust were such that I did not risk laying a hand on him then. But I resolved to win him if it were possible. His tragic eyes haunted me. There was a story in them I could not read. He always seemed to be looking afar. On this occasion I came to the conclusion that he hated Jones.

Buckskin Forest was well named. It appeared to be full of deer, the large black-tailed species known as mule deer. This species must be related to the elk. The size and beauty of them, the way they watched with long ears erect and then bounded off as if on springs, never failed to thrill me with delight.

As we traveled on, the forest grew wilder and more beautiful. In the park-like glades a bleached white grass waved in the wind and bluebells smiled wanly. Wild horses outnumbered the deer, and that meant there were some always in sight. A large gray grouse flew up now and then, and most striking of the forest creatures to fascinate me was a magnificent black squirrel, with a long bushy white tail, and tufted ears, and a red stripe down its glossy sides.

We rode for several days through this enchanting wilderness, gradually ascending, and one afternoon we came abruptly to a break in the forest. It was the north rim of the Grand Canyon. My astounded gaze tried to grasp an appalling abyss of purple and gold and red, a chasm too terrible and beautiful to understand all at once. The effect of that moment must have been tremendous, for I have never recovered from it. To this day the thing that fascinates me most is to stand upon a great height—canyon wall, or promontory, or peak—and gaze down into the mysterious colorful depths.

Our destination was Powell's Plateau, an isolated cape jutting out into the canyon void. Jones showed it to me—a distant gold-rimmed, black-fringed promontory, seemingly inaccessible and unscalable. The only trail leading to it was a wild-horse hunter's trail, seldom used, exceedingly dangerous. It took us two days over this canyon trail to the Saddle—a narrow strip of land dipping down from the Plateau and reaching up to the main rim. We camped under a vast looming golden wall, so wonderful that it kept me from sleeping. That night lions visited our camp. The hounds barked for hours. This was the first chance I had to hear

Don. What a voice he had! Deep, ringing, wild, like the bay of a wolf!

Next morning we ascended the Saddle, from the notch of which I looked down into the chasm still asleep in purple shadows; then we climbed a narrow deer trail to the summit of the Plateau. Here indeed was the grand, wild, isolated spot of my dreams. Indeed, I was in an all-satisfying trance of adventure.

I wanted to make camp on the rim, but Jones laughed at me. We rode through the level, stately forest of pines until we came to a ravine on the north side of which lay a heavy bank of snow. This was very necessary, for there was no water on the Plateau. Jones rode off to scout while the rest of us pitched camp. Before we had completed our task a troop of deer appeared across the ravine, and motionless they stood watching us. There were big and little deer, blue-gray in color, sleek and graceful, so tame that to me it seemed brutal to shoot at them.

Don was the only one of the dogs that espied the deer. He stood up to gaze hard at them, but he did not bark or show any desire to chase them. Yet there seemed to me to be a strange yearning light in his dark eyes. I had never failed to approach Don whenever opportunity afforded, to continue my overtures of friendship. But now, as always, Don turned away from me. He was cold and somber. I had never seen him wag his tail or whine eagerly, as was common with most hounds.

Jones returned to camp jubilant and excited, as far as it was possible for the old plainsman to be. He had found lion trails and lion tracks, and he predicted a great hunt for us.

The Plateau resembled in shape the ace of clubs. It was perhaps six miles long and three or four wide. The body of it was covered with a heavy growth of pine, and the capes that sloped somewhat toward the canyon were thick with sage and cedar. This lower part, with its numerous swales and ravines and gorges, all leading down into the jungle of splintered crags and thicketed slopes of the Grand Canyon, turned out to be a paradise for deer and lion.

We found many lion trails leading down from the cedared broken rim to the slopes of yellow and red. These slopes really constituted a big country, and finally led to the sheer perpendicular precipice, three thousand feet lower.

Deer were numerous and as tame as cattle on a range. They

grazed with our horses. Herds of a dozen or more were common. Once we saw a very large band. Down in the sage and under the cedars and in ravines we found many remains of deer. Jones called these lion-kills. And he frankly stated that the number of deer killed yearly upon the Plateau would be incredible to any one who had not seen the actual signs.

In two days we had three captive lions tied up to pine saplings near camp. They were two-year-olds. Don and I had treed the first lion; I had taken pictures of Jones lassoing him; I had jumped off a ledge into a cedar to escape another; I had helped Jones hold a third; I had scratches from lion claws on my chaps, and— But I keep forgetting that this is not a story about lions. Always before when I had told it I have slighted Don.

One night, a week or more after we had settled in camp, we sat round a blazing red fire and talked over the hunt of the day. We all had our parts to tell. Jones and I had found where a lioness had jumped a deer. He showed me where the lioness had crouched upon a little brushy knoll, and how she had leaped thirty feet to the back of the deer. He showed me the tracks the deer had made—bounding, running, staggering with the lioness upon its back—and where, fully a hundred paces beyond, the big cat had downed its prey and killed it. There had been a fierce struggle. Then the lioness had dragged the carcass down the slope, through the sage, to the cedar tree where her four two-year-old cubs waited. All that we found of the deer were the ragged hide, some patches of hair, cracked bones, and two long ears. These were still warm.

Eventually we got the hounds on this trail and soon put up the lions. I found a craggy cliff under the rim and sat there watching and listening for hours. Jones rode to and fro above me, and at last dismounted to go down to join the other men. The hounds treed one of the lions. How that wild canyon slope rang with barks and bays and yells! Jones tied up this lion. Then the hounds worked up the ragged slope toward me, much to my gratification and excitement. Somewhere near me the lions had taken to cedars or crags, and I strained my eyes searching for them.

At last I located a lion on top of an isolated crag right beneath me. The hounds, with Don and Ranger leading, had been on the right track. My lusty yells brought the men. Then the lion stood up—a long, slender, yellowish cat—and spat at me. Next it leaped off that crag, fully fifty feet to the slope below, and bounded down, taking the direction from which the men had come. The hounds gave chase, yelping and baying. Jones bawled at them, trying to call them off, for what reason I could not guess. But I was soon to learn. They found the lion Jones had captured and left lying tied under a cedar, and they killed it, then took the trail of the other. They treed it far down in the rough jumble of rocks and cedars.

One by one we had ridden back to camp that night, tired out. Jim was the last in and he told his story last. And what was my amazement and fright to learn that all the three hours I had sat upon the edge of the caverned wall, the lioness had crouched on a bench above me. Jim on his way up had seen her, and then located her tracks in the dust back of my position. When this fact burst upon me I remembered how I had at first imagined I heard faint panting breaths near me somewhere. I had been too excited to trust my ears.

"Wal," said Jones, standing with the palms of his huge hands to the fire, "we had a poor day. If we had stuck to Don there'd have been a different story. I haven't trusted him. But now I reckon I'll have to. He'll make the greatest lion dog I ever had. Strikes me queer, too, for I never guessed it was in him. He has faults, though. He's too fast. He outruns the other hounds, an' he's goin' to be killed because of that. Some day he'll beat the pack to a mean old Tom lion or a lioness with cubs, an' he'll get his everlastin'. Another fault is, he doesn't bark often. That's bad, too. You can't stick to him. He's got a grand bay, shore, but he saves his breath. Don wants to run an' trail an' fight alone. He's got more nerve than any hound I ever trained. He's too good for his own sake—an' it'll be his death."

Naturally I absorbed all that Buffalo Jones said about dogs, horses, lions, everything pertaining to the West, and I believed it as if it had been gospel. But I observed that the others, especially Jim, did not always agree with our chief in regard to the hounds. A little later, when Jones had left the fire, Jim spoke up with his slow Texas drawl:

"Wal, what does he know about dawgs, I'll tell you right heah, if he hadn't shot Don we'd had the best hound that ever put his nose to a track. Don is a wild, strange hound, shore enough. Mebbe he's like a lone wolf. But it's plain he's been mistreated by men. An' Jones has just made him wuss."

Emmet inclined to Jim's point of view. And I respected this giant Mormon who was famous on the desert for his kindness to men and animals. His ranch at Lee's Ferry was overrun with dogs, cats, mustangs, burros, sheep and tamed wild animals that he had succored.

"Yes, Don hates Jones and, I reckon, all of us," said Emmet. "Don's not old, but he's too old to change. Still, you can never tell what kindness will do to animals. I'd like to take Don home with me and see. But Jones is right. That hound will be killed."

"Now I wonder why Don doesn't run off from us?" inquired Jim.

"Perhaps he thinks he'd get shot again," I ventured.

"If he ever runs away it'll not be here in the wilds," replied Emmet. "I take Don to be about as smart as any dog ever gets. And that's pretty close to human intelligence. People have to live lonely lives with dogs before they understand them. I reckon I understand Don. He's either loved one master once and lost him, or else he has always hated all men."

"Humph! That's shore an idee," ejaculated Jim, dubiously. "Do you think a dog can feel like that?"

"Jim, I once saw a little Indian shepherd dog lie down on its master's grave and die," returned the Mormon, sonorously.

"Wal, dog-gone me!" exclaimed Jim, in mild surprise.

One morning Jim galloped in, driving the horses pell-mell into camp. Any deviation from the Texan's usual leisurely manner of doing things always brought us up short with keen expectation.

"Saddle up," called Jim. "Shore that's a chase on. I seen a big red lioness up heah. She must have come down out of the tree whar I hang my meat. Last night I had a haunch of venison. It's gone. . . . . Say, she was a beauty. Red as a red fox."

In a very few moments we were mounted and riding up the ravine, with the eager hounds sniffing the air. Always over-anxious in my excitement, I rode ahead of my comrades. The hounds trotted with me. The distance to Jim's meat tree was a short quarter of a mile. I knew well where it was and, as of course the lion trail would be fresh, I anticipated a fine opportunity to watch Don. The other hounds had come to regard him as their leader.

When we neared the meat tree, which was a low-branched oak shaded by thick silver spruce, Don elevated his nose high in the air. He had caught a scent even at a distance. Jones had said more than once that Don had a wonderful nose. The other hounds, excited by Don, began to whine and yelp and run around with noses to the ground.

I had eyes only for Don. How instinct he was with life and fire! The hair on his neck stood up like bristles. Suddenly he let out a wild bark and bolted. He sped away from the pack and like a flash passed that oak tree, running with his head high. The hounds strung out after him and soon the woods seemed full of a baying chorus.

My horse, Black Bolly, well knew the meaning of the medley and did not need to be urged. He broke into a run and swiftly carried me up out of the hollow and through a brown-aisled pine-scented strip of forest to the canyon.

I rode along the edge of one of the deep indentations on the main rim. The hounds were bawling right under me at the base of a low cliff. They had jumped the lioness. I could not see them, but that was not necessary. They were running fast towards the head of this cove, and I had hard work to hold Black Bolly to a safe gait along that rocky rim. Suddenly she shied, and then reared, so that I fell out of the saddle as much as I dismounted. But I held the bridle, and then jerked my rifle from the saddle sheath. As I ran toward the rim I heard the yells of the men coming up behind. A the same instant I was startled and halted by sight of something red and furry flashing up into a tree right in front of me. It was the red lioness. The dogs had chased her into a pine the middle branches of which were on a level with the rim.

My skin went tight and cold and my heart fluttered. The lioness looked enormous, but that was because she was so close. I could have touched her with a long fishing-pole. I stood motionless for an instant, thrilling in every nerve, reveling in the beauty and wildness of that great cat. She did not see me. The hounds below engaged all her attention. But when I let out a yell, which I could not stifle, she jerked spasmodically to face me. Then I froze again. What a tigerish yellow flash of eyes and fangs! She hissed. She could have sprung from the tree to the rim and upon me in two bounds. But she leaped to a ledge below the rim, glided along that, and disappeared.

I ran ahead and with haste and violence clambered out upon a jutting point of the rim, from which I could command the situation. Jones and the others were riding and yelling back where I had left my horse. I called for them to come.

The hounds were baying along the base of the low cliff. No doubt they had seen the lioness leap out of the tree. My eyes roved everywhere. This cove was a shallow V-shaped gorge, a few hundred yards deep and as many across. Its slopes were steep, with patches of brush and rock.

All at once my quick eye caught a glimpse of something moving up the opposite slope. It was a long red pantherish shape. The lioness! I yelled with all my might. She ran up the slope and at the base of the low wall she turned to the right. At that moment Jones strode heavily over the rough loose rocks of the promontory toward me.

"Where's the cat?" he boomed, his gray eyes flashing. In a moment more I had pointed her out. "Ha! I see. . . . Don't like that place. The canyon boxes. She can't get out. She'll turn back."

The old hunter had been quick to grasp what had escaped me. The lioness could not find any break in the wall, and manifestly she would not go down into the gorge. She wheeled back along the base of this yellow cliff. There appeared to be a strip of bare clay or shale rock against which background her red shape stood out clearly. She glided along, slowing her pace, and she turned her gaze across the gorge.

Then Don's deep bay rang out from the slope to our left. He had struck the trail of the lioness. I saw him running down. He leaped in long bounds. The other hounds heard him and broke for the brushy slope. In a moment they had struck the scent of their quarry and given tongue.

As they started down Don burst out of the willow thicket at the bottom of the gorge and bounded up the opposite slope. He was five hundred yards ahead of the pack. He was swiftly climbing. He would run into the lioness.

Jones gripped my arm in his powerful hand.

"Look!" he shouted. "Look at that fool hound! . . . Runnin' up-hill to get to that lioness. She won't run. She's cornered. She'll meet him. She'll kill him. . . . Shoot her! Shoot her!"

I scarcely needed Jones's command to stir me to save Don, but it was certain that the old plainsman's piercing voice made me tremble. I knelt and leveled my rifle. The lioness showed red against the gray—a fine target. She was gliding more and more slowly. She saw or heard Don. The gunsight wavered. I could not hold steady. But I had to hurry. My first bullet struck two yards below the beast, puffing the dust. She kept on. My second bullet hit behind her. Jones was yelling in my ear. I could see Don out of the tail of my eye. . . . Again I shot. Too high! But the lioness jumped and halted. She lashed with her tail. What a wild picture! I strained —clamped every muscle, and pulled trigger. My bullet struck right under the lioness, scattering a great puff of dust and gravel in her face. She bounded ahead a few yards and up into a cedar tree. An instant later Don flashed over the bare spot where she had waited to kill him, and in another his deep bay rang out under the cedar.

"Treed, by gosh!" yelled Jones, joyfully pounding me on the back with his huge fist. "You saved that fool dog's life. She'd have killed him shore. . . . Wal, the pack will be there pronto, an' all we've got to do is go over an' tie her up. But it was a close shave for Don."

That night in camp Don was not in the least different from his usual somber self. He took no note of my proud proprietorship or my hovering near him while he ate the supper I provided, part of which came from my own plate. My interest and sympathy had augmented to love.

Don's attitude toward the captured and chained lions never ceased to be a source of delight and wonder to me. All the other hounds were upset by the presence of the big cats. Moze, Sounder, Tiger, Ranger would have fought these collared lions. Not so Don! For him they had ceased to exist. He would walk within ten feet of a hissing lioness without the slightest sign of having seen or heard her. He never joined in the howling chorus of the dogs. He would go to sleep close to where the lions clanked their chains, clawed the trees, whined and spat and squalled.

Several days after that incident of the red lioness we had a long and severe chase through the brushy cedar forest on the left wing of the Plateau. I did well to keep the hounds within earshot. When I arrived at the end of that run I was torn and blackened by the brush, wet with sweat, and hot as fire. Jones, lasso in hand, was walking round a large cedar tree under which the pack of hounds was clamoring. Jim and Emmet were seated on a stone, wiping their red faces.

"Wal, I'll rope him before he rests up," declared Jones.

"Wait till—I get—my breath," panted Emmet.

"We shore oozed along this mawnin'," drawled Jim.

Dismounting, I untied my camera from the saddle and then began to peer up into the bushy cedar.

"It's a Tom lion," declared Jones. "Not very big, but he looks mean. I reckon he'll mess us up some."

"Haw! Haw!" shouted Jim, sarcastically. The old plainsman's imperturbability sometimes wore on our nerves.

I climbed a cedar next to the one in which the lion had taken refuge. From a topmost fork, swaying to and fro, I stood up to photograph our quarry. He was a good-sized animal, tawny in hue, rather gray of face, and a fierce-looking brute. As the distance between us was not far, my situation was as uncomfortable as thrilling. He snarled at me and spat viciously. I was about to abandon my swinging limb when the lion turned away from me to peer down through the branches.

Jones was climbing into the cedar. Low and deep the lion growled. Jones held in one hand a long pole with a small fork at the end, upon which hung the noose of his lasso. Presently he got far enough up to reach the lion. Usually he climbed close enough to throw the rope, but evidently he regarded this beast as dangerous. He tried to slip the noose over the head of the lion. One sweep of a big paw sent pole and noose flying. Patiently Jones made ready and tried again, with similar result. Many times he tried. His patience and perseverance seemed incredible. One attribute of his great power to capture and train wild animals here asserted itself. Finally the lion grew careless or tired, on which instant Jones slipped the noose over its head.

Drawing the lasso tight, he threw his end over a thick branch and let it trail down to the men below. "Wait now!" he yelled and quickly backed down out of the cedar. The hounds were leaping eagerly.

"Pull him off that fork an' let him down easy so I can rope one of his paws."

It turned out, however, that the lion was hard to dislodge. I could see his muscles ridge and bulge. Dead branches cracked, the tree top waved. Jones began to roar in anger. The men replied with strained hoarse voices. I saw the lion drop from his perch and, clawing the branches, springing convulsively, he disappeared from my sight.

Then followed a crash. The branch over which Jones was lowering the beast had broken. Wild yells greeted my startled ears and a perfect din of yelps and howls. Pandemonium had broken loose down there. I fell more than I descended from that tree.

As I bounded erect I espied the men scrambling out of the way of a huge furry wheel. Ten hounds and one lion comprised that brown whirling ball. Suddenly out of it a dog came hurtling. He rolled to my feet, staggered up.

It was Don. Blood was streaming from him. Swiftly I dragged him aside, out of harm's way. And I forgot the fight. My hands came away from Don wet and dripping with hot blood. It shocked me. Then I saw that his throat had been terribly torn. I thought his jugular vein had been severed. Don lay down and stretched out. He looked at me with those great somber eyes. Never would I forget! He was going to die right there before my eyes.

"Oh, Don! Don! What can I do?" I cried in horror.

As I sank beside Don one of my hands came in contact with snow. It had snowed that morning and there were still white patches in shady places. Like a flash I ripped off my scarf and bound it round Don's neck. Then I scraped up a double handful of snow and placed that in my bandana handkerchief. This also I bound tightly round his neck. I could do no more. My hope left me then, and I had not the courage to sit there beside him until he died.

All the while I had been aware of a bedlam near at hand. When I looked I saw a spectacle for a hunter. Jones, yelling at the top of his stentorian voice, seized one hound after the other by the hind legs and, jerking him from the lion, threw him down the steep slope. Jim and Emmet were trying to help while at the same time they avoided close quarters with that threshing beast. At last they got the dogs off and the lion stretched out. Jones got up, shaking his shaggy head. Then he espied me and his hard face took on a look of alarm.

"Hyar—you're all—bloody," he panted plaintively, as if I had been exceedingly remiss.

Whereupon I told him briefly about Don. Then Jim and Emmet

approached and we all stood looking down on the quiet dog and the patch of bloody snow.

"Wal, I reckon he's a goner," said Jones, breathing hard. "Shore I knew he'd get his everlastin'."

"Looks powerful like the lion has aboot got his, too," added Jim.

Emmet knelt by Don and examined the bandage round his neck. "Bleeding yet," he muttered, thoughtfully. "You did all that was possible. Too bad! . . . The kindest thing we can do is to leave him here."

I did not question this, but I hated to consent. Still, to move him would only bring on more hemorrhage and to put him out of his agony would have been impossible for me. Moreover, while there was life there was hope! Scraping up a goodly ball of snow, I rolled it close to Don so that he could lick it if he chose. Then I turned aside and could not look again. But I knew that tomorrow or the following day I would find my way back to this wild spot.

The accident to Don and what seemed the inevitable issue weighed heavily upon my mind. Don's eyes haunted me. I very much feared that the hunt had reached an unhappy ending for me. Next day the weather was threatening and, as the hounds were pretty tired, we rested in camp, devoting ourselves to needful tasks. A hundred times I thought of Don, alone out there in the wild brakes. Perhaps merciful death had relieved him of suffering. I would surely find out on the morrow.

But the indefatigable Jones desired to hunt in another direction next day and, as I was by no means sure I could find the place where Don had been left, I had to defer that trip. We had a thrilling, hazardous, luckless chase, and I for one gave up before it ended.

Weary and dejected, I rode back. I could not get Don off my conscience. The pleasant woodland camp did not seem the same place. For the first time the hissing, spitting, chain-clinking, tail-lashing lions caused me irritation and resentment. I would have none of them. What was the capture of a lot of spiteful, vicious cats to the life of a noble dog? Slipping my saddle off, I turned Black Bolly loose.

Then I imagined I saw a beautiful black long-eared hound enter the glade. I rubbed my eyes. Indeed there was a dog coming.

Don! I shouted my joy and awe. Running like a boy, I knelt by him, saying I knew not what. Don wagged his tail! He licked my hand! These actions seemed as marvelous as his return. He looked sick and weak, but he was all right. The handkerchief was gone from his neck but the scarf remained, and it was stuck tight where his throat had been lacerated.

Later Emmet examined Don and said we had made a mistake about the jugular vein being severed. Don's injury had been serious, however, and without the prompt aid I had so fortunately given he would soon have bled to death. Jones shook his gray old locks and said: "Reckon Don's time hadn't come. Hope that will teach him sense." In a couple of days Don had recovered and on the next he was back leading the pack.

A subtle change had come over Don in his relation to me. I did not grasp it so clearly then. Thought and memory afterward brought the realization to me. But there was a light in his eyes for me which had never been there before.

One day Jones and I treed three lions. The larger leaped and ran down into the canyon. The hounds followed. Jones strode after them, leaving me alone with nothing but a camera to keep those two lions up that tree. I had left horse and gun far up the slope. I protested; I yelled after him, "What'll I do if they start down?"

He turned to gaze up at me. His grim face flashed in the sunlight.

"Grab a club an' chase them back," he replied.

Then I was left alone with two ferocious-looking lions in a piñon tree scarcely thirty feet high. While they heard the baying of the hounds they paid no attention to me, but after that ceased they got ugly. Then I hid behind a bush and barked like a dog. It worked beautifully. The lions grew quiet. I barked and yelped and bayed until I lost my voice. Then they got ugly again! They started down. With stones and clubs I kept them up there, while all the time I was wearing to collapse. When at last I was about to give up in terror and despair I heard Don's bay, faint and far away. The lions had heard it before I had. How they strained! I could see the beating of their hearts through their lean sides. My own heart leaped. Don's bay floated up, wild and mournful. He was coming. Jones had put him on the back trail of the lion that had leaped from the tree.

Deeper and clearer came the bays. How strange that Don should

vary from his habit of seldom baying! There was something un-
canny in this change. Soon I saw him far down the rocky slope.
He was climbing fast. It seemed I had long to wait, yet my fear
left me. On and up he came, ringing out that wild bay. It must
have curdled the blood of those palpitating lions. It seemed the
herald of that bawling pack of hounds.

Don espied me before he reached the piñon in which were the
lions. He bounded right past it and up to me with the wildest demeanor. He leaped up and placed his forepaws on my breast. And
as I leaned down, excited and amazed, he licked my face. Then he
whirled back to the tree, where he stood up and fiercely bayed the
lions. While I sank down to rest, overcome, the familiar baying
chorus of the hounds floated up from below. As usual they were
far behind the fleet Don, but they were coming.

Another day I found myself alone on the edge of a huge cove
that opened down into the main canyon. We were always getting
lost from one another. And so were the hounds. There were so
many lion trails that the pack would split, some going one way,
some another, until it appeared each dog finally had a lion to himself.

It was a glorious day. From far below, faint and soft, came the
strange roar of the Rio Colorado. I could see it winding, somber
and red, through the sinister chasm. Adventure ceased to exist
for me. I was gripped by the grandeur and loveliness, the desolation and loneliness, of the supreme spectacle of nature.

Then as I sat there, absorbed and chained, the spell of enchantment was broken by Don. He had come to me. His mouth was
covered with froth. I knew what that meant. Rising, I got my canteen from the saddle and poured water into the crown of my
sombrero. Don lapped it. As he drank so thirstily I espied a bloody
scratch on his nose.

"Aha! A lion has bated you one, this very morning," I cried.
"Don—I fear for you."

He rested while I once more was lost in contemplation of the
glory of the canyon. What significant hours these on the lonely
heights! But then I only saw and felt.

Presently I mounted my horse and headed for camp, with Don
trotting behind. When we reached the notch of the cove the hound
let out his deep bay and bounded down a break in the low wall. I
dismounted and called. Only another deep bay answered me. Don

had scented a lion or crossed one's trail. Suddenly several sharp deep yelps came from below, a crashing of brush, a rattling of stones. Don had jumped another lion.

Quickly I threw off sombrero and coat and chaps. I retained my left glove. Then, with camera over my shoulder and revolver in my belt, I plunged down the break in the crag. My boots were heavy soled and studded with hobnails. The weeks on these rocky slopes had trained me to fleetness and surefootedness. I plunged down the sliding slant of weathered stone, crashed through the brush, dodged under the cedars, leaped from boulder to ledge and down from ledge to bench. Reaching a dry stream bed, I espied in the sand the tracks of a big lion, and beside them smaller tracks that were Don's. And as I ran I yelled at the top of my lungs, hoping to help Don tree the lion. What I was afraid of was that the beast might wait for Don and kill him.

Such strenuous exertion required a moment's rest now and then, during which I listened for Don. Twice I heard his bay, and the last one sounded as if he had treed the lion. Again I took to my plunging, jumping, sliding descent; and I was not long in reaching the bottom of that gorge. Ear and eye had guided me unerringly, for I came to an open place near the main jump-off into the canyon, and here I saw a tawny shape in a cedar tree. It belonged to a big Tom lion. He swayed the branch and leaped to a ledge, and from that down to another, and then vanished round a corner of wall.

Don could not follow those high steps. Neither could I. We worked along the ledge, under cedars, and over huge slabs of rock toward the corner where our quarry had disappeared. We were close to the great abyss. I could almost feel it. Then the glaring light of a void struck my eyes like some tangible thing.

At last I worked out from the shade of rocks and trees and, turning the abrupt jut of wall, I found a few feet of stone ledge between me and the appalling chasm. How blue, how fathomless! Despite my pursuit of a lion I was suddenly shocked into awe and fear.

Then Don returned to me. The hair on his neck was bristling. He had come from the right, from round the corner of wall where the ledge ran, and where surely the lion had gone. My blood was up and I meant to track that beast to his lair, photograph him if possible, and kill him. So I strode on to the ledge and round the point of wall. Soon I espied huge cat tracks in the dust, close to the base. A well-defined lion trail showed there. And ahead I saw the ledge—widening somewhat and far from level—stretch before me to another corner.

Don acted queerly. He followed me, close at my heels. He whined. He growled. I did not stop to think then what he wanted to do. But it must have been that he wanted to go back. The heat of youth and the wildness of adventure had gripped me and fear and caution were not in me.

Nevertheless, my sensibilities were remarkably acute. When Don got in front of me there was something that compelled me to go slowly. Soon, in any event, I should have been forced to that. The ledge narrowed. Then it widened again to a large bench with cavernous walls overhanging it. I passed this safe zone to turn on to a narrowing edge of rock that disappeared round another corner. When I came to this point I must have been possessed, for I flattened myself against the wall and worked round it.

Again the way appeared easier. But what made Don go so cautiously? I heard his growls; still, no longer did I look at him. I felt this pursuit was nearing an end. At the next turn I halted short, suddenly quivering. The ledge ended—and there lay the lion, licking a bloody paw.

Tumultuous indeed were my emotions, yet on that instant I did not seem conscious of fear. Jones had told me never, in close quarters, to take my eyes off a lion. I forgot. In the wild excitement of a chance for an incomparable picture I forgot. A few precious seconds were wasted over the attempt to focus my camera.

Then I heard quick thuds. Don growled. With a start I jerked up to see the lion had leaped or run half the distance. He was coming. His eyes blazed purple fire. They seemed to paralyze me, yet I began to back along the ledge. Whipping out my revolver I tried to aim. But my nerves had undergone such a shock that I could not aim. The gun wobbled. I dared not risk shooting. If I wounded the lion it was certain he would knock me off that narrow ledge.

So I kept on backing, step by step. Don did likewise. He stayed between me and the lion. Therein lay the greatness of that hound. How easily he could have dodged by me to escape the ledge! But he did not do it.

A precious opportunity presented when I reached the widest

part of the bench. Here I had a chance and I recognized it. Then, when the overhanging wall bumped my shoulder, I realized too late. I had come to the narrowing part of the ledge. Not reason but fright kept me from turning to run. Perhaps that might have been the best way out of the predicament. I backed along the strip of stone that was only a foot wide. A few more blind steps meant death. My nerve was gone. Collapse seemed inevitable. I had a camera in one hand and a revolver in the other.

That purple-eyed beast did not halt. My distorted imagination gave him a thousand shapes and actions. Bitter despairing thoughts flashed through my mind. Jones had said mountain lions were cowards, but not when cornered—never when there was no avenue of escape!

Then Don's haunches backed into my knees. I dared not look down, but I felt the hound against me. He was shaking, yet he snarled fiercely. The feel of Don there, the sense of his courage, caused my cold thick blood to burst into hot gushes. In another second he would be pawed off the ledge or he would grapple with this hissing lion. That meant destruction for both, for they would roll off the ledge.

I had to save Don. That mounting thought was my salvation. Physically, he could not have saved me or himself, but this grand spirit somehow pierced to my manhood.

Leaning against the wall, I lifted the revolver and steadied my arm with my left hand, which still held the camera. I aimed between the purple eyes. That second was an eternity. The gun crashed. The blaze of one of those terrible eyes went out.

Up leaped the lion, beating the wall with heavy thudding paws. Then he seemed to propel himself outward, off the ledge into space —a tawny spread figure that careened majestically over and over, down—down—down to vanish in the blue depths.

Don whined. I stared at the abyss, slowly becoming unlocked from the grip of terror. I staggered a few steps forward to a wider part of the ledge and there I sank down, unable to stand longer. Don crept to me, put his head in my lap.

I listened. I strained my ears. How endlessly long seemed that lion in falling! But all was magnified. At last puffed up a sliding roar, swelling and dying until again the terrific silence of the canyon enfolded me.

Presently Don sat up and gazed into the depths. How strange

to see him peer down! Then he turned his sleek dark head to look at me. What did I see through the somber sadness of his eyes? He whined and licked my hand. It seemed to me Don and I were more than man and dog. He moved away then round the narrow ledge, and I had to summon energy to follow. Shudderingly I turned my back on that awful chasm and held my breath while I slipped round the perilous place. Don waited there for me, then trotted on. Not until I had gotten safely off that ledge did I draw a full breath. Then I toiled up the steep rough slope to the rim. Don was waiting beside my horse. Between us we drank the rest of the water in my canteen, and when we reached camp night had fallen. A bright fire and a good supper broke the gloom of my mind. My story held those rugged Westerners spellbound. Don stayed close to me, followed me of his own accord, and slept beside me in my tent.

There came a frosty morning when the sun rose red over the ramparts of colored rock. We had a lion running before the misty shadows dispersed from the canyon depths.

The hounds chased him through the sage and cedar into the wild brakes of the north wing of the Plateau. This lion must have been a mean old Tom, for he did not soon go down the slopes.

The particular section he at last took refuge in was impassable for man. The hounds gave him a grueling chase, then one by one they crawled up, sore and thirsty. All but Don! He did not come. Jones rolled out his mighty voice, which pealed back in mocking hollow echoes. Don did not come. At noonday Jones and the men left for camp with the hounds.

I remained. I had a vigil there on the lofty rim, along where I could peer down the yellow-green slope and beyond to the sinister depths. It was a still day. The silence was overpowering. When Don's haunting bay floated up it shocked me. At long intervals I heard it, fainter and fainter. Then no more!

Still I waited and watched and listened. Afternoon waned. My horse neighed piercingly from the cedars. The sinking sun began to fire the Pink Cliffs of Utah, and then the hundred miles of immense chasm over which my charmed gaze held dominion. How lonely, how terrifying that stupendous rent in the earth! Lion and hound had no fear. But the thinking, feeling man was afraid. What did they mean—this exquisitely hued and monstrous canyon—the setting sun—the wildness of a lion, the grand spirit of a dog—and the wondering sadness of a man?

I rode home without Don. Half the night I lay awake waiting, hoping. But he did not return by dawn, nor through the day. He never came back.

GEORGE PATTULLO

CORAZON

Anyone who has had experience in "breaking" a horse, or who has watched the process, will appreciate this exciting but precise account by George Pattullo. A "buster" must be, as Mullins was, a man of courage and delicate skill, for he must master the wild pony of the plains without killing its spirit.

WITH manes streaming in the wind, a band of bronchos fled across the grama flats, splashed through the San Pedro, and whirled sharply to the right, heading for sanctuary in the Dragoons. In the lead raced a big sorrel, his coat shimmering like polished gold where the sun touched it.

"That's Corazon," exclaimed Reb. "Head him or we'll lose the bunch."

The pursuers spread out and swept round in a wide semi-circle. Corazon held to his course, a dozen yards in advance of the others, his head high. The chase slackened, died away. With a blaring neigh, the sorrel eased his furious pace and the entire band came to a trot. Before them were the mountains, and Corazon knew their fastnesses as the street urchin knows the alleys that give him refuge; in the cañons the bronchos would be safe from man. Behind was no sign of the enemy. His nose in the wind, he sniffed long, but it bore him no taint. Instead, he nickered with delight, for he smelled water. They swung to the south, and in less than five minutes their hot muzzles were washed by the bubbling waters of Eternity Spring.

Corazon drew in a long breath, expanding his well-ribbed sides, and looked up from drinking. There in front of him, fifty paces away, was a horseman. He snorted the alarm and they plunged into a tangle of sagebrush. Another rider bore down and turned them back. To right and left they darted, then wheeled and sought desperately to break through the cordon at a weak spot, and failed. Wherever they turned, a cowboy appeared as by magic. At last Corazon detected an unguarded area and flew through it with the speed of light.

"Now we've got 'em," howled Reb. "Don't drive too close, but keep 'em headed for the corral."

Within a hundred yards of the gate, the sorrel halted, his ears cocked in doubt. The cowboys closed in to force the band through. Three times the bronchos broke and scattered, for to their wild instincts the fences and that narrow aperture cried treachery and danger. They were gathered, with whoops and many imprecations, and once more approached the entrance.

"Drive the saddle bunch out," commanded the range boss.

Forth came the remunda of a hundred horses. The bronchos shrilled greeting and mingled with them, and when the cow ponies trotted meekly into the corral, Corazon and his band went too, though they shook and were afraid.

For five years Corazon had roamed the range—ever since he had discovered that grass was good to eat, and so had left the care of his tender-eyed mother. Because he dreaded the master of created things and fled him afar, only once during that time had he seen man at close quarters. That was when as a youngster, he was caught and branded on the left hip. He had quickly forgotten that; until now it had ceased to be even a memory.

But now he and his companion rovers were prisoners, cooped in a corral by a contemptible trick.

They crowded around and around the stout enclosure, sometimes beneath the boards. And not twenty feet away, the dreaded axis of their circlings, sat a man on a horse, and he studied them calmly. Other men, astride the fence, were uncoiling ropes, and their manner was placid and businesslike. One opined dispassionately that "the sorrel is shore some horse." "You're whistlin'," cried the buster over his shoulder, in hearty affirmation.

Corazon was the most distracted of all the band. He was in a frenzy of nervous heat, his glossy coat wet and foam-flecked. He would not stand still for a second, but prowled about the wooden barrier like a jungle creature newly prisoned in a cage. Twice he nosed the ground and crooked his forelegs in an endeavor to slide through the six inches of clear space beneath the gate, and the outfit laughed derisively.

"Here goes," announced the buster in his expressionless tones. "You-all watch out, now."

At that moment Corazon took it into his head to dash at top speed through his friends, huddled in a bunch in a corner. A rope whined and coiled, and when he burst out of the jam, the noose was around his neck, tightening so as to strangle him. Madly he ran against it, superb in the sureness of his might. Then he squalled with rage and pain and an awful terror. His legs flew from under him, and poor Corazon was jerked three feet into the air, coming down on his side with smashing force. The fall shook a grunt out of him, and he was stunned and breathless, but unhurt. He staggered to his feet, his breath straining like bellows, for the noose cut into his neck and he would not yield to its pressure.

Facing him was the man on the bay. His mount stood with feet braced, sitting back on the rope, and he and his rider were quite collected and cool and prepared. The sorrel's eyes were starting from his head; his nostrils flared wide, gaping from the air that was denied him, and the breath sucked in his throat. It seemed as if he must drop. Suddenly the buster touched his horse lightly with the spur and slackened the rope. With a long sob, Corazon drew in a life-giving draught, his gaze fixed in frightened appeal on his captor. "Open the gate," said Mullins, without raising his voice. He flicked the rope over Corazon's hindquarters, and essayed to drive him into the next corral, to cut him off from his fellows. The sorrel gave a gasp of dismay and lunged forward. Again he was lifted from the ground, and came down with a thud that left him shivering.

"His laig's done bust!" exclaimed the boss. "No; he's shook up, that's all. Wait awhile."

A moment later Corazon raised his head painfully; then, life and courage coming back with a rush, he lurched to his feet. Mullins waited with unabated patience. The sorrel was beginning to respect that which encircled his neck and made naught of his strength, and when the buster flipped the rope again, he ran through the small gate, and brought up before he had reached the end of his tether.

Two of the cowboys stepped down languidly from the fence, and took position in the center of the corral.

"Hi, Corazon! Go it, boy!" they yelled, and spurred by their cries, the horse started off at a trot. Reb tossed his loop,—flung it carelessly, with a sinuous movement of the wrist,—and when Corazon had gone a few yards, he found his forefeet ensnared. Enraged at being thus cramped, he bucked and bawled; but, before Reb could settle on the rope, he came to a standstill and sank his teeth into the strands. Once, twice, thrice he tugged, but could make no impression. Then he pitched high in the air, and——

"*Now!*" shrieked Reb.

They heaved with might and main, and Corazon flopped in the dust. Quick as a cat, he sprang upright and bolted; but again they downed him, and while Reb held the head by straddling the neck, his confederate twined dexterously with a stake-rope. There lay Corazon, helpless and almost spent, trussed up like a sheep for market: they had hog-tied him.

It was the buster who put the hackamore on his head. Very deliberately he moved. Corazon sensed confidence in the touch of his fingers; they spoke a language to him, and he was soothed by the sureness of superiority they conveyed. He lay quiet. Then Reb incautiously shifted his position, and the horse heaved and raised his head, banging Mullins across the ear. The buster's senses swam, but instead of flying into a rage, he became quieter, more deliberate; in his cold eyes was a vengeful gleam, and dangerous stealth lurked in his delicate manipulation of the strands. An excruciating pain shot through the sorrel's eye: Mullins had gouged him.

"Let him up." It was the buster again, atop the bay, making the rope fast with a double half-hitch over the horn of the saddle.

Corazon arose, dazed and very sick. But his spirit was unbreakable. Again and again he strove to tear loose, rearing, falling back, plunging to the end of the rope until he was hurled off his legs to the ground. When he began to weary, Mullins encouraged him to fight, that he might toss him.

"I'll learn you what this rope means," he remarked, as the broncho scattered the dust for the ninth time, and remained there, completely done up.

In deadly fear of his slender tether, yet alert to match his strength against it once more, should opportunity offer, Corazon followed the buster quietly enough when he rode out into the open. Beside a sturdy mesquite bush that grew apart from its brethren, Mullins dismounted and tied the sorrel. As a farewell he waved his arms and whooped. Of course Corazon gathered himself and leaped—leaped to the utmost that was in him, so that the bush vibrated to its farthest root; and of course he hit the earth with a jarring thump that temporarily paralyzed him. Mullins departed to put the thrall of human will on others.

Throughout the afternoon, and time after time during the interminable night, the sorrel tried to break away, but with each sickening failure he grew more cautious. When he ran against the rope now, he did not run blindly to its limit, but half wheeled, so that when it jerked him back he invariably landed on his feet. Corazon was learning hard, but he was learning. And what agonies of pain and suspense he went through!—for years a free rover, and now to be bound thus, by what looked to be a mere thread, for he knew not what further tortures! He sweated and shivered, seeing peril in every shadow. When a coyote slunk by with tongue lapping hungrily over his teeth, the prisoner almost broke his neck in a despairing struggle to win freedom.

In the chill of the dawn they led him into a circular corral. His sleekness had departed; the barrel-like body did not look so well nourished, and there was red in the blazing eyes.

"I reckon he'll be mean," observed the buster, as though it concerned him but little.

"N-o-o-o. Go easy with him, Carl, and I think he'll make a good hoss," the boss cautioned.

While two men held the rope, Mullins advanced along it foot by foot, inch by inch, one hand outstretched, and talked to Corazon in a low, careless tone of affectionate banter. "So you'd like for to kill me, would you?" he inquired, grinning. All the while he held the sorrel's gaze.

Corazon stood still, legs planted wide apart, and permitted him to approach. He trembled when the fingers touched his nose; but they were firm, confident digits, the voice was reassuring, and the gentle rubbing up, up between the eyes and ears lulled his forebodings.

"Hand me the blanket," said Mullins.

He drew it softly over Corazon's back, and the broncho swerved, pawed, and kicked with beautiful precision. Whereupon they placed a rope around his neck, dropped it behind his right hind leg, then pulled that member up close to his belly; there it was held fast. On three legs now, the sorrel was impotent for harm. Mullins once more took up the blanket, but this time the gentleness had flown. He slapped it over Corazon's backbone from side to side a dozen times. At each impact the horse humped awkwardly, but, finding that he came to no hurt, he suffered it in resignation.

That much of the second lesson learned they saddled him. Strangely enough, Corazon submitted to the operation without fuss, the only untoward symptoms being a decided upward slant to the back of the saddle and the tucking of his tail. Reb waggled his head over this exhibition.

"I don't like his standing quiet that a-way; it ain't natural," he vouchsafed. "Look at the crick in his back. Jim-in-ee! he'll shore pitch."

Which he did. The cinches were tightened until Corazon's eyes almost popped from his head; then they released the bound leg and turned him loose. What was that galling his spine? Corazon took a startled peep at it, lowered his head between his knees, and began to bawl. Into the air he rocketed, his head and forelegs swinging to the left, his hindquarters weaving to the right. The jar of his contact with the ground was appalling. Into the air again, his head and forelegs to the right, his rump twisted to the left. Round and round the corral he went, bleating like an angry calf; but the thing on his back stayed where it was, gripping his body cruelly. At last he was fain to stop for breath.

"Now," said Mullins, "I reckon I'll take it out of him."

There has always been for me an overwhelming fascination in watching busters at work. They have underlying traits in common when it comes to handling the horses—the garrulous one becomes boldly watchful, the Stoic moves with stern patience, the boaster soothes with soft-crooned words and confident caress. Mullins left Corazon standing in the middle of the corral, the hackamore rope loose on the ground, while he saw to it that his spurs were fast. We mounted the fence, not wishing to be mixed in the glorious turmoil to follow.

"I wouldn't top ol' Corazon for fifty," confessed the man on the adjoining post.

"Mullins has certainly got nerve," I conceded.

"A buster has got to have nerve." The range boss delivered himself laconically. "All nerve and no brains makes the best. But they get stove up and then——"

"And then? What then?"

"Why, don't you know," he asked in surprise. "Every buster loses his nerve at last, and then they can't ride a pack-hoss. It must be because it's one fool man with one set of nerves up ag'in a new hoss with a new devil in him every time. They wear him down. Don't you reckon?"

The explanation sounded plausible. Mullins was listening with a faintly amused smile to Reb's account of what a lady mule had done to him; he rolled a cigarette and lighted it painstakingly. The hands that held the match were steady as eternal rock. It was maddening to see him stand so coolly while the big sorrel, a dozen feet distant, was a-quake with dread, blowing harshly through his crimson nostrils whenever a cowboy stirred—and each of us knowing that the man was taking his life in his hands. An unlooked-for twist, a trifling disturbance of poise, and, with a horse like Corazon, it meant maiming or death. At last he drew the cigarette from him and walked slowly to the rope.

"So you're calling for me?" he inquired, gathering it up.

Corazon was snorting. By patient craft Reb acquired a grip on the sorrel's ears, and, while he hung there, bringing the head down so that the horse could not move, Mullins tested the stirrups and raised himself cautiously into the saddle.

"Let him go."

While one could count ten, Corazon stood expectant, his back bowed, his tail between his legs. The ears were laid flat on the head and the forefeet well advanced. The buster waited, the quirt hanging from two fingers of his right hand. Suddenly the sorrel ducked his head and emitted a harsh scream, leaping, with legs stiff, straight off the ground. He came down with the massive hips at an angle to the shoulders, thereby imparting a double shock; bounded high again, turned back with bewildering speed as he touched the earth; and then, in a circle perhaps twenty feet in diameter, sprang time after time, his heels lashing the air. Never had such pitching been seen on the Anvil Range.

"I swan, he just misses his tail a' inch when he turns back!" roared a puncher.

Mullins sat composedly in the saddle, but he was riding as never before. He whipped the sorrel at every jump and raked him down the body from shoulder to loins with the ripping spurs. The brute gave no sign of letting up. Through Mullins' tan of copper hue showed a slight pallor. He was exhausted. If Corazon did not give in soon, the man would be beaten. Just then the horse stopped, feet a-sprawl.

"Mullins,"—the range boss got down from the fence,—"you'll kill that hoss. Between the cinches belongs to you; the head and hindquarters is the company's."

For a long minute Mullins stared at the beast's ears without replying.

"I reckon that's the rule," he acquiesced heavily. "Do you want that somebody else should ride him?"

"No-o-o. Go ahead. But, remember, between the cinches you go at him as you like—nowhere else."

The buster slapped the quirt down on Corazon's shoulder, but the broncho did not budge; then harder. With the first oath he had used, he jabbed in the spurs and lay back on the hackamore rope. Instead of bucking, Corazon reared straight up, his feet pawing like the hands of a drowning man. Before Mullins could move to step off, the sorrel slung his head round and toppled backward.

"No, he's not dead." The range boss leaned over the buster and his hands fumbled inside the shirt. "The horn got him here, but he ain't dead. Claude, saddle Streak and hit for Aqua Prieta for the doctor."

When we had carried the injured man to the bunk-house, Reb spoke from troubled meditation:

"Pete, I don't believe Corazon is as bad as he acts with Mullins, he didn't——"

"You take him, then; he's yours," snapped the boss, his conscience pricking because of the reproof he had administered. If the buster had ridden him his own way, this might not have happened.

That is how the sorrel came into Reb's possession. Only one man of the outfit witnessed the taming, and he would not talk;

but when Reb came to dinner from the first saddle on Corazon, his hands were torn and the nail of one finger hung loose.

"I had to take to the horn and hang on some," he admitted.

Ay, he had clung there desperately while the broncho pitched about the river-bed, whither Reb had retired for safety and to escape spectators. But at the next saddle Corazon was less violent; at the third, recovering from the stunning shocks and bruisings of the first day, he was a fiend; and then, on the following morning, he did not pitch at all. Reb rode him every day to sap the superfluous vigor in Corazon's iron frame and he taught him as well as he could the first duties of a cow-horse. Finding that his new master never punished him unless he undertook to dispute his authority, the sorrel grew tractable and began to take an interest in his tasks.

"He's done broke," announced Reb; "I'll have him bridle-wise in a week. He'll make some roping horse. Did you see him this evening? I swan——"

They scoffed good-naturedly; but Reb proceeded on the assumption that Corazon was meant to be a roping horse, and schooled him accordingly. As for the sorrel, he took to the new pastime with delight. Within a month nothing gave him keener joy than to swerve and crouch at the climax of the sprint and see a cow thrown heels over head at the end of the rope that was wrapped about his saddle-horn.

The necessity of contriving to get three meals a day took me elsewhere, and I did not see Corazon for three years. Then, one Sunday afternoon, Big John drew me from El Paso to Juárez on the pretense of seeing a grand and extraordinary, a most noble bullfight, in which the dauntless Favorita would slay three fierce bulls from the renowned El Carmen ranch, in "competency" with the fearless Morenito Chico de San Bernardo; and a youth with a megaphone drew us both to a steer-roping contest instead. We agreed that bull-fighting was brutal on the Sabbath.

"I'll bet it's rotten," remarked Big John pessimistically, as we took our seats. "I could beat 'em myself."

As he scanned the list, his face brightened. Among the seventeen ropers thereon were two champions and a possible new one in Raphael Fraustro, the redoubtable vaquero from the domain of Terranzas.

"And here's Reb!" roared John—he is accustomed to converse in the tumult of the branding-pen—"I swan, he's entered from Monument."

Shortly afterwards the contestants paraded, wonderfully arrayed in silk shirts and new handkerchiefs.

"Some of them ain't been clean before in a year," was John's caustic comment. "There's Slim; I *know* he hasn't."

They were a fine-looking body of men, and two of my neighbors complained that I trampled on their feet. The horses caught the infection of excitement from the packed stands and champed on their bits and caracoled and waltzed sideways in a manner highly unbecoming a staid cow-pony.

There was one that did not. So sluggish was his gait and general bearing, in contrast to the others, that the crowd burst into laughter. He plodded at the tail-end of the procession, his hoofs kicking up the dust in listless spurts, his nose on a level with his knees. I rubbed my eyes and John said, "No, it ain't—it can't be——"; but it was. Into that arena slouched Corazon, entered against the pick of the horses of the Southwest; and Reb was astride him.

We watched the ropers catch and tie the steers in rapid succession, but the much-heralded ones missed altogether, and to John and me the performance lagged. We were waiting for Reb and Corazon.

They came at last, at the end of the list. When Corazon ambled up the arena to enter behind the barrier, the grandstand roared a facetious welcome; the spectacle of this sad-gaited nag preparing to capture a steer touched its risibilities.

"Listen to me," bawled a fat gentleman in a wide-brimmed hat, close to my ear. "You listen to me! They're all fools. That's a cowhorse. No blasted nonsense. Knows his business, huh? You're whistlin'!"

Assuredly, Corazon knew his business. The instant he stepped behind the line he was a changed horse. The flopping ears pricked forward, his neck arched, and the great muscles of his shoulders and thighs rippled to his dainty prancing. He pulled and fretted on the bit, his eyes roving about in search of quarry; he whinnied an appeal to be gone. Reb made ready his coil, curbing him with light pressure.

Out from the chute sprang a steer, heading straight down the arena. Corazon was frantic. With the flash of the gun he breasted the barrier-rope and swept down on him in twenty strides. Reb stood high in the stirrups; the loop whirled and sped; and, without waiting to see how it fell, but accepting a catch in blind faith, the sorrel started off at a tangent.

Big John was standing up in his place, clawing insanely at the hats of his neighbors and banging them on the head with his programme.

"Look at him—just look at him!" he shrieked.

The steer was tossed clear off the ground and came down on his left side. Almost before he landed, Reb was out of the saddle and speeding toward him.

"He's getting up. *He's getting up.* Go to him, Reb!" howled John and I.

The steer managed to lift his head; he was struggling to his knees. I looked away, for Reb must lose. Then a hoarse shout from the multitude turned back my gaze. Corazon had felt the slack on the rope and knew what it meant. He dug his feet into the dirt and began to walk slowly forward—very slowly and carefully, for Reb's task must not be spoiled. The steer collapsed, falling prone again but the sorrel did not stop. Once he cocked his eye, and seeing that the animal still squirmed, pulled with all his strength. The stands were rocking; they were a sea of tossing hats and gesticulating arms and flushed faces; the roar of their plaudits echoed back from the hills. And it was all for Corazon, gallant Corazon.

Reb stooped beside the steer, his hands looping and tying with deft darting twists even as he kept pace with his dragged victim.

Then he sprang clear and tossed his hands upward, facing the judges' stand. After that he walked aimlessly about, mopping his face with a handkerchief; for to him the shoutings and the shifting colors were all a foolish dream, and he was rather sick.

Right on the cry with which his master announced his task done, Corazon eased up on the rope and waited.

"Mr. Pee-ler's time," bellowed the man with the megaphone presently, "is twenty-one seconds, ty-ing the world's record."

So weak that his knees trembled, Reb walked over to his horse. "Corazon," he said huskily, and slapped him once on the flank.

Nothing would do the joyous crowd then but that Reb should ride forth to be acclaimed the victor. We sat back and yelled ourselves weak with laughter, for Corazon having done his work refused resolutely to squander time in vain parade. The steer captured and tied he had no further interest in the proceedings. The rascal dog-trotted reluctantly to the center of the arena in obedience to Reb, then faced the audience; but all the time Reb was bowing his acknowledgments Corazon sulked and slouched and he was sulking and shuffling the dust when they went through the gate.

"Now," said John, who is very human, "we'll go help Reb spend that money."

As we jostled amid the outgoing crowd, several cowboys came alongside the grandstand rail, and Big John drew me aside to have a speech with them. One rider led a spare horse and when he passed a man on foot, the latter hailed him:

"Say, Ed, give me a lift to the hotel?"

"Sure," answered Ed, proffering the reins.

The man gathered them up, his hands fluttering as if with palsy, and paused with his foot raised toward the stirrup.

"He won't pitch nor nothing, Ed?" came the quavered inquiry. "You're shore he's gentle?"

"Gentler'n a dog," returned Ed, greatly surprised.

"You ain't fooling me, now, are you, Ed?" continued the man on the ground. "He looks kind of mean."

"Give him to me!" Ed exploded. "You kin walk."

From where we stood, only the man's back was visible. "Who is that fellow?" I asked. "Who? Him?" answered my neighbor. "Oh, his name's Mullins. They say he used to be able to ride anything with hair on it, and throw off the bridle at that. I expect that's just talk. Don't you reckon?"

NARRATIVES

FREDERICK R. BECHDOLT

THE FIRST COWBOY

Smoothly written, and swift-moving as the almost incredible game of chance and battle it describes, this narrative of fact reads like fiction. The author is an authority on the Old West. (From *Tales of the Old-Timers*, Appleton-Century, 1924.)

IN THE days when Texas was a nation, when farmer boys along the Trinity and Brazos were carrying rifles to their evening chores for fear of lurking Indians and the men of the Southwestern settlements were constantly under arms against invading Mexicans, a number of young fellows drifted down into the country between the lower Nueces and the Rio Grande. The most of them had lost their fathers at the Alamo and in the massacre of Fannin's men at Goliad. They came hither to seek adventure and to make their livings, two projects which were at that time compatible.

The land was wild; great grass-grown pampas intersected by wide river bottoms where dense thickets of mesquite and cat's-claw grew. Here in former years there had been enormous ranches, but the Mexican owners had migrated beyond the Rio Grande with the unsettled conditions of the Texan revolution; the Indians had burned their homes; nothing remained of that pastoral civilization save a few crumbling adobe walls and the bands of cattle, which had lapsed to wildness like the land. These roved the prairies and browsed in the timber, shy as the antelope which wandered in the hills, lean-bodied, swift as mustangs.

The youths hunted them down. They knew nothing of the reata's uses; such few of them as had seen the rawhide ropes scorned them as they scorned everything Mexican. But all of them were expert horsemen. They made their expeditions during the periods of the full moon. By day and night they chased the wild long-horns across the open plateaus and through the timbered bottoms, relaying their ponies when they got the chance, outwearing the fear-maddened herds until, through sheer exhaustion, the brutes became half tractable. Then they corralled them in stout pens and drove them eastward to the markets.

They dressed in smoke-tanned buckskin, for in this land where there were neither women nor looms a man must get his raiment as he got his meat, with his long-barreled rifle. A few wore boots, but most of them were shod in moccasins. They were among the first in Texas to use the slouching wide-brimmed hat which afterward became universal throughout the cattle country. Some of them had built cabins and dugouts near the streams, but they seldom saw their habitations. Save when the snow was on the ground they spent their days and nights in the open.

It was a period of Indian raids, and Santa Anna's troops were constantly crossing the Rio Grande to make brief forays against the isolated border towns. Scarcely a month went by which did not witness the galloping of horsemen who brought to ranch and village and budding frontier metropolis the call to arms. Every district had its ranger company, commanded by some local veteran, whose members were ready to seize their rifles and sling on their long powder-horns at a moment's notice. The young fellows from the Nueces were well known among the other bands for their iron endurance in the saddle, their faultless marksmanship, the boldness of their fighting.

So it came that they received a name from those with whom they rode pursuing Indians or Mexicans. And the term by which men called them stuck to them through the years. It fell to them quite naturally because of their vocation. They were known as the "Cowboys."

It was the first time that the word was used west of the Mississippi, and always thereafter it retained its peculiar significance; it was handed down by these riders of the later thirties to the booted herders who succeeded them, and so it spread all over the West.

Cameron's Cowboys was the way that most men put it. For as his men stood out among the Texans, the leader whom they had chosen stood out among them.

Ewen Cameron. They say that he was handsome in a fine rugged way. He stood straight as an arrow, and he weighed more than two hundred pounds. Six feet two in his moccasins, dark-haired, with clear gray eyes and heavy brows; you may picture him in his broad-brimmed hat, his buckskin shirt and breeches worn from long riding; his powder-horn slung by his side, and in his belt the bowie-knife which was as invariable in those days as the forty-five single-action revolver was later on. He came from the Highlands of Scotland, and there was a burr in his speech. But what may help you best to see him is the love his men had for him. He had led them so boldly against both Mexicans and Indians that, as they were wont to put it, they would have followed him into the depths of hell.

In 1839, spurred on by the example of the Texans, a considerable proportion of the people in northern Chihuahua formed a government of their own and rebelled against the dictator, Santa Anna. They named their new-born state the Republic of the Rio Grande, and Licentiate Canales, a suave lawyer, was given command of their troops. Some three hundred Texans crossed the river and joined the movement, among them Ewen Cameron and his cowboys. There was good fighting and plenty of it. In time the armies of Santa Anna triumphed. The men from Texas went back to their homes. The leaders of the unsuccessful movement made their peace with the dictator. Which has its significance in this story because, during those days of stress and battle, Canales and Ewen Cameron had quarreled bitterly. The lawyer never forgot it. Time passed. He grew strong in the good graces of Santa Anna. And with the rancor that smoldered in his heart begins the glorious last chapter of the Scotchman's life.

On the afternoon of Sunday, September 25, 1842, Ewen Cameron stood among one thousand Texans before the ruins of the Alamo. The call to arms had brought them here to resist a Mexican incursion: farmer boys from the Trinity, the Colorado, and the Brazos; high officials from the capital at Austin; border rangers from the southwestern counties; lawyers, ministers, schoolteachers, and gamblers from a dozen towns. They wore no uniforms. Long marches, battles, and the hardships of living tentless in the open had left the most of them ragged and weatherstained until it would be hard to tell the settler whose home was a dugout from the statesman who was famous for his oratory. Now, while they were waiting for the event that had brought them together in this spot after weeks of campaigning, a private clapped his captain on the back and called him by his first name; a major paused before a group of his men to beg a chew of tobacco from a tow-haired farm lad. But this spirit of democracy, which was perhaps stronger among the Texans than it has been in any other nation before or since, could not erase certain fundamental distinctions; and as they moved among the throng there was that in the leaders which proclaimed their standing as unmistakably as shoulder-bars. So, if you had been there, you could have picked out Captain John C. Hays, the famous ranger who had led a score of forays against hostile Indians; old Matthew Caldwell, scout and plainsman just back from months in a Mexican prison after last year's ill-fated expedition to Santa Fé; Thomas J. Green, a fiery South Carolinian, a graduate of West Point and a brigadier-general in the war for Texan independence; and Colonel William Fisher who had served with distinction at San Jacinto. Among them all there was none who got more man-to-man respect from his followers than Ewen Cameron; none who looked more like a leader than the tall Scotchman in his smoke-tanned buckskin.

Of the throng that filled the space before the Alamo's shattered walls, his forty cowboys were a distinctive element. Although they had been campaigning out here on the western frontier ever since the previous April, they looked fresher and more fit than the companies that had marched into the town less than a week ago. Of all they were the most impatient for the beginning of this day's business.

The yellow September sunlight was slanting across the square when a man appeared in a gap that had been a chapel window. At once the murmur of voices died away. For a moment he stood there, enframed by the riven walls, and looked down upon the crowd in silence. His form was lean; gray threads were beginning to show in his lank dark hair; his face was slender, and his eyes were piercing black. It was Edward Burleson, vice-president of the Republic of Texas, who had led his regiment to capture Santa Anna's cannon at the battle of San Jacinto. By their votes these fighting men had made him their commander within the past week. He was about to outline a plan of campaign.

His head went back. He began speaking. He was reminding them of what had taken place that summer.

San Antonio lay on the uttermost frontier, sixty miles from the nearest town, with one hundred and eighty miles of wilderness between it and the Rio Grande. In April fourteen hundred of Santa Anna's troops had swooped down upon the place, to retreat across the border when the first ranger companies came hither against them. Within the last month they had returned, to take a dozen of the most prominent citizens prisoners. Three hundred Texans had hurried here and fought them to a standstill just outside the town. The speaker paused; his voice rang as he went on to describe the fate of Captain Dawson's company of fifty, who had found themselves surrounded by odds of ten to one during the battle and had surrendered—to be massacred as soon as they laid down their arms. Then the invaders had fled across the Rio Grande.

These things had taken place. They would, he said, take place again; the towns of western Texas would never be safe from such invasions—until the men of Texas put a stop to it. They could do that; and now the time was come. Let them go to their homes and recruit fresh horses; then in a month return—and he himself would lead them across the Rio Grande where they would put such fear in the hearts of the Mexicans as would keep them within their own borders.

Burleson ceased speaking, and a thousand voices roared applause. He had promised them the thing they wanted. And the next morning the companies began departing from San Antonio to prepare for the coming expedition.

The weeks went by. All through Texas men talked of the projected invasion; recruits blocked the towns; the ranger companies were gathering at San Antonio. But all the time a power greater than opposing armies was at work against them.

The dickerings of nations, which for the sake of euphemism we still call diplomacy, were as potent in those days as they are now. Texas was bankrupt. Only a European loan or annexation to the United States could save her from disintegration. England, on whose friendship a loan depended, was secretly eager that Mexico retake the country north of the Rio Grande. And our administration at Washington demanded that the young republic remain at peace with Santa Anna. Every skirmish helped to jeopardize the hopes for annexation.

President Sam Houston knew these things. He knew also the temper of his people. Disruption would follow his refusal to sanction the expedition. So he acted, and when the companies had gathered in San Antonic they found that Burleson had been virtually forced out of the command. By proclamation of the chief executive, General Alexander Somerville was to lead the expedition.

It was on the morning of November 22 that they marched out from San Antonio on the old Laredo road. There were more than seven hundred men in line. Two hundred pack-animals and three hundred head of cattle followed the column. Even Cameron and his cowboys, who had been chafing at the multitude of recent delays, ceased fretting on that Indian summer morning, for they knew that there were not enough troops in all of northern Mexico to stop them.

The fine weather lasted less than a week. The rains came. General Somerville moved his little army in a manner that was beyond the understanding of men or officers. For nearly three months he marched and countermarched them through boggy river bottoms and over the wild prairies. When Mexican troops were reported in one direction he took another. They used up their meat; their clothing was in tatters. The howling northers cut them to the bone. There was no fighting, and it seemed as if they would never reach the Rio Grande.

Several companies became disgusted and departed for their homes. At last Ewen Cameron got a number of the officers together, and they made so formidable a protest that the commander reluctantly moved the troops to the boundary. But on December 14, when they had been dallying for a week or so along the river's banks, Somerville astonished them all by ordering that they disperse to their homes.

Two hundred of them went back. There remained three hundred. Five days after the departure of their companions they elected William Fisher as their commander and prepared to invade Mexico.

When one remembers that only four years before one hundred and twelve Texans under Captain S. W. Jordan had defeated

two thousand Mexican troops at Saltillo and had retreated all
the way to the Rio Grande with a total loss of five men, the project
does not seem so mad. The whole world boasted no better marksmen than these six tattered companies who were encamped at their
country's border on December 19, 1842. Their long-barreled muz-
zle-loading rifles were the deadliest small arms in modern warfare;
there were those among their number who had killed more than a
score of Mexicans. Moreover, they belonged to a breed which never
did like to turn back.

So they went on. Fisher, their colonel, had fought in this section
during the brief-lived Republic of the Rio Grande. Thomas A.
Murray was his adjutant. Colonel Thomas J. Green, the West
Pointer, was put in command of a flatboat flotilla. The captains
of the companies were Ewen Cameron, William M. Eastland, J.
G. W. Pierson, William N. Ryan, Claudius Buster, and C. K.
Reese. They moved downstream, took the town of Mier without
opposition, and levied on its people for food and clothing.

On the afternoon of Christmas day, while they were waiting for
the arrival of these promised supplies on their own side of the
Rio Grande, they learned that twenty-four hundred Mexican
troops had entered the village. The officers went into council and
unanimously decided to attack the enemy.

Mier lies on the right bank of the Alcantra River, seven miles
or so from the point where it empties into the Rio Grande. The
town has not changed much with the years; you may still see the
same flat-topped adobe buildings whose thick gray-brown walls
gave shelter to the men of Texas on that December day of 1842;
the same narrow streets which literally ran red with the blood of
Santa Anna's soldiers. But through the idiosyncrasies of American historians the glory of that day has been well-nigh forgotten. The name of Mier means nothing when men hear it spoken
now.

It was four o'clock in the afternoon when the officers arrived at
their decision. They left forty-two men to guard their camp,
crossed the Rio Grande, and marched up the Alcantra. At seven
in the evening they halted on the summit of a high bluff just
across the river from the town. It was black dark; a drizzling
rain was falling.

Mexican outposts held the opposite bank. A quarter of a mile
or so beyond, the lights of the first houses glowed faintly through

the dampness. Colonel Green took a dozen riflemen down a narrow
path which wound along the bluff's sheer side to the river, and,
while these held the attention of the pickets, the others felt their
way along the trail; they reached the bank, stole upstream to the
ford, and crossed without discovery.

In the confusion of the advance Joseph Berry had fallen over
the bluff and broken his leg. So nine men were detailed to remain
with him. In the events that were to follow, this little party had
its own large share.

If one believed in such things he would surely be justified in
saying that Fate was busy arranging matters from the very beginning. General Ampudia and General Canales shared the joint
command of the Mexicans. In the days of the Republic of the
Rio Grande Ampudia and Colonel Fisher had become firm friends.
It has been told how Canales hated Ewen Cameron.

That was the situation at midnight when the Texans lined up
on the river bank in the darkness and started toward the town. It
was so black that a man could barely see his hand before his face.
When they had gone a hundred yards or so a dense mass seemed to
emerge from the night before them and a voice called:

"Quién vive?"

Three of the captains answered at the same time, and with the
same sharp order:

"Fire!"

A hundred rifle-flashes cut the darkness. Then they heard the
Mexican colonel who was in command of the outpost calling on
his men to charge. There had been one hundred of those men. Now
there were not a dozen left to obey him.

A few moments later the Texans reached the outskirts of the
town. According to old custom the enemy should be occupying the
plaza. So they felt their way between the adobe buildings toward
the square, and as they were crossing one of the narrow streets at
the end of a block, there came a great flash off to their left; the
night was shaken with the roar of a field-piece. They knew where
the plaza was now.

They halted as they were, half of them on one side of the street
and half on the other. Colonel Green took a dozen riflemen into
the roadway. They fired, and before the artillery company had
reloaded they fell back into the shelter of the buildings. The cannon's flare made the night red again. The Texans leaped into the

street and let go another volley. They kept this up for something like half an hour. In the meantime their companions were entering the houses on both sides of the thoroughfare.

Low structures, some of limestone and some of adobe, they lined the street to the plaza's edge. The captains sent their best marksmen to the windows and roof-tops. They put the others to work at battering down the intervening walls. Thus they went slowly on from one room to another; and as the riflemen established themselves in each new stronghold, the pioneers attacked the next barrier.

The field-piece bellowed in the plaza. The lean and sunburned marksmen lay along the roofs lining their sights when its flashes gave them light, aiming by guesswork in the intervening periods of darkness. Swarthy foot-soldiers swarmed to the building-tops beyond the open square, and the rattle of musketry grew into a long roll. The rifles answered slowly; and when dawn began to creep up over the sky-line, leaking down upon the landscape, the Texans saw the bodies drooping over the low parapets and damming the shallow gutters by the roadway.

The morning dragged on. They gained the last buildings fronting the plaza. While the men in the close rooms sweated at their picks and crowbars to open loopholes, the field-piece battered the thick walls from without. The riflemen leaped to each growing aperture. And now the heaps of corpses grew fast about the cannon. Some time toward noon sixteen Mexicans made a last rush to serve the piece, and when the little spurts of smoke cleared away from window and parapet fifteen of them lay dead. The artillery was silenced for good now.

Noon passed. There came a lull in the fighting. A bugle sounded in a side street; the riflemen atop of the buildings heard the beat of hoofs, the tramp of feet. The Mexicans were gathering for a charge. In the last rooms on both sides of the roadway the dust rose thick, shrouding the forms of the sharp-shooters by the loop-holes. Here one was busy cleaning his rifle; another doled the black-grained powder from the long horn, then tamped the wadding down upon it with his ramrod. Grime stained their faces, and the sulphurous smell of old volleys was heavy on the air. A wounded man was moaning in a corner.

A shout came from the roof-tops. An officer hurried forth to learn what new development had come, and dallied on the parapet,

held by the spectacle that had provoked the cheering. Less than
a half mile away, across the river on the bluff they had occupied
the night before, a stirring drama was being enacted.

The nine men who had been left with Joseph Berry at the beginning of the advance, had taken shelter in a little stone building.
Ten Mexican cavalrymen forded the stream on reconnaissance
and approached the place. The Texans opened fire. Two of the
troopers remained alive when the smoke had cleared away. They
fled back to the town.

Now three hundred horsemen and a field-piece crossed the Alcantra, and while the artillery was taking a roundabout course
toward the summit of the bluff the cavalry deployed. They began
closing in on the stone building. The Texans waited until the
circle had grown narrow. Then they came forth, nine men against
three hundred, and charged straight upon the advancing line.
They fired as they drew near; then broke full speed for the gap
their bullets had made for them. Four of them fell dead. Berry
was slain in the bed where he was lying helpless. Two survived to
reach their companions in the adobe buildings by the plaza. And
three were taken prisoners. The men who were watching the struggle from the housetops never dreamed of the part one of those
captives was unwittingly to play against them within the hour.

Now the bugles sounded again in the hidden streets. Eight hundred Mexicans swept around a corner and, as they advanced into
the plaza, divided into two charging columns. So it fell that Ewen
Cameron and Colonel Fisher found themselves on opposite sides
of the street, each in command of his own detachment, repelling
separate attacks.

Cameron took his cowboys from the building they had been
holding into a yard beside the plaza. A low wall of loose rocks inclosed the place. They dropped on their knees behind it.

Four hundred of Ampudia's picked infantry advanced toward
them at the double-quick. Half-way across the plaza they
slackened their pace; a curtain of smoke unrolled before the front
ranks; musket-balls spattered against the wall and snarled above
the heads of the kneeling Texans. The crash of the volley died
away; the smoke-cloud cleared. They saw a thick mass of blue
and red whose front bristled with leveled bayonets sweeping upon
them.

"Now, boys," said Ewen Cameron, "we will go at it."

They fired at will. Gaps showed in the advancing lines. They wavered briefly; then the gaps closed, and the mass swept on.

"To the stones, boys," Cameron shouted. They tore the loose rocks from the wall and met the charge with such a rain of missiles that the hundreds broke and fled before it. That evening, when there was time for noting such things, men counted a dozen dead who lay with their brains dashed out from the deadly rain. The cowboys were reloading when the rout began. But the column did not rally.

Meantime another force atacked the building on the opposite side of the roadway, and Colonel Fisher took twenty picked men, who hurled themselves upon the Mexicans in a countercharge so savage that the enemy turned and fled.

It was mid-afternoon now. A second lull came in the fighting. The Texans had lost ten killed and twenty-three wounded. The Mexican casualties numbered eight hundred. The cannon was silenced. But Colonel Fisher was lying in his headquarters, racked with nausea. A musket-ball had severed his thumb at the joint and torn a nerve-center. Body and mind and will were limp from agony.

Just at this time the cavalrymen who had made the sortie across the river brought their prisoners before General Ampudia. Dr. Sinnockson, the surgeon of the expedition, was one of the trio. He knew nothing of the battle's progress or where the advantage lay.

"You will take a white flag," General Ampudia instructed him, "and go to Colonel Fisher. Tell him that his old friend Ampudia sends him this message: 'You are outnumbered ten to one, and seventeen hundred fresh troops are on their way to me. These reinforcements are already close to the town. If you fight on, you and all your men will surely be killed. If you surrender I will grant you all proper treatment as prisoners of war. I will give you five minutes for decision.' "

That was the purport of the message. Dr. Sinnockson found Colonel Fisher in the throes of nausea. The other officers were called into conference, and while they stood there, astonished at the demand, the sick man raised himself with great effort.

"I think," he said, "it is our only hope." Then Ewen Cameron cried out that he would die first, and Thomas Green turned around to face the soldiers who stood close by.

"If a hundred of you will go with me, I'll take you back across the Rio Grande," he shouted.

Fisher was on his feet now.

"Let the men be brought to attention," he ordered. And when this had been done he asked them for a vote.

But there was no vote. There was nothing but a great confusion, a medley of upraised voices, oaths of astonishment, shouts of anger.

Then several of the overwearied threw down their rifles. There was, they said, no use in going on. Two or three started off toward the Mexican lines. Cameron's cowboys yelled in derision.

"Go," one called after them, "and rot in chains. You belong there." But Fisher had already sent back word that he would sign a capitulation. And so, by the chain of strange coincidence, in the moment of their victory, these men of Texas became prisoners.

That night Licentiate Canales came to the town church where they lay under guard and saw his old enemy Ewen Cameron among them. The next day the lawyer-general set forth for the City of Mexico to bring the news to Santa Anna. That was his official mission, but he had a private errand with the dictator.

Five days later the prisoners started on the long march to the City of Mexico. General Ampudia and his staff went on ahead with Colonel Fisher, Thomas J. Green, Murray the adjutant, and two or three privates who were to act as servants for the captive officers. Colonel Barragon and two hundred and fifty soldiers followed with the rest. The six captains remained with their companies. So it came about that Ewen Cameron was henceforth the leader of the Texans.

Ewen Cameron was leader. None chose him; there was no word spoken of captains or command. For a long time there was no talk of plans. Fifteen to twenty miles a day, they marched along the highway between the lofty arid mountains. At every town their guards conducted them, as the ancient armies used to lead their captives, in triumphal procession through the streets all hung with banners; and some in the crowds spat upon them as they passed. At night they slept in thick-walled cuartels or in the cattle corrals at the outskirts of the dreary villages. The swarthy soldiers who watched them marveled at their songs and laughter. Always it was the cowboys of the Nueces who sang loudest. They danced in couples on the earthen floors of musty jails. They dropped on all fours in the stock-pens, with lowered heads, and pretended they were bulls. They pawed the earth and bellowed challenges; they fought mock battles while the others roared with mirth. They were the first to whisper the word that was in every man's mind now:

"Escape."

At first a word; the time came when it was a definite project. The cowboys were its foremost advocates; and Ewen Cameron was the man who planned its details.

The days dragged on, one weary march after another, and every night-time saw them further from the Rio Grande. Cameron waited for a favorable opportunity. They reached Monterrey, where ten of their countrymen who had been taken prisoners in other border forays were added to their number. On February 10 they came to the Hacienda Salado, one hundred miles beyond Saltillo. And here, when Cameron had talked with the five other captains, he gave out word that the next morning they should rush the guards.

The Hacienda Salado lay in the depths of a narrow valley. On either side steep mountains rose to the sky. Only the Spanish bayonet and cactus grew on those peaks; their flanks were earthless. A savage sun had stripped them bare. They were the skeletons of mountains. Under their inclosing sides the hamlet of flat-topped adobes was almost indiscernible, a few scattered specks lost to the eye in the enormous confusion of arid granite.

As the cold twilight of dawn seeped down from the sky's whitening rim, revealing the infolded ridges, wiping away the shadows in which the cliffs lurked, to crawl at last along the valley's floor, there came the beat of hoofs, the tramp of infantry; somewhere a horse neighed; a bugle-call climbed from the depths, growing fainter as it mounted from rock to rock. The guards were gathering for the day's march.

The building where the Texans were confined was the only one of any size in the place. A tall stone wall inclosed an outer courtyard, in whose center the prison stood. A company of foot-soldiers came down the narrow road and halted before the wall's main gate; a troop of cavalry drew up beside them, dismounted, and stood at ease among the horses. Within the courtyard one hundred and fifty infantrymen were smoking their after-breakfast cigarettes, awaiting the order to form at attention. Their muskets were stacked; the cartridge-boxes hung in clusters from the bayoneted muzzles. Two sentries were pacing back and forth across the outer gateway; two others stood within the building's open door with loaded muskets at their shoulders.

Inside the long earthen-floored room the Texans awaited their great moment; two hundred and fourteen ragged men, unarmed, gaunt from underfeeding, foot-sore from weeks of marching. Ewen Cameron was to give the signal by throwing his hat in the air. Then they would attack two hundred and fifty soldiers with their bare hands. Like cattle stirring on the holding ground they moved about. They talked in low tones; now and again one laughed or clapped his fellow on the back in passing. The light crept through the barred windows, and as it grew within the room Cameron began to approach the doorway. Samuel H. Walker was lounging near the threshold smoking a cigarette; he was to rush one sentry while the Scotchman fell upon the other.

Now Cameron stopped to speak a word to one of his cowboys, who grinned with the marvelous serenity of youth, making some careless answer. Now he came on as one indifferent to where he strays. He paused again to chat with a fellow-captain. He took a few steps toward the threshold. Then he halted and glanced around at his followers.

"Well, boys," he said coolly, "we will go at it." And with that he flung his hat to the ceiling.

He sprang upon the nearest sentry, and Walker made his leap in the same instant. They were big men, these two; the clipping thud of their great fists came distinct and sharp into the silence; the soldiers went down before them like a pair of pole-axed oxen. And now the leaders bounded back from the senseless forms, brandishing the captured muskets. The whole roomful surged after them through the doorway.

They poured into the courtyard where the companies of infantry were lounging in the pallid sun-rays. Some in those swarthy groups glanced about at the noise of footfalls and ran to the stacked muskets. They seized the first pieces that their hands fell upon and turned to face the rush. The sentries at the outer gate fired into the mass; and the place was filled with eddying confusion of swiftly moving forms; a score of hand-to-hand fights were raging at once. A tall farmer boy from the Bexar country had got hold of a bayonet and was stabbing desperately at an infan-

tryman who was sweeping about him with his clubbed gun. Young
Captain Barragon, son of the guard's commander, was standing
with his back to the wall waving a broken sword in defiance at a
group of cowboys who had surrounded him and were demanding
his surrender. His soldiers were already beginning to scatter. The
roar of voices swelled, then died, and the sound of blows on bare
flesh succeeded it. The most of the Mexicans were in full flight
now. Four or five bodies lay before the gateway.

Ewen Cameron broke through the group who were closing in on
the beardless captain.

"I surrender only to an officer," the boy was shouting.

"I am an officer," Cameron answered and took the broken sword.
He turned to his men. "To the gate, boys." They followed him and
were in the forefront in the rush.

The soldiers in the street had formed, the cavalry afoot beside
the infantry. Their muskets flamed. Dr. R. F. Brenham and Patrick
Lyons fell before the volley. The others swept on. Some of them
bore captured guns, and some were fighting with brickbats. They
charged with the desperation of men who had rather die than not,
and the troopers fled before them, abandoning their horses. The
infantry fell back around a corner. Captain Fitzgerald called
for volunteers. Fifty fell in behind him and rushed the companies
as they were re-forming. A spattering of shots sounded as they
turned the corner. Fitzgerald fell dead. The rest hurled themselves upon the close-formed ranks and scattered them.

It was all over now. Two hundred and fourteen unarmed men
had defeated two hundred and fifty who were equipped for battle.
The Mexican officers surrendered formally. The Texans gathered
up all the horses and muskets in the village. By ten o'clock they
all were in the saddle; all save the wounded, whose proper care
had been made the main condition of the capitulation. The Rio
Grande lay four hundred miles away. After what they had done
that distance seemed a little thing.

There were one hundred and ninety-three of them when they
started northward that morning. They rode for fifty miles and
halted at midnight long enough to water their horses. They then
swung into the saddles and went twelve miles further. Here they
slept for two hours while the wearied animals got a bite to eat.

The sun was rising when they resumed their journey. Now and
again that day they passed a ranch or hacienda. Soldiers were

guarding all of these places. Toward evening they saw a few small squads of cavalry in their rear. But the troopers hung back beyond rifleshot, for all the world like bands of coyotes that follow a herd of sheep, awaiting a favorable opportunity to make a dash on some lagging animal when the shepherd is looking elsewhere. The road wound through steep-walled defiles, mounting the flanks of the inclosing peaks to pass from one cañon to the next. The country all about was waterless, a nest of savage mountains.

On the morning of February 12 they left the highway to avoid Saltillo. For twenty-four hours they climbed among the granite ridges. During that time they did not see a drop of water. They found no food. Huge buzzards sailed overhead, keeping pace with their slow advance, biding their time. At dawn on the thirteenth they struck the road again. Two hours later they found a little spring. There was a sup for every man, and every horse was allowed a single swallow.

That day they passed more ranches, and at every one they saw a detachment of red-capped soldiers. Rather than risk the delay of an engagement they kept on, although thirst was beginning to torture all of them. It was evident that the alarm had gone before them. Evening was coming on when they met a Scotchman who had been in the country for a year or two. He told them they were on the main road and advised them to stick to it; but several of the officers feared treachery and prevailed on Cameron to leave the highway. That night they struck off into the mountains again.

The little trail that they had taken dwindled out before they crossed the first ridge, and when they reached its summit they rested among the rocks till dawn came revealing a dead world of naked peaks whose scorched sides stood out scarred by avalanches. A Mexican shepherd met them as they began their march that morning. They asked him of the country. He shook his head. There was no water in this part of the range, he told them.

They had been twenty-four hours without a drink. The horses were staggering from weakness. The shoes of the men were torn to pieces. That day they killed the animals and drank the blood. They stripped the meat from the bones. They made rude sandals from the saddle-flaps. They started on; and a cloud of buzzards settled down upon the place before they had fairly left it.

There was no pretense at formation now; there were no orders

from the officers. Cameron and one or two companions kept to
the front, looking over the savage ridges and the sun-baked cañons
from every high point, to pick the route. The others straggled
along behind them. Some of those in the rear were throwing away
their captured muskets. Now one dropped out, and now two or
three departed up a branch cañon, lured away by fancies that the
defile might hide water. So they toiled on for three days. Many were
holding pebbles in their mouths; some were chewing leaves of nig-
gerhead and prickly pear; and others were staggering aimlessly
along, talking to themselves in thirst's delirium.

Cameron had sent three of his cowboys ahead to search for a
spring. On the fourth day they returned and reported that there
was not a drop of water in the country. The Scotchman looked
about him. He saw some whose swollen tongues were protruding
between their lips and some who were scooping dry dirt into their
mouths.

He gave the order to return to the road. Better to risk the soldiers than to die out here.

That evening they came out of the last cañon and saw the road
ahead of them. Cameron was in the lead; some fifty-odd men hung
close behind him. The rest were scattered along for miles in little
groups.

One of his cowboys pointed to a column of smoke that wound
into the sky. The captain bade two go on and reconnoiter. They
were back within a few hours with the news that squads of cavalry
were patrolling the highway and a troop was guarding the next
pass.

The last chance was gone. They waited for the dawn; and with
the sunrise came the soldiers. The Scotchman called his men together; they loaded their muskets and deployed to receive the
enemy.

They were barely able to stand from weakness. But when an
officer rode out before the column and ordered them to surrender
Cameron replied:

"On one condition only. We shall be treated as prisoners of
war."

And on that condition General Mexía, the governor of the province, received their arms. It is only fair to say that he did all a man
could to see the promise was kept.

For a week the cavalry were busy gathering in the last stragglers, until they had one hundred and eighty-one in custody. Four
had escaped to make their way to the Rio Grande. Eight had died
out in the sun-baked mountains. Within the next few days five
more succumbed to what they had gone through.

Mexía saw to it that they were humanely treated. By his orders
the thirst-stricken captives were at first given a few sips of water
and a few morsels of food. As time went on the allowance was increased. They were taken back to Saltillo and were held there
pending the arrival of instructions from Santa Anna.

It has been told how the lawyer Canales had an errand of his
own with Mexico's ruler when he set forth to bring the news from
Mier. Now after all these weeks of waiting he saw his opportunity
to carry out his private mission. He did it so effectively that Santa
Anna sent an order to execute the prisoners to the last man.

A storm of protest rose in Saltillo. A score of letters went to
the dictator from prominent Mexicans who cried out against the
black injustice. Governor Mexía wrote that he would resign his
commission rather than do this thing. The American and British
ministers in Mexico City added their voices to the clamor.

Then Santa Anna modified the sentence. Let one man out of
every ten be led out and shot, was the purport of his new instructions. He sent Colonel Domingo Huerta northward to carry them
out; and before Huerta left the capital Canales had a quiet word
with him.

On March 25, 1843, the thing was done. The Texans had
been brought to the Hacienda Salado. In the room from which
they had escaped more than a month before, they were lined up,
and Alfred S. Thurmand interpreted the dictator's written order
to his companions.

Chance would decide on the victims; so said the document
which Thurmand read. Two soldiers brought a jar; they poured
into its mouth one hundred and fifty-nine white beans and seventeen black ones.

Colonel Domingo Huerta had done his work neatly, down to the
last detail. No lottery ever looked fairer than this grim game that
he had set before the Texans. The officers were to have the first
choice. Cameron's name headed the list.

But William F. Wilson had been standing near the jar from the
beginning and had observed something that had escaped the eyes

of the others. Now, when Cameron stepped forward to plunge in his hand:

"Dip deep, Captain," Wilson whispered. For he remembered that the black beans had been poured in last, and there had been no stirring.

Cameron glanced about the room.

"Well, boys, we have to draw," he said. "Let's be at it." He thrust his fingers into the jar's mouth. Whether he had heard Wilson no man knows; it may have been blind luck. But when he withdrew his hand he held a white bean, and the cheers of his companions shook the rafters.

So Canales lost for the time being.

Then Wilson, who had some days since refused a proffer of intervention from the British consul at Saltillo, saying that he meant to share whatever fate came to the Texans, took his turn and won his life. In after years the State of Texas named a county for him.

Captain Eastland was the first officer to get a black bean. He held it up for all to see, shrugged his shoulders, and stepped back for the next man without changing his expression.

"Boys, I told you so," Major Cook said when his turn was done and he had his death-sentence between his fingers, "I never failed to draw a prize." He shook his head and smiled. "Well, they only rob me of forty years." He had just passed his thirtieth birthday.

When one plucked a white bean from the jar, those awaiting turns cheered his luck which jeopardized their own chances by that much more.

"This," said one who had been a well-known gambler in Austin the previous spring, "beats raffling all to hell." He was looking at his bean when he spoke, and it was black.

"Ruther draw for a Spanish hoss and lose him," shouted Talking Bill Moore and won the right to live.

Two brothers by the name of Beard quarreled because one insisted that if he should get a white bean and his brother a black one, they must trade. The Mexican corporal in charge of the jar cut them short and both drew white. When Henry Whaling saw his fate between his fingers:

"They don't make much off of me," he said lightly. "I've killed more'n twenty-five of the yellow bellies."

So it went on until the last black bean was shown; and then the shackles were knocked off from the luckless ones. They were taken out to die.

News moved slowly in those times. When the details of the execution reached the City of Mexico the captives were on the road far south of the Hacienda Salado. Canales heard how Ewen Cameron had escaped, and he went again to Santa Anna. The dictator sent out another order. It met the procession of shackled prisoners one evening at a little hamlet within a hundred miles of the capital.

That night Ewen Cameron was taken from the room where they were housed; and in the morning when they were departing the Texans heard the volley of the firing-squad, which he was facing, as he had faced all his enemies in days gone by, with head erect, unflinching.

So he died. But his memory lived after him. It helped to steel the nerves of twenty of his cowboys, who tunneled through the thick walls of the fortress of Perote a few months later under the noses of the guards. The most of them were recaptured; but a few managed to make their way back to their own country.

Months went by. The prisoners were kept at making roads and cleaning up the streets about the palace of Santa Anna. They never lost heart. And the bitterness that grew within them was made sterner every time the name of Ewen Cameron was spoken. There came a day when the efforts of the American and British ministers and the pleas of Santa Anna's wife resulted in an order from the dictator releasing those who still remained in custody.

So they returned to Texas, and they told the story. Thomas J. Green, who was among the party escaping from Perote, wrote down the details of the whole expedition. There was a time when all the Southwest rang with the name of Ewen Cameron.

The Mexican War came on. Major Walter P. Lane of Texas, who was leading a number of troops on a scouting expedition toward San Luis Potosí, crossed the mountains to the Hacienda Salado. Here he compelled the *mayordomo* to exhume the bones of the seventeen who had drawn black beans on that March afternoon five years before, and to furnish mules to transport them back across the Rio Grande. They were buried with full honors of war at La Grange, Texas.

But the grave of Ewen Cameron remained unmarked. So he

sleeps, like many a one of the bold young riders who succeeded him and his companions of the Nueces, without so much as a headboard to remind men of his resting-place. Had he a monument, perhaps the most fitting inscription on its face would be:

EWEN CAMERON
THE FIRST COWBOY

RUTH LAUGHLIN BARKER

GENTLEMEN-ON-HORSEBACK

Here again is the thunder of the hoofs of old Santa Fe, the color and dash of the Spanish Caballeros. Here is the picturesque, romantic, old Southwest, excitingly re-created by an able historian. (From *Caballeros,* Appleton-Century, 1931.)

SANTA FE's main street is the calle de San Francisco. At the western end there are houses of an older day with small native shops opening on the street and sunny patios beyond the open doorways. Yesterday I was walking there as two Caballeros passed each other. Both had reached an age where a cane is a comforting assurance. Don Pedro's face, as he came toward me on his way to the Plaza, had a full, somber dignity. His gray mustache and hair set off the brown skin of heavy jowls and large, arrogant nose. Eyebrows bushed over dark eyes, watchful and yet aloof to passing motors and the paved street. His clothes were as gray as his hair, and an old-fashioned gold watch chain dangled across his vest. I followed Don Miguel's tall spare figure in the black suit with the coat settled into old wrinkles from the stooped shoulders. As they passed, each raised his hand to his broad-brimmed black hat with a single word of greeting:

"Caballero!"

"Caballero!"

In that single Spanish word—Gentlemen!—there was all the history of their people. It implied pride of race, aristocratic recognition, innate courtesy, and punctilious formality. As the oldest European title in the Americas it merited respect. More than four hundred years ago Cortés brought it to North America when he unloaded the first horses at Vera Cruz. Caballeros were horsemen, those who rode caballos. But because the luxury of a horse was the outward and visible sign of a gentleman of means, Caballero took on the meaning of Gentleman-on-Horseback.

Now Don Pedro and Don Miguel ride only their canes, yet the old title springs to their lips. Horsemanship has faded in this day of motors, but the significance of Gentleman remains.

New Mexico is characteristically the country of the Caballeros, particularly northern New Mexico, the old division of the upper Rio Grande and Chama valleys that was known as the Rio Arriba. Here is the last stand of Spain in North America. It is a mark left upon the land as indelible as the one-fifth quinta mark on old Spanish silver.

This life naturally focuses in Santa Fe, flowing into it from a wide radius. For more than two centuries the City of the Holy Faith was the northernmost seat of royal rule in the Kingdom of New Spain, the headquarters of a province whose vast boundaries extended from the Mississippi river to the Pacific and from the Mexican city of Parral to the unknown north. It is the oldest capital in what is now the United States, with a Spanish heritage that is as important in the American scene as the English tradition is on the Atlantic coast. Its prestige was due not only to vested Spanish authority but to its importance as a hub of western trails. The Chihuahua Trail, the Spanish trail to California, the fur trappers' trail from north of Taos, and the Santa Fe Trail ended here, bringing cargoes to be redistributed to the western half of a continent.

Yet the trails of those early days were too hazardous for any but the most necessary trade and rare official notices. A fifteen-hundred-mile trek over blazing deserts and grim mountains left the northern province to an isolation that must be self-contained if it continued to exist. Oñate's entrada in 1598 brought four hundred colonists to settle in the Rio Grande Valley. They formed the nucleus of a purely Spanish culture whose traditions were so intensified in their isolation that the Andalusian folkways of 1900 were not so different from those of 1600. They flavored life with the sal andaluz—the salt of Andalusian wit and character retained in their speech to-day with pithy proverbs and the grandiloquence of Don Quixote.

It is a curious fact that this province has remained more Spanish than the rest of New Spain, as Mexico was called. Spaniards conquered the Aztecs, who had attained a high state of civilization and a simplified government under Montezuma. An abundance of gold and silver, emeralds and pearls gave the conquered people a certain material authority in treasure-seeking Spanish eyes. Caballeros married chieftains' daughters, starting the mestizo class who would later rule Mexico. There the Indian strain is a proud heritage, but in New Mexico it is ignored for a valiant upholding of Spanish purity.

The northern Indians were less advanced. Navajos, Apaches and Comanches were living in the aboriginal, hunting stage. The Pueblos, as the Spaniards called the town-dwelling Indians, had progressed to agriculture and architecture. None of the tribes had ever heard of gold. Since they had no material wealth, Spaniards discounted them as ignorant, lowly vassals, taking their women only as slaves and disqualifying the men's voice in government.

These Indians had no conception of a centralized government, united against a common foe. The first and only time they joined in the Pueblo rebellion of 1680 they ousted the Conquistadores in three days. For, a century before that, a few Spaniards had subdued unnumbered red men, scattered and defenseless in their own country. The nomadic tribes fought each other and preyed upon the Pueblos. Each pueblo defended itself as a small, independent city republic. Though the villages were separated by only a few miles up and down the rivers, they were entirely separated from thought communication by four different language groups—the Tano, Piro, Tewa and Keres. Distrust, bred by fear and ignorance of each other, brought ceaseless intertribal wars.

For three centuries the Spaniards ruled the land by quelling one tribe after another. Perhaps they lacked the grace of ruling a subject people wisely, for theirs was a day when might made right. Even in peace, Indian subjects gave only a negative submission and were never a coöperative factor in government.

In our present warless days we appreciate the Indian's right of self-defense in his own country and forget the bitter struggle of life and death that surrounded the Spaniards. Even fifty years ago men remember that they dared not take their families as far as Española without an armed escort. Scalping raids were seared into their memory so vividly that they marvel to-day at our careless picnic parties. Now the Indians are our friends. They have shrunk into their picturesque pueblos like strange, anachronous islands in our overflowing civilization. Clinging to their ancient self-respecting standards, they survive to teach us lessons interpreted in art and spiritual poise and even in government, for the Pueblos are the most successful of all communists.

Since written history began on this continent, this has been Spanish domain. Those first Spaniards were heroic men of a heroic time. The stock was so virile that it still characterizes half the population of the state as a vital, living element, not yet diluted to romantic memories and bygone glories. The quick changes taking place before our eyes now are not as remarkable as the fact that Indians and Spaniards have remained intact through so many centuries.

In the long judgment of time the Caballero is more important to this country than the Conquistador. The Conquerors cleared the land with fierceness and force, but the Gentleman-on-Horseback planted it with the seeds of faith, art and tradition. The cruelties of the Conquistadores have vanished, but the harvest of the Caballeros' culture flourishes to-day.

The Caballeros carried three symbols into this Kingdom of New Spain—gold, the cross, and the horse. The search for gold, that lure that drew Spaniards across oceans and deserts, is a part of the mystery of the mountains and the legends of the land. Every placita has its chapel with the cross set above it to show the march of Christ in a pagan land. More than either, the horse is the symbol of the Caballeros. Where the horse has vanished before the inroads of a mechanical age, Spanish backgrounds have vanished. But where the horse still brings men home in the sunset to warm, adobe placitas, the old folkways continue and the horse's trot echoes in the rhythm of love songs and the click of high heels in the Varsoviana.

Columbus started the gossip of gold in the Indies and made it a reality when he returned to Sevilla in a triumphal procession with Indians gleaming in golden ornaments and forty sailors carrying forty gorgeous parrots. Every Spanish port swarmed with men whose eyes sparkled with the get-rich-quick dream of finding gold, eager to cross the seas as fast as slow sails would carry them. Spain was Queen of the Seas and the most powerful nation in their world. With a typical far-flung gesture the distant rich lands were included as Spanish possessions. Conquering them and gaining their gold was part of the high adventure and daring that stirred men in a day when little Spanish ships had accomplished the tremendous feat of crossing an ocean and finding a new world. To these primitive adventurers gold was a tangible reality to be exchanged for the luxuries of the Orient—cloth of gold, taffetas, gauze and brocades, heavy perfumes, numberless slaves, and spices to flavor rich foods. Of these spices pepper was the most precious and rare; pepper that was forever after to color the food of Mexico and New Mexico with hot, red chile.

Contrasted with the greed for material wealth was the devout faith of Christians who had succeeded after eight centuries in conquering the infidel Moors. The cross of Christ and the banners of Castilla had led the victorious army against the crescent. Now they would go forward in a pagan land and redeem it for the Saviour. With faith to absolve them as proselyting overlords and national pride, greed and adventure to spur them on, a small band of Caballeros overcame Montezuma and the fertile land of the Aztecs.

Horses were the unexpected factor of greatest consequence in the conquest after Hernán Cortés landed at Vera Cruz in 1519. Before he burned his ships to impress upon his handful of men that the march to Mexico City meant conquest or death, he unloaded sixteen Spanish horses. The Indians, seeing horses for the first time, believed that man and horse were "all in one part." Even more than arquebuses and "sticks that shot thunder and lightning," horses terrified them into fleeing before this new supernatural monster. Medicine men hid in the jungle thickets to dispel the evil magic. By the time they discovered that horses were unsaddled at night and that man and horse could not be one animal, since a captain had pitched over his horse's head on a coast trail, it was too late to stop them. In two years the strange, pale-skinned, bearded conquerors had taken the white temples of Mexico City.

Cortés riding his rose-garlanded stallion there was a magnificent Gentleman-on-Horseback. The first Spanish word the Aztecs learned was caballo, the name for the awe-inspiring animal the Conquerors rode. Soon the Spaniards found that the distinction of being Caballeros brought more homage from Indian chiefs than the proud Castilian title of Hidalgos. Hidalgo had been shortened from Hijo de Algo, Son of a Somebody. These Somebodies might be powerful princes in far-away Spain but in Mexico the Caballero had his horse under him to prove his leadership.

Of the sixteen horses there were eleven snorting stallions and five high-stepping mares. They were Arabian barbs whose colors of chestnut, sorrel and silver gray were to be repeated indefinitely in the mustang breed of western horses. Each boatload of restless younger sons of the Castilian court brought more horses to Mexico. They were richly caparisoned with tooled leather saddles and bridles ornamented with silver, yet this extravagant equipment was not worth one-tenth the price of a five-thousand-dollar horse. Horses were not for sale, even for money worth three times its value to-day. One cavalier refused a ten-thousand-dollar offer for his horse and slave.

But within a century, the increase of horses lowered their price to ten dollars a head. Turned out to forage for themselves, they strayed away and formed the bands of horses who would overrun the western plains. Stallions, leading their mares, were as wild as though their sires had never known a Spanish bridle. Surviving in spite of short mountain grasses and winter blizzards, they became stunted and sturdy, like all semi-arid growth. Piebalds and pinto ponies had the curious marks of inbreeding. Acclimated to a dry country, the small, tough successors of the Arabian barbs were to carry the Caballeros up and down the farthermost trails.

From that day to this the Spanish domain of the wide Southwest has been known as the horse country. Sentiment and necessity made horses preëminent figures in its story, first as the symbol of Spanish conquest, then as means to "run meat" by buffalo hunters, later pulling covered wagons and carrying cowboys over unfenced ranges and now reverting to the luxury class as swift-turning polo ponies. Navajos riding across red deserts and Spanish-Americans intent on a local horse race owe their mounts to the original Spanish horses. They belong to a day of romance and individualism that is lost before a standardized, twelve-cylinder motor.

The first explorers to penetrate the Southwest failed, perhaps because they were not mounted. Alvar Núñez Cabeza de Vaca had lost his horse in Florida. With two companions and the black slave Estevan he made the first difficult trip across the continent on foot. After nine hard years of wandering, captured by Indians and escaping to push their way to the Pacific as medicine men and jugglers, they reached Mexico in 1536. Cortés and the Viceroy Don Antonio de Mendoza received them to hear from Cabeza de Vaca's own lips an account of the country to the north. They had heard reports of fabulous gold there which would rival Alvarado's explorations in Central America. Cabeza de Vaca told of the country of the Seven Cities of Cíbola—seven terraced cities, larger than the City of Mexico, and so rich that doorways were encrusted with gold and precious stones. The cíbola, or buffalo, blackened the plains in vast herds, providing an unlimited meat supply.

Within the next year the shrewd Mendoza sent a small scouting party north to verify these extravagant reports. If he had equipped them with horses, these first two men to discover New Mexico might have had a happier fate. But the chief scout was friar Marcos de Niza, and frailes were accustomed to go afoot into their wilderness field, armed only with their breviary and cross. His guide was the black slave Estevan of Cabeza de Vaca's party. It was not fitting to mount a slave on a master's horse. So the two, accompanied by six Indian interpreters, set out on foot for the trackless northern wilderness.

Black Steven, used to nine years of foot travel, went ahead. He was to send back a small cross if the land was poor, a larger one if it was good. Indians staggered under the man-sized cross they brought back to Friar Marcos. The cross was typical of the grandiose visions the slave threw around himself, once he was free from his masters. He traveled ahead in state, decked in gaudy feathers and followed by credulous Indians and their prettiest women. His vanity was his undoing. When he reached Hawikuh, the first of the Seven Cities near modern Zuñi, the caciques killed him as an evil man and a spy. Friar Marcos, hurrying to overtake his guide, was warned not to approach the pueblo. Like Moses he looked at the Promised Land from the height of a mesa, planted a cross in this new "Kingdom of St. Francis" and made his lonely, discouraged way home.

He wrote a faithful report of the Cíbola country for the Viceroy, but the gente did not read it. They heard and repeated, and each telling grew more golden, the tale of the barber who

shaved the fraile after his return. Not even a Franciscan mission-
ary should have been held too responsible for anything he might
have told a barber mowing off a three-months' beard, and the
barber lost no glory in talking of the illustrious patron who had
visited his little shop. "There," the barber cried, "the people are
shrewd and marry only one wife at a time. The cities are populous
and surrounded by walls. The women wear golden beads and the
men girdles of gold, and white woolen dresses."

Perhaps the barber's gossip had more to do with the expedition
that was to claim one-half of the Western continent than the
truthful but uninteresting report of the Friar. Mendoza himself
was taken with the gold fever and ordered a tremendous royal
subsidy to outfit an expedition to the Seven Cities. Within a few
days three hundred men had signed up for the gold rush.

There was no question of this expedition going on foot. They
were mounted on the best Spanish horses. Many of the captains
were young Castilian nobles whose restless energy had stirred up
intrigues and fights in Mendoza's capital. Don Antonio blessed
them fervently and gratefully as they rode off to the north,
scarlet and gold banners flying, the cross upraised. At their head
rode their leader, Francisco Vásquez Coronado, the sun glinting
on his golden helmet and the polished flanks of his horse. Their
valor would repay the huge royal subsidy by finding mountains of
gold; and the Church, the King and his Viceroy, Don Antonio,
would profit with a vast new kingdom.

After months of riding they came to the land of the Seven
Cities to find primitive mud and stone huts instead of rich palaces.
Yet Hawikuh was not conquered before arrows had pierced Coronado's golden helmet and killed many of his horses. They camped
for the winter in a broad valley of the Rio Grande y Bravo at
Tiguex, near Bernalillo. From there they rode as far west as the
Grand Canyon and east to the Gran Quivira in Kansas. But they
failed to search the mountains within twenty miles of their camp,
where future generations were to pick up gold nuggets as thick as
piñones after the first frost. Nor did they find the hill of Chal-
chihuites near Los Cerrillos where Indians burrowed for their
sacred turquoise. Adventure blinded them to nearby opportunities
and romance led them to chase the rainbow.

After two years of disappointments, the bedraggled Caballeros
mutinied and Coronado was forced to lead them back to Mexico,

riding now with drooping head. He cursed Friar Marcos as a faith-
less liar, yet Coronado had found just what the friar had officially
reported—terraced towns beside each river, people whose jewels
were turquoise, and many buffalo. But he had not found that
which lent magic to the barber's tale—gold.

What traces did the Caballeros leave on this first entrada?
The country reverted to the Indians as worthless, yet they left
a geographical imprint upon it, setting boundaries for Spain far
beyond their imaginations. It was worth indeed a thousand times
the royal subsidy, but Coronado died in humiliated poverty because he had not found mountains of gold.

The cross was left with its dawning influence, for three friars
refused to return with Coronado. Padre Juan de la Cruz and the
lay brother Luis Descalona were martyred before Coronado
reached Mexico. Padre Juan de Padilla went back to the Gran
Quivira and lived long enough for a legend to form around him.
It is said that his body is buried at Isleta, the sunny pueblo below
Albuquerque. How he came to rest there, so far from Kansas, no
one knows. But according to the legend, Padre Padilla rises in
his coffin, hollowed out of a cottonwood log, every twenty years.
Some say that his emaciated body is as dry as a mummy and his
brown gown crumbling, as well it might after four centuries,
but when his coffin bursts the mud floor before the altar, it is
the blessed omen of a good year.

The two years' stay left the Indians with corroding memories
which would influence them for the next three hundred years.
To them the bearded strangers were not Caballeros, but buccaneers
attacking peaceful villages, burning alive two hundred Indians at
Pecos, turning the Tewas out of their warm, winter homes so that
the soldiers might be comfortable at Tiguex. They looked with
pitying wonder at the babies born to their women that year,
babies with pale eyes and reddish glints in their hair. These were
not their ruddy Children of the Sun but the bleached Children of
the Moon. The ancient prophecy that a strange white people
would conquer them had been fulfilled.

Horses and perhaps a few sheep were left behind by the Caballeros. Being miraculous and unknown creatures, horses were soon
woven into the Indian's rich mythology. Johano-ai was the god
who carried the golden disk of the sun from east to west. Now,
on this daily journey, he rode one of five great horses—a horse

of turquoise, a horse of white shell, a horse of pearl shell, a horse of red shell and a horse of coal black. The Children of the Sun knew which horse he had chosen, for at dawn, if the sky was blue and clear, he had mounted the turquoise horse or the one of white or pearl shell. But if there was the sweep of the dust-red wind or black clouds piled up, he was riding the fiery red horse or the one of coal black.

Other legends told of a white stallion with flowing mane and tail ridden swiftly by a mysterious unknown god and never overtaken. He was seen only in the twilight, fleeing toward the horizon and followed by his band of black mares.

Horses were to change the entire life of the American Indians. Before the coming of the Caballeros, Indians had carried heavy burdens by dog teams and depended upon their own swift feet in the hunt. By lassoing the wild Spanish horses, and riding them bareback with a noose for a bridle, the roving tribes of Apache, Navajo, the dreaded Comanche and the Plains Indians could ride to distant hunting grounds. These encroachments were always a cause for war and brought further strife to keep the Indians from uniting.

Coronado's failure to find gold pricked the balloon of northern hopes. The King and his viceroys refused to grant further large subsidies for explorations. If other men were foolhardy enough to seek this golden will-o'-the-wisp, they must do so at their own expense. This phrase was so impressed upon the colonial mind that all further chronicles included it. "This, I accomplished at my own expense" became the customary appendage to all documents, whether they related to outfitting an army, exploring new territory, or building and repairing churches.

Three years after Coronado returned, the first great silver mine was discovered by the Spaniards in Bolivia and another at Cerro de Pasco in Perú. In northern Mexico, Zacatecas was the silver bonanza of 1548. Here was silver in such quantities that wine goblets, forks and spoons, wash basins and pitchers, mirror frames and chandeliers were pounded out of the gleaming, white metal. Por supuesto, the luxurious horses, were outfitted with it! There were solid silver horns and stirrups, bits and spurs, silver buttons to ornament the leather of saddles and bridles, silver shoes for the captains' horses.

If there was so much silver, surely there must be some of the precious gold north of Zacatecas, so pure that little energy would be lost in refining it. With the Spaniards the dream of gold could not die. These pioneer prospectors had the same malady that is chronic with all men who seek riches from the earth— the faith that on the next trip they will discover pay dirt. They refused to be stopped by the hardships and disappointments of Coronado.

For the next sixty years miners, explorers and missionaries rode to the north—always at their own expense. Some expeditions, failing to find gold, made up for their expenses as slave-catching raids. In 1561 Francisco Ibarra came back to tell the homefolk of a new land he had seen, "as marvelous as a new Mexico." New Mexico was advertised under her own name for the first time. Fourteen years later Chamuscado and two friars marked the north trail with their bleached bones. In 1583 Antonio de Espejo and his fourteen men were the first tourists to see New Mexico and return in ten months. Espejo was a practical promoter and made his trip pay by trading with the Indians. He returned with a promoter's enthusiasm for the mineral wealth and colonization possibilities of New Mexico.

Mañana is a word that is characteristic of Spaniards anywhere. In spite of Espejo's rosy propaganda, the colonizing scheme was put off until mañana. The viceroy was too busy keeping his own seat to start a northern colony. He was beset with plots and intrigues, for the highly individualistic Spaniard chafed at being under any one man's authority. Finally Don Juan de Oñate volunteered to lead a colonizing expedition to New Mexico "at his own expense."

The unstinted magnificence of spending a million pesos on this project came from silver mines in Zacatecas—a magnificence to be trebled from the gold mines he hoped to find on the thousands of acres of land the King would grant him in the new province, where he would rule as governor and captain-general. His wife, Doña Isabel, helped him to the royal reward, for she was the granddaughter of the great Cortés. The Gentlemen-on-Horseback in his company were the rich and distinguished nobility of Spain, a different type of men from the impoverished religious refugees who were to land on Plymouth Rock twenty-two years later.

The poetic glamour and adventure of a quest worthy of the dramatic Golden Age attracted friars, with names as old as

Spanish history, and illustrious men of letters. One of his captains was Don Marcos Farfán, the first dramatist who produced a play in what is now the United States, a comedy given by soldier-actors on the banks of the Rio Grande at El Paso del Norte. Another captain, Don Gaspar de Villagrá, wrote the log of the expedition as an epic poem. Its thirty-two cantos give New Mexico the unique honor of having a poem as the original and accurate authority for its dawning history.

They left Mexico in 1598, a gay and brilliant company, dressed as befitted Caballeros in satin and slashings of scarlet taffeta in their puffed sleeves. Long curling plumes waved from their velvet hats. Lacy ruffles fell from their throats and wrists and garters. In a final bold gesture of leavetaking they buckled on their shining armor and helmets. Their horses were snorting and eager to be off, the best high-spirited steeds that silver could buy.

Don Juan placed his twelve-year-old son Cristóbal on the charger the child was to ride at the head of the troop, saluted the proud Doña Isabel and leaped on his stallion. There were music and songs, trumpets calling, the quick trot of horses' feet, roses and carnations thrown in their path by excited women, and tearful cries of "Adios! Vaya con Dios." The historic migration had started north.

Behind Don Juan there were resplendent captains and soldiers, somber friars fingering their rosaries, four hundred colonists driving seven thousand cattle and sheep in the clouds of dust. Eighty-three teams of oxen pulled the heavy solid-wheeled carretas, loaded with the luxuries of the day to pleasure Don Juan and his gentlemen. Perched on top of the high-piled wagons were children too small to walk. Beside them trudged their mothers and older children, for one hundred and thirty colonists had brought their families whose pioneer courage would make homes in the wilderness.

Oñate's entrada was a long six months' journey, testing high spirits with hardships and dangers. Forbidding mountain crags and burning deserts offered them no easy welcome, for it is characteristic of this land to hold itself impenetrable to strangers. Sheep, cattle and horses foraged for themselves. The colonists depended upon the never-plentiful provisions in the Indian villages they passed. There was always the dreaded fear of failing to find water—a fear that materialized in the parched wastes called in desperation the Jornada del Muerto—the Journey of the Dead. With swollen tongues and blistered feet they found at the other side of this death valley a pueblo where the Indians succored them, and gratefully named the place for Nuestra Señora de Socorro.

Day by day the sun blazed on the heavy armor, creaking wagons and footsore colonists. They followed the Rio Grande y Bravo del Norte, for the river was an active source of life in this semi-arid land. A wall of purple lava overflow at La Bajada divided the big and fierce river of the north into the warm lowlands of the Rio Abajo and the high, timbered mesas of the Rio Arriba. It was a natural division destined to be important always in New Mexican history.

From the crest of each mesa they searched the clear, blue distance for gold, silver and precious stones glinting in the doorways. In spite of the reports of the earlier travelers, they hoped to reach the fabled Seven Cities where there would be luxurious ease for their tired bodies and gold pouring into their eager hands. Instead they too found clumps of primitive mud houses where Indians wore homespun cotton mantas. Their only wealth was shelled corn and crudely cut sky stones.

Don Juan rode north of Coronado's camp at Tiguex until the river widened into a fertile, green valley, a welcome sight to hungry men and beasts. As had been the custom with earlier trail blazers, the padres set up a great cross in the nearby village of Kay-pa and blessed it with the new name of a helpful saint. Who was more appropriate for this final stopping place than San Juan de Los Caballeros, Don Juan's patron Saint John, who had aided the Gentlemen-on-Horseback?

The camp remained here three years and was then moved across the river to San Gabriel. Though Oñate had found no gold mines, he realized the importance of governing and colonizing so large a province. It was not an easy job, for the colonists were discouraged and the Indians unruly. The Pueblo Indians submitted outwardly to Spanish rule and Christianity, but inwardly they were festering spots of hostility. The roving tribes were openly rebellious, pillaging the settlements as much as they dared for horses and provisions.

With typical Spanish courage, small bands of Caballeros left the headquarters for explorations east and west. At Acoma, Oñate stormed the high rocky citadel of this city in the sky, seventy soldiers against fifteen hundred angry Indians. The Acomans guarded their pueblo on the high mesa of solid rock with bows and arrows, timbers, stones and boiling water, ready to destroy any invader brave enough to climb the steep trail. Their horses were of no use, but by a ruse the Spaniards gained the mesa up the back trail. The battle wavered on the dizzy edge of the cliff. The Indians barricaded themselves inside their houses, but the Spaniards drove them from room to room, setting fire to the houses behind them. There were only six hundred inhabitants of haughty Acoma left to submit to the Spanish crown. The strongest fortress in the Indian country had met defeat.

Following the road to the sun, west of Acoma, Oñate's horses were stopped by the waves of the "South Sea," as he called the Pacific. On his return he rested at the towering red sandstone pinnacle, thrust up through the plains between Zuñi and Acoma. There he carved his record into the enduring rock—"Pasó por aquí el Adelantado Don Juan de Oñate, del descubrimiento de la mar del sur, a 16 de abril, 1605." It is the earliest historical record to be found in the United States. Oñate's memoir was followed by other famous conquerors for the next two hundred and fifty years, making "El Morro" the huge stone autograph album of western history.

Oñate returned to find his headquarters at San Gabriel confused by disheartened colonists and rebellious Indians. The petty jealousies that beset every leader raised the young Don Cristóbal in his father's place as governor. About 1609 Don Pedro de Peralta was appointed as the third governor of the province with orders to found a "new villa," the future Santa Fe.

Early Spanish explorers were required to keep a minute journal of their expeditions. Many of these journals may be studied to-day in the Federal Building archives, yellowed paper showing the quaint lettering in unfaded black ink. Every expense was itemized from the three pairs of sandals allowed each padre to the elaborate wardrobe of Oñate, the salaries, rations and ammunition for the army. Each Indian village was recorded with its new Christian name.

Yet in no record up to 1614 is there a mention of Santa Fe.

Historians who have delved through the archives of "the Indies" believe that the journals between 1609 and 1614 might

have been lost in their long-ago travels between New Mexico and
Spain or may be hidden among the old manuscripts in Mexico
City. Peralta's order to establish a "new villa" was without doubt
the cause of the founding of Santa Fe. The records of such an
important undertaking as building a permanent capital to be the
center of authority in the limitless northern province must have
been sent to the king and viceroy. Probably some day this historic
file will be found to give the oldest capital an authentic birthday.
Until then we must be content with such reliable facts that Oñate's
camp was moved from San Gabriel after he came back from the
"South Sea" and that Peralta's "new villa," Santa Fe, was established between 1609 and 1614.

There is a tradition that Santa Fe was built upon the site
of the pre-Columbian pueblo of Kwa-po-ge. The old men of San
Ildefonso tell that in the "long since" this was the place where
the Virgin Mother of the Sun and Moon was tossed about in
the angry waters of the deluge. Resting upon the high loma, she
gave birth here to the twin gods of war.

Whether the fighting twins eventually destroyed their mother's
home or whether pestilence wiped it out, as it did the pueblo of
Pecos, is all a surmise into that dim past. The skeletons dug
up each year in the construction of city foundations tell no
tales except that their skulls are narrow like those of the Pajarito
peoples.

The tradition of Kwa-po-ge is all that remains to give an inkling
of the life of people living here half a thousand years ago. Kwa-
po-ge, meaning the Place of the Shell-Bead People, suggests
that even then this little valley at the foot of the mountains must
have been a center of trails coming up from the sea-washed countries, where shells were traded and polished into beads to give
their name to a tribe.

The terraced walls of Kwa-po-ge had crumbled to the earth
probably two hundred years before Oñate's entrada, leaving no
trace of a living pueblo to be listed in the explorer's journals. Yet
the location which had attracted the wise Indians later appealed
to the Caballeros. Oñate may have noted it as he rode the trail
between Pecos and Tesuque and suggested it for the permanent
capital.

It had many advantages to recommend it. It was nine miles
away from the strife of the nearest pueblo at Tesuque. It was

higher than the Rio Grande Valley, giving it a strategic military position and cooler summers. It was surrounded by a high forest, good farm lands and a river to irrigate them. This rio, which mercifully never ran dry, was of importance in a land where the gift of water was mentioned in every one's prayers. To the north and east the valley was protected by snowy peaks, at first called by the Spaniards the "Sierra Nevada." But the seventeenth century was a time when lifeblood was offered and spilled in the name of Christ. Later when devout Caballeros watched the crimson radiance of the afterglow of sunset suffuse the mountains, they likened it to the mystical stain of the blood of Christ, and called the mountains the Sangre de Cristo. Clouds with rain-filled sails floated up from the golden plains to the south and broke on these peaks with life-giving moisture for the new villa. From the watchtower of Atalaya Hill sentinels could give warning of any approach from the plains.

To any one who is familiar with long, euphonious Spanish names "Santa Fe" is too short and impersonal for the title of a royal city. Spanish towns needed the protection of some patron saint who would look after his namesake place in time of trouble. Old records show that Santa Fe was named in accordance with this tradition, but the hurry of the last American century has clipped it to one-fourth its original dignity. The Caballeros had time to roll sonorously over their tongues and print upon their fine manuscripts the full name—"La Villa Real de la Santa Fe de San Francisco de Assisi"—the Royal City of the Holy Faith of St. Francis of Assisi. From the beginning the town had to live up to such a name as that.

There was no haphazard chance about building this royal city. The rules of city planning of three hundred years ago were ordered in detail in Spain and followed as strictly in this far-away frontier as though King Phillip might ride in any day to inspect the villa real. In this way Spanish towns attained the permanent design of dignified architectural units, instead of becoming an ungainly ramble of shacks on either side of a wide place in the road.

Town plans followed the home feeling of houses built around a patio and centered around a plaza. The Plaza Mayor in Santa Fe was laid out and blessed with a cross and the pomp of royal investiture. It was a rectangle half again as long as it was wide "making it better for horses used upon fiestas and other occasions." At the east end, the church and monastery of San Francisco was begun by Friar Benavides, "raised and set apart from other buildings, so that it might be seen and venerated." Shops and houses filled the southern and western sides of the hollow square, with the "Capilla Militar," or soldiers' chapel, on the south side.

The entire northern side was occupied by the Royal Palace, a long, low adobe building with towers at either end. The west tower guarded the arsenal and the east tower the officers' chapel, "La Hermita de Nuestra Señora." High adobe walls formed a compound of several blocks behind the palace, enclosing the Plaza de las Armas and the officers' homes in the Casas Reales. A zaguán was the one wide entrance into the compound where Caballeros might ride inside and ox-teams could be unloaded. With adobe walls thick enough to be arrowproof and only the few necessary doors and windows, the Palacio Real looked like an Arabian desert fortress. It had a simple, massive dignity essentially different from the ornate colonial palaces of the south. Its stark exterior expressed the necessities of a frontier outpost, a huge, solid protectress in a hostile land. But the inner sales and patios had the grace and beauty of this nucleus of Spanish life, doubly precious to the exiled settlement. Like the Indian pueblos the buildings were projections of the brown earth, moulded from mud by conscripted Indian laborers and Spanish artisans. It basked in the sun as the one European official building in all the oceans-bounded continent north of Mexico.

Across the river a smaller settlement was built for the Tlascaltecan slaves brought along with the colonists. It was called the Barrio Analco, from the Aztec words meaning a Little Suburb across the Water. Its chapel was dedicated to the dragon-slaying San Miguel as the slaves' church.

By 1621 the Mission Supply Service established the first time-tables for freight trains between Mexico and the distant missions at Santa Fe. Financed by the Crown it carried north padres and supplies, including oysters, conserves, copper bells, oil paintings of the saints, nails and axes for the lifetime exile in a pagan field. These freight trains of mules were far from being a daily service. As Friar Benavides wrote in 1631, "Though it is true this dispatch is assigned to be made punctually every three years, five and six years are wont to pass without the royal officials bethinking themselves about us. And God knows what it costs to remind them!" Three years were allowed for the round trip, a year and half for actual travel and the same time for loading and unloading at either end.

Like smaller cousins, the Spanish ass or burro followed the mules up the trail. Leaving Mexico they were loaded with kegs of golden pesetas and bullion. Returning from Santa Fe the kegs were filled with salt, as scarce and precious as gold and found only in the dried salt lakes of the Estancia Valley. A trickle of colonists came up the Camino Real, hauling the few necessities to start homes in the wilderness in crude carretas. The first wagons had been brought into the province in 1590 with the unlicensed expedition of Castaño de Sosa. The creaking of these first wheels to turn in the future United States was the prelude to the death knell of the Spaniard's horse. Later he was not necessary for iron wheels propelled by steam, for gas-driven motors nor for airplanes darting through the sky like dragonflies. But for two and a half centuries horses, ox-drawn carts, packtrains of mules and burros were to be the only transportation between the civilized world and the isolated province.

There in the blue and silver of the far mountain valley the city of Oñate's Caballeros put down its roots. The colonists grappled with the problems of the frontier, fighting for life not only against the Indians but against the forces of nature in a semi-arid country. The Spanish settlement counted only a few armed men against the uncounted hordes of Indians. They held Spanish rule supreme during that dangerous day because the Indians were constantly at war among themselves. In the great rebellion of 1680 they united as a red race for the first and last time. Even their complete victory could not teach them the lesson of a united Indian nation.

A spirit of antichrist quickened the rebellion. The Indians had added the new Christian God to their galaxy of nature gods but He had not brought them happiness or peace. Added to the enforced Christian practices was the age old incentive for war— taxation without representation. The head of each family was required to bring to the royal treasury one vara of cotton cloth and one fanega of corn—the Indian's chief wealth and means of barter. Yet for more than two generations they had had no voice in governing the land that belonged to them.

Witchcraft played its part in the rebellion, made dramatic by the medicine man, Po-pé of Taos. In 1675 he had been put in prison with three other medicine men and was only released upon the insistent demand of the Indians. They had suffered already from years of drought and famine. Now they were terrified for fear some new evil would befall them if their priests of nature magic were executed.

Po-pé proclaimed that he was under the guidance of three dark underworld spirits who commanded him to free the Indians from the tyranny of the Christians. For the next five years he went from tribe to tribe using the one universal language for his propaganda. By signs and war shields painted with symbols as old as pictographs on the rocks, he incited them to reclaim their own land and their own gods.

By 1680 they were ready for the rebellion. It was to be the last great battle between men with horses and men without horses. In their final plans the Indians scorned the symbol of the Caballeros and used their fastest runners who ran the long distance from Taos in the north to western Zuñi and the southern Rio Grande villages. These runners, Omtua and Cantua, carried cords whose knots signified how many days would elapse before the general uprising.

But Omtua and Cantua were betrayed and brought to Governor Otermín in Santa Fe. Not to be balked in their break for freedom, other runners were hastily sent forth from Tesuque. One knot in each cord was untied, hastening the rebellion by one day.

On that day, August 11, 1680, every Indian in the province rose to attack the Spaniards. After murdering the padres and colonists in the outlying missions, they hurried over all the trails to Santa Fe. The Spaniards from the ranches and slaves from the Barrio Analco gathered within the protection of the Palace compound. Cannons were set up in the zaguán doorway, men with arquebuses took their precarious positions in the towers.

Governor Otermín asked for a parley. The war cacique met him, barbaric in bright paint and feathers, with a scarlet taffeta sash tied around him that he had snatched from a dying Caballero in the monastery at Galisteo. The cacique offered Otermín two crosses —a white cross signifying that the Spaniards would be allowed to depart peacefully from the Indian country; the red cross symbolizing the blood that would flow if they stayed. Otermín chose the red cross and prepared for battle, realizing for the first time that the entire province echoed with the murderous war cry.

In the battles the Indians lost more warriors than the Spaniards. But the Indian force was growing hourly as new tribes joined them. The trick that quickly decided the victory came when the Indians cut off the water supply for the Palace, an acequia running from the river through the Casas Reales. Horses and cattle began to die from thirst; men, women and children went mad with swollen tongues. The Indians had blocked any help that might have come from Mexico. To-morrow the savage Apaches would come, for once joining the Pueblos in battle.

Governor Otermín took the only alternative between life and death from thirst and butchery and abandoned Santa Fe. The altar of La Hermita was stripped of its chalices and saints, colonists grabbed their few belongings and the Governor divided the provisions among them. The great doors of the zaguán swung open as the dejected Caballeros rode out on their horses, followed by frightened colonists and the remaining cattle and sheep. The Indians watched them go without assault. Not a living Spaniard could be found on the long march south to El Paso where the refugees made their home for the next twelve years.

As the Caballeros rode away, the Indians danced the drama of victory in the plaza and cried "God, the Father of the Spaniards and Mary, their Mother, are dead. But our own gods, whom we obey, have never died." They plunged into the river, scrubbing off the taint of Holy Water with amole lather. They tore down the buildings around the Palace and built in their place terraced communal houses. Two large underground kivas near the plaza were dedicated to the return of the old gods. A high adobe wall with only one doorway surrounded the town. Horses, crosses and the greed for gold were gone. A pueblo flourished once more on the ruins of Kwa-po-ge.

The Indians were not used to a capital. The Tano tribe lived in the Palace and communal buildings in Santa Fe, and other tribes began to quarrel over the spoils of the Spaniards. Return to the old freedom meant also a return to more tribal jealousies and raids. But they held the province against invasion for more than a decade.

It was not easy for Spanish pride to relinquish its stronghold. The ex-Santa Feans, huddled beside the Rio Grande at El Paso, were humiliated and restless in their defeat. Several expeditions started bravely north but were forced to turn back. Finally in

1692 Don Diego de Vargas y Luján Ponce de Leon gathered together an army for the reconquest of Santa Fe "at his own
expense."

Horses and Gentleman-on-Horseback again rode•up the Camino
Real. The success of this third entrada was due more to Caballero
kindness than to the firearms of the Conquistadores. Diplomat as
well as general, de Vargas ordered his soldiers not to harm any
Indian on the march. They arrived before the high adobe walls
surrounding the Santa Fe pueblo in the dawn of September 13,
1692. Sunrise was a happy portent for the colors of Castilla
seemed to have permanently stained the land—crimson cliffs rose
above the southern plain, a spreading cloth of gold of flowering
chamisa and yellow sand.

But war-painted Indians crowded the terraced roofs of the
three- and four-story houses. From the inner plaza came the sounds
of war whoops and the deep beat of drums. Trenches had been
dug before the walls, and four round towers were armed with captured Spanish cannon. The Spaniards' massive Palacio Real had
been turned against them as an impregnable fortress.

De Vargas cautiously camped to the west of the town and began
a parley with the Indians. They jeered at him until his soldiers
repaid the Indians' trick by cutting off the acequia bringing
water into the pueblo. By dawn of the next day the Indians were
ready to talk with de Vargas if he would come inside the walls.
His captains pleaded with him not to go alone through the one
narrow doorway into a death trap of a thousand treacherous
Indians.

"That is nothing," exclaimed de Vargas. "Who will not risk
himself in order to secure perpetual glory and an illustrious
name?" With the Padre Custodio and six soldiers he went through
the door.

Individual bravery was the quality Indians most admired. The
war cacique mét the general with equal dignity. De Vargas explained they had not come to punish the Indians but to forgive and
rebaptize them and to offer them the protection of Spain. "Spain"
was the most formidable word in all the world at that time. Even
in this wilderness frontier it brought submission. De Vargas took
possession of the province again in the name of Carlos Segundo,
and the Padre Custodio blessed the great cross soon erected in the
plaza.

The walled pueblo was left to the Indians while the Spaniards tactfully camped beside the river to the west. A week later the leader Tu-pa-tú, who had succeeded Po-pé, came to pay his respects to de Vargas. Tu-pa-tú was as grand as any Caballero with a mother-of-pearl crown upon his head and a splendid horse under him, for the Indians now exulted in their fine Spanish mounts.

For more than a year de Vargas used the camp as headquarters. In the last cold days of December 1693 Father Farfán came up from Mexico with many colonists. De Vargas could not care for them in camp and the Indians refused to quarter them in the warm adobe houses around the plaza. The general decided that the generosity of the Caballeros had been wasted, and it was time for the Conquistadores to retake their Royal City.

The siege of Santa Fe began the next day. For two days the Indians succeeded in holding their strong walled pueblo. Before dawn of the third day the Spaniards attended mass in the camp chapel, and de Vargas raised aloft the image of his patron saint "La Conquistadora," vowing a yearly celebration in Her honor if She would aid them in a victorious assault. With the zeal of crusaders and the cry of "Santiago" on their lips the soldiers rushed the walls in the dawning light and drove the pagans out of the City of the Holy Faith. By New Year's day of 1694, "La Conquistadora" was established in the hastily refurnished tower chapel of La Hermita, and the Spaniards attended a solemn mass of thanksgiving for having regained for Catholic Spain the capital of the northern province.

De Vargas had little time to rebuild the Royal City, for the last ten years of his life were spent in constant effort to subdue the Indians. He died in the Sandia mountains in 1704, asking that his body be buried under the altar of the church in Santa Fe. In his will he acknowledged his illegitimate son and two daughters, dividing four thousand pesos between them. To his friend Don Antonio Maldonado Zapata he left "one pair of yellow silk stockings embroidered in silver and one pair of socks." Jewels, silverware and the many suits belonging to the aristocratic Caballero were sold to pay the debts he had incurred in reconquering Santa Fe.

When the Marqués de la Peñuela was appointed Governor-General, he began a thorough restoration of the capital. The terraced Indian buildings around the plaza were torn down to make way for Spanish shops, houses and patios. In 1710 the slaves' church of San Miguel was restored by the energetic Marqués "at his own expense," as the carved beam states, and the parish church of San Francisco was rebuilt over the monastery begun by Friar Benavides in 1622 and partially destroyed in the rebellion.

The Indians appreciated the solid construction of the Palace of the Governors too much to destroy it. The Marqués repaired what damage had been done in the fourteen years of Indian occupancy and established himself in the Casas Reales behind the Palace walls. The Palacio continued to be the most important stronghold of the wide province. Within its salas the Caballeros carried on all the pomp of an isolated court with the colorful costumes and strict etiquette characteristic of Spanish rule. In the Sala de Justicia rebellious Indian chiefs were brought before Spanish authority, prisoners were condemned to the dungeon or sent up the hill to La Garita to be hanged, maneuvers were planned, secret treaties sealed and expeditions outfitted to carry Gentle-men-on-Horseback on still further trails.

The eighteenth century was the long era of Spanish colonization for the province. Military men were constantly busy with keeping the King's rule supreme, five thousand Spaniards against the unnumbered foes of roving Indians, besides the sixty populous pueblos. Padres went out unarmed to establish twenty-eight missions far away from the settlements. A site on the Rio Grande, named for the Duke of Albuquerque, in 1705, with La Cañada de Santa Cruz to the north, were the only Spanish towns in the entire province besides Santa Fe.

But up and down the Rio Grande y Bravo the seeds of Spain were sown in smaller clusters. Land could be had for the asking, in a petition to the governor, viceroy and king. The greed for gold persisted in the hope that the dry grants of land might hide veins of pure yellow metal. New Mexico became a patchwork quilt of Spanish grants. They were of odd sizes and, since the surveyor's compass was unknown, natural boundaries of trees, rocks and cañons were confusing in a land that was all trees, rocks and cañons. Adding to the confusion of the titles was the Spanish custom of dividing the land among the numerous children into narrow strips, sometimes only a half a mile wide on the river frontage but running back over the mountains for twenty miles. The vague descriptions of these thirty-five million acres were not to be settled until two hundred years had passed and another army of American conquerors came with their laws to establish the Court of Private Land Claims.

To the colonists of the 1700's it mattered very little if the holdings overlapped in the vast unknown continent. A Spanish grandee might ride for days on his own estate, larger than the state of Connecticut. From his hacienda he could look to any horizon and know that it included his grant from the King.

With such distances to cover, his horse was his most valuable possession. He was the Caballero, luxuriously mounted, owning great cattle and sheep ranges, and master of a home like a feudal castle, where a hundred peons worked at his command. By military force he had conquered his Indian foes, but the daily fear of raiding parties kept him and his horse on their mettle.

Settling the province, living on the frontier upon what provisions they could raise, molding a new pattern of life in the wilderness, could be accomplished only by men and women of great faith, vitality and resourcefulness. Time moved slowly, endured with a patience that is now called the mañana habit. It was in this century that the culture of the Caballeros took permanent root in a province so isolated that no other influence came in to change it.

HENRY HOWE

THE EXPEDITIONS OF
FREMONT,
LEWIS AND CLARK AND
Z. M. PIKE

These narratives of the exploration of the wilderness, now
grim, now exultant, are inspiring examples of the great pioneering spirit traditional in America. Mr. Howe quotes freely
from the reports made by the explorers themselves, courageous
men, pathfinders of our country. (From *The Great West,*
1858.)

FREMONT'S EXPEDITIONS

JOHN C. FREMONT, originally a lieutenant of the United
States Topographical Engineers, made three expeditions to the
Far West under the authority of the general government, a
fourth and a fifth being on private account. The object of the *First
Expedition*—made in 1842—was to explore the country between
the frontiers of Missouri and the *South Pass* in the Rocky Mountains, on the line of the Great Platte and Kansas Rivers. His party
was almost entirely made up in the vicinity of St. Louis, and numbered twenty-eight, including himself. It consisted principally of
Creole and Canadian *voyageurs* of French descent, and familiar

with prairie life from having been in the service of the fur companies in the Indian country. The noted Christopher or *Kit Carson* was engaged as guide. On the 10th of June, the party left Choteau's trading-house, near the Missouri, four hundred miles above St. Louis, on the route of their intended explorations.

The journey was one of much interest, and occasionally enlivened by buffalo hunts and interviews with the Indians of the plains. On the 10th of July, they reached Vrain's Fort, on the south fork of the Platte, and four days after, Fort Laramie, on Laramie's River. This latter post belonged to the American Fur Company, and was inhabited by a motley collection of traders with their Indian wives and parti-colored children. After passing beyond the Hot Spring and the Devil's Gate, two narrow and lofty rocky passages in the mountains, on the 8th of August, they came to the *South Pass* of the Rocky Mountains. On the 15th, Fremont ascended the loftiest peak in this part of the range, which is about one hundred miles north of the southern boundary of Oregon. It is now called *Fremont's Peak*, and rises 13,570 feet above the Mexican Gulf, and is in the part termed the Wind River Mountains.

"We rode on," says Fremont, in describing the ascent, "until we came almost immediately below the main peak, which I denominated the *Snow Peak*, as it exhibited more snow to the eye than any of the neighboring summits. Here were three small lakes of a green color, each perhaps a thousand yards in diameter, and apparently very deep. We managed to get our mules up to a little bench, about a hundred feet above the lakes, where there was a patch of good grass, and turned them loose to graze. Having divested ourselves of every unnecessary incumbrance, we commenced this time like experienced travelers. We did not press ourselves, but climbed leisurely, sitting down so soon as we found breath beginning to fail. At intervals, we reached places where a number of springs gushed from the rocks, and about eighteen hundred feet above the lakes, came to the snow line. From this point our progress was uninterrupted climbing. Here I put on a pair of light thin moccasins, as the use of our toes became necessary to a further advance. I availed myself of a sort of a comb of the mountain, which stood against the wall as a buttress, and which the wind and solar radiation, joined to the steepness of the smooth rock, had kept almost entirely free from snow. Up this I made

my way rapidly. In a few minutes we reached a point where the
buttress was overhanging, and there was no other way of sur-
mounting the difficulty than by passing around one side of it,
which was the face of a vertical precipice of several hundred feet.

"Putting hands and feet in the crevices between the rock, I succeeded in getting over it, and when I reached the top, found my
companions in a small valley below. Descending to them, we
continued climbing, and in a short time, reached the crest. I
sprang upon the summit, and another step would have precipitated
me into an immense field below. As soon as I had gratified the
first feelings of curiosity, I descended, and each man ascended in
his turn; for I would only allow one at a time to mount the un-
stable and precarious slab, which, it seemed, a breath would hurl
into the abyss below. We mounted the barometer in the snow of
the summit, and fixing a ramrod in a crevice, unfurled the national
flag to wave in the breeze where never a flag waved before. A
stillness the most profound and a terrible solitude forced themselves constantly on the mind as the great features of the place.
The day was sunny and clear, but a bright shining mist hung over
the lower plains, which interfered with our view of the surrounding
country. On one side, we overlooked innumerable lakes and streams,
the springs of the Colorado of the Gulf of California, and on
the other, was the Wind River Valley, where were the heads of
the Yellow Stone branch of the Missouri; far to the north, we
could just discover the snowy heads of the *Trois Tetons* (a clus-
ter of high pointed mountains covered with perpetual snow, rising
almost perpendicularly ten thousand feet), where were the sources
of the Missouri and Columbia Rivers; and at the southern extremity of the ridge, the peaks were plainly visible, among which
were some of the springs of the Nebraska or Platte River. Around
us the whole scene had one main striking feature, which was that
of terrible convulsion. Parallel to its length, the ridge was split
into chasms and fissures, between which rose the thin, lofty walls
terminating with slender minarets and columns. We had accomplished an object of laudable ambition and beyond the letter of
our instructions. We had climbed the loftiest peak of the Rocky
Mountains, and looked down upon the snow below, and standing
where human feet had never stood before, felt the exultation of
first explorers." Soon after, the party set out on their return,
and on the 17th of October arrived at St. Louis.

Fremont's *Second Expedition* was made to Oregon and California in the years 1843-44. His corps numbered thirty-nine men, consisting principally of Creoles, Canadian French, and Americans. The party started from the little town of Kansas, on the Missouri frontier, on the 29th of May. Their route was up the valley of the Kansas to the head of the Arkansas and to some pass in the mountains, if any could be found at the sources of that river.

In the early part of their journey, trains of emigrant wagons were almost constantly in sight on their way to Oregon. On the 10th of July, they came in full sight of Pike's Peak. It looked grand and luminous, glittering with snow at the distance of forty miles. On the 13th of August, they crossed the Rocky Mountains at the South Pass. This is on the common traveling route of emigration to Oregon, and about half way between the Mississippi and the Pacific Ocean. On the 6th of September, they ascended an eminence from which they beheld the object of their anxious search—the waters of the Great Salt Lake, "the Inland Sea, stretching in a still, solitary grandeur far beyond the limits of their vision."

After the party had visited the lake, they resumed their route to the mouth of the Columbia, where they arrived on the 25th of October, at the Nez Perces Fort, one of the trading establishments of the Hudson's Bay Company, at the junction of the Wallawalla with the Columbia River.

On the 4th of November, they came to the termination of their land journey westward, from which point they proceeded down the river in boats to *Fort Vancouver*, on the Columbia, about one hundred miles from its entrance into the Pacific. There they were hospitably received by Dr. McLaughlin, the executive officer of the Hudson Bay Company west of the Rocky Mountains. They set out on their return, on the 25th of November, by a southern route. They passed to the south, easterly of the Cascade Mountains, to the Pass in the Sierra Nevada, on whose summit they encamped on the 20th of February, 1844. From this point they proceeded in a southwesterly direction toward San Francisco. The party suffered severely while on this mountainous range. Nearly the whole journey had been made over ground covered with snow, without forage for the cattle, which, when they were starved to death, were eaten by their famished owners. The Indian guides would pilot them for short distances, and pointing with their hands the direction they should take, then desert them. With too good a leader to go in any other direction than that pointed out by duty, too brave men to be discouraged by hundreds of miles of untrodden snow, too familiar with death to quail at his embrace, they persevered and murmured not. But among even these iron-hearted travelers, such were their sufferings, that some became deranged, and plunged into the icy torrents, or wandered in the forests. Well might Fremont have said, "That the times were hard when stout men lost their minds from extremity of suffering; when horses died; and when mules and horses, ready to die from starvation, were killed for food."

On the 10th of January, Fremont discovered the Pyramid Lake in California, about three hundred and fifty miles westerly from the Great Salt Lake. It is about forty miles long and twenty broad, and was named from a huge rock of about six hundred feet in height, rising from the water, and presenting a close resemblance in form to the great pyramid of Cheops. It appeared to the party like a gem in the mountains—its dark-green waves curling in the breeze. The position and elevation of this lake make it an object of great geographical interest. It is the nearest lake to the western rim, as the Great Salt Lake is to the eastern rim, of the *Great Basin,* which lies between the Rocky Mountains and the Sierra Nevada, and has a length and breadth of about five hundred miles. The Great Basin is thus described by Fremont: "Elevation between four thousand and five thousand feet; surrounded by lofty mountains; contents almost entirely unknown, but believed to be filled with rivers and lakes, which have no communication with the sea; deserts and oases, which have never been explored; and savage tribes, which no traveler has seen or described."

On the 20th of February, they encamped on the summit of the Pass, on the dividing ridge of the Sierra Nevada (*i.e.* Snowy Mountain), which rises several thousand feet higher than even the Rocky Mountains.

"On the 6th of March," says Fremont, "we came unexpectedly into a large Indian village, where the people looked clean, and wore cotton shirts, and various other articles of dress. They immediately crowded around us, and we had the inexpressible delight to find one who spoke a little indifferent Spanish, but who at first confounded us by saying that there were no whites in the country; but just then a well dressed Indian came up and made his salutations in very well spoken Spanish. In answer to our inquiries, he informed us that we were upon the *Rio de los Americanos*—the River of the Americans—and that it joined the Sacramento about two miles below. Never did a name sound more sweetly! We felt ourselves among our countrymen; for the name of American, in these distant parts, is applied to citizens of the United States. To our eager inquiries, he replied: 'I am a *vaquero* (cowherd), in the service of Captain Sutter, and the people in this *ranche* work for him.' Our evident satisfaction made him communicative; and he went on to say, that Captain Sutter was a very rich man, and always glad to see his country people. We asked for his house. He answered, it was just over the hill before us, and offered, if we would wait a moment, to take his horse and conduct us to it. We readily accepted his civil offer. In a short distance we came in sight of the fort; and passing on the way the house of a settler on the opposite ridge (a Mr. Sinclair), we forded the river; and in a few miles were met, a short distance from the fort, by Captain Sutter himself. He gave us a most frank and cordial reception, conducted us immediately to his residence, and under his hospitable roof we had a night of rest, enjoyment and refreshment, which none but ourselves could appreciate."

The route homeward was resumed on the 24th of March. They passed along the valley of the San Joaquin southward to its headwaters, where there was a pass through the mountains to the east. "When at this point," says Fremont, "our cavalcade made a strange and grotesque appearance, and it was impossible to avoid reflecting upon our position and composition in this remote solitude. Within two degrees of the Pacific Ocean; already far south of the latitude of Monterey, and still forced on south by a desert on the one hand, and a mountain range on the other; guided by a civilized Indian, and attended by two wild ones from the Sierra; a Chinook from Columbia; and our own mixture of American, French and German—all armed; four or five languages heard at once; above a hundred horses and mules half wild; American, Spanish and Indian dresses intermingled—such was our composition. Our march was a sort of procession; scouts ahead and on the flanks; a front and rear division; the pack animals, baggage and horned cattle in the center; and the whole stretching a quarter of a mile along our dreary path."

On the 18th of April, Fremont struck the *Spanish Trail*, the great object of their search. From the middle of December, they had been forced south by mountains and by deserts, and now would have to make six degrees of *northing* to regain the latitude on which they wished to recross the Rocky Mountains. They followed the Spanish Trail to New Mexico, four hundred and forty miles, and then struck off in a northern direction toward Utah Lake—the southern limb of the Great Salt Lake—which they reached on the 25th of May, having traveled in eight months an immense circuit of three thousand five hundred miles. They crossed the Rocky Mountains about the middle of June, about one hundred and ninety miles south of the South Pass. On the 1st of July, they arrived at Bent's Fort, and on the 31st of July, again encamped on the Kansas, on the frontiers of Missouri.

Fremont was accompanied, as previously mentioned, in this expedition by the celebrated Christopher Carson, commonly called "Kit Carson." Although scarcely thirty winters had passed over him, yet no name was better known in the mountains from Yellow Stone to 'Spanish Peaks, from Missouri to Columbia River. Small in stature, slender limbed, but with muscles of wire, with a fair complexion—to look at Kit, one would not suppose that the mild looking being before him was noted in Indian fight, and had "raised more hair" (*i.e.* scalped) from Redskins, than any two men in the western country. Fremont relates a desperate adventure in which Carson and another mountaineer were engaged, which illustrates the daring bravery of the mountain men.

"While encamped on the 24th of April, at a spring near the Spanish Trail, we were surprised by the sudden appearance among us of two Mexicans; a man and a boy—the name of the man was Andreas Fuentas, and that of the boy (a handsome lad eleven years old) Pablo Hernandez. With a cavalcade of about thirty horses, they had come out from Pueblo de los Angelos, near the Pacific; had lost half their animals, stolen by Indians, and now sought my camp for aid. Carson and Godey, two of my men, volunteered to pursue them, with the Mexican; and, well mounted, the three set off on the trail. In the evening Fuentas returned, his horse having failed; but Carson and Godey had continued the pursuit.

"In the afternoon of the next day, a war whoop was heard, such as Indians make when returning from a victorious enterprise; and soon Carson and Godey appeared driving before them a band of horses, recognized by Fuentas to be a part of those they had lost. Two bloody scalps dangling from the end of Godey's gun, announced that they had overtaken the Indians as well as the horses. They had continued the pursuit alone after Fuentas left them, and toward night-fall entered the mountains into which the trail led. After sunset the moon gave light, and they followed the trail by moonlight until late in the night, when it entered a narrow defile, and was difficult to follow. Here they lay from midnight until morning. At daylight they resumed the pursuit, and at sunrise discovered the horses; and immediately dismounting and tying up their own, they crept cautiously to a rising ground which intervened, from the crest of which they perceived the encampment of four lodges close by. They proceeded quietly, and had got within thirty or forty yards of their object, when a movement among the horses discovered them to the Indians. Giving the war shout, they instantly charged in the camp, regardless of the numbers which the *four* lodges might contain. The Indians received them with a flight of arrows, shot from their long bows, one of which passed through Godey's shirt collar, barely missing the neck. Our men fired their rifles upon a steady aim, and rushed in. Two Indians were stretched upon the ground, fatally pierced with bullets; the rest fled, except a lad, who was captured. The scalps of the fallen were instantly stripped off, but in the process, one of them who had two balls through his body, sprung to his feet, the blood streaming from his skinned head, and uttered a hideous howl. The frightful spectacle appalled the stout hearts of our men; but they did what humanity required, and quickly terminated the agonies of the gory savage. They were now masters of the camp, which was a pretty little recess in the mountain, with a fine spring, and apparently safe from all invasion. Great preparations had been made for feasting a large party, for it was a very proper place for a rendezvous, and for the celebration of such orgies as robbers of the desert would delight in. Several of the horses had been killed, skinned, and cut up—for the Indians living in the mountains, and only coming into the plains to rob and murder, make no other use of horses than to eat them. Large earthen vessels were on the fire, boiling and stewing the horse beef; and several baskets containing fifty or sixty pairs of moccasins, indicated the presence or expectation of a large party. They

released the boy, who had given strong evidence of the stoicism,
or something else of the savage character, by commencing his
breakfast upon a horse's head, as soon as he found he was not to
be killed, but only tied as a prisoner.

"Their object accomplished, our men gathered up all the surviving horses, fifteen in number, returned upon their trail, and
rejoined us at our camp in the afternoon of the same day. They
rode about one hundred miles in the pursuit and return, and all
in thirty hours. The time, place, object and numbers considered,
this expedition of Carson and Godey may be considered among the
boldest and most disinterested which the annals of western adventure, so full of daring deeds, can present. Two men, in a savage
wilderness, pursue day and night an unknown body of Indians
into the defiles of an unknown mountain—attack them on sight
without counting numbers—and defeat them in an instant—and
for what? to punish the robbers of the desert, and revenge the
wrongs of Mexicans whom they did not know. I repeat, it was
Carson and Godey who did this—the former an *American*, born in
Boone County, Missouri; the latter a Frenchman, born in St.
Louis—and both trained to western enterprise from early life."

In the fall of 1845, Fremont started on his *Third Expedition*.
His object was, if possible, to discover a new route to Oregon,
south of the one usually traveled. But his expedition ultimately
became diverted from its intended object by the breaking out of
hostilities between the United States and Mexico, and he became
an active participant in the conquest of California, where he had
arrived in January, 1846.

In June of 1847, he commenced his return to the United States
across the country by the South Pass, in company with General
Kearney, and other officers and privates, to the number of about
forty. At Fort Leavenworth, on the Missouri frontier, he was
arrested by General Kearney, tried, and condemned to lose his
commission, on account of some alleged breach of military etiquette. The President, however, pronounced his pardon; but
Fremont, in June (1848), resigned; maintaining that he had done
no wrong, and desired no clemency.

The fourth and last expedition of Fremont was a private enterprise. His objects were multifarious, but he appears to have had
in view, the discovery of a proper route for the great highway
connecting the Mississippi with the Pacific. The termination of

this expedition was disastrous to all concerned, the history of which has been given in two private letters of Fremont.

On the 25th of November, 1848, Fremont with his party, left the Upper Pueblo Fort, near the head of the Arkansas. They had upward of one hundred and thirty good mules, and one hundred and thirty bushels of shelled corn, intended as a support for their animals in the deep snows of the high mountains. The great error of the expedition appears to have been in engaging, as a guide, an old trapper, well known as "Bill Williams," who spent some twenty-five years of his life in trapping, in various parts of the Rocky Mountains. He proved never to have known, or to have entirely forgotten the country through which they were to pass.

"The 11th of December," says Fremont in his first letter, "we found ourselves at the mouth of the Rio del Norte canon, where that river issues from the Sierra San Juan—one of the highest, most rugged, and impracticable of all the Rocky Mountain ranges, inaccessible to trappers and hunters, even in summer. Across the point of this elevated range, our guide conducted us; and having great confidence in this man's knowledge, we pressed onward with fatal resolution. Even along the river bottoms, the snow was breast deep for the mules, and falling frequently in the valley, and almost constantly in the mountains. The cold was extraordinary. At the warmest hours of the most pleasant day, the thermometer stood at zero. Judge of the night and the storms!

"We pressed up through the summit, the snow deepening as we rose, and in four or five days of this struggling and climbing, all on foot, we reached the naked ridges which lie above the line of the timbered region, and which form the dividing heights between the Atlantic and Pacific Oceans. Along these naked heights it storms all winter, and the winds sweep across them with remorseless fury. On our first attempt to cross, we encountered a *pouderie* —dry snow driven thick through the air by violent wind, and in which objects are visible only a short distance—and were driven back, having some ten or twelve men variously frozen—face, hands, or feet. The guide came near being frozen to death here, and dead mules were lying about the camp fires. Meantime, it snowed steadily. The next day (December) we renewed the attempt to scale the summit, and were more fortunate, it then seemed. Making mauls, and beating down a road or trench through the deep snow, we forced the ascent in spite of the driving *pouderie*, crossed the crest, descended a little, and encamped immediately below in the edge of the timbered region. The trail showed as if a defeated party had passed by—packs, pack-saddles, scattered articles of clothing, and dead mules strewed along. We were encamped about twelve thousand feet above the level of the sea. Westward the country was buried in snow. The storm continued. All movement was paralyzed. To advance with the expedition was impossible. To get back was impossible. Our fate stood revealed. We were overtaken by sudden and inevitable ruin. The poor animals were to go first.

"It was instantly apparent that we should lose every one. I took my resolution immediately, and determined to recross the mountain back to the valley of the Rio del Norte, dragging or packing the baggage by men. With great labor the baggage was transported across the crest to the head springs of a little stream leading to the main river. A few days were sufficient to destroy that fine band of mules. They would generally keep huddled together; and as they froze, one would be seen to tumble down and disappear under the driving snow. Sometimes they would break off, and rush down toward the timber until stopped by the deep snow, where they were soon hidden by the *pouderie*. The courage of some of the men began to fail."

In this situation Fremont determined to send a party to New Mexico for provisions, and for mules to transport their baggage. King, Brackenridge, Creutzfeldt, and the guide, Williams, were selected for this purpose; the party being placed under the command of King. Now came on the *tedium* of waiting for the return of this relief party. Day after day passed, and no news from them. Snow fell almost incessantly in the mountains. The spirits of the camp grew lower. Life was losing its charms to those who had not reasons beyond themselves to live. Proue lay down in the trail and froze to death. On a sunshiny day, and having with him the means to make a fire, he threw his blanket down on the trail, lay down upon it, and lay there till he froze to death!

Sixteen days passed away, and no tidings from the party sent for relief. Weary with delay and oppressed with anxiety, Fremont determined to go in person in search of the absent party and for relief in the Mexican settlements. Leaving the camp employed with the baggage, under the command of Vincent Haler, with injunctions to follow in three days Fremont set off down the river with

Godey, Preuss, and Saunders, a colored servant, leaving in camp provisions only for a few meals.

"On the sixth day after leaving camp," says Fremont, "about sunset, we discovered a little smoke in a grove of timber off from the river, and thinking it might be our express party (King and his men on their return), we went to see. This was the twenty-second day since that party had left us. We found them—three of them: Creutzfeldt, Brackenridge, and Williams—the most miserable objects I had ever beheld. I did not recognize Creutzfeldt's features when Brackenridge brought him up and told me his name. They had been starving. King had starved to death a few days before. His remains were some six or eight miles above, near the river. By the aid of the Indian horses, we carried these three with us down the valley, to the Pueblo on the Little Colorado, which we reached on the fourth day afterward, having traveled in snow and on foot one hundred and sixty miles. I looked upon the feelings which induced me to set out from the camp as an inspiration. Had I remained there, waiting the return of poor King's party, every man of us must have perished.

"The morning after reaching the Little Colorado Pueblo—horses and supplies not being there—Godey and I rode on to the Rio Hondo, and thence to Taos, about twenty-five miles, where we found what we needed; and the next morning, Godey, with four Mexicans, thirty horses or mules, and provisions, set out on his return to the relief of Vincent Haler's party."

Fremont waited in much anxiety for the successful return of those left behind, from the 17th of January until February 5, when Vincent Haler came in. In a subsequent letter, written the next day at Taos, some eighty miles north of Santa Fe, he gives the following account of the terrible calamities that befell those that were left behind:

"You will remember that I left in the camp twenty-three men, when I set off with Godey, Preuss, and my servant, in search of King and succor, with directions about the baggage, and with occupation sufficient to employ them about it for three or four days; after which they were to follow me down the river. Within that time I expected relief from King's party, if it came at all. They remained seven days and then started, their scant provisions about exhausted, and the dead mules on the western side of the great *Sierra*, buried under snow.

"Manuel—you will remember Manuel, a Christian Indian of the Cosumne tribe, in the valley of the San Joaquin—gave way to a feeling of despair, after they had moved about two miles, and begged Vincent Haler, whom I had left in command, to shoot him. Failing to find death in that form, he turned and made his way back to camp, intending to die there. The party moved on, and at ten miles Wise gave out, threw away his gun and blanket, and at a few hundred yards further, fell over into the snow and died. Two Indian boys, countrymen of Manuel, were behind. They came upon him, rolled him up in his blanket, and buried him in the snow on the bank of the river.

"No other died that day. None the next.

"Carver raved during the night—his imagination wholly occupied with images of many things which he fancied himself to be eating. In the morning he wandered off, and probably soon died. He was not seen again. Sorel on this day—the fourth from camp—laid down to die. They built him a fire, and Morin, who was in a dying condition and snow-blind, remained with him. These two probably did not last until the next morning. That evening—I think it was—Hubbard killed a deer. They killed here and there a grouse, but nothing else, the deep snow in the valley having driven off the game. The state of the party became desperate, and brought Haler to the determination of breaking it up, in order to prevent them from living upon each other. He told them that he had done all that he could for them—that they had no other hope remaining for them than the expected relief—and that the best plan was to scatter and make the best of their way, each as he could, down the river; that for himself, if he was to be eaten, he would at all events be found traveling when he did die. The address had its effect. They accordingly separated.

"With Haler, continued five others—Scott, Hubbard, Martin, Bacon, Roher, and the two Cosumne boys. Roher now became despondent and stopped. Haler reminded him of his family and urged him to try and hold out for their sake. Roused by this appeal to his tenderest affections, the unfortunate man moved forward, but feebly, and soon began to fall behind. On a further appeal he promised to follow and to overtake them at evening. Haler, Scott, Hubbard, and Martin now agreed that if any of them should give out, the others were not to wait for him to die, but to push on and try to save themselves. Soon this mournful covenant had to be kept.... At night Kerne's party encamped a few hundred yards from Haler's, with the intention, according to Taplin, of remaining where they were until the relief should come, and in the meantime to live upon those who had died and upon the weaker ones as they should die. With this party were the three brothers Kerne, Chaplin, Cathcart, McKie, Andrews, Stepperfeldt, and Taplin.

"Ferguson and Beadle had remained together behind. In the evening, Roher came up and remained in Kerne's party. Haler learnt afterward from some of the party, that Roher and Andrews wandered off the next morning and died. They say they saw their bodies. Haler's party continued on. After a few hours, Hubbard gave out. According to the agreement, he was left to die, but with such comfort as could be given him. They built him a fire, and gathered him some wood, and then left him—without turning their heads, as Haler says, to look at him as they went off.

"About two miles further, Scott—you remember him, he used to shoot birds for you on the frontier—he gave out. He was another of the four who had covenanted against waiting for each other. The survivors did for him as they had done for Hubbard, and passed on.

"In the afternoon, the two Indian boys went ahead—blessed be these boys!—and before nightfall met Godey with the relief. He had gone on with all speed. The boys gave him the news. He fired signal guns to notify his approach. Haler heard the guns and knew the crack of our rifles, and felt that relief had come. This night was the first of hope and joy. Early in the morning, with the first gray light, Godey was in the trail, and soon met Haler with the wreck of his party slowly advancing. I hear that they all cried together like children—these men of iron nerves and lion hearts when dangers were to be faced or hardships to be conquered! They were all children in this moment of melted hearts. Succor was soon dealt out to these few first met, and Godey with his relief, accompanied by Haler who, turning back hurriedly, followed the back trail in search of the living and the dead scattered in the rear. They came to Scott first. He was alive, and is saved! They came to Hubbard next. He was dead, but still warm. These were the only ones of Haler's party that had been left. From Kerne's party, next met, they learnt the deaths of Andrews and Roher; and a little further on, met Ferguson, who told them that

Beadle had died the night before. All the living were found and saved, Manuel among them—which looked like a resurrection—and reduced the number of the dead to TEN—one-third of the whole party which a few days before was scaling the mountain with me, and battling with the elements twelve thousand feet in the air.

"How rapid are the changes of life! A few days ago, and I was struggling through snow in the savage wilds of the Upper Del Norte—following the course of the river in more than Russian cold, no food, no blanket to cover me in the long frozen nights—uncertain at what moment of the night we might be roused by the Indian rifle—doubtful, very doubtful, whether I should ever see you or friends again. Now, I am seated by a comfortable fire, alone, pursuing my own thoughts, writing to you in the certainty of reaching you—a French volume of Balzac on the table—a colored print of the landing of Columbus before me—listening in safety to the raging storm without!

"You will wish to know what effect the scenes I have passed through have had upon me. In person none. The destruction of my party and the loss of friends are causes of grief, but I have not been injured in body or mind. Both have been strained and severely taxed, but neither hurt. I have seen one or the other, and sometimes both, give way in strong frames, strong minds, and stout hearts; but as heretofore, I have come out unhurt. I believe that the remembrance of friends sometimes gives us a power of resistance which the desire to save our own lives could never call up."

In about a fortnight after writing the foregoing account, Fremont made up a party at Santa Fe, and started for California overland by the old Gila route, where he arrived early in the succeeding spring, his family having preceded him by the Panama route.

LEWIS AND CLARK'S AND PIKE'S
EXPLORING EXPEDITIONS

Expedition of Lewis and Clark.—Just before the transfer of Louisiana to the United States, in 1803, President Jefferson was preparing to have explored what now comprises the northwestern part of our country, of which then but little was known. In January, 1803, Congress having approved of his suggestions, he commissioned Captains Meriwether Lewis and William Clark, to explore the Missouri and its principal branches to their sources, and then to seek and trace to its termination in the Pacific, some stream which might give the most direct and practicable water communication across the continent, for the purposes of commerce. Other persons, were, at the same time, appointed to examine the Upper Mississippi and its principal western tributaries below the Missouri; exact information being desired as soon as possible of the newly acquired territories from France, that power having previously possessed the country west of the Mississippi, under the general name of Louisiana.

Shortly after Lewis had received his instructions, the news of the conclusion of the treaty for the cession of Louisiana, reached the United States. In May, 1804, the party of Lewis and Clark commenced the ascent of the Missouri in boats. Their ascent being slow, they did not arrive at the country of the Mandan Indians, sixteen hundred miles from the Mississippi, near lat. 48 deg., until the latter part of October.

Remaining in their encampment in the Mandan country until the 7th of April, following, Lewis and Clark, with thirty men, commenced their voyage westward up the Missouri, and about the 1st of May, reached the mouth of the principal branch, called by the French traders, the *Roche Jaune*, or Yellow Stone River. Thence continuing their progress westward on the main stream, their navigation was arrested on the 13th of June, by the *Great Falls of the Missouri*, a series of cataracts extending about ten miles in length, in the principal of which, the whole river rushes over a precipice of rock eighty-seven feet in height. Again embarking in canoes, they on the 19th of July, passed through the *Gates of the Rocky Mountains*, where the Missouri, emerging from that chain, runs for six miles in a narrow channel between perpendicular, black rocky walls of twelve hundred feet in height. Beyond this, they ascended its largest source, named by Lewis, Jefferson River, near lat. 44 deg., where the navigation of the Missouri ends near three thousand miles from its entrance into the Mississippi. While the canoes were ascending Jefferson River, Lewis and Clark, with some of their men, proceeded through the mountains, and soon found streams flowing to the west, and meeting several parties of Indians belonging to a nation called Shoshonee, they were satisfied from their accounts, that those streams were the head waters of the Columbia. They then rejoined their

men at the head of Jefferson, and having *cached* (concealed in
pits) their canoes and goods, and procured some Shoshonees for
guides, and some horses, the whole party pursued their journey
overland, and on the 30th of August, entered the Rocky Mountains.

Up to this time their difficulties and privations were comparatively small; but during the three weeks they were passing through
the mountains, they underwent every suffering which hunger, cold,
and fatigue could impose. The mountains were high, and the
passes through them rugged and in many places covered with
snow; and their food consisted of berries, dried fish, and the meat
of dogs or horses, of all which the supplies were scanty and
precarious.

About four hundred miles by their route from Jefferson River
they reached the Kooskooske, and on the 7th of October, began its
descent in canoes which they constructed. In three days they
entered the principal southern branch of the Columbia, which they
named Lewis, and in seven more reached its junction with its
larger northern branch, which was called by them Clark. They
were then fairly launched on the *Great River of the West*, and
passing down it through many dangerous rapids, they, on the 31st,
arrived at the *Falls of the Columbia*, where it rushes through the
lofty chain of mountains nearest the Pacific. On the 15th of November, they landed on Cape Disappointment, at the mouth of the
Columbia, after having passed over about six hundred miles on its
waters, and reaching a point of more than four thousand miles
from the mouth of the Missouri.

The winter, or rather rainy season, soon setting in, they built a
dwelling in that vicinity, which they named *Fort Clatsop*, where
they remained until March 23d, 1806. Then they commenced
their return by ascending the Columbia in their canoes. Proceed-
ing carefully up the stream they discovered the *Cowelitz* and the
Willamette, the latter now noted for having on its banks the most
flourishing settlements in Oregon.

At the Falls of the Columbia they abandoned their canoes, and
proceeded on horses to their point of embarkation on the Kooskooske in the preceding year; thence due eastward through the
Rocky Mountains to Clark River, which flows for some distance
in a northerly direction from its sources before turning southward to join the other branches of the Columbia. There, on the 3d

of July, in latitude forty-seven degrees, Lewis and Clark separated to meet at the mouth of Yellow Stone.

Lewis with his party proceeded northward some distance down the Clark, and then, quitting it, crossed the Rocky Mountains to the headwaters of the *Maria*, which empties into the Missouri just below the falls. There they met a band of Indians belonging to the numerous and daring race, called the *Blackfoot*, who infest the plains at the base of the mountains, and are ever at war with all other tribes. These savages attempted to seize the rifles of the Americans, and Lewis was obliged to kill one of them before they desisted. The party then hastened to the Falls of the Missouri, and thence floated down to the mouth of the Yellow Stone, which is scarcely inferior in length to the main branch of the Missouri.

Meanwhile, the party under Clark rode southward up the Clark to its sources; and after exploring several passes in the mountains between that and the headwaters of the Yellow Stone, they embarked on it in canoes, and descending, joined Lewis and his men at its mouth on the 12th of August. From thence the whole body floated down the Missouri, and on the 23d of September, 1806, arrived in safety at St. Louis after an absence of more than two years, during which they had traveled over nine thousand miles.

The Missouri had been ascended to the mouth of the Yellow Stone by the French and Spanish Indian traders, long before this expedition, but no correct information had been obtained of the river and country. With regard to the country between the Great Falls of the Missouri and those of the Columbia, we have no accounts earlier than those furnished by this exploring expedition. Their journal is still the principal source of information, respecting the geography, natural history, and the aboriginal inhabitants of that region.

Politically, the expedition was an announcement to the world of the intentions of the American government to occupy and settle the countries explored, and they thus virtually incurred the obligation to prosecute and fulfill the great ends for which the labors of Lewis and Clark were preparatory.

A few years since there was residing at Brown's Hole, in Oregon, an old Shoshonee Indian, who was the first of his tribe who saw the cavalcade of Messrs. Lewis and Clark, on the headwaters of the Missouri, in 1805. He appears to have been galloping from place to place in the office of sentinel to the Shoshonee camp, when he suddenly found himself in the very presence of the whites. Astonishment fixed him to the spot. Men with faces as pale as ashes had never been seen by him or his nation. "The head rose high and round, the top flat; it jutted over the eyes in a thin rim; their skin was loose and flowing, and of many colors." His fears at length overcoming his curiosity, he fled in the direction of the Indian encampment. But being seen by the whites, they pursued and brought him to their camp, exhibited to him the effect of their fire-arms, loaded him with presents, and let him go. Having arrived among his own people, he told them he had seen men with faces pale as ashes, who were makers of thunder and lightning, etc. This information astounded the whole tribe. They had lived many years, their ancestors had lived many more, and there were many legends which spoke of many wonderful things, but a tale like this they had never before heard. A council was, therefore, held to consider the matter. The man of strange words was summoned before it, and he rehearsed in substance what he had before told others, but was not believed. "All men were red, and there-fore, he could not have seen men as pale as ashes. The Great Spirit made the thunder and lightning; he, therefore, could not have seen any men of any color that could produce it. He had seen nothing—he had lied to his chief, and should die." Upon this, the culprit produced some presents which he had received from the pale men. These being quite as new to them as pale faces were, it was determined "that he should have the privilege of lead-ing his judges to the place where he had declared he had seen these strange people; and if such were found there, he should be excul-pated; if not, these presents were to be considered as conclusive evidence that he dealt with evil spirits, and that he was worthy of death by the arrows of his kinsfolks." The pale men—the thunder makers were found, and were witnesses of the poor fellow's story. He was released, and was ever after much honored and loved by his tribe and every white man in the mountains. He was then about eighty years old, and poor, but was never permitted to want.

Pike's Expedition.—During the absence of Lewis and Clark, the United States prosecuted other explorations in different parts of Louisiana. Lieutenant Z. M. Pike—afterward the celebrated

General Pike, who fell at York, Upper Canada, in 1813—was sent, in 1805, to explore the sources of the Mississippi. Having set out late in the season, he proceeded to the mouth of the Crow Wing, where, winter having overtaken him, he erected a blockhouse for the protection of his men and stores, and proceeded in snow-shoes with a small party to Leech Lake and other places in that vicinity, and returned on the opening of navigation in the spring, without having fully accomplished the objects of his journey. During his absence he purchased of the Indians the site where Fort Snelling, the first American establishment in Minnesota, was founded in 1819.

In the year 1806, he was sent on another exploring expedition by the United States Government with a party of men, in the course of which he traveled southwestward from the mouth of the Missouri up the Arkansas, with directions to pass to the sources of that stream, for which those of the Canadian were then mistaken. He, however, even passed around the head of the latter, and crossing the mountain with an almost incredible degree of peril and suffering, descended upon the Rio del Norte with his little party, then but fifteen in number. Believing himself now upon Red River within the then assumed bounds of the United States, he erected a small fortification for his company until the opening of the spring of 1807 should enable him to continue his descent to Natchitoches.

As he was within the Mexican Territory, however, and but about seventy miles from the northern settlements, his position was soon discovered, and a force sent out to take him into Santa Fe, which, by a treacherous maneuver, was effected without opposition. The Spanish officer assured him that the governor, learning that he had missed his way, had sent animals and an escort to convey his men and baggage to a navigable port on Red River (Rio Colorado), and that his excellency desired very much to see him at Santa Fe, which might be taken on their way. As soon, however, as the governor had him in his power, he sent him with his men to the Commandant-General at Chihuahua, when most of his papers were seized and he and his party were sent under an escort, via San Antonio de Bexar, to the United States.

The Red and Washita Rivers were at the same time explored to a considerable distance from the Mississippi, by Messrs. Dunbar,

Hunter, and Sibley, whose journals, as well as those of Pike, Lewis, and Clark, were subsequently published, and contain many interesting descriptions of those parts of America.

Thus within three or four years after Louisiana came into the possession of the United States, it ceased to be an unknown region, and the principal features of the country drained by the Columbia were displayed.

WASHINGTON IRVING

THE CAMP OF THE WILD HORSE

There is a great deal of pathos in this narrative of the capture and subjugation of a wild horse (or The Pacing Mustang, as he is known in the folk tale of the Western frontier) "one day, a prince of the prairies—the next day, a pack-horse!" Irving comments, "The transition in his lot was such as sometimes takes place in human affairs, and in the fortunes of towering individuals." (From *Tour on the Prairies*, the first volume of *The Crayon Miscellanies*, 1835.)

WE HAD encamped in a good neighborhood for game, as the reports of rifles in various directions speedily gave notice. One of our hunters soon returned with the meat of a doe, tied up in the skin, and slung across his shoulders. Another brought a fat buck across his horse. Two other deer were brought in, and a number of turkeys. All the game was thrown down in front of the captain's fire, to be portioned out among the various messes. The spits and camp kettles were soon in full employ, and throughout the evening there was a scene of hunter's feasting and profusion.

We had been disappointed this day in our hopes of meeting with buffalo, but the sight of the wild horse had been a great novelty, and gave a turn to the conversation of the camp for the evening. There were several anecdotes told of a famous gray horse, which

363

has ranged the prairies of this neighborhood for six or seven years, setting at naught every attempt of the hunters to capture him. They say he can pace and rack (or amble) faster than the fleetest horses can run. Equally marvelous accounts were given of a black horse on the Brazos, who grazed the prairies on that river's bank in Texas. For years he outstripped all pursuit. His fame spread far and wide; offers were made for him to the amount of a thousand dollars; the boldest and most hard-riding hunters tried incessantly to make prize of him, but in vain. At length he fell a victim to his gallantry, being decoyed under a tree by a tame mare, and a noose dropped over his head by a boy perched among the branches.

The capture of a wild horse is one of the most favorite achievements of the prairie tribes; and, indeed, it is from this source that the Indian hunters chiefly supply themselves. The wild horses which range those vast grassy plains, extending from the Arkansas to the Spanish settlements, are of various forms and colors, betraying their various descents. Some resemble the common English stock, and are probably descended from horses which have escaped from our border settlements. Others are of a low but strong make, and are supposed to be of the Andalusian breed, brought out by the Spanish discoverers.

Some fanciful speculatists have seen in them descendants of the Arab stock, brought into Spain from Africa, and thence transferred to this country; and have pleased themselves with the idea that their sires may have been of the pure coursers of the desert that once bore Mahomet and his warlike disciples across the sandy plains of Arabia.

The habits of the Arab seem to have come with the steed. The introduction of the horse on the boundless prairies of the Far West changed the whole mode of living of their inhabitants. It gave them that facility of rapid motion, and of sudden and distant change of place, so dear to the roving propensities of man. Instead of lurking in the depths of gloomy forests, and patiently threading the mazes of a tangled wilderness on foot, like his brethren of the North, the Indian of the West is a rover of the plain; he leads a brighter and more sunshiny life; almost always on horseback, on vast flowery prairies and under cloudless skies.

I was lying by the captain's fire, late in the evening, listening to the stories about those coursers of the prairies, and weaving speculations of my own, when there was a clamor of voices and a loud cheering at the other end of the camp; and word was passed that Beatte, the half-breed, had brought in a wild horse.

In an instant every fire was deserted; the whole camp crowded to see the Indian and his prize. It was a colt about two years old, well grown, finely limbed, with bright prominent eyes and a spirited yet gentle demeanor. He gazed about him with an air of mingled stupefaction and surprise, at the men, the horses, and the campfires; while the Indian stood before him with folded arms, having hold of the other end of the cord which noosed his captive, and gazing on him with a most imperturbable aspect. Beatte, as I have before observed, has a greenish olive complexion, with a strongly marked countenance, not unlike the bronze casts of Napoleon; and as he stood before his captive horse with folded arms and fixed aspect he looked more like a statue than a man.

If the horse, however, manifested the least restiveness, Beatte would immediately worry him with the lariat, jerking him first on one side, then on the other, so as almost to throw him on the ground; when he had thus rendered him passive, he would resume his statue-like attitude and gaze at him in silence.

The whole scene was singularly wild; the tall grove, partially illumined by the flashing fires of the camp, the horses tethered here and there among the trees, the carcasses of deer hanging around, and in the midst of all, the wild huntsman and his wild horse, with an admiring throng of rangers, almost as wild.

In the eagerness of their excitement, several of the young rangers sought to get the horse by purchase or barter, and even offered extravagant terms; but Beatte declined all their offers. "You give great price now," said he, "to-morrow you be sorry, and take back, and say d—d Indian!"

The young men importuned him with questions about the mode in which he took the horse, but his answers were dry and laconic; he evidently retained some pique at having been undervalued and sneered at by them; and at the same time looked down upon them with contempt as greenhorns, little versed in the noble science of woodcraft.

Afterward, however, when he was seated by our fire, I readily drew from him an account of his exploit; for, though taciturn among strangers, and little prone to boast of his actions, yet his taciturnity, like that of all Indians, had its times of relaxation.

He informed me that, on leaving the camp, he had returned to the place where we had lost sight of the wild horse. Soon getting upon its track, he followed it to the banks of the river. Here, the prints being more distinct in the sand, he perceived that one of the hoofs was broken and defective, so he gave up the pursuit.

As he was returning to the camp, he came upon a gang of six horses, which immediately made for the river. He pursued them across the stream, left his rifle on the river bank, and putting his horse to full speed, soon came up with the fugitives. He attempted to noose one of them, but the lariat hitched on one.of his ears, and he shook it off. The horses dashed up a hill, he followed hard at their heels, when, of a sudden, he saw their tails whisking in the air, and they plunged down a precipice. It was too late to stop. He shut his eyes, held in his breath, and went over with them —neck or nothing. The descent was between twenty and thirty feet, but they all came down safe upon a sandy bottom.

He now succeeded in throwing his noose round a fine young horse. As he galloped alongside of him, the two horses passed each side of a sapling, and the end of the lariat was jerked out of his hand. He regained it, but an intervening tree obliged him again to let it go. Having once more caught it, and coming to a more open country, he was enabled to play the young horse with the line until he gradually checked and subdued him, so as to lead him to the place where he had left his rifle.

He had another formidable difficulty in getting him across the river, where both horses stuck for a time in the mire, and Beatte was nearly unseated from his saddle by the force of the current and the struggles of his captive. After much toil and trouble, however, he got across the stream, and brought his prize safe into camp.

For the remainder of the evening the camp remained in a high state of excitement; nothing was talked of but the capture of wild horses; every youngster of the troop was for this harum-scarum kind of chase; every one promised himself to return from the campaign in triumph, bestriding one of these wild coursers of the prairies. Beatte had suddenly risen to great importance; he was the prime hunter, the hero of the day. Offers were made him by the best mounted rangers to let him ride their horses in the chase, provided he would give them a share of the spoil. Beatte bore his honors in silence, and closed with none of the offers. Our stammering, chattering, gasconading little Frenchman, however, made up for his taciturnity by vaunting as much upon the subject as if it were he that had caught the horse. Indeed he held forth so learnedly in the matter, and boasted so much of the many horses he had taken, that he began to be considered an oracle; and some of the youngsters were inclined to doubt whether he were not superior even to the taciturn Beatte.

The excitement kept the camp awake later than usual. The hum of voices, interrupted by occasional peals of laughter, was heard from the groups around the various fires, and the night was considerably advanced before all had sunk to sleep.

With the morning dawn the excitement revived, and Beatte and his wild horse were again the gaze and talk of the camp. The captive had been tied all night to a tree among the other horses. He was again led forth by Beatte, by a long halter or lariat, and, on his manifesting the least restiveness, was, as before, jerked and worried into passive submission. He appeared to be gentle and docile by nature, and had a beautifully mild expression of the eye. In his strange and forlorn situation, the poor animal seemed to seek protection and companionship in the very horse which had aided to capture him.

Seeing him thus gentle and tractable, Beatte, just as we were about to march, strapped a light pack upon his back, by way of giving him the first lesson in servitude. The native pride and independence of the animal took fire at this indignity. He reared, and plunged, and kicked, and tried in every way to get rid of the degrading burden. The Indian was too potent for him. At every paroxysm he renewed the discipline of the halter, until the poor animal, driven to despair, threw himself prostrate on the ground, and lay motionless, as if acknowledging himself vanquished. A stage hero, representing the despair of a captive prince, could not have played his part more dramatically. There was absolutely a moral grandeur in it.

The imperturbable Beatte folded his arms, and stood for a time, looking down in silence upon his captive; until seeing him perfectly subdued, he nodded his head slowly, screwed his mouth into a sardonic smile of triumph, and, with a jerk of the halter, ordered him to rise. He obeyed, and from that time forward offered no resistance. During that day he bore his pack patiently, and was led by the halter; but in two days he followed voluntarily at large among the supernumerary horses of the troop.

I could not look without compassion upon this fine young animal, whose whole course of existence had been so suddenly reversed. From being a denizen of these vast pastures, ranging at will from plain to plain and mead to mead, cropping of every herb and flower, and drinking of every stream, he was suddenly reduced to perpetual and painful servitude, to pass his life under the harness and the curb, amid, perhaps, the din and dust and drudgery of cities. The transition in his lot was such as sometimes takes place in human affairs, and in the fortunes of towering individuals. One day, a prince of the prairies—the next day, a pack-horse!

HENRY HOWE

LIFE AMONG THE TRAPPERS

A portrait from life of the Rocky Mountain trapper, "strong, active, hardy . . . expert in the use of weapons . . . depending upon his instinct for the support of life," is presented in the following narrative, another selection from Henry Howe's *The Great West*.

THE trappers of the Rocky Mountains belong to a "genus" more approximating to the primitive savage, than, perhaps, any other class of civilized men. Their lives being spent in the remote wilderness of the mountains, with no other companion than Nature herself, their habits and character assume a most singular cast of simplicity, mingled with ferocity, appearing to take their coloring from the scenes and the objects which surround them. Knowing no wants, save those of Nature, their sole care is to procure sufficient food to support life, and the necessary clothing to protect them from the vigorous climate. This, with the assistance of their trusty rifles, they are generally able to effect, but sometimes at the expense of great peril and hardship. When engaged in their avocation, the natural instinct of primitive men is ever alive to guard against danger and provide food.

Keen observers of nature, they rival the beasts of prey in discovering the haunts and habits of game, and in their skill and cunning in capturing it. Constantly exposed to perils of all kinds, they become callous to any feeling of danger, and destroy human, as well as animal life, with as little scruple, and as freely as they expose their own. Of laws, human or divine, they neither know nor care to know. Their wish is their law, and to attain it, they do not scruple as to ways and means. Firm friends and bitter enemies, with them it is "a word and blow," and the blow often first. They may have good qualities, but they are those of the animal; and people fond of giving hard names, call them revengeful, blood-thirsty, drunkards—when the wherewithal is had—gamblers, regardless of the laws of *meum* and *tuum*—in fact, "white Indians." However, there are exceptions, and we *have* met honest mountain men. Their animal qualities, nevertheless, are undeniable. Strong, active, hardy as bears, daring, expert in the use of weapons, they are just what uncivilized white men might be supposed to be in a brute state, depending upon his instinct for the support of life. The majority of the trappers and mountain hunters are French Canadians and St. Louis French Creoles.

Not a hole, or a corner of the "Far West," but has been ransacked by these hardy men. From the Mississippi to the mouth of the Colorado of the West, from the frozen regions of the North to the Gila in Mexico, the beaver trapper has set his traps in every stream. Most of this vast country, but for their daring enterprise, would be, even now, a *terra incognita* to geographers. The mountains and the streams still retain the names assigned to them by the rude hunters; and these alone, are the hardy pioneers who braved the way for the settlement of the western country.

Trappers are of two kinds—the "hired hand," and the "free trapper"; the former is hired for the hunt by the fur companies; the latter supplied with animals and traps by the company is paid a certain price for his furs and peltries. There is, also, the trapper "on his own hook"; but this class is very small. He has his own animals and traps, hunts where he chooses, and sells his peltries to whom he pleases.

On starting for a hunt, the trapper fits himself out with the necessary equipment, either from the Indian trading forts, or from some of the petty traders—*coureurs des bois*—who frequent the western country. This equipment consists usually of two or three horses or mules—one for saddle, the others for packs—and six traps, which are carried in a bag of leather, called a *trap-sack*. Ammunition, a few pounds of tobacco, dressed deer-skins for moccasins, etc., are carried in a wallet of dressed buffalo-skin, called a *possible pack*. His "possibles" and "trap-sack" are generally carried on the saddle mule while hunting, the others being packed with the furs. The *costume* of the trappers is a hunting-shirt of dressed buck-skin, ornamented with long fringes; pantaloons of the same material, and decorated with porcupine quills and long fringes down the outside of the leg. A flexible felt hat and moccasins clothe his extremities. Over his left shoulder and under his right arm, hang his powder-horn and bullet-pouch, in which he carries his balls, flint, steel, and odds and ends of all kinds. Round the waist is a belt, in which is stuck a large butcher-knife in a sheath of buffalo-hide, made fast to the belt by a chain or guard of steel, which, also, supports a little buck-skin case containing a whetstone. A tomahawk is often also added; and, of course, a long heavy rifle is part and parcel of his equipment. Around his neck hangs his pipe holder, and is generally a *"gage d'amour,"* and a triumph of squaw workmanship, in shape of a heart garnished with beads and porcupine quills.

Thus provided, and having determined the locality of his trapping-ground, he starts to the mountains, sometimes alone, sometimes three or four in company, as soon as the breaking up of ice allows him to commence operations. Arrived on his hunting-ground, he follows the creeks and streams, keeping a sharp lookout for "sign." If he sees a prostrate cotton-wood tree, he examines it to discover if it be the work of beaver—whether "thrown" for the purpose of food, or to dam the stream. The track of the beaver on the mud or sand under the bank, is also examined; and, if the "sign" be fresh, he sets his trap in the run of the animal, hiding it under water, and attaching it by a stout chain to a picket driven in the bank, or to a bush or tree. A "float stick" is made fast to the trap by a cord a few feet long, which, if the animal carry away the trap, floats on the water, and points out its position. The trap is baited with "medicine," an oily substance obtained from a gland in the scrotum of the beaver, but distinct from the testes. A stick is dipped into this, and planted over the trap; and the beaver, attracted by the smell, and wishing a close inspection, very foolishly puts his leg into the trap, and is a "gone beaver."

When a lodge is discovered, the trap is set at the edge of the dam, at the point where the animal passes from deep to shoal water, and always under water. Early in the morning, the hunter always mounts his mule and examines the traps. The captured animals are skinned, and the tails, which are a great dainty, carefully packed into camp. The skin is then stretched over a hoop, or frame-work of osier twigs, and is allowed to dry; the flesh and fatty substance being carefully scraped (grained). When dry, it is folded into a square sheet, the fur turned inward, and the bundle, containing about ten to twenty skins, lightly pressed and corded, is ready for transportation.

During the hunt, regardless of Indian vicinity, the fearless trapper wanders far and near in search of "sign." His nerves must ever be in a state of tension, and his mind ever present at his call. His eagle-eye sweeps around the country, and in an instant, detects any foreign appearance. A turned leaf, a blade of grass pressed down, the uneasinesss of wild animals, the flight of birds, are all paragraphs to him, written in Nature's legible hand and plainest language. All the wits of the subtile savage are called into play to gain an advantage over the wily woodsman; but with the instinct of primitive man, the white hunter has the advantage of a civilized mind, and thus provided, seldom fails to outwit, under equal advantage, the cunning savage.

Sometimes following on his trail, the Indian watches him set his traps on a shrub-belted stream, and passing up the bed, like Bruce of old, so that he may leave no track, he lies in wait in the bushes until the hunter comes to examine his carefully set traps. Then waiting until he approaches his ambush within a few feet, *whiz*, flies the home-drawn arrow, never failing at such close quarters to bring the victim to the ground. For one white scalp, however, that dangles in the smoke of an Indian lodge, a dozen black ones, at the end of the hunt, ornament the camp-fire of the rendezvous.

At a certain time, when the hunt is over, or they have loaded their pack animals, the trappers proceed to their "rendezvous," the locality of which has been previously agreed upon; and here the traders and agents of the fur companies await them with such assortment of goods as their hardy customers may require, including generally a fair supply of alcohol. The trappers drop in singly and in small bands, bringing their packs of beaver to this mountain market, not unfrequently to the value of a thousand dollars each, the produce of one hunt. The dissipation of the "rendezvous," however, soon turns the trapper's pocket inside out. The goods bought by the traders, although of the most inferior quality, are sold at enormous prices—coffee twenty and thirty shillings a pint cup, which is the usual measure; tobacco fetches ten and fifteen shillings a plug; alcohol from twenty to fifty shillings a pint; gunpowder sixteen shillings a pint cup; and all other articles at proportionably exorbitant prices.

The "beaver" is purchased at from two to eight dollars per pound; the Hudson's Bay Company alone buying it by the pluie or "pluew," that is, the whole skin, giving a certain price for skins, whether of old beaver or "kittens."

The rendezvous is one continued scene of drunkenness, gambling, brawling, and fighting, so long as the money and credit of the trappers last. Seated Indian fashion around the fires, with a blanket spread before them, groups are seen with their "decks" of cards playing at "euchre," "poker," and "seven up," the regular mountain games. The stakes are "beaver," which is here current coin; and when the fur is gone, their horses, mules, rifles, and shirts, hunting packs, and breeches are staked. Daring gamblers make the rounds of the camp, challenging each other to play for the trapper's highest stake—his horse, his squaw (if he have one), and as once happened, his scalp. A trapper often squanders the produce of his hunt, amounting to hundreds of dollars, in a couple of hours; and supplied on credit with another equipment, leaves the rendezvous for another expedition, which has the same result, time after time, although one tolerably successful hunt would enable him to return to the settlements and civilized life with an ample sum to purchase and stock a farm, and enjoy himself in ease and comfort the remainder of his days.

These annual gatherings are often the scenes of bloody duels, for over their cups and cards, no men are more quarrelsome than your mountaineers. Rifles, at twenty paces, settle all differences, and as may be imagined, the fall of one or other of the combatants is certain, or as sometimes happens, both fall at the word "fire!"

CAPTAIN WILLIAM BANNING
and GEORGE HUGH BANNING

STAGE-COACH

We have all seen in the motion-picture and in the museum, the stage-coach of the West. But little is known of its origin and history. Certainly almost nothing is known of Jim Birch, the man who "put an empire on wheels." In the following excerpt from *Six Horses* (Appleton-Century Company, 1928) is an exciting account of the coach and the men who rode and ruled it. It is a breathtaking chapter in the history of American transportation and one of the most colorful stories in our nation's history.

I THE MAN WHO WOULD BE KING

STAGES, with their teams of six, are backed up in long rows, sweating porters and baggage-masters in front and behind. John Chinaman, with long tail wound at the back of his head, is running distractedly through the crowd in search of a lost bundle; anxious women, prolific in crinoline and gorgeous in silks and satins, are fretting and scolding over crushed bandboxes; and stern-looking men of an official cast are shouting fiercely:

"This way, gents! Over here with your baggage! Bring it along if you want it weighed; if you don't, it won't go—that's all!"

And there is the machine that weighs; and there stands the inexorable gentleman that marks off the weights—ten, forty, sixty, ninety pounds per passenger—thirty pounds allowed; all extra baggage twenty-five cents per pound.

"Fifteen dollars for you, sir." "Twenty-five for you, sir." "Forty-six for you, madam." "Seventy-five for you, miss—heavy trunk that, miss."

"Oh, dear! Oh, goodness gracious! Must I pay seventy-five dollars for my trunk?"

"Yes, miss—sorry for it—no getting over it."

"Oh!"

"Quick, if you please, ladies and gents! Stages behind time—won't get to Placerville before dark."

"All aboard!" and off goes stage No. 1.

"Pile in, gents. Get down from that front seat, you, sir—place engaged. All aboard!" and off goes stage No. 2.

"Pitch in, Cap—all set!" and stage No. 3 follows through the dusty clouds that cover the road and the hillsides. And so on till we are all fairly in and off, looking back with fervent thanks that we are clear at last. . . .

It was as J. Ross Browne found and described it on a lively day in the middle sixties when there existed a daily stage-coach service across the plains—a distance of nearly two thousand miles, coursed within seventeen days.

It is certain [he writes] there is no such a country in the world for feats of horse-flesh. . . . The length of our stage routes, the rapidity with which we travel upon them, and the facilities afforded by the expresses, are matters of astonishment to the people of Europe, who have not the faintest idea of the real difficulties to be overcome in carrying enterprises into effect in a wild country like ours.

During my sojourn in Germany, I received a letter from California by Pony Express in less than four weeks after it was written; and it was not until I showed the date and express stamp and carefully explained the whole matter that I was enabled to overcome the incredulity of my Teutonic friends. The idea of such a feat being accomplished by horse-flesh was something they could not comprehend. Nor could they quite reconcile their notions of the practicable that we had spanned the continent with our stages—crossing deserts and mountains, from San Francisco to Missouri, as they would cross the cultivated plains and well-graded hills of their native country.[1]

[1] "Adventures in the Apache Country," 308-315.

Such enterprise was, moreover, unparalleled in the world's annals; for the world had never, perhaps, made such demands. It was a natural development, and a naturally rapid development with, not unlikely, the continued unity of the very nation at stake.

The prodigious gold rush of forty-nine was followed by a period of some thirteen years before any Pacific Railroad measure became a law, not to mention the seven additional years required for the law to become a railroad. It was in spite of the fact that the earliest floods of westward emigration had put the project rather clearly in the light of an exigency. As early as 1850, with California's admission into statehood, alarmists were not alone in their misgivings that the retention of perhaps half the new Western empire might depend upon the immediate driving of spikes and the clenching of iron bands across the continent.

Stage lines, real stage lines with regular and frequent relays over the wilderness to fill the temporary need, might have been vaguely suggested by the crude night-camping mule wagons that trekked with the mail and occasional passengers from the Missouri frontiers to Santa Fe or to the Mormon city at Salt Lake; but for all that any system of horse transportation might have meant toward the preservation of national ties, there was to choose, it seemed, between the utterly inadequate and the utterly fantastic or impossible. The delay of the railroad was not to be taken lightly.

The very wilderness, with its unconquered nations of Indians, its deserts, its Continental Divide, its coastal barriers—the vast, vague map of the future—presented such uncertainties that it was not difficult to fancy as many national boundaries as those over the Continent of Europe. The virtual principality of Mormons, which often appeared to be waiting for the day—*der Tag*—when Uncle Sam might see fit to take issue with its attitude of independence—here was a slight manifestation of possibilities. But the youthful State of California, with her appalling increase of population, with her heavy infusion of foreign blood, young blood, and with her national barriers and resources—here were real potentialities; and they could not be overlooked.

Ties with the new State of the Pacific were more sound, no doubt, than all of the East was prepared to believe; but they were based to a considerable extent upon the promise of benefits which were being everlastingly withheld. The bond, though perhaps stanchly elastic, was stretching; and it was a stretch more like that of a hopeful imagination than of any pervading sense of national allegiance.

But this situation was not the most ominous one. The extended delay of rail legislation was a far lesser menace in itself than the circumstances causing the delay. For the same conditions of broadly divided national interests, leading rapidly and surely toward civil war, were likewise throwing one political faction against the other on the question of what overland route should be favored by Federal appropriations. Any feasible line of communication which happened to pass through Northern territories was sure to be condemned by the South and *vice versa*.

Thus, at a critical time when the ties between the North and the South were being tensed toward their point of breaking, those between the East and the West were being put to an unwonted test. Something had to be done; and suffice it to say that *perhaps* the stage-coach did it, idle though it may be to speculate on what might have been the history and geography of any country had worse come to worst. But considering the tremendous rôle that the old vehicle assumed, and the visionary aspect which that rôle first presented, one is apt to look for a genius among the pioneers —some one who perceived the opportunity, asked for no precedent but simply drove in to fill the breach.

There was such a genius—a man, broadly, whom nobody knows. Not as many as two consecutive pages of history or biography have heretofore been devoted to his memory; but he died as the emperor of the whole West-American stage-coach institution; and it may be said of him fairly that he put an empire on wheels. He was Jim Birch, a Yankee. He was James E. Birch, with middle name lost even to his surviving kin, although some of them dwell in the mansion which he built from the gold-dust that swirled up from the fast wheels of his pioneer stage.

It was with the creaking of ox-yokes and the slogging of cloven hoofs that he made his first journey to the Pacific Coast. And from the big muddy Missouri, along the green of the Platte, over the passes of the Rocky Mountains, and across deserts beyond, there were moving the fleets of young men like himself, the Argonauts of forty-nine—one white, monotonous, almost endless file. It was contracting and expanding, stopping here and starting there, yet in the grip, it would seem, of but one irresistible power, winding in such fiber as the maps of empires are made of, such stuff as romance is spun from—material like Birch, and also like Frank Shaw Stevens, who was fairly a part of Birch.

Now, in the course of their four months' journey from Providence, Rhode Island, to Sacramento, California, they were rocking in their saddles, side by side, relaying the cries from other horsemen in advance, and inhaling the dust of an interminable caravan. Dust and more dust, but they enjoyed it; they were dusty by trade—they were, or had been, stage drivers.

Whether or not they would ever "drive stage" again they could not have predicted with much certainty. But once a man had learned to hold the whip, to wield it and to handle the multiple lines; once he had trained his foot to the delicate manipulation of the brake and gloried in the sight of four or six horses pattering along before him, responding by shades of movement to his every whim, he was married to an art and could not hope to abandon it without surrendering much of himself. There was an infinite glamour to his calling. His whip had been his scepter and his box a throne. He had held the sway of the road and all that fringed it, from the little boys that tossed their caps as he passed, or the guests of the tavern who hung on his words, or the farmer's wife who urged him to sample her biscuits and cider, to the eyes that peeped at him from upstairs windows and the small handkerchief that sometimes waved. Knight of the Reins! Here he comes! There he goes! He knew what it was to be king.

Young Birch and Stevens were not, therefore, of any very humble origin, although now they were learning what it was to be looked upon simply as any mere Tom, Dick, or Harry. What was a driver, or even a reinsman, a master out here in this wilderness where the need of him as yet was wholly nil?

It was true—not a coach wheel turned in any land from the Missouri River to the Pacific shores. Some day, perhaps, some one would lay on the whip; but now travelers shifted for themselves and cared not so long as they "got there." The whole affair seemed only as a temporary fling. The New West, the new waste, was to be shorn of its gold; then . . . home again!

Thus Birch may have been thinking in rather broad transcontinental terms even at this early date; and if already his visionary travels involved in a stage route of his own across this wild expanse, perhaps he was not alone in his fancies. There were rumors, for one thing, of a firm in St. Louis, bent on establishing a wagon service of a kind to ply between the Missouri frontiers and California, carrying some hundred and twenty passengers to the trip at $200 a head. It was an enterprise which, like several others of the kind, was destined to die in the embryo; and Birch was too practical a stageman to think of operating a mere passenger mule train with any hope of success.

But there were many other stagemen bumping along somewhere or other in the line—Charles McLaughlin, perhaps, and Warren F. Hall, J. B. Crandall, John Dillon, other whips not incapable of driving between the lines of history. In short, here in this caravan were embodied all the potentialities—the modes and methods, the habits and traditions—the best blood of New England's old stage-coach order. It was flowing toward a fertile field, the richest soil for which it could possibly have hoped. It was moving toward a land where it was bound to flourish independent of mail contracts—of government, politics—and to flourish to such an extent that a line extended eastward across the continent would appear not only as practicable but as a natural growth. The transplanted Yankee system was to know an eastward rather than a westward progression. From California, as more than a predominating influence, an improved New England school was to become the school of the plains.

All this could scarcely have been foreseen by the many whips now on their way to the new El Dorado. But dreams were at large, and there were probably few more glittering than those which accompanied the train of Birch and Stevens. Twenty-one years being the age of them both, they were apt to have had great expectations; yet Stevens appeared as sophisticated and deliberate as the typical driver of New England, openly suspicious of anything that glittered, to say nothing of the yarns from El Dorado. Birch was different—electrical, his eyes burning and sparkling as from a runaway dynamo within him. But he had himself well in control; and his mastery cannot be more clearly demonstrated than by his actions upon reaching the Gold Coast with the wild men of forty-nine.

Here, amid the carnival whirl of what-not in big boots and scraggly or braided beards, in sombreros and flaming serapes, in raven coats and craven stovepipes, in pig-tails and silken jackets

—amid all that gyrated between Sacramento and Hangtown, between gambling-houses and churches, between temporary distraction and permanent dementia—Birch, by his equanimity, must have appeared madder than them all. He began doing only what he had done at home. He commenced "driving stage."

Stevens seemed also to be underestimating possibilities. He had invested in a wooden shack, a hotel in the center of Sacramento City—the center, that was, so long as two merchant vessels, retailing ware from their decks, remained in their present berths along the river bank. There were other rival establishments. "Eating is Done Here" was the sign on one; "Tip-top Accommodations for Men and Beasts" was the boast of another; "Rest for the Weary and Storage for Trunks" was the appeal of the building of Stevens.

Here James Birch may have stored a saddle roll and wished his old friend well; but he, just now at least, was not seeking rest. There were relay stations to organize and stock to buy; and, while his route was to be only about thirty miles in extent, the investment and responsibilities were considerable. Several sporadic attempts at the staging business by rancheros and others (who knew nothing about it) had already resulted in so many failures. There was that to consider. Still, there was reason to believe that he, Birch, an experienced driver, was not taking quite their chances.

There was, moreover, a certain Alexander Todd, pioneering in the Western express business, just as Birch was pioneering along stage lines. Todd, too, could point back to premature efforts and failures of others; but having invested in a rowboat on the Rio San Joaquin, now he was prospering. If Todd could deliver mail to Stockton at a rate of four dollars per letter, carry gold-dust back in butter kegs at other such rates of profit, tax his oarsmen (his power plant) sixteen dollars a head, going and coming, and divide sometimes as much as a thousand dollars a day with his partner, surely the prospects were bright enough in the business of transportation. And thirty dollars a passenger would be no presumptuous rate of fare for a thirty-mile drive by stage.

In any event, Birch appeared one morning in September with an old rancho wagon. He was perched upon it in as stately a manner as though on the box of a Concord coach fresh from the shops of Abbot Downing. Holding some bull-whacker's lash as a true linesman would hold a stage-whip, he humored four nervous mustangs, four Mexican broncos that were apparently stage-struck before the gathering throngs. But it was:

"All aboard for Mormon Island! Forks of the American River! All aboard!"

It was all aboard for the maiden trip; all aboard, incidentally, for the very inception of everything which was to be regarded in days to come as West-American staging. He had conceived the embryo of a colossus; it was to become a giant even under his patronage, and stand prepared to meet a national crisis before passing from his control.

Blanket rolls, guns, and boots; picks and shovels and tin pans; hairy faces and war whoops; wild horses but master reins. . . .

"All aboard!"

II THE EARLY STAGES

There was to be established in the following year (1850), over an old mail route between Independence, Missouri, and Santa Fe, an isolated and rather forlorn mule-wagon concern which, even after more than a decade of operation, would boast only several relay stations over a distance of about 850 miles! A few other similar but still more primitive systems for the carriage of mail in various parts of the plains region were forthcoming shortly; but they were to be purely trekking institutions. And at present these camping-out lines could no more suggest a solution to the overland problem than did Birch's line of stock in California. The railroad was the project. One heard nothing but railroad.

There were arguments on the subject of routes for the laying of tracks, and of negotiable passes through the high Sierra Nevadas, as though the locomotive were just outside, whistling for some one to open a gate. During 1849, and a brief several years thereafter, there was a locomotive attached to the general train of thought from the Atlantic Coast to California.

We want the railroad [cried the "New York Tribune" while the year was yet 1850] and cannot have it an hour too soon. If it were done to-morrow the difficulty would not be to find business enough, but to do all that would offer. California is a State of this Union, but is 40 days' journey from the seat of government. She should not be above ten days; she must not be if we would have our Republican Empire hold together and realize in the future all the greatness we so fondly imagine.[2]

The South had recently made another of her periodic gestures toward secession. As for California—"each year, and she grows more powerful, populous and wealthy," the "Tribune" concluded; "the tie that binds her to the confederation will become weaker unless it be strengthened by iron bands."

Roaring steam of this nature was being let off with equal force in Washington, St. Louis, New Orleans, and elsewhere, not to mention the volumes of it that were generated in the various meetings, conventions, newspaper offices, and all spheres of common converse on the Pacific Coast.

Albeit, nearly two decades were to pass before the advent of rails across the continent. There was strife ahead, and enough of it without a civil war—more than enough arising from the railroad itself. Coveted by the South to serve Southern territory and by the North to serve its own, the project was soon to become so involved in sectional wrangling as to be classed with hopes deferred. If visible ties of union were required to meet the pending crisis, there was meaning to the crack of a pioneer's whip, to his cry of "All aboard!"

To Birch himself, it seems, there was a far-reaching significance involved; but it was of a rather personal and private nature. It had to do with a young girl in New England, Julia Chase, stepdaughter of his former employer, Otis Kelton of Providence. It had to do with ways and means of returning to her with what fortune in gold would be needed to support a wife.

Thus Birch was bound to the country he had left by a wisp of hair. California, as the "New York Tribune" might well have considered along with its fears of disunion, was likewise bound to the nation that claimed it by myriads of similar wisps—dark ones, light ones, red, white, and all but blue ones; but of all these, there was one to warrant some special regard.

The romance involved in the life of Birch (which was also the romance of Stevens) was to have a peculiar but positive bearing upon his public career and hence, providentially, even upon the development of overland transportation throughout the West.

[2] Quoted by the "California Courier," November 6, 1850.

Frank Stevens did not join his friend Birch at once in the business of staging; and in fact his national significance as a stageman is of a rather singular nature.

It is true that his biography might accord him a conspicuous place among the earlier and later proprietors of important lines; that it might recall him, for instance, as having formed apparently the first and most perfect link in one of the later great overland chains, or as having served many years as an active vice-president, and later as a mainstay, of what was at one time the largest stage-coach firm in the world, or as having been a financial power behind one early overland line. All this was a part of his career; but it was the least of it. Alone, it would have placed him in a class of splendid pioneer whips who, though they served to put an empire on wheels, are all too numerous to name. And his other —his greater enterprises—unfortunately are not to be found in Stagedom. But this fact remains:

Frank Stevens was a friend of Birch; his life is inextricable from the romantic saga of Birch; and to Birch—first and last— belongs the story of a very noteworthy pioneer phase.

Now, however, Stevens was merely saving a few generous pinches of "dust," trying to content himself, perhaps, with "Rest for the Weary and Storage for Trunks," while stages went clattering off to the mines and back with a share of their gold. Birch, having led off in the race, had been joined by others. The rumble of his wheels had been accompanied by a prospering jingle and attracted men of his calling from many parts of the country. Never before, in the world of hoofs and wheels, had there appeared such unbounded opportunities.

Travel—it was the impulse and the act and the life. There were fairly no moorings: neither home nor bonnet nor bib. There were restless young men in droves; there was the atmosphere of adventure with prospects everywhere. Be it slump or boom here or there in the gold-fields, the stages packed them coming and going. They sheared the gold fleece from their will-o'-the-wisps at a rate as high as a dollar to the mile. Soon there was scarcely a place in the whole mining region where four and six horse teams were not leaving their tracks.

Down the craggy mountains, loaded with passengers and express, came the stage, the driver with one foot, two arms, both shoulders, and all fingers working, his body swaying like a sailor's to the motion of a ship, his leaders dancing at the brink of damnation, wheels striking sparks out of granite, flicking chips into space, while passengers stared out over the blue tops of pines, chewing their cigars to a pulp. It was a common spectacle; miles by the hundreds were being rolled out every day.

The precocious nature of the yearling institution is suggested in part through the "Recollections" of California's first American governor, Peter Burnett. News of "the Department's" leap into statehood during the fall of 1850 had already thrown San Francisco into happy riot, but had yet to be despatched to the capitol at San José. The governor himself joined the race among bearers, his vehicle a stage-coach, his driver one J. B. Crandall,[3] a new part-owner with Warren Hall of the line.

"He was one of the celebrated stagemen," observes Burnett, who might have added, by the way, that Crandall, after a very enviable career among the pioneers of his kind, was to be the first to span the Sierra Nevadas with a stage route. But at this early juncture he was regarded only as "a most excellent man . . . a cool, kind but determined and skillful driver."

"There were two rival lines to San José," Burnett goes on. And their quaint advertisements, to interrupt the late governor again, may be appropriately reprinted here so that we may select our own vehicle or driver in the race to San José. These notices appeared in the "Pacific News" during the latter months of 1850.

This was a time [says Peter Burnett] to test their speed.

After passing over the sandy road to the mission, there was some of the most rapid driving that I have ever witnessed. . . . The people flocked to the road to see what caused our fast driving and loud shouting, and without slackening our speed in the slightest degree, we took off our hats, waved them around our heads, and shouted at the top of our voices:

"California is admitted to the Union!"

Thus flew Crandall's team over the dry, hard prairie lands, and onward, through lightning relays, toward the capitol of the State. And there was Crandall himself, known as "the prince of drivers," with the governor beside him, racing on through the dust, through

[3] In some of the advertisements of the day this name was spelled Crandal, and is so printed in the accompanying reproduction.

the yellow, whisking grasses and glades of oaks, neck and neck at times with a rattling rival, yet calmly watching his horses with a knowledge of their separate capacities, calling them by name, holding them in, telling each what to do, signaling with the most precise movements of individual or multiple lines, urging them at last, forging ahead. . . .

Ackley & Maurison's opposition advertised "60 miles, in about Six hours," but Ackley & Maurison were to taste the dust of "Berford"—of Hall & Crandall. Crandall had passed. It was fitting that he should have. It was fitting that the governor should be the first to bring the news to his seat of government. But it was perhaps more fitting that it should have been driven home thus to the heart of the new State aboard a stage-coach, and with such a splendid reinsman, and future blazer of overland roads, upon the box.

They had stretched on into San José. California admitted to the Union! Steamer news! California admitted!

Almost literally she had come in on wheels. And it may have been aboard the typical American coach from Concord, New Hampshire; for the first of an endless succession of them to be imported by clipper around Cape Horn had already appeared, drawn by six splendid bays, in San Francisco (June 24, 1850) several months before Crandall's race.

Upon that occasion—the advent, it appears, of the first real coach of all Trans-Mississippi Stagedom[4]—large crowds had turned out to marvel and to reminisce, to be carried, as one editor was already able to imagine, "several thousand miles over the hills and far away" to the States.

Long since recognized there as the only perfect passenger vehicle in the world, it was an epoch-making Yankee creation whose excellence, in the light of its purpose, had never been, and was never to be, duplicated by other manufacturers. Abbot, Downing & Company alone knew how to make them. With a record (now mostly lost) dating back to 1813, it is not surprising that by 1858 this historic firm, covering four acres of ground in Concord, New Hampshire, was to boast "the largest factory in the United States,"[5] with buyers in Mexico, South America, and the colonies

[4] See (San Francisco) "Alta California," June 25, 1850—a date exactly five days before a coach, probably of the Troy or Concord make, is said to have pulled out on a maiden trip from Independence, Missouri, for Santa Fe.

[5] "Sacramento Union," July 31, 1858.

even of coach-building England, including Australia and South
Africa, one fourth of the yearly output being marked for export.
There were reasons for this popularity.

The conveyance itself, as one cannot be reminded too often, was
not the worn, torn, dead thing of our museums, much less the grotesque rattletrap of our fiction, drama, and other oft-profaning
arts, but a resplendent and proud thing—a heavy but apparently
a light thing of beauty and dignity and life. It was as tidy and
graceful as a lady, as inspiring to the stagefaring man as a ship
to a sailor, and had, incidentally, like the lady and the ship,
scarcely a straight line in its body.

With trim decking and panels of the clearest poplar, and with
stout frame of well-seasoned ash, this body, in all of its tri-dimen-
sional curves, fairly held itself together by sheer virtue of scientific design and master joinery, for very little iron was used; and
this, where needed, was iron only of the best Norway stock.

It was a body design evolved as a pleasing modification from
the early nineteenth-century types, shaped somewhat like an egg,
but surviving in this period only as "cuts" for advertisements.
The newer type, the typical, was, among other things, far more
commodious, having ample and well-upholstered space inside for
nine passengers. Outside there was room for at least a dozen more,
while the "boots"—the cargo holds of the front and rear—de-
voured mail bags, express boxes, and baggage, if not an occasional
stowaway or some passenger desiring to curl up for a little nap.

"Thorough-braces"—two lengths of manifold leather straps
of the thickest steer hide—suspended this heavy structure, allowed it to rock fore and aft, and, incidentally, to perform a vital
duty beyond the province of any steel springs. It was a function
of such importance to the Western staging world that we may
hazard the contention that an empire, as well as the body of its
coach, once rocked and perhaps depended upon thorough-braces.

Without them, at least, there could have been no staging to
meet a crying need. Without them over the rugged wilderness, any
vehicle carrying the loads that had to be carried, maintaining
such speed as the edicts of staging demanded, would have been
efficient only as a killer of horses. For thorough-braces, while they
served the purpose of springs to a very adequate extent, had the
prime function of acting as shock-absorbers for the benefit of
the team. By them violent jerks upon the traces, due to any ob-

struction in the road, were automatically assuaged and generally eliminated. It was the force of inertia—the forward lunge and the upward lurch of the rocking body—that freed the wheels promptly from impediment, and thus averted each shock before it came upon the animals. Passengers could tolerate a little buffeting, while the coach itself had been made to withstand any shock that any road could impose, and to survive this punishment through a lifetime at least, given the usual care.

Each spoke of the Concord wheel, hand-hewn from the clearest ash, was the result of a series of painstaking selections, carefully weighed and balanced in the hand, and fitted to rim and hub (where eyes could not stray) as snugly as any surface joint in the best of joinery. So well seasoned was the whole that it was practically insensible to the climatic changes in any part of the world. Africa proved the fact for Major Frederick R. Burnham, who saw the wheels of many wagons shrink, warp, and go to pieces, the Concord wheel standing alone and holding its shape. Such qualities of durability in a coach weighing about 2,500 pounds may not appear at once to be the soundest boast, but when it is added that no other vehicle of equal capacity, and few enough of any capacity, ran as easily over the average road, there is little more to be said.

It is no wonder that California, with the rugged mining zones of her mountains to face, began importing Concords before the year of 1850 was half done, and no wonder that scores of them were to follow, though it were by the route of Cape Horn. The growing demand was everywhere apparent. Fifteen months of existence, and the local system could count at least fifteen busy stage firms and a mileage sufficient to extend suggestively well-nigh to the Rocky Mountains.

It was in 1851 when Frank Stevens sprang into the race and founded the "Pioneer Line" from Sacramento to Hangtown or Placerville—the same line which later old Crandall was to project beyond the Sierra Nevada to a point not six hundred miles from Salt Lake City.

Birch had extended his route considerably and was adding two more. He was out to conquer along with a dozen other rising firms in whose dusty tracks opposition rose and fell. The traveler of 1851 had only to visit one of the larger staging centers— Marysville, Stockton, or, above all, Sacramento—in order to appreciate their numbers and the competition involved.

In Sacramento, for example, he might have stopped at the Crescent City Hotel—a new establishment of seventy-five rooms, extra bunk space, and with coffee, beans, and venison for breakfast by candle-light at five in the morning. But even at this early hour, there was always consolation in the fact that some hundred other travelers had also been routed from their blankets. By disposing hurriedly of breakfast, moreover, he could spend time to advantage at the bar.

This room, before the stages pulled away, was crowded with red- or blue-shirted miners in boots, with their guns and various accouterments, with their patchwork trousers and fiery complexions, all bound for various diggings; and what a tremendous circus parade of vehicles was required to take them there! Outside this morning, as every morning, the congestion was a hub-rubbing and swearing affair. Stages stood four abreast, occupying the whole wide street for a distance of some sixty-five yards. And despite this very early date, though the four-horse ranch wagon still prevailed, there were many real Concord coaches among them, and teams—to quote J. D. Borthwick, an Englishman who viewed the scene—"as good as ever galloped with her Majesty's mail."[6]

The animals were pawing and snorting, grooms at the leaders' heads trying to quiet them. Drivers were humoring them and calling out the towns of their devious routes. Runners were living up to their names, hustling here and there, yelping and shouting:

"This way, sir! Nevada City! Over here for Nevada! Over there for Stockton and Sonora! Birch stages connect for Sonora and the Southern Mines!"

"Shasta! Here! Shasta, sir, and Tehama! Baxter & Munroe stages for Tehama and Shasta! . . . One-Horsetown, you say!"

"No. Georgetown!"

"Horsetown! You bet! That's us! One-Horsetown!"

And the Georgetown aspirant, carpet-bag and all, was fairly boosted into the Horsetown and Shasta coach, while the runner

[6] "American horses" from Ohio, Kentucky, and elsewhere, driven in from over the plains, were rapidly supplanting the native mustangs in the staging world. Borthwick says that at this time dray horses were being imported from Sydney; cab horses were the finest—worth from $1,000 to $1,500 each; that a three-minute horse was the "slowest worth driving," that a two-forty horse was not considered fast, and that stage-coaches sometimes covered "60 miles in about five hours" (which of course *was* considered fast). See Borthwick, "Three Years in California."

went leaping off to catch another and ship him to parts unknown.

Then with a firing-off of whips in the lead, the great mass of stages began to move. There were the sounds of cavorting hoofs and the shouting of miners. Hostlers cleared away as best they could. The rolling mass gained speed, such speed at last that it appeared unable to remain any longer intact. Off flew the many component parts over the arc of an open fan, and in nearly as many directions as a fan has ribs. There was a waving of "wide-awake" hats— Good-by! *Au revoir! Adiós!* and the same perhaps in Chinese, Norwegian, Hawaiian, German, Portuguese, and half the languages of the civilized world; for these stages were loaded to the utmost with nearly everything. Away they went over a vast sea of green sprayed over with wild flowers on a straight course for the still-invisible mountains. Roadless, fenceless, postless, hedgeless, houseless—it was, says Mr. Borthwick, like going to sea with a fleet of small vessels. They spread rapidly away from one another, and farther away till they were all hull-down on the horizon.

Then it was:

> Creeping through the valley, crawling o'er the hill,
> Splashing through the branches, rumbling o'er the mill;
> Putting nervous gentlemen in a towering rage.
> What is so provoking as riding in a stage?
>
> Spinsters fair and forty, maids in youthful charms,
> Suddenly are cast into their neighbors' arms;
> Children shoot like squirrels darting through a cage—
> Isn't it delightful, riding in a stage?
>
> Feet are interlacing, heads severely bumped,
> Friend and foe together get their noses thumped;
> Dresses act as carpets—listen to the sage:
> "Life is but a journey taken in a stage."

It was the impression, at least, of some local bard of the day whose inspiration, to judge from its domestic flavor, must have sprung from the old Spanish *Camino* to San José. Otherwise it might have come from any or all roads in the State. They were all rather bumpy. A driver did well to avoid them whenever it was possible, and for this reason they often appeared to be hundreds of feet in width. But in the mountains the way was so narrow that only at certain known points could two vehicles pass. A Mrs. D.

B. Bates, telling of the trying conditions to be encountered by women on the Gold Coast in the early fifties, calls staging in the mountains "perfectly awful":

One night about eleven o'clock [she writes] a lady came into the hotel [at Marysville] looking more dead than alive. She was leading a little girl of about seven years of age, who was in the same plight as her mother. They were both covered with bruises, scratches and blood, with their garments soiled and torn. They were coming back from Bidwell's Bar, a place about forty miles from Marysville, in a stage-coach in which were nine Chinamen. The coach was all closed, as it was rather cool in the mountains in the evening. All at once they found themselves turning sommersets.

The coach was overturned down a steep bank. All the Chinamen with their long cues reaching to their heels, were rolling and tumbling about in the most ungraceful manner imaginable. They were vociferating at the tops of their voices in a language which, if spoken calmly . . . is harsh and disagreeable in extreme. "And," said she, "such a horrid din of voices as raged in my ears, it was scarcely possible to conceive of; which, together with the fright, was almost sufficient to deprive me of my reason." The driver was seriously hurt, and so were some of the horses; but the inside passengers escaped without having any of their limbs broken, but their cues were awfully disarranged.[7]

Stage-coach accidents, according to all sound experience as well as careful statistics, were, however, extremely rare,[8] but there is no doubt that riding was rough, generally, over the whole staging West. In certain regions at certain times, where and when nature granted, this was not the case; and it is true that the building and maintenance of a few highways in later days might have done credit to the work of Sir James and Mr. John Louden McAdam as happily known to the wheels of the old British mail; but it would scarcely do for a Western stageman to boast of his roads— especially in the presence of some coaching enthusiast from England.

He might better confine his boasting to the fact that his roads,

---

[7] Mrs. Bates. "Four Years on the Pacific Coast."

[8] Early California daily journals seldom failed to note even the slightest of stage-coach mishaps. One deliberate count of them all covered a period of five years—1855-60—and indicated that, certainly, there was not an average of one accident per month—forty of them over a period of sixty months being the actual findings. All these entailed about twenty-five mentionable injuries and but one consequent death.

however scientifically graded, were terrible, his country rough enough to shake passengers out of their wits, hills steep enough to frighten them into distraction, turns of such a nature that six horses and coach might cover, all at one time, the essential curvatures of the letter S; and so on. Then, not only would he be rather close to the truth, but at the business end of the stage-coach horn. He would be in the position of the seaman from around Cape Horn confronting the mariner from Lake Lucerne: "You've never seen nasty weather, m'lad, and you'll never be a sailor till you do."

In short, there is no warranted comparison between the old British and the later American institutions. The vastness of the latter's country, and the brevity of its life therein, put the problem of good roads almost beyond consideration. It became necessary for the Yankee to develop his equipments, his methods, his men in a manner to surmount obstacles which neither the British coach, the British methods, nor the British coachman was ever obliged to contemplate. The Englishman was happily able to make his ways suit his means; the Yankee was forced to do the opposite. Two very different systems naturally evolved.

One Western driver of the early fifties may be recalled from Horace Bell's "Reminiscences" as having driven a six-horse coach, for certain reasons, over "a precipice"—it was, no doubt a very steep grade. "Down! down! down! Rickety clatter bang! Sometimes the horses ahead of the stage, sometimes the stage ahead of the horses, all, however, going down! down with a crash!"

The driver, it seems, was simply proving to an unbelieving world that a stagecoach and team could traverse this particular mountain; that the pass was worthy of improvement. The hope was to stimulate popular subscription for the construction of a road; and in this light, as it proved, the demonstration was "a complete success."

The enterprising linesman, having extricated himself and animals from the wreckage, promptly despatched riders with news that the coach had successfully gone over—gone over, in fact, with flying colors. Appropriations from merchants and business houses were forthwith advanced. A small army of men, armed with shovels and picks, were soon on hand "to repair parts of the road" which the coach in its descent had "knocked out of joint." Overland trade—freighting and staging—followed between two parts of

California which had formerly depended on the sea for all such intercourse; and it was by the route thus blazed that there later passed the first transcontinental stages into northern California as a precursor of the Southern Pacific Railroad.

Thus pathfinding of a kind was sometimes an important part of the Western stageman's business; and, as it may be seen, similar feats to promote the construction of negotiable mountain transits belong with far-reaching significance to the annals of these pioneers. Their ways, in one sense, were rough; but on the whole they were rough in one sense only. There are apparently many misconceived notions with regard to the old order as it ranged in its prime through the West.

STANLEY VESTAL

WINDWAGON

Like the stage-coach, the "windwagon," or prairie schooner, is for us another symbol of the hardiness and enterprise of our ancestors. Stanley Vestal (whose real name is W. S. Campbell), a gifted exponent of the Southwest, describes here Windwagon Thomas and his sail-bearing prairie craft. It is an authentic piece of Americana, almost folklore, and it is a story that might readily lend itself to song and ballad. (From *The Old Santa Fe Trail*, Houghton Mifflin, 1939.)

THE trail to Santa Fe led from Missouri almost a thousand miles across the Great Plains to the Spanish settlements at the foot of the Rocky Mountains.

Those plains were like the ocean, a region of magnificent distances, of desolate and barren wastes, strange, solitary, unexplored. Sometimes that ocean was a sea of grassy hillocks, sometimes level with the flatness of dead calm, oftener rolling in long swells to the far-off horizon, green, tumultuous, tossing its waves of grass under the driving winds, changing shape and color as swift cloud shadows sped over the uneven surface.

Like the sea, those plains were swept by masses of living things: vast shoals of shaggy bison, antelope, and other game, which appeared and disappeared without warning. Birds, sometimes even gulls, flapped and soared above it. And like the sea, the plains were subject to violent storms, sudden variations of temperature, ter-

rific gales, cruel frosts, tornadoes, and drenching cloudbursts.
Here and there that empty sea was broken by buttes like islands,
sterile promontories.

The emptiness, the loneliness, the pathetic solemnity of the
region oppressed some men, and all women, to the verge of mad-
ness. Many, on first emerging from their familiar woodlands, became physically sick. Even Coronado's hard-boiled Spanish
troopers were terrified by a country where one could see the sky
under a horse's belly.

But for those hardy tempers who could love great spaces, where
one spot was no more important than another, experience of
the sea of grass was glorifying. On the Great Plains a man of
strong identity stood always at the center of his world, a king of
infinite space.

Today we think of the Santa Fe Trail in terms of wagons:
wagons creaking up long prairie slopes; wagons rolling down
hills; wagons grinding through heavy sand, sucking through
sticky mud, swishing through tall grass; wagons with locked
wheels plunging down steep river-banks; wagons snaked through
clinging quicksands, or jiggling over ribbed sandbars rough as
cobblestones; wagons hauled yard by painful yard up the forbidding rocks of the Raton Pass, two slow miles a day; wagons
corralled against the attacks of treacherous redskins; wagons
broken down, abandoned, stranded by the loss of animals stolen
by raiding savages; wagons burned in prairie fires; wagons warped
and shrunken by the heat and drouth. Wagons crammed with
rich furs, Mexican silver, gold bullion.

But in the old days, travellers on those plains spoke habitually of "making port," urged Congress to enact navigation laws
for the "prairie ocean." Their covered wagons, appropriately
dubbed "prairie schooners," were in fact watertight boats mounted
on wheels, rising high at prow and stern. They thought of the
plains in terms of seafaring, and felt the glamour of them as a
magic of the sea. They named the jumping-off place in Missouri
Westport!

In Westport, fittingly enough, a company was actually formed
to navigate the uncharted plains in wagons rigged with sails and
steering-gear.

One spring day in 1853, the citizens of that frontier town were
amazed to see a light vehicle steering down the street, driven by

the wind which filled its white sail. Horses reared and ran away, women and children fled into their houses, dogs scuttled for safety, and the men of Westport stood with open mouths, watching that strange craft come sailing in.

Its pilot lowered the sail, locked his brakes, and rolled to a stop before the entrance to the Yoakum Tavern. He disembarked, and the startled citizens gathered to inspect his bark and question him.

They learned that his name was Thomas, that he had come from somewhere east, and that his sole cargo consisted of a compass, a water butt, and a carpetbag. He walked like a seafaring man, and they suspected that he was tattooed under his faded monkey jacket. Was he a whaler, had he ever struck a fish? They could not tell, for Thomas wasted few words in telling of himself. He announced that he had come as the Navigator of the Prairies, and invited them to join with him and form a company to engage in the Santa Fe trade!

In Yoakum's Tavern, leading citizens split a bottle with him, while he diverted them by explaining his plan. He proposed to build—with their backing—a fleet of large prairie clippers to carry cargo to the cussed Spaniards. The advantages of wind-power were numerous, according to the nautical stranger. Speed, economy, freedom from expense of buying and the trouble of feeding draft animals, freedom to leave the Trail along the Arkansas River (since there would be no animals requiring water) and sail on the high prairies by compass. Westport was the outfitting place for all travellers bound west; it would be easy to have the wagons built there. Injuns would be scared of the strange craft. And there would never be any lack of wind to drive them.

But the men of Westport were not to be taken in by any clever Yankee. They dubbed the stranger Windwagon, hooted at his scheme for a "dryland navy," and kept their money in their pockets. And so, when the bottle was empty, Windwagon left the Tavern, not at all cast down by their ridicule. "I'll l'arn ye," he declared. "I'll sail to Council Grove and back. Then maybe you'll listen to reason."

With that, undaunted and imperturbable, he embarked in his wagon, hoisted sail, and left the staring citizens of Westport in his dusty wake. Once beyond the town, he tacked out upon the open prairie, and laid his course to the setting sun. The wiseacres returned to the Tavern, laughing at his folly. It was close upon one hundred and fifty miles to Council Grove. They thought they had seen the last of Windwagon Thomas.

His coming might have remained a nine days' wonder, had he not come sailing into port again before the nine days had elapsed, bringing with him a letter from a well-known man, who managed the blacksmith shop at the Grove. Once more he cast anchor before Yoakum's door, rolled into the Tavern, and proceeded to talk turkey to the men of Westport.

That same day the men who had made fun of him chipped in and financed the building of a super-windwagon. The Overland Navigation Company included among its members and directors Doctor J. W. Parker, a leading physician; Benjamin Newson, the Indian agent; J. J. Mastin, a young lawyer; Henry Sager; Thomas W. Adams, and the inventor, Windwagon. Under his supervision, the first ship of the plains was built and launched.

The result was a mammoth wagon, constructed after the fashion of a Conestoga prairie schooner. It was fully twenty-five feet from stem to stern, seven-foot beam, and mounted upon four huge wheels, each twelve feet in diameter, with hubs as big as barrels. The sides of the wagon-box, or cabin, rose to the top of the wheels, and above that was the deck. The craft was rigged like a catboat, with the mast stepped well forward, and carried only a mainsail.

Specifications for the steering-gear are lacking, but it is certain that the craft was intended to move backwards; that is, the tail-gate of the wagon was the prow of the ship, and the tongue was brought up and over the stern to serve as tiller. When the craft was completed, the directors gathered in Yoakum's bar and fortified themselves. Then they adjourned to witness the inventor's demonstration.

Two yoke of oxen hauled the huge contrivance out upon the open prairie, and the directors of the Company—with one exception—climbed aboard. Doctor Parker, who knew what broken bones meant, preferred to watch the maiden voyage from the hurricane deck of his saddle mule. Windwagon Thomas, elated by his importance, and perhaps by his potations, took his place on deck, hoisted the mainsail, and grasped the helm.

Slowly, the wagon creaked into motion. A strong wind caught the sail, and away it went, rolling high over all obstacles, scooting

over hill and dale, tacking and veering over the plain. The passengers were at first amazed, then delighted, and at last alarmed
at the speed of their craft. Doctor Parker, who had thoughtfully filled his saddlebags with necessaries for any accidents,
whipped his mule into a run, and lumbered after. The windwagon
made the wagons drawn by oxen seem like snails.

The directors shut up in the cabin were frightened, unaccustomed as they were to anything faster than a horse and buggy.
They dared not abandon ship, and began to call upon the pilot to
shorten sail.

But Windwagon Thomas was riding the waves. He paid no heed
to their clamor, steering before the gale. Instead of obeying his
partners, he began to show his seamanship, and yelled down to
his helpless passengers, "Watch me run her against the wind." He
put the helm over, and the heavy craft came round grandly.

But then, somehow, something went wrong. The wind caught
her, and in spite of all the pilot could do, the windwagon went
into reverse. Doctor Parker and his mule narrowly escaped being
run down, and had to turn and fly before the monster. The steering-
gear locked, and the craft went sailing round and round in a circle
a mile wide.

By this time the passengers, thoroughly scared, decided to
abandon ship. High as they were above ground, the jump was
risky. But they risked it, rather than stay in that crazy ship with
its confused hunk of a sea-captain. One by one they dropped to
the ground, miraculously unhurt except for a few bruises and
considerable fright.

But Windwagon Thomas was made of sterner stuff. He was
evidently determined to go down with the ship, colors flying. He
remained on deck, clutching the useless helm, until the mammoth
wagon jolted him off as it brought up against a stake-and-rider
fence on the bank of Turkey Creek.

Nothing Windwagon could say would induce the Company to
build the rest of the fleet. The lubbers had no heart for prairie
seafaring. They went back to their shops and their offices, put the
venture down to profit and loss, and thanked heaven that they were
still alive and sound. What else could be expected of men who had
halted on the edge of the sea of grass?

But Windwagon remained undaunted. He embarked once more
in the small, light craft in which he had come to Westport, made

sail, and vanished as swiftly and mysteriously as he had come. History has no more to tell of him.

Maybe he sailed away to shoot buffalo from the afterdeck, or harpoon redskins daring enough to run afoul of him on their cruising ponies. Perhaps he ran hard aground in some deep valley or ravine, where no wind came to fill his sail, and no bull-whacker blundered in to haul him out upon the windy plain. Perhaps the cussed Injuns found him thus becalmed, and hung his hair upon some pony's bridle. There are legends among the Indians of a vehicle seen on the prairie, a wagon that was bigger than any wagon, which moved without horses or oxen to draw it, and carried a white "flag" as tall as a tipi. What became of the Navigator of the Plains will never be known.

But, in two respects, his story is significant, showing us how men of those days thought of the Plains, with all the beauty and mystery of the sea, and also illustrating the dauntless character of the men who crossed them, made them their home.

For the Great Plains of the West were man's country. Women and weaklings shrank from the vastness, the sameness, where there was nothing to give shelter, no bower of trees, no security, no nest. The women either persuaded their men to halt and build at the edge of their familiar woodlands, or scuttled fearfully across the prairies to the snug forests of Oregon, the cozy valleys of California. Even later, when those plains were settled, and lone nesters dotted the grass with sod houses and dugouts, women still hated the lonesome, wind-bitten land. Everything there was different, strange, and frightening. Many and many a settler's wife went crazy on the plains.

But not the men. Not men of the old North European stock, hard-drinking, hard-fighting warriors and wanderers, gamblers and explorers. They loved those plains, delighted in vague, receding horizons, in the loneliness, the sand and the silence, the independence and chancy emergencies of that romantic country. There was Valhalla come to earth, a region where men might do impromptu battle, and ride away to fight again some other day. The moods of the plains were moods of violence, and the men who loved them shared that moodiness. Not since the day of the Vikings had the virile white man found a country so congenial to his heart's desire.

DANE COOLIDGE

COLONEL CHARLES GOODNIGHT—TRAIL-MAKER

In Texas, the home of the subject of this authentic biography, the title of Colonel is conferred only on "a first-class fighting man." And in Texas, Charles Goodnight was "Colonel" Goodnight "from the time he could climb up a saddle-string." An extraordinary man in many other ways (at the age of ninety he took a young wife), his history makes exciting reading. (From *Fighting Men of the West*, Dutton, 1932.)

DOWN in Texas they have two honorary titles which they confer upon their favorite sons—Judge and Colonel. A Judge may be a lawyer, a leading citizen, or merely a good judge of whisky; but to earn the title of "Colonel" you must be a first-class fighting man. The Lone Star State has had no more loyal citizen than Charles Goodnight, but no one ever called him Judge. He was always Colonel Goodnight, for from the time he could climb up a saddle-string Uncle Charley was on the warpath.

First for four long years, while the Civil War was raging, he served as guide and scout for Captain Jack Cureton's famous company of Texas Rangers. Then, blazing a new trail across the Staked Plains, he took herd after herd of Texas cattle through the land of the Comanches and Apaches. When the Indians were tamed and he had settled in the Panhandle he devoted the rest of his life to a battle against rustlers and outlaws.

It is a curious fact, though, that this Texan of Texans was a Northerner, born in Illinois in 1836. At the age of nine his parents moved to Texas when it was still an independent republic, and in the turbulent times that followed the Mexican War he grew up with a gun in his hands. When nineteen years old he took the trail for California but turned back when he had crossed the Brazos River and went into the cattle business, on shares.

This was right in the heart of the Indian country and for the next six years he fought off the Comanches while he built up his little herd. Then the Civil War broke out, and with it came a great moral problem. Young Goodnight was a Northerner by birth and tradition and while he was loyal to his adopted State he did not wish to join the Confederate Army and fight against his own people. The pressure to enlist became stronger, stripping the border counties of their men, and while he hesitated the wild tribesmen of the Plains decided for him. Seeing so many isolated homes left defenseless, the Comanches swept down upon the settlements; and when Captain Jack Cureton and his company of Rangers rode in, young Goodnight joined them as a scout.

Here was a job to his liking, defending the wives and families of his old neighbors and friends, and to it he brought a training in Indian warfare which won the respect even of the Rangers. He had learned to follow a straight course, by day or night; he knew every bush and shrub that indicated water. He could tell by the flight of birds whether they were going far to water or whether it was close. When he looked at a track he could tell how old it was, for he knew that only at night did the minute desert insects come out and leave their tiny trails.

For these and other qualities he was made guide and scout, and every day as they went into the unknown wilderness he rode on ahead of the command. Ten Tonkaway scouts followed behind him, and behind them the company of Rangers; and as a dare to his Indian enemies he wore a vest made of leopard skin. Soon the hostile Comanches came to know that spotted garment and the man who led off alone, and they named him Leopard Coat. Then, thinking he was the chief of this band which dealt them so much misery, they gave him a second name—Dangerous Man.

All this the Colonel learned long afterwards when, at his great ranch in Palo Duro Canyon, his former enemies came to visit him. At first he was surprised that these men whom he had harried, whose brothers he had killed and whose people he had chased, should come in and want to shake hands. He even doubted their good faith, but they insisted upon being friends. One old man rode hundreds of miles to see him, and in the long talk that followed Colonel Goodnight discovered that he had shot this very warrior in a fight and left him for dead. The Comanche showed the wound where the bullet had gone through him, but he bore Dangerous Man no ill will. It was from him that Leopard Coat learned that the Indians had no respect for a coward, or even a peaceable man, but they loved a fighter, even if his bullet had crippled them.

As the war went on and the Mexican settlers in the Pecos Valley discovered how weak and unprotected the outlying settlements were, they engaged big bands of Comanches to help them round up Texas cattle and drive them west into New Mexico. Around 300,000 head were thus run off before the end of the Civil War, and when the Rangers crossed the desert after them they found hundreds of Texas steers yoked up in Mexican ox-teams.

The Indians had no use for cattle, except to kill a few for beef, but they stole and sold them to the Mexicans. This traffic was broken up years later when a Captain of the United States Army, after watching this Rustler Trail and arresting several bands of thieves, finally cut the Gordian knot by killing all the stolen cattle wherever he found them, thus taking the profits out of the business.

In all the years that he was riding this country Colonel Goodnight stored away in his retentive memory every trail that he travelled, every landmark, every water-hole. That was his business, and he did it thoroughly, and when the war was over he turned it to a very useful purpose. Returning to his old home in Palo Pinto county, where he had been handling cattle on shares, he found thousands of cows on his range. His herds had increased, and there were mavericks everywhere, but absolutely no market for beef. A steer had a "hide and tallow" value of around $3.00, but Leopard Coat thought he saw a way out.

Besides being a warrior of note, Colonel Goodnight was a very good business man. Not the kind that is described as safe, sane and conservative, but up-and-coming, aggressive, taking long chances. During his lifetime he amassed two large fortunes, but his methods

were always daring. Where others were afraid to venture he led
the way, but at the same time he was careful and systematic.

In 1859 when the Comanches were peaceful, Oliver Loving, a
Texas cattleman, had driven a herd of cattle through their country
to the north and on into Colorado. But now they were on the war-
path. Shortly after his return the valiant Leopard Coat moved
3000 cattle beyond the settlements and lost two-thirds of them to
his old enemies. This satisfied him that, without an army to protect
him, the old Loving route was impractical. But he had located in
his travels a potential market for Texas cattle in the Army Posts
of New Mexico and, undeterred by his losses, he determined to
cut a trail west.

While in the Pecos Valley he had encountered Mr. Loving and
heard the story of his first trip north. They had, in fact, returned
to Texas together with the idea of repeating the drive and the
only effect of this initial disaster was to make them change their
plans. From his work in the Ranger service Colonel Goodnight
knew that the Comanches generally kept to the north part of their
range, where there was more grass and water for their ponies
and great herds of buffaloes to prey on. He, therefore, laid off a
new trail to the southwest across the Staked Plains, a rolling
stretch of prairie absolutely without water for a distance of ninety-
six miles.

To make this trip doubly dangerous, there were on the way a
series of salt or alkali lakes, the waters of which, if drunk, would
kill a cow in twenty minutes. It was a three-day-and-night drive
from the headwaters of the South Concho River to the Pecos River
in New Mexico, and on his first trip to the north Loving had lost
half his herd, either from thirst or from drinking alkali water. So
crazed did the cattle become that they could smell the sunken lakes
for miles, and at the first whiff of water a stampede would follow
which no human power could stop. Still, if the lakes could be located and the herd kept to windward, this danger could be avoided.

It was in 1866, a year before the first trail-herds went north,
that Colonel Goodnight made this daring attempt to find a market
for Texas cattle. The ranges were covered with them, they could
be purchased on credit for almost nothing, while at Fort Sumner
in New Mexico the Government was buying beef for 11,000 Indians,
and paying an exorbitant price. The prize was worth trying for
and, in partnership with Loving, he gathered the cattle for his

drive. Each partner put up his share, making a mixed herd of about a thousand, and in June the start was made.

A huge chuck-wagon had been built, requiring twenty oxen to haul it, and provisions for a six hundred mile trip were provided, that being the distance from Young County, Texas, to Fort Sumner, New Mexico, where they expected to sell their cattle. Eighteen picked men were hired for the drive and these were thoroughly drilled regarding their places and duties. A *remuda* of sixty good horses was provided and, owing to the danger from Indian attacks, they were always kept between the herd, with its attendant riders, and the equally well-guarded wagon. The Colonel had found that if men were held together they would fight, but if permitted to separate they would scatter before an attack. He therefore kept his trail hands bunched up.

For several weeks, while they trailed their cattle southwest to the jumping-off place on the Concho nothing happened to break the monotony of the trip. Then, after filling the cattle up with grass and water, the perilous drive across the desert was begun. The herd strung out slowly, its speed absolutely controlled by the well-disciplined trail-hands. When they wished it to move faster the men on the sides closed in, and when slower they moved further away. The weak cattle in the drag were protected by the rear men, who pushed the stronger animals out of their way; and so, day and night, they toiled on across the plain towards the water of the distant Pecos.

But as the cattle became foot-weary, and crazed by heat and thirst, a difference of opinion developed. Loving, an old and experienced cow-hand, wanted to stop and rest the herd, while Goodnight was for pressing on. The steers had become so fractious they would fight like rattlesnakes. The cows that had lost their calves would turn back, and for three days and nights, until they reached the Pecos River, the cowboys were constantly in the saddle. The chuck-wagon was sent ahead and as the weary men trooped past they were handed out food and a drink, but no one had any sleep except on the back of his horse.

On the third day, when the cattle began to give out and the controversy flared up again, the partners divided their herd. Loving stayed behind to let his cattle rest and Goodnight shoved his on. In the night he came to a box canyon, not far from the Pecos River, and there he held them till dawn. Before him in broken country lay the sunken lake of salt which threatened the safety of his herd and, plucking a few hairs from his horse, he dropped them to note the direction of the wind.

At daylight the half-dead cattle were driven out of the canyon and taken far to the windward of the lake, and while still eight miles from the river the leaders smelled its water and ran. In vain the weary cowboys attempted to hold them back. They rushed on across the flat until they came to the ten-foot cut-bank, and there the leaders went in. Others followed over their bodies until they bridged the river, a distance of some sixty feet, and doubled back for a drink; and still they piled in until the stream was full of cattle, some drinking, others feeding on the cane that grew along the brink.

For three days the cowboys were kept busy, towing them down the stream to where they could climb up the bank, and most of this herd was saved. But when Goodnight went back to help bring up the drag he found that some three hundred had got to the alkali lake and perished from drinking salt water. The remainder were brought in to the river, where a crossing had been made, and allowed to drink and rest.

In this desperate manner the Goodnight Trail was blazed across the Staked Plains, from water to water, and in the years that followed over 250,000 head of cattle followed after them and then on to the North. But though the bulk of the herd was saved, many weary miles lay before them as they followed up the Pecos, with the cattle closely guarded against Indians. When Goodnight reached Fort Sumner in July, dressed beef was selling at sixteen cents a pound and the Government could not get enough to feed the Indians properly. The partners received eight cents a pound on the hoof, closing out what they had to various Army Posts and Indian Reservations and going clear to Denver.

The following year Loving and Goodnight assembled a herd of twenty-five hundred head, all steers. These animals could travel faster than a mixed herd with cows and calves and they found a readier market at the forts. Everything looked propitious for a successful drive, but disaster attended them from the first. On the clear fork of the Brazos the Comanches stampeded the herd, wounding one man in the fight that followed; and on the lower Pecos in a second attack they ran off about four hundred head.

There were Indians everywhere, and so numerous had they become that the cattle could not be recovered.

The drive across the desert, on the other hand, was executed without any loss. The cattle were started about noon, after filling up with water, and for three days and nights without a stop they were pushed on until they reached the Pecos. Every detail was systematized, and this at a time when the great northern drives had not begun. Certain men took the point, others rode at the sides, others shoved along the "corners" toward the rear of the herd to protect the weaker "drag" behind. All orders were given by signal and in case of a stampede each man knew just what to do. They even had steer leaders, with ox-bells on their necks, the only case on record.

In order to avoid the Indians who lived near the river, the herd was driven along the high ground to the east, out of sight behind the rim of the Staked Plains, and taken down only to drink. In this way over a hundred miles was covered without a sign of Indians, and after passing the eastern spurs of the Guadalupe Mountains, the stronghold of the Mescalero Apaches, Oliver Loving became restless to go on, for the contracts for furnishing beef would soon be let at Santa Fe.

Once more a difference of opinion developed between the partners, Loving being of a reckless disposition, but as he insisted upon going Goodnight extracted a promise from him that he would travel only by night. With a single companion Loving took the trail north, and for two nights all went well. Then, seeing no Indians, he kept on by day and was surrounded by six hundred Comanches. A long siege followed, under the bank of the Pecos, in which Loving was wounded twice; and after holding out for days he was finally rescued and taken to Fort Sumner, where he died.

The death of his partner, whom he loved very dearly, made a great impression on Goodnight, but it did not alter his purpose. He kept on to Colorado with the cattle, which he sold for a very good price. Then, returning to Fort Sumner, he took the body of Loving, according to his dying request, six hundred miles back to Texas to be delivered to his family. The following year he turned over to the estate the sum of $40,000, Loving's share in the profits of the trip.

When he trailed his first herd into Colorado, Colonel Goodnight encountered in Raton Pass the redoubtable Dick Wooten who, on the strength of a toll-road he had constructed, was collecting ten cents a head for all stock that went through the pass. In order to avoid a long and dangerous detour the Colonel bargained for some time to get a rate, threatening to find another way through the mountains unless a reduction was granted. Wooten dared him to do so and, much to his surprise, Goodnight found one better than Wooten's, which saved him around a hundred miles, besides the toll. At this Wooten offered to cross him free, in order to keep others from following him; but the young trail-maker refused to accept, pushing his way on the next year to Cheyenne and the Chugwater, in Wyoming.

Shortly after Loving's death, Goodnight formed a new partnership with John Chisum, who in later years became the cattle king of the Pecos country, owning 60,000 head. The money with which Chisum bought these cattle—those that he did buy— was the profits of their three years together, working on the following basis: He was to deliver to Goodnight at Bosque Grande on the Pecos River all the cattle he could bring in from Texas, being paid a dollar a head above Texas prices to compensate him for his risk, as in that time he lost two herds to the Indians. After driving the cattle north to Colorado and Wyoming, Colonel Goodnight divided the profits with him equally, to the advantage of them both.

In 1866, Chisum had followed after the first Loving and Goodnight herd with six hundred head of Jingle Bob steers, which he wintered at Bosque Grande and sold the next spring to Army contractors. He was therefore a pioneer in the country and the business; and, being a good hand with cattle, was making money. But at the end of three years his brother Pitzer, in bringing a herd of cattle from Texas, was attacked by the Apaches near Guadalupe Mountains and lost everything but the horses his men rode. Pitzer and his cowboys rode five miles from the herd to the chuck-wagon and as a result of their own carelessness lost 1100 head of steers. Being under contract to deliver the cattle, Chisum returned to Texas, rounded up the first 1100 steers he came across, and tried to deliver them to Goodnight.

In the three years of their partnership there had never been a disagreement between them, but when Goodnight saw the brands on the stolen stuff he absolutely refused to accept them and called their agreement off. Up to this time John Chisum had been perfectly honest, delivering nothing but straight brands, but after they parted company he went from bad to worse, gathering such a hard bunch of cowboys around him that they intimidated the whole country, finally bringing on the Lincoln County War by their aggressions upon their neighbors.

But until Billy the Kid and his gang took charge, the Colonel himself saw to it that indiscriminate killings were discouraged. By that time he was out of the country, nicely located in the Texas Panhandle. But it might be mentioned that as President of the Canadian River Cattlemen's Association, it was Colonel Goodnight who sent John Poe, the cattle detective, into Lincoln County and was thereby instrumental in bringing William Bonney to justice. All his life he hated a thief and a murderer, and Billy the Kid was both.

It was part of the Colonel's code that a trail boss was morally responsible for the lives of his men, and before starting on a drive he drew up an article of agreement, setting forth what each was to do. The main clause was that if one shot another he was to be tried by the outfit and hanged on the spot—if found guilty. He never had a man shot on the trail, but at Horsehead Crossing where they struck the Pecos there were thirteen graves, all but one the result of pistol shots.

On the first Chisum round-up, while receiving the cattle wintered at Bosque Grande, a brutal murder was committed by one of the Jingle Bob men called Curly Tex. He was really from Kansas, one of those border toughs who wished to get the name of a killer, and his victim was a quiet young fellow named James who had a wife and two children in Kansas City. One morning while they were on herd Curly accused James of lying to the boss about the cattle, and when he protested that he didn't want any trouble Curly Tex drew his gun and killed him.

Both men were Chisum hands, but Goodnight took it upon himself to demand justice. Chisum however was reluctant to interfere, since it would break up his round-up to have so many men summoned as witnesses to the distant county seat of Las Vegas.

"All right, then," said the ex-Ranger, "we'll have a trial right here, before any more murders are committed."

"But who's going to arrest Curly Tex?"

"I'll attend to that," promised Goodnight.

He had a good man in his employ who felt competent for the job and, refusing the aid of a posse, rode out to the murderer alone.

"You come on in," he said, "and if you offer to draw your gun I'll be only too glad to kill you."

So Curly Tex surrendered, a jury was selected and men appointed for prosecution and defense. Then witnesses were called, the last being Nigger Frank, Chisum's colored horse-wrangler, who had been present at the killing. After he had given his testimony the jury found the defendant guilty and he was hung from the end of a wagon-tongue, which had been propped up for that purpose. That stopped all killings for several years, until Billy the Kid broke loose.

After his break with John Chisum, who nevertheless remained his friend, Colonel Goodnight played a lone hand—and against a crooked game, at that. In the minds of the Army officers at Fort Sumner the Texans were all "rebels" and, though they had needed the first herd of Loving and Goodnight cattle, they had held out the pay until Goodnight, who was a Mason, had gone over their heads to the General at Santa Fe. A ring was now formed composed of crooked officers and certain contractors, who underbid Goodnight on the cattle to be delivered the following summer.

The Colonel had wintered his herd on the Pecos, expecting to sell them at the fort, but the contractors sent word back to Texas to have two more herds brought in. When the contract was nearly due the news came that the Indians had got both herds. That broke the contract, and incidentally the contractors, and the cattle would have to be bought in at high prices on the local market.

Outside of Goodnight's, there were only two bunches of cattle in the country—a herd of eight hundred on the Rio Hondo and a trail herd belonging to Jack Burleson, who was on his way up the Pecos. The first that Colonel Goodnight knew of the Indian raids was when the contractors drove past on the run, to buy the eight hundred head on the Hondo. After he had verified the report Goodnight followed them, but in their haste the contractors had got bogged at a quick-sand crossing and had been compelled to camp.

Coming by in the night, Goodnight saw their predicament and, keeping discreetly out of sight, he rode up to the only safe crossing and bought the eight hundred cows himself. Then, riding on down the trail, he met the genial Burleson and purchased his whole herd on sight. After that he stuck the officers for a tremendous price for all his cattle, they having over 10,000 Indians to feed, and cleaned up a mint of money.

This Jack Burleson was a queer character, a great gambler and sport, who took with him on the trail a pair of fine race horses and three baskets of game cocks, to match against those of the Mexicans. He also carried along several cases of fine liquors, but his Mexican herders were afoot and he took no precautions against the Indians. Most of his men were entirely unarmed and the rest only poorly provided, but in some mysterious way he had got through unharmed while the two herds of the contractors were driven off.

Another curious character whom Goodnight encountered under equally auspicious circumstances was Honey Johnson, a man who used to gather pecans and wild honey along Devil River and the Llano and sell them to the soldiers at Fort Sumner. Although he drove his huge wagon alone through the heart of the Indian country he was never molested in any way, as he was entirely un-afraid. When they visited his camp he fed them with honey, of which they were very fond, and his very lack of fear won their superstitious respect.

While returning from Fort Sumner with $12,000 in specie on a mule, Goodnight and his party were attacked just at dark, and during a storm, by a band of ambushed Indians. They finally fought their way out but in the excitement all their provisions were lost. In order to get through a box canyon before it was closed against them the cattlemen rode all night but in the morning, with the ninety-mile desert before them, they felt the pangs of hunger and thirst.

Pressing forward in a very low mood they beheld on the great plain to the east a long, straight line of dust, approaching them. It had every appearance of a war party of Comanches and the majority were for turning back, but the Colonel insisted upon going ahead, with very happy results. As they rode in closer they discovered beneath the dust the trail wagons of Honey Johnson, who was hauling a load of watermelons across the country to sell to the Mexicans of a salt caravan. They stopped him right there and, according to Colonel Goodnight, they "mighty nigh ate the whole load."

So for several years with many ups and downs he followed the historic trail named after him, finally marrying in 1870 and settling down in Colorado. All the money he had made, and it was a small-sized fortune, he invested or loaned out in Pueblo; but the panic of '73 wiped out all his savings except a few thousand dollars. He paid off all his debts and, with the 1600 cattle he had left, set forth to blaze his second trail—that from Pueblo to the Texas Panhandle, at that time entirely uninhabited except by bands of roving Indians.

During his service with the Rangers, Goodnight had scouted through the Panhandle and had noticed in particular the deep Palo Duro Canyon and the fertile acres above and below it. In those days it was a stronghold of the Comanche Indians and the wintering place of thousands of buffalo, which sought the shelter of its sunken bottomlands to escape the sweep of the blizzards. But there was no road, not even a trail, and once more he blazed his way.

It was in the fall of 1875 that he started his herd south. They were mostly grade Durhams and Texas cattle mixed, with about a hundred pure Durhams among them, probably the first ever brought into Texas. His outfit consisted of only six or seven men and, on account of the fear of Indian raids, they wintered in the brakes just across the Texas line, pushing on again the following fall. Coming at last to the high bluffs of Palo Duro Canyon, they drove their cattle down the old Comanche Trail, halting at the place which later became the headquarters for the famous JA Ranch.

During the entire trip they did not meet a single Indian or lose a single cow; but, though the country was still open, the time had come when land was being taken up. In Colorado, Goodnight had met John Adair, a wealthy English Lord, with a burning desire to go into the cattle business. So, just to accommodate him, he took about $12,000 of his money, accepted a salary of $2500 a year and signed a contract to start the JA Ranch, with Adair's money, for a one-third interest. At the time it looked like a terrible gamble, but at the end of five years, when they figured up their profits, it turned out that Uncle Charley had earned seventy-odd per cent per year, every year, counting in the profit on the land.

Shortly after Goodnight located in Palo Duro Canyon a land speculator named Jot Gunter came out and surveyed him in by laying a blanket filing on the surrounding country. This he did under a law which he had put through the Legislature himself, giving a man the privilege of taking up a whole county if he wanted it at an expense of a dollar and a half. Having shut him in, Gunter went first to Adair and then to Goodnight with a proposition to sell them land, and after some shrewd bargaining on both sides 12,000 acres were purchased for a dollar an acre.

It was stipulated by the Colonel, however, that he should be allowed to pick the land and when the lines were run he took nothing but the best, scattering his locations all over Palo Duro Canyon and including every place that any other man was likely to occupy. Then, in return for a tip on another good stretch of country, Goodnight exacted an option on a second 12,000 acres and a promise from Mr. Gunter not to sell any land to nesters— only to cattlemen who wanted to buy a big ranch. In this way he avoided the possibility of a swarm of trouble-making neighbors and at the end of five years the JA Ranch covered 650,000 acres of land.

It was quite a ranch, even for Texas, and at one time the Colonel had two million acres under his control and nearly 100,000 head of cattle. He imported purebred Durham bulls to breed up the rangy Texas stock and, to provide a market for his beef steers, he laid off a third trail—the Palo Duro-Dodge City Trail, 250 miles in length, across the vast plains of the Texas Panhandle. In later years he domesticated the last of the wild buffaloes and crossed them with cows to produce his famous cattaloes, a beef animal hard to surpass.

But with all these cattle under his care in a new and lawless country it is not to be imagined that he entirely escaped the attention of rustlers and outlaws. Until the day he died the Colonel hated a thief—and especially a cow thief. Although it was not generally known, he had an accountant who reported to him the number of calves branded, the number of steers shipped, and the number of range cattle reported to the assessor by most of the big cattlemen in Texas; and any marked discrepancy in the ratio between calf-crop and cows made a difference in his attitude towards that cattleman.

Shortly after the rustlers started working on him he sent secretly to San Francisco and bought three powerful marine or night glasses, which were carefully kept out of sight and brought disaster to more than one cow thief. About the time the rustler

got his calves in the corral and began his nocturnal brand-burn-
ing a deputy sheriff would drop over the ridge and arrest him for
grand larceny. A stock detective whom Colonel Goodnight sent
among the rustlers in the guise of a fellow cow thief was solemnly
warned against his boss:

"You want to look out for that old scoundrel. He can *smell*
a rustler further than you can see one."

They never did catch on to those night glasses.

One day, following the custom of his Ranger days, he was
scouting the range alone when he came in sight of a new town to
the north which he had never visited. It was a farming community
whose inhabitants had given him no trouble but some hunch im-
pelled him to ride towards it. When he came into town he saw
a mob of armed men about to lynch a prisoner in their midst.
From his horse, the Colonel looked over their heads and recognized
an Indian that he knew—an old Taos chief who had helped him
in his early drives.

The Indian was repeating over and over in agonized accents
the Spanish name by which the Colonel was known: "*Buena
Noche!*" But no one could understand. Then above the crowd he
saw Goodnight's face and knew he had found a friend.

Upon inquiry, Goodnight was told by the crowd that the Indian
was a desperate character and they were going to kill him, forthwith.

"You are mistaken," he answered. "I know this man well, and
I want you to turn him loose. He has been asking for me, all the
time. *Buena Noche*, in Spanish, means Good Night."

Like so many of the early settlers, many members of this rabble
wanted to kill the poor Indian just so they could say they had
got one; but the Colonel talked them out of that idea with a six-
shooter and took his old friend away. For several days he remained
at the JA Ranch while they talked about old times and then Buena
Noche started him home. He had been trying for days to get
back towards Taos, but all the old trails had been fenced with
barbed wire and he had found himself hopelessly shut in.

Many, many years passed and the Chief died. Colonel Goodnight was over ninety years old. But one day with his big automobile he drove into the pueblo of Taos to enquire about his
friends. One time he had found two Taos Indians who were
stranded at a town in Texas and had staked them and paid their

way home. They had sent back presents, word had passed back and forth but for many years he had heard nothing of them. In his car he had brought a present, a beautiful buffalo robe such as they used in their ancient ceremonies, but no one came out to meet him.

Every door was closed, for the Indians were worn out with tourists, and at last the Colonel got out and knocked.

"I am Buena Noche," he said, "the friend of your old chief."

"*Buena Noche!*" shouted the Indian, rushing up to the house-top and rousing the whole village with his outcries. "Buena Noche has come to see us!"

Then the doors which had seemed so unfriendly were suddenly all thrown open. The son of the old chief appeared and intro-duced him to all the people. Every Indian in the pueblo crowded in to shake hands with him, and when he spread out the fine buffalo hide they knelt down and stroked it reverently. The only one they had left for their ceremonies was so worn it was almost hairless. Then one by one they returned to their houses and brought out their most precious gifts. If he had accepted a tenth part of what was laid at his feet he could not have piled it in his car. They gave him their very best, for his name had been known to them for years as a good friend of their tribe.

But Buena Noche, with his wide knowledge of Indians, knew just how to refuse this great outpouring of presents without giv-ing offense to his hosts. From the son of the chief he accepted an ancient bois d'arc bow which he had carried in many a battle and, waving his hand, he was driven away leaving every man his friend.

There were few Indians in the country who had not heard of the great Buena Noche, who always fed them when they came to visit him and talked with their old men for days. There were few white men also in the great State of Texas who did not know his name and love to do him honor. He was a good neighbor, a good friend —even to the poor nesters who sometimes stole his beef. But if any of them ever took more than they needed for their families and began to run off his stock, they found him a bad man to monkey with. Until the day he died the old Colonel hated a cow thief and he put the fear into many a black heart.

In appearance Colonel Goodnight was a little over middle height, but of very rugged build. He had dark eyes, a mane of hair and a stern cast of countenance; but with children and those he loved his voice was always gentle and socially he had very courtly manners. What marked him off from the average run of humanity was the absolute integrity of his character. If there ever was a cowman who never ate his neighbor's beef or branded another man's calf, Charles Goodnight was that paragon. He was honest, and he expected others to be honest.

At the age of ninety Colonel Goodnight lost his wife, and he too seemed close to death. In the empty old ranch-house, far from town and doctors, he lay at last almost alone, waiting grimly for the reaper to come. But instead there came another woman who gave him a new lease of life. The similarity of their names, she being Corinne Goodnight, had started a correspondence between them; and on her way back to Montana from Florida she had stopped off to pay him a visit.

Week after week she stayed to take care of him and nurse him back to health. He would not let her go, and she on the other hand would not leave the old man to die. A devotion sprang up between them such as is rarely seen and even more rarely understood; but in the end they were married, the Colonel gained back his strength, and after a long lifetime of turmoil and conflict he entered an interlude of idyllic peace. The stern old warrior and the young, dark-eyed wife had many qualities in common and for three and a half years they lived on happily, visiting old friends and making new ones, until at last the reaper came. So passed from this world the greatest trail-maker in Texas—a man who left his mark on the West.

WILLIAM McLEOD RAINE

"STICK 'EM UP"

Offered here is an exciting narrative concerned with some of the more notorious gentry who earned their livelihood with "trigger-talk." Here are the progenitors of the modern gangster, the Youngers, the James and the Daltons, desperadoes who inspired numberless tales and legends in the literature of the West. (From *Guns of the Frontier*, Houghton Mifflin, 1940.)

DURING the generation following the Civil War a profitable way of life financially was train robbery with bank "stickups" as a side line. The occupation had two drawbacks. Those who did well at it could not keep their easily acquired wealth from slipping swiftly through their fingers. The second disadvantage was more serious. Night riders who took up the business did not live long. Nine out of ten of them came to sudden violent ends.

The first eminent practitioners of the "Hands up!" fraternity were Jesse James and his gang. In spite of efforts to make a Robin Hood out of him, this bandit leader was a cold-blooded killer who had learned under Quantrell utter ruthlessness. His associates the Youngers held more closely to the code of the frontier, to the clan spirit which taught a man to "go through" for his comrades.

After a dozen daring and successful bank and train robberies the James-Younger outlaws made the mistake of leaving their own

terrain to rob a bank in Minnesota, five hundred miles from the
district they knew, with the thickly settled state of Iowa between
the scene of the holdup and home. The adventure would probably
have come to grief in any case, but the cashier of the bank, J. L.
Haywood, gave his life to make failure certain.

There were eight of the robbers. The two James brothers and
Bob Younger went into the bank to get the money. Jim Younger
and Pitts guarded a bridge across which they had to retreat.
Chadwell, Miller, and Cole Younger stayed with the horses and
watched the street.

Though they had twice before this killed bank cashiers during
holdups—at Liberty and at Gallatin, both in Missouri—the
raiders expected no trouble at Northfield. But when Frank James
ordered Haywood to open the safe the cashier faced him boldly
and refused.

"We'll kill you if you don't," Jesse warned.

"I know that, but I won't help you if I die for it," the obstinate
man flung back.[1]

He was shot down instantly. The teller bolted for a side
door, was hit in the shoulder, but made his escape.

In the building opposite the bank a Doctor Wheeler had his
office. He was a hunter, and from a rack he picked up a gun loaded
for big game. Through the office window he began firing. His first
shot dropped Bill Chadwell from the saddle. He sent a bullet
tearing into Pitts, and when the bandits in the bank came out
wounded Bob Younger.

Word spread like a prairie fire that there was a bank holdup.
Men snatched up their rifles—for this was close to a game
country where most of these pioneers hunted—and from doors and
street corners peppered at the outlaws. With the exception of the
James brothers all the rest of the gang were hit. The robbers clat-
tered out of town, leaving their dead behind them. Far out on the
prairie they pulled up to tie to their saddles the sagging bodies
of those who were worst hurt.

The fugitives reached Mankato, greatly hampered in their
flight by the desperate condition of Bob Younger. Jesse James
made a callous proposal to Cole Younger bluntly.

"Bob is going to die anyhow," he said. "We'll be caught if

[1] The assistant cashier testified to the words at the coroner's inquest.

we stay with him. Let's finish the job they started in town. He'll be out of his misery then."

Cole looked at him, chill anger in his eyes. "Go ahead and save yourself if you like. Jim and I are sticking with Bob."

The bandits separated. Frank and Jesse James rode away. Clem Miller elected to stay with the Youngers. Perhaps he was afraid that his wounds might hamper him and Jesse would rid himself of the encumbrance. After half a dozen close calls Frank and Jesse reached Missouri.

The pursuit centered on the rear guard of the robbers. The Youngers and Miller hid in a swampy wood to spend the night. When morning broke they realized they were surrounded.

All day the battle lasted, four hundred against four. Miller exposed himself to get a better shot. A bullet crashed into his head. Jim and Cole were both hit again. Bob was in very bad condition. Cole talked the situation over with Jim. They tied a white handkerchief to the barrel of a rifle and surrendered.

They were tried and given life in the Minnesota Penitentiary. When I was a college boy selling books at Stillwater I visited the prison and saw them. Cole was librarian. He was soft-voiced and gentle of manner. Only the steadiness of the steel-barred eyes gave hint of the manner of man he was.

After twenty-five years Cole and Jim were pardoned. Bob had died in prison. He never fully recovered from his wounds. Outside the walls of the prison Jim found no place for him. He shot himself. Cole had been converted to religion. He lived the rest of his life quietly. Occasionally he preached, his own misspent life the text.

Long before this time Jesse James had been treacherously killed by one of his band, Bob Ford, who in turn was shot down at Creede, Colorado, by "Red" O'Kelley without warning. Charley Ford committed suicide. Only Frank James was left to be stared at by weak-minded admirers.

Of the Collins-Bass gang, Heffridge, Collins, Berry, Bass, and Barnes went out to the sound of roaring guns in the hands of law officers. The others slipped away into obscurity. The proportionate mortality in the Dalton-Doolin gang was even greater. With the settling up of the country and the coming of the rural telephone, chances for escape were constantly diminishing. Oklahoma and the Indian Territory were still wild, rough country, but the deputy United States marshals knew the Cherokee Strip almost as well as the bandits. Such officers as Bill Tilghman, Heck Thomas, Chris Madsen, and Bud Ledbetter were first-class trailers, expert shots, and game to the core. They were the leaders of a group who stamped out the bad man and made law respected in the borderland.

The Daltons were cousins to the Youngers, and in spite of their wild lawlessness were far removed from the Jesse James type of outlaw. None of them were killers from choice, except as this was forced on them from their manner of life. Daring and reckless frontiersmen, when guns came out they fought in the open to kill to ensure their own safety, but in all their long record there is no evidence of cold-blooded murder or treachery.

Louis and Adeline Dalton had fifteen children. They were a stalwart outdoor breed. The daughters married neighboring farmers. Some of the sons took up land, married, and lived close to the soil, good citizens all the days of their lives. But five of the boys had the love of adventure stirring unquenchably in their blood. The legends which had gathered around their notorious cousins and the still better-known James brothers were part of the family heritage. As youngsters they had seen Jesse James on their place. After his death the favorite horse of the outlaw chief came into the possession of the boys.

Like their neighbors, the Daltons ran cattle. All the lads were cowboys. They rode the range with other hardy cowhands, all good riders and excellent shots. Working on the Bar-X-Bar and the neighboring Turkey Track Ranch were Bill Powers, George Newcomb, Charley Bryant, Dick Broadwell, Charley Pierce, and Bill Doolin, all of them later associated with the Dalton and Doolin gangs. Four out of the five wild Daltons, and all the cowboys named above, went out of life violently and suddenly, shot to death by officers or citizens supporting the law. If they learned anything at all from the experience of others, they must have known that they would come with unexpected swiftness to the end of the crooked trails they were following, that for them there could be no future for which to plan.

It must be remembered that in the Indian Territory at this time there was no law except that which was enforced by the deputy United States marshals operating from Fort Smith, Arkansas, under the direction of federal officers in conjunction with Judge Isaac C. Parker's court. Never before or since has there been such a judicial set-up as this one. The marshals were hard, grim men, and many of them died in the performance of their duty. The judge was firm and harsh. Before him at one time or another stood twenty-eight thousand criminals dragged there to receive justice. During the twenty-five years of his incumbency one hundred and sixty-eight men were sentenced to the gallows, of whom eighty-eight were actually hanged. In such an environment as surrounded those in the Cherokee Strip, though there were many bad men the good citizens far outnumbered them. The parents of thousands of youths watched them anxiously as they grew up, for they knew there came an hour when spirited lads stood at the forking of the trails, one branch leading to an upright and constructive life, the other to crooked paths that could have no safe ending. Each of the Daltons came in turn to that place of dividing roads. Some took the plodding way of hard work and respectability. Grat, Bob, Emmett, and Bill Dalton followed the other trail.

There was an older brother, Frank, in whose blood the call to adventure also sang. But Frank lined up on the side of the law. He was one of the deputy United States marshals who went out from Fort Smith to run down the whiskey-smugglers and the other criminals who infested the Indian Territory. In a desperate battle, during which several outlaws were killed, Frank Dalton came to his death. Grattan was chosen to fill his brother's place, and shortly afterward Bob joined the force. Young Emmett also served as guard.

But Grattan and his younger brothers lacked the disciplined self-control of Frank. They went wild, first in California and later on their home terrain. Having left the government service, it was not long until they were outside the law. Bob and Emmett Dalton, with George Newcomb and Charley Bryant, robbed a Santa Fe train at Whorton in the Strip. They made a haul of fourteen thousand dollars and a safe getaway. Newcomb, Pierce, Broadwell, and Powers were with the Daltons when they held up an M. K. & T. train near Wagoner. The take this time was nineteen thousand dollars, not counting non-negotiable paper. Then came the Red Rock robbery.

One of the gang had already "handed in his checks," as the

border phrase went. Charley Bryant had been captured by Ed Short, one of the old fighting marshals of the border. The outlaw was put on a train by the officer, who was careless enough to let his handcuffed prisoner get his fingers on a revolver. The two men stood in a baggage car and blazed away at each other. Both were killed.

It was on a pleasant July evening in 1892 when the Dalton gang stopped the "Katy" train near Adair, Oklahoma. Some hint of the attack had reached the authorities and a posse was on board the train. There was a sharp battle, in which three of the guards were badly wounded. The bandits robbed the express car and departed into the night. It was not the custom of the Daltons to rob the passengers.

There is vanity in train and bank holdups. A bandit gets the hero complex. The Daltons decided to outdo the James-Younger gang by robbing two banks at the same time. They picked the Condon and the First National Banks at Coffeeville, Kansas. There were five of the band present, Broadwell, Powers, and Grat, Bob, and Emmett Dalton. A negro with supplies waited in the Cherokee Strip for the return of the robbers after their exploit. He waited, but they never came. At last word reached him that four of the lusty riders were dead, the fifth dying from twenty wounds, many of them made by buckshot.

The bank "stickups" went wrong from the first. Before a gun was fired the adventure was doomed. Somehow the word spread that the Daltons were robbing the Condon. Coffeeville was on the edge of a hunting country. The citizens found their guns, and when the Oklahoma men came out with their loot the battle began. Bob and Emmett reached the hitching rack where the horses had been left. They waited for their accomplices to come. At last Broadwell, Powers, and Grat Dalton appeared. From all directions bullets poured upon the robbers, and they returned the fire.

The town marshal, Charles T. Connelly, went down, dead. Bob and Grat Dalton were down. Powers, Broadwell, and Emmett had been wounded. All three of them reached their saddles, but Powers was killed before his second foot had touched the stirrup. Broadwell wheeled and spurred away. Just outside of town he dropped from the saddle lifeless. Emmett rode back through the lane of fire to pick up his brother Bob. A shotgun in the hands of Carey

Seaman, a barber, sent eighteen buckshot into the back of Emmett as he stooped for the leader of the band. He slid to the ground.

Four citizens were dead, four bandits. Several others were wounded. Amazingly Emmett Dalton recovered. He went to the penitentiary, was paroled, and finished his life as a Los Angeles business man.

The rest of the band took no warning. Under Bill Doolin they reorganized. Tilghman captured Doolin. He escaped, to go on more forays. As I have written, he came to a sudden violent end, as did Newcomb, Pierce, and Bill Dalton.

The bad man never learns from the experience of others. The Dalton and the Doolin gangs were hardly out of the way before other desperate men were organizing to try their luck at the same hazardous game, this time in the rough country of Wyoming. They were called the Hole-in-the-Wall gang, this bunch of former cowboys who preyed not only on Wyoming but on a great stretch of country that included bits of Montana, Nevada, Utah, Idaho, Colorado, New Mexico, and Oklahoma.

Leaders of this group were "Kid" Curry, whose real name was Harvey Logan, and "Butch" Cassidy, also known as George Parker. Two other Logan brothers, John and Loney, and a cousin named Bob Lee were members of the outfit, as was also Harry Longabaugh, a big, bow-legged fellow who was often dubbed "the Sundance Kid." O. C. Hanks, Tom O'Day, Ben Kilpatrick, Will Carver, and Elza Lay rode with "the Wild Bunch" on their raids, though it was seldom that the whole party was together at any one time. "Flat-Nosed" George Curry (no relative of the Logans) was a prominent member of the party.

This part of the Northwest was always a wild district. Ten years before Butch Cassidy arrived on the scene, the Montana Stock Association, of which Granville Stuart was president, in alliance with the Wyoming cattlemen, held a drive of rustlers which lasted for two or three months and resulted in the death of seventy of the thieves, according to the evidence of some of those engaged in it. This had been an effective lesson, but the rustlers were back at their old ways again. Cassidy was convicted and sent to the penitentiary at Laramie, Wyoming. He was well liked, and at that time had no reputation as a bad man. His friends induced Governor Richards to pardon him. Shortly after this the bank and train robberies began.

The headquarters of the gang was at Lost Cañon, sixty miles from Thermopolis, though they shifted their habitat frequently. Sometimes they were at Robbers' Roost, sometimes in Brown's Park. Utah saw a good deal of them. Occasionally some of them drifted into Idaho.

They robbed a bank at Belle Fourche, South Dakota, and another at Montpelier, Idaho. In June, 1899, the Wild Bunch robbed the eastbound Union Pacific express at Wilcox, Idaho. The trail was picked up quickly, and they were pursued as far as Casper, Wyoming, by Sheriff Hazen of Converse County. The escaping men turned suddenly on the posse, and in the exchange of shots the sheriff was killed, the outlaws "holing up" in the mountains.

The "Black Jack" Ketcham gang was operating in New Mexico, and its membership was more or less interchangeable with that of the Hole-in-the-Wall group. With Elza Lay and Ben and George Kilpatrick, Butch Cassidy and the Ketchams held up a train at Folsom, New Mexico, in the course of which the conductor killed George Kilpatrick and wounded Black Jack. The sheriff of Huerfano County, Colorado, was hot on the trail of the fleeing robbers. A bullet finished the life of Will Ketcham. Lay's arm was shot off, and he and Black Jack were captured, but not before they had mortally wounded the sheriff, Jeff Farr. Black Jack was tried and hanged. Lay was given twenty years in the penitentiary at Santa Fe.

In August, 1900, Harvey Logan and Ben Kilpatrick held up a Union Pacific train at Tipton, Wyoming, after which they retired for a time to Fort Worth, Texas, where Cassidy and Longabaugh were taking a holiday. It was not too long a rest, for on September 19 of the same year they stopped and robbed the First National Bank at Winnemucca, Nevada. In making a getaway the fugitives divided forces. A posse caught up with one group as far away from the scene as Texas and Will Carver was killed. A year or two prior to this time Carver had shot down a law officer named George Scarborough, who had put an end to John Selman, who had assassinated John Wesley Hardin, who had a record by his own admission of having killed more than thirty men. The homicide chain could be carried back much farther without a break.

Not long after this Harvey Logan (Kid Curry), Ben Kilpatrick, and O. C. Hanks "stuck up" a Great Northern train at Wagner, Montana. Pinkerton men took the trail. Ben Kilpatrick was arrested at St. Louis, November 5, 1901, and Kid Curry at Knoxville, Tennessee, after a desperate resistance in the course of which he wounded two officers. Curry was given a short sentence of one hundred and thirty-five years in all, but he overpowered a guard and escaped without serving any of it.

The Wild Bunch was getting near the end of its trail. Charles Siringo, "Doc" Shores, and a dozen other officers and sheriffs were watching for them any time they made an appearance. Siringo claims in his book that he followed these law-breakers twenty-five thousand miles. A reward of $6500 was offered by the Pinkertons after the Wagner holdup. The circular explained that a man had boarded the blind baggage as the train was léaving Malta, Montana, and that he had crawled over the engine tender and covered the two of the crew who were in the cab, forcing them to stop the engine at the point they wished.

The territory of the different "bandit" belts throughout the western part of the United States was pretty well defined. One stretched across Texas to Arizona. Another zigzagged through the Rockies in Colorado to the district about the famous Robber's Roost. A third crossed Wyoming in the sparsely settled country adjacent to the Hole-in-the-Wall district. Here for many years skulked a nomadic population of rustlers, stage-robbers, and fugitives from justice. Among the foothills southeast of the Big Horn Mountains, with the nearest railroad a hundred miles distant, where the gulches and mountain pockets offered natural hiding-places, law officers had small chance to pick up the trail soon enough after the train-robbers had struck.

The Union Pacific Railroad organized a band of rangers to protect its line. Every train carried with it armed guards. Tim Keliher, chief of the Wyoming branch of the Union Pacific secret service, was put in charge of this. He picked as deputies Jeff Carr, a well-known law-enforcer of Wyoming, Pat Lawson and Tom Meggeson, noted trailers, and Joe La Fors, the deputy United States marshal who brought to justice the notorious Tom Horn. Headquarters were at Cheyenne. A baggage car was specially fitted up for the rangers and an engine put at their service. At one end of the car the horses were tied, at the other canteens, tin stoves, cots, and supplies of food were kept ready for the call.

Inside of ten minutes the rangers' car could be on the way to the scene of any holdup.

Wyoming did not look so good to Butch Cassidy and his friends after that. They shifted to Colorado for their next raid. At Parachute a train was held up, but little booty was secured. Doc Shores, a hawk-eyed oldtimer, took up the chase. He trapped the robbers in a gulch near Rifle, Colorado. Kid Curry, badly wounded, was heard to call to his companions, "Good-bye, boys. Don't wait for me." A moment later he sent a bullet from a .45 revolver into his brain.

One after another the Hole-in-the-Wall bad men were arrested or "rubbed out." George Kilpatrick had been shot to death near Folsom, New Mexico, and his brother Ben was serving a long sentence at the Columbus Penitentiary. (It may be mentioned that after his release Ben returned to his evil ways and lost his life at Sanderson, Texas, March 13, 1912, while attempting to hold up a train.) Two minor members of the gang, named Madden and Bass, were breaking rocks for their share in a Great Northern Railroad robbery. At Laramie Bob Lee was behind bars and at Santa Fe Elza Lay. Flat-Nosed George Curry had come to the end of the trail at Thompson Springs, Utah, and O. C. Hanks at San Antonio, Texas, both shot while resisting arrest. While resting at his old home in Dobson, Missouri, Loney Logan had been trapped and destroyed trying to fight his way out. His brother John had "gone west" years before this. A turbulent fellow, John had an arm filled with slugs as he "hurrahed" a town, and it was later amputated. The wound was hardly healed before he ordered a ranchman named Winters to leave his homestead. The nester declined, was threatened, and saved his life temporarily by shooting John before the latter did as much by him. Kid Curry took care of the Winters' account later.

Only Butch Cassidy and Harry Longabaugh were left. Both of them could see the writing on the wall. No matter how they dodged and backtracked there was no safety for them now in the West. They slipped down to New Orleans and took boat for the Argentine. For years little was heard of them, though rumors came up of their troubles with the authorities there. At last Arthur Chapman verified a story that they had been killed. In 1909 they held up a mine payroll near Quechisla in southern Bolivia. With the pursuit closing in on them, they flitted from place to place hurriedly. In the course of their flight they stole a mule to help them escape.

At San Vicente they stopped to rest at a drinking-place. At last they had made a clean getaway, they thought. By sheer chance a stranger in the place recognized the mule. A Bolivian captain walked into the *tendejon* to make inquiries. One of the fugitives killed him. The troops, now under the command of a sergeant, besieged the place.

The desperadoes had left their rifles in the room they had taken across the patio. After emptying their revolvers it was clear that they had to get the rifles to save themselves. Longabaugh tried to cross the square and fell, desperately wounded. Cassidy dragged him back to cover. Two cartridges were left in the dead captain's revolver. The outlaws decided not to let the soldiers capture them. When the attackers broke in five minutes later they found both the gringos dead.

Roughly speaking, the old-time Western outlaws ran true to type. Most of them had been cowboys before they started to follow crooked trails. When they rode the range there was no outward difference between them and their fellow-punchers, unless it was in the restlessness which always kept them moving and in the recklessness that made them undependable. But within them was an impatience at the steady grind of work, an urgent impulse to take short cuts to easy money. So far they were all alike, but within the type individuals differed. In the terrible Plummer gang Steve Marshland was unique. He would rob, but he would not kill. Other road agents have shared this characteristic. It is said that Butch Cassidy never killed a man until the last day of his life.

In this respect he differed from his co-leader Kid Curry, who left behind him the record of a trail of homicides. At Knoxville, Tennessee, he quarreled with a saloonkeeper and killed him. In revenge for his brother John's death he cut down the nester Winters with a bullet sent from the brush as the homesteader was brushing his teeth. The most famous of his victims was Pike Landusky, trapper, freighter, cowboy, Indian fighter, and saloonkeeper, from whom a town in northern Montana derives its name.

Landusky would have been out of place in any setting except that of the frontier West. He was a long, rangy man, broadshouldered and strong, and never in his life did he sidestep a fight. A born leader, he had a large following among those with whom he lived. Generous to a fault, he was ready at any time to share all he had with a friend. But he could be a bitter enemy, one so blunt and impulsive that trouble followed him all his life. His chief weakness was a temper so little under control that he was likely on small provocation to fly into furious rages.

For more than twenty years he was an outstanding figure in his part of Montana. For a time he was employed by the Diamond R freight outfit, but later went on his own as a trapper. Dan R. Conway tells a characteristic story of him. In partnership with John Wirt he had acquired a fine lot of furs, which they cached on the Musselshell while they went to town for supplies. In their absence a party of Sioux Indians found the furs and at once appropriated them for personal use. The trappers returned, to find themselves prisoners, but captives who declined to give up their arms. The braves gave them some buffalo meat, which Landusky cooked in a fry-pan for himself and partner. He was boiling with rage but realized the folly of giving way to it.

One of the warriors reached over Landusky's shoulder and snatched up the meat. Pike went berserk. He slammed the pan against the face of the brave, spattering him with hot grease, then drove the barrel of his rifle into the stomach of the Indian and doubled him up. Tearing off the man's breech-cloth, he whipped him over the head with it, an unforgivable offense to the Sioux. Wirt cocked his gun and waited. His opinion was that both he and his partner would be dead inside of five minutes.

The Sioux chief rushed across to Wirt and ordered him to make Landusky stop at once. "The hearts of my men are bad and they will kill you both," he warned.

Fortunately one of the braves called out that Landusky was crazy. There could be no other explanation of a rage so wild which must result in death for himself. The other Indians agreed, and the tribes never injured a madman. This was ingrained in them as a part of their religion. The war party caught up their horses and departed. They were on their way to the Crow country to steal riding-stock. On their return they stopped to present Landusky and Wirt with sixteen horses, to pay for the stores they had destroyed.

There was enmity between Landusky and Kid Curry. How it started is not known, but there is a story that Pike was appointed a deputy sheriff to take Curry to Fort Benton for trial prior to his conviction for rustling and that Pike grew angry and abused his prisoner. Curry was a sullen fellow, and he nursed his desire for revenge.

He rode to Landusky and tied his horse at the rack in front of the place of "Jew Jake," who was himself a hard character. In a gunfight with the marshal at Great Falls Jake had lost a leg, and he now carried a rifle as a crutch.

Pike stood in front of the bar, an elbow leaning on it, when Kid Curry pushed through the swing door into the gambling-house. Curry walked to his foe, lashed at his face with a doubled fist, and before Landusky could recover slammed down on his head with the barrel of a revolver. Already shaken and jarred, Pike tried to close with the outlaw. Curry fought him off, beating his opponent to the floor with more crashing blows. Still on the ground, Pike reached for a handkerchief to wipe the blood out of his eyes. The kid pumped a bullet through his heart, claiming afterward that he thought Landusky was about to draw a pistol.

Kid Curry's eyes lifted from the lax body of the man he had just killed and let them sweep the room. "Anybody want to take this up?" he demanded.

Jew Jake hobbled forward on his rifle-crutch. "Everybody satisfied, I reckon," he said amiably.

That was stretching the truth. A good many were not pleased at what Harvey Logan, alias Kid Curry, had done, though they admitted that Pike Landusky's violent explosive temper had brought him close to death a dozen times. Pike had his faults and his virtues. Both were of an outstanding kind. Reckless and undisciplined though he had been, a host of friends regretted his murder.

More than a decade after the Hole-in-the-Wall gang had been exterminated, a road agent of an entirely new kind appeared in Wyoming. He played a lone hand and robbed the coaches from the inside while the train was still traveling across country. After he had mulcted the passengers of two trains of their cash a guard was sent to protect them. The robberies occurred west of Laramie on the Union Pacific. A reward of $6500 was offered for his capture.

The bandit was a country boy brought up near Greeley, Colorado, named William L. Carlisle. Evidently he robbed for the sake of the excitement and the notoriety as much as for the money.

After the second holdup he wrote a letter to the Denver *Post* which shows his vanity and love of the limelight. It ran as follows:

> I am sending you the watch chain that I took from a passenger on my last holdup. I'll return the watch on my next. I'll hold up the Union Pacific west of Laramie just to convince the police that they have not got the right party. Please return the chain to its owner with my compliments.
>
> I remain, sincerely,
> THE WHITE MASKED BANDIT

On April 21, 1916, a passenger boarded the Denver-Salt Lake Limited at Laramie. He was a man of about twenty-eight years of age, six feet two in height, and weighed one hundred and ninety-eight pounds. Nobody paid any attention to him. He was just another cowboy on the move, evidently a garrulous chap, for he talked with the guard, the brakeman, and the conductor. Half an hour after the train had left Laramie he prodded the guard in the back with a revolver.

"All right," he said. "Time for the holdup. I'll take your gun first."

The startled guard could make no resistance. In fact, under the urge of the revolver he walked down the aisle in front of the outlaw and held his hat for the passengers to make their contributions in it. Carlisle and his unwilling assistant passed into a second car and continued the levy on travelers' assets. Before the next station was reached the bandit made the conductor stop the train. He descended from it and vanished into the night, after handing to the guard the watch he had promised to return.

The country was full of posses searching for the daring bandit. A member of one of them came upon Carlisle hiding in a boulder field. To the surprise of the officer, the robber flung his revolvers to the ground.

"I'm not a killer," he called to his hunter. "If I have to shed blood to get away I would rather surrender."

Carlisle spent many years in the penitentiary. When he was released not very long ago he bought a cigar stand in a Wyoming town and sold magazines and tobacco to the public. Long since he had lost his craving for grandstanding.

During the 1920's there was a recrudescence of bank "stickups," owing to the discovery that the automobile made swift escape possible. When the James-Younger gang held up the gate receipts at the Kansas City Fair before a thousand witnesses they had to depend upon fast horses to get away. But by the time the Hole-in-the-Wall gang was operating the rural telephone made bank and train holdups highly hazardous. The automobile brought a new factor into the problem of putting an end to such raids. All over the West there was a temporary outbreak of bank robberies. It became possible to strike unexpectedly, deflect from the main thoroughfares, and dodge from one country road to another until the hideout was reached.

One of the most spectacular of these raids was the one upon the First National Bank at Lamar, Colorado. Just before noon, on May 23, 1928, a blue sedan drove up to the bank, and from it descended four men, not masked. They left the engine of the car running and walked into the building. The leader, a tall, brown-faced man, snapped out an order to the staff and to the customers present.

"Stick 'em up!"

Eight or nine pairs of arms stretched ceilingward. The president of the bank, A. N. Parrish, an old man of seventy-seven, was frontier stock and had always said that if an attempt was made to rob his bank he would resist. He jumped for a revolver and fired at the nearest bandit, the bullet hitting the man in the jaw. A moment later Parrish went down, drilled through and through. Several slugs had struck him, and he was dead before his body slumped to the floor. His son snatched up another gun, to come to the aid of his father. He too was instantly killed.

The voice of one of the outlaws cut into the panic. "Lie down on the floor, every last one of you," it ordered.

From the vault was taken more than two hundred thousand dollars in gold, notes, and securities. Within three minutes of the sound of the first shot the robbers moved back to the blue sedan, taking with them as a protection against attack Cashier Kesinger and Teller Lundgren. The car raced into the country, and because it was crowded one of the bank officials was pushed out.

Sheriff Alderman of Lamar was already in pursuit in a fast car. He overhauled the robbers, who presently stopped their sedan. One of them got out and fired with a rifle from behind Kesinger. As Alderman had only his six-guns with him he had to give up the chase for the moment.

A dozen posses took the field in automobiles. Planes flew above the road ribbons. Guards picketed the exits of towns. The bandits made a clean getaway. No positive clews of their line of travel could be picked up except the tragic ones of dead bodies. Kesinger was found in an old shack near Liberal, Kansas. He had been shot through the back.

At Dighton, Kansas, on the night of the robbery two men came to the door of Doctor W. W. Wineinger and asked him to come into the country to attend a young man who had been hurt by a tractor. They proposed to take him in their car and bring him back, but Wineinger said he preferred to go in his own. One of the men rode beside him. The doctor suggested that since the weather was muggy the right-hand window might be opened. His companion put a finger against the pane and pushed it out. That one fingerprint cost four men their lives and probably saved four others from the gallows.

The body of Doctor Wineinger was found a week later in a deep gully. His car had been pushed into it after him. The automobile had been gone over with a greased rag to wipe out fingerprints. The one mark on the windowglass was the only one left. An expert dusted, developed, and photographed it.

Meanwhile many arrests were made. Some showed perfect alibis. The evidence pointed to four suspects. Brought to Lamar, they were identified by the witnesses. Feeling against them ran high, and there seemed to be little doubt of a conviction.

The fingerprint had been sent to Washington. Months passed, and one day the discovery was made that this print was identical with another made in 1916 at the Oklahoma Penitentiary of Convict 6591. The convict was William Harrison Fleagle, commonly nicknamed Jake. Chief of Police Hugh Harper went to Garden City, Kansas, to get his man. Jake had been warned and had fled, but Harper picked up his brother, Ralph Emerson Fleagle.

It was found that the Fleagles had surprisingly large bank accounts. The two brothers and some companions lived intermittently on what they called a horse ranch, but they did little business in horses. Confronted with this and other evidence, after a long grilling Ralph Fleagle talked. One of the bandits, the same man whose jaw had been shattered by the old banker's bullet, was Howard L. Royston, and he was living in California. After Wineinger had given first aid and been murdered Royston was hurried to an undercover doctor at St. Paul, Minnesota. An apartment had been rented and George J. Abshier, the fourth robber, looked after him until he was well. Royston and Abshier were arrested and brought to Colorado. The case against the former suspects was dropped. Fleagle, Abshier, and Royston were convicted and hanged. Detectives followed Jake Fleagle and caught up with him on a train at Branson, Missouri, and when he reached for his pistol shot him to death.

There was nothing romantic about the Fleagles, Dillinger, or "Pretty Boy" Floyd. They were gangsters of the most cold-blooded types, just as Capone and his associates were. Like the bandits of a generation ago, they had their little day and ceased to be. If there is one point that stands out like a bandaged thumb, it is that in the end the law will catch up with all of them. The aphorism that crime does not pay is trite but true.

C. B. GLASSCOCK

THE NAMING OF
DEATH VALLEY

The terrible hardships of the early pioneers in their struggle
to explore and conquer the West are starkly set forth by Mr.
Glasscock. That the conquest was achieved is history; it is
also history that men and women died cruelly in the achieve-
ment. "Death Valley" was an inevitable name for this "pit,
130 miles long, shaped and colored in spots like a Gila monster. . . ." (From *Here's Death Valley*, Bobbs-Merrill, 1940.)

SEATED in the sun, his back against a wall, his leathern face
alight, Indian George gazed back through ninety years to the
one great event of his childhood.

"Yes," he said, "me and my papa, we see. We live Panamint
side. What you call Emigrant Spring. We go up on hill. Long time
ago. I'm little boy."

He held out a gnarled hand, blotched and blackened by a hundred years of Death Valley and Panamint sun. The palm was perhaps three feet from the ground.

"I'm little boy. You savvy. Mebbe ten year old. Injun boy ten
year old little. No get much eat. My papa stop. I see three men
down canyon. I point. I say, 'Papa, what those?' I scared. Those
men all long hair down front." He gestured to indicate untrimmed
beards. "I no see nothing like that before. I start run. My papa,

432

he grab. Say, 'No run. They see run, they shoot.' He hold me down. Hide. Those men go on. No see us."

He paused, took a last long drag at his cigarette, held it so that I could see it was down to its last half-inch, and regretfully heeled it into the dirt. When another cigarette was burning he looked at me with filmed old eyes.

"How long time ago that?" he demanded abruptly.

"Mebbe so ninety years," I said.

He nodded with satisfaction. Evidently my estimate of the time agreed with others he had heard. It confirmed the opinion of his importance that he has acquired since he became known to a few zealous students of western history as the one living human being who actually saw the advance guard of the first recorded party of white men ever to encounter Death Valley.

"I'm plenty old man," he said proudly, after a pause. "Long time, I remember."

He settled back comfortably. The utter quiet of a windless day upon the desert, with neither sound nor movement, closed upon us. I handed over cigarettes and matches, and waited. After a time there came forth other memories. They were memories which illuminate the history of ninety desert years. Some were slow years through which Death Valley itself waited, less concerned than its stolid native Indians, for the movements of the white men.

Indian George has no doubt about what he saw. He has even helped to correct an error of many years' standing as to the precise route taken by the historic Jayhawker party in their escape from what the Indians through centuries had called Tomesha, meaning ground afire. That has earned George some honors and many cigarettes. But one frightened little Indian boy could never have suspected all the tragedy, heroism and accomplishment centering in the valley of ground afire on that December day in 1849.

The three hairy men whom he saw were a detachment of the Jayhawkers who had burned their wagons to smoke the meat of their starved oxen on the valley crossing a few miles north of what is now known as Furnace Creek Ranch. George and his papa were plenty scared. After they had watched the hairy men disappear into a rocky canyon they took to the hills and saw no more. Tomesha was to burn through ten more summers before the boy encountered his next group of hairy men. He found that adventure so pleasing that he took for himself the name of their leader.

All that was just as well. Possibly the undernourished little Indian boy might have been frightened literally to death if he had seen the scores of other hairy men, their women, their children, their great horned beasts and covered wagons moving in the depths of Tomesha. For there were more white men in the region in that Christmas week of 1849 than there were to be through the next quarter of a century, and they were the first ever to be seen by the local Indians.

To the whites, Death Valley was merely another and more terrible hazard than any they had encountered on a wandering, unmapped desert journey of eighty days southwestward from the recently established Mormon settlement of Salt Lake City. It was too vast to visualize in its entirety from any point they had yet climbed. It was a pit 130 miles long, shaped, and colored in spots somewhat like a Gila monster, stretching near the southeast slanting line of what was later to be defined as the California border.

Nearly half of that great pit lay below sea level. The emigrants, approaching through a narrow canyon near the center of its eastern wall, could see only that its lower surfaces, almost flat, were streaked and smeared as if by a colossal whitewash brush, carelessly wielded. The mountain barriers which formed its sides towered a mile above the depths, and changed from deep blue in the shades of dawn and sunset to brilliant yellows and dull reds, slashed with dark shadows, in the gleaming sunlight. From the feet of the mountain walls, at the narrow mouth of each barren canyon, alluvial deposits, a mile and more wide and long, laid their slate-blue fans down to the soiled white expanses below the level of the sea.

At dawn and sunset the fires of heaven—or hell—mantled the mountains and sometimes spread across the entire dome of the sky. Exhausted by the hardships of their long journey from the rendezvous near Salt Lake City, the travelers knew only that they must cross the barren sink before them and climb the forbidding heights beyond, with more ranges, visible, snow-capped, still farther to the westward. The gold-laden streams above the fertile valleys of California had been their goal for almost a year. The bitter waters in the sink below threatened to be their reward.

But they were men and women of the stock that had been conquering the frontiers of America for more than two hundred years. Their wagon train from Salt Lake City had been broken by disagreements as to routes and policies. Their only remaining ties were personal, family and group loyalties, and an unyielding will to reach their goal.

Largest of the groups was that known as the Jayhawkers— thirty-six young men who had set out from Galesburg, Illinois, ten months earlier. The Rev. James Welch Brier and his valiant wife and three small sons, with a few stragglers, traveled on the trail of the Jayhawkers. Detachments of men from Georgia and Mississippi, numbering about twenty-five, moved under the general direction of James Martin and "Captain" Towne. There were also some twenty men in the Coker party.

Choosing a different route from their point of entrance into the valley proper was the group of two families and their associates that has gone down in history as the Bennett-Arcane party, followed by the Wade family, consisting of father, mother and four children ranging in age from six to fourteen years. A few single men were attached to the Bennett-Arcane group, led by the heroic William Lewis Manly.

Group by group, held within a few days' march of each other not so much by intent as by the slow advance of leaders who sought a passable way, they had crossed the Amargosa, desert of bitterness, and headed downward into the desert of death.

Picture that broken caravan, you who may follow its course today on a smooth oiled road from the Amargosa Hotel down Furnace Creek wash. Pause a moment in your fifty-mile-an-hour flight—just long enough to permit the boulders beside the highway to assume their true significance. They were barriers to the movement of broken-hoofed oxen and lumbering, heaving, straining covered wagons. On either side of you, extending to the high and low rocky walls of this sloping wash, is precisely the sort of roadway down which those hardy Americans journeyed.

Furnace Creek wash has not changed in these years. It has merely been smoothed in a narrow ribbon for the passage of automobiles. One cloudburst, of which it has known scores since the passage of the emigrants, will restore it to precisely the same condition in which they found it. Be happy that you will not have to make the journey then—that you can wait until the CCC boys roll away the boulders, scrape away the gravel, and restore the oiled strip of motor-smooth surface.

The emigrants could not wait. Death waited. They must roll

away their own boulders, or hoist their wagons, jarring, over the rocks. And so they did.

First moved the Jayhawkers, young men, once strong, once well-equipped and well-supplied, once singing, fiddling, joking around their campfires. But they were no longer strong, nor well-supplied, nor gay. Life for them had been reduced to its two fundamentals—food and water. Reduced almost to the primitive condition of the naked savages who watched from hiding, they were far less well-equipped with the needed wisdom of the desert.

All felt the imminent danger of death from starvation and thirst. None appreciated how fortunate they were to be entering the ground afire when its flames had been cooled by the ideal weather of the Christmas season. If it had been the Fourth of July, in the conditions of those days not one could have lived to tell the tale. As it was, the great majority came safely through their ordeal.

The Jayhawkers with their wagons and starving oxen turned northward from the valley's entrance at the mouth of Furnace Creek wash. They camped at a brackish spring which nourished a little coarse grass for their animals, near what later became known as the Salt Creek crossing, near the present east-west road between Daylight Pass and Towne's Pass. The Georgians and Mississippians, arriving in the same neighborhood, had already burned their wagons and packed their few belongings on their oxen. The Jayhawkers decided to do the same thing.

When Manly, scouting ahead of the Bennett-Arcane party, which he had left back in Furnace Creek wash, arrived at the pitiful camp the Jayhawkers were already burning wagons to smoke the stringy meat of a few slaughtered oxen. At a distance which they estimated as fifteen or twenty miles to the westward they could see a depression in the mountain wall which they had named Martin's Pass, but which scouts had told them was impassable for wagons. They advised Manly of that, and went on with their preparations.

From that point, marked for many years by parts of wagons, iron work and discarded ox-yokes, the various groups moved as best they could, westward across the valley, and up the wide alluvial slope upon which Stovepipe Wells Hotel now welcomes travelers. At the top of the gravel fan the parties divided as their judgment suggested.

How harrowing were their experiences, even in the balmy winter of the deep desert valley, may be best revealed in the brief diary records attributed to Asa Haynes, as captain of one of the divisions of the Jayhawkers. Undated day after day he recorded their movements and their hardships in items of not more than half a dozen words each: "South 12 miles, no water." "Then southeast 8 miles, got weak."

In a single entry of seven words, without mention of the scene or dates, he crowded the whole story of the Jayhawkers' experience in Death Valley. "Left wagons, packed cattle, six days wandering." And those six days brought the Jayhawkers only over the first mountains to the westward, into a maze of other desert ranges and valleys.

In five short entries Haynes has left a suggestion of the following weeks of struggle. A man named Fish died. "Starvation." No detail. No further comment. William Isham died. Luther Richards found water. Two men, Frank and Townshend, wandered away. One man collapsed, and when Haynes returned to him with coffee he was dead. No name is given. William Robinson and McGowan passed the desert only to die "at the foot of the mountains." Townshend found dead. "Scalped." And all that after Death Valley itself had been left behind.

It is not a clarifying record but it is as illuminating as the desert sun, as harsh and stark as the Death Valley sink and mountains.

From subsequent research we know that a man named Fish, identified by Haynes as from Iowa, by Manly as from Indiana, and by Carl I. Wheat as from Illinois, died near the summit of the Argus Range, some two weeks' travel from the pit of the valley. We know that William Isham, from Rochester, New York, died on the same day, far to the southward near the bitter Searles Lake. That distance indicates the wide scattering of the emigrants. No record except that of Haynes mentions the finding of Townshend "scalped," and Townshend has never been adequately identified under that name. There has been no identification of the man whom Haynes mentions as having died while Haynes had gone to fetch him coffee. William Robinson died four weeks' distance from Death Valley. McGowan's death or identity has never been established. Captain Culverwell alone died in the valley.

Possibly a few were lost and never identified. Indians eventually reported finding the body of a white man in the mountains to the west with a broken leg and a bullet hole in his forehead. It sug-

gests a mercy killing by friends who could do nothing better to
save him from death by thirst and starvation. Manly's record,
written many years after the events, mentions a "Dale" family,
but Carl I. Wheat, who has compiled the most comprehensive
census of the emigrants to date, believes that that was either a
misprint or an error in memory.

For nearly ninety years the route of the Jayhawkers from the
valley proper was commonly believed to be through what has
long been known as Emigrant Canyon. Only in 1936 did Farland
Wells and Rocky Cochran of the Death Valley CCC camp, with
an Indian, Tom Wilson, born in the vicinity, find a boulder in
a smaller canyon a short distance west of Emigrant, bearing
convincing evidence that the Jayhawkers passed that way.

Inscribed on the rock were names, initials and dates. Some were
almost obliterated by the action of the elements. "W B R, 1849"
may have been the inscription of W. B. Roods, listed in the original
Jayhawker party. A faint "lar" may have been the imprint of
Andrew Larken, the only Jayhawker with that syllable in his
name. Brier may have found strength to scratch his name, of
which only the "rier" can be deciphered. A few later dates and
names are comparatively clear. "J. Hitchens 1860 Boston" is
known to have been a member of Dr. Darwin French's prospecting
and exploration party of that year. "Frank L. Weston 1861"
appears. "T. G. Beasley" added no date to his inscription, but
is known to have been a member of the French party.

The inscriptions and the date of 1849 are conclusive evidence
that some of the emigrants passed that way instead of the slightly
easier route that came to be known as Emigrant Canyon. Further
verification has been obtained from Indian George, who saw them.
Diplomatically put on the grill by T. Ray Goodwin, superintendent of Death Valley National Monument, who likes to have
everything under his direction well defined, George admitted that
the three hairy men whom he saw as a boy did not go up Emigrant
Canyon.

"Why you always say they go that way, George?"

George grinned. "White man always say that way," he said. "I
lettum go."

"But you saw them go next canyon west." It was not a question.
Goodwin was bearing down in the interest of accuracy.

"Yes," said George. "Next canyon they go."

George is always willing to oblige his white friends. So Superintendent Goodwin has named the next canyon Jayhawker Canyon. My friend Carl I. Wheat, who happily chronicles painstaking corrections of long-established errors for the California Historical Society Quarterly, has accepted and approved this finding. He has also, with the assistance of Mr. Goodwin and Donald Curry in the field, made numerous corrections of the precise routes taken by the scattered emigrants before and after they entered Death Valley, and has published a brochure which is the last word on the subject.

If that inscribed rock had not been found, or Indian George had not been so accommodating, everything would be much simpler. Tourists could drive on an excellent road, as they do drive, up Emigrant Canyon, and picture the emigrants stumbling, struggling, over that identical boulder-strewn terrain. And now they will have to walk up the neighboring Jayhawker Canyon, or the Park Service will have to build another road.

Perhaps, to obtain a more accurate idea of what those emigrants encountered, they had better walk. They should go on a diet of starved beef, rice, unleavened bread and tea or coffee made with alkaline water, for several weeks of training. They should drive ahead of them the hide-covered skeleton of a steer carrying the pitiful remnants of their food, and to serve as lunch when the other food is exhausted. To make it quite realistic they might even carry a nine-year-old boy, wasted to the weight of a three-year-old, as Mrs. Brier did.

It may be safer for them to drive the Emigrant Canyon route. Possibly some of the emigrants went that way. The whole assembly at Salt Creek had broken up with the final abandonment of the wagons. They turned aside or moved ahead as strength, judgment, or desperation dictated.

Two divisions of the Jayhawkers, led by Edward Doty and Asa Haynes, with the Brier family and others following, catching up, falling behind and catching up again, eventually found their way across the Mojave desert to the fertile San Francisquito Ranch, near what is now Newhall. The hospitality of the *hacienda-dos* awaited them—water, food, rest, life, and the beginning of fame. The date was February 4, 1850. Forty days from Death Valley. To them it must have been like the forty years of the Israelites. I drove from the valley to Newhall on February 26,

1939, in six hours, and stopped for an hour to hear from Indian George how he had seen them go by.

"How long time ago, that?"

"Ninety years."

Ninety years, and Death Valley is unchanged. Only the man-made threads of road upon its ruggedness have opened the way to its wonders, beauties, and history.

If you doubt, try camping for a month where the Bennett-Arcane party camped for a month in that winter of 1849-50, while the occasional companions of the eighty days preceding the ordeal struggled out upon various routes. But remember, to get the true effect you should limit your accommodations to the old-fashioned covered wagons, not the modern trailer. You should limit your food to emaciated ox-meat, and flour—not much flour —and a spoonful of rice a day. You should forget that there are roads and maps. You should see only the waiting carrion ravens.

Seeing the valley from the spot where Mrs. Bennett and Mrs. Arcane crouched in the meager shade of their wagons, helplessly watching their little ones sink nearer and nearer to death from starvation and illness through days and weeks of waiting, one can understand how little it has changed.

Seeing it from the mile-high point of Dante's View a few miles to the eastward, a mile straight up from the lowest spot of land upon this continent, one can understand how little it has changed. Only a tiny man-made thread of road here and there upon its unearthly beauty emphasizes the fact that man may come and go, but Death Valley waits, inviolable.

The Bennett-Arcane party knew only that man might come. In agony and terror they doubted that man, once in the clutches of Death Valley, could ever go.

Before his conference with the Jayhawkers at the Salt Creek crossing where he found them burning their wagons, Manly had scouted down Furnace Creek wash ahead of the Bennett-Arcane party and had seen an Indian silhouetted upon a distant butte, "so far away he looked no taller than my finger." And he saw far more than that. His book of memoirs, published half a century after the events, remains the most coherent, complete and readable record of those incredible experiences.

He records that it was Christmas Day, 1849. He was made aware of the date when he found the Brier family encamped beside some feeble springs far down the wash which was their route into the valley. The Rev. James Welch Brier was celebrating the occasion by giving a lecture. More than fifty years later, his son, the Rev. John Wells Brier, in memoirs published in *Out West*, thus described that celebration:

"The best we could do for Christmas was to slaughter an ox free for all. The men wanted something to remind them of other days, and my father gave a lecture on education. It was grave, humorous and reminiscent."

Manly mentions no one at that camp except the Briers. There may or may not have been stragglers from other groups.

After watching the Briers away from the Furnace Creek encampment the next morning, the scout returned to his own party and guided their footsore oxen and lumbering wagons down the last eight boulder-strewn miles of the wash. On the following day he scouted the floor of the valley. A minor shock of that day was his discovery of a mummy-like Indian hidden in the sand hills beyond the mouth of the canyon.

"He was not dead for I could see him move as he breathed, but his skin looked very much like a well-dried venison ham." A greater shock was the discovery that the valley to the southward appeared to be paved with practically impassable blocks and pinnacles of rock salt.

"After this discovery I took my way back to the road made by the Jayhawkers and found it quite level, but sandy. Following this I came to a campfire soon after dark at which E. Doty and mess were camped. . . . I inquired of them about Martin's Pass, as they were now quite near it. They said it was no pass at all. No wagon could get over it. . . . Before daylight I was headed back on the trail."

Returning to his own company, Manly met two companions of the long journey whom he identifies as "oldish men, perhaps fifty years old, one a Mr. Fish of Indiana and another named Gould." Fifty was old indeed for such undertakings. The great majority of gold-rush emigrants were under thirty. Manly left his acquaintances with the feeling that he would never see them again. He never did—alive.

Joining his people at the Furnace Creek encampment, he advised them that the Jayhawkers and others in advance, had burned their wagons to smoke their ox-meat for an attempted escape through the mountains to the northwest. The company agreed to try a southwesterly route, and Manly led them across the valley, probably on the approximate line of the corduroy road which was built many years later to give safe and dry access from Furnace Creek Ranch to the Panamint Mountains. He remembered half a century later that they crossed through shallow water, while he waded ahead, prodding with a mesquite stick to make sure of depth and solidity of the bottom.

They attempted a climb up one of the precipitous Panamint canyons and found it hopeless. On the second night they found fresh water with a little overflow nourishing enough coarse grass to keep their oxen alive.

Precisely where that point may have been is now also a question in dispute. For decades it was accepted as being the harsh oasis of mesquite and salt grass known as Bennett's Well. More recently some students of history have placed it a few miles farther north, at a spot known as Tule Spring, or somewhere between the two, where thirty years later the Eagle Borax Works flourished briefly. The fact that Manly's memoirs refer to the wagons as the only shade available cast the chief doubt upon the Bennett's Well location. A wide thicket of mesquite trees, certainly more than a hundred years old, provides sparse natural shade in that area.

The point of immediate importance to the travelers was that there was enough potable water for their requirements and enough feed to keep their oxen alive. On the first day in that camp, four men who had made the long journey as ox-drivers and helpers with Bennett and Arcane refused to remain. Each of the four packed ten days' provisions on his back and moved northward to find the trail of the Jayhawkers.

The Bennetts and Arcanes, with the two little Bennett girls, Melissa and Martha, the Bennett boy, George, and little Charley Arcane, settled into camp. Half the night they debated, and at last decided that Manly and John Rogers should go out on foot to find a route, and return with help. Another ox was killed, and the meat dried to supply the scouts. Later Manly wrote that some idea of the emaciated condition of their cattle could be obtained from the fact that seven-eighths of all the flesh of that ox was carried away in the two men's knapsacks.

With their dried meat, two spoonfuls of rice and tea, a small tin cup and a quart tin kettle and sheath knife each; with a shotgun and rifle, half a blanket, and thirty-odd dollars between them, the two men moved out upon their journey. Heavier than their physical burdens were their spirits, and their responsibility.

I shall not attempt to tell in detail the story of that journey. William Lewis Manly himself has written it, in all its harrowing and heroic features. Beside his unadorned tale any other must fade into insignificance.

Bennett expected them to be gone ten days. Manly believed they would require fifteen. They did, in fact, consume twenty-six. Climbing, plodding, thirsting, they blundered upon the trail of the Jayhawkers. They found the body of Fish, unburied. They came by night to the campfire of the Jayhawker group captained by Doty. They heard of the death of Isham, and that the Brier family was somewhere behind and the Haynes detachment somewhere ahead.

Struggling onward the next day they caught up with the Haynes party. They found and fed the Bennett-Arcane teamsters who were waiting like scavengers for scraps from a slaughtered ox of which even the intestines were prized as food. Leaving that camp at daybreak they broke a new trail southward, carrying with them the names and addresses of eastern families to be notified if the men behind them trudged to death instead of life. On and on, mountain and desert, starvation and thirst.

At last, a day of days, the first game encountered for weeks, a crow, a hawk and a quail fell before their guns. A mountain brook completed their happiness, and restored their strength. Another day and Heaven itself opened before them—a grassy, tree-studded valley, with a grazing yearling steer within rifle shot. It fell, and they pounced upon it with the hunger of wolves.

Another day, and they were in the settlements. Another, at San Fernando Mission. Two or three more, and with a little one-eyed mule packed with beans, flour and other provisions, and a horse each to ride, they turned their backs once more upon life, and headed toward Death Valley.

Would they be in time? Would their starving friends, the ailing children, have waited so many days beyond the time set for their return. If they had not waited, as seemed probable, the scouts were undertaking another month of tortuous, useless travel. But they put that thought aside and hurried out again across the desert.

But the horses could not survive one half the journey that the two men had made on foot. Exhausted, they could no longer climb. Weeping in their own weakness and disappointment, the men abandoned them. Heart-wrenching whinnies followed the men, clambering up a canyon.

And so, in time, with only the little mule and its pitiful supply of provisions, and their own hard-won knowledge of routes and far-spaced water holes to show for their weeks of torture, Manly and Rogers came again down the steep slope of a Panamint canyon toward the camp of their friends.

Rogers, in advance, halted abruptly. Stretched upon the ground, face upward, lay the body of a white man. It was Captain Culverwell whom they had last seen weeks ago on the morning of their departure from the encampment. One strayed from camp. One dead. How many more might they find, or never find?

Cautiously now they moved onward. Not a sound, not a movement welcomed them. Four wagons in the distance where they had left seven, and the four had been stripped of their coverings. They knew a sudden stunning fear that the friends for whom they had been risking their lives had been massacred by raiding Indians. The Indians might still be there, in ambush, waiting to kill the only two white men who had ever returned to Tomesha after having once escaped.

Within rifle shot, beyond arrow shot, they consulted. Seven charges in Manly's rifle, two in Rogers' shotgun. One shot from the rifle would still leave a total of eight with which to repulse the Indians if the alarm brought them from hiding. Manly fired.

Out from beneath a distant wagon crawled a man. He came painfully to his feet and looked around. A white man!

Even today, ninety-one years later, speeding smoothly by, or stopping, in the luxury of our cars, beside the scene of that drama, we must feel its soul-shaking force.

Remember; two mothers, two fathers, four sick and starving children, had waited amid that desolation for twenty-six agonizing days for this moment. And here it was. Black despair ended with the abruptness of that rifle shot. Here, suddenly, in the hands of two loyal men, freely offered, were the gifts of life. In an instant all the terrors of an unknown future fled before this great new hope.

Four adults and four children only were left to profit by that moment. The other groups, of the Wade family and the single men, had lacked the faith of the Bennett-Arcane party in the loyalty and stamina of Manly and Rogers. Within a week after the scouts' departure, the others had started to move away, some dragging their wagons with them, some abandoning the wagons and carrying meager packs upon their weakened oxen. The last of them had gone two weeks before the return of Manly and Rogers, seeking any route which might appear in the wilderness. They preferred to die in a struggle for life rather than in an idle waiting for death.

How many of those desperate wayfarers survived is not definitely recorded. But eighty-nine years later two elderly women ascended the broad stone terraces of Furnace Creek Inn, and stood and gazed silently for a long time, away to the south. Perhaps it was the strain of trying to distinguish the small dark blot of the Bennett's Well mesquite thicket in the long expanse of whiteness that made them press their handkerchiefs to their eyes.

Later, within the luxury of the Inn, they told of the hardships of a little girl of nine, encamped at that dim spot upon Death Valley's floor to the southward, eighty-nine years earlier. That little girl was Almira Wade. Almira Wade was their mother. They were Mrs. John Quincy White of Ukiah and Mrs. J. A. Hunter of Santa Clara. The Death Valley known to its first white travelers was very real to those white-haired women. They had heard about it from a mother who had known it all too well.

They had heard about it from William Lewis Manly, in repeated conferences with their mother, Mrs. Ortley, at their home in Alviso. There Manly frequently arrived from his own home in Santa Clara to discuss details while he was writing his memoirs for publication in 1894. They were able to state with authority that the Wade family, father, mother, and three children had found their own way out to life while the Bennetts and Arcanes waited for the return of Manly and Rogers.

Why Manly omitted that important detail from his book will remain a mystery. That he was under some obligations to Almira Wade Ortley for contributory recollections about the emigrants' experiences is beyond doubt. Almira Wade's daughters remember twitting their widowed mother about her white-bearded boy friend from Santa Clara.

At the moment, in Death Valley, the first blinding light of hope, which had brought the women in tears to their knees, and left the men speechless, faded a little before Manly's practical information. There were 250 miles of barren desert and mountain still between them and safety.

But those were women and men of stamina seldom equaled in the modern generation of dependence upon formulas of relief. Daylight found them cutting and sewing the stout canvas of their wagon covers into pack harness for their oxen. Two hickory shirts with tails sewed together and necks tied, flung over the back of an ox, could carry the two smallest children, while the two others rode astride. Each of the women could mount an ox, and do the best she could. The little mule, for best insurance, could carry the new provisions. Other oxen could carry what their strength permitted, and be available for butchering when necessary.

And so they did. It is not necessary to repeat all the harrowing details of that journey. The point is that they made it, in spite of hell and high mountains. The children screamed with illness and pain, or moaned with weariness and thirst. The mothers, helpless to give relief or comfort, tottered into whatever camps Manly could arrange in advance. In camp they collapsed upon the blankets laid out for them, to eat a soup of stringy ox-meat if providence gave them a camp beside water. They lay in a coma of exhaustion until daylight drove them on. The men did what they could. Day after day, day after day, week after weary week, they staggered on.

And, by God! they made it!

Every man, woman and child of that pitiful party, four oxen remaining, the dog Cuff, and the little one-eyed mule came, thanking God, into the paradise of San Francisquito rancho.

On the crest of the Panamints, looking back and down into the pit where they had waited, despairing, for the return of Manly and Rogers, they had spoken a heartfelt farewell.

"Good-by, Death Valley!"

Tomesha had been rechristened, with tears and blood.

Death Valley waited for the years and the men to come.

THEODORE ROOSEVELT

A PECCARY-HUNT IN THE NUECES

Teddy Roosevelt, famous sportsman, writer, and, incidentally, one-time President of the United States, became acquainted with the West as a boy. His writings of the West are
based on both a love and first-hand knowledge of the country.
In the following narrative, we are introduced to a little-known
species of sportsman's game, the peccary, a small, vicious-
appearing wild hog. The Nueces is a river in Texas emptying
into the Gulf of Mexico. (From *Hunting Adventures in the
West*.)

IN THE United States the peccary is only found in the southern-
most corner of Texas. In April, 1892, I made a flying visit to the
ranch country of this region, starting from the town of Uvalde,
with a Texan friend, Mr. John Moore. My trip being very hurried, I had but a couple of days to devote to hunting.

Our first halting-place was at a ranch on the Frio; a low, wooden
building, of many rooms, with open galleries between them, and
verandas round about. The country was in some respects like, in
others strangely unlike, the northern plains with which I was
so well acquainted. It was for the most part covered with a scattered growth of tough, stunted mesquite-trees, not dense enough
to be called a forest, and yet sufficiently close to cut off the view.

447

It was very dry, even as compared with the northern plains. The bed of the Frio was filled with coarse gravel, and for the most part dry as a bone on the surface, the water seeping through underneath and only appearing in occasional deep holes. These deep holes or ponds never fail, even after a year's drouth; they were filled with fish. One lay quite near the ranchhouse, under a bold rocky bluff; at its edge grew giant cypress-trees. In the hollows and by the watercourses were occasional groves of pecans, live-oaks, and elms. Strange birds hopped among the bushes; the chaparral-cock—a big, handsome ground-cuckoo of remarkable habits, much given to preying on small snakes and lizards—ran over the ground with extraordinary rapidity. Beautiful swallow-tailed king-birds with rosy plumage perched on the tops of the small trees, and soared and flitted in graceful curves above them. Blackbirds of many kinds scuttled in flocks about the corrals and outbuildings around the ranches. Mocking-birds abounded, and were very noisy, singing almost all the daytime, but with their usual irritating inequality of performance, wonderfully musical and powerful snatches of song being interspersed with imitations of other bird notes and disagreeable squalling. Throughout the trip I did not hear one of them utter the beautiful love-song in which they sometimes indulge at night.

The country was all under wire fence, unlike the northern regions, the pastures, however, being sometimes many miles across. When we reached the Frio ranch a herd of a thousand cattle had just been gathered, and two or three hundred beeves and young stock were being cut out to be driven northward over the trail. The cattle were worked in pens much more than in the North, and on all the ranches there were chutes with steering gates, by means of which the individuals of a herd could be dexterously shifted into various corrals. The branding of the calves was done ordinarily in one of these corrals and on foot, the calf being always roped by both forelegs; otherwise the work of the cow-punchers was much like that of their brothers in the North. As a whole, however, they were distinctly more proficient with the rope, and at least half of them were Mexicans.

There were some bands of wild cattle living only in the densest timber of the river bottoms, which were literally as wild as deer, and moreover very fierce and dangerous. The pursuit of these was exciting and hazardous in the extreme. The men who took

part in it showed not only the utmost daring but the most con-
summate horsemanship and wonderful skill in the use of the rope,
the coil being hurled with the force and precision of an iron quoit;
a single man speedily overtaking, roping, throwing, and binding
down the fiercest steer or bull.

There had been many peccaries, or, as the Mexicans and cowpunchers of the border usually call them, javalinas, round this
ranch a few years before the date of my visit. Until 1886, or thereabout, these little wild hogs were not much molested, and abounded
in the dense chaparral around the lower Rio Grande. In that year,
however, it was suddenly discovered that their hides had a market
value, being worth four bits—that is, half a dollar—apiece; and
many Mexicans and not a few shiftless Texans went into the
business of hunting them as a means of livelihood. They were
more easily killed than deer, and, as a result, they were speedily
exterminated in many localities where they had formerly been
numerous, and even where they were to be found only in greatly
diminished numbers. On this particular Frio ranch the last little
band had been killed nearly a year before. There were three of
them, a boar and two sows, and a couple of the cowboys stumbled
on them early one morning while out with a dog. After half a
mile's chase the three peccaries ran into a hollow pecan-tree, and
one of the cowboys, dismounting, improvised a lance by tying his
knife to the end of a pole, and killed them all.

Many anecdotes were related to me of what they had done in
the old days when they were plentiful on the ranch. They were
then usually found in parties of from twenty to thirty, feeding
in the dense chaparral, the sows rejoining the herd with the young
very soon after the birth of the latter, each sow usually having
but one or two at a litter. At night they sometimes lay in the
thickest cover, but always, where possible, preferred to house in
a cave or big hollow log, one invariably remaining as a sentinel
close to the mouth, looking out. If this sentinel were shot, another
would almos´ certainly take his place. They were subject to
freaks of stupidity, and were pugnacious to a degree. Not only
would they fight if molested, but they would often attack entirely
without provocation.

Once my friend Moore himself, while out with another cowboy
on horseback, was attacked in sheer wantonness by a drove of
these little wild hogs. The two men were riding by a grove of live-

oaks along a wood-cutter's cart track, and were assailed without
a moment's warning. The little creatures completely surrounded
them, cutting fiercely at the horses' legs and jumping up at the
riders' feet. The men, drawing their revolvers, dashed through
and were closely followed by their pursuers for three or four
hundred yards, although they fired right and left with good
effect. Both of the horses were badly cut. On another occasion
the bookkeeper of the ranch walked off to a water-hole but a
quarter of a mile distant, and came face to face with a peccary on
a cattle-trail, where the brush was thick. Instead of getting out of
his way, the creature charged him instantly, drove him up a small
mesquite-tree, and kept him there for nearly two hours, looking
up at him and champing its tusks.

I spent two days hunting round this ranch, but saw no peccary
sign whatever, although deer were quite plentiful. Parties of wild
geese and sand-hill cranes occasionally flew overhead. At night-
fall the poorwills wailed everywhere through the woods, and coyotes yelped and yelled, while in the early morning the wild turkeys
gobbled loudly from their roosts in the tops of the pecan-trees.

Having satisfied myself that there were no javalinas left on
the Frio ranch, and being nearly at the end of my holiday, I was
about to abandon the effort to get any when a passing cowman
happened to mention the fact that some were still to be found on
the Nueces River, thirty miles or thereabout to the southward.
Thither I determined to go, and next morning Moore and I started
in a buggy drawn by a redoubtable horse, named Jim Swinger,
which we were allowed to use because he bucked so under the saddle that nobody on the ranch could ride him. We drove six or
seven hours across the dry, waterless plains. There had been a
heavy frost a few days before, which had blackened the budding
mesquite-trees, and their twigs still showed no signs of sprouting.
Occasionally we came across open spaces where there was nothing
but short brown grass. In most places, however, the leafless, sprawling mesquites were scattered rather thinly over the ground, cutting off an extensive view and merely adding to the melancholy
barrenness of the landscape. The road was nothing but a couple
of dusty wheel 'tracks; the ground was parched, and the grass
cropped close by the gaunt, starved cattle. As we drove along
buzzards and great hawks occasionally soared overhead. Now and
then we passed lines of wild-looking long-horned steers, and once

we came on the grazing horses of a cow outfit, just preparing to start northward over the trail to the fattening pastures. Occasionally we encountered one or two cow-punchers; either Texans, habited exactly like their brethren in the North, with broad-brimmed gray hats, blue shirts, silk neckerchiefs, and leather leggings; or else Mexicans, more gaudily dressed, and wearing peculiarly stiff, very broad-brimmed hats, with conical tops.

Toward the end of our ride we got where the ground was more fertile and there had recently been a sprinkling of rain. Here we came across wonderful flower prairies. In one spot I kept catching glimpses through the mesquite-trees of lilac stretches which I had first thought must be ponds of water. On coming nearer they proved to be acres on acres thickly covered with beautiful lilac-colored flowers. Farther on we came to where broad bands of red flowers covered the ground for many furlongs; then their places were taken by yellow blossoms, elsewhere by white. Generally each band or patch of ground was covered densely by flowers of the same color, making a great vivid streak across the landscape; but in places they were mixed together, red, yellow, and purple, interspersed in patches and curving bands, carpeting the prairie in a strange, bright pattern.

Finally toward evening we reached the Nueces. Where we struck it first the bed was dry, except in occasional deep, malarial-looking pools, but a short distance below there began to be a running current. Great blue herons were stalking beside these pools, and from one we flushed a white ibis. In the woods were reddish cardinal-birds, much less brilliant in plumage than the true cardinals and the scarlet tanagers; and yellow-headed titmice which had already built large domed nests.

In the valley of the Nueces itself, the brush grew thick. There were great groves of pecan-trees, and evergreen live-oaks stood in many places, long, wind-shaken tufts of gray moss hanging from their limbs. Many of the trees in the wet spots were of giant size, and the whole landscape was semi-tropical in character. High on a bluff shoulder overlooking the course of the river was perched the ranch-house toward which we were bending our steps; and here we were received with the hearty hospitality characteristic of the ranch country everywhere.

The son of the ranchman, a tall, well-built young fellow, told me at once that there were peccaries in the neighborhood, and that he had himself shot one but two or three days before, and volunteered to lend us horses and pilot us to the game on the morrow, with the help of his two dogs. The last were big black curs with, as we were assured, "considerable hound" in them. One was at the time staying at the ranch-house, the other was four or five miles off with a Mexican goat-herder, and it was arranged that early in the morning we should ride down to the latter place, taking the first dog with us and procuring his companion when we reached the goat-herder's house.

We started after breakfast, riding powerful cow-ponies, well trained to gallop at full speed through the dense chaparral. The big black hound slouched at our heels. We rode down the banks of the Nueces, crossing and recrossing the stream. Here and there were long, deep pools in the bed of the river, where rushes and lilies grew and huge mailed gar-fish swam slowly just beneath the surface of the water. Once my two companions stopped to pull a mired cow out of a slough, hauling with ropes from their saddle-horns. In places there were half-dry pools, out of the regular current of the river, the water green and fetid. The trees were very tall and large. The streamers of pale-gray moss hung thickly from the branches of the live-oaks, and when many trees thus draped stood close together they bore a strangely mournful and desolate look.

We finally found the queer little hut of the Mexican goat-herder in the midst of a grove of giant pecans. On the walls were nailed the skins of different beasts, raccoons, wildcats, and the tree-civet, with its ringed tail. The Mexican's brown wife and children were in the hut, but the man himself and the goats were off in the forest, and it took us three or four hours' search before we found him. Then it was nearly noon, and we lunched in his hut, a square building of split logs, with bare earth floor, and roof of clapboards and bark. Our lunch consisted of goat's meat and *pair de mais*. The Mexican, a broad-chested man with a stolid Indian face, was evidently quite a sportsman, and had two or three half-starved hounds, besides the funny, hairless little house dogs, of which Mexicans seem so fond.

Having borrowed the javalina hound of which we were in search, we rode off in quest of our game, the two dogs trotting gaily ahead. The one which had been living at the ranch had evidently fared well, and was very fat; the other was little else but skin and bone, but as alert and knowing as any New York street boy, with the same air of disreputable capacity. It was this hound which always did most in finding the javalinas and bringing them to bay, his companion's chief use being to make a noise and lend the moral support of his presence.

We rode away from the river on the dry uplands, where the timber, though thick, was small, consisting almost exclusively of the thorny mesquites. Mixed among them were prickly-pears, standing as high as our heads on horseback, and Spanish bayonets, looking in the distance like small palms; and there were many other kinds of cacti, all with poisonous thorns. Two or three times the dogs got on an old trail and rushed off giving tongue, whereat we galloped madly after them ducking and dodging through and among the clusters of spine-bearing trees and cactus, not without getting a considerable number of thorns in our hands and legs. It was very dry and hot. Where the javalinas live in droves in the river bottoms they often drink at the pools; but when some distance from water they seem to live quite comfortably on the prickly-pear, slaking their thirst by eating its hard, juicy fibre.

At last, after several false alarms, and gallops which led to nothing, when it lacked but an hour of sundown we struck a band of five of the little wild hogs. They were running off through the mesquites with a peculiar hopping or bounding motion, and we all, dogs and men, tore after them instantly.

Peccaries are very fast for a few hundred yards, but speedily tire, lose their wind, and come to bay. Almost immediately one of these, a sow, as it turned out, wheeled and charged at Moore as he passed, Moore never seeing her but keeping on after another. The sow then stopped and stood still, chattering her teeth savagely, and I jumped off my horse and dropped her dead with a shot in the spine over the shoulders. Moore meanwhile had dashed off after his pig in one direction, and killed the little beast with a shot from the saddle when it had come to bay, turning and going straight at him. Two of the peccaries got off; the remaining one, a rather large boar, was followed by the two dogs, and as soon as I had killed the sow I leaped again on my horse and made after them, guided by the yelping and baying. In less than a quarter of a mile they were on his haunches, and he wheeled and stood under a bush, charging at them when they came near him, and once catching one, inflicting an ugly cut. All the while his teeth kept going like castanets, with a rapid champing sound. I ran up close and killed him by a shot through the back-bone where it joined the neck. His tusks were fine.

The few minutes' chase on horseback was great fun, and there was a certain excitement in seeing the fierce little creatures come to bay; but the true way to kill these peccaries would be with the spear. They could often be speared on horseback, and where this was impossible, by using dogs to bring them to bay they could readily be killed on foot; though, as they are very active, absolutely fearless, and inflict a most formidable bite, it would usually be safest to have two men go at one together. Peccaries are not difficult beasts to kill, because their short wind and their pugnacity make them come to bay before hounds so quickly. Two or three good dogs can bring to a halt a herd of considerable size. They then all stand in a bunch, or else with their sterns against a bank, chattering their teeth at their antagonists. When angry and at bay, they get their legs close together, their shoulders high, and their bristles all ruffled, and look the very incarnation of anger, and they fight with reckless indifference to the very last. Hunters usually treat them with a certain amount of caution; but, as a matter of fact, I know of but one case where a man was hurt by them. He had shot at and wounded one, was charged both by it and by its two companions, and started to climb a tree; but as he drew himself from the ground, one sprang at him and bit him through the calf, inflicting a very severe wound. I have known of several cases of horses being cut, however, and dogs are very commonly killed. Indeed, a dog new to the business is almost certain to get very badly scarred, and no dog that hunts steadily can escape without some injury. If it runs in right at the heads of the animals, the probabilities are that it will get killed; and, as a rule, even two good-sized hounds cannot kill a peccary, though it is no larger than either of them. However, a wary, resolute, hard-biting dog of good size speedily gets accustomed to the chase and can kill a peccary single-handed, seizing it from behind and worrying it to death, or watching its chance and grabbing it by the back of the neck where it joins the head.

Peccaries have delicately moulded short legs, and their feet are small, the tracks looking peculiarly dainty in consequence. Hence, they do not swim well, though they take to the water if necessary. They feed on roots, prickly-pears, nuts, insects, lizards, etc. They usually keep entirely separate from the droves of half-wild swine that are so often found in the same neighborhoods; but in one case, on this very ranch where I was staying, a peccary deliberately joined a party of nine pigs and associated with them. When the owner of the pigs came up to them one day the peccary manifested great suspicion at his presence, and finally sidled close up and threatened to attack him, so that he had to shoot it. The ranchman's son told me that he had never but once had a peccary assail him unprovoked, and even in this case it was his dog that was the object of attack, the peccary rushing out at it as it followed him home one evening through the chaparral. Even around this ranch the peccaries had very greatly decreased in numbers, and the survivors were learning some caution. In the old days it had been no uncommon thing for a big band to attack, entirely of their own accord, and keep a hunter up a tree for hours at a time.

MARQUIS JAMES

DICK YEAGER

Here is an enjoyable, nostalgic piece concerned with the "growing up" of young Marquis in the Cherokee Strip in the '90's. It is the first of many fascinating chapters contained in the book, *The Cherokee Strip* (Viking, 1945), by the well known Pulitzer Prize biographer.

I FLOPPED in a patch of new grass on the rim of the bluff in the horse lot and Prince trotted up and flopped by me. Prince was never very far from where I was. At nights he slept at the foot of my bed on an old lap robe which every morning I had to hang in the air. Prince had been after a cottontail. He was panting with his tongue out.

The rim was about my favorite place on the whole claim. You could look and look, for there was, indeed, much to see. Below lay the dark, plowed earth of West Bottom, which we sometimes called the Horseshoe from the way Boggy Creek curved around it. Lazying in from the Schrock claim on the other side of the Bottom, old Boggy's winding course was defined by a string of elms and cottonwoods whose branches the opening buds bathed in a pale green haze.

Mr. Schrock worked early and late. He had built himself a little house of lumber and turned the sod house into a stable. His whole hundred-and-sixty was under fence, and a good half of it

broken and in crops. Later on you would see Mrs. Schrock helping her husband plant corn with a hand drill, a hill at a time.

"I declare," Mama would say, "there's a couple bound to get on
in a new country."

Today Mr. Schrock was plowing, diminished by distance to a
toy man with a toy plow and a toy team raising a plume of brown
dust. I could have picked up all three and held them in my
hand.

The claim north of Mr. Schrock's was Mr. Howell's. Mr.
Howell had no fence, and he did not plow. From his dugout in the
side of a little rise near the creek the prairie tilted gently until
it met the northwestern sky. Bright islands of new grass were blot-
ting out the winter-gray of this sloping plain. Out of sight beyond
the crest was South Town—and all that went on there. Some days
you could see the smoke of a Rock Island train and hear the
whistle, too. Other times you could just see the smoke; other
times just hear the whistle.

The new grass was soft to lie in. It tickled my legs and feet because this was the first time I'd had my shoes off. The sun felt good
on my back. A glance down the face of the bluff at Boggy's green
bosom made you think of swimming.

Prince pricked up his ears: cowbird on a hackberry limb beneath
us. You know what a claim-jumper a cowbird is—laying its eggs
in other birds' nests and all. That's what this cowbird was fixing
to do. It was a robin's nest. I was fishing in my pocket for the
nigger-shooter Mr. Howell had made me when I happened to look
around, and there was Ad Poak coming over the rise in our pasture. He was riding Pat and he came from the direction of the
East Draw.

The cowbird forgotten, I watched Ad let himself, without dismounting, through the far gate of the horse lot and then through
the near gate. At the tie rail by the house he swung down and tied
up. Pat was a stallion and would not stand without tying.

Mama was feeding the chickens. She beckoned Ad to come
around in back. Ad walked toward her as if taking time to think.
The wind was the wrong way to hear what they said but pretty
soon it was plain, from the motions her sunbonnet made, that
Mama was giving it to Ad for some reason. When she scolded,
Mama talked so fast that her head would bob up and down.

The fact that it looked as if Ad had come from the East Draw was a matter of interest in itself, let alone maybe having done something there to be scolded by Mama. The East Draw was where the outlaws camped while waiting for Papa to come home. Sometimes one would be there for days. Arkansas Tom was supposed to be there now. That was what Ad Poak and the hired man had said. I wasn't allowed to go to the Draw and see for myself.

Just the same Prince and I *had* gone there, no more than two, three days before I heard about Arkansas Tom. I had looked down from the rim but I never saw any outlaw, only the ashes of an old fire by the plum thicket. I was good and winded by the time I topped the rise in the pasture which first brought in sight the top of the Big Tree, and then the hip roof of the barn, and then the roof of our house. As these friendly objects met my eyes I slowed to a walk, feeling more comfortable: not so much because I had been afraid of encountering an outlaw as of being caught doing something that wasn't allowed. Even Papa had told me not to go to the Draw alone.

"It would worry your mama, son," he said.

By and by I couldn't stand not hearing what Mama and Ad were saying; and so I started for home running gingerly to favor my tender feet. As I ran I snatched off my hat and shook out my hair. Mama liked to see my hair down about my shoulders, though it was sure a bother to me, catching every briar and twig. Away from the house I kept it twisted up under my hat. Prince bounced ahead, his feathery tail riffled by the wind. Prince was a black dog, part spaniel. You should have seen him swim and dive.

It was just as I thought. Ad had been to the Draw, and he was wearing his gun. But the rest was something nobody would have thought: he had put Arkansas Tom off the claim!

Mama seldom stayed mad very long. Shucks, she was getting over it already, and just pretending. One brown hand brushed at the bonnet strings the wind whipped about her face. The other hand cradled a pan of kaffir corn against her hip.

"I still say that's no way to carry on around an outlaw. Dick Yeager seems to have gone to your head. You'll get it shot off your shoulders one of these days."

"Not by Tom Conway I won't; no, ma'am." Ad was a slow talker, different from Mama. He held on to his words as if sorry to see them go. "Too much of a cloud on his reputation."

"Ad Poak, will you be serious for once? 'Cloud on his reputation.' Now what am I to gather from that?"

"What I been driving at, Miz James, is that outlaw's just a courtesy title in Tom's case. Something picked up as a character reference here in the Strip. The judge can't be bothered with such trash."

Mama raised her eyes toward heaven, and tried hard not to smile. "Strikes me," she said, "this Arkansas Tom has no monopoly on courtesy titles. Mr. Poak, just what have you done around here today? Now, Ad, I want you to put Pat up, fill Martha's water buckets, get some cobs for the cook-stove, and hear Marquis's reading lesson. Then it will be time to help the man with the chores."

"Yes, ma'am," said Ad. "What'll it be, Markey? *Robinson Crusoe* or *Tom Sawyer?*"

When we were out of Mama's hearing I said, kind of whispering to be on the safe side:

"Just tell me about the time you captured Dick Yeager. I'll go get the shell."

It made it more real to hold in my hand the brass shell which had contained the bullet with which Ad Poak had ended Dick Yeager's career. It belonged to Mr. Howell's .40-.70 single-shot Winchester, his bear gun. Ad had given the shell to Mama as a keepsake. She kept it in a drawer of the sewing machine.

Two or three days later when Papa came home he said that Mama and Ad were both right, but Mama the righter of the two. A client was a client these days and entitled to considerate treatment. Papa talked slowly, too, and he never talked nearly enough. When Papa spoke I always stopped what I was doing to listen.

"But Ad meant well," he went on. "Aims to improve the tone of my practice. Like those city lawyers in St. Louis: clerk in the ante-room to shoo off callers who look like they might turn out to be nuisances. The Draw's my ante-room. And yet there's such a thing as an excess of zeal on the part of a law clerk. Ad brought in Dick Yeager, all right. But he brought him in in too poor condition to stand trial."

Martha entered with a pitcher of buttermilk. Martha knew how Papa loved fresh buttermilk. This time it was a part of her preparation to ask him to do something for Jerry.

Papa read Martha's mind. After thanking her for the buttermilk he went on talking to Mama and Ad. But the words were
intended for Martha. "There's a client I mean to hold on to.
Better put in my time keeping Jerry in jail than Tom Conway
out. When that no-good nigger's locked up Martha can keep her
mind on her work."

A shadow crossed Martha's round face—if you can imagine a
shadow on a black face, as I can, having seen it so often. She set
down the pitcher and silently returned to the kitchen.

Martha's name was not really Martha. It was Victoria, but
Papa thought Martha more appropriate for the wife of Jerry
Washington. Jerry was a dressy-up nigger who never worked, and
the only colored person Mama permitted me to speak of as a
nigger. When Jerry was in jail or carrying on with some high
yellow on Two Street in South Town, Martha lived with us.
When Jerry was loose and broke he would carry Martha off to
Two Street where she would take in washing to provide him with
a fresh supply of pocket money. By and by Jerry would get in
trouble again or just go off and Martha would be back, looking
melancholy and down.

II

I missed Martha the times she was away but I missed Mr.
Howell more, and he had been gone a long while now—driving
stage out of Fort Reno. No smoke came from the stovepipe which
crooked from the dugout's window. Mr. Howell said the window
was the place for the stovepipe in a dugout. Poke it through the
roof and your roof would leak water when it rained. Mr. Howell's
dugout didn't leak. In the winter it was snug and cozy; and in
summertime as cool and nice as our cyclone cellar in the creek
bank beneath the Big Tree. Prince and I went over there often,
but the padlock was still on the door and everything hushed and
lifeless. Before he went away Mr. Howell had no lock for his
door. Prince and I could come and go, making ourselves at home
on the neatly made bunk. Now I tried to peer through the window
to see if the familiar room was the same, but it was too dark inside
to make out anything.

Mr. Howell was the only person I knew who was always doing
something interesting and would let me do it with him: hunting

and fishing; laying and tending traps for muskrat along Boggy Creek; cooking and eating in the dugout—or wherever we were when we got hungry. A trotline and a gun provided Mr. Howell with most of his victuals. He prepared them with the hunting knife he wore in a leather scabbard at his waist. Mr. Howell could cook as well on the embers of a fire outdoors as on the jack-stove in the dugout. He carried salt with him in a leather sack about half the size of Papa's tobacco pouch. Mr. Howell ate with the hunting knife. There was no fork in the dugout, and when Mr. Howell ate at our house Mama said he regarded a fork as an unfamiliar weapon. When Mr. Howell and I ate together I would use my pocket knife like he used his hunting knife. At home Mama not only made me use a fork but I had to hold it a certain way.

Mr. Howell taught me to have no fear of snakes, and how to kill them.

"They'll all run from you, never arter you; *sabe?*—don't keer what folks say. Allus carry a stick and just go at 'em. Rattlers an' moccasins the only pizen snakes in these parts."

We killed snakes nearly every day. The ones I killed I dragged back of the barn. Papa would count them and pay me a bounty of one cent each. One day I got a whole litter of nine little black-snakes, no longer than your finger. Papa paid just the same. While not actually afraid of rattlers, I never went out of my way to look for one. Mr. Howell knew a cow-camp cook in Colorado who was bitten on the thumb by a rattler. He went to the chuck wagon and took a cleaver and whacked off the thumb. They seared the stump with a branding iron.

Mr. Howell and I would visit the old cowhand who worked for Mr. Jim Utsler. His face was creased and leathery. He walked as if it hurt him—I don't know whether from stiff joints or tight boots. But he could sure ride. He and Mr. Howell would squat on their heels in the shade of the big Utsler barn and talk about how the Strip was before the Run: all cattle range. The different brands they would trace on the ground with sticks. Right here along Boggy was the Circle J H outfit; down by the Cimarron the 2 S; over west toward the Salt Plains the Half Diamond R.

Mr. Howell and the old puncher talked about Nigger Green, a colored cowboy who followed the ranges from Old Mexico to Canada. Nigger Green had surmounted the barrier of race and adorned his name with bunkhouse legend. Without previous promise or later boast he performed superior feats. "Think *you* can ride him, Nigger?" partners would ask, indicating an outlaw bronc. "Mos' likely not, but might have a try." Nigger Green could ride about anything you could saddle.

Whatever their more obvious conceits, cowboys bragged of their horsemanship by understatement. Ask a cowhand if he rode and the answer would be: "Couldn't rightly say I do; take a stab at it sometimes, though." Any other reply was the mark of a tenderfoot. Good riders by eastern standards turned up in the West looking for jobs with cow outfits for the fun of it. They came from England, even—young fox-hunting gentlemen, good at five-bar gates. If, in all innocence, a tenderfoot would admit to experience in the saddle, the foreman would observe: "Now that's fine. Boys, here's a man who can ride. Suppose you bring out something and let him limber up." You can imagine what the boys would bring.

Most of all I missed Mr. Howell for the stories he told. It might be a wet day when he was tinkering with his traps, loading shotgun shells, greasing his boots or mending his clothes. Mr. Howell had two guns, the Winchester and the muzzle-loader. Papa's 10-gauge shotgun was at the dugout much of the time, an arrangement which kept our table supplied with small game. But usually it seems that Mr. Howell and I were out of doors when he talked—following the course of the creek, or resting on the slope of a buffalo wallow on the prairie.

He told how buffalo wallows were made and how he had seen buffalo on the plains as thick as blackbirds in the sky, and how he had made his living as a buffalo hunter, taking only the pelts and leaving the carcasses by the hundred for the buzzards. He told me about hunting grizzly bear in the Bitter Root Range, and about mountain lions. He told me about a fish he called a salmon that could jump as high as the dugout—up a waterfall, to get where it was going. I didn't know what a waterfall was until he took a stick and made a little one for me at our spring. Bears, he said, could catch fish—flip them out of the water with their paws, which was more than a man could do.

Mr. Howell had many Indian stories to tell. The bluish scar on his leg had been made by a Blackfoot arrow. Mr. Howell hadn't always fought the Indians, though. He'd hunted and trapped with them. He'd wintered in a Sioux village. That was a good tale, though nothing much happened.

Of course, you saw a good many Indians there in the Strip. They were usually on hand at our place at butchering time, looking for offal and scraps. They would pitch their tepees beside the creek along the section-line road which bordered our claim on the east. Mr. Howell and I often visited their camps.

"*How!*" Mr. Howell'd say and hold up one hand, with the palm toward the Indian he was speaking to.

"*How!*" I'd say after him.

Mr. Howell would squat on his heels and talk in the Indian sign language, mixed with grunts and ughs. This was the language Indians of different tribes used to talk to each other. He'd pick out a wrinkled old Indian who knew no English at all. I'd squat and watch.

"They's Injuns an' Injuns, Marquis," Mr. Howell told me. "Excusin' the old men, yore Cherokees, here, 'ud starve to death in the Comanche country. Fergittin' how to hunt. Leased their huntin' grounds to the cattlemen for cash money an' et store grub too long."

For Comanches, with their lean, sinewy bodies and straight, resentful glances, Mr. Howell showed more respect. "Finest hunters on the plains." Mr. Howell said that, despite its name, the Cherokee Strip was Comanche country, really; and so the unforgiving Comanches still regarded it. Away back, the Gov'mint had taken it from the Comanches and their friends the Kiowas and had given it to the Cherokees in trade for other lands taken from the Cherokees. As with all the history that he knew, Mr. Howell had this pretty close first-hand—from old Comanche and Kiowa and Cherokee bucks.

Comanches didn't come by our place so often, but when they did Mr. Howell always went over and talked to them in Spanish. "Bad *hombres*, yore Comanches," he informed me, and summed the matter up: "Wouldn't trust one no further'n I could spit— excusin' Quanah Parker." Against Quanah Parker Mr. Howell had fought at 'Dobe Walls. But later on they had become friends. When Quanah left the warpath the Gov'mint was so glad that it fixed him up a big ranch near Anadarko on the Comanche reservation. Mr. Howell used to visit Quanah there.

Mr. Howell told how Quanah Parker had received his name— from his mother, Cynthia Ann Parker, a white woman, carried off by the Indians when she was a child in Texas.

Visiting a Comanche camp I'd stay close to the side of Mr.
Howell long after the conversations, which I could not understand, had become tedious. There was no poking about on my
own to explore the interiors of tepees, or to peer in the stew
kettles the squaws stirred with sticks.

This circumspection amused Mr. Howell. "Marquis, they ain't
stealin' young'uns no more." As far as that went, Mr. Howell
allowed that Cynthia Ann hadn't had such a bad time at all, until
the battle in which the Texas Rangers killed her husband and
captured her. When the Rangers found out who their captive
was, they took her to Austin and made a big to-do of restoring her
to her people. For this Cynthia Ann did not thank them. The
Comanches were her people then, and she wanted only to return
to them and find out what had become of her boy Quanah. The
whites wouldn't let her and Cynthia Ann pined away and died.

"I tell you, Marquis, it's the whites that's had a heap to do
with making yore Comanche what he is, an' that's the way of it.
Mind as how when I was on the high plains in the fifties, 'fore the
Rebellion. Greatest run a' game I ever see in open country, an' the
Comanches troublin' nobody. The cowmen an' the nesters had
ought to let them be."

The story of Cynthia Ann Parker was well known in our part
of the country. The fact is I was more interested in the less familiar
narrative which concerned her brother, John, on whose ranch
in Old Mexico Mr. Howell had stayed for a spell. Captured
the same time Cynthia was, John had grown up with a different
Comanche band. He received a young Comanche's training as a
hunter and a warrior. As described by Mr. Howell, this seemed a
desirable mode of life. The Comanches hunted and fought on
horseback with lances and arrows; and there was nothing they
could not do on a horse. By and by this band of Comanches
captured a Mexican girl. John married her and finally she persuaded him to leave the tribe and go to Old Mexico and set up
as a rancher. To my mind that was quite a comedown.

Mr. Howell told other good tales about prospecting for gold in
Colorado and in Californy; and about the big trees in Californy.
Surely Mr. Howell had seen more wonderful things than any
other man on earth. Our Big Tree was a cottonwood with bark
so old and gnarly that a barefooted boy could go up the trunk
like he could go up a ladder. The first crotch was almost as high

as our chimney. As long as I could keep the top of the Big Tree in sight, I always knew which way home was. Strangers measured the distance around the trunk. It was fourteen feet and something. I heard Papa tell Doctor Fairgrieve that the Big Tree was the oldest living thing in the Cherokee Strip. Even Mr. Howell was stumped to think of anything larger on the plains, but I judged that beside trees in Californy the Big Tree wasn't much more than a bush.

Nor were Oklahoma outlaws, not even Dick Yeager or Jack Dalton, to be mentioned in the same breath with Mr. Howell's acquaintances, Billy the Kid (who was left-handed) and Sam Bass. And then there were tales of the cattle drives up the Chisholm Trail, and about the pony express, and about the Run, and about the North Town War.

Before Mr. Howell told about the Run and the North Town War, I used to think that nothing interesting had ever happened to Papa. Now I knew better, for Mr. Howell let it out that Papa had made the Run and that he had been in the North Town War. Yet I could never get Papa to tell about them—a regular story, that is. Of course, there was no one like Mr. Howell, always with a tale on the tip of his tongue. I comforted myself with the thought that Papa just wasn't ready with his story yet. Therefore I listened whenever he spoke, so as not to miss his story when he should get around to telling it.

The North Town War was also called the Railroad War. The Rock Island Railroad wanted the town of Enid to be three and a half miles north of the place where the South Town people wanted it. The railroad owned most of the northern townsite. The Rock Island called its town Enid and the South Town people called their town Enid. So people could tell one Enid from the other nobody around where we lived said Enid at all. We said South Town and North Town. Papa was for South Town because our town lots were there and because it was closer to our claim.

The railroad would not stop trains at South Town. People had to get off at North Town. They were told that they were in Enid, the place they were looking for. If they insisted on going on to South Town they would have to get a rig, and no rigs could be hired for that purpose in North Town. When South Town people went to get the travelers, North Towners would try to upset the rigs and cut the harness. It was hard for Mr. Peter Bowers to get things for his store. For a while it looked as if South Town was a goner. Then the people decided that passengers and freight left at North Town should reach South Town whether or no. Every mule-freight was furnished with an armed guard, and a regular stage was sent to meet the passenger trains. Mr. Howell drove the stage, and he carried the Winchester in a holster beside his high seat.

In that way the passengers and freight got to South Town, though not without a ruckus now and then, as when a committee of South Town citizens had to throw a hint in the direction of Mr. Nat Campbell. Mr. Campbell was a lawyer. The word got around that he was a secret agent of North Town. When the committee called on Mr. Campbell he shut himself in the shack which served as his office and residence. The citizens pulled down the shack. They had a rope and I have heard Mr. W. O. Cromwell, another lawyer, say that one end of the rope was around Mr. Campbell's neck. Others who were present don't remember that part so well. Pretty soon Mr. Cromwell came to the conclusion that the committee might get worked up and do something to hurt the name of South Town as a peace-loving community. He asked the citizens to let Mr. Campbell go. When they refused Mr. Cromwell got a dry-goods box from Meibergen & Godschalk's and climbed on it. Pulling a paper from his pocket, he began making out to read the names of the citizens who were interviewing Mr. Campbell. Mr. Cromwell said that already he had started a copy of the list on the way to Guthrie, and if Mr. Campbell wasn't turned loose somebody would go to the pen as sure as shooting. They turned Mr. Campbell loose.

Still, Rock Island trains whistled through South Town without stopping. Red lanterns and dynamite caps on the track failed to stop them. Bullets failed to stop them: conductors would draw the window blinds and tell passengers to scrooch down away from the glass. One night someone sawed the pilings of the trestle and a freight train went into the south branch of Boggy. That was the first train to stop in South Town. If you know the right parties in Enid you can see the saw that was responsible. Some day it may go to the Oklahoma Historical Society.

South Town held a jollification at which there was a lot of talk about having the Rock Island licked. Mr. W. O. Cromwell went to my father. "James," he said, "this is bad medicine. If railroad detectives aren't in that crowd already they'll be there in a jiffy and sooner or later one of these blowhards is going to talk too much with his mouth. See what you can do to break up the meeting." Papa requested to be heard. He asked if the crowd wasn't overlooking something. This train which for reasons unfathomable had proved too heavy for the bridge contained a car filled with fine seed wheat. The car was smashed and the wheat spilled. Now everyone knew how dear and scarce seed wheat was. Didn't this look like a chance for a settler to get some real reasonably? The meeting broke up and the people went to get the seed wheat. Mr. Cromwell told me this story. As I say, Papa himself never mentioned such things.

Pretty soon the Rock Island agreed to stop its trains at South Town and the Railroad War was over—unfortunately, I thought —before Mr. Howell got a chance to plug anyone with his Winchester. Our Enid became Enid in fact, and the railroad Enid, North Enid. No love was lost between the two towns for a long time thereafter, though.

I remember driving to North Town with my father and sitting alone in the buggy and being terrified at the sight of some children who trooped by. I expected them to cut the harness and set upon me. Children usually frightened me because I so rarely saw a child on the claim.

III

With Mr. Howell gone, there seemed to be more coyotes yapping around at night and getting the chickens. That was what Mama said. Mr. Howell kept the coyotes down, though personally he didn't have a very high opinion of coyote-killing. He bothered to shoot them only as a favor to Mama. "Take yore gray wolf, now. Mind as how in the early eighties they was so bad the cattlemen got the bounty up to twenty dollars. . . . "

My efforts to keep the image of Mr. Howell and the sound of his words before me were earnest efforts. Sitting in the dusty hay in the stable loft, I would draw up one knee and clasp my hands about it, as Mr. Howell did when leaning back on his bunk in the dugout. I would tell Mr. Howell's stories to Prince, pretending I was Mr. Howell and Prince was me.

"Reminds me, Marquis, of mule-freightin' outa Dodge City 'cross No Man's Land into the Panhandle. . . . "

That story was easy. All we did was catch and hang the Mexican horse thief. "Pulled out an' left him standin' on nothin' lookin' up a rope. Yessiree."

"Back in the winter of '75, Marquis, when me and my podner was scoutin' for Crook on the Tongue. . . ."

I had trouble remembering all that one and had to make up stretches as I went along. Once I got the hang of it, though, this making up wasn't so hard as a body might think. Moreover, it was a wonderful convenience. Sometimes when I really remembered the way Mr. Howell had told it I would make up differently because I liked the story better that way. It was the only way I had of saving the life of Mr. Howell's podner, who, unlike the Mexican horse thief, had not deserved to die.

You see, General Crook had told Mr. Howell and his podner to go up the river, ahead of the army, and look for signs of Crazy Horse. Pretty soon they came to a branch with steep rocky banks. Mr. Howell said he would scout the head of the branch and double back and meet his podner on the main stream. He didn't see any Injuns, but when he got back to the Tongue he found his podner lying on a flat rock, dead and scalped and his rifle and his belt gone. I would change that part so that it was Mr. Howell's podner who had kilt the Injuns instead of the other way around.

Thinking about Mr. Howell so much caused me to recollect a remark Papa had made, and it bothered me. It bothered me so badly that I asked Mama:

"Is it so, what Papa says about Mr. Howell?"

"What's that, Marquis?"

" 'If old man Howell'd done all he says he's done he'd be a hundred and ten years old.' "

Mama laughed. "Mr. Howell's a good, kindly old man who's lived a rough and a lonely life. Lonely people have large imaginations sometimes."

Her words made me very sad. So it was true, after all. Mr. Howell, too, made up parts of his stories. That's what Mama meant, even if she didn't come out and say so. Suddenly I felt very angry at my father and mother. I told myself I would not, *would* not believe what they said about Mr. Howell.

Mama must have seen that something was the matter.

"You mustn't mind what your father says. It's the stairs, you know. It may be as your father tells it: that Mr. Howell was stumped and didn't know how to build a staircase after talking pretty big about the carpentering he'd done. And it may be as Mr. Howell says: that your father forgot to put a staircase in the plans."

Ever since I could remember I'd heard the grown people talk about our house not having any stairs, only a ladder that went up from the south porch. But Papa mostly joked about it, it seemed.

"Here I plan to build the first two-story residence in Garfield County. Get the lumber, only slightly less dear than good bourbon. Get it hauled from North Town. Carpenters scarcer than hens' teeth, owing to everyone in town wanting to build at once. Along comes old man Howell. By that time, I knew he'd advised Sherman at Atlanta and won most of our Indian campaigns and dug most of the gold in the West. But I didn't know he claimed to be a carpenter until I mentioned the fix I was in. Then it appeared that he was fresh from the Cripple Creek boom where he'd laid off digging gold in order to erect palaces for those who'd struck it rich already. So I turn him loose on my lumber and go to Guthrie for a jury trial. Come back and what have I? A two-story dwelling without a stairway."

"That was three years ago, Houstin," Mama would say. "Other carpenters have since been available, and we've no stairway yet."

"Too busy getting in our tobacco—twenty acres of the best tobacco in the Cherokee Strip."

"The only tobacco in the Cherokee Strip, unless I'm misinformed," Mama would say.

"A new country, Rachel. Twenty acres in tobacco, and when that tobacco goes to market I'll put a little something to it and throw that new addition across the front of the house and put the stairway in *it*."

"You've a lot of confidence in that tobacco."

"Naturally. This is the latitude of North Carolina, the finest tobacco country in the world."

The promise of a staircase in the new front addition kindled my interest in staircases, with which I had not enough experience for the novelty to wear off. Most of the stairways in Enid—we didn't

say South Town so much any more—were on the outsides of the
buildings where you could get a good look at them. But some
were on the insides, as in the Rex Hotel and the Cogdal-McKee
building where Papa had his office. I rather hoped ours would
be on the outside. People would see it and stop talking about the
James house which had an upstairs and no way to get there.

IV

A trip to Enid was surely a marvelous treat, the stairways one
saw being the very least of it. First off, on the edge of the
prairie was a house here and a house there—and not so many of
them sod houses, either. Quite a few were even painted. There
was Doctor Field's and across the road no farther than I could
shy a rock was the house of Mr. Marshall who owned the lumber
yard. Those little girls swinging on the gate would be the Marshall twins no one could tell apart. A little farther was the house
of Mr. B. T. Thompson who had the Racket Store on the
Square. Then there was Banker Fleming's and Doctor McKenzie's
and Colonel John C. Moore's. Papa said Colonel John C. Moore
had the best building site in Enid: on a bluff overlooking Boggy
Creek and the whole town. The house was painted yellow, like
ours. It had an upstairs. As I could see no ladder (and I looked
sharply) there must have been a staircase *inside*.

Once we saw a lady milking a Jersey cow in Banker Fleming's
yard.

"It's Mrs. Fleming," said Mama. "For all their money she
gives herself no airs."

About some of the houses were planted little locust and maple
trees. Instead of a picket fence Doctor McKenzie's house was
enclosed by the tidiest row of bushes.

"That is a hedge," said Mama, "a hard thing to grow in this
country; and the doctor'll need his windmill to keep up that
lawn."

What Mama called a lawn was a front yard of grass no higher
than buffalo grass but a prettier green.

The road from our claim was one of several roads leading from
the flat prairie into Enid from the east. They all came together
like the ribs of Mama's black fan and made one big straight road
which was E Street. On E Street the houses were so numerous

and so near each other that it would be hard to speak particularly of any one of them, unless Mr. Rick Messall's. Mr. Rick Messall was a saloonkeeper and, of course, very rich.

"At least he has the *manners* of a gentleman," Mama said of him.

Then you crossed the railroad and if very, very lucky got to see a train of cars pass. "Stop, Look and Listen!" said the white sign which was in the shape of an X. No one ever stopped. Enid people were not going to let the Rock Island tell them what to do. Pretty soon the stores began, with the buildings *touching* each other and no front yards at all, only board sidewalks shaded by wooden awnings. Then you came to the Square.

By this time my head would be in such a whirl that I'm afraid it would have been beyond me to tell you, all at once, about the Square. You never saw so many rigs or so many people. Rigs of all kinds: buggies and carriages, tops up and tops down; farm wagons of all kinds, from light spring wagons to big red and green Studebakers; enormous hayracks; movers' covered wagons; closed town hacks; the weatherbeaten yellow stage which now ran only from the Square to the Rock Island depot at train times; buckboards, carts, broad-tired drays, the splendid brewery trucks, and, oh, yes, the Moore phaeton with its colored driver handling the bays, and the colonel's daughter, Miss Mabel, leaning back with a folded parasol on her lap, looking like a picture in a book. Once I got close enough to see that Miss Mabel was freckled.

Behind a settler's wagon a calf or a steer or a colt might walk in the dust at the end of a lead rope. In the bed might be a few oinking shoats on their way to market; or chickens or turkeys or guineas with wings clipped and feet tied. Or a bed might be piled with watermelons, turnips or roasting ears; with fence posts or with jack rabbits dressed with the fur on. The fence posts and the jack rabbits usually told you a settler came from "the jacks," where jack oaks and jack rabbits were about all that grew. On the other hand a load of cedar posts would have been hauled, at some risk to the hauler, all the way from the Gyp Hills. The Hills were Government land, where you weren't supposed to cut timber. A cedar hauler had to keep an eye peeled for deputy marshals on the make for a little mileage money. I always looked twice at a cedar hauler out of respect for the chances he took. The fence posts on our claim were cedar.

Sometimes we sent a wagonload of watermelons to town. In the back of the buggy Mama would stow baskets of eggs packed in hay and crocks of butter to trade at Mr. Peter Bower's. I made it a point to be present when she did her trading. After figuring with a pencil Mr. Bowers would shove his glasses up on his forehead.

"Mrs. James, I make it so and so much—not mentioning the usual little something extra. A bit of that nice China tea you like and—"

The storekeeper's glance would fall on me and his arm would reach into the showcase filled with candy. My eyes would follow the hand of the reaching arm. The trigger finger was missing at the middle joint: Dick Yeager had shot it off. Ah, the hand moved toward a big striped stick, a *big* one. Sometimes it stopped at a smaller stick.

Tie rails where people tied their teams and their buggies and their saddle horses ran nearly around the bare dust-blown five-acre Square. Considerate people moved their animals from one side to another to catch the shade of the buildings. When Mama or Papa sent me to move Tom it was an important thing. For a moment I could pretend that I'd driven to Enid all by myself. Inside the Square campers, with teams unhitched and stamping flies in the dust, made themselves at home about their covered wagons, cooking and toting water from the land-office pump or the courthouse pump, whichever was nearer.

On one street corner a crowd gathered about Colonel Joshua Mathis, the horse auctioneer. "Forty-five dollars I'm bid for this lively little mare. Do I hear a fifty?" A smaller crowd listened to a blind Negro in front of Jim Utsler's saloon and gambling house. The blind Negro was playing a guitar and singing a doleful song about Sam Bass.

Once Papa took me inside Jim Utsler's. Behind the bar was the biggest looking glass in the world. You could have seen a house in it. The floor was covered with sawdust and there were brass spittoons two feet high. On the walls were the horns of steers and snakeskins and old reward posters: "WANTED DEAD OR ALIVE." And there was a big picture of an Indian fight. I spelled out the words: "Custer's Last Stand." That must have been the very fight Mr. Howell told me about. But none of these was what Papa wanted to show me. He wanted to show me the fans that were attached to the ceiling. They were turned by little leather belts running from a wheel on a steam engine in a shed in the back, and they kept the place nice and cool.

Mama didn't fancy Papa's taking me into a saloon.

"But Jim Utsler's; you know you like Jim," Papa said.

Mama did like Jim Utsler, of whom she couldn't say, as she did of Mr. Rick Messall, that he had the manners of a gentleman. Jim Utsler was a rough and tough customer. With a scraggly mustache, tobacco-stained teeth, and rumpled clothes, he looked more like a cattleman than a high-toned saloonkeeper. He'd bought the claim north of us from the old cowpuncher who'd staked it, built a fine house and the largest red barn I'd ever seen. He'd loan anything: farm machinery, horses to draw it, a side of meat from his smokehouse, his white-faced Hereford bull.

"A lot of settlers are better off for Jim Utsler, and that's a fact. I reckon it makes up a little for those worse off on his account."

Mama's remark would bring before me a likeness of God, with a great beard like that of Colonel Joshua Mathis, the horse auctioneer. God would be bending over a thick book, balancing the good marks against the bad opposite the name of Jim Utsler.

Bullfights were occasionally held in a ring in the Square. The bullfighters were Mexicans. Though Mama would not go to a bullfight, Papa took me to more than one. But Mama loved the horse races, as she did everything that had to do with horses. The sin she said was betting. For a long while that was all I knew about betting. One time some man who was with us said such-and-such horse should win when I was sure that Mr. Ed Weatherly's filly would. The man offered to bet a nickel. He explained how it was to bet. The Weatherly filly won going away. Thus it was that I had two nickels to rub against each other in my pocket. Such a pity it was a sin.

It seems odd that I cannot recall ever having seen Ad Poak ride his own horse, Pat, in a race. Had I done so perhaps my career as a gambler would have made swifter if less fortunate progress. Surely I could not have refrained from betting on the big sorrel stallion no matter what other horses were running. I remember Mama returning from the Fair Grounds saddened because Pat had lost, or, if he had won, because Ad was unwilling to leave well enough alone. For Ad would keep on racing until in the end he had lost all his money and more besides. With Pat, he would return to the claim to clear away his debts. So Ad Poak, like Martha, was with us only on and off. For that matter so were Papa, Mr. Howell, and Will or Ira or whatever happened to be the name of the hired man. They came and went. Only Mama stayed all the time.

Besides reading to me and listening to me read and explaining the new words, Ad's duties about the claim were something Mama said she had never got clear in her mind. Mostly they seemed to consist of currying and clipping Pat and exercising him in the West Bottom. Ad was not a hired man. He did not sleep in the "boys' house." He was the only occupant of our upstairs.

All the same Mama and Ad got along fine. My mother had spent half her life in parts of the country where more men carried firearms than carried timepieces. Yet she had never fired a gun, which Ad declared to be a scandal. Ad spent a good deal of the time he could spare from Pat at pistol practice, fixing his marks to the chopping block in the back yard. He shot a bone-handled, double-action, nickel-plated Smith & Wesson .38. Mama said that was about the only use Ad made of the chopping block.

One time he came in with a little 16-gauge shotgun he had borrowed and began teasing Mama to shoot it. He told what shots his mother and his sister were—the sister who could "make a *git*-tar just talk." Finally he said that if Mama could hit her dishpan at twenty feet he'd buy her a new one. Mama sure surprised him.

"Happens I need a new dishpan, Ad. I'll just take you up on that."

Ad propped the pan against the chopping block.

As Mama aimed Ad kept giving her advice.

"Shut *one* eye, Miz James. Look the *same* way you point the gun—*toward* the dishpan."

With both eyes closed and her face turned from the target, Mama blazed away. She blew a hole in the dishpan you could have thrown a cat through.

Mama would say to Ad: "Why don't you go back to the good home you left and marry some nice Missouri girl and settle down instead of running wild in this forsaken part of the world?" Ad would read us his mother's letters. They seemed mostly about the colts they were raising on their farm in Missouri.

Getting back to my trips to Enid, I'd rather go with Papa than with Mama because he would let me twist my hair under my hat so that I did not look like a girl. Papa wouldn't get my hair cut off, though.

"It would displease your mama," he said. "Wait until you start school, son."

Best of all the ways to go to town was to sneak a trip in the wagon with Ad Poak. Barefooted, in the clothes I wore at home and with Prince at my side, I wasn't so fearful of the boys I saw in the streets. Once Ad and I ran smack into Papa, pitching horseshoes in the shade of the courthouse. With a happy shout he swung me to his shoulder.

"Gentlemen, I have the honor of presenting the Strip's own Huck Finn!"

Grateful for the welcome after my forbidden journey and enchanted to be the center of attention, I shook hands with Judge McAtee, Colonel John C. Moore, Mr. Sturgis, Doctor Fairgrieve and one or two gentlemen whose names were strange to me.

At one of them I must have looked closely, for his hair fell about his shoulders in glistening ringlets, as mine would have done were it not twisted up.

"Temple," Papa said, "this is my son. Marquis: Mr. Temple Houston."

Mr. Temple Houston made such an impression on my mind that I mentioned him to Mr. Howell.

"Temple Houston? Why, shore. Knowed his pappy, ol' Sam. Yessiree, knowed ol' Sam Houston, Bigfoot Wallace, an' all them early *Tejanos*. When I was a young squirt in the Rangers, 'fore the Rebellion."

V

Most memorable of my early excursions to Enid was the time I shook hands with Dick Yeager. Far from erasing a single detail of that meeting, or of the events which made it possible, I find by consulting the record that the intervening years have added details and performed other useful services.

This suggests that Mr. Howell's talent for elevating truth above the range of the familiar has not been lost on his most entranced listener. Indeed, I was all prepared to grace these pages with a story of Dick Yeager's pursuit and capture, and of my subsequent audience with him purporting to be based on my own recollections. I was almost as certain that I remembered those things as I am of anything. Then I looked up the date. Dick was taken on August 4, 1895. He died in the Garfield County jail on September 7. My fourth birthday was August 29, 1895.

So, the story I tell you now is of events I cannot remember, really. I pass it on from my memory (corrected by the record, where that is possible) of the accounts of others which were told to me, and told so often that they have come to seem a part of actual experience. My father's and Ad Poak's associations with Dick Yeager, and my meeting with him, embodied a claim to distinction which a child will keep bright.

Dick Yeager was any Cherokee Strip youngster's ideal of what an outlaw should be and do—an almost mythological figure, difficult to realize within the confines of acceptable evidence. The saga of how they hunted him down I must have heard a hundred times —from Ad Poak who fired the last shot; from other participants (who weren't hard to find since a thousand men took part in the chase first and last); and from Mama, who probably knew as many of the actors in the drama as any woman in Oklahoma Territory. Though too great a slave to facts to compete with Mr. Howell, Mama lived in a day and in a part of the world where storytelling was still an important art.

Dick's end came as a result of one thing leading to another. First was only the holdup at the Cimarron River bridge of a Rock Island train which was carrying gold for the Army payroll in Texas. Bill Doolin's gang did that, and the best testimony does not place Dick on the scene. Later, in the Garfield County jail, Dick said he was there, but during his residence in our jail Dick said a lot of things. The Cimarron bridge holdup caused no great indignation in Enid. The Railroad War was too recent a memory for us to get worked up over the misfortunes of the Rock Island. That was distinctly something for Chris Madsen to worry about. Mr. Chris Madsen was the United States Marshal, the head of the Federal Government's law-enforcement establishment in the Territory.

Federal officers, appointed in Washington and sent down to tell us what and what not to do, were not popular with the rank and file of settlers. For instance, we didn't like the way they used the cedar haulers. Cedar haulers were products of the droughts and general hard times in the early years after the Opening. They were settlers who would drive into the Gyp Hills, cut a load of fire-killed cedar, light and easy to handle, drive thirty-five miles to Enid or to Alva, and sell the load for eight or ten dollars. The Gyp Hills, rising abruptly from the plain, were also called the Gloss Mountains from the way the shiny rocks in the steep red slopes caught the sun and glistened. Unfit for homesteading, the Hills were Government-owned and rarely visited except by cedar haulers or by outlaws on the dodge.

The law against cutting timber on Government land was a law settlers had no use for when in need of a little cash money. United States deputy marshals enforced the law spasmodically for the same reason. Deputies drew fees on a mileage basis—ten cents a mile as I recall—for the distance traveled with prisoners after an arrest. They were paid by the head. Escorting ten prisoners one mile was the same as escorting one prisoner ten miles. A couple of deputies would ride into the Hills, arrest a few outfits of cedar haulers, take them to Alva, the county seat of Woods County, thirty-five miles away, and put in for mileage on each man in custody. The vouchers approved, prisoners would be turned loose —inconvenienced only by the confiscation of their loads and the loss of their time. This leniency was not appreciated, however: settlers definitely didn't like the marshals' way of piecing out their incomes. So, after the Rock Island holdup, if Chris Madsen wanted to catch Bill Doolin that was Chris's affair.

Mr. Madsen accepted the challenge and got right busy. He was at the head of a small posse which killed a man the newspapers said was Rattlesnake Jim, a member of the Doolin gang. The publication of this item proved a boon to the real Rattlesnake Jim, whom they never got at all. Years later I saw him in my father's law office. When I left Oklahoma he was still above ground leading a different life.

One of Madsen's deputies, Bill Banks, killed Dan Clifton and Charlie Pierce, known, respectively, as Dynamite Dick and Tulsa Jack. They had been at the Cimarron bridge. Doolin and six companions reached the Gyp Hills but were not permitted the undisturbed enjoyment of that haven. Deputy Hec Thomas cornered the leader in a dugout and shot him to death. Of Bill Doolin I cannot pretend to speak from the best information. I still think of certain old-time Oklahoma outlaws in connection with attorneys

who defended them, and from whom in later years I got some of
the particulars that are related here. Bill Doolin's attorney was
Mr. Scott Denton, with whom my father was on such distant terms
that I never had a chance to hear him talk about Bill. But my
impression is that Hec Thomas terminated the career of a southwestern highwayman to whom history has done less than justice.

Bill Radler was wounded and captured. Buck Wateman, Dick
West, and Arkansas Tom got away. Retribution caught up with
Buck and Dick shortly after. Buck was killed while robbing a
Wells-Fargo express box in Woods County and Dick West after
a Rock Island holdup at Siding Number One near Chickasha, in
the Chickasaw Nation. Dick was killed by Mr. William D. Fossett, a friend of my father whom I came to know very well. Mr.
Fossett was one of the great, though unpublicized, peace officers of
the powder-stained Southwest: a man to mention with Wild Bill
Hickok and Bat Masterson. Dick West's reputation likewise has
failed to survive, though in the nineties he was regarded as a
highwayman who had reached the top of his calling.

Arkansas Tom, the third of the trio to escape from the Gyp
Hills, was the only one the law never got its hands on. His reputation as a desperado didn't amount to much at the time and thereafter he was careful not to enhance it. Maybe this was because he
was smart, and maybe because he'd had a scare thrown into him.
Ad Poak's opinion of Arkansas Tom is recorded earlier in this
chapter, and Ad wasn't a bad judge of such matters. In any event,
the year I left the Strip Mr. Fossett told me Tom was still living
in Oklahoma under a different name.

With Doolin dead, Radler caught, and Wateman, West, and
Arkansas Tom on the loose, none of the party who had held up the
train remained in the Hills. Yet the deputies and their small posses
had quarry before them: Dick Yeager and Ike Black. It was
thought then (and for that matter long after) that Dick and Ike
had been at the Cimarron with Bill Doolin. Supporting this was
the fact that they had been with the Doolin band at the time of
the fight in which the leader was killed and Radler wounded and
run down. Yet the most dependable evidence denies Yeager and
Black any part in the Rock Island holdup. Their presence in the
Gyp Hills with Doolin was a coincidence.

Ike Black was an outlaw of so little account as to be hardly
worth the trouble of arresting except for mileage. Dick Yeager

stood in a different light. Having killed a Kansas sheriff and twice broken jail in Guthrie, the Territorial capital, he had a price on his head. After the second jail-delivery, Dick had gone so thoroughly into seclusion that people about forgot to look for him. Well these two, Yeager and Black, were on their way from a hideout in Kansas to the Hills to lay low some more, when what should happen but they meet up with Bill Doolin and colleagues. After Bill had been killed and his band scattered, the officers kept right on going—in pursuit of Dick Yeager and Ike Black. At any rate that is how Mr. Fossett, who was in one of the original posses, explained the matter to me. He never did believe Dick Yeager as big a man as his reputation. Mr. Fossett entertained deep convictions on that subject, or he would not have mentioned it to me —knowing that Dick had been a client of my father and a childhood hero of mine. A strict constructionist in the rating of outlaws according to their merits, Mr. Fossett's point was that it had not been established that Dick ever held up a bank or a railroad train.

The pursuit of Dick Yeager might have continued as the pursuit of Bill Doolin had begun—a professional limited-participation affair with the Federal officers on one side and the outlaws on the other and the public taking little more than a spectator interest— had not Dick and Ike the poor judgment to kill a settler who got in their way. Kill one settler and you rouse up a swarm of settlers. That was what turned the chase of Dick Yeager into the greatest man-hunt Oklahoma ever had. The almost unbelievable endurance, the wiliness and the bravado of Yeager made it so. That's the rock on which his reputation rests.

VI

The aim of Yeager and Black was to escape from the Gyp Hills to the Cherokee Nation. Time and again they ventured upon the intervening prairie and fought incredible pitched battles, the two of them against whole posses. They failed to break through; but the posses failed to take them. In these fights Dick seemed to bear a charmed life. Time and again men swore they had seen him knocked down by the impact of their bullets. On one of his captured horses was a saddle with nine holes in it. Dick stole other horses and kept on. But always he and Black were driven back to the Hills.

Ad Poak was with a posse, thus leaving Mama and me alone much of the time. Mama was not afraid. In her day she had met Jesse James and had known Cole Younger's whole family. She had never heard of an outlaw harming a woman. Certainly Dick Yeager would not have bothered us, though he knew the East Draw well.

Nearly every day brought fresh news of the hunt. Mr. Sam Campbell's posse came by our place and, after scouting the Draw, unsaddled and watered their horses, fed and rested them. Some of the men sat around and cleaned their guns. Others stretched out under the Big Tree and slept with their hats over their eyes. A few moonlight nights later this posse came on Dick and Ike sleeping beside their picketed horses. One man fired too soon. He missed, awakening the outlaws who shot their way out of the trap. Yeager used only one pistol, carrying his boots in the other hand. A few days after that a man in a decrepit spring wagon, driving a seventeen-year-old horse and playing a mouth organ, rode through a line of vigilantes. Too late they learned that he was Dick Yeager. That happened on Skeleton Creek not far east of our claim. The occurrence made the posses more suspicious. When two men traveling south in a light covered wagon refused to explain themselves promptly enough, they were shot and one of them killed. It was printed in the papers that the victims were Dick Yeager and Ike Black. They turned out to be young farmers, brothers, from Old Oklahoma, who had been looking for gold along Boggy Creek. A little later a posse concealed in an angle of a corn field ambushed the right men as they dismounted at a settler's shack to ask for grub. Ike was killed, Dick wounded again and his horse captured.

At the point of a gun Dick got a fresh horse belonging to a settler named Blakely. Mr. Blakely described the fugitive as in no condition to ride far. Presently the horse was found. The bed of a dry creek revealed the track of a man who stopped frequently to rest and who appeared to be lame. It led into Alvin Ross's stand of corn. Sheriff Thralls of Enid spread his posse around the field and sent Ad Poak and Tom Smith to follow the track through the corn. The tassels were more than head high. Not a breath of air was stirring. This made it impossible for Ad and Tom Smith to move without rustling the corn. They kept their Winchesters ready. The track was very fresh and it twisted as if the person who made it did not know where he was going.

The track led to a small bare mound of bad soil where no corn would grow. Stretched out on this mound was the enormous form of Dick Yeager, apparently asleep. His clothes were tattered and stained with blood. He wore one boot and one shoe. At his right side lay a six-shooter and a rifle. Ad and Tom Smith raised their rifles. Ad said.

"Let's give the poor devil a chance."

With guns still leveled Ad called out:

"Put up your hands, Dick. We've got you."

The bandit opened his eyes and blinked. He did not say a word. His right hand moved toward his pistol.

Ad and Tom Smith fired. Dick rolled over one complete turn. But he had his pistol.

"Drop that gun," yelled the men.

Dick dropped it and stiffly raised his right hand.

"Both hands!"

"I can't, boys," said Dick Yeager. "That arm's broke."

The county jail was in the Square slantwise across the street from the Rex Hotel. A tight, slate-colored fence with four or five strands of barbed wire on top enclosed it. At each corner of the fence a deputy sheriff armed with a Winchester sat on a box.

There was always a crowd about the jail. People came on the cars from long ways off to see the celebrated desperado. Admirers brought hampers of fried chicken and cold bottles of beer. Dick enjoyed this attention, held court from a cot in his cell and entertained everybody. He admitted every crime that had been committed in the Strip since the Opening. He joshed the lawyers, saying they weren't worth the powder to blow them to hell. The lawyers were kind of disappointed because Doctor McKenzie said from the first that there would be no trial. Dick had been shot in almost every part of his huge body. He couldn't possibly get well.

Ad Poak had been given a job on the jail fence. He talked his way out of the hot sun and became the famous prisoner's personal cell-guard and chamberlain. He introduced visitors, helped Dick along with his tall stories, and consumed a share of the delicacies an appreciative public showered on the prisoner.

I had gone to town with Mama on one of her regular trips to Mr. Bowers's store when a little colored boy came to say that Papa would like to see us at the jail.

As Mama suspected, the message had come from Ad Poak. Papa wasn't at the jail at all. We waited until a crowd of sight-seers cleared out of the cell and Ad took us in.

Ad Poak was a small neat man with a silky yellow mustache Mama made fun of because it was so puny. About his neck was usually a figured silk handkerchief held by a ring made by cutting the center from a poker chip. I don't think Ad was much taller than Mama, whose head came little higher than Papa's shoulder. Any man taller than my father I knew to be real big. Well, you should have seen Dick Yeager. He was lying on his bunk, covered by a clean white sheet. But you could tell how tall he was. His feet stuck over the foot of the bunk. The cell smelled of medicine. Wet blankets were hung against the walls to keep down the heat. The brindle jail pup, with which Dick had made friends, was lying on the damp floor, panting. Dick's head was by the barred window. He was sucking a lemon.

"Dick Yeager, I hope you are comfortable," said Mama after Ad had said who we were.

Mama stood by the door of the cell.

"I am; tol'ably so; thank you, ma'am," said Dick Yeager.

Dick held out his hand. I marched to the bunk and took it. Mama stayed where she was.

"Young man," said Dick Yeager, "you can tell 'em you've shook hands with the bigges' outlaw Oklahoma ever had."

"Yes, sir," said I.

There was a chair in the cell, Ad's chair. He invited Mama to sit down.

"I'll stand; thank you, Ad," she said.

Mama was looking at Dick Yeager's face. It was covered with a reddish stubble of beard. His eyes were bright blue. In a moment Mama said:

"Dick Yeager, I hope you rest comfortably while you are here. Now, Ad, if you will excuse us."

Mama took my hand. While Ad was unlocking the door I looked at the gigantic figure on the cot. I wanted to say some-thing, but it was Dick who spoke.

"Bub, jus' you recollec' what I tol' you: bigges' outlaw the Territory ever had."

When we got outside Ad said:

"Well, Madam, that was the coolest reception Dick's had so far."

The look of sadness in my mother's gray eyes stopped Ad's banter.

"What a tragic sight to see," she said, and added, "I reckon outlaws sometimes are just made by what happens to them."

Mama may have been talking to Doctor McKenzie. He, too, knew how outlaws sometimes were made: a cowboy who likes to brag gets in bad company and one thing leads to another. Could Doctor McKenzie have healed Dick Yeager's wounds it would have been only so they could have hanged him. Consequently the doctor, who wore an Old Testament beard and was a pillar of the Baptist church, tried to do something for Dick's soul. Dick wasn't interested.

Doctor McKenzie told Mama how Dick Yeager died. For a while Dick had seemed to fool the predictions of the doctors. He got stronger and spryer. Then one evening his fever began to rise fast.

"Dick," said the doctor, "this is your last night on earth. Is there anyone you wish to see or anything you wish to say?"

"Nobody to see, Doc; an' nothin' to say."

In the shallow top drawer of the rolltop desk in his office Papa kept Dick Yeager's revolver. It was the one he had carried through the one hundred and twenty-five days of the great pursuit. The pistol stayed there for years. One time after we had left the claim and moved to Enid, I opened the drawer to show the gun to a crony. It was gone.

"I gave it to a lady," Papa explained, "a rather nice-looking countrywoman I'd never seen before. She convinced me that she was a sister of Ellsworth Wyatt. That was Dick Yeager's true name. She wanted something to remember him by."

The gun was a cedar-handled, single-action, long-barreled Colt .45, with the "dog" filed for fanning the hammer. Dick's sister carried it away wrapped in a newspaper.

DAVID LAVENDER

CRAZY AS A SHEEPHERDER

This account of the physiology, psychology, and economics of sheepherding is terse and factual; the implications are poetic. The sheepherder may be a little "crazy," but the word takes on a special meaning, and not at all a derogatory one, after you read what Mr. Lavender has to say. (From *One Man's West*, Doubleday, Doran, 1943.)

SHEEP cannot be avoided on the Western ranges. They are more numerous today in Colorado than cattle. Sooner or later every cowboy comes up against them, no longer as enemies, necessarily, but often as creatures he must be able to handle. All of us on different occasions spent many a night in sheep camps between Paradox and the high country, and there we learned that this trade, too, has its fine, rich moments and its black disappointments.

On its face, however, sheepherding is plain misery:

Wintertime. Out on the bleak Wyoming prairie a canvas-covered wagon, looking like the old Conestoga schooners of pioneer fame, hunches on a snow-cased hill, its chimney smoke streaking across a cold yellow sunset. A dirty gray mass of sheep huddles near by, blatting hungrily. A man walks around them, headed for the only home he knows, his sheepskin collar turned against the wind. He climbs into the wagon. The door bangs shut behind him. An empty sound in an empty world.

"Good God," a person thinks, "only a half-wit would live like that!"

Such is the common assumption. A standard simile throughout the stock-raising West is, "crazy as a sheepherder"—never shepherd; that word apparently has too idyllic a connotation. Everywhere the same old yarns are told about them. One perennial favorite says that three herders happened into town at the same time. They sat on the steps of the store, munching apples and talking earnestly. But not to each other, not even to the apples. To themselves. And then there's the tale about the poor fellow who died of exhaustion while trying to make his bed—he couldn't figure out the long way of a square blanket.

If the impact of environment is enough to drive a man insane, then those stories would seem to be well founded. For the impact of sheepherding is terrific. You can never, not for an instant throughout the year, escape it. From the minute— But let's go back to that lonely wagon on the prairie and take a look.

The quarters are not as unbearable as they appear. The bed is off the ground; the canvas reflects the heat of the roaring sheet-iron stove. The wagon sides contain built-in cupboards for food, dishes, clothes, and books—except for the Mexicans, many herders do a surprising amount of reading. When the camp mover takes the equipment to new grazing grounds, as he does every few days, he simply hitches a team to the wagon and goes, while the herder follows with the sheep, unworried about packing up—until the wagon tips over in an arroyo, which always happens sooner or later.

Things are more complicated if the herder lives in a tent, as he must in the mesa lands of Colorado and Utah, or wherever the terrain is too rough for wagons. Every four or five days his entire household is put on muleback and relocated. He can't accumulate any little comforts; traveling light is too important. He sleeps on the frozen earth. Heaps of dirt banked around the edges of the canvas are the only means of keeping drafts out and heat in.

Whether his home is wagon or tent, the herder spends little time in it. The sheep are up at dawn, hungry and on the move for the thin feed—the cured rice grass, shad scale, even the bitter sagebrush tips—of the winter range. Their guardian must make sure they move together, where he can keep an eye on them. For a sheep is the most helpless of animals. Its only teeth are grinders far back in its upper jaw, useless for fighting. It does not have fleetness enough to run from attack, or sufficient size and endurance to buck a storm or flooded gully. Whatever chance at life it has, the herder gives it.

At nights, especially when the moon shines and you think you can see frost dancing in the air, the coyotes are bold. Their yap-yapping trembles over the hills—a sort of sarcastic laugh, it sounds—but you don't worry so long as they are noisy. Then they fall silent. Your wise, shaggy dog, lying by the tent entrance, lifts his head and growls. A frightened bleat runs through the bedded herd. You grab a rifle and pile out into the cold. You shoot to frighten the marauders away. Sometimes you set off firecrackers. The echoes fade, and it grows terribly still. You listen until you are shivering too hard to hear and go back to bed.

The utmost vigilance isn't always enough. One morning you find several carcasses near the bed ground. This is the work of a killer coyote. He has cut a bunch of ewes from the main herd, struck one down, eaten her warm liver, and raced after the others, killing for the sheer lust of it. A furious desire to hunt him down rises in your throat, but you cannot leave the herd. When the camp mover comes you send for the government trapper.

The man is apt to use more poison than traps. All the carrion he finds he shoots full of strychnine, working on a canvas spread from horseback before he dismounts and wearing canvas gloves so as to leave no warning scent. The coyotes are wily, but they are hungry too; the poison gets a lot of them.

You keep an eye on your dog, but one afternoon he wanders off and does not come back for supper. You stay up until midnight, whistling and calling. The next morning he is outside the tent, dead, frozen hard. You can see where he has dragged himself through the snow, trying to get back on the job. You dig a grave, roll him in, and go on after the herd. A few days later the camp mover brings you another pup, full of ambition and mischief. Training him lightens the monotony. But you don't forget; you don't think any better of poisoning, even when the trapper boasts that he got six coyotes last week and the killer visits you no more.

Always you watch the horizon, smell the wind, study the way birds fly, drawing on every bit of lore and superstition you have gleaned for predicting storms. When dawn comes with that still, steel-gray look you keep the sheep in the trees or behind a protecting ridge. A blizzard catching you in the open can be catastrophic. No sheep will face wind-driven snow. They turn and drift before it, knowing only fear and the need to escape this thing they cannot fight. They pile blindly into arroyos, one on top the other, until there is a bridge of dead for the living to cross. They jam into dead-end pockets, crushing each other, smothering each other.

You drift with them, cursing them, fighting them, hating them, doing your best to save them. Finally you get them stopped in a sheltered basin, build a fire with numbed fingers, and hunker down to wait out the storm. Your belly is hollow; you are cold and lonely. You know the boss will say plenty, not about the animals you have saved, but about the ones you lost. . . . At last the wind feathers out. You start working the listless herd back toward the bed ground. There are drifts to buck now, worries about the feed buried deep under this new fall. The nights seem longer. Your thoughts turn in on yourself, and that is not so good. . . .

But it ends. Spring is on the way. You can smell it in the thawing earth, hear it in the soft whistle of bluebirds, come suddenly from you don't know where. You feel it in the new resiliency of willow shoots, see it in the swelling abdomens of the ewes. Even the camp mover softens into a smile now and then. You begin to step livelier. You need to; the hardest, dirtiest part of your work lies ahead.

Shearing comes first. Here the machine age has intruded. Smaller outfits own or hire ancient automobiles which can move from camp to camp, where their engines furnish power for mechanical clippers not unlike, except in size, the ones used by a town barber. Larger operators have a regular shearing "factory": a long frame shed roofed with corrugated iron and surrounded by a maze of corrals. From it rises a whir like a hundred egg beaters working at once. Toward it a dozen herds creep, traveling on schedules timed to the hour, though some have come half a hundred miles, three or four miles a day.

You ease your bunch along in turn. Through the trees you can see other sheep in the pens around the shed. Shorn of their mattress of wool, they appear different animals entirely. Their heads seem too big for their gaunt, ungainly bodies. Their hides have a bluish tinge, spotted here and there with blood where the hurrying shears have nipped too close.

You shiver in the raw wind, thinking how you would like to be turned out naked to the unpredictable mercies of the weather. For months the strange tyranny of man's economics has let you alone, and now it has found you out again. There is nothing you can do about it. You walk on, kicking at stones, angry without really understanding why. Protecting your sheep for the shearer and the butcher is part of your job, isn't it? The justification of all you've done and will keep on doing.

Generally the shearing is contracted to professionals who move from ranch to ranch. Piece payment, averaging twenty-five cents for a ewe, half a dollar for a big, husky ram. Their job folds on them with the season, and so they have developed astonishing skill. A good man can make twenty dollars a day.

Inside the shed a gasoline motor drives an overhead shaft, powering a line of a dozen or so clippers, one man to a clipper. Behind each worker is a small pen, kept filled with sheep. He reaches into it, seizes an animal by the hind leg, drags it out, wrestles it into a sitting position, and kneels by its left side, using his left hand to hold its underjaw.

The sheep lies helpless on the round of its rump, dumb terror in its yellow eyes. *Snip-snip-snip.* Along the neck and side from back to belly travel the shears. Sweat pours from the operator. This is work, holding a ninety-pound mutton with one hand while the other races against time. *Snip-snip-snip.* The fleece comes off in one unbroken greasy mass. The shearer—his hands are always debutante-soft from the lanolin in the wool—folds it with the clean hair inside and tosses it onto a conveyor belt running overhead. He pushes the shorn animal through a door in the outside wall, reaches back for another.

The conveyor belt dumps the fleece in a huge burlap bag taller than a man. A Mexican boy is in the bag, tramping the wool tight. When the sack is full it is removed for another. Its open end is laced and it is piled with a score more on a loading dock, waiting for the snorting trucks that will take it to the railroad, to the busy textile mills of New England. Great business, sheep raising. The rancher gets two cracks at the market, where other stock raisers get only one. Foolproof—on paper.

Next come the lambs. Your stomach begins to tighten as you think of all the things that can happen. Not enough feed on the lambing grounds. Not enough water. Or too much water: a cold rain, a late snow. Coyotes. Bears. Stampedes. One or all these things, striking when the newborn lambs are utterly helpless, can break an outfit overnight.

Breeding is controlled so that the lambs all arrive in the spring. When this mass motherhood is due you hurry to a protected spot. You split the herd up (you have helpers now), letting each bunch graze slowly along. Each day's and night's drop is left behind. As mother and child get acquainted (by smell first, by voice later) you put them with others until at last the herd is reassembled, double its former size—on paper again.

Actually it is an appalling event. You've had to drive nineteen hours a day to reach the lambing grounds. You marshal your forces and decide you'll have time for one good night's sleep before things start. Unutterably weary, you crawl into bed. An hour later you are up. The stork (two thousand storks for the average herd) never waits—and he's brought an icy fog with him.

You light your lantern and stumble off through the mist. You are a midwife now: straightening twisted heads, changing positions in case of breached presentations, delivering the stillborn. The drizzle is chilling the live lambs to death. The mother won't— can't—do anything to help. You take the feeblest to the tents, give them a warm bath, dry them, wrap them in sheets, feed them canned milk from a small-necked bottle with a rag tied over the mouth. You dare not keep one too long, for the ewe will forget its smell and refuse to own it. You hustle it back, though it still seems pitifully weak. You stand it up by a ewe. But you have made a mistake; she's not the mother. She butts the lamb flat. You try another. The same thing happens. You want to kill them all. They are butting back to death this frail little life you've struggled so to save. At last you find the right one. She snuffs the lamb over with maddening suspicion, then accepts it.

Sometimes a mother will refuse her child for no apparent reason. You resort to subterfuges to wake the maternal instinct: rub the lamb's head with the ewe's own milk, or drag its tail through her mouth. Sometimes you have to build a pen and lock them up together before she will decide this really is Junior after all.

Your opinion of a sheep's character sinks to the nadir. A ewe now and then doesn't even seem to know whether her lamb is born or not. Often she will get up before the event transpires and start looking around for what is not yet there. Old ewes or weak ewes with no milk will walk off and leave their young. Apologists say this is smartness; the ewe knows she can't raise her offspring and isn't going to wear herself out to no gain. But somehow you think she ought at least to try.

You'd think, too, that a ewe whose lamb is born dead would be willing to adopt one which has been orphaned. But no, she has to be tricked into it. You slip her dead lamb onto a canvas and, by a rope attached to the canvas, drag it off. The ewe associates this movement with the lamb and not with you, since you aren't touching it. She thinks it must be alive. She calls for it to come back. When it doesn't she runs after it, bleating and stamping the ground in anxious bewilderment.

You get the dead lamb out of sight, skin it quickly, and fasten the hide over an orphan. You take the orphan, thus disguised, back to the ewe. Now she is in a quandary. She snuffs the little thing over inch by inch while you watch and hold your breath. She walks away, the lamb tottering after her and blatting hungrily. She looks back. This does not seem to be her child. And yet—the smell is there. She emits a tentative rumbling noise, and you breathe again. (It is a strange noise, this sound of affection between sheep: a sort of deep grumble made well down in the throat without opening the mouth. It must be affection. Ewes talk so to their lambs; bucks to the ewes at mating time.)

The enforced parent is likely to remain doubtful for several days. But gradually the odors—particularly the tail odors—of the dead lamb and the live one intermingle until she can't detect one from the other. By the time the disguise has lost its potency and you take it away she is convinced.

When you reassemble the herd to move on each ewe has learned the voice of its lamb, and the lamb its mother's. It is their salvation. In the evening the sheep mill on the bed ground in indescribable confusion. The lambs gang up in companies along the edge of the herd, race back and forth, and suddenly spring high into the air in their glee at being alive. Gradually they grow hungry and begin to hunt their mothers. The din is terrific: thousands of throats, each calling for one particular object. It seems impossible they can mate. Yet out of the bedlam a lamb or ewe will pick the proper call. It starts running. Hundreds of others are also running every which way. Suddenly there is a quiet island in the turmoil. Lamb and ewe have joined. Down on his front knees goes the lamb, sucking greedily, his tail bobbing in ecstatic jerks.

Late spring blizzards are tragic now. The tiny lambs are help-less; the shorn ewes have no resistance to cold. Fortunately, though dust-lashing winds are usual, there is little snow. But sometimes it comes. One May a three-day storm howled down from the San Juans, catching the herds moving toward the forests near Mount Sneffels and Telluride. Half a thousand blinded sheep, stampeding before it, piled into the water reservoir above the railway junction of Ridgeway and drowned. Other herds were trapped on the main automobile highway between Placerville and the top of Dallas Divide. When clear weather at last came the tight-lipped herders threw corpses out of the road into piles higher than a man's head, soaked them in kerosene, and set them afire. . . .

On you go. The sheep must be dipped: prodded one by one through a vat of foul creosote mixture which rids them of para-sites. The lambs must have their tails docked (cut off) and be castrated. Brands must be painted on. And always feed and water be found. Days and nights merge into a blur of sheep, dust, smell, and noise.

Many sheep are ranged in one section throughout the year. But more are moved tremendous distances with each shift of the seasons—to the comparatively snow-free desert in winter; to the high country, the fringes of timber line and above, in summer. Every mountain is a focal point; Colorado, because of its abun-dance of hills, draws hundreds and hundreds of thousands. How many sheep are on the trail throughout the Western United States each spring is hard to say. Government estimates indicate close to twenty million head.

That many sheep eat a lot of grass. They are bound to encroach on range claimed by someone else. In the old days of swift expan-sion quarrels inevitably passed from violent words to violent deeds, occasionally to open warfare that swept whole counties.

Here again the fights have been exaggerated in countless fiction stories. Trouble was there, however. Even after Colorado became a state in 1876 little attempt was made to extend the supervision of courts and law officers to the grazing lands. The country was thinly settled and deemed valueless except for pasturage. Here the range users ruled supreme; if controversy arose they settled it between themselves and to the devil with legal procedure.

The first move toward organization had come in 1872, when the proprietor of the Bull's Head Corral in Denver called a meeting of all agriculturists "to protect the interests alike of stockmen, ranchers, and farmers, and to harmonize whatever might be conflicting." The dice were loaded from the start. Cattlemen controlled the organization, and the farmers did not bother to show up and watch them pass resolutions for their own benefit. An attempt was actually made by the Colorado association and others to have Congress set aside as pasture land a thousand-mile stretch of continent between the one hundredth meridian, which passes through Kansas, and the Sierra Nevada Mountains of California! Farming was to be forbidden on these hundreds of millions of acres, and vast tracts were to be leased or sold to stockmen at a nominal sum. President Hayes himself told Congress that such a sweeping act would "be a source of profit to the United States, while at the same time *legalizing* the business of cattle raising." (The italics are mine.)

For a few years sheepmen were admitted as members of the Colorado Stock Growers Association, but antagonism between the groups soon flared hot, and the sheep raisers withdrew. Public sentiment favored cattle, and violence against sheep was blandly shrugged aside. Rewards were offered for the perpetrators, but there is not a single record of a man being arrested for molesting sheep. And molested they were. Near Pueblo, Colorado, eight hundred of a flock of sixteen hundred were killed with poisoned bran; other hundreds were clubbed to death or had their throats cut. A reward of three thousand dollars for information leading to the arrest of those responsible went begging. Goat Creek, near Beaver Park, received its name when several masked cowboys charged into a mixed herd of sheep and goats and stampeded several hundred animals to death over a high cliff.

Naturally the sheepmen fought back, often with success, for there was money to be made in the business, and its followers were by no means without influence or ability. On many occasions there was bloodshed and even death. After such a fracas both the cattle and sheep associations passed pious resolutions of "deep regret," but that did not solve the problem. Indeed, it was never solved until the "free" range was brought under outside control and the so-called "rights" of the competing factions were established by official supervision, first through the national forests and, more recently, over the rest of the public domain through the Taylor Grazing Act.

One of the first decrees of the grazing boards set up stock driveways for the herds of migrant sheep. The width of these driveways varies from many miles to as little, in places, as a few hundred yards, depending on the terrain and the lay of adjoining deeded land. Each herder naturally tries to reach his particular driveway ahead of other outfits. The early flocks grub out the grass; the laggards are often hard put to escape starvation. Some men (not you, of course) have been known to resort to such skulduggery as stealing supplies, destroying bridges, etc., to delay their rivals.

Sooner or later you stray onto some cattleman's range. You may do it innocently enough, but the cattleman never believes it. Up he rides, purple with rage. He no longer dares shoot you, but, nonetheless, he makes you squirm in spite of yourself. There is something of the old feudal lord-serf setup inherent in facing afoot an angry man on horseback; you can't help feeling you ought to doff your hat.

The cattleman roars at you to get those blankety-blank sheep out of there pronto, and a lot he cares that you have neither feed nor water to take them to. Your maddening sense of inferiority makes you sore. You've read enough magazines to know you should invite him down for a punch in the nose. Indeed, you consider it. But you don't act. If you do he'll sue your boss. Probably he will sue him anyhow. Since there are four or five court actions coming out of this trip at best, you swallow your pride and spend half the night fighting your herd off all that good grass to a bare 'dobe flat. It's things like this, rather than lambing troubles or blizzards, that make you resolve never to look at another sheep.

But you keep on and at last you reach the mountains. Tough herding now: thick brush, down timber, raging streams. A forest ranger generally shows you where you may establish bed grounds. You grumble only as a matter of principle, for you realize that a bed ground, with thousands of sheep jammed on it every night for a week, takes a terrible beating, and public policy demands restraint in its location. In the main the ranger is considerate. He may not give you that flat, lush meadow you've been eyeing by the trout stream, but if possible he will pick a spot that's not too steep, that has some open ground with firewood and water near by and a few tall, straight aspens you can cut down and hollow out for troughs to hold the salt crystals you feed the sheep.

Tourists—you meet a lot of them during the summer: fishermen, mountain climbers, campers—wonder how you can be sure you haven't lost some of your sheep in the tumbled hills. You can't count them all each day to check, of course. But you know, anyhow, and it is not so mysterious as it seems. Sheep are clannish. As a herd feeds it breaks up into subherds, each with a leader. Goats make good leaders, so you use a few of them. Also, you bell the aggressive wethers. (You soon get to know the sound of these bells and can tell with surprising accuracy whether your sheep are feeding or resting or growing nervous and where, though to all outward appearances you are snoozing under a bush.) In addition you spot markers in each clan: black or spotted sheep. You can count these animals—the goats, the bell-wethers, the markers—as you drive the herd to the bed ground at night. If one of them is gone it is a cinch that others have strayed with it, and you set out to track them down.

Higher and higher you go, onto range too rough and too near the peak tops for even cattle to follow. Now you are in the wide green basins above timber line. Splintered, snow-creased peaks rear on every hand. It is the climax of your year. Soon trouble will start again: shoving back down the mountain, separating the terrified lambs from their mothers, driving them to the loading pens at the railroad, and betraying them with Judas goats into the cars that will take them to the slaughterhouses. Then winter again. But you don't think about that now. The nights are crisp, star-hung, the days an indolent delight. Everything is open, everything clear. From yonder pinnacle you can see your whole fattening flock without stirring. You lie on a warm grass bank, chewing a flower stem and dreaming with the clouds.

In such moments you are apt to kid yourself. You like to think that the freedom of these clouds and these mountains is your freedom too. Actually, of course, you are shackled to your job as no other wage earner is to his. Some states even have laws making it a penitentiary offense for a herder to leave his band without notice. You can't so much as set your own pace in moving from spot to spot. You've got to be at the next bed ground when the camp mover and his pack train arrive or you will go hungry and shelterless.

Yet there is something to the craft. The strange assortment of men in it indicates that. College graduates, unlettered Mexicans, engineers, writers, farmers' sons, paroled convicts, merchants—it seems no sheepherder ever started life as one. Perhaps they chose the profession as an escape from the spirit-bruising facts of the modern world. It is not a complete flight, however. The job takes too much courage and resourcefulness, too much faith and responsibility. No one makes decisions for you when trouble strikes; no one fights your fights. Come what may, it is squarely in your own two hands.

Maybe that is the freedom of it. You have been the slave of this flock, but you have been its god too. You have made the weak strong, have led the timid and the faltering. Only sheep, to be sure, but part of creation. Your creation. And you have done it alone. Aloneness is your habit and your reliance.

Are you crazy? You really don't know. Nor do you care. Because whatever else you may or may not be, you're still a damn good sheepherder.

FREDERIC F. VAN DE WATER

CUSTER

George Armstrong Custer, American soldier and Indian fighter, met his tragic end at the hands of the Sioux, at Little Big Horn, on June 25, 1876. Mr. Van de Water presents the grim drama with simplicity and with power, and achieves, in my opinion, one of the greatest of all battle-stories in modern literature. (From *Glory Hunter,* Bobbs-Merrill, 1934.)

THE 7th Cavalry was coming up the valley with massed trumpeters in advance. Forked star-and-stripe guidons were uneasy specks of color above the dark river of horsemen, and low dust blew away beneath the trampling hoofs. The head of the column vanished in a hollow, emerged magnified, and behind it, marching fours flowed interminably down the farther slope.

Custer's men were on the move once more, riding from the glamour of the past into legend. Their chief smiled proudly as the splendid regiment drew near. The red-faced trumpeters swung out of line, and, still sounding their hosannahs, halted beside the reviewing party to play the regiment through.

Young Charley Varnum, chief of scouts, leads his followers past —the swarthy Bouyer in half-Indian garb; Reynolds with his felon-infected right hand in a sling; Herendeen, the courier who is there to carry back Custer's tidings to Terry; the bearded Fred Girard, the grinning black Isaiah Dorman, interpreters; Mark Kellogg, the correspondent, astride a mule; Bloody Knife and the twenty-four Arikara scouts, sullen men with loose black hair blowing beneath bandeaus of cloth or buckskin; the tall merry Crows lent by Gibbon—Goes Ahead, White Man Runs Him, Curly, Half Yellow Face, White Swan, Hairy Moccasin. These pass above the low blowing dust and behind them like the clangor of the bugles made flesh, with jangling arms and squeaking leather, moves the rippling blue and yellow mass of the regiment.

Dry brown men who remember Washita, sunburned recruits whose saddle soreness is still an acute memory, faces that grin, faces that frown in the shadows of the slouch hat's brims—these, and the chargers' tossing heads that sweep past, four by four; these and the flickering guidons and the beat of carbines against the burdened saddles; these, and the mincing mules whose packs even now are slipping askew, all are to be part of their leader's fame. Past him and Terry and Gibbon they ride to become eternal satellites to the glory, heart-stirring as the shouting trumpets, of George Armstrong Custer. Terry takes the salutes of officers riding at the head of their troops and calls to each a kindly word of farewell.

The last fours swing past. The last rebellious mule is shepherded along. The trumpeters hush their clamor and fall in behind as the column moves up the ridge whose farther slope leads into the Rosebud Valley. Custer smiles at the compliments of Terry and Gibbon, clasps hands with them and wheels to follow the regiment whose boasted power is enough to abolish all Indians on the plains. Gibbon, in jest or out of his knowledge of the man, calls after him:

"Now, Custer! Don't be greedy! Wait for us!"

The buckskin clad horseman raises a hand in acknowledgment.

"No," he calls back cryptically, "I won't," and gallops off. Under the gray sky, the cold wind sings through the sage as Terry, Gibbon and the rest ride back to the *Far West*.

He was committed to the flood. George Armstrong Custer rode over the ridge his regiment had crossed and down to the rising tide of ordained calamity, which was to be the agent, but not the author, of his death.

The twelve troops, with their lagging mules, splashed through a ford near the mouth of the Rosebud, a clear, pebbly-bottomed, slightly alkaline stream, and marched up its far bank. Above, the clouds split and showed blue sky. Sunlight, blazing through, turned the dust of the march to gold. Men, who repacked the burdens that slipped from mules or prodded the lagging creatures onward, sweated while they swore.

For eight miles, the valley was broad. Thereafter, for the additional four they marched that day, bluffs shouldered in on either hand. They bivouacked in timber at the foot of a rocky height. Grass was plentiful and there were many fish in the stream. Men found, when camp had been made, that the strange mood which had oppressed their leader the day before, the gloom which the excitement of departure had banished, now had returned and again possessed him.

The valley was roofed by sunset when a trumpet stuttered officers' call. The regiment's sole major, its captains and lieutenants, assembled about their leader's camp-bed and those who in the past had been fired by, and those who had mocked at, Custer's flaring elation when a trail led toward battle, were depressed by his dismal air even before he spoke officially.

"It was not," Godfrey recalls, "a cheerful assemblage."

Nor was it the headlong, sublimely self-confident Custer of old who talked to his subordinates in a singularly placating tone. Custer spoke of his reliance on his officers—he who heretofore had felt the need of dependence on no one. The sad voice professed trust in their judgment, discretion and loyalty.

It recited instructions for the marches ahead—no further trumpet calls, "boots and saddles" at five A. M., each troop commander to be responsible for the welfare of his command in all things except the start and the camping place on each day's journey. These were to be ordered by Custer himself. The pack-mules attached to each troop hereafter were to be herded together in the column's rear under command of Lieutenant E. C. Mathey.

Thereafter, with a puzzling air of self-justification, Custer explained to his astounded officers, who never had been informed of reasons for his acts, why he had refused the offer of Brisbin's Squadron of the 2nd Cavalry. Godfrey's report of that confidence reveals his chief's blindness to logic.

Custer told the uneasy circle about him that he expected to meet not more than fifteen hundred Indians. He believed that the 7th Cavalry alone could defeat these. If they could not, there was no regiment in the service that could. Wherefore, the addition of a squadron under Brisbin—equal in strength to at least a third of Custer's present force—could not affect the issue. Furthermore, the inclusion of four troops of the 2nd would be certain to mar the harmony of the 7th and cause jealousy. It was for the same shaky reason that he had refused the offer of Low's Gatlings.

After this strange baring of a normally reticent spirit, the plaintive voice revealed a startling purpose. Godfrey reports it thus:

"Troop officers were cautioned to husband their rations and the strength of their mules and horses, as we might be out for a great deal longer time than that for which we were rationed, as he intended to follow the trail until we could get the Indians, even if it took us to the Indian agencies on the Missouri River or in Nebraska."

The council ended on the identical note of appeal that had launched it. Custer begged his officers to bring him either then or later, whatever suggestions they might have for expediting the march. Dazedly, the men rose and walked away. Lieutenant Wallace strode beside Godfrey and at length broke the silence.

"Godfrey," said Wallace, "I believe General Custer is going to be killed. I have never heard him talk in that way before."

Stars appeared in the crooked strip of sky above the valley. The voice of the river grew as sleep settled over the bivouac and darkness intensified the mental gloom of those still awake. Red men, as well as white, were subject to the oppressive dread. About their camp-fire, Bouyer, the half-breed Sioux, Half Yellow Face, the Crow, and Bloody Knife conversed in sign talk. As Godfrey passed, Bouyer checked him with apprehensive questions. The guide heard without conviction the soldier's boast that the 7th Cavalry could whip the Sioux.

"Well," he shrugged. "I can tell you we're going to have a God-damned big fight."

Stars swung above the sleeping regiment; above the *Far West*, tied for the night a few hours' run up-stream from the Rosebud's mouth; above the bivouac of Gibbon's column, en route for the Bighorn. Reveille did not sound in the 7th Cavalry's camp on the morning of June twenty-third. At three o'clock, the horse guards shook the troopers from their slumbers.

Sunlight slanted through smoke of spent camp-fires when the column moved at five A. M. Already a screen of scouts—Arikaras,

Crows and whites—had gone forward under Varnum. Custer led
the regiment out. The reorganized pack-train was massed at the
column's tail and Benteen's H Troop brought up the rear. Mules
strayed and straggled and lost their packs.

Encroaching bluffs blocked the regiment's advance. In the first
three miles, the column forded the Rosebud five times. Then, on the
right, the valley widened. Five miles farther along the timber-
dotted level bank Custer found the trail he sought.

There were many circles of packed earth where lodges had stood.
Bent brush showed where wickiups—temporary shelters—had been
fashioned. Grazing ponies had "clipped the grass, almost like a
lawn mower," and beyond the litter of the camp, a broad trail ran
up-stream churned by hoofs, raked by dragging lodge-poles.

Scouts gathered about Custer. He shook his head and turning to
Lieutenant Varnum, said:

"Here's where Reno made the mistake of his life. He had six
troops of cavalry and rations enough for a number of days. He'd
have made a name for himself if he'd pushed on after them."

The hunt was up. The buckskin-clad horseman pushed forward
and behind him the mounting metallic roar told of the cavalry's
quickened pace. Five miles they hurried and then were forced to
halt and wait for the pack-train to catch up. When the mules at
last rejoined the column, it pushed on, forded the Rosebud, rode
fifteen miles up the left bank, crossed the stream again and camped
in the old wreckage of Indian travel on the right shore. On either
side the stream, hills rolled back, lightly timbered, scored by
deep ravines. There was scant grazing that night for horses that
had done thirty-three miles.

Fires were extinguished after supper. Men slept soddenly beneath the sparkling sky. This arched above the Gibbon column,
in bivouac on the Yellowstone's north bank opposite the Bighorn's mouth; above the *Far West*, tied up farther down-stream.
The stern-wheeler came abreast of Gibbon's command on the
morning of June twenty-fourth shortly after the 7th Cavalry had
resumed its march.

At daybreak, Crow scouts had reported to Custer that the trail
ahead was broader and fresher. In the face of these tidings he
could not bear to match his pace to the deliberation of the mule-
hampered column. He took two troops and rode far in advance.
Almost every loop of the river now was stamped with the circles

of vanished lodges. Broken branches and pony droppings and the ashes of fires told him how swiftly he was overhauling the quarry.

Custer and his escort passed the lashed sapling framework of a dance lodge and a brown withered object swung therefrom in the wind. Crows identified it as a white man's scalp, probably of a 2nd Cavalry trooper killed in a brush with the Sioux during Gibbon's march down the Yellowstone. Crows also reported that over the ridge to the right lay the headwaters of Tullock's Creek and that they had seen what looked like smoke signals down its valley.

At noon, Custer halted and when his regiment rejoined him, ordered coffee made. Varnum and the scouts had ridden on ahead. While the column rested on the Rosebud's right bank, Custer summoned his officers. They gathered where his headquarters flag, staff thrust in the earth, whipped in the steady blast of a south wind, and again at this conference something was wrong. It may have been the nervousness of their leader; it may have been prescience of impending disaster. Whatever its source, many of the officers were in the jumpy state of mind that is receptive to ill omen.

They heard their commander's tidings. The trail was freshening hourly. Custer believed the smoke reported from the Tullock's Valley to be only mist. When scouts in the advance sent back word, the regiment would move on, but with increased caution. Each troop would take a separate course so as to diminish the dust of the march.

The officers were dismissed. As Godfrey started to leave, the wind blew over Custer's headquarters flag. It fell toward the rear. Godfrey recovered and replanted it. It fell toward the rear. He picked it up and dug its staff into the earth, supporting it against a sage-brush. It stood now but some of those who had marked its double fall saw an augury of defeat.

At four, scouts returned and reported to Custer. He led his regiment forward and again they forded the Rosebud. The stream's left bank was ridged by the passage of unnumbered lodge poles. Hourly, the wide trail of the Sioux grew heavier and fresher. The regiment camped at seven-forty-five below a bluff. It had marched twenty-six miles. Fires were small and soon extinguished. Horses were not unsaddled. Mules retained their packs. The whisper ran through the bivouac that scouts still were following the trail, which had left the river's edge and now inclined westward. If it crossed the divide into the valley of the Little Bighorn, so rumor muttered, the regiment would march that night. Meanwhile, weary men rolled up in their blankets and caught what sleep they could. At the mouth of Tullock's Creek, forty-five miles distant in a bee-line, Terry camped with the men of Gibbon's column.

Gibbon himself lay on the *Far West* while the boat worked her way up the Bighorn. He had been stricken with intestinal colic and did not rejoin his command until June twenty-sixth.

A company of infantry and a Gatling had been left on the Yellowstone's north bank to guard the command's surplus stores. The rest of the infantry, Brisbin's Squadron of the 2nd Cavalry and two Gatlings had been ferried across the stream and had marched up the Bighorn to the Tullock's mouth.

Earlier in the day, twelve of the bravest of Gibbon's Crows had been sent to scout up Tullock's Creek. They had gone ten miles, seen a wounded buffalo and had stampeded back. They were afraid of the Sioux.

In Custer's camp men slept and horses and mules had grazed. Beyond the wide scar of the Indian trail, grass was abundant, for the Sioux had not tarried here. At nine that night the scouts returned. Reno's earlier report had been correct. The trail ran over the divide into the valley of the Little Bighorn.

Circumstance deals Custer one more thrust. It had small subsequent part in the development of the tragedy. His own hands, his own headstrong, headlong spirit contrived it. Yet fate intervenes here, as accessory.

The trail he has followed has been made, so his scouts have told him, by four hundred lodges. There have been wickiups too. In all, perhaps fifteen hundred warriors have crossed the Wolf Mountains into the Little Bighorn Valley. This is the estimate Custer has given his officers. It is probably accurate. But these fifteen hundred warriors are only a fraction of the host assembled on the Little Bighorn. A portion, and only a portion, of the greatest mobilization of Indian might this continent ever saw had met Crook on the upper reaches of the Rosebud June seventeenth and had beaten him back. The Indians whom Custer followed had taken no part in that fight. They were additional reenforcements to the hostiles, but the man who followed them had no knowledge of this.

Circumstance or the luck whose darling Custer had been, turns against him now as his scouts report and he sends his orderlies to wake and summon his officers. He does not know that Crook has been defeated. He is rashly certain that the Sioux he follows are all his regiment will have to face. This is fate's part in his destruction.

Officers, roused by the questing orderlies, stumbled through windrows of slumbering men and toward the bright speck in the gloom that was a candle on Custer's table. The conference was brief.

Custer told his blinking and disheveled subordinates the course of the trail and his intention of getting as close to the top of the divide as possible before daybreak, there to hide and attack on the twenty-sixth. He ordered them to be ready to march at eleven-thirty. Varnum with Reynolds, Bouyer, the Crows and some Arikaras had been sent to a peak overlooking the farther valley. Lieutenant Hare of Troop K was detailed to command the remaining scouts.

The officers returned to their troops. Gradually, as the hour for the march approached, the valley filled with clamor. Soldiers, freshly wakened, found their mounts and sought their places in the column by a universal and noisy game of blind man's buff. Mules brayed and horses whinnied. Officers bawled for strayed members of their troops and these shouted back. The clatter of arms and equipment, the tumult of voices filled the black valley with confused and doleful sound.

They were to march at eleven-thirty. They did not get under way till after midnight. The reassembling of the regiment took time. There was renewed difficulty with the mules and it was an interminable job for Mathey and Keogh, who had the rear-guard, to collect the beasts and start them forward. At last Custer, with Fred Girard, interpreter, and Half Yellow Face, the Crow, moved out at the head of his command.

Girard was of the many who warned his chief of the Indian might. While they waited for the column to get under way, Custer asked the interpreter how many hostiles they were likely to meet. Girard told him at least twenty-five hundred but the estimate was offered to a man apparently deaf.

Once the regiment marched, the clamor and the confusion multiplied. The column's actual course is not certain, but the best evidence indicates that it strove to follow the valley of Davis Creek, a tributary of the Rosebud, up to the divide. The sky was clouded and darkness was curdled further by the mounting dust. No man could see the rider ahead of him. The blind column proceeded chiefly by scent and hearing. Men who no longer breathed dust knew that they had strayed from the line of march. Some troopers beat their tin cups against their saddles to aid those who followed. There was shouting and much heartfelt swearing and now and then an explosive rattle and thumping as a horse fell. Any Indian in a range of several miles and not stone deaf must have heard that uproarious advance.

At length, even Custer perceived the vanity of further tumultuous groping. Scouts assured him he could not possibly reach the ridge before daybreak and word was passed back, halting the disrupted column which had marched ten miles. Dawn found its scattered elements in the valley of the dwindling stream. Its water was so bitter with alkali that horses and mules would not drink it. Coffee made therefrom scored men's throats.

Dawn also found Varnum and his men asleep at the foot of the rocky pinnacle on the ridge's crest that red men called the Crow's Nest. As the dim mass took form against the paling sky, Hairy Moccasin, the smallest and most alert of the Crows, left his slumbering companions and climbed to its top. Varnum was wakened by his voice and saw the Indian stamped against gray heaven.

The Lieutenant and the others swarmed up the peak. On either hand, earth fell away in fir-dappled slopes of gray rock. Far down the eastern slant, the smoke of the 7th Cavalry's fires crept up across a watery daybreak and the Crows snarled. Did Custer think, they asked, that the Sioux were blind?

To the West, the land went down in broken steps to a wide valley where night still dwelt. They watched one another's faces grow sharper in the quickening light. They saw the timber-shielded Little Bighorn snaking its way across the plain. Then, one by one, the Indians exclaimed and stared to the north.

The morning mist seemed thicker and darker there and beneath it was the sense rather than the sight of movement, a confused wide-spread stirring. The Crows jabbered in awed voices and Reynolds said mildly: "That's the biggest pony herd any man ever saw."

"Biggest village," Bouyer amended. "A heap too big."

Light grew stronger. The sun was coming up behind gray clouds. Varnum's strained eyes were bleared by seventy hours' scouting with scant sleep.

"Look for worms," Bouyer advised him, for the movement of the vast and distant pony herd was like the pulsating and twitching of tangled angleworms. Still Varnum saw nothing, but the excitement of those about him left no room for doubt. He scribbled a hasty note to Custer and sent it down-hill by an Arikara.

The regiment, when the messenger reached it shortly before eight A. M., still rested in the valley where it had made its fires. Custer, on receiving Varnum's note, leaped bareback on his horse and rode through his command shouting to his officers to be ready to march by eight o'clock. When he returned to the column's head, Bloody Knife approached him, face glowering with earnestness.

There were too many Sioux yonder, Custer's favorite scout told his chief. It would take days to kill them all. The Glory-Hunter laughed. The imminence of an enemy had restored his pre-battle elation.

"Oh," he retorted tolerantly, "I guess we'll get through them in one day," and swinging into the saddle, gave the order for the advance.

For two hours and a half, the regiment crawled up the hostile slope, gray rock below, gray sky above. Clouds still hid the sun's brilliance but not its heat. The air grew sultry so that the upward scrambling men and horses sweltered under an ash white sky. The regiment marched ten miles and then, a mile or so from the ridge's summit, hid in a ravine at Custer's order while he himself rode ahead to the Crow's Nest.

Varnum and his scouts still kept vigil there. Custer listened skeptically to their report of a colossal village to northward and with scarcely more credulity to the tale of Sioux who had been seen, scouting along ridges above the cavalry's advance. He stared into distance that swam in plum-colored haze and shook his head; clapped field-glasses to his eyes and looked long again. Despite the insistence of the Indians, despite the efforts of Reynolds and Bouyer to help him see, Custer rasped at last:

"I've been on the plains a good many years. My eyesight is as good as yours. I can't see anything that looks like Indian ponies."

Bouyer blurted: "If you don't find more Indians in that valley than you ever saw before, you can hang me."

"All right, all right, all right," Custer rattled with a short laugh. "It would do a damned lot of good to hang you, wouldn't it?"

In the distance hung the blue haze of lodge smoke. Dim beneath its veil crawled the enormous pony herd. Custer left the lookout, still insisting that he saw no sign of Indians; that he believed none were there. The waiting regiment had gained meanwhile more definite evidence of the presence of the Sioux.

Sergeant Curtis of Troop F had lost clothing from his saddle roll on the march up-hill. While the regiment sweated in the ravine, waiting its chief's return, Curtis obtained permission from Captain Yates to ride back in search of the missing raiment. Presently, he came galloping to report to Yates that he had found, not what he sought, but a breadbox, dropped from one of the mules. About the box had been Indians, Sioux, who had fled at his approach.

Yates told Keogh who informed Cook, the adjutant, who, when Custer returned to the hiding regiment, informed his chief.

That morning of June twenty-fifth, Terry lingered on Tullock's Creek, expecting Custer's courier. He marched three and a third miles up the valley in hope of meeting him and sent Lieutenant Bradley and fifteen mounted infantry still farther. The Crows would not go. They feared the Sioux.

From the concealing ravine on the eastern slope of the Wolf Mountains, where weary men drowsed and thirsty horses stood with drooping heads, a trumpet spoke. That brazen voice, silent for sixty hours past, tore through the sultry air, bounced echoing from the gray cliffs. It shouted officers' call, and those who had not already gathered about Custer scrambled up the ravine's side and joined him.

It was then about eleven-thirty on the morning of June twenty-fifth.

Men who had marched all the day before and most of the night were too weary for many questions; too spent perhaps to see the paradox in their leader's orders. Despite the insistence and the warnings of his scouts, Custer did not believe there were Indians in the Valley of the Little Bighorn. Since scouts and Sergeant Curtis had seen the Sioux, it would be useless to hide here any longer. The regiment would move at once toward a foe in whose existence its commander disbelieved. Each troop would march as it made ready. Benteen's men were the first to lurch up out of the ravine.

The others followed. Behind them, Mathey with seven soldiers from each troop and five or six civilian packers herded along the one hundred and sixty mules of the train. McDougall's B Troop, forty-five strong, brought up the rear.

The cloudy sky burned white before the vertical sun. Heat soaked into dusty men and sweating horses as the re-formed column toiled up to the divide and went over its ridge. Five hundred and ninety-odd soldiers, plus scouts, interpreters and packers, rode down beneath a pillar of dust to the Little Bighorn.

They caught, as they crossed the summit, glimpses of an olive green valley, fifteen miles away. They marked where, to the north, heat haze was tinged with blue and wondered dully at Custer's skepticism. That surely was smoke. It was now seven minutes past twelve P. M. and the trail they followed went down-hill.

There was ground for further wonder immediately thereafter. Custer spoke to Benteen whose troop was foremost in the column. The white-haired Captain turned in his saddle, bawled an order and swung left oblique out of the line of march, moving toward a line of bluffs four miles away with Troops H, D and K—his own, Weir's and Godfrey's.

Reno, still without command, unconsulted by Custer and aggrieved, flung a question at Benteen as he passed.

"Going to those hills to drive everything before me," the Captain replied dryly and led his squadron onward. The Major had scant time to brood over this new evidence of neglect, for Cook, Custer's adjutant, rode up to him and announced:

"The General directs that you take specific command of Companies M, A and G."

"Is that all?" Reno asked as the Adjutant turned and Cook flung assent over his shoulder.

The Chief Trumpeter galloped away on the course Benteen had taken and, overhauling him, delivered additional directions from Custer. If no Indians were found on the first line of bluffs, the Captain should proceed to another farther line.

The column, meanwhile, scraped and slithered down the irregular folds of the mountainside. It followed still the Indian trail that bordered the course of a little stream, called Sundance then and later renamed Reno Creek. The Major had assumed command

of Moylan's, McIntosh's and French's troops. He led them along
the left bank of the watercourse. Custer, with his brother's Troop
C, Smith's E, Yates's F, Keogh's I and Calhoun's L, went down
along the right bank. Apprehensive Arikaras and Crows under
Varnum and Hare moved before the twin columns. With Custer
rode his brother Boston, his young nephew and namesake, Armstrong Reed, and Mark Kellogg, the correspondent.

Benteen was out of sight now, but Custer turned and spoke to
Sergeant-Major W. W. Sharrow who trotted off, to bear to the
senior Captain further elaboration of the original orders. If
neither line of bluffs yielded Indians, Benteen was to move into
the valley beyond and if this proved barren into the valley beyond that.

Meanwhile, in columns of twos, Custer's five troops and Reno's
three rode toward the Little Bighorn. The sunless heat weighed
down the men. Dust plastered the flanks and barrels of reeking
horses. Ridges on either hand had closed in upon the command so
that, as they descended, they caught no further sight of the valley. Stunted firs were aromatic in lifeless air that shook to the
dull sound of hoofs, the quarreling voices of leather and steel, the
mumbling speech of tired soldiers. Already the pack-train with
all supplies and reserve ammunition had lagged behind.

So they rode for eight or ten miles, dazed by fatigue, wilted by
heat—Reno's one hundred and twelve, Custer's two hundred and
twenty-five men—while the stream that parted them deepened and
grew vocal and the sharp pitches of the ridges flattened. Rocks
and dwarfed firs crept past and vanished. Bare rolling foot-hills
succeeded them, curved earthen surges, olive with the browning
grass of spring. Through these the stream twisted and the trail
still followed it.

When they had marched ten or twelve miles, the Indian trail
ran wholly along the creek's right bank. Custer signaled with his
white hat for Reno to cross. The Major obeyed. His three troops
followed. The two commands moved down the stream's right side,
parallel and fifty yards apart. Lieutenant Wallace, who kept the
column's itinerary, looked at his watch. It was two P. M.

They had seen no Indians. The nervous scouts who preceded
the column on a trail now alarmingly fresh had caught no glimpse
of the Sioux. Then, in the valley before them, they saw the brown

lonely cone of a single lodge. Its smoke vent was empty. No dogs, no children moved about its latched door-flaps.

Arikaras approached it with increasing boldness, at last tore open its entrance. A dead warrior lay with his gear beside him, a brother of Circling Bear, Sioux chief. He had died in the fight with Crook eight days before. As a spiteful blow against their enemies, the Arikaras set fire to the lodge.

The columns had halted. Girard, scout and interpreter, rode to a knoll. The lodge burned reluctantly with pallid flames and a towering smoke. Girard from his lookout yelled to Custer.

"Thar go yore Injuns, runnin' like devils."

Custer joined him and saw beyond the knoll some forty Sioux warriors cantering their ponies toward the river and yelping derision. He shouted for the Arikaras to follow them. They glowered and refused, nor could his scornful suggestion that they turn in their weapons and go home shake them free from terror.

There were at least some Indians in this valley despite the scoffing of Custer. He had seen them. His eager voice stiffened aching spines and tightened faces that had sagged with weariness. The twin column lunged forward at a trot, at a gallop. Side by side they roared down the valley, and Cook, veering from Custer's side, ranged his horse alongside Reno's. Orders jolted from him:

"The Indians," Cook shouted, long black whiskers streaming, "are about two and a half miles ahead and on the jump. Follow them as fast as you can and charge them and we will support you."

Reno galloped on with the Adjutant and Keogh who had followed on his charger, Comanche. Custer slackened pace so that the distance between the Major's column and his increased. It was then two-fifteen P.M.

The Indian trail the 7th had followed for days crossed to the left bank of the creek. Reno's three troops pursued it. A hill thrust in between them and Custer's command, blocking further views of the laggards. Ahead were trees and the glitter of moving water. Above foliage, a great dust-cloud rose in the northwest.

Cook and Keogh accompanied Reno's command to the river. Girard rode to another knoll that gave him clear view downstream. There was delay at the ford. The horses waded into the Little Bighorn's flow and thrust parched muzzles deep. They would not cross until they had drunk. The Arikara scouts were unwilling to cross at all. They listened sullenly to Varnum's exhortations and some of them vanished.

Gradually Reno got his command to the farther bank. Cook and Keogh shouted, "Good luck," and turned to rejoin Custer. Girard rode down from the knoll. He had seen the source of the great dust. Beneath it were Indians, many Indians, rushing upstream along the river's left bank. The scout hailed Cook and told of his discovery.

Cook replied: "All right. I'll go and report."

The Adjutant rode back to Custer. On the stream's far bank, Reno was forming. Varnum, half frantic, shouted to Girard that the Arikaras refused to go farther. In their own tongue, Girard lashed them and a dozen crossed the river with him, Varnum and Hare, Reynolds, Dorman, the negro, and other scouts.

Bellowing officers subdued confusion on the Little Bighorn's left bank. Troopers guided their dripping mounts into place. The command solidified. Reno took his place at its head and gathered in his charger's rein. Nervous horses reared. The Major called:

"Take your time. There are enough ahead for all of us."

Before him rolled a plain, bordered on the left by shelving higher ground, on the right by timber-shielded loops of the river. Farther to the right, across the stream, were brown cliffs, ravine scored, and above their broken perpendiculars, treeless hills went back toward the gray, fir stippled ridges of the Wolf Mountains.

Ahead of the Major for two miles, the plain ran drab, undulant and empty. Then a peninsula of timber, thrust out to the left from the river bank, cut off more distant view and above the leafy barrier, the dust-cloud towered. Reno looked at the ranked column behind him. Beyond it, the ford was empty. No brilliant figure in buckskin led five troops into support. The Major turned to Trooper McIlargy, his striker, and bade him ride to Custer with news that the Indians were coming in force. Then, rising in his stirrups, he shouted his orders:

"Left into line. Guide center. Gallop."

The column woke. Fours shifted and wove. The line spread out across the valley and moved forward. Presently when through dust behind him, the Major still could see no sign of support, he sent Trooper Mitchell, a cook, back with a further, more urgent message to Custer.

Neither McIlargy nor Mitchell ever was seen again. They were killed in passage or else they died on the heights with Custer.

The Glory-Hunter had not followed Reno to the ford. He had led his men at a trot on the Major's trail. Then, for reasons no man may ever know, Custer had swung sharply to the right and had ridden up into the brown hills to the north. The men of Keogh and Smith, Yates, Calhoun and Tom Custer had followed him down-stream above the bluffs that walled the Little Bighorn's right bank; down-stream behind the flutter of the familiar blue and red pennant; down-stream, away from Reno and into a nation's Valhalla.

Across the river in the valley below, Girard thought he glimpsed Yate's gray horse troop, riding hard along the ridges, and Lieutenant De Rudio insisted that later Custer had appeared on a height above the plain and had waved his hat.

Meanwhile, Reno went down the valley before his line and looked often over his shoulder for the promised support. Behind him galloped Moylan's Troop A and French's M, strung out across the plain with Varnum's scouts and reluctant Indians on the left against the higher ground. In the rear McIntosh's Troop G rode in reserve.

The squadron swung around the peninsula of timber that obscured the lower valley. Before them, as though earth were ablaze, the dust-cloud smoked to heaven. Above the roar of the advance, men could hear from that bilious murk high voices—Sioux voices—screeching like souls in torment, and where the dust thinned, momentarily, horsemen moved and feathers were slivers of light in the haze.

Out of that prototype of later smoke-screens, Indians darted, screaming, to fire and vanish. Up from before the charging line, sprang a Cadmean crop of warriors. Ahead of the troopers, a ravine split the plain. It was full of Sioux. And the valley behind Reno was empty of support.

Facing the half-hidden host before him, one hundred and twelve troopers seemed dauntingly few to Reno. He had not even the dubious aid of his Indian allies now. At the first whoop of the Sioux, all these save Bloody Knife and one or two more had vanished, leaving Varnum and Hare to hold the left flank with a handful of scouts. G Troop was thrown into line to fill that gap.

Reno marked the ravine ahead. Military· training, or more human caution, told him the Sioux who advanced only to retreat were not afraid. They were luring him into ambuscade. He flung up his hand and dragged on his charger's rein.

"Halt," Reno shouted before his charge had struck a single enemy, or his troopers had fired a shot. "Halt! Prepare to fight on foot."

There was a moment of plunging confusion. At least one unhappy recruit was carried on by his bolting mount into the shrill obscurity ahead, to return no more. The horse-holders, veterans all, each galloped four steeds back into the shelter of the timber. The thin line of footmen wavered and shrank from the crackle of bullets overhead, the sibilant flight of arrows. Then it steadied and began earnestly to bang away at yelping horsemen who swooped and wheeled like swallows in the yellow gloom.

The line plodded forward a hundred yards. A breath of air lifted the dust-screen an instant and men saw a host of horsemen and beyond them unnumbered lodges. The line advanced no farther. It knelt or lay and shot as rapidly as it might into the cloud ahead that hid no man knew what enormity. Sergeant Hynes of Troop A was dead. One or two more had been hit. The Sioux wheeled and came closer, blazing away at the troopers who replied quickly and blindly. The accuracy of both reds and whites was deplorable. The rapid fire heated the trooper's Springfields and cartridges jammed in the breeches. Men had to cut out the empty shells before they could shoot again.

Word came from the timber that Sioux were massing on the stream's far bank, that Sioux were crossing to get at the horses. Reno withdrew G Troop from the firing line and sent it back to protect the animals. Still, there was no sign of Custer and through the Major's mind may have crept the recollection of the scandalous regimental legend concerning another Major of the 7th Cavalry, Elliot by name.

Others were conscious of Custer's betrayal of his promise. Wallace, who had heard Cook's orders to Reno and who had remained on the firing line when McIntosh, his commander, had withdrawn his troop to the timber, bawled to Captain Moylan that some one ought to be sent to hurry up support. Both officers pled with Billy Jackson, a half-breed scout. He shook his head and waved to the rear.

"No one," he shouted, "could get through that."

There were Sioux behind as well as before the line now and more were sweeping around the weak left flank or pouring down from the heights on the left. The troopers were being surrounded on the open plain. There still was equivocal safety in the timber. The line went back to the shelter of brush and the few large trees.

Here was confusion. Officers lost their commands in the thickets. Horses plunged. Sioux bullets slashed through foliage or smacked against solid wood. Mounted Indians swarmed about the timbered peninsula, firing and screaming in high fierce voices. Others on foot worked up from the river and set the wood on fire.

Reno's ammunition was growing low, thanks to recruits who fired more for the comfort of the sound than for marksmanship. The Sioux were filtering through a line too thin to defend the entire grove. The defense bent backward from the river side of the wood. The Indians crawled forward. Dust billowed in from the plain, where screeching Sioux circled. The tangle of brush and cottonwoods filled with a brawling, fearful sound—panicky banging of guns, white shouting and savage screeching, screams of horses and the harsh rip of bullets through foliage. One hundred-odd men were surrounded by thrice their number and more Indians continually were arriving from the village. It was now about three-thirty P. M. Where was the promised support? Where was Custer?

History cannot see him. Glory, for whom he rode northward through the hills, is mute. Even the route over which he led two hundred and twenty-five men to death is in dispute. All men ever will know surely of that last red hour is contained in the brief recitals of two who saw only its dawn—Daniel A. Kanipe, of Carolina, sergeant in Tom Custer's Troop C, and Trumpeter John Martin, born Giovanni Martini and a Garibaldi veteran, who had been detailed from Benteen's Troop H, to serve as orderly to the Regiment's commander.

When Custer turned toward the hills, two ways were open to him. Beyond the first ridge that crowned the bluffs above the Little Bighorn, a shallow valley runs northward. Beyond a second ridge to the east of this valley, is another ravine, and many hold it was along this that the five troops rode. Since men with Reno believed they saw Custer and portions of his command on the heights and since, furthermore, he twice rode to a promontory to survey the valley below, it is probable that he led his men along the westerly ravine. They rode at a gallop. The pace was so hard that some of the weary horses gave out. The riders of two of these later joined Reno.

Somewhere, early in that rush northward, the troopers caught a glimpse of the dust-enveloped Little Bighorn. Kanipe says they cheered at the sight and Custer cried: "Hold your horses, boys. There's plenty down there for all of us."

The rounded hills cut off their view. They galloped farther. In a breathing space, Tom Custer called Kanipe, who, long after, remembered his instructions thus:

"Go to Captain McDougall. Tell him to bring the pack train straight across country. If any packs come loose, cut them and come on quick. A big Indian village. If you see Captain Benteen, tell him to come quick. A big Indian village."

Kanipe swung his horse out of line and spurred it back. The column launched into a gallop again. At its head, the Glory-Hunter rode. Behind his bright sorrel, Vic, pounded the horse of his orderly, Trumpeter Martin. Here is the testimony of the last white survivor to see George Armstrong Custer alive:

"There was a big bend on the hill; he turned these hills and went on top of the ridge. All at once, we looked on the bottom and saw the Indian village. At the same time we could only see children and dogs and ponies—no Indians at all. General Custer appeared to be glad and supposed the Indians were asleep in their tepees. We could not see the timber because it was under the hill—nor anything of Reno's column. I rode about two yards from General Custer.

"After he saw the village he pulled off his hat and gave a cheer and said: 'Courage, boys, we will get them and as soon as we get them, then we will go back to our station.'

"We went more to the right from the ridge and down to a ravine that led to the river. It the time General Custer passed the high place on the ridge, or a little below it, he told his adjutant to send an order back to Captain Benteen. I don't know what it was. Then the Adjutant called me—I was right at the rear of the General—and said, 'Orderly, I want you to take this dispatch to Captain Benteen and go as fast as you can.' "

Martin, the second messenger, rides back along the trail Kanipe already has taken. Behind him Custer and the five troops vanish, with pounding hoofs and the roar of equipment, in a dust-cloud that is the forerunner of eternal glory.

From the ridge Custer has looked down upon a myriad brown cones of lodges, stippling for more than three miles the Little Bighorn's western bank. He has seen the earlier warnings of his scouts made manifest. He who had scoffed at these discovers they had been underestimates. This is the village whose existence he has doubted and it is incredibly vast.

A year later, General Hugh L. Scott, then a lieutenant in the 7th Cavalry, came to the Little Bighorn Valley on the expedition sent to rebury the dead. Scott counted along the stream the sites of eighteen hundred lodges and never completed his tally. There were many wickiups as well. Men have estimated the strength of the host that broke the 7th Cavalry at all the way from twelve hundred and fifty to eight thousand warriors. Scott's count proves that there must have been at least four thousand and against them Custer rode with a total force of less than six hundred troopers.

At first sight of that village, he should have read omen in its sinister quiet. He knew Indians too well to believe that at midday they were sleeping, as Martin reports. The trumpeter's English was faulty. Custer probably said that he had "caught the enemy napping." Elation rather than alarm seems to have possessed him, yet he sent at once to recall Benteen and the note Cook scribbled and Martin bore has the disjointed haste of panic. It read:

"Benteen, come on—big village—be quick—bring packs.
                                         W. W. Cook.
"P. S. Bring packs."

With that frantic message, the history of George Armstrong Custer ends. In the blank that intervenes before men found his stripped body, unnumbered theories flourish.

In the river bottom, Reno with three troops strives to hold back a rising red tide.

Miles away to the southeast, Benteen with three troops is growing weary of a "wild-goose chase" that reveals only more and more broken land and no Indians.

Miles up the trail from the divide, Mathey and eighty men struggle with the lagging pack-train.

Behind this, McDougall and his troop fume.

Martin sees the dust smoke up as Custer leads his two hundred and twenty-five down toward the Valley of the Little Bighorn. The rest of his last pursuit of glory is hidden from men.

One more adherent rides hard to join George Armstrong Custer in death. A mile or so back along the trail, Martin, his last messenger, encounters Boston Custer. Earlier in the day the young man's horse had failed him and he had returned to the pack-train for another. He flings a question at Martin who grins and points the way. Boston spurs his mount along the endless road his brothers and nephew, Reed, and brother-in-law, Calhoun, already have taken.

Benteen had grown tired of "valley hunting." His choleric mouth grew ever tighter about the stem of his pipe. Lieutenant Gibson of his troop and six skirmishers preceded his column. Part of the time, the Captain rode ahead even of them. There had been no Indians beyond the first line of bluffs, or the second, and continually the country grew rougher, pushing him out of his original line of march toward the down-hill trail Reno and Custer had followed.

Benteen at last gave up the hunt, technically disobeying his commander's orders, and definitely turned back to rejoin Custer. The column came out of the badlands where Sundance Creek spread a marshy pool beside the trail Custer and Reno had traveled about two hours earlier. It halted there to water suffering horses. These had marched some thirty miles in fifteen hours without a drink. It was now three-thirty P. M.

As Benteen's command moved off from the pool, the first mules of the pack-train came charging down-hill, attendant troops cursing horribly, and plunged into the water. Benteen moved on, passing the smoldering tepee that Custer's scouts had fired. Kanipe came riding. He grinned as the troopers cheered, shouted that the Indians were "on the run" and after reporting to Benteen, went on to the pack-train.

Two miles from the ford where Reno crossed, Trumpeter Martin approached, spurring a weary horse. Indians had fired on him and a bullet had wounded his mount. He had not known this till Benteen pointed it out. The Captain read Cook's message. Martin smiled confidently in response to his questions:

"Eenjuns," he reported, "eesa skedaddling."

Benteen scribbled a note to McDougall and sent Martin on up the trail, showed Cook's message to Captain Weir whose troop was in advance, and then went down toward the river at a smart trot. The valley was filled with smoke and dust and the squadron heard the far popping of gun-fire. An Indian came up from the ford, driving captured ponies ahead of him. It was Half Yellow Face, the Crow, who, when Benteen bawled a question about the soldiers, pointed toward a bluff on the column's right.

Meanwhile dust and smoke had darkened the grove where Reno's three troops were besieged. The banging of Springfields had a panicky sound. There was the lilt of imminent triumph in the Indians' yells. No responsive, reassuring cheer echoed the shouts of beleagured officers and men. No trumpet split the tumult to signal approach of Custer's promised support. No trumpet proclaimed to the scattered troops Reno's determination to leave the timber. The Major gave the order which some heard and some did not.

Those who obeyed led their horses into a clear space in the grove's center and mounted there. As the column was forming Sioux fired pointblank from a thicket. A trooper of M screamed, "O God, I've got it!" and pitched from his horse. Bloody Knife, the valiant Arikara, was at Reno's side. The Major heard the thwack of the bullet that split his skull. Reno launched his "charge" from the timber.

He left his dead and wounded. A dozen troopers and Lieutenant De Rudio of Troop A, Herendeen, Reynolds and other scouts were deserted in the grove. At the head of Troop A in column of fours, with part of G following and M in the rear, Reno rode out and made for the ford by which he had crossed.

The plain swarmed with Indians, "thick as trees in an orchard," who gave way, wolf fashion, before the column's head, and, wolf-like, ranged along its right flank to pull down the weak and laggard. Painted bodies burned dimly in the dust. The haze shook with shrill yelling and the uneven roar of gun-fire. Sioux laid their rifles across their ponies' withers and pumped lead into the fleeing column. Sioux watched until men had emptied their revolvers, then closing in, shot or stabbed them. Lieutenant Donald McIntosh of Troop G, the half-breed Indian, was killed close to the timber. Lonesome Charley Reynolds died therein and those who later found his headless body counted sixty empty cartridges about it. Isaiah Dorman, the negro interpreter, was slain there too.

More and more Sioux ranged along the column's right flank as though the desperate troopers were buffalo. The catlike ponies leaped in toward soldiers whose guns were empty, the screaming riders slipped from sight behind their mounts when cavalrymen aimed at them.

Varnum, aghast at the mounting panic of the retreat, ran his horse to the head of Troop A, shouting:

"For God's sake, boys, don't run. Don't let them whip us."

A voice replied sharply: "I am in command here, sir!"

It was Reno's. He rode in the forefront of the retreat.

The head of the column kept fair order, but the rear frayed and was increasingly lashed by terror. The pressure of the Sioux forced the command away from the ford by which it had entered the valley. The war yell soared higher, Indian guns blazed as Troop A swung to the left and led by the Major, who had lost his hat, went over a five-foot bank into belly-deep water of the Little Bighorn.

The stream at this point was some twenty-five feet wide, and running full. The farther bank was eight feet high with a fissure therein whereby active horsemen might scramble up. Above, the bluff rose steeply, with narrow ravines scoring its high brown wall. There were Indians on the heights firing down at the troopers. There were ever more Indians on the west bank, shooting into their backs.

No effort was made to guard the ford, or to control the order in which terrified troopers plunged their mounts into the river. The breadth of water became a stew of thrashing horses, screaming men, foam and the small brief fountains struck by bullets. The fugitives could ascend the far bank only one by one. The stream was jammed with fear-roweled cavalry fighting for that single passage, while from the rear the Sioux poured in their fire. Many died there.

Doctor De Wolf, assistant surgeon, reached the far bank and there was killed. Lieutenant Benny Hodgson, Reno's adjutant and a favorite in the regiment, was wounded as he reached the west shore. He caught the stirrup of a trooper and was towed across, only to be shot through the head as he reached the east bank.

Spurring and lashing their horses, the survivors rode them up the ravine with ungainly rabbit-like jumps. On the plateau above, the breathless, hatless Major strove to reorganize the remaining half of his command. Men saw Benteen's three troops come riding toward them through the hills. It was now about four-thirty.

Reno, a handkerchief bound about his head, was firing his revolver at Indians far out of range when Benteen's column joined the remnants of his own. Varnum, wild with grief at the death of his friend Hodgson, was blazing away, equally vainly, with a carbine.

If the Sioux had followed, they might have rolled up over the Major and Benteen as well, but the gun-fire from the valley slackened and died, save for occasional snipers' shots. The horsemen began a quick movement down the valley.

Benteen, the grimly efficient, shared his troop's cartridges with Reno's survivors and organized the defense. A semicircle of higher peaks blocked view of the village and whatever down-stream event summoned the victorious Sioux. On the hill, nerve-shattered men cursed the name of Custer. Lieutenant Hare on Godfrey's horse rode back to the pack-train to hurry it in and to bring back with him ammunition mules.

Down-stream, to the north, men heard the brawl of guns. Not all those on the hill heard volleys, though to De Rudio and others, still trapped in the timber and saved later by the withdrawal of the Indians, the concerted blasts were plain. The firing rolled away to the north, and Captain Weir of Troop D muttered to his lieutenant, Edgerly, that Reno ought to move to the support of Custer.

Edgerly assented and Weir asked whether, if Reno permitted, the Lieutenant would follow his Captain toward Custer with Troop D. Edgerly agreed and when Weir, without authorization, rode out alone over the hills toward the north, Edgerly, presuming permission had been granted, led Troop D after its commander.

They reached a height from which they could look down the valley and saw the lodges standing along the stream and the unbelievably wide and slowly shifting carpet of the pony herd. On the hill three miles away, Indians swarmed like disturbed ants. There was no sign of Custer. It was now close to five P. M.

Hare had brought in two ammunition mules, with a trooper guiding each by the bridle and another behind, lashing the stubborn brute along. McDougall's troop, Mathey and the rest of the train, arrived about five o'clock. So few Indians remained that

Herendeen and eleven troopers abandoned in the timber were able to rejoin the command.

The reorganized column moved out in the direction Weir had taken, slowly and with difficulty for there were wounded and each of these had to be borne in a horse blanket by four men. At about six P. M. when the command reached the promontory where D Troop lingered, the Indians had completed the mission that had called them down-stream and were returning.

The column fell back toward its original position with French's A and Weir's D covering the retreat. The impatient Weir here learned the power of the Sioux. These came on so fast and in such numbers that the covering force turned into fugitives. Troops A and D went back like hunted rabbits. Godfrey's Troop K, dismounted, checked the pursuit and then retired. What remained of the 7th Cavalry stood at bay.

Benteen took charge of the defense, routing out skulkers, thrusting the troopers into line, barking orders with magnificent self-possession.

"Wallace," he shouted. "Form your troop here."

"Troop?" Wallace panted, grinning shakily, "I've got just three men."

"Very good. Form your three men here."

From higher ridges and peaks, that ringed the plateau where the soldiers lay, guns began to talk. The reports quickened, then blurred into a steady daunting roar. Bullets blew sand about the troopers and killed or wounded men and horses. The storm of lead continued while the sun went down, a red lacquer disk slipping through a rift in the cloud. The firing ebbed with dusk and ceased with darkness.

All night long, while the besieged fortified their position, a witches' sabbath endured in the valley. Great fires blazed and there rose wild yelling, the wailing minors of Indian song and the flat rhythm of many drums. There were trumpet calls, too, sounded in derision by some gifted Sioux, on an instrument taken from Custer's command. Troopers believed that their leader was returning or that Crook was riding to their rescue. It was a night of dread and of blasted hope, worse than terror. No one seems to have thought of going down to the river for the water they were to need so sorely on the morrow.

Some of the beleaguered were so utterly weary that they slum-

bered. Edgerly, waking, encountered Major Reno in the darkness
and remembered how the unhappy man exclaimed: "Great God,
I don't see how you can sleep!"

Up through the Bighorn Valley, Terry was marching that night
of June twenty-fifth. The *Far West* was moving up-stream with
Gibbon, still ill, on board. Terry had led the column across country
from the valley of Tullock's Creek. His attempt at a short-cut had
been disastrous. The command had become entangled in terrific
badlands. Terry's Crows were frightened and more useless with
every mile. There were no white guides with the column. Herendeen was with Reno's besieged command and Bouyer, who knew this
country like the palm of his hand, lay dead with Custer. The infantry halted at length, completely spent. Terry pressed on with
his cavalry. He had promised Custer, Terry told his staff, that he
would be at the foot of the Little Bighorn Valley on June twenty-
sixth.

They rode through blackness, intensified by rain. In the crooked
country, Low's Gatlings got lost and were found again and the
cavalry at last was stalled on a bluff above the Bighorn, from
which they were guided to camp on the shore by Little Face, one
of the less timorous Crows. Terry's men barely had gone to sleep
when the day began for Reno's.

The seven remaining troops of the 7th Cavalry had had scant
slumber. Through the hours of darkness, they had entrenched
desperately, digging rifle-pits with the three spades in the command, with knives and tin cups; piling dead animals and the packs
into redoubts. The horses and mules had been taken with the
wounded into a hollow on the plateau. The line the troops established was horseshoe shape, with the open end toward the bluff.
The ridges commanded it. When those to eastward grew sharp
against a faintly paling sky, the first Indian rifle heralded dawn.

All that morning, while showers came and went, a lead storm
beat upon the position. The troopers saw few Indians but a horde
waited in the valley for place on the firing-line, and within carbine
range hundreds invisible screeched and yelped and wreathed the
peaks with the smoke of a steady fusillade that battered against
barricades and frail earthworks; that killed mules and horses and
hit not a few men crouched behind inadequate protections. Reno
lost sixteen killed and forty-odd wounded on that hill.

Throughout the deadly blizzard, it was Benteen who best kept

head and heart. It was he who by direct action and by prompting
his Major, controlled the defense. The Indians crept close to his
side of the horseshoe. Benteen insisted that Reno lend him French's
troop from the other side of the defense and led H and M in a
charge that drove back the Sioux. White-haired, erect, imperturbable, he was immune to bullets and fear.

"Captain, sorr," Sergeant Mike Madden objected, "ye tell us
to keep down. It's yourself should keep down. They'll git ye."

"Oh, pshaw," Benteen grinned. "They can't hit me."

Madden later was wounded and lost a leg. It was Benteen who
gave the order for a charge that Reno led to clear the other side
of the horseshoe of an inward creeping enemy.

At ten that morning, the firing abated, dwindling into occasional sniping through which hardy souls stole down to the river,
dived under fire across a little beach and obtained precious water
for the wounded. Thereafter, the gusts of bullets came fitfully like
a failing storm. There was another heavy outburst at two, with
many flights of arrows, but this faded, and after three there was
no firing at all. Grimed and haggard men, who long had looked
at death, now stared without belief at life's incredible fairness.

Below them the valley filled with smoke. The Indians had fired
the grass. At seven that evening, the handful on the hill beheld
the awesome passage of the military might of the Sioux. Through
the shifting smoke-screen, the Indian host moved up-stream in
an enormous compact column, three miles in length, almost a mile
in breadth. They marched with the deliberation of the retreating
grizzly. The massed dark horsemen passed and vanished, followed by thin cheering from the survivors of the regiment that,
alone, could whip all hostiles on the plains.

That noon, June twenty-sixth, Terry, the convalescent Gibbon, the cavalry and guns, reached the Valley of the Little Bighorn and waited impatiently for the infantry to catch up. Bradley and the scouts had talked that morning to three Crows, Hairy
Moccasin, Goes Ahead and White Man Runs Him, who had called
across the bank-full Bighorn to the disbelieving troops that
Custer and all his men were dead. Thereafter all Indians still
remaining with the Terry-Gibbon column had deserted.

When the infantry joined him, Terry moved ahead. It was
Bradley, scouting in advance, who marked how the Sioux gathered
in the distance to contest farther passage. Toward dark, the

column bivouacked in hollow square. Two white scouts, Bostwick and Muggins Taylor, who had been sent to establish contact with Custer, returned angrily swearing that the country was "stiff with Sioux." In Terry's camp, the General and some others felt dread at which the rest of the officers scoffed. Nothing, the skeptical insisted, could happen to Custer, the eternally fortunate.

On the morrow, the Sioux were gone. Toward noon, Bradley and his scouts found on a hill, east of the Little Bighorn and opposite the northern end of the vanished village, the stripped bodies of many men.

Custer lay toward the northern end of a ridge whose slope went down to the river. He had fallen, not at the summit but a little way below it, and down the slope and along the ridge to the south were scattered the fragments of the command that had been burst apart and abolished by the power of the Sioux.

Some thirty men, including his brother, his nephew and most of his officers, had died close to Custer. Many of them were stripped. A few were mutilated. He himself had been shot in the left side and temple. With his dead about him he lay as, eight years earlier, the young and eager Major Elliot had lain, center of a ring of slain, on the frosty grass above the Washita.

The wounds that had killed George Armstrong Custer, Lieutenant-Colonel, 7th Cavalry, Brevet Major-General, United States of America, were not apparent. Among the blasted bodies that still bore impress of the fury which had passed over them, his was unmarred by agony or terror. He who found it wrote:

"His expression was rather that of a man who had fallen asleep and enjoyed peaceful dreams."

George Armstrong Custer well may have lain content. Glory, sought all his stormy life, was his at last and forever.

PIÑONES

The author of this charming sketch calls the piñon tree "a disarming and perfect creation of nature's." Dwarfed, dark blue-green, with henna-colored flaring cones, it bears fruit whose taste is "pine and sunshine and popcorn, and peanuts too in a way." At harvest time it provides abundant food and festival for the natives throughout the Southwest. (From *Piñon Country,* Duell, Sloan and Pearce, 1941.)

THE piñon tree is a disarming and perfect creation of nature's. I first touched and smelled it some twenty years ago, when my train was delayed for two hours on a February afternoon near Laguna Pueblo. I stepped down into the freshness and vastness of the diminutive forest and as I walked about among the blue-green odorous trees I felt like a giant, for over their heads was the horizon of the mountains. On a near-by hill was the ancient Indian town, the first pueblo I had ever seen. I was pleased that houses could be so unpretentious, built simply of the earth and leaving nothing to be improved upon. So with the little trees: they gave me the pleasure that comes of small perfect things which adapt their forces without scattering or waste. With the strength of their roots they plainly held the earth tight in its fight against erosion.

The piñon (Pinus edulis) is the most prominent characteristic of the Upper Sonoran life-zone, and does not occur outside it.

So you encounter the piñon chiefly in New Mexico and northern Arizona, but also to some extent in southern Utah and Colorado, west Texas, and northern Mexico when you reach an elevation of five thousand feet and pass from the hot shadeless plains to the coolness of rolling slopes and sharp inclines on the northern side of which snow lingers. In among the trees the blue grama grass begins to grow; for miles in every direction the land is spick and span as a well-cared-for park. You ride horseback through the dwarf groves for hours finding no more clutter than the occasional woodcutter leaves. Near a native or Indian town, the piñones and their constant companions, the sabinas (junipers), will be harvested for firewood, but generally without endangering their future growth.

Three-quarters of New Mexico and a great part of northern Arizona are Upper Sonoran, and so piñones are widespread. But in these regions you can quickly ascend from the Upper Sonoran to the Transition zone (where there is fishing and hunting among the big pines), or descend to the Lower Sonoran, where the mesquite and creosote plants cling to life with their elaborate leaflessness. Above the Transition zone come the aspens of the Canadian belt, the tiny mountain flowers of the Hudsonian, and then the gaunt summits of the Arctic-Alpine. These states have all varieties of climate, tree life, bird life; what is true in one place is false in another. You can watch apricot trees blossom day after day if you follow them up different gradations of climate.

It is in the piñon country near river valleys or springs that man has for centuries done best with his life. For piñon country is grazing country. In and through the trees go the flocks of sheep and goats, from the western boundary of the Navajo reservation to Raton and its mesas on the east. Neither piñon nor sabina will ever create a generation of lumber millionaires. There is no money in them, and they will stay to carpet hundreds of miles with their green. Sabina wood is impossible for open fireplaces because it snaps and throws sparks, but it makes a quick and lasting heat for cooking, and keeps flues free of soot. The sabina takes a long time to rot, and so is good for fence posts. If I use the expression "U. S. American" for people coming to New Mexico and Arizona from the other states, it is only to avoid the common usage that refers to them, whether they are

Jewish, German, Irish, Yankee or Greek, as "Americans," "Nordics," or "Anglos."

The piñon nut (called also the pine nut and the Indian nut) has always been an important food to Indians and natives. They harvest only a small fraction of the crop, for piñones stretch mile after mile, and the demand is less than the supply. In good years the crop may be worth a million dollars, and the pickers get perhaps a third of this amount. About four-fifths of the crop is sold outside the state, most of it going to the east side of New York. There the pushcart vendors sell the nuts to people who miss the Russian pine nuts and the Italian pistachios of their homelands. The piñon is a good nut, quite small, higher in protein and carbohydrates than pecans, but lower in fat. It keeps well; if unshelled it can go a year without turning rancid.

Every year there are piñon nuts to gather. But the heavy crop comes every third, fifth, or seventh year, according to what you like to think. The nuts require two years to mature; drought shrivels them. To gather them is an occasion for the whole family to work together, and if relatives are visiting, to get some work out of the relatives. Cars and wagons lie like beetles along the highways and byways. You hear people and children chattering not far away, with as much noise as the piñon-jays whose blue wings flash among the branches. The dwarf trees are suddenly a vineyard; the barren land turns fruitful and calls for pickers. Little children run from tree to tree picking up the nuts that have fallen. Sometimes they find the cache of a squirrel and get ten or fifteen pounds at a stroke. Against the dark green of the tree the cones are a beautiful henna inside and flare out in ever wider clusters of dark little coffee berries, until they literally bend backward. The taste is pine and sunshine and popcorn, and peanuts too in a way. Grown-up people spread a sheet underneath the tree and beat the nuts down with an old broom. They take along stout flour-sacks, and when they return to town in the October dusk after a long day and two meals in the open, the sacks are full, and they have made sure of one source of food for the winter.

The country is at its best when the piñons ripen. The Upper Sonoran ranges are comparatively free of pests at any season, but you have to look out for the red ants, which sting diabolically, and for the little black-tailed rattler (not the diamond-back, he lives in the Lower Sonoran). By October snakes and ants have gone. The ground is warm, the little trees make everything cosy; you can lie down anywhere and take a nap. It is a kind of Garden of Eden.

Even U. S. Americans become expert in cracking the shells with their teeth. But it takes an old Indian or native to show what can be done. Piñons go in one corner of the mouth and the shells come out the other. Sitting against a warm wall in the winter sun, people can keep it up for hours. Political speakers grow used to the cracking and munching of their audiences. After the broadcasts of the world series in the plazas of many towns, the pavements close to the curbs are deep with shells, and tires of cars make a noise like tearing cloth. At the public and parochial schools the janitors begin to hate the young human squirrels who leave such a litter in their desks.

The piñon crop, being a free gift of God and an occasion for families to go into the country together in the perfect weather (for October in the Southwest is a dream), fills thousands of people with memories that make life good and worth living, not just endurable. It is a special and dear experience.

Occasionally some visitor is repelled by the piñon landscape. I remember Stanley Vestal's saying of the landscape between Santa Fe and Tesuque, "those strangely depraved hills studded with stunted piñon, hills pink and salmon in color, dead hills or dead alive, looking like hams stuck with cloves." His remark is as accurate as it is vivid about places where erosion is at work. But in those very places the dwarf trees are doing their greatest favor to man; they are keeping the hills from slipping away.

In a country where the winds keep pushing and often bear sand or snow or rain, all elevated shapes tend to become pyramids sooner or later, cones of earth that look like triangles reaching their apexes to the sky. The little trees cling desperately to these cones, and only give up when the battle is lost. From the mesas which they forest thickly you see them thin out as they approach a stretch of badly eroded lands, from thousands to hundreds, then to dozens. When the white lightning forks into these towers and tombs of erosion, or a sunspot plays on them, you see revealed a few dark spots that are trees fighting for their life and for the earth's life.

These scenes have been the same for ages. So it is odd to read in the paper that old-timers are to hold a banquet, with tall tales of cowboy and trail days; that the cowboy poet will be there and sing ballads; that the widow of the hero of a famous Indian fight is to talk.

Such people would, of course, be old-timers in a sense the country east of the Mississippi would not know about, for that country can no longer recall its frontier days. Still, they are not old-timers here in the sense that the Spanish Americans are, whose people go back three centuries, or the Navajo and the Apache, who go back to 1200 at least, or the Pueblo Indians who are immemorial. The stubborn continuance of these other groups foreshortens in our view the old-timer who had his day only a couple of generations since, when the pony express came over the Santa Fe trail. A Southwest newspaper is like the surface of a lake, and all the fish in the lake from the beginning of time to the minnows dumped into it yesterday, have a way of coming to the surface, or of floating along near it so you can see them.

Our American landscape has two major themes—forests and grass plains. The Southwest entwines the two strangely and memorably, by turning plains into deserts, and forest trees into bushes. The stories of the men who explored the virgin lands east of the Mississippi are not like the stories of Southwest exploration. The landscape of piñones remains as it always was, for man is not able to change mountains and mesas; and although he can change semi-arid regions to an extent, it is only to an extent, and one that may not last. But the characteristic of the virgin lands in the East was the great forest. We cannot visualize today the white man's early days there, for the forest has gone. With its going the streams have changed that carried the voyageurs and the explorers. The animals they lived upon, and the tribes of Indians they mingled with or fought with, have also disappeared. It has all changed. Patches of tall evergreens remain in the protection of hills or mountains, and remnants of the delicate hardwood forests in the woodlot of farms. They suggest something of what the land was in its entirety and the abundant life of the first inhabitants, in the vast damp shade and the occasional spaces of sun. There were no vistas in the East in the sense that the piñon country is full of vistas. That very early eastern life as it came westward down the rivers seems night-covered, half-blind, unrestrained, licentious, cruel. On the other hand, the early life of the Southwest was much as it is today, sun-filled and wide-eyed, yet trembling with mirage and shifts of altitude; cautious, yet unworldly and visionary.

The early East must have been a remarkable and beautiful scene of physical life. There was interconnection and interdependence of man and the birds and animals, of streams, grasses, bushes, and forests, with everything dependent on the forest humus. But when the ax felled the first tree, when the Indian drank his first bottle of whiskey, the whole fabric of existence began to unravel and nothing could be done about it. In the piñon country what interdependence there is centers about the water supply; there is no lack of physical life, only one grows less aware of it than of distance, dearth, death, timelessness. Call the Southwest a spiritual experience or not, it has forced people to face the realities of existence. This is noticeable not only in the Indian, though he has felt the regional influences longest. It comes out in the first Europeans who ever entered the region.

ROBERT FROTHINGHAM

THE GRAND CANYON
OF THE COLORADO

The armchair adventurer will feel, I am sure, that Mr. Frothingham's description of the Grand Canyon is so vivid and realistic, that, notwithstanding the reluctance to venture beyond his threshold, he will involuntarily begin making plans for an actual visit to Colorado. (From *Trails Through the Golden West,* McBride, 1932.)

WHEN enthusiastic travelers compare notes on the sights that have impressed them most in various parts of the world, they are likely to find themselves at a loss for adjectives that they can trust to convey their feelings adequately. So many places defy their vocabularies to produce the exact word, and so many of the words that naturally come to mind have been misused until they no longer mean anything. But everybody who sees the Grand Canyon of the Colorado agrees that in this instance the adjective is precisely right. What is more, when we come face to face with such immensity—an immensity that is actually shocking —we are likely to feel that if "grand" is the right term here, then it ought never to be applied to anything else among the natural wonders of the world. For it must henceforth mean to us something that is unique, indescribable in its majesty, its terrible beauty, its power to strike awe to the soul.

He who has not seen the Grand Canyon may ask how it is possible for a thing to be lovely and at the same time terrible. For his answer he must go and see it. Then he will know. The Canyon is like an ancient oracle: it replies to your questions, but the interpretation of its replies rests with you—it depends on what kind of person you are. I do not mean literally, of course, that you will do any "asking" as you stand and look out over this tremendous spectacle; indeed, you are far more likely to be struck speechless, overcome by such emotions as you never felt before. What you see is so utterly unexpected. You may have been all over the world and have looked on hundreds of natural marvels; you may have been told about the Canyon, or read about it, or seen pictures of it. You may have vivid imagination that has created for you what you think must be a pretty adequate vision of what the Grand Canyon really looks like. No matter. None of this is any good, as you will discover when you get there. Whatever your anticipations, the reality will dwarf them.

There is nothing especially interesting or remarkable about the last few miles of the approach to the Canyon. When your train reaches the southern verge there is a sharp drop of a hundred feet or so back to the level of the plain over which you have been speeding since daylight. While you were asleep the car in which you have been riding ever since you left Chicago was shunted off the Santa Fe main line to a side track at Williams, Arizona—that once wild-and-woolly cowtown—with fifty miles left to go before reaching the Grand Canyon. As you look out of the car-window over that wide expanse of sagebrush desert on the left-hand side of the train, you will hardly realize that, hidden completely by the steep grade and by the magnificent conifers of Coconino Forest, there lies one of the wonders of the world. And when the train comes to a stop at the hotel, things still seem rather commonplace. You alight at the back door of El Tovar and walk up several flights of stairs to the lobby. It is just breakfast time. You are looking forward to a nice table at a window from which you can see the Grand Canyon. Your first set-back arrives when you learn that the dining-room overlooks the desert, not the gorge. However, after breakfast will do. You finish your meal, light a cigar, and complacently stroll out on the plaza to see what may be seen. Near the parapet there are some seats; you take one, and proceed to look.

And look. And look. Presently you note subconsciously that your cigar has gone out, or fallen from your fingers—something; anyhow, you haven't the mind—now—to get it going again. For mind and heart and body are tense with incredulous astonishment. All your attention is needed to assure you that what you are looking at is real.

Stretching before your eyes for miles and miles is a flame-tinted void. Your eyes are blurred, and when you rub them they descry something far down in the depths, away off to the left— a silver thread glinting in the sun's rays. Yes—that's the Colorado River, and it lies a trifle more than one mile below the spot where you are sitting. Directly opposite and etched against the startling blue of the Arizona sky are the cliffs that form the northern rim of the Canyon. They look all of five or six miles away. They are twelve miles away. Just in front of you is a crimson cliff—now, *that* is close; you could toss a pebble and hit it. You toss the pebble—it falls at your feet, and somebody nearby informs you that the cliff is more than a hundred yards from your seat.

It is all very upsetting, however large your preconceptions have been. You begin to understand why the hotel people did not put the dining-room on the Canyon side of the building. The sunlight is a little hard on your eyes, so you go in and get your dark glasses and come out again and look. Just sit there and look. If anybody speaks to you he goes unanswered. Either you don't hear him, or else you can't bear the sound of a human voice. At this moment, the biggest fact in the world to you is silence, imponderable but overwhelming silence. Not even a bird-note is to be heard. After a while it begins to dawn on you that people were right when they confessed that they could not describe the Grand Canyon. You won't be able to, yourself, now that you have seen it.

A hotel attendant comes along and asks whether you want to take a motor ride along the rim. Tell him no—not today, anyway. You have got to give your senses and your nerves a chance to get used to this miracle. It would be a little too much for your self-control to have to listen to some Hermione call the Canyon "swell," and certainly you would strangle that idiot who has just sauntered out from the breakfast table, toothpick in mouth, and who would be sure to tell the world that the Canyon was "some ditch, believe me." Moreover, you do not have to take a motor-car; some of the spots that are best worth seeing can be reached only on foot. The motor cannot approach them; the lazy will not. Find one of these, and you will be safe from the crowd.

At some of these places you can sit down and let your feet hang over—if you have nerve enough to go right to the brink of that precipice; and when you drop a pebble down from the side of your knee it will fall twenty-five hundred feet without touching anything. You wonder how on earth anybody ever manages to get down to the bottom of that pit—alive. But it appears that other people have done it, quite a lot of them; so you can decide that you will try it.

The painter of the Canyon is the sun and his "brushes of comet's hair" are in use every hour of the day. Since every picture that he and the clouds paint is different, we might change the figure of speech to the kaleidoscope. The atmosphere, too, is a potent factor in this amazing play of light and shadow and color. Some of it you will be able to catch with your camera. Indeed, if you are a camera enthusiast you will have the time of your life here. But you must confine your efforts to early morning and late afternoon, avoiding midday, especially for taking pictures along the rim—when the sun is overhead everything flattens out, photographically speaking.

But you must take your camera work seriously if you want good results. A good many amateurs have been heartbroken because their cameras have served them well everywhere else during their summer holiday, only to betray them when they reached the Grand Canyon. They have not learned that in Arizona the danger lies in under-exposure, and that the safest rule is to take time-exposures. Brilliant sunlight does not always imply a clear atmosphere. If you haven't the patience for time-exposures and prefer instantaneous work, then set your camera at not more than 25, or even 20, in point of time. Under normal conditions the difference between 25 and 50 is so infinitesimal that you would have difficulty in determining which was which in the appearance of either negative or print. But where you encounter red rays in the sunlight, as is so frequently the case in desert country, you'll find that 25 in time and 8 in the diaphragm will prove the salvation of many a good shot that would otherwise be lost to you. This advice is not meant for the "sharks"; it is intended for folk like

me who never could find the time to take their photography seriously until driven to it by tragic losses.

Again, choose your subjects with care. There is such an embarrassment of scenic riches here that a little selection on your
part will yield great rewards. This is, too, another argument
for your wandering off by yourself instead of following the crowd,
most of whose photographic longings are satisfied by an Indian
who looks as if he had been intercepted on his way to a masquerade
ball, compelled to mount into the saddle, shade his eyes with his
hand, and point dramatically across the Canyon. Either that or
the cowboy who has ascertained that the Open Sesame to popularity with a certain brand of tourist is to pose nonchalantly with
cigarette, sombrero, snaky silk handkerchief, and chaps beside his
faithful bronc, just returned from "night-herding" and ready to
brave the dangers of a descent into the Canyon. Under pressure he
will admit that it's a great life if you don't weaken. But you will
learn to take that cowboy a lot more seriously when you see him
start down the trail to the river with a string of horses on which
are mounted a heterogeneous lot of men and women and young
folk, all of whom are going to be perfectly safe under his guidance.

The sun is setting. Scarlet flames creep up the sides of the
Canyon walls in one direction; in another the deep shadows are
apparently dropping down, down, down into bottomless depths.
Where a few moments ago the river was winding its silvery and
tortuous way there is now only a purple path between towering
walls, shot through here and there with an errant gleam that has
escaped through a cranny in those erosion-bitten peaks in the
gorge. Faraway ranges light up, one by one, with an unearthly
luminosity as the foreground becomes less and less distinct and
the middle distance is suddenly metamorphosed from a blazing
inferno into sharply silhouetted, ragged ramparts of innumerable
peaks fringed with fire. Overhead the sky is banked with fleecy,
billowing clouds. It seems hardly possible that a mere human
being could behold such ineffable glory and live to tell the tale.
An awful solemnity pervades the place, and a silence that is
almost palpable.

At home, the coming of night is just nightfall. In the Grand
Canyon it is a miracle.

SONGS AND BALLADS

JOHN A. LOMAX

COLLECTOR'S NOTE

Perhaps one of the richest and most rewarding fields open to the explorer of the literary West is the song and ballad literature of this region. While the West has produced no Keats or Whitman or Frost, it has given us a great wealth of material rich in tradition, humor and folklore. Out of the great abundance of songs and ballads available, I have selected from a number of sources the following twenty-nine pieces. Only limitation of space prevented me from following a strong urge to include a good many more. It gives me pleasure to present here, as a Foreword to this section, an abridgment of John A. Lomax's "Collector's Note" to his own book, *Cowboy Songs and Other Frontier Ballads* (Macmillan), for which my deepest thanks are due this authority and lifelong devotee of Western song.

Out in the wild, far-away places of the big and still unpeopled West,—in the cañons along the Rocky Mountains, among the mining camps of Nevada and Montana, and on the remote cattle ranches of Texas, New Mexico, and Arizona,—yet survives the Anglo-Saxon ballad spirit that was active in secluded districts in England and Scotland even after the coming of Tennyson and Browning. This spirit is manifested both in the preservation of the English ballad and in the creation of local songs. Illiterate people, and people cut off from newspapers and books, isolated and lonely,—thrown back on primal resources for entertainment and for the expression of emotion,—utter themselves through somewhat the same character of songs as did their forefathers of perhaps a thousand years ago. In some such way have been made and preserved the cowboy songs and other frontier ballads contained in this volume. The songs represent the operation of instinct and tradition. They are chiefly interesting to the present generation, however, because of the light they throw on the conditions of pioneer life, and more particularly because of the information they contain concerning that unique and romantic figure in modern civilization, the American cowboy.

The profession of cow-punching, not yet a lost art in a group of big western states, reached its greatest prominence during the first two decades succeeding the Civil War. In Texas, for example, immense tracts of open range, covered with luxuriant grass, encouraged the raising of cattle. One person in many instances owned thousands. To care for the cattle during the winter season, to round them up in the spring and mark and brand the yearlings, and later to drive from Texas to Fort Dodge, Kansas, those ready for market, required large forces of men. The drive from Texas to Kansas came to be known as "going up the trail," for the cattle really made permanent, deep-cut trails across the otherwise trackless hills and plains of the long way. It also became the custom to take large herds of young steers from Texas as far north as Montana, where grass at certain seasons grew more luxuriant than in the south. Texas was the best breeding ground, while the climate and grass of Montana developed young cattle for the market.

A trip up the trail made a distinct break in the monotonous life of the big ranches, often situated hundreds of miles from where the conventions of society were observed. The ranch community consisted usually of the boss, the straw-boss, the cowboys proper, the horse wrangler, and the cook—often a negro. These men lived on terms of practical equality. Except in the case of the boss, there was little difference in the amounts paid each for his services. Society, then, was here reduced to its lowest terms. The work of the men, their daily experiences, their thoughts, their interests, were all in common. Such a community had necessarily to turn to itself for entertainment. Songs sprang up naturally, some of them tender and familiar lays of childhood,

others original compositions, all genuine, however crude and un-
polished. Whatever the most gifted man could produce must
bear the criticism of the entire camp, and agree with the ideas
of a group of men. In this sense, therefore, any song that came
from such a group would be the joint product of a number of
them, telling perhaps the story of some stampede they had all
fought to turn, some crime in which they had all shared equally,
some comrade's tragic death which they had all witnessed. The
song-making did not cease as the men went up the trail. Indeed
the songs were here utilized for very practical ends. Not only
were sharp, rhythmic yells—sometimes beaten into verse—employed to stir up lagging cattle, but also during the long watches
the night-guards, as they rode round and round the herd, improvised cattle lullabies which quieted the animals and soothed
them to sleep. Some of the best of the so-called "dogie songs"
seem to have been created for the purpose of preventing cattle
stampedes,—such songs coming straight from the heart of the
cowboy, speaking familiarly to his herd in the stillness of the night.

The long drives up the trail occupied months, and called for
sleepless vigilance and tireless activity both day and night. When
at last a shipping point was reached, the cattle marketed or
loaded on the cars, the cowboys were paid off. It is not surprising
that the consequent relaxation led to reckless deeds. The music,
the dancing, the click of the roulette ball in the saloons, invited;
the lure of crimson lights was irresistible. Drunken orgies, reac-
tions from months of toil, deprivation, and loneliness on the ranch
and on the trail, brought to death many a temporarily crazed
buckaroo. To match this dare-deviltry, a saloon man in one
frontier town, as a sign for his business, with psychological in-
genuity painted across the broad front of his building in big black
letters this challenge to God, man, and the devil: *The Road to
Ruin.* Down this road, with swift and eager footsteps, has trod
many a pioneer viking of the West. Quick to resent an insult real
or fancied, inflamed by unaccustomed drink, the ready pistol
always at his side, the tricks of the professional gambler to
provoke his sense of fair play, and finally his own wild recklessness to urge him on,—all these combined forces sometimes brought
him into tragic conflict with another spirit equally heedless and
daring. Not nearly so often, however, as one might suppose, did he
die with his boots on. Many of the most wealthy and respected

citizens now living in the border states served as cowboys before settling down to quiet domesticity.

A cow-camp in the seventies generally contained several types of men. It was not unusual to find a negro who, because of his ability to handle wild horses or because of his skill with a lasso, had been promoted from the chuck-wagon to a place in the ranks of the cowboys. Another familiar figure was the adventurous younger son of some British family, through whom perhaps became current the English ballads found in the West. Furthermore, so considerable was the number of men who had fled from the States because of grave imprudence or crime, it was bad form to inquire too closely about a person's real name or where he came from. Most cowboys, however, were bold young spirits who emigrated to the West for the same reason that their ancestors had come across the seas. They loved roving; they loved freedom; they were pioneers by instinct; an impulse set their faces from the East, put the tang for roaming in their veins, and sent them ever, ever westward.

That the cowboy was brave has come to be axiomatic. If his life of isolation made him taciturn, it at the same time created a spirit of hospitality, primitive and hearty as that found in the mead-halls of Beowulf. He faced the wind and the rain, the snow of winter, the fearful dust-storms of alkali desert wastes, with the same uncomplaining quiet. Not all his work was on the ranch and the trail. To the cowboy, more than to the goldseekers, more than to Uncle Sam's soldiers, is due the conquest of the West. Along his winding cattle trails the Forty-Niners found their way to California. The cowboy has fought back the Indians ever since ranching became a business and as long as Indians remained to be fought. He played his part in winning the great slice of territory that the United States took away from Mexico. He has always been on the skirmish line of civilization. Restless, fearless, chivalric, elemental, he lived hard, shot quick and true, and died with his face to his foe. Still much misunderstood, he is often slandered, nearly always caricatured, both by the press and by the stage. Perhaps these songs, coming direct from the cowboy's experience, giving vent to his careless and his tender emotions, will afford future generations a truer conception of what he really was than is now possessed by those who know him only through highly colored romances.

The big ranches of the West are now being cut up into small farms. The nester has come, and come to stay. Gone is the buffalo, the Indian war whoop, the free grass of the open plain;—even the stinging lizard, the horned frog, the centipede, the prairie dog, the rattlesnake, are fast disappearing. Save in some of the secluded valleys of southern New Mexico, the old-time round-up is no more; the trails to Kansas and to Montana have become grass-grown or lost in fields of waving grain; the maverick steer, the regal long-horn, has been supplanted by his unpoetic but more beefy and profitable Polled Angus, Durham, and Hereford cousins from across the seas. The changing and romantic West of the early days lives mainly in story and in song. The last figure to vanish is the cowboy, the animating spirit of the vanishing era. He sits his horse easily as he rides through a wide valley, enclosed by mountains, clad in the hazy purple of coming night,—with his face turned steadily down the long, long road, "the road that the sun goes down." Dauntless, reckless, without the unearthly purity of Sir Galahad though as gentle to a pure woman as King Arthur, he is truly a knight of the twentieth century. A vagrant puff of wind shakes a corner of the crimson handkerchief knotted loosely at his throat; the thud of his pony's feet mingling with the jingle of his spurs is borne back; and as the careless, gracious, lovable figure disappears over the divide, the breeze brings to the ears, faint and far yet cheery still, the refrain of a cowboy song:

> Whoopee ti yi, git along, little dogies;
>   It's my misfortune and none of your own.
> Whoopee ti yi, git along, little dogies;
>   For you know Wyoming will be your new home.
> —John A. Lomax

A HOME ON THE RANGE*

OH, give me a home where the buffalo roam,
Where the deer and the antelope play,
Where seldom is heard a discouraging word
And the skies are not cloudy all day.

Home, home on the range,
Where the deer and the antelope play;
Where seldom is heard a discouraging word
And the skies are not cloudy all day.

Where the air is so pure, the zephyrs so free,
The breezes so balmy and light,
That I would not exchange my home on the range
For all of the cities so bright.

The red man was pressed from this part of the West,
He's likely no more to return
To the banks of Red River where seldom if ever
Their flickering camp-fires burn.

How often at night when the heavens are bright
With the light from the glittering stars,
Have I stood here amazed and asked as I gazed
If their glory exceeds that of ours.

Oh, I love these wild flowers in this dear land of ours,
The curlew I love to hear scream,
And I love the white rocks and the antelope flocks
That graze on the mountain-tops green.

Oh, give me a land where the bright diamond sand
Flows leisurely down the stream;
Where the graceful white swan goes gliding along
Like a maid in a heavenly dream.

* From John A. Lomax's *Cowboy Songs and Other Frontier Ballads.*

Then I would not exchange my home on the range,
Where the deer and the antelope play;
Where seldom is heard a discouraging word
And the skies are not cloudy all day.

> Home, home on the range,
> Where the deer and the antelope play;
> Where seldom is heard a discouraging word
> And the skies are not cloudy all day.

I RIDE AN OLD PAINT*

I RIDE an old Paint, I lead an old Dan,
I'm goin' to Montan' for to throw the hoolian.
They feed in the coulees, they water in the draw,
Their tails are all matted, their backs are all raw.

> Ride around, little dogies,
> Ride around them slow,
> For the fiery and snuffy are a-rarin' to go.

Old Bill Jones had two daughters and a song,
One went to Denver and the other went wrong.
His wife she died in a poolroom fight,
Still he sings from mornin' till night.

> Ride around, little dogies,
> Ride around them slow,
> For the fiery and snuffy are a-rarin' to go.

Oh, when I die, take my saddle from the wall,
Put it on my pony, lead him out of his stall.
Tie my bones to his back, turn our faces to the West,
And we'll ride the prairie that we love the best.

> Ride around, little dogies,
> Ride around them slow,
> For the fiery and snuffy are a-rarin' to go.

* From Carl Sandburg's *The American Songbag.*

WHEN BOB GOT THROWED

THAT time when Bob got throwed
I thought I sure would bust;
I liked to died a-laffin'
To see him chewing dust.

He crawled on that pinto bronc
And hit him with a quirt,
The next thing that he knew
He was wallerin' in the dirt.

Yes, it might 'a' killed him,
I heard the hard ground pop,
But to see if he was injured
You bet I didn't stop.

I jest rolled on the ground
And began to kick and yell;
It liked to tickled me to death
To see how hard he fell.

'T warn't more than a week ago
That I myself got throwed;
But that was from a meaner horse
Than old Bob ever rode.

D' you reckon Bob looked sad and said
"I hope that you ain't hurt"?
Naw; he just laughed and laughed
To see me chewin' dirt.

I've been prayin' ever since
For his horse to turn his pack,
And when he done it I'd 'a' laughed
If it had broke his back.

So I was still a-howlin'
When Bob he got up lame;
He seen his horse had run clear off,
And so for me he came.

He first chucked sand into my eyes,
With a rock he rubbed my head,
Then he twisted both my arms:
"Now, go fetch that hoss," he said.

So I went and fetched him back,
But I was feelin' good all day;
For I sure enough do love to see
A fellow get throwed that way.

THE DREARY BLACK HILLS*

KIND friends, you must pity my horrible tale,
I am an object of pity, I am looking quite stale,
I gave up my trade selling Right's Patent Pills
To go hunting gold in the dreary Black Hills.

Don't go away, stay at home if you can,
Stay away from that city, they call it Cheyenne,
For big Walipe or Comanche Bills
They will lift up your hair on the dreary Black
    Hills.

The round-house in Cheyenne is filled every night
With loafers and bummers of most every plight;
On their backs is no clothes, in their pockets no bills,
Each day they keep starting for the dreary Black
    Hills.

I got to Cheyenne, no gold could I find,
I thought of the lunch route I'd left far behind;

* From John A. Lomax's *Cowboy Songs and Other Frontier Ballads*.

Through rain, hail, and snow, frozen plumb to the
    gills,—
They call me the orphan of the dreary Black Hills.

Kind friend, to conclude, my advice I'll unfold,
Don't go to the Black Hills a-hunting for gold;
Railroad speculators their pockets you'll fill
By taking a trip to those dreary Black Hills.

    Don't go away, stay at home if you can,
    Stay away from that city, they call it Cheyenne,
    For old Sitting Bull or Comanche Bills
    They will take off your scalp on the dreary Black
    Hills.

SWEET BETSY FROM PIKE*

OH don't you remember sweet Betsy from Pike,
    Who crossed the big mountains with her lover Ike,
With two yoke of cattle, a large yellow dog,
    A tall Shanghai rooster, and one spotted hog;

    Refrain:
    Saying goodbye, Pike County,
        Farewell for a while;
    We'll come back again
        When we've panned out our pile.

One evening quite early, they camped on the Platte,
    'Twas near by the road on a green shady flat;
Where Betsy, quite tired, laid down to repose,
    While with wonder Ike gazed on his Pike County Rose.
    Refrain:

* From Carl Sandburg's *The American Songbag.*

They soon reached the desert, where Betsy gave out
  And down in the sand she lay rolling about;
While Ike in great tears looked on in surprise,
  Saying, "Betsy get up, you'll get sand in your eyes."
Refrain:

Sweet Betsy got up in a great deal of pain,
  And declared she'd go back to Pike County again.
Then Ike heaved a sigh and they fondly embraced,
  And she traveled along with his arm 'round her waist.
Refrain:

The Shanghai ran off and the cattle all died,
  The last piece of bacon that morning was fried;
Poor Ike got discouraged, and Betsy got mad,
  The dog wagged his tail and looked wonderfully sad.
Refrain:

One morning they climbed up a very high hill,
  And with wonder looked down into old Placerville;
Ike shouted and said, as he cast his eyes down,
  "Sweet Betsy, my darling, we've got to Hangtown."
Refrain:

Long Ike and Sweet Betsy attended a dance,
  Where Ike wore a pair of his Pike County pants,
Sweet Betsy was covered with ribbons and rings,
  Quoth Ike, "You're an angel, but where are your wings?"
Refrain:

A miner said, "Betsy, will you dance with me?"
  "I will, old hoss, if you don't make too free;
But don't dance me hard. Do you want to know why?
  Dog on ye, I'm chuck full of strong alkali."
Refrain:

Long Ike and Sweet Betsy got married, of course,
  But Ike getting jealous obtained a divorce;
And Betsy, well satisfied, said with a shout,
  "Goodbye, you big lummox, I'm glad you backed out."

Last Refrain:
Saying goodbye, dear Isaac,
　　Farewell for a while.
But come back in time
　　To replenish my pile.

SAGE-BRUSH*

WHEN I'm sleepin', seems like I can hear the mules
　　a coughin'——coughin' in the dust.
All at once, I'll be sittin' up, pullin' in the sheets,
　　thinkin' that I'm takin' up a little jerkline slack.
Then I wake up, and life is all a bust, with somethin'
　　gnawin' at my vitals, talkin' to me, chantin' like an
Injun, till it's drove me half insane.
　　　　And I know what it's sayin'——talkin', whisperin', prayin',
. . . God! I've got to smell the sage again!

High up among the purple hills I want to smell it, when
　　it's wet with rain and my horse is wading through it,
Belly-deep and happy, drinkin' with me of its fragrance as
　　he tramps it down into the dark brown earth.
Lonely cañons beckon to me——there's a mesa high above the
　　King's, and trout holes in the Santa Rosas, of which
The phantom voices sing: "There are night-camps in the valleys——
　　don't you know them?——can't you see them——
Little fires with hazy smoke wreaths driftin' 'round in rings?"

Know them? . . . Say!——just like I know the way the smell
　　o' bacon hits you in the open, 'bout the time the
Sun is makin' up his mind to rise. And no one needs to tell me
　　that the mountain-quail are flyin'——nor mention any of
The forty kinds of lyin' a cowhand can employ to get a whirl
　　　　　　　　　　　　　　　　　　　　　　　　at them,

* By permission of the author, Harry Sinclair Drago.

Even though it's round-up time and the bunch is
Poundin' leather fourteen hours a day—sweatin', swearin',
     ropin'—anythin' to get the stuff aboard the cars.

"Thought you were comin' back again this fall?" those little
                              desert voices taunt me.
     "Thought you were goin' to ride the range again just for
                              a spell,
And fill your eyes and ears with sights and sounds the city
                              never knows?"

     Oh! I want to go—I've *got* to go before white winter
Comes to choke the draws and blot the trails from sight.
     I've got to smell the sage again—or die!

SAM BASS*

Sam BASS was born in Indiana, it was his native home,
And at the age of seventeen young Sam began to roam.
Sam first came out to Texas a cowboy for to be,—
A kinder-hearted fellow you seldom ever see.

Sam used to deal in race stock, one called the Denton mare,
He matched her in scrub races, and took her to the Fair.
Sam used to coin the money and spent it just as free,
He always drank good whiskey wherever he might be.

Sam left the Collins' ranch in the merry month of May
With a herd of Texas cattle the Black Hills for to see,
Sold out in Custer City and then got on a spree,—
A harder set of cowboys you seldom ever see.

On their way back to Texas they robbed the U. P. train,
And then split up in couples and started out again.
Joe Collins and his partner were overtaken soon,
With all their hard-earned money they had to meet their doom.

* From John A. Lomax's *Cowboy Songs and Other Frontier Ballads.*

Sam made it back to Texas all right side up with care;
Rode into the town of Denton with all his friends to share.
Sam's life was short in Texas; three robberies did he do,
He robbed all the passenger, mail, and express cars too.

Sam had four companions—four bold and daring lads—
They were Richardson, Jackson, Joe Collins, and Old Dad:
Four more bold and daring cowboys the rangers never knew,
They whipped the Texas rangers and ran the boys in blue.

Sam had another companion, called Arkansas for short,
Was shot by a Texas ranger by the name of Thomas Floyd;
Oh, Tom is a big six-footer and thinks he's mighty fly,
But I can tell you his racket,—he's a deadbeat on the sly.

Jim Murphy was arrested, and then released on bail;
He jumped his bond at Tyler and then took the train for
    Terrell;
But Mayor Jones had posted Jim and that was all a stall,
'Twas only a plan to capture Sam before the coming fall.

Sam met his fate at Round Rock, July the twenty-first,
They pierced poor Sam with rifle balls and emptied out his
    purse.
Poor Sam he is a corpse and six foot under clay,
And Jackson's in the bushes trying to get away.

Jim had borrowed Sam's good gold and didn't want to pay,
The only shot he saw was to give poor Sam away.
He sold out Sam and Barnes and left their friends to mourn,—
Oh, what a scorching Jim will get when Gabriel blows his horn.

And so he sold out Sam and Barnes and left their friends to
    mourn,
Oh, what a scorching Jim will get when Gabriel blows his horn.
Perhaps he's got to heaven, there's none of us can say,
But if I'm right in my surmise he's gone the other way.

BRIGHAM YOUNG. I.*

I'LL sing you a song that has often been sung
About an old Mormon they called Brigham Young.
Of wives he had many who were strong in the lungs,
Which Brigham found out by the length of their tongues.
Ri tu ral, lol, lu ral.

Oh, sad was the life of a Mormon to lead,
Yet Brigham adhered all his life to his creed.
He said 'twas such fun, and true, without doubt,
To see the young wives knock the old ones about.
Ri tu ral, lol, lu ral.

One day as old Brigham sat down to his dinner
He saw a young wife who was not getting thinner;
When the elders cried out, one after the other,
By the holy, she wants to go home to her mother.
Ri tu ral, lol, lu ral.

Old Brigham replied, which can't be denied,
He couldn't afford to lose such a bride.
Then do not be jealous but banish your fears;
For the tree is well known by the fruit that it bears.
Ri tu ral, lol, lu ral.

That I love one and all you very well know,
Then do not provoke me or my anger will show.
What must be our fate if found here in a row,
If Uncle Sam comes with his row-de-dow-dow.
Ri tu ral, lol, lu ral.

Then cease all your quarrels and do not despair,
To meet Uncle Sam I will quickly prepare.
Hark! I hear Yankee Doodle played over the hills!
Ah! here's the enemy with their powder and pills.
Ri tu ral, lol, lu ral.

* From John A. Lomax's *Cowboy Songs and Other Frontier Ballads.*

BRIGHAM YOUNG. II.*

NOW Brigham Young is a Mormon bold,
And a leader of the roaring rams,
And shepherd of a lot of fine tub sheep
And a lot of pretty little lambs.
Oh, he lives with his five and forty wives,
In the city of the Great Salt Lake,
Where they breed and swarm like hens on a farm
And cackle like ducks to a drake.

   Chorus:—
Oh Brigham, Brigham Young,
It's a miracle how you survive,
With your roaring rams and your pretty little lambs
And your five and forty wives.

Number forty-five is about sixteen,
Number one is sixty and three;
And they make such a riot, how he keeps them quiet
Is a downright mystery to me.
For they clatter and they chaw and they jaw, jaw, jaw,
And each has a different desire;
It would aid the renown of the best shop in town
To supply them with half they desire.

Now, Brigham Young was a stout man once,
And now he is thin and old;
And I am sorry to state he is bald on the pate,
Which once had a covering of gold.
For his oldest wives won't have white wool,
And his young ones won't have red,
So, with tearing it out, and taking turn about,
They have torn all the hair off his head.

* From John A. Lomax's *Cowboy Songs and Other Frontier Ballads.*

Now, the oldest wives sing songs all day,
And the young ones all sing songs;
And amongst such a crowd he has it pretty loud,—
They're as noisy as Chinese gongs.
And when they advance for a Mormon dance
He is filled with the direst alarms;
For they are sure to end the night in a tabernacle fight
To see who has the fairest charms.

Now, if any man here envies Brigham Young
Let him go to the Great Salt Lake;
And if he has the leisure to enjoy his pleasure,
He'll find it a great mistake.
One wife at a time, so says my rhyme,
Is enough,—there's no denial;—
So, before you strive to be lord of forty-five,
Take two for a month on trial.

THE BOOZER

I 'M a howler from the prairies of the West!
If you want to die with terror look at me!
I'm chain-lightning—if I ain't, may I be blessed!
I'm the snorter of the boundless prairie!

He's a killer and a hater!
He's the great annihilator!
He's a terror of the boundless prairie!

I'm the snoozer from the upper trail!
I'm the reveler in murder and in gore!
I can bust more Pullman coaches on the rail
Than any one who's worked the job before.

He's a snorter and a snoozer!
He's the great trunk line abuser!
He's the man who puts the sleeper on the rail!

I'm the double-jawed hyena from the East!
I'm the blazing bloody blizzard of the States!
I'm the celebrated slugger; I'm the Beast!
I can snatch a man bald-headed while he waits!

He's a double-jawed hyena!
He's the villain of the scena!
He can snatch a man bald-headed while he waits!

AS I WALKED OUT IN THE STREETS OF LAREDO*

As I walked out in the streets of Laredo,
As I walked out in Laredo one day,
I spied a poor cowboy wrapped up in white linen,
Wrapped up in white linen and cold as the clay.

"I see by your outfit that you are a cowboy,"
These words he did say as I boldly stepped by.
"Come sit down beside me and hear my sad story;
I was shot in the breast and I know I must die.

"Let sixteen gamblers come handle my coffin,
Let sixteen cowboys come sing me a song,
Take me to the graveyard and lay the sod o'er me,
For I'm a poor cowboy and I know I've done wrong.

"It was once in the saddle I used to go dashing,
It was once in the saddle I used to go gay.
'Twas first to drinking and then to card playing,
Got shot in the breast, I am dying today.

"Get six jolly cowboys to carry my coffin,
Get six pretty girls to carry my pall;

* From Carl Sandburg's *The American Songbag.*

Put bunches of roses all over my coffin,
Put roses to deaden the clods as they fall.

"O beat the drum slowly and play the fife lowly
And play the dead march as you carry me along,
Take me to the green valley and lay the sod o'er me,
For I'm a young cowboy and I know I've done wrong."

We beat the drum slowly and played the fife lowly,
And bitterly wept as we bore him along;
For we all loved our comrade, so brave, young, and handsome,
We all loved our comrade although he'd done wrong.

THE TENDERFOOT*

ONE day I thought I'd have some fun,
And see how punching cows was done;
So when the roundup had begun
I tackled the cattle king.
Says he, "My foreman's gone to town,
He's in a saloon and his name is Brown;
If you see him he'll take you down."
Says I, "That's just the thing."

We started out to the ranch next day.
Brown talked to me most all the way.
Says, "Punching cows is nothing but play,
It is no work at all."
Oh jimminy krissmas, how he lied!
He had a hell of a lot of gall,
He put me in charge of the cavvy hole,
Says Brown, "Don't work too hard."

Sometimes those cattle would make a break
And across the prairie they would take,

* From Carl Sandburg's *The American Songbag.*

Just like they was running for a stake.
To them it was nothing but play.
Sometimes they would stumble and fall,
Sometimes you couldn't head 'em at all,
And we'd shoot on like a cannonball
Till the ground came in our way.

They saddled me up an old gray hack
With a great big seat fast on his back.
They padded him down with gunny sack
And with my bedding too.
When I got on him he left the ground,
Went up in the air and circled around
And when I came down I busted the ground.
I got a terrible fall.

They picked me up and carried me in
And rubbed me down with a picket pin.
Says, "That's the way they all begin."
"You're doing fine," says Brown.
"To-morrow morning if you don't die
I'll give you another hoss to try."
Says I, "Oh can't I walk? . . ."
Says Brown, "Yep, back to town."

I've travelled up, I've travelled down,
I've travelled this wide world all around,
I've lived in city, I've lived in town;
I've got this much to say:
Before you go to punching cows,
Go kiss your wife, get a heavy insurance upon your life,
And shoot yourself with a butcher knife,
For that is the easiest way.

THE LONE STAR TRAIL*

I'M a rowdy cowboy just off the stormy plains,
My trade is girting saddles and pulling bridle reins.
Oh, I can tip the lasso, it is with graceful ease;
I rope a streak of lightning, and ride it where I please.
My bosses they all like me, they say I am hard to beat;
I give them the bold standoff, you bet I have got the cheek.
I always work for wages, my pay I get in gold;
I am bound to follow the longhorn steer until I am too old.

 Ci yi yip yip yip pe ya.

I am a Texas cowboy and I do ride the range;
My trade is cinches and saddles and ropes and bridle reins;
With Stetson hat and jingling spurs and leather up to the knees,
Gray backs as big as chili beans and fighting like hell with fleas.
And if I had a little stake, I soon would married be,
But another week and I must go, the boss said so to-day.
My girl must cheer up courage and choose some other one,
For I am bound to follow the Lone Star Trail until my race is run.

 Ci yi yip yip yip pe ya.

It almost breaks my heart for to have to go away,
And leave my own little darling, my sweetheart so far away.
But when I'm out on the Lone Star Trail often I'll think of thee,
Of my own dear girl, the darling one, the one I would like to see.
And when I get to a shipping point, I'll get on a little spree
To drive away the sorrow for the girl that once loved me.
And though red licker stirs us up we're bound to have our fun,
And I intend to follow the Lone Star Trail until my race is run.

 Ci yi yip yip yip pe ya.

* From John A. Lomax's *Cowboy Songs and Other Frontier Ballads.*

I went up the Lone Star Trail in eighteen eighty-three;
I fell in love with a pretty miss and she in love with me.
"When you get to Kansas write and let me know;
And if you get in trouble, your bail I'll come and go."
When I got up in Kansas, I had a pleasant dream;
I dreamt I was down on Trinity, down on that pleasant stream;
I dreamt my true love right beside me, she come to go my bail;
I woke up broken hearted with a yearling by the tail.

    Ci yi yip yip yip pe ya.

In came my jailer about nine o'clock,
A bunch of keys was in his hand, my cell door to unlock,
Saying, "Cheer up, my prisoner, I heard some voice say
You're bound to hear your sentence some time to-day."
In came my mother about ten o'clock,
Saying, "O my loving Johnny, what sentence have you got?"
"The jury found me guilty and the judge a-standin' by
Has sent me down to Huntsville to lock me up and die."

    Ci yi yip yip yip pe ya.

Down come the jailer, just about eleven o'clock,
With a bunch of keys all in his hand the cell doors to unlock,
Saying, "Cheer up, my prisoner, I heard the jury say
Just ten long years in Huntsville you're bound to go and stay."
Down come my sweetheart, ten dollars in her hand,
Saying, "Give this to my cowboy, 'tis all that I command;
O give this to my cowboy and think of olden times,
Think of the darling that he has left behind."

    Ci yi yip yip yip pe ya.

WESTWARD HO*

I LOVE not Colorado
Where the faro table grows,
And down the desperado
The rippling Bourbon flows;

Nor seek I fair Montana
Of bowie-lunging fame;
The pistol ring of fair Wyoming
I leave to nobler game.

Sweet poker-haunted Kansas
In vain allures the eye;
The Nevada rough has charms enough
Yet its blandishments I fly.

Shall Arizona woo me
Where the meek Apache bides?
Or New Mexico where natives grow
With arrow-proof insides?

Nay, 'tis where the grizzlies wander
And the lonely diggers roam,
And the grim Chinese from the squatter flees
That I'll make my humble home.

I'll chase the wild tarantula
And the fierce cayote I'll dare,
And the locust grim, I'll battle him
In his native wildwood lair.

Or I'll seek the gulch deserted
And dream of the wild Red man,
And I'll build a cot on a corner lot
And get rich as soon as I can.

* From John A. Lomax's *Cowboy Songs and Other Frontier Ballads.*

WHEN THE WORK'S ALL DONE THIS FALL[*]

A GROUP of jolly cowboys, discussing plans at ease,
Says one, "I'll tell you something, boys, if you will listen, please.
I am an old cow-puncher and hyer I'm dressed in rags,
I used to be a tough one and go on great big jags.
But I have got a home, boys, a good one, you all know,
Although I have not seen it since long, long ago.
I'm going back to Dixie once more to see them all,
Yes, I'm going to see my mother when the work's all done this fall.

"After the round-up's over and after the shipping's done,
I am going right straight home, boys, ere all my money is gone.
I have changed my ways, boys, no more will I fall;
And I am going home, boys, when the work's all done this fall.
When I left home, boys, my mother for me cried,
Begged me not to go, boys, for me she would have died;
My mother's heart is breaking, breaking for me, that's all,
And with God's help I'll see her when the work's all done this fall."

That very night this cowboy went out to stand his guard;
The night was dark and cloudy and storming very hard;
The cattle they got frightened and rushed in wild stampede,
The cowboy tried to head them, riding at full speed.
While riding in the darkness so loudly did he shout,
Trying his best to head them and turn the herd about,
His saddle horse did stumble and on him did fall,
The poor boy won't see his mother when the work's all done this fall.

His body was so mangled the boys all thought him dead,
They picked him up so gently and laid him on a bed;
He opened wide his blue eyes and looking all around
He motioned to his comrades to sit near him on the ground.

[*] From Carl Sandburg's *The American Songbag*.

"Boys, send my mother my wages, the wages I have earned,
For I am afraid, boys, my last steer I have turned.
I'm going to a new range, I hyer my Master's call
And I'll not see my mother when the work's all done this fall.

"Bill, you may have my saddle; George, you may take my bed;
Jack may have my pistol, after I am dead.
Boys, think of me kindly when you look upon them all,
For I'll not see my mother when the work's all done this fall."
Poor Charlie was buried at sunrise, no tombstone at his head,
Nothing but a little board and this is what it said,
"Charlie died at daybreak, he died from a fall,
The boy won't see his mother when the work's all done this fall."

WESTERN LIFE

I BUCKLED on a brace of guns and sallied to Wyoming,
And thought I'd kill some Indians ere day had reached the
    gloaming;
But the first red-skin that came to view upon the reservation
Said: "Ah, my dear old college chum, I give you salutation!"

For Western life ain't wild and woolly now;
They are up on Wagner, Ibsen,
And adore the girls of Gibson—
For Western life ain't wild and woolly now!

I struck a little prairie town and saw two cowboys greet,
And thought: "Now there'll be powder burnt when these two bad
    men meet";
But the first one says to Number Two: "You beat me, Dick, at
    tennis:
Now come along, old chap, and read the finish of 'Pendennis.' "

For Western life ain't wild and woolly now;
The cowboy knows a lot besides more cow;

He can two-step, do hemstitching,
And do hay or baseball pitching—
For Western life ain't wild and woolly now!

So in despair I turned into a busy Western town,
And hoped to see the gun-fighters a-mowing of men down;
But while I loitered on the street to see blood by the flagon,
I fell before a green-goods man and then a devil wagon.

For Western life ain't wild and woolly now;
There is no daily gunpowder powwow;
There are bunco games galore
And the chauffeur holds the floor—
But Western life ain't wild and woolly now!

THE COWMAN'S PRAYER*

NOW, O Lord, please lend me thine ear,
The prayer of a cattleman to hear,
No doubt the prayers may seem strange,
But I want you to bless our cattle range.

Bless the round-ups year by year,
And don't forget the growing steer;
Water the lands with brooks and rills
For my cattle that roam on a thousand hills.

Prairie fires, won't you please stop?
Let thunder roll and water drop.
It frightens me to see the smoke;
Unless it's stopped, I'll go dead broke.

As you, O Lord, my herd behold,
It represents a sack of gold;

* From John A. Lomax's *Cowboy Songs and Other Frontier Ballads.*

I think at least five cents a pound
Will be the price of beef the year around.

One thing more and then I'm through,—
Instead of one calf, give my cows two.
I may pray different from other men
But I've had my say, and now, Amen.

WHOOPEE, TI YI YO, GIT ALONG, LITTLE DOGIES*

As I walked out one morning for pleasure,
I spied a cow-puncher all riding alone;
His hat was throwed back and his spurs was a-jingling,
As he approached me a-singin' this song,

Whoopee ti yi yo, git along, little dogies,
It's your misfortune, and none of my own.
Whoopee ti yi yo, get along, little dogies,
For you know Wyoming will be your new home.

Early in the spring we round up the dogies,
Mark and brand and bob off their tails;
Round up our horses, load up the chuck-wagon,
Then throw the dogies upon the trail.

It's whooping and yelling and driving the dogies;
Oh how I wish you would go on;
It's whooping and punching and go on, little dogies,
For you know Wyoming will be your new home.

Some boys goes up the trail for pleasure,
But that's where you get it most awfully wrong;
For you haven't any idea the trouble they give us
While we go driving them all along.

* From John A. Lomax's *Cowboy Songs and Other Frontier Ballads.*

When the night comes on and we hold them on the bedground,
These little dogies that roll on so slow;
Roll up the herd and cut out the strays,
And roll the little dogies that never rolled before.

Your mother she was raised way down in Texas,
Where the jimson weed and sand-burrs grow;
Now we'll fill you up on prickly pear and cholla
Till you are ready for the trail to Idaho.

Oh, you'll be soup for Uncle Sam's Injuns;
"It's beef, heap beef," I hear them cry.
Git along, git along, git along, little dogies
You're going to be beef steers by and by.

BILLY VENERO*

BILLY VENERO heard them say,
In an Arizona town one day,
That a band of Apache Indians were upon the trail of death;
Heard them tell of murder done,
Three men killed at Rocky Run,
"They're in danger at the cow-ranch," said Venero, under breath.

Cow-Ranch, forty miles away,
Was a little place that lay
In a deep and shady valley of the mighty wilderness;
Half a score of homes were there,
And in one a maiden fair
Held the heart of Billy Venero, Billy Venero's little Bess.

So no wonder he grew pale
When he heard the cowboy's tale
Of the men that he'd seen murdered the day before at Rocky Run.

* From John A. Lomax's *Cowboy Songs and Other Frontier Ballads.*

"Sure as there's a God above,
I will save the girl I love;
By my love for little Bessie I will see that something's done."

Not a moment he delayed
When his brave resolve was made.
"Why man," his comrades told him when they heard of his daring
    plan,
"You are riding straight to death."
But he answered, "Save your breath;
I may never reach the cow-ranch but I'll do the best I can."

As he crossed the alkali
All his thoughts flew on ahead
To the little band at cow-ranch thinking not of danger near;
With his quirt's unceasing whirl
And the jingle of his spurs
Little brown Chapo bore the cowboy o'er the far away frontier.

Lower and lower sank the sun;
He drew rein at Rocky Run;
"Here those men met death, my Chapo," and he stroked his glossy
    mane;
"So shall those we go to warn
Ere the coming of the morn
If we fail,—God help my Bessie," and he started on again.

Sharp and clear a rifle shot
Woke the echoes of the spot.
"I am wounded," cried Venero, as he swayed from side to side;
"While there's life there's always hope;
Slowly onward I will lope,—
If I fail to reach the cow-ranch, Bessie Lee shall know I tried.

"I will save her yet," he cried,
"Bessie Lee shall know I tried,"
And for her sake then he halted in the shadow of a hill;
From his chapareras he took
With weak hands a little book;
Tore a blank leaf from its pages saying, "This shall be my will."

From a limb a pen he broke,
And he dipped his pen of oak
In the warm blood that was spurting from a wound above his heart.
"Rouse," he wrote before too late;
"Apache warriors lie in wait.
Good-bye, Bess, God bless you darling," and he felt the cold tears
    start.

Then he made his message fast,
Love's first message and its last,
To the saddle horn he tied it and his lips were white with pain,
"Take this message, if not me,
Straight to little Bessie Lee";
Then he tied himself to the saddle, and he gave his horse the rein.

Just at dusk a horse of brown
Wet with sweat came panting down
The little lane at the cow-ranch, stopped in front of Bessie's door;
But the cowboy was asleep,
And his slumbers were so deep,
Little Bess could never wake him though she tried for evermore.

You have heard the story told
By the young and by the old,
Away down yonder at the cow-ranch the night the Apaches came;
Of that sharp and bloody fight,
How the chief fell in the fight
And the panic-stricken warriors when they heard Venero's name.

And the heavens and earth between
Keep a little flower so green
That little Bess had planted ere they laid her by his side.

THE COWBOY'S DREAM

LAST night, as I lay on the prairie,
And looked at the stars in the sky,
I wondered if ever a cowboy
Would drift to that sweet by and by.

I hear there's to be a grand round-up
Where cowboys with others must stand,
To be cut out by the riders of judgment
Who are posted and know all the brands.

The trail to that great mystic region
Is narrow and dim, so they say;
While the one that leads down to perdition
Is posted and blazed all the way.

Whose fault is it, then, that so many
Go astray, on this wild range fail,
Who might have been rich and had plenty
Had they known of the dim, narrow trail?

I wonder if at the last day some cowboy
Unbranded and unclaimed should stand,
Would he be mavericked by those riders of judgment
Who are posted and know all the brands?

I wonder if ever a cowboy
Stood ready for that Judgment Day,
And could say to the Boss of the Riders,
"I'm ready, come, drive me away"?

For they, like the cows that are locoed,
Stampede at the sight of a hand,
Are dragged with a rope to the round-up,
Or get marked with some crooked man's brand.

And I'm scared that I'll be a stray yearling,
A maverick, unbranded on high,
And get cut in the bunch with the "rusties"
When the Boss of the Riders goes by.

For they tell of another big owner
Who's ne'er overstocked, so they say,
But who always makes room for the sinner
Who drifts from the straight, narrow way.

They say he will never forget you,
That he knows every action and look;
So for safety you'd better get branded,
Have your name in the great Tally Book.

My wish for all cowboys is this:
That we may meet at that grand final sale;
Be cut out by the riders of judgment
And shoved up the dim, narrow trail.

WINDY BILL*

WINDY BILL was a Texas man,—
Well, he could rope, you bet.
He swore the steer he couldn't tie,—
Well, he hadn't found him yet.
But the boys they knew of an old black steer,
A sort of an old outlaw
That ran down in the malpais
At the foot of a rocky draw.

This old black steer had stood his ground
With punchers from everywhere;
So they bet old Bill at two to one
That he couldn't quite get there.

* From John A. Lomax's *Cowboy Songs and Other Frontier Ballads.*

Then Bill brought out his old gray hoss,
His withers and back were raw,
And prepared to tackle the big black brute
That ran down in the draw.

With his brazen bit and his Sam Stack tree
His chaps and taps to boot,
And his old maguey tied hard and fast,
Bill swore he'd get the brute.
Now, first Bill sort of sauntered round
Old Blackie began to paw,
Then threw his tail straight in the air
And went driftin' down the draw.

The old gray plug flew after him,
For he'd been eatin' corn;
And Bill, he piled his old maguey
Right round old Blackie's horns.
The old gray hoss he stopped right still;
The cinches broke like straw,
And the old maguey and the Sam Stack tree
Went driftin' down the draw.

Bill, he lit in a flint rock pile,
His face and hands were scratched.
He said he thought he could rope a snake
But he guessed he'd met his match.
He paid his bets like a little man
Without a bit of jaw,
And 'lowed old Blackie was the boss
Of anything in the draw.

There's a moral to my story, boys,
And that you all must see.
Whenever you go to tie a snake,
Don't tie it to your tree;
But take your dolly welters
'Cordin' to California law,
And you'll never see your old rim-fire
Go drifting down the draw.

THE COWBOY'S MEDITATION

At midnight, when the cattle are sleeping,
On my saddle I pillow my head,
And up at the heavens lie peeping
From out of my cold grassy bed;—
Often and often I wondered,
At night when lying alone,
If every bright star up yonder
Is a big peopled world like our own.

Are they worlds with their ranges and ranches?
Do they ring with rough-rider refrains?
Do the cowboys scrap there with Comanches
And other Red Men of the plains?
Are the hills covered over with cattle
In those mystic worlds far, far away?
Do the ranch-houses ring with the prattle
Of sweet little children at play?

At night, in the bright stars up yonder,
Do the cowboys lie down to their rest?
Do they gaze at this old world and wonder
If rough riders dash over its breast?
Do they list to the wolves in the canyons?
Do they watch the night owl in its flight,
With their horses their only companions
While guarding the herd through the night?

Sometimes, when a bright star is twinkling
Like a diamond set in the sky,
I find myself lying and thinking,
It may be God's heaven is nigh.
I wonder if there I shall meet her,
My mother whom God took away;

If in the star-heavens I'll greet her
At the round-up that's on the Last Day.

In the east the great daylight is breaking,
And into my saddle I spring;
The cattle from sleep are awaking,
The heaven-thoughts from me take wing;
The eyes of my bronco are flashing,
Impatient he pulls at the reins,
And off round the herd I go dashing,
A reckless cowboy of the plains.

THE COWBOY*

ALL day long on the prairies I ride,
Not even a dog to trot by my side;
My fire I kindle with chips gathered round,
My coffee I boil without being ground.

I wash in a pool and wipe on a sack;
I carry my wardrobe all on my back;
For want of an oven I cook bread in a pot,
And sleep on the ground for want of a cot.

My ceiling is the sky, my floor is the grass,
My music is the lowing of the herds as they pass;
My books are the brooks, my sermons the stones,
My parson is a wolf on his pulpit of bones.

And then if my cooking is not very complete
You can't blame me for wanting to eat.
But show me a man that sleeps more profound
Than the big puncher-boy who stretches himself on the
        ground.

* From John A. Lomax's *Cowboy Songs and Other Frontier Ballads.*

My books teach me ever consistence to prize,
My sermons, that small things I should not despise;
My parson remarks from his pulpit of bones
That fortune favors those who look out for their
    own.

And then between me and love lies a gulf very wide.
Some lucky fellow may call her his bride.
My friends gently hint I am coming to grief,
But men must make money and women have beef.

But Cupid is always a friend to the bold,
And the best of his arrows are pointed with gold.
Society bans me so savage and dodge
That the Masons would ball me out of their lodge.

If I had hair on my chin, I might pass for the goat
That bore all the sins in the ages remote;
But why it is I can never understand,
For each of the patriarchs owned a big brand.

Abraham emigrated in search of a range,
And when water was scarce he wanted a change;
Old Isaac owned cattle in charge of Esau,
And Jacob punched cows for his father-in-law.

He started in business way down at bed rock,
And made quite a streak at handling stock;
Then David went from night-herding to using a sling;
And, winning the battle, he became a great king.
Then the shepherds, while herding the sheep on a hill,
Got a message from heaven of peace and goodwill.

THE RANGE RIDERS*

COME all you range riders and listen to me,
I will relate you a story of the saddest degree,
I will relate you a story of the deepest distress,—
I love my poor Lulu, boys, of all girls the best.

When you are out riding, boys, upon the highway,
Meet a fair damsel, a lady so gay,
With her red, rosy cheeks and her sparkling dark eyes,
Just think of my Lulu, boys, and your bosoms will rise.

While you live single, boys, you are just in your prime;
You have no wife to scold, you have nothing to bother your minds;
You can roam this world over and do just as you will,
Hug and kiss the pretty girls and be your own still.

But when you get married, boys, you are done with this life,
You have sold your sweet comfort for to gain you a wife;
Your wife she will scold you, and the children will cry,
It will make those fair faces look withered and dry.

You can scarcely step aside, boys, to speak to a friend
But your wife is at your elbow saying what do you mean.
With her nose turned upon you it will look like sad news,—
I advise you by experience that life to refuse.

Come fill up your bottles, boys, drink Bourbon around;
Here is luck to the single wherever they are found.
Here is luck to the single and I wish them success,
Likewise to the married ones, I wish them no less.

I have one more request to make, boys, before we part.
Never place your affection on a charming sweetheart.
She is dancing before you your affections to gain;
Just turn your back on them with scorn and disdain.

* From John A. Lomax's *Cowboy Songs and Other Frontier Ballads.*

THE GOL-DARNED WHEEL*

I CAN take the wildest bronco in the tough old woolly West.
I can ride him, I can break him, let him do his level best;
I can handle any cattle ever wore a coat of hair,
And I've had a lively tussle with a tarnel grizzly bear.
I can rope and throw the longhorn of the wildest Texas brand,
And in Indian disagreements I can play a leading hand,
But at last I got my master and he surely made me squeal
When the boys got me a-straddle of that gol-darned wheel.

It was at the Eagle Ranch, on the Brazos,
When I first found that darned contrivance that upset me in
   the dust.
A tenderfoot had brought it, he was wheeling all the way
From the sun-rise end of freedom out to San Francisco Bay.
He tied up at the ranch for to get outside a meal,
Never thinking we would monkey with his gol-darned wheel.

Arizona Jim begun it when he said to Jack McGill
There was fellows forced to limit bragging on their riding skill,
And he'd venture the admission the same fellow that he meant
Was a very handy cutter far as riding bronchos went;
But he would find that he was bucking 'gainst a different kind
   of deal
If he threw his leather leggins 'gainst a gol-darned wheel.

Such a slam against my talent made me hotter than a mink,
And I swore that I would ride him for amusement or for chink.
And it was nothing but a plaything for the kids and such
   about,
And they'd have their ideas shattered if they'd lead the critter
   out.
They held it while I mounted and gave the word to go;
The shove they gave to start me warn't unreasonably slow.

* From John A. Lomax's *Cowboy Songs and Other Frontier Ballads.*

But I never spilled a cuss word and I never spilled a squeal—
I was building reputation on that gol-darned wheel.

Holy Moses and the Prophets, how we split the Texas air,
And the wind it made whip-crackers of my same old canthy
    hair,
And I sorta comprehended as down the hill we went
There was bound to be a smash-up that I couldn't well prevent.
Oh, how them punchers bawled, "Stay with her, Uncle Bill!
Stick your spurs in her, you sucker! turn her muzzle up the
    hill!"
But I never made an answer, I just let the cusses squeal,
I was finding reputation on that gol-darned wheel.

The grade was mighty sloping from the ranch down to the
    creek
And I went a-galliflutin' like a crazy lightning streak,—
Went whizzing and a-darting first this way and then that,
The darned contrivance sort o' wobbling like the flying of a
    bat.
I pulled upon the handles, but I couldn't check it up,
And I yanked and sawed and hollowed but the darned thing
    wouldn't stop.
Then a sort of a meachin' in my brain began to steal,
That the devil held a mortgage on that gol-darned wheel.

I've a sort of dim and hazy remembrance of the stop,
With the world a-goin' round and the stars all tangled up;
Then there came an intermission that lasted till I found
I was lying at the ranch with the boys all gathered round,
And a doctor was a-sewing on the skin where it was ripped,
And old Arizona whispered, "Well, old boy, I guess you're
    whipped,"
And I told him I was busted from sombrero down to heel,
And he grinned and said, "You ought to see that gol-darned
    wheel."

THE TEXAS COWBOY*

OH, I am a Texas cowboy,
Far away from home,
If ever I get back to Texas
I never more will roam.

Montana is too cold for me
And the winters are too long;
Before the round-ups do begin
Our money is all gone.

Take this old hen-skin bedding,
Too thin to keep me warm,—
I nearly freeze to death, my boys,
Whenever there's a storm.

And take this old "tarpoleon,"
Too thin to shield my frame,—
I got it down in Nebraska
A-dealin' a Monte game.

Now to win these fancy leggins
I'll have enough to do;
They cost me twenty dollars
The day that they were new.

I have an outfit on the Mussel Shell,
But that I'll never see,
Unless I get sent to represent
The Circle or D. T.

I've worked down in Nebraska
Where the grass grows ten feet high,

* From John A. Lomax's *Cowboy Songs and Other Frontier Ballads.*

And the cattle are such rustlers
That they seldom ever die;

I've worked up in the sand hills
And down upon the Platte,
Where the cowboys are good fellows
And the cattle always fat;

I've traveled lots of country,—
Nebraska's hills of sand,
Down through the Indian Nation,
And up the Rio Grande;—

But the Bad Lands of Montana
Are the worst I ever seen,
The cowboys are all tenderfeet
And the dogies are too lean.

If you want to see some bad lands,
Go over on the Dry;
You will bog down in the coulees
Where the mountains reach the sky.

A tenderfoot to lead you
Who never knows the way,
You are playing in the best of luck
If you eat more than once a day.

Your grub is bread and bacon
And coffee black as ink;
The water is so full of alkali
It is hardly fit to drink.

They will wake you in the morning
Before the break of day,
And send you on a circle
A hundred miles away.

All along the Yellowstone
'Tis cold the year around;

You will surely get consumption
By sleeping on the ground.

Work in Montana
Is six months in the year;
When all your bills are settled
There is nothing left for beer.

Work down in Texas
Is all the year around;
You will never get consumption
By sleeping on the ground.

Come all you Texas cowboys
And warning take from me,
And do not go to Montana
To spend your money free.

But stay at home in Texas
Where work lasts the year around,
And you will never catch consumption
By sleeping on the ground.

OLD TIME COWBOY*

COME all you melancholy folks wherever you may be,
I'll sing you about the cowboy whose life is light and free.
He roams about the prairie, and, at night when he lies down,
His heart is as gay as the flowers in May in his bed upon the
    ground.

They're a little bit rough, I must confess, the most of them, at
    least;
But if you do not hunt a quarrel you can live with them in peace;
For if you do, you're sure to rue the day you joined their band.
They will follow you up and shoot it out with you just man to man.

* From John A. Lomax's *Cowboy Songs and Other Frontier Ballads.*

Did you ever go to a cowboy whenever hungry and dry,
Asking for a dollar, and have him you deny?
He'll just pull out his pocket book and hand you a note,—
They are the fellows to help you whenever you are broke.

Go to their ranches and stay a while, they never ask a cent;
And when they go to town, their money is freely spent.
They walk straight up and take a drink, paying for every one,
And they never ask your pardon for anything they've done.

When they go to their dances, some dance while others pat.
They ride their bucking bronchos, and wear their broad-brimmed
    hats;
With their California saddles, and their pants stuck in their boots,
You can hear their spurs a-jingling, and perhaps some of them
    shoots.

Come all soft-hearted tenderfeet, if you want to have some fun;
Go live among the cowboys, they'll show you how it's done.
They'll treat you like a prince, my boys, about them there's
    nothing mean;
But don't try to give them too much advice, for all of them ain't
    green.

THE PECOS QUEEN*

WHERE the Pecos River winds and turns in its journey to the
    sea,
From its white walls of sand and rock striving ever to be free,
Near the highest railroad bridge that all these modern times have
    seen,
Dwells fair young Patty Morehead, the Pecos River queen.

She is known by every cowboy on the Pecos River wide,
They know full well that she can shoot, that she can rope and ride.

* From John A. Lomax's *Cowboy Songs and Other Frontier Ballads.*

She goes to every round-up, every cow work without fail,
Looking out for her cattle, branded "walking hog on rail."

She made her start in cattle, yes, made it with her rope;
Can tie down every maverick before it can strike a lope.
She can rope and tie and brand it as quick as any man;
She's voted by all cowboys an A-1 top cow hand.

Across the Comstock railroad bridge, the highest in the West,
Patty rode her horse one day, a lover's heart to test;
For he told her he would gladly risk all dangers for her sake—
But the puncher wouldn't follow, so she's still without a mate.

THE DYING COWBOY*

O BURY me not on the lone prairie,"
These words came low and mournfully
From the pallid lips of a youth who lay
On his dying bed at the close of day.

He had wailed in pain till o'er his brow
Death's shadows fast were gathering now;
He thought of his home and his loved ones nigh
As the cowboys gathered to see him die.

"O bury me not on the lone prairie
Where the wild cayotes will howl o'er me,
In a narrow grave just six by three,
O bury me not on the lone prairie.

"In fancy I listen to the well known words
Of the free, wild winds and the song of the birds;
I think of home and the cottage in the bower
And the scenes I loved in my childhood's hour.

* From John A. Lomax's *Cowboy Songs and Other Frontier Ballads.*

"It matters not, I've oft been told,
Where the body lies when the heart grows cold;
Yet grant, Oh grant this wish to me,
O bury me not on the lone prairie.

"O then bury me not on the lone prairie,
In a narrow grave six foot by three,
Where the buffalo paws o'er a prairie sea,
O bury me not on the lone prairie.

"I've always wished to be laid when I died
In the little churchyard on the green hillside;
By my father's grave, there let mine be,
And bury me not on the lone prairie.

"Let my death slumber be where my mother's
          prayer
And a sister's tear will mingle there,
Where my friends can come and weep o'er me;
O bury me not on the lone prairie.

"O bury me not on the lone prairie
In a narrow grave just six by three,
Where the buzzard waits and the wind blows free;
Then bury me not on the lone prairie.

"There is another whose tears may be shed
For one who lies on a prairie bed;
It pained me then and it pains me now;—
She has curled these locks, she has kissed this brow.

"These locks she has curled, shall the rattlesnake
          kiss?
This brow she has kissed, shall the cold grave press?
For the sake of the loved ones that will weep for me
O bury me not on the lone prairie.

"O bury me not on the lone prairie
Where the wild cayotes will howl o'er me,
Where the buzzard beats and the wind goes free,
O bury me not on the lone prairie.

"O bury me not," and his voice failed there,
But we took no heed of his dying prayer;
In a narrow grave just six by three
We buried him there on the lone prairie.

Where the dew-drops glow and the butterflies rest,
And the flowers bloom o'er the prairie's crest;
Where the wild cayote and winds sport free
On a wet saddle blanket lay a cowboy-ee.

"O bury me not on the lone prairie
Where the wild cayotes will howl o'er me,
Where the rattlesnakes hiss and the crow flies free
O bury me not on the lone prairie."

O we buried him there on the lone prairie
Where the wild rose blooms and the wind blows free,
O his pale young face nevermore to see,—
For we buried him there on the lone prairie.

Yes, we buried him there on the lone prairie
Where the owl all night hoots mournfully,
And the blizzard beats and the winds blow free
O'er his lowly grave on the lone prairie.

And the cowboys now as they roam the plain,—
For they marked the spot where his bones were lain,—
Fling a handful of roses o'er his grave,
With a prayer to Him who his soul will save.

"O bury me not on the lone prairie
Where the wolves can howl and growl o'er me;
Fling a handful of roses o'er my grave
With a prayer to Him who my soul will save."

THE OLD CHISHOLM TRAIL*

COME along, boys, and listen to my tale,
I'll tell you of my troubles on the old Chisholm trail.

    Coma ti yi youpy, youpy ya, youpy ya,
    Coma ti yi youpy, youpy ya.

I started up the trail October twenty-third,
I started up the trail with the 2-U herd.

Oh, a ten dollar hoss and a forty dollar saddle,—
And I'm goin' to punchin' Texas cattle.

I woke up one mornin' on the old Chisholm trail,
Rope in my hand and a cow by the tail.

I'm up in the mornin' afore daylight
And afore I sleep the moon shines bright.

Old Ben Bolt was a blamed good boss,
But he'd go to see the girls on a sore-backed hoss.

Old Ben Bolt was a fine old man
And you'd know there was whiskey wherever he'd land.

My hoss throwed me off at the creek called Mud,
My hoss throwed me off round the 2-U herd.

Last time I saw him he was going cross the level
A-kicking up his heels and a-running like the devil.

It's cloudy in the West, a-looking like rain,
And my damned old slicker's in the wagon again.

* From John A. Lomax's *Cowboy Songs and Other Frontier Ballads.*

Crippled my hoss, I don't know how,
Ropin' at the horns of a 2-U cow.

We hit Caldwell and we hit her on the fly,
We bedded down the cattle on the hill close by.

No chaps, no slicker, and it's pouring down rain,
And I swear, by God, I'll never night-herd again.

Feet in the stirrups and seat in the saddle,
I hung and rattled with them long-horn cattle.

Last night I was on guard and the leader broke the
    ranks,
I hit my horse down the shoulders and I spurred him
    in the flanks.

The wind commenced to blow, and the rain began to
    fall,
Hit looked, by grab, like we was goin' to lose 'em all.

I jumped in the saddle and grabbed holt the horn,
Best blamed cow-puncher ever was born.

I popped my foot in the stirrup and gave a little yell,
The tail cattle broke and the leaders went to hell.

I don't give a damn if they never do stop;
I'll ride as long as an eight-day clock.

Foot in the stirrup and hand on the horn,
Best damned cowboy ever was born.

I herded and I hollered and I done very well,
Till the boss said, "Boys, just let 'em go to hell."

Stray in the herd and the boss said kill it,
So I shot him in the rump with the handle of the
    skillet.

We rounded 'em up and put 'em on the cars,
And that was the last of the old Two Bars.

Oh, it's bacon and beans most every day,—
I'd as soon be a-eatin' prairie hay.

I'm on my best horse and I'm goin' at a run,
I'm the quickest shootin' cowboy that ever pulled a
    gun.

I went to the wagon to get my roll,
To come back to Texas, dad-burn my soul.

I went to the boss to draw my roll,
He had it figgered out I was nine dollars in the hole.

I'll sell my outfit just as soon as I can,
I won't punch cattle for no damned man.

Goin' back to town to draw my money,
Goin' back home to see my honey.

With my knees in the saddle and my seat in the sky,
I'll quit punching cows in the sweet by-and-by.

    Coma ti yi youpy, youpy ya, youpy ya,
    Coma ti yi youpy, youpy ya.

* From John A. Lomax's *Cowboy Songs and Other Frontier Ballads.*

A GLOSSARY OF WESTERN WORDS

acequia, irrigation ditch.

adobe, unburnt brick dried in sun: used for building material in Central America and Mexico; house built of adobe brick.

angoras, chaps made of goat hide with hair retained.

arroyo, watercourse or rivulet; dry bed of small stream.

badlands, arid country; land suffering from erosion.

brand, to impress the mark of owner's identity on an animal's hide with a hot iron; mark or identification so made.

break, to tame by force.

broncho-busting, horse-breaking.

bronco, broncho, unbroken Mexican, or Californian, horse.

buckaroo, buccaroo, cowboy (Northwest).

bucker, pitching or bucking horse.

burn, to brand; mark so made.

bushwhack, to ambush.

caballada, band of horses.

caballero, Spanish knight or horseman; gay cowboy; expert horseman.

caballo, horse.

cabestro, rope; horsehair-rope halter.

California pants, heavy wool pants worn by cowboys on the range.

caracole, to make a half turn to the right or left on horseback.

cattaloes, cross-breed of cattle and buffaloes.

centre-fire saddle, saddle that fastens on horse's back with only one girth at middle.

chapparral, chaparral, shrubs or thicket of thorny shrubs.

chaps, chaparheras, chaparejos, leather breeches: worn by cowboys at work.

cholla, type of large cactus with sharp spines.

cocktail hours, between 5 and 8 in the evening, before first guard on night herd: term used when men are with roundup wagon.

Colt, pistol with revolving cylinder, holding six cartridges (from name of inventor).

compadre, boon companion; pal.

conchas, silver disks worn for decoration on chaps, hats, saddles, etc.

Conestoga wagon, covered wagon.

corral, pen for livestock.

corral dust, lies; false, boastful stories.

coulee, ravine; dry creek; depression in the earth.

cow, general name in common use by cowboys for all cattle of any age or sex.

cowboy, rider employed by stockman or rancher, to look after herds, keep them from wandering, see to the brandings, and attend to the general roundup for buyers and ranchers.

cowpuncher, cowboy.

coyote, small type of prairie wolf; cowardly sneak.

cutter, pistol.

dab a loop on, to rope or lasso (an animal).

diggins, lodgings; living-quarters.

dinero, money.

dogie, calf; ill-fed, undernourished, motherless calf.

drag, young or weak animals bringing up rear of column.

drift fence, range fence built to prevent wandering away of cattle.

dude ranch, ranch operated for recreation; pleasure resort.

dude wrangler, guide on dude ranch.

equalizer, pistol.

fence-rider, cowboy who patrols and maintains property boundaries.

filly, young mare.

forty-five, gun of .45 caliber.

forty-four, gun of .44 caliber.

forty-niner, participant in 1849 California gold rush.

freighter, sixteen-foot wagon, with hooped top covered with canvas.

frijole, frijol, type of bean much cultivated in Mexico as an article of food.

full stamped saddle, saddle engraved with decorative designs.

gelding, young, castrated horse.

grama, type of pasture grass.

grapplin' irons, spurs.

grave-yard shift, from midnight till 2 A.M.: term used when men are with roundup wagon.

greaser, disrespectful name for Mexican or Spanish American.

gringo, in Spanish America, a foreigner; especially, a native of the U.S.

grubstake, supplies or money advanced to a prospector on share basis; to advance such.

hacienda, in Spanish America, a large plantation on which the owner is resident; an establishment for raising stock.

hackamore, halter provided with loop which may be tightened around the nose: used chiefly in breaking horses.

hairbrand, brand in which the hair alone, and not the skin, is burned; to brand in this fashion.

hasta la vista, Spanish expression meaning a friendly farewell; freely translated: "till we meet again."

haze, to lead or drive (an animal) slowly.

heifer, young cow.

hell-for-leather, at a furious pace.

hemp, rope.

hen-skin, comforter filled with feathers.

hightail, to leave quickly and abruptly.

hogleg, large pistol.

hog-tie, to rope both hind legs and one forefoot of an animal, making it helpless.

hole up, to hide out.

hunker, to sit on one's haunches.

iron, branding iron; pistol.

jacal, small hut or cabin.

javalina, peccary, or wild boar.

jerky, wagon without springs; strips of dried beef.

junta, business meeting.

Justin's, cowboy boots (from name of manufacturer).

kaffir corn, type of grain sorghum grown in dry regions.

keno, general expletive meaning "O.K.!" or "The end!"

lariat, rope.

lasso, rope with sliding noose.

latigo, leather strap attached to girth and used to fasten saddle on horse's back.

law wrangler, lawyer.

leppy, orphan calf.

Levis, overalls (from name of manufacturer).

lobo, wolf.

loco, crazy, foolish.

lone-wolf, person who lives or works alone, avoiding others.

longhorn, breed of cattle with long horns.

long rope, cattle thief.

maguey, rope made of the fibers of the century plant or of some other Agave.

mañana, tomorrow; later.

mantas, type of blanket or wrap.

maverick, unbranded animal; calf that has wandered away from its mother.

maverick brand, false brand put on cattle by one who has no right or claim to the animals.

mesa, elevated tableland.

mesquite, mesquit, thorny shrub of the bean family common to Southwestern U.S.

mestizo, half-breed.

mustang, the small, hardy, semi-wild horse of the prairies.

mustanger, one who catches mustangs.

muzzle-loader, gun that must be loaded through the muzzle.

navvy, Indian pony.

nester, homesteader or squatter who settles on government land.

nubbin, saddle horn.

one-ear bridle, bridle formed of a single strap which is kept in place by fitting it over one ear of the animal.

paint, horse whose color is irregular or showy.

palomino, golden-yellow horse with cream-colored mane and tail.

pampas, large barren plains.

pan, to wash gravel or sand in order to separate the gold particles in mining.

patio, courtyard.

peewees, short-topped cowboy boots.

peso, Mexican dollar; hence, any dollar.

picket pin, small stake to which a horse may be hitched at night on the range.

piñon, pinion, dwarf pine.

pinto, piebald; small calico horse of the Western plains; Mexican Indian.

pluie, pleuw, the whole skin of the beaver, as sold.

possible pack, wallet of dressed buffalo-skin for carrying ammunition, food, etc.

prickly pear, type of cactus plant or its edible fruit.

prairie schooner, covered wagon.

pueblo, building or group of buildings constructed by Indians of Southwest.

pull bog, to pull cattle out of mud.

quirt, whip made of leather strips woven together.

ranchero, rancher; especially, Mexican rancher.

range rider, cowboy whose job is to ride the range at random

to guard and protect his employer's property.

rawhide, cowhide; cowhide whip; untanned skin.

reata, leather rope; lariat.

remuda, band of saddle horses; extra mounts.

riatta, see *reata.*

rim-fire saddle, saddle with a single girth at the front.

road agent, stagecoach robber.

rodeo, a gathering together of cattle on a ranch; roundup; exhibition of riding and buck-jumping on broncos or bulls.

romal, whip fashioned from leather thongs, and attached to bridle or saddle.

roundup, gathering cattle together on a range by riding around them and driving them to a common center, as for branding.

rustler, cattle thief.

sagebrush, tough, stunted wiry shrub that covers vast tracts of the alkali plains of Southwestern U.S.

savvy, to understand; comprehension.

scrub, inferior grade of animal.

serape, blanket worn as cloak by Mexicans.

Sharps, single-shot, breech-loading rifle of heavy caliber.

shorthorn, cattle with short horns; tenderfoot.

sidewinder, type of rattlesnake that strikes by swinging its head to the side.

six-gun, the pistol as commonly called in the West.

snaffle, bridle bit consisting of a joint in the middle and rings at the ends.

snake, unruly steer; hence, term of opprobrium.

sombrero, broad-brimmed felt hat.

sorrel, horse of reddish-brown color.

sourdough, cook; bachelor; prospector.

spurs, rowel with sharp points on the heel of a boot for inciting a horse.

stampede, sudden panic seizing a herd of animals causing them to run violently away.

stake-rope, rope used to hitch horses to a stake.

Stetson, hat (from name of manufacturer).

stomp, dance.

strong on pretty, dressed in fancy style.

sudaderos, leather lining on underside of saddle.

sugans, suggans, bed comforters, blankets.

swamper, cook's assistant.

tapaderos, leather covers over front of stirrups to protect rider's feet.

tarantula juice, whisky.

teepee, tepee, the wigwam of the American Indian: a conical-shaped hut, formerly made of skins.

tenderfoot, person new to the life of a mining region, ranch, or frontier district.

thorough-braces, two lengths of manifold leather straps of thickest steer hide to suspend body of stagecoach.

tinhorn, silly dude; cheap sport or gambler.

toad-sticker, knife.

tumbleweed, a thistle which rolls to great distances in the wind.

vaquero, cowpuncher, cowboy.

vara, Spanish measure of length equal to about a yard.

waddie, waddy, cowpuncher.

wickiup, rude hut or cabin.

Winchester, light repeating rifle.

wipes, cowboy's neckerchief.

wrangler, person who herds saddle horses and cares for their equipment.

yearling, an animal one year old, or in its second year: applied to cattle, sheep, and horses.

Yucca country, the Southwest generally.

ACKNOWLEDGMENTS

The Publishers wish to acknowledge with thanks permission to use the following material contained in this volume:

"The Story of the Lucky Louse, or, Blood Will Tell," by G. Ezra Dane and Beatrice J. Dane, from *Ghost Town*, Alfred A. Knopf, copyright, 1941. Reprinted by permission of the publishers.

"The Phantom Fence Rider of San Miguel," by Henry Yelvington, from *Ghost Lore*. Reprinted by permission of The Naylor Company.

"Millionaires," by Mark Twain, from *Roughing It*, copyright, 1872. Reprinted by permission of Harper & Brothers.

"Speakin' of Cowpunchers," by Charles M. Russell, from *Trails Plowed Under*, copyright, 1927, by Doubleday, Doran and Company, Inc. Reprinted by permission of the publishers.

"The Sun-Dog Trail," by Jack London. Reprinted by permission of Charmian K. London.

"The Two-Gun Man," by Stewart Edward White, from *Arizona Nights*, copyright, 1907, by Doubleday Page & Company, copyright 1935, by Stewart Edward White. Reprinted by permission of Brandt & Brandt.

"The Bride Comes to Yellow Sky," by Stephen Crane, from *Twenty Stories*, Alfred A. Knopf, copyright, 1941. Reprinted by permission of the publishers.

"The Square Piano," by Conrad Richter, from *Early Americana*, Alfred A. Knopf, copyright, 1936. Reprinted by permission of the publishers.

"Higher Education," by Oliver La Farge, from *All The Young Men*, Houghton Mifflin Company, copyright, 1930. Reprinted by permission of the publishers.

"Ghost of the Cimarron," by Harry Sinclair Drago, from *Fifty Thrilling Wild West Stories*. Reprinted by permission of the author.

"Riding Bog," by Will James, from *Home Ranch*, Charles Scribner's Sons, copyright, 1935. Reprinted by permission of the publishers.

"Spoil the Child," by Howard Fast, from *The Saturday Evening Post*, August 6, 1938. Reprinted by permission of the author.

"A Pigeon Hunt," by Andy Adams, from *A Texas Matchmaker*, Houghton Mifflin Company. Reprinted by permission of the publishers.

"The Come-On," by Eugene Manlove Rhodes, from *The Saturday Evening Post*, November 23, 30, 1907. Reprinted by permission of Mrs. Eugene Manlove Rhodes.

"Bar-Nothing's Happy Birthday," by Eugene Cunningham. Published with the permission of the author.

"We Can't All Be Thoroughbreds," by Irvin S. Cobb, from *Faith, Hope and Charity*, The Bobbs-Merrill Company, copyright, 1934. Reprinted by permission of the publishers.

"The Mystery of the Palo Duro," by J. Frank Dobie, from *Coronado's Children*. Reprinted by permission of the author.

"A Call Loan," by O. Henry, from *Heart of the West*, Doubleday, Doran and Company, Inc., copyright, 1907. Reprinted by permission of the publishers.

"Don; The Story of a Lion Dog," by Zane Grey. Harper & Brothers, copyright, 1925. Reprinted by permission of Mrs. Zane Grey.

"Corazon," by George Pattullo. Reprinted by permission of the author.

"The First Cowboy," by Frederick R. Bechdolt, from *Tales of the Old-Timers*, D. Appleton-Century Company, copyright, 1924. Reprinted by permission of the publishers.

"Gentlemen-On-Horseback," by Ruth Laughlin Barker, from *Caballeros*, D. Appleton-Century Company, copyright, 1931. Reprinted by permission of the publishers.

"Stage-Coach," by Captain William Banning and George Hugh Banning, from *Six Horses*, D. Appleton-Century Company, copyright, 1928. Reprinted by permission of the publishers.

"Windwagon," by Stanley Vestal, from *The Old Santa Fe Trail*, Houghton Mifflin Company, copyright, 1939. Reprinted by permission of the publishers.

"Colonel Charles Goodnight—Trail-Maker," by Dane Coolidge, from *Fighting Men of the West*, E. P. Dutton & Company, Inc., copyright, 1932. Reprinted by permission of the publishers.

"Stick 'Em Up," by William McLeod Raine, from *Guns of the Frontier*, Houghton Mifflin Company, copyright, 1940. Reprinted by permission of the publishers.

"The Naming of Death Valley," by C. B. Glasscock, from *Here's Death Valley*, Bobbs-Merrill Company, copyright, 1940. Reprinted by permission of the publishers.

"A Peccary-Hunt in the Nueces," by Theodore Roosevelt, from *Hunting Adventures in the West*. Reprinted by permission of the Guaranty Trust Company of New York for the Edith K. Roosevelt Trust.

"Dick Yeager," by Marquis James, from *The Cherokee Strip*, The Viking Press, copyright, 1945. Reprinted by permission of the publishers.

"Crazy as a Sheepherder," by David Lavender, from *One Man's West*, Doubleday, Doran & Company, Inc., copyright, 1943. Reprinted by permission of the publishers.

"Custer," by Frederic F. Van de Water, from *Glory Hunter*, copyright, 1934; used by special permission of the publishers, the Bobbs-Merrill Company.

"Piñones," by Haniel Long, from *Pinon Country*, Duell, Sloan and Pearce, copyright, 1941. Reprinted by permission of the publishers.

"The Grand Canyon of the Colorado," by Robert Frothingham, from *Trails Through the Golden West*, Robert M. McBride & Company, copyright, 1932. Reprinted by permission of the publishers.

The following are reprinted from *Cowboy Songs and Other Frontier Ballads* (Macmillan, 1916) by permission of John A. Lomax: "Collector's Note" (abridged); "A Home on the Range"; "The Dreary Black Hills"; "Sam Bass"; "Brigham Young. I"; "Brigham Young. II"; "The Lone Star Trail"; "Westward Ho"; "The Cowman's Prayer"; "Whoopee, Ti Yi Yo, Git Along, Little Dogies"; "Billy Venero"; "Windy Bill"; "The Cowboy"; "The Range Riders"; "The Gol-Darned Wheel"; "The Texas Cowboy"; "Old Time Cowboy"; "The Pecos Queen"; "The Dying Cowboy"; "The Old Chisholm Trail."

The following are reprinted from *The American Songbag*, by Carl Sandburg (Harcourt, Brace & Company, 1927) by permission of the publishers: "I Ride an Old Paint"; "Sweet Betsy from Pike"; "As I Walked Out in the Streets of Laredo"; "The Tenderfoot"; "When the Work's All Done This Fall."

"Sage-Brush," by Harry Sinclair Drago, is reprinted by permission of the author.